AMERICAN

POPULAR
MUSIC

AMERICAN POPULAR MUSIC

FROM MINSTRELSY TO MTV

Larry Starr

Christopher Waterman

New York   Oxford
Oxford University Press
2003

Oxford University Press

Oxford   New York
Auckland   Bangkok   Buenos Aires   Cape Town   Chennai
Dar es Salaam   Delhi   Hong Kong   Istanbul   Karachi   Kolkata
Kuala Lumpur   Madrid   Melbourne   Mexico City   Mumbai
Nairobi   São Paulo   Shanghai   Taipei   Tokyo   Toronto

Published by Oxford University Press, Inc.
198 Madison Avenue, New York, New York 10016
http://www.oup-usa.org

Oxford is a registered trademark of Oxford University Press

Library of Congress Cataloging-in-Publication Data
Starr, Larry.
    American popular music : from minstrelsy to MTV / Larry Starr and
Christopher Waterman.
        p. cm.
Includes bibliographical references (p.) and index.
    ISBN-13: 978-0-19-510854-5
    ISBN-10: 0-19-510854-X
    1. Popular music—United States—History and criticism.   I. Waterman, Christopher Alan,
1954- II. Title.
    ML3477 .S73 2002
    781.64'0973—dc21   2002000699

Text design by Cathleen Bennett

Printing number: 9 8 7 6 5

Printed in the United States of America
on acid-free paper

CONTENTS

PREFACE

In presenting this survey of the rich terrain of American popular music, we hope to have created a book capable of serving a number of purposes. It may be used as a text for introductory college-level courses, obviously, as it assumes a mature and literate reader but not one who necessarily has any specific background in music or in this particular area of musical study. These same assumptions will also make this book useful to the general reader who wishes a broad-based introduction to our subject. In addition, the comprehensive scope of this volume will serve the interests of specialists—musicians, graduate students, teachers, and scholars—who need a one-volume overview, or review, of the topic. We have kept this wide potential audience constantly in mind as we strove to keep our book accessible and inviting, while always reflecting our own deep involvement in the music and in contemporary scholarly issues surrounding it.

What distinguishes our book from others in its rapidly growing field is that it combines two perspectives not often found in the same place: the study of cultural and social history on the one hand, and the analytical study of musical style on the other. Lest this sound disconcertingly heavy, let us assure our readers at the outset that we have brought to the treatment of our subject years of experience in teaching courses for a general student population and in lecturing on musical subjects to general audiences. This experience has taught us that it is neither necessary nor desirable to talk down, write down, or think down to such groups. People love music and can quickly grasp all kinds of intricacies and subtleties concerning music, so long as jargon is avoided and explanations kept clear and unpretentious. We love American popular music ourselves—that is why we have written this book—and we have attempted to foreground this love for the subject in our writing, realizing that it is the most valuable common bond we share with all potential readers of our work.

We fully expect that students, teachers, and readers of all kinds will enter into a creative dialogue with the material in this book. No general overview of a complex subject can begin to satisfy everyone. And since passions run high in the field of popular music, we anticipate that our particular perspectives, and particularly our choices of artists to emphasize and of specific examples to study, may well provoke some controversy at times, whether in the classroom or simply in the mind of the reader. We have felt it better to identify clearly our own viewpoints and enthusiasms than to try to hide behind a scrim of apparent "objectivity." The opening chapter outlines particular *themes* and *streams* that serve as recurring reference points throughout the book, so that our narrative focus and our strategy are put forward at the outset. While we feel that this text provides a sound and reliable starting point for the study and appreciation of American popular music, we claim no more than that. We hope and expect that teachers who use this book will share supplementary and contrasting perspectives on the material with their students, and that individual readers will use the bibliography as an enriching source of such perspectives as well. As white males who came to maturity in the days of rock 'n' roll and 1960s rock, we inevitably bring certain limitations, along with our passions, to the understanding of the broad trajectory of American pop, and it is certainly desirable for all readers to seek out other perspectives and modes of understanding as they pursue this subject further.

A brief word concerning methodology. We have sought to limit the use of specialized terms, to employ them only when clearly necessary, and to define them as they arise naturally in the course of study. The most important and frequently employed of these terms appear in **boldface,** and are given extensive definitions in the glossary at the end of the book. The glossary is reserved for terms that recur throughout the book and that would not be defined adequately for our purposes in a standard college dictionary. (This means that terms like **producer,** which have a special meaning in popular music, will be found in the glossary, along with other expected terms such as **blues** and **syncopation.**) Significant terms that are relevant only to a limited section of material are *italicized* when they first occur, are defined in context, and may also be located by using the book's index.

An analogous strategy has been used for musical analyses. Rather than being separated out, or introduced independently, the main musical discussions are integrated into the text at the points where they become relevant to the developing narrative; this approach seemed to us both logical and functional. Listening charts are used to represent and summarize, in outline form, the most important elements of recordings that are discussed in some detail in the text. The fact that we are dealing here to an overwhelming extent with *songs*—texted music—has enabled us to treat musical issues with some sophistication without having to employ actual musical notation, since lyrics may be used as points of specific orientation in the musical discussions. This keeps the focus on *listening* and opens the musical analyses to the widest possible audience of readers without compromising depth of treatment.

Boxes are used occasionally in this book to provide further insight and information on significant individuals, recordings, and topics in cases where such material—albeit useful—would interrupt the flow of narrative. Important names are <u>underlined</u> throughout the book.

We are pleased to offer with this book a two-CD set presenting many important songs discussed in its pages. Obviously, due to both practical and licensing restrictions, we are unable to present a number of specific selections we wished to include, or to present as many selections as we would have liked. Although many songs analyzed in considerable detail are present on the CDs, not all of them are. (It especially pains us that we could not license any recordings issued by Atlantic Records and its subsidiaries during the 1950s and 1960s—an essential body of rhythm & blues and soul music—or any recordings by Frank Sinatra, Elvis Presley, the Beatles, Ray Charles, and Bob Dylan. It relieves us somewhat to realize that much of this material is widely available in libraries and stores.) Even with these limitations, the CD set offers a "soundtrack" that ranges from the second through the penultimate chapter in the book, beginning with a song written in the 1850s and concluding with one written and recorded in 1995. We should note here that all song lyrics quoted in the text are designed to be quotations of what is actually sung on the recordings under discussion.

We would like to thank our families, who put up with a great deal as this book underwent its extensive prenatal development: Leslie, Dan, Sonya, and Gregory Starr; and Glennis and Max Waterman. We extend our gratitude to Maribeth Payne, our initial, ever-patient editor at Oxford University Press; to her gifted associates Maureen Buja and Ellen Welch; to Peter M. Labella, senior editor at OUP; to Christine D'Antonio, senior project editor at OUP; and to Larry Hamberlin for his superb job of copyediting. Many thanks also to Peter L. Kohan, Premium Sales Manager at Universal Music Special Markets, for his dedicated work on the CD package. We owe a substantial debt to the many anonymous readers who offered extensive and helpful comments on the manuscript in its various stages. At the University of Washington, our valued colleague Tom Collier has been a consistent and selfless source of assistance and encouragement. The course on American popular music out of which this book grew was shaped not only by faculty members, but by graduate students as well—among whom we especially wish to cite Jon Kertzer, Peter Davenport, Stuart Goosman, and Jun Akutsu. The many students who "road-tested" drafts of several chapters and offered their reactions to them also merit our sustained thanks. Graduate assistants Timothy Kinsella and Nathan Link at the University of Washington, and Sabrina Motley, Mark Eby, and Ann Mazzocca at UCLA gave invaluable and generous editorial assistance. We also owe a debt of gratitude to the folks at Joel Whitburn's Record Research for their series of books containing *Billboard* chart data. We could readily go on, like those CD inserts thanking everybody from the Almighty on down, but there's a story waiting to be told, and we'd best get on with it. If there's anybody out there we neglected to thank, let us know, and pray for a second edition so that we can do it next time!

Larry Starr, University of Washington
Christopher Waterman, UCLA

LYRIC CREDITS

CHAPTER ONE

THEMES AND STREAMS OF AMERICAN POPULAR MUSIC

Welcome to Seattle! Let's tune to the left end of the FM band and hit the scan button:

- 88.7—KPLU, jazz and public radio
- 90.3—KCMU, alternative/eclectic
- 91.3—KBCS, jazz/eclectic
- 92.5—KLSY, adult contemporary ("The Best Mix of the Eighties, Nineties, and Now.")
- 93.3—KUBE, contemporary hits (mix of rock music and urban contemporary)
- 94.1—KMPS, country ("The Sound of New Country")
- 94.9—KUOW, public radio
- 95.7—KJR, 1960s and 1970s rock ("Super Hits of the Sixties and Seventies")
- 96.5—KYPT, 1980s rock
- 97.3—KBSG, oldies (1950s–70s) ("Your Oldies Station: Fun, All the Time!")
- 98.1—KING, classical music
- 98.9—KEZX, easy listening ("Smooth 99")
- 99.9—KISW, album-oriented rock ("More Pure Rock, No Useless Talk")
- 101.5—KPLZ ("Star 101.5: Today's Best Variety")
- 102.5—KZOK, classic rock
- 103.7—KMTT, adult alternative ("The Mountain: We've Got Your Music")
- 105.3—KCMS, Christian music ("The Music Speaks for Itself")
- 106.1—KISS, contemporary rock ("For All of Today's Best Music")
- 107.7—KNDD, modern rock ("The End: Some People Like Things the Way They Used to Be; and Then Again, Some Don't")

Having made this quick pass over the FM radio landscape of Seattle, you probably know immediately which stations you'd want to program on your automatic tuner. There are doubtless some stations that you might try only on occasion, and a few that you'd remove permanently from your radio if you knew how. That's the way popular music is, after all: some types of music attract us, others incite us to pitch the radio out the window, and yet others, to borrow a Brazilian phrase, don't smell bad or good, they just don't smell like anything at all.

But think for a moment. Why all these stations? Who listens to them? Why are adjectives such as "smooth" and "hard" applied to music? How do radio formats such as "new country," "classic rock," "album-oriented rock," and "adult alterna-tive" take shape? What does this dividing up of styles and audiences tell us about contemporary American culture? Who's making money from all this?

We hope that this book will help you to think creatively and critically about such questions. Our goal is to get you to listen closely to popular music and to learn some-thing about its history and about the people and institutions that have produced it. We cover a wide range of music, starting in the nineteenth century and continuing up through the 1990s. Listening to music is an important part of this study, and we hope that you will enjoy the recordings that we have chosen to highlight. But be forewarned—we cannot possibly do justice to all the music you like, or all the mu-sicians you admire (nor can we adequately denigrate the music you hate).

It is difficult to come up with a satisfactory definition of "popular music." In many cases popular music is defined by its difference from other types of music, especially "art music" or "classical music," on the one hand, and "folk music," on the other. One problem with such categories is that they seem less reasonable when you get to grips with particular examples. In some ways the "garage band" tradi-tion of rock music—in which a bunch of people get together to play music for fun, sometimes copying songs from records and sometimes composing their own—is more like "folk music" than "popular music." In other cases—say, the ragtime pi-ano pieces of Scott Joplin or the Beatles' album *Sgt. Pepper's Lonely Hearts Club Band*—it is not easy to separate the "artistic" from the "popular." Much of the music that people regard today as "folk music"—the records of the Weavers, the Kingston Trio, or Peter, Paul, and Mary—has been profoundly shaped by market forces. In many cases stylistic categories are themselves partly the product of marketing strategies by record companies, who in defining types of music hope to define types of fans to whom they can sell the music.

In this book we use the term "popular music" broadly, to indicate music that is mass-reproduced and disseminated via the mass media; that has at various times been listened to by large numbers of Americans; and that typically draws upon a variety of preexisting musical traditions. It is our view that popular music must be seen in relation to a broader musical landscape, in which various styles, audiences, and institutions interact in complex ways. This musical map is not static—it is al-ways in motion, always evolving.

THEME ONE: LISTENING

Although this book covers a wide range of performers, styles, and historical peri-ods, it is unified by several themes. First and foremost, we hope to encourage you to *listen critically* to popular music. The word "critical" doesn't imply adopting a negative attitude. Rather, critical listening is listening that consciously seeks out meaning in music, drawing on some knowledge of how music is put together, its cultural significance, and its historical development.

Even if you don't think of yourself as a musician, and don't have much—or any—experience at reading musical notation, it is likely that you know much more about music than you think. You know when a chord sounds "wrong," a note "out of tune," or a singer "off key," even if you can't come up with a technical explanation for your reaction. You have learned a lot about music just growing up as a member of society, although much of that knowledge rests below the level of conscious awareness.

In everyday life, people often do not think carefully about the music they hear. Much popular music is in fact designed not to call critical attention to itself (a good example of this is the multimillion-dollar "environmental music" industry, pioneered by the Muzak Corporation). Other types of popular music—big band swing, funk, punk rock, hard rap, thrash metal—seek to grab your attention, but do not by and large encourage you to engage them analytically. The point of analyzing popular music is not to ruin your enjoyment of it. Rather, we want to encourage you to expand your tastes, to hear the roots of today's music in earlier styles, and in the final analysis, to be a more critically aware "consumer" of popular music.

Formal analysis—listening for musical structure, its basic building blocks and the ways in which they are combined—can tell us a lot about popular music. We can, for example, discover that recordings as different as Glenn Miller's 1939 big-band hit "In the Mood," Little Richard's rock 'n' roll anthem "Tutti Frutti," James Brown's "I Got You (I Feel Good)," The Doors' "Riders on the Storm," and the theme song of the 1960s TV show *Batman* all share the same basic musical structure, the twelve-bar blues form (to be discussed in Chapter 5). Similarly, tunes as diverse as George Gershwin's 1930 song "I Got Rhythm," the Penguins' 1955 doo-wop hit "Earth Angel," and the theme of the 1960s cartoon show (and the 1993 film) *The Flintstones* all have an AABA melodic structure. You don't have to worry about such technicalities yet; there will be ample opportunity to discuss them later on. The point here is simply to suggest that a lot of popular music draws on a limited number of basic formal structures.

Structure is not the only important dimension of music. In order to analyze the way popular music actually sounds—the grain of a singing voice, the flow of a dance groove, or the gritty sound of an electric guitar—we must complement formal analysis with the analysis of *musical process*. To adopt a biological analogy, there is an important difference between understanding the *structure* of an organism—its constituent parts and how they are related—and the *processes* that bring these parts and relationships to life. Popular songs may be analyzed not only as composed "works" with their own internal characteristics but also as interpretations by particular performers: in other words, one must understand not only *song* but also *singing*.

Traditional musicology, which focuses on the written scores that serve as the model for performances in classical music, is often of little relevance in helping us to understand popular music. In this book we frequently use concepts directly relevant to popular music itself: for example, **riff,** a repeated pattern designed to generate rhythmic momentum; **hook,** a memorable musical phrase or riff; and **groove,** a term that evokes the channeled flow of "swinging" or "funky" or "phat" rhythms.

Another important aspect of musical process is **timbre,** the quality of a sound, sometimes called "tone color." Timbre plays an important role in establishing the "soundprint" of a performer. Play just five seconds of a recording by Louis Armstrong, Frank Sinatra, Johnny Cash, Aretha Franklin, Neil Diamond, Bruce Springsteen, Bonnie Raitt, Dr. Dre, or Eddie Vedder, and any knowledgeable listener will be able to identify the singer by the "grain" of his or her voice.

Instrumental performers may also have highly memorable "soundprints." Some—for example, Jimi Hendrix, Eric Clapton, Eddie Van Halen, or Kenny G— have become superstars. Others remain unknown to the general listening public, although their soundprints are very familiar: for example, James Jamerson, the master bassist of Motown; King Curtis, whose gritty tenor saxophone is featured on dozens of soul records from the 1960s; and Steve Gadd, studio drummer par excellence, who played on records by Aretha Franklin, Stevie Wonder, Barbra Streisand, Steely Dan, and Paul Simon during the 1970s.

Recording engineers, producers, arrangers, and record labels may also develop unique "soundprints." We will encounter many examples of this: the distinctive **"slap-back"** echo of Elvis Presley's early recordings on Sun Records; the quasi-symphonic teen pop recordings produced by Phil Spector; the stripped-down, "back to basics" soul sound of Stax Records in Memphis; and the immense sampled bass drum explosions used by engineer Steve Ett of Chung House of Metal, one of the most influential hip-hop studios. You will learn more about the creative contributions of arrangers, engineers, and producers as we go along; for now, you should simply note that the production of a particular "sound" often involves many individuals performing different tasks.

Lyrics—the words of a song—are another important aspect of popular music. In many cases words are designed to be one of the most immediately accessible parts of a song. In other cases—for example, the songs of Robert Johnson, Bob Dylan, John Lennon and Paul McCartney, David Byrne, Kurt Cobain, or Ice-T—the lyrics seem to *demand* interpretation, and fans take a great deal of pleasure from the process of figuring them out.

Dialect has also been a crucial factor in the history of American popular music. Some musical genres are strongly associated with particular dialects (country music with southern white dialects, rap music with certain urban black dialects, 1970s punk rock with working-class British dialects). The ability of African American artists such as Nat "King" Cole, Chuck Berry, and Diana Ross to "cross over" to a white middle-class audience was to some degree predicated upon their adoption of a dialect widely used in the mass media. In other cases, the mutual incomprehensibility of varieties of English has been consciously emphasized, particularly in recordings aimed at consumption within ethnic communities. There are sometimes very good reasons not to be understood by the majority.

These are some of the dimensions of popular musical style to keep in mind as you work your way through this book. Think about what attracts you to the music you like: the texture of a voice, the power of a guitar, the emotional insight of a lyric, the satisfying predictability of a familiar tune, the physical momentum of a rhythm. This is what makes popular music important to people: its sound, the sense it makes, and the way it feels.

THEME TWO: MUSIC AND IDENTITY

None of us is born knowing who we are—we all *learn* to be human in particular ways, and music is one important medium through which we formulate and express our identity. Think back to the very first pop song you remember hearing as a little kid, when you were, say, five years old. Odds are you heard it at home, or maybe in a car, or (depending on your age) over a transistor radio or a portable CD player at the beach. The person playing it may have been one of your parents, or an older brother or sister. These are often the people who influence our early musical values, and it is they whose values we sometimes emphatically reject later in life. In elementary school, other kids begin to influence our taste, a development closely connected with the ways in which we form social groups based on gender, age, and other factors (boys versus girls, fifth graders versus first graders, cool kids versus nerds).

As we move into adolescence, popular music also enters our private lives, providing comfort and continuity during emotional crises and offering us the opportunity to fantasize about romance and rebellion. Pop music provides images of gender identity, culturally specific ways of being masculine and feminine. Ethnicity and race—including notions of how to act "white" or "black" or "Latino"—are also powerfully represented in popular music.

As you grow older, a song or a singer's voice may suddenly transport you back to a specific moment and place in your life, sometimes many decades earlier. Like all human beings, we make stories out of our lives, and music plays an important role in bringing these narratives to life. Some popular songs—for example, Frank Sinatra's version of "It Was a Very Good Year," Dolly Parton's "Coat of Many Colors," and Don McLean's "American Pie"—are really *about* memory and the mixed feelings of warmth and loss that accompany a retrospective view of our own lives.

Popular music in America has from the very beginning been closely tied up with *stereotypes*, convenient ways of organizing people into categories. It is easy to find examples of stereotyping in American popular music: the common portrayal in song lyrics and music videos of women as sexual objects, and the association of men with violence; the image of African American men as playboys and gangsters; the stereotype of southern white musicians as illiterate, backwoods "rednecks"; the association of songs about money with supposedly Jewish musical characteristics; and the caricatures of Asian and Latin American people found in many novelty songs from the 1920s through the 1960s.

Stereotyping is often a double-edged sword. In certain cases popular performers have helped to undermine the "commonsense" association of certain styles with certain types of people: the black country singer Charley Pride and the white blues musician Stevie Ray Vaughan are just two examples of performers whose styles challenge stereotyped conceptions of race and culture. The history of popular music in the United States is also replete with examples of minority groups who have reinterpreted derogatory stereotypes and made them the basis for distinctive forms of musical creativity and cultural pride—"Say It Loud, I'm Black and Proud," "Okie from Muskogee," "The Happy Polak Polka," "[At the] YMCA."

Why do people make and listen to music? What do they want from it, and what does it give them? These questions take us beyond the central concern of classic aesthetic theory, the creation and appreciation of "beauty for beauty's sake." People value music for many reasons, including a desire for beauty, but also a great deal more: they use music to escape from the rigors of the work week, to celebrate important events in their lives, to help them make money, war, and love. In order to understand the cultural significance of popular music, we must examine both the music—its tones and textures, rhythms and forms—and the broader patterns of social identity that have shaped Americans' tastes and values.

THEME THREE: MUSIC AND TECHNOLOGY

From the heyday of printed sheet music in the nineteenth century through the rise of the phonograph record, network radio, and sound film in the 1920s, right up to the present era of digital recording, computerized **sampling,** and fiber-optics networks, technology has shaped popular music and has helped disseminate it, more and more rapidly, to more and more people. Technology doesn't determine the decisions made by a musician or an audience, but it can make a particular range of choices available to them.

It has often been argued that the mass media create a gap between musicians and their audiences, a distance that often encourages us to forget that the music we hear is made by other human beings. To what degree has technology affected our relationship to music and, more importantly, to other people? This is by no means a simple issue. Some critics of today's musical technology would say that a much higher percentage of Americans were able to perform music for their own enjoyment a century ago, when the only way of experiencing music was to hear it performed live or to make it yourself. This decline in personal music making is generally attributed to the influence of mass media, which are said to encourage passive listening. However, nationwide sales figures for musical instruments—including electronic instruments such as MIDI synthesizers—suggest that millions of people in the United States *are* busy making music.

In addition, although the mass media can encourage passivity, people aren't always passive when they listen to recorded music. Have you ever pretended to *be* a favorite musician while listening to music by yourself, perhaps even mimicking onstage movements (playing "air guitar" or "virtual drums")? Have you ever embarrassed yourself by unconsciously singing along with your Walkman in a public setting? When you listen over headphones, don't you enter into the music in your imagination and in an important sense help to "make" the music?

Although we tend to associate the word "technology" with novelty and change, older technologies often take on important value as tokens of an earlier—and, it is often claimed, better—time. Old forms of musical "hardware" and "software"— music boxes, player pianos, phonographs, sheet music, 78s, 45s, and LPs—become the basis for subcultures made up of avid collectors. In some cases, older music technologies are regarded as qualitatively superior to the new. For example, some contemporary musicians make a point of using analog rather than digital recording technology. This decision is based on the aesthetic judgment that analog recordings—which directly mirror the energy fluctuations of sound waves—"sound better" than digital recordings—which break sound waves down into packets of information. Musicians who prefer analog recording say that it is "warmer," "richer-sounding," and somehow "more human" than digital recording.

Sometimes the rejection of electronic technology functions as an emblem of "authenticity," as, for example, in MTV's *Unplugged* series, where rockers such as Eric Clapton, R.E.M., and Nirvana demonstrate their "real" musical ability and sincerity by playing on acoustic instruments. However, there are also many examples of

One of the earliest FM radio stations, Alpine, New Jersey, 1948. Courtesy Library of Congress.

technologies being used in ways that *encourage* active involvement, including the manipulation of multiple record turntables by hip-hop **DJs** and the increasing popularity of *karaoke* singalong machines and computer software in American nightclubs and homes. If it is true that technology has been used in cynical ways to manipulate the public into buying certain kinds of music, it is also the case that people often exert creative control over the role of musical machines in their own lives.

THEME FOUR: THE MUSIC BUSINESS

In order to understand the history of American popular music, it is necessary that we learn about the workings of the music business. The production of popular music typically involves the work of many individuals performing different roles. From the nineteenth century until the 1920s, sheet music was the principal means of disseminating popular songs to a mass audience. This process typically involved a complex network of people and institutions: the composer and lyricist who wrote a song; the publishing company that bought the rights to it; song pluggers, who promoted the song in stores and convinced big stars to incorporate it into their acts; the stars themselves, who often worked in shows that toured along a circuit of theaters controlled by yet other organizations; and so on, right down to the consumer, who bought the sheet music and performed it at home.

The rise of radio, recording, and movies as the primary means for popularizing music added many layers of complexity to this process. Today hundreds of people will have had a hand in producing the music you listen to. In mainstream pop music, the **composer** and **lyricist** are still important; the songs they write are reworked to complement a particular performer's strengths by an **arranger,** who decides which instruments to use to accompany them, what key the song should be in, how many times it should be repeated, and a host of other details. The **A&R** (artists and repertoire) personnel of a record company seek out talent, often visiting nightclubs and rehearsals to hear new groups. The **producer** of a record plays several roles: convincing the board of directors of a record company to back a particular project, shaping the development of new "talent," and often intervening directly in the recording process. Engineers work in the studio, making hundreds of important decisions about the balance between voice and instruments, the use of effects such as echo and **reverb,** and other factors that shape the overall "sound" of a record. The publicity department plans the advertising campaign, and the public relations department handles interactions with the press.

This is only the barest outline of the interlocking roles involved in the production and promotion of popular music today. Business agents, video producers, graphic artists, copy editors, record stores, stage hands, truck drivers, T-shirt companies, and the companies that produce musical hardware—often owned by the same corporations that produce the recordings—also play vital roles in this process. It is hard to know where to draw the boundaries of an industry that has extended itself into so many aspects of commerce and culture.

In addition, many of the roles described above have become intermingled in complex ways. A person like Quincy Jones, for example, is a performer, a songwriter, an arranger, a producer (who makes lots of engineering decisions), and a record label executive. And the wider availability of digital recording equipment means that some performers may also act as their own arranger, producer, and engineer (Stevie Wonder and Prince are good examples of this kind of collapsing of roles).

Theodor Adorno, a German philosopher who wrote in the 1940s and 1950s, powerfully criticized the effects of capitalism and industrialization on popular music. He suggested that the music industry promotes the *illusion* that we are all highly independent individuals defined by our personal tastes—"I'm a country music fan," "You're a metalhead." In fact, Adorno argued, the industry manipulates the notion of personal taste to sucker us into buying its products. Emotional identification with the wealthy superstars portrayed on television and in film—the "Lifestyles of the Rich and Famous" syndrome—is, in Adorno's view, a poor substitute for the humane and ethical social relations that typify healthy communities.

In some ways Adorno was right: Americans are probably less individualistic than they like to think, and it is often true that record companies con us into buying the latest thing on the basis of tiny differences in musical style, rather like the little design changes that mark off different kinds of automobiles or tape decks or tennis shoes. And it is true that the private experience of listening over head-phones—like the experience of driving alone in an automobile with the windows rolled up—can isolate people from one another.

But there's more to it than that. Just ask anyone who's worked in the music busi-ness and developed an ulcer trying to predict what the next trend will be. Com-pared to other industries that produce consumer products, the music business is quite unpredictable. Today, only about one out of eight recordings makes a profit. One platinum record—something like Michael Jackson's *Thriller*, Madonna's *Like a Virgin*, Nirvana's *Nevermind*, or Dr. Dre's *The Chronic*—must compensate for liter-ally hundreds of unprofitable records made by unknown musicians or faded stars. As record company executives seek to guarantee their profits by producing varia-tions on "the same old thing," they also nervously eye the margins to spot and take advantage of the latest trends.

The relationship between the "majors"—large record companies with lots of cap-ital and power—and the "indies"—small independent labels operating in marginal markets—has been an important factor in the development of American popular music. In most cases, the majors have played a conservative role, seeking to ensure profits by producing predictable (some would say "bland") music for a large middle-class audience. The indies, run by entrepreneurs, have often had to be more daring, searching out new talent, creating specialized niches, and feeding new styles into the musical mainstream. It is mostly these small labels that initially popular-ized blues, country music, rhythm & blues, rock 'n' roll, funk, soul music, reggae, punk rock, rap, grunge, worldbeat, and other "alternative" styles. In some cases, indie labels have grown large and powerful; one example of this is Atlantic Records, which began as a small **R&B** label in the late 1940s and grew into a multimillion-dollar corporation.

Today, the relationship between indies and majors has been extended over the globe—five corporations (only one of them actually based in the United States) now control around 90 percent of the world's legal trade in commercially recorded mu-sic. Each of these transnational corporations has bought up many smaller labels, us-ing them as incubators for new talent, a system reminiscent of the relationship be-tween major and minor league teams in baseball.

THEME FIVE: CENTERS AND PERIPHERIES

The distinction between major and minor labels leads us to a final theme: the idea that the history of American popular music may be broadly conceptualized in terms of a center-periphery model. The "center"—actually several geographically distinct centers, including New York, Los Angeles, and Nashville—is where power, capi-tal, and control over mass media are concentrated. The "periphery" is inhabited by smaller institutions and by people who have historically been excluded from the political and economic mainstream. This distinction is by no means intended to sug-gest that the center is "normal" and the periphery "abnormal." Rather, it is a way of clarifying a process that has profoundly shaped the development of popular mu-sic in the United States: that is, the role of the musical "margins" in shaping main-stream popular taste and the workings of the music industry.

The stylistic mainstream of American popular music was, until at least the mid-1950s, largely oriented toward the tastes of white, middle- or upper-class, Protestant, urban people. In economic terms, this makes perfect sense, since it was these people who for many years made up the bulk of the expanding urban market for mass-reproduced music. From whom have the vital "peripheral" musical impulses of which we have been speaking come? The evidence, as you shall see, is abundant: from African Americans, poor southern whites, working-class people, Jewish and Latin American immigrants, adolescents, gays, and various other folks whose "difference" vis-à-vis the mainstream has at times weighed upon them as a burden.

The history of popular music in the United States shows us how supposedly marginal musics and musicians have repeatedly helped to invigorate the center of popular taste and the music industry. Regrettably, it has sometimes also been the case that the people most responsible for creating the music that people in the United States and elsewhere consider quintessentially American have not reaped an equitable share of the profits accumulated from the fruits of their labor.

STREAMS OF TRADITION: THE SOURCES OF POPULAR MUSIC

In 1937 the anthropologist Ralph Linton published an article entitled "One-Hundred Percent American." "There can be no question about the average American's Americanism or his desire to preserve his precious heritage at all costs," wrote Linton. "Nevertheless, some insidious foreign ideas have already wormed their way into his civilization without his realizing what was going on." These "insidious ideas"—derived from the cultures of Asia, the Near East, Europe, Africa, and Native America—include pajamas, the toilet, soap, the toothbrush, the chair, shoes, the mirror, coffee, fermented and distilled drinks, the cigar, and even the newspaper. On the train to work, Linton's "average American" reads the news of the day, imprinted in characters invented by the ancient Semites by a process invented in Germany on a material invented in China. As he scans the latest editorial pointing out the dire results to our institutions of accepting foreign ideas, he thanks a Hebrew God in an Indo-European language that he is 100 percent (decimal system invented by the Greeks) American (from Americus Vespucci, Italian geographer).

Similarly, every aspect of popular music that is today regarded as American in character has sprung from imported traditions. These source traditions may be classified into three broad "streams": European American music, African American music, and Latin American music. Each of these streams is made up of many styles of music, and each has profoundly influenced the others.

The European American Stream

Until the middle of the nineteenth century, American popular music was almost entirely European in character. The cultural and linguistic dominance of the English meant that their music—including folk ballads, popular songs printed as sheet music, and various types of dance music—established early on a kind of "mainstream" around which other styles circulated.

At the time of the American Revolution, professional composers of popular songs in England drew heavily upon **ballads,** a type of song in which a series of **verses** telling a story, often about a historical event or personal tragedy, are sung to a repeating melody (this sort of musical form is called **strophic**). Originally an oral tradition, passed down in unwritten form, ballads were eventually circulated on large sheets of paper called *broadsides*, the ancestors of today's sheet music. While some broadside ballads were drawn from folk tradition, many were urban in origin and concerned with current events (much like today's tabloid newspapers). In most cases only the words were provided, with an indication of a traditional melody—for example, "Greensleeves"—to which they were to be sung. Ballad-mongers hawking the broadsides sang them on the streets, an early form of commercial song promotion. Composers of broadside ballads often added a catchy **chorus,** a repeated melody with fixed text inserted between verses.

The *pleasure garden*, a forerunner of today's theme parks, was the most important source of public entertainment in England between 1650 and 1850. Large urban parks filled with meandering tree-lined paths, the pleasure gardens provided an idyllic rural experience for an expanding urban audience. The pleasure gardens became one of the main venues for the dissemination of printed songs by professional composers, and many of the first widely popular songsheets were illustrated with sketches of the gardens and other romanticized rural scenes. In the 1760s the first American pleasure gardens opened in Charleston, New York, and other cities.

The English *ballad opera* tradition was also extremely popular in America during the early nineteenth century. These stage productions drew upon ballads, some

Castle Garden, New York City, in 1848, as depicted in a lithograph by Nathaniel Currier. Courtesy Library of Congress.

of which had previously been circulated as broadsides. Perhaps the best known of the English ballad operas is John Gay's *The Beggar's Opera* (1728), designed to counter the domination of the British stage by Italian composers and musicians. The main characters in ballad operas were common people, rather than the kings and queens of imported operas; the songs were familiar in form and content; and the lyrics were all in English rather than Italian.

The pleasure gardens and ballad operas both featured songs produced by professional composers for large and diverse audiences. Melodies were designed to be simple and easy to remember, and the lyrics focused on romantic themes.

The English folk ballad tradition thrived in America, and songs were reworked to suit the life circumstances of new immigrants. In the early twentieth century folklorists interested in continuities with English traditions were able to record dozens of versions of old English ballads in the United States. While today these songs are preserved mainly by folk music enthusiasts, the core of the tradition—including its musical forms and storytelling techniques—lives on in contemporary country and western music. In addition, vocal qualities derived from the Anglo-American tradition—notably the thin, nasalized tone known as the "high lonesome sound"—continue today as markers of southern white identity.

Irish, Scottish, and Italian songs also influenced early American popular song. Copies of Thomas Moore's multivolume collection of *Irish Melodies* (a collection of Moore's poems set to Irish folk melodies, published in London and Dublin between 1808 and 1834) were widely circulated in the United States, and Scottish songs such as "Auld Lang Syne" (probably written in the late seventeenth century and still performed today on New Year's Eve) also enjoyed wide popularity. By the first decades of the nineteenth century, the Italian opera was also very popular in the United States. Songs by Rossini, Bellini, Donizetti, and other Italian composers were published as sheet music, and the *bel canto* style of singing—light, clear, flexible, and intimate—had a major effect on the development of popular singing style.

Dance music was another important aspect of the European influence on American popular music. Until the late nineteenth century European American dance was closely modeled on styles imported from England and the Continent. Country dances—in which dancers arranged themselves into circles, squares, or opposing rows—were popular. In the United States the country dance tradition developed into a plethora of urban and rural, elite and lower-class, black and white variants. It continues today in country and western line dances and in the contradances that form part of the modern folk music scene.

The nineteenth century also saw a move toward couple dances, including the waltz, the galop, the schottische, and the ballroom polka, the last based on a Bohemian dance that had already become the rage in the ballrooms of Paris and London before coming to America. Later, in the 1880s, a fast dance called the one-step, based in part on marching band music, became popular. These couple dances are direct predecessors of the African American–influenced popular dance styles of the early twentieth century, including the two-step, fox trot, bunny hug, and Charleston.

In addition to songs and dance music produced by professional composers for a largely urban audience, immigration brought a wide variety of European *folk music* to America. The mainstream of English-dominated popular song and dance music was from early on surrounded by a myriad of folk and popular styles brought by immigrants from other parts of Europe. The descendants of early French settlers in North America and the Caribbean maintained their own musical traditions. Millions of Irish and German immigrants came to the United States during the nineteenth century, seeking an escape from oppression, economic uncertainty, and—particularly during the potato famine of the 1840s—the threat of starvation. Between 1880 and 1910 an additional seventeen million immigrants entered the United States, mostly from eastern and southern Europe. These successive waves of migration contributed to the diversity of musical life in the United States. European-derived musical styles such as Cajun (Acadian) fiddling, Jewish *klezmer* music, and the Polish polka—an energetic dance, quite different from the "refined" style of polka discussed above—have each contributed to mainstream popular music while maintaining a solid base in particular ethnic communities.

The African American Stream

Not all immigrants came willingly. Between one and two million people from Africa, about 10 percent of the total transatlantic traffic in slaves, were forcibly brought to the United States between the seventeenth and nineteenth centuries. The areas of western and central Africa from which slaves were drawn were home to hundreds of distinct societies, languages, and musical traditions.

The genesis of African American music in the United States involved two closely related processes. The first of these was *syncretism*, the selective blending of traditions derived from Africa and Europe. The second important process was the creation of *institutions* that became important centers of black musical life—the family, the church, the voluntary association, the school, and so on.

It is misleading to speak of "black music" as a homogeneous entity. African American culture took different forms in Brazil, Cuba, Haiti, Jamaica, and the United States, shaped by the particular mix of African and European (and in some cases American Indian) source traditions, and by local social conditions. In the United States, people from the Senegambia region of West Africa—the Wolof, Mandinka, and other groups—appear to have made up a large part of the slave population. Kunta Kinte, the ancestor of *Roots* author Alex Haley, was a Wolof man from what is today the nation of Gambia; the banjo, an African American invention, was developed from stringed instruments common in the Senegambia region; and certain aspects of blues singing, including the role of the musician as a social critic, are derived from the *griot* (praise singer) traditions of the West African savannah.

Certain features of African music form the core of African American music and, by extension, of American popular music as a whole. *Call-and-response* forms, in which a lead singer and chorus alternate, the leader being allowed more freedom to elaborate his part, are a hallmark of African American musical traditions. In much African musicmaking *repetition* is regarded as an aesthetic strength, and many forms are constructed of relatively short phrases—often two to eight beats in length—that recur in a regular cycle. These short phrases are combined in various ways to produce music of great power and complexity. In African American music such repeated patterns are often called **riffs.**

The aesthetic interest of much African music lies in the *interlocking* of multiple repeating patterns to form dense **polyrhythmic** textures (textures in which many rhythms are going on at the same time). This technique is evident in African American styles such as funk music, particularly the work of James Brown, and the instrumental accompaniments ("beats") for contemporary rap recordings. One common West African rhythm pattern has generated many variants in the Americas, including the "hambone" riff popularized during the rock 'n' roll era by Bo Diddley, Johnny Otis, and Buddy Holly.

In contrast to the aesthetics of Western art music, in which a "clear" tone is the ideal, African singers and instrumentalists often make use of a wide palette of **timbres**. *Buzzing tones* are often created by attaching a rattling device to an instrument, and singers frequently use growling and humming effects, a technique that can also frequently be heard in African American genres such as blues, gospel, and jazz. In West African drumming traditions the lead or master drummer often plays the lowest-pitched drum in the group. This *emphasis on low-pitched sounds* may be a predecessor of the prominent role of the bass drum in Mississippi black fife-and-drum ensembles and of the "sonic boom bass" aesthetic in rap music (the *whoooomp!* created by heavily amplified low-frequency signals). Kurtis Blow, a rap performer and producer, described the rap producer's goal in terms of breaking car speakers, house speakers, and boom boxes, identifying this as "African music"!

The influence of African musical aesthetics and techniques on American popular music has been profound. The history of this influence, which we shall examine in some detail, reveals both the creativity of black musicians and the persistence of racism in the music business and American society as a whole. The origins of a distinctively American style of popular entertainment lie in the minstrel show of the mid-nineteenth century, in which white performers artificially darkened their skin and mimicked black music, dance, and dialect. In the early twentieth century African American ragtime and blues profoundly shaped the mainstream of American popular song. The "jazz age" of the 1920s and the "swing era" of the 1930s and 1940s involved the reworking of African American dance music so it would appeal to a predominantly white middle-class audience.

Although country music is typically identified as a "white" style, some of its biggest stars—for example, Ray Charles and Charley Pride—have been black, and the styles of influential country musicians such as Jimmie Rodgers, Hank Williams, and Willie Nelson were strongly influenced by African American music. One could cite many more examples of the influence of black music on the musical "mainstream" of America: 1950s rock 'n' roll was, in large part, rhythm & blues (**R&B**) music reworked for a predominantly white teen music market; the influence of 1960s soul music, rooted in black gospel and R&B, is heard in the vocal style of practically every pop singer, from Bonnie Raitt and Whitney Houston to Bruce Springsteen and Michael Jackson; the virtuoso guitar style of heavy metal owes a large debt to the urban blues of Muddy Waters and Howlin' Wolf; and rap music, based on African-derived musical and verbal traditions, continues to provide many white Americans with a vicarious experience of "listening in" on black urban culture.

We could say, then, that with every passing year American popular music has moved closer to the core aesthetic values and techniques of African music. Yet this way of phrasing the matter is somewhat misleading, for it directs attention away from the fact that African Americans are Americans, that the ancestors of black Americans arrived in the United States *before* the forebears of many white Americans. The complex history of interaction between European American and African

American styles, musicians, and audiences demonstrates the absurdity of racism, just as it attests to the unfortunate tenacity of racial thinking in America.

The Latin American Stream

As in the United States, musicians in Latin America developed a wide range of styles blending African music with the traditions of Europe (including colonial powers such as Spain, Portugal, and France). Caribbean, South American, and Mexican traditions have long influenced popular music in the United States.

The first Latin American style to have a major international impact was the Cuban *habanera*, an African-influenced variant of the European country-dance tradition that swept the United States and Europe in the 1880s. The characteristic *habanera* rhythm—an eight-beat pattern divided 3–3–2—influenced late nineteenth-century ragtime music and was an important part of what the great New Orleans pianist Ferdinand "Jelly Roll" Morton called the "Latin tinge" in American jazz.

The next wave of Latin American influence on the music of the United States came from Argentina. The *tango*, initially played by musicians in the capital city of Buenos Aires, was influenced by the Cuban *habanera* rhythm, Italian and Spanish songs, and the songs of *gauchos* (cowboys). The tango reached Europe in the 1910s, where it was popularized by Carlos Gardel, a film and recording star who is today regarded as a national hero in Argentina. In the United States the ballroom version of the tango, a couple dance featuring close contact between partners and an insistent rhythm, was popularized around 1914 by dance stars Irene and Vernon Castle (see Chapter 3). One of the first big tango stars was Rudolph Valentino, whose film persona somewhat indiscriminately mixed the stereotypes of the "Latin lover" and the proud and independent Middle Eastern sheik.

The next wave of Latin American musical influence was the *rumba*. The roots of the ballroom rumba style that became popular in the United States lie in 1920s Cuba. The rural *son*—a Cuban parallel of "country music"—moved to the city of Havana, where it was played by professional dance bands. These musicians created a more exciting style by adding rhythms from the *rumba*, an urban street drumming style strongly rooted in African traditions.

A "refined" version of *rumba*, developed by musicians working at tourist hotels in Cuba, was introduced to the world by Don Azpiazú and his Havana Casino Orchestra. Azpiazú's 1929 recording of "El Manicero" ("The Peanut Vendor") became a huge international hit. Within a few months of its release many dance orchestras in the United States had recorded their own versions of the song, a phenomenon later known as "covering" a hit song. The *rumba* reached a height of popularity in the United States during the 1930s and was succeeded by a series of Cuban-based ballroom dance fads, including the *mambo* (1940s) and *cha-cha-chá* (1950s).

Variants of Cuban-based music in the United States ranged from the exciting blend of modern jazz and *rumba* pioneered by Machito and Dizzy Gillespie in the 1940s to the tourist-oriented style performed by Desi Arnaz's orchestra on the *I Love Lucy* television show. The 1960s saw the emergence of *salsa*, a *rumba*-based style pioneered by Cuban and Puerto Rican migrants in New York City. The stars of *salsa* music include the great singer Celia Cruz and bandleader Tito Puente. In the 1980s Miami Sound Machine created a commercially successful blend of *salsa* and disco music, and "world beat" musicians such as Paul Simon and David Byrne began to experiment with traditional Afro-Cuban rhythms.

The Brazilian *samba* is another dance style strongly rooted in African music. The variant of samba that had the biggest influence in the United States was the *carioca*, a smooth style developed in Rio de Janeiro. The *carioca* was boosted in the 1940s by the meteoric career of Carmen Miranda, who appeared in a series of popular musical films. A cool, sophisticated style of Brazilian music called the *bossa nova* ("new trend") became popular in United States during the early 1960s, eventually spawning hit songs such as "The Girl from Ipanema" (1964).

Mexican music has long had a symbiotic relationship with styles north of the Rio Grande. At the end of the nineteenth century Mexican musicians visited the World's Columbian Exposition in Chicago (an early example of the world's fair) and later toured throughout the United States. The two best-known Mexican-derived styles today are *conjunto acordeon* ("accordion band") music, played in northern Mexico and Texas; and *mariachi* ("marriage") music, a staple of the Mexican tourist trade, performed by ensembles made up of guitars, violins, and trumpets. Country and western music has been influenced by Mexican styles since at least the 1930s. Mexican immigrants in California (*Chicanos*) have also played an important role in the development of rock music. This continuing influence is exemplified by Ritchie Valens's 1959 hit "La Bamba," based on a folk tune from Veracruz; the mixture of *salsa* and guitar-based rock music developed in the late 1960s by guitarist Carlos Santana; recordings of traditional Mexican songs by Linda Ronstadt; and the hard-rocking style of the Los Angeles–based band Los Lobos.

In this chapter we have discussed some unifying themes that run through the history of American popular music and described some of the diverse traditions that have contributed to this rich history. Now we want to get more specific, beginning with the nineteenth century, when the music business and the first distinctively American styles of popular music began to take shape.

CHAPTER TWO

"AFTER THE BALL"

Popular Music of the Nineteenth and Early Twentieth Centuries

In this chapter we turn our attention to popular music of the nineteenth and early twentieth centuries. This period saw the birth of minstrelsy, the first distinctively American form of popular culture; the rise of the modern music industry; rapid expansion of the audience for popular music; changes in technology that supported the dissemination of music to a national audience; and the emergence of song and dance music styles that were to influence profoundly the subsequent development of popular music in the United States.

THE MINSTREL SHOW

The *minstrel show*, the first form of musical and theatrical entertainment to be regarded by European audiences as distinctively American in character, featured mainly white performers who artificially blackened their skin and carried out parodies of African American music, dance, dress, and dialect. Today blackface minstrelsy is quite reasonably regarded with embarrassment or anger. Yet there is good reason to believe that the common interpretation of minstrelsy as an unvarying expression of white racism oversimplifies the diverse and sometimes ambiguous meanings that this form of popular culture held at different times and for various audiences. In any case, it would be difficult if not impossible to understand subsequent developments in the history of American popular music without some knowledge of the minstrel show.

Recent scholarship on the evolution of blackface minstrelsy suggests that this seminal form of American popular culture emerged from rough-and-tumble, predominantly working-class neighborhoods such as New York City's Seventh Ward, commercial urban zones where interracial interaction was common. From this point of view, early blackface performers were the first expression of a distinctively American popular culture, in which working-class white youth expressed their own sense of marginalization through an identification with African American cultural forms. This does not mean that minstrelsy cannot also be read as a projection of white racism—in fact, this interpretation makes even more sense in the later years of minstrelsy (1840s–1880s), when, as we shall see, the portrayal of black characters became more rigidly stereotypical. But, as is often the case with popular cultural forms, the meanings of blackface minstrelsy were neither fixed nor unambiguous.

Black characters had been played by white actors in British comic operas of the eighteenth century, some of which became popular in America before the Revolutionary War. Most of the songs sung by these characters were European in character and written in a childishly simple style; they often drew upon Irish or Scottish melodies ("exotic" styles available to English composers). George Washington Dixon was the first white performer to establish a wide reputation as a "blackface" entertainer. He made his New York debut in 1828, and two of the earliest "Ethiopian" songs to enjoy widespread popularity—"Long Tail Blue" and "Coal Black Rose"—were featured in his act. Like their English predecessors, they were simple melodies in a European mold.

Thomas Dartmouth Rice (1808–60), a white actor born into a poor family in New York's Seventh Ward, demonstrated the potential popularity (and profitability) of minstrelsy with the song "Jim Crow" (1829), which became the first international American song hit. Rice sang this song in blackface while imitating a dance step called the "cakewalk," an Africanized version of the European quadrille (a kind of square dance). Ironically, the cakewalk was first developed by slaves as a parody of the "refined" dance movements of the white slave owners. An ex-slave, interviewed in 1901, recalled the slave dances of the 1840s, the same period in which minstrelsy rose to mass popularity among whites:

> Us slaves watched the white folks' parties where the guests danced a minuet and then paraded in a grand march, with the ladies and gentlemen going different ways and then meeting again, arm in arm, and marching down the center together. Then we'd do it, too, but we used to mock 'em, every step. Sometimes the white folks noticed it, but they seemed to like it. I guess they thought we couldn't dance any better! (Levine 1977, p. 17)

One could scarcely imagine a more striking example of the ironies of racial relations in mid-nineteenth-century America—the slaves performing a delicious parody of European dance styles, while the whites watch with fascination, oblivious to the fact that they themselves are being ridiculed! (Beginning in the 1850s, a version of the cakewalk became popular among whites as a ballroom dance step. The rhythms of the music used to accompany the cakewalk exemplify the principle of **syncopation;** such "irregular" rhythms later became one important source of ragtime music, discussed later in this chapter.)

Soon after Rice introduced his Jim Crow character to New York in 1832, there was a veritable explosion of blackface performance in venues ranging from formal theaters to saloons, the latter often patronized by a racially mixed audience of urban workers and craftsmen. Contrary to much of what has been written about early minstrelsy, which suggests that the performers were exclusively white, recent research suggests that black and mixed-race performers were on view in most of the local "dives" that featured minstrel performances. The musical and linguistic heritage of early minstrelsy was just as mixed as its audience and practitioners. Scholars have suggested that the most likely inspiration for "Jim Crow" was not an African American song but an Irish folk tune that had subsequently been transformed into an English stage song. Although sheet music arrangements suggest that Rice's song bore only an indirect relationship to African American folk music, we have no direct evidence of the musical aspects of his stage performances.

"Daddy" Rice's Jim Crow character spoke and sang in a dialect that was partly based on preexisting white rural characters (such as the Kentucky rifleman, Davy Crockett) and partly on the variety of black and creole dialects heard by Rice as a youngster growing up by the docks in New York's Seventh Ward.

> Come, listen all you gals and boys, I'se just from Tuckyhoe
> I'm goin to sing a little song, My name's Jim Crow
> Weel about and turn about and do jis so
> Eb'ry time I weel about I jump Jim Crow

The Jim Crow character used this hybrid dialect—neither black nor white but something in between—to make fun of pretentious politicians and social elites, mangling their fancy words and introducing a satirical subtext that Rice's high-class targets found somewhat threatening:

> I make my infernal sensibilifications yieldify to de "Fox popular," as I tinks dey call de people's breath at de Walnut street Te-atre. . . . I am gwaing in short time to do like oder great hactors, publish my account ob men and manners in dese blessed States, and I trus I shall be inable to do dem as much justice as dey desarve, on account ob my debility to use falsificationority as de foreignificated deatrical ladies do. (Lhamon 1998, pp. 188–89)

This speech, from the introduction to Rice's 1835 autobiography *The Life of Jim Crow*, captures the subversive, trickster-like quality of the Jim Crow character, a quality lost sight of in the subsequent furor over minstrelsy's role in promulgating racist stereotypes. Arbiters of public taste and morals, including newspaper and magazine publishers, politicians, and the clergy, ridiculed minstrelsy as an indicator of the depraved state of the lower classes, and urged its rejection in favor of more refined (i.e., European-derived) forms of entertainment. For their part, the racially mixed, relatively impoverished audience for early minstrelsy must have found Jim Crow's lampooning of the pretensions and "falsificationority" of the "foreignificated deatrical ladies" ("high society" critics of minstrelsy) richly satisfying.

When Thomas Dartmouth Rice toured England in the 1830s, he became the first native-born American performer to export a type of music *perceived* abroad as quintessentially American in style and content. There is a terrible irony in the fact that the title of Rice's "Jim Crow"—arguably the origin point of American popular music—was soon transformed into a derogatory epithet for African Americans, and, from the 1870s until the 1950s, for the segregationist laws that excluded blacks from white theaters, cemeteries, hospitals, restaurants, and schools.

The next big "Ethiopian" song hit was "Zip Coon," published in New York in

Cover of the published sheet music for "Zip Coon." Foster Hall Collection.

1834. The song was in the familiar verse-chorus ballad form, its verses sprinkled with images of banjo playing, wild dancing, and barnyard animals. The chorus consisted of the nonsense syllables "Zip a duden duden duden zip a duden day" (direct ancestor of the song "Zip a Dee Doo Dah," featured in Walt Disney's 1947 cartoon *Song of the South*). Like "Jim Crow," the melody of "Zip Coon" is more closely related to Irish or Scottish than to African American song. The same melody was adopted by both black and white country fiddlers, rearranged, and given the title "Turkey in the Straw." This is a good example of the continually evolving relationship between popular and folk music in the nineteenth century. (Early minstrel songs still surface occasionally in popular music; for example, Michelle Shocked's medley entitled "Jump Jim Crow/Zip a Dee Doo Da" on her 1992 CD *Arkansas Traveler*).

From the 1840s through the 1880s blackface minstrelsy rose to become the predominant genre of popular culture in the United States. As the genre was reworked for mass appeal by theatrical entrepreneurs and promoters and transformed into the more formally organized and predictable "minstrel show," much of its original subversive quality was lost. As the scholar W. T. Lhamon Jr. has phrased it, "the early Jim Crow was not the late Jim Crow. Jim Crow went from fond alliance to hateful segregation as the Civil War approached and then as the Nadir replaced Reconstruction" (Lhamon 1998, p. 191). As the fires of white racism were stoked, first by the escalating conflict between the states and then by postbellum fears of black backlash and economic competition, minstrelsy both reflected and helped to promulgate the national obsession with symbols of racial difference. It was during this period that the most pernicious stereotypes of black people—the old faithful slave (a.k.a. the "good negro") and the big-city knife-toting dandy (the "bad negro")—became enduring images in mainstream American popular culture, disseminated by an emerging entertainment industry and patronized by a predominantly white mass audience.

Beginning in 1843 with the first appearance of the Virginia Minstrels (led by the white banjo virtuoso Dan Emmett), more lengthy performances featuring a standardized group of performers became popular. This became the classic minstrel show, organized around a sequence of more or less independent sketches and songs, and featuring characters such as Mr. Interlocutor, a lead performer who sang and provided patter between acts, and Bones and Tambo, who sat at either end of the line of performers.

By the mid-nineteenth century minstrel songs had become an important influence on the mainstream of American popular song. Many of these "plantation songs" were very successful as sheet music, and they were a dominant force in the development of nineteenth-century popular music. Some of these later minstrel tunes do show evidence of African American influence, particularly in their irregular syncopated rhythms, but there is good reason to believe that few minstrel performers were able to capture the rhythmic and textural complexity of the black musical traditions they purported to represent. The typical minstrel song of the early 1840s was sung by one member of the troupe, accompanied by a fiddle, one or more banjos, a tambourine, and a pair of rib bones held in one hand and clacked together to create a syncopated rhythmic pattern.[1] Despite the adoption of instruments used by some black musicians, this type of performance still had little to do with African American musical traditions of the American South. Nonetheless, minstrel troupes competed with one another on the basis of their attention to "authentic" details of southern black culture.

Although the biggest celebrities of minstrelsy were white during the form's rise to national popularity, African American performers continued to appear in

---

1. Examples of minstrel performance, reenacted in the early 1980s, can be heard on *Early Minstrel Show* (New World Records NW 338).

minstrel shows. In a practice that shows the arbitrariness of social distinctions based on race, light-skinned African American minstrels had to apply blackface in order to prepare themselves for their stage roles as "authentic negroes." This development adds yet one more twist to the complex and often ironic feedback between African American and European American cultures. In this later stage of the evolution of minstrelsy, a parody of white culture, initially created by African slaves and later incorporated into a popular theatrical genre that developed in urban working-class neighborhoods, was in turn propagated by negroes whose physical appearance apparently did not match white stereotypes of blackness. We might cite this as an example of the importance of popular culture as a key to understanding the development of racial identity in the United States, including contemporary notions of whiteness and blackness. Suffice it for now to say that in this regard as in others, minstrelsy left a lasting imprint on American popular consciousness.

In the formation and rise of the nineteenth-century minstrel show we encounter many of the basic themes that will concern us throughout our survey of the history of American popular music. Minstrelsy arose during the 1830s as an expression of a predominantly white urban youth culture, which sought to express its independence through the appropriation of black style. As minstrelsy became a mass phenomenon in the decades just before and after the American Civil War, its form became routinized, and its portrayal of black characters more rigidly stereotyped. This basic pattern, in which a new genre of music arises within a marginalized community and then moves into the mainstream of mass popular culture, in the process losing much of the rebellious energy that gave rise to it in the first place, will be encountered many times in this book.

Minstrel troupes toured the United States constantly from the 1840s until the 1870s, helping to create an embryonic national popular culture. Minstrels borrowed from the diverse traditions they encountered, adopting aspects of English, Irish, German, and African music, dialect, and dance and continually crossing the boundaries between folk and popular, rural and urban, southern and northern culture. The minstrel show is also the direct ancestor of *vaudeville*, a kind of variety show that became the dominant form of popular entertainment in late nineteenth- and early twentieth-century America (see Chapters 3 and 4). And while the mass success of the blackface minstrel show doubtless helped to reinforce racist attitudes among whites, minstrelsy also established a mobile performance tradition within which influential black musicians such as W. C. Handy, Ma Rainey, and Bessie Smith could later flourish (see Chapter 5).

THE FIRST POP SONGWRITER: STEPHEN FOSTER

Stephen Collins Foster (1826–64), who composed around two hundred songs during the 1840s, 1850s, and early 1860s, is regarded as the first important composer of American popular song. He was probably the first person in the United States to make his living as a full-time professional songwriter, surviving on the fees and royalties generated by sales of sheet music for songs such as "Oh! Susanna," "Old Folks at Home," "My Old Kentucky Home, Good Night," "Jeanie with the Light Brown Hair," and "Beautiful Dreamer." His earliest musical experiences, growing

Advertising lithographs for minstrel (c. 1879) and vaudeville (1899) shows. Courtesy Library of Congress.

up on the western frontier near Pittsburgh, were dominated by the sentimental song tradition, derived from England and considered a mark of gentility by upwardly mobile Americans. Foster also knew and incorporated into his work the various song styles popular in midcentury America: ballads, Italian light opera, Irish and German songs, and minstrel songs.

LISTENING AND ANALYSIS   "JEANIE WITH THE LIGHT BROWN HAIR"

Jeanie with the Light Brown Hair is an example of Foster's sentimental "Irish" style, strongly reminiscent of the songs of Thomas Moore (see Chapter 1). The most typical realization of this song would have featured a high male tenor, employing a slight Irish accent. "Jeanie" is also a prototypical example of a form that would become increasingly common in American popular music: the four-section song with an AABA melodic structure. The A sections begin identically, although their endings vary slightly (this is why we have chosen to call them A^1, A^2, and A^3; see the listening chart). The B section introduces a new melody and chords and acts as a musical "bridge" that leads us to the final A section. This basic structure, with its economical and easily comprehended balance between repetition and variation, was to become one of the most important popular song forms of the early twentieth century.

Forms such as AABA are not just technical features or blueprints for the composer. They also become the basis for listening habits. Once you have learned to hear a kind of song form, you expect things to happen in a certain order. The *arrangement* of a song—that is, the way in which the song is actually presented in a particular performance—may delay things or speed them up. A performer or arranger may even vary the order of the sections to create a certain effect. But these variations make sense only against the background of the listener's learned expectations.

The melody of "Jeanie" contains hints of its origin in Irish popular song. In melodic terms, there is plenty of conjunct (that is, step-by-step) movement, which is contrasted with dramatic leaps up or down. See if you can identify the large melodic leaps as you listen: "*I dream of Jeanie with the light* [downward leap →] *brown hair, Borne like a* [upward leap →] *vapor on the summer air.*"

LISTENING CHART "JEANIE WITH THE LIGHT BROWN HAIR"

Music and lyrics by Stephen Foster; published 1854

FORM	LYRICS	DESCRIPTIVE COMMENTS
A¹	*I dream of Jeanie with the light brown hair . . .*	Here is the main melody, meant to "hook" your ear.
A²	*I see her tripping where the bright streams play . . .*	The melody repeats, with new words and a different ending.
B	*Many were the wild notes her merry voice would pour . . .*	New melody, new chords, and new words.
A³	*I dream of Jeanie with the light brown hair . . .*	This final A section has a new ending, which produces an effect of finality (this is called a **cadence**).

[The form repeats itself, with new words.]

"Jeanie with the Light Brown Hair," a product of the nineteenth-century genteel song tradition, reemerged onto the Hit Parade during World War II, performed by several swing era dance bands. And it was still well-enough remembered in the 1960s to lend its name—or, to be more precise, a pun built on its first line—to a popular television series, *I Dream of Jeannie.*

Although Foster was not the wealthiest popular songwriter of the nineteenth century, he was the most influential. He was a master at creating the simple but compelling combinations of melody and text that later popular composers would refer to as "hooks" (i.e., the basic musical or verbal idea that "hooks" the listener's ear). Foster's compositions were heard almost everywhere—in saloons, theater productions, variety shows, and band concerts. His biggest hit, a plantation song called "Old Folks at Home," sold some 100,000 copies of sheet music during the year it was published (1851). On a per capita basis, this is equal to a million-seller in today's terms. Some of Foster's songs became part of American oral tradition, passed from generation to generation without the aid of musical notation.

Foster's success was supported by a number of social and technological factors. Minstrel troupes performed his songs on their tours, popularizing them across the country. In addition, the sheet music publishing business expanded during the mid-nineteenth century, fueled in part by the rapid growth of public music education, which allowed many more people to read and play the simple piano arrangements that accompanied popular songs. This trend was also encouraged by expanded domestic production of cheap pianos. The piano became a standard feature of the middle-class parlor—a cozy room outfitted with sofas, paintings, books, kerosene lamps and candles, and, if the family in question could afford it, a piano or reed organ. The parlor was a center of family life, a place for entertainment, conversation, and courting.

Foster's success as a "hit maker" occurred well before the rise of electronic mass media and was dependent on the ability of the public to read and perform the arrangements of his songs published on sheet music and in songbooks. During this period, people often performed music in their homes. Amateur piano playing was widely considered a female specialization, an attractive feature in a prospective wife. The piano remained a center of domestic music making in the United States until the 1920s, when commercial radio was introduced.

Foster's life—which ended in obscurity and poverty at the age of thirty-seven—illustrates the state of copyright enforcement in the mid-nineteenth century. His first success, the plantation song "Oh! Susanna" (1847), was sold outright to a music publisher for one hundred dollars. The publisher subsequently made thousands of dollars from the worldwide hit, but no more money for the music went to Foster. This was a typical situation, for the law covered the rights of music firms but not those of the composers of songs bought by the firms. A study of various arrangements of "Oh! Susanna" published between 1848 and 1851 indicates the ways in which numerous publishers might profit from a single song. "Susanna" was published sometimes as a minstrel song but more often in wordless piano arrangements in the style of popular dance steps, including the quadrille, the quickstep, and the polka (the latest fashionable dance from Paris and London). All in all, twenty different arrangements appeared during the three-year period, copyrighted by eleven different publishers.

DANCE MUSIC AND BRASS BANDS

From its very inception, American popular music has been closely bound up with the dance and with the varied social functions of dancing, including courtship, entertainment, celebration of community, and the communication of ethnic and class identity. The earliest examples of published dance music in the United States were modeled strongly on styles popular in England, as was the case with popular song. Until the early twentieth century, social dancing among white Americans was dominated by offshoots of the contradance or country dance tradition (in which teams of dancers formed geometric figures such as lines, circles, or squares) and by dances such as the waltz, mazurka, schottische, and polka, performed by couples. Many of these dances were originally modeled on the traditions of rural peasants, although the music and movements often bore little resemblance to the folk traditions from which they sprang. The adoption of country dances by the urban elite was an aspect of the romantic fascination with rural themes that we have already described in connection with the pleasure gardens (see Chapter 1).

The typical setting for dancing among the upper classes (and the upwardly mobile) was the ball, organized around a program of preselected music played by an orchestra and arranged to accompany a specific sequence of dances. A typical dance program of the late nineteenth century might include a waltz, a mazurka or polka, and a cotillion, itself a sequence of dances during which couples would continuously exchange partners. This succession of dances would be overseen by a dance master, who called out the sequences of movements, sometimes referring to a book of instructions called a dance manual.

The Grand Ball, originally modeled on the aristocratic occasions of European royalty, provided an important public venue for Americans desiring to demonstrate their refinement and knowledge of high culture. These rules for male dress, published in a dance instruction book in 1867, give some sense of the close relationship between ballroom dancing and public demonstrations of gentility:

> The dress should be studiously neat, leaving no impression other than that of a well-dressed gentleman. Black dress coat, black or white vest, black trousers, white necktie, patent leather boots or pumps and black or white stockings, white kid gloves, hair well-dressed. Coats of fancy character and colors, velvet collars, and metal buttons are not proper for the opera or ball. (Stephenson and Iaccarino 1980, p. 31)

In general, ballroom dancing focused more on uniformity and restraint than improvisation or the expression of emotion. Another nineteenth-century dance manual suggests that

> the upper part of the body should be slightly inclined forward, the hips backward—the forward inclination just enough to cause a tendency in the heels to rise from the floor; the head erect, legs straight, arms hanging by the sides, elbows very slightly turned outward so that the arms will present gently curved lines to the front. (Dodworth 1885, p. 24)

As the nineteenth century progressed, there was a shift away from the more formal dances based on the contradance and toward an increased emphasis on couple dancing, a change that was regarded with alarm by some dance masters (perhaps because it threatened to put them out of a job!). Even the **waltz,** which first rose to popularity in the United States in the 1820s, was initially regarded as an "indecorous exhibition" of intimacy between men and women, and a threat to public morality. By the end of the century, however, the waltz, with its lilting triple-meter accompaniment, circular movements, and smooth, graceful lines, had become the ultimate symbol of sophistication and romance.

As was the case with other adopted European customs, local variants of the Grand Ball tradition in America reflected the tastes and cultural values of particular communities. Uniquely American versions of the ball included the rough-and-ready miners' balls of the California Gold Rush—often accompanied by drinking and general rowdiness—and the slave balls held on southern plantations, which satirized the elite dances of the white slave owners (recall our discussion of minstrelsy earlier in this chapter). In addition, occupational and ethnic groups in big cities such as New York held their own imitations of the elite grand balls.

Throughout the nineteenth century there was a continual feedback between urban and rural, "high-class" and "low-class" dance styles. Urban professional musicians arranged folk dances and their associated music for mass consumption, and some of the popular songs published by big New York City music companies were adopted into rural dance traditions such as the square dance. (Minstrel songs such as "Turkey in the Straw" and Stephen Foster's "Camptown Races" are good examples of the latter process.) The diversity of American popular dance was reinforced by waves of European immigrants, who brought distinctive dance music styles with them. Some of these were maintained solely in ethnic enclaves, while others circulated into the popular mainstream. And the mass influence of African American dance, which began in the 1830s with the cakewalk steps performed by white minstrels, intensified, rising to become the dominant force in American popular dance during the first few decades of the twentieth century (see Chapter 3).

From the Civil War through the 1910s *brass band concerts* were one of the most important musical aspects of American life. Although military bands made up of brass instruments (e.g., trumpets, cornets, trombones, and tubas) had been around since the birth of the United States, they spread rapidly during and after the Civil War (1861–65). One conservative estimate suggests that at one point the Union Army had five hundred bands and nine thousand players, to which must be added the probably only marginally smaller number of musicians who served in the Confederate Army. While a number of these regimental bands continued to flourish after the war, many of the musicians who were decommissioned formed bands in their home communities. In addition, many colleges and high schools formed bands during this period. By 1889 a journalist wrote that there were over ten thousand brass bands in the United States. Almost every town of note had a park with a band shell in it, and bands were formed in association with city governments, schools, churches, and business enterprises. As one contemporary observer wrote in 1878, "a town without its brass band is as much in need of sympathy as a church without a choir. The spirit of a place is recognized in its band" (Camus 1986, p. 133).

The brass band movement of the late nineteenth century drew energy from the interaction of patriotism and popular culture, and from the growing force of American nationalism. The lion's share of a band's repertoire generally consisted of patriotic marches, a type of music that in the wake of the Civil War became an important symbol of the unity of the nation. Marches stirred the emotions and were used to foster public support for the assertion of American military and economic power overseas (including the Panama Canal project and the Spanish American War of 1898). Then, as today, brass bands are associated with national holidays such as the Fourth of July, and their music often holds a special significance for those who have served in the armed forces during times of war. Many bands, however, also played arrangements of the popular sheet music hits of the day, music for dance styles such as the cakewalk, polka, and waltz, and adaptations of classical music. This ability to move between patriotic music and the popular styles of the day reinforced the brass band's role as a community institution.

The most popular bandleader from the 1890s through World War I was John Philip Sousa (1854–1932), popularly known as America's "March King." The son of a trombonist in the U.S. Marine Band, Sousa eventually became its conductor and later formed a "commercial" concert band, which toured widely in America and Europe. This band, arguably the first American pop "supergroup," made two dozen hit phonograph recordings between 1895 and 1918 (Sousa himself despised "canned

John Philip Sousa (center) in uniform as leader of the U.S. Marine Band. Courtesy Library of Congress.

music," and many of the recordings made under his name were actually directed by Arthur Pryor, who later became the most prolific conductor of brass band music). The Sousa band's repertoire included stirring patriotic marches by Sousa such as "El Capitan," "The Washington Post," and "The Stars and Stripes Forever" (the official march of the United States), and popular songs such as "In the Good Old Summer Time," complete with vocals. Sousa toured constantly, and the appearance of his band, with more than fifty members, in cities and towns across the country created a sensation that could only be surpassed by a presidential "whistlestop" tour. In addition to his activities as a bandleader, conductor, and composer, Sousa was one of the first musicians to negotiate royalty payments (based on a percentage of total sales of his compositions) with publishers, and he was an important advocate of copyright reform.

"Business bands"—touring bands not connected to government institutions— were an important part of the American music business. Italian concert bands, led by charismatic conductors, were among the most popular groups of the 1890s. A newspaper headline that appeared in New York City in 1899 described the excitement and athletic appeal of an Italian brass band as follows: "WOMEN ON TABLES IN HYPNOTIC FRENZY. Broadway pleased by Exhibition of Athletic Leadership" (Schwartz 1975, p. 216). Although we do not usually think of brass bands as purveyors of popular music, the American passion for bands was a truly national phenomenon and a powerful shaper of musical taste during the late nineteenth century. The brass band tradition also contributed to later developments in popular music, particularly the development of jazz, as we shall see in Chapter 3.

THE BIRTH OF TIN PAN ALLEY

By the end of the nineteenth century the American music publishing business, formerly distributed among a number of cities on the eastern seaboard and in the Midwest, had become centered in New York City. The established publishers, who had made their fortunes in classical music and genteel parlor songs, were, from around 1885 on, challenged by smaller companies specializing in the more exciting popular songs performed in dance halls, beer gardens, and theaters.

These new publishing firms—many of them founded by Jewish immigrants from Eastern Europe—had offices in a section of lower Manhattan, a dense hive of small rooms with pianos where composers and "song pluggers" produced and promoted popular songs. This stretch of 28th Street became known as *Tin Pan Alley*, a term that evoked the clanging sound of many pianos simultaneously playing songs in a variety of keys and tempos.

The 1890s saw the rise of the modern American music business, an industry aimed at providing "hits" for an expanding urban mass market. For the first time, a single song could sell more than a million copies. Sheet music sold for between twenty-five and sixty cents, and the wholesale value of printed music in the United States more than tripled between 1890 and 1909. Publishing firms such as T. B. Harms and Witmark and Sons hired teams of composers and lyricists to crank out new songs.

Popular songs, printed as sheet music, were promoted by song pluggers, whose job it was to promote a given company's product. Sheet music was sold by specialized music outlets, by mail order houses such as Sears, Roebuck, and Co., and in large department stores such as Macy's and Montgomery Ward. A song plugger's typical workday might begin with a visit to a big department store, where he would deliver bundles of sheet music and sing the company's latest songs over and over in the store to get customers' attention. It would typically end late at night in a saloon, where he might perform from his table, or backstage at a theater, trying to convince a popular singer to adopt one of the company's songs into his act. The promotional strategies of the music publishers were evidently quite successful: by 1910 annual sales of sheet music in the United States had reached thirty million copies.

By the turn of the century *vaudeville*, a popular theatrical form descended from music hall shows and minstrelsy, had become the most important medium for popularizing Tin Pan Alley songs. Unlike minstrel shows, where the entire cast remained onstage for the whole performance, vaudeville shows typically consisted of a series of performances—singers, acrobats, comedians, jugglers, dancers, animal acts, and so on—presented one after the other without any overarching narrative theme. Every city in the country had at least one large vaudeville theater, and the music publishing firms sent representatives out along the theater circuit to make sure that performers lived up to the terms of their contracts and that local music stores had a sufficient stock of sheet music for the songs being promoted. By 1915 more than half a million dollars was being paid every year to vaudeville performers for song boosting.

Most performers had to provide their own transportation, lodging, costumes, songs, and arrangements; they were dependent on the whims of powerful booking agents, to whom they paid substantial fees. Racial segregation meant that there was a separate chain of theaters for black performers and audiences, and a separate booking agency, the Theatre Owners Booking Agency (TOBA, known informally as "Tough On Black Asses").

Tin Pan Alley songs—their forms, themes, and performance styles—were to dominate the mainstream American music industry for almost seventy years. The principles of popular songwriting established by Stephen Foster in the 1840s were further developed by Tin Pan Alley composers. The romantic parlor song remained popular, as did "Irish" and waltz songs. One of the most popular composers of the early Tin Pan Alley period was Paul Dresser (1857–1906), who wrote a series of sentimental and nostalgic songs, including "The Letter That Never Came" (1885) and "On the Banks of the Wabash, Far Away" (1899; later adopted as the official state song of Indiana). Harry von Tilzer (1872–1946), sometimes referred to as the "Daddy of Popular Song," was another successful turn-of-the-century songwriter; his big hits included "A Bird in a Gilded Cage" (1900) and "I Want a Girl (Just Like the Girl That Married Dear Old Dad)" (1911). Von Tilzer was a calculating composer: one of his hints for aspiring songwriters was to keep the tunes to a limited range so that even a baby could hum them. The songs of Dresser and von Tilzer represent the commercial peak of the nineteenth-century parlor song.

"Plantation songs," descended from the minstrel song tradition, were also popular. One of the best-known and most successful composers of plantation songs was James A. Bland (1854–1911), the first successful black songwriter. An ex-minstrel show performer from a middle-class background, Bland wrote some seven hundred songs, including "Carry Me Back to Old Virginny" (published in 1878, for a long time the official state song of Virginia) and "Oh, Dem Golden Slippers" (published 1879). He became popular in Europe, where he performed concerts for large fees. It has been argued that Bland's plantation songs featured a somewhat more dignified portrayal of American blacks than the crude "Ethiopian" songs but it is not easy to distinguish his lyrics of "In the Evening by the Moonlight" (1880) from those written by other composers of plantation songs:

> *All dem happy times we used to hab' will ne'er return again,*
> *Eb'rything was den so merry gay and bright,*
> *And I neber will forget it, when our daily toil was ober,*
> *How we sang in de ebening by de moonlight.*

In stylistic terms also, Bland's songs are similar to those of his white contemporaries. Although Bland has been criticized by some later observers for pandering to white misconceptions about blacks and lionized by others for his supposed championing of "authentic" African American music, the real situation is more complex. Bland, the product of a comfortable middle-class home, was determined to achieve the same level of economic success as his white contemporaries. Like many other black musicians who have sought to gain access to mass markets, he had to work through the imagery of blackness already established in mainstream popular music.

LISTENING AND ANALYSIS "AFTER THE BALL"

"After the Ball," published in 1892, was the first "mega-hit" pop song, eventually selling over five million copies in sheet music. The song's history reveals certain facets of the music business around the turn of the century. Its composer, Charles K. Harris (1867–1930) was a self-taught banjo player from Wisconsin who could not write down music; he dictated his songs to a professional musician. Aware that his new song needed boosting by a popular performer, Harris paid a well-known singer in a traveling theater production to incorporate "After the Ball" into his performance. It soon became the most popular part of the play, and audiences requested that it be repeated several times during each performance.

"After the Ball" became even more popular after it was performed by John Philip Sousa's band at the World's Columbian Exposition in Chicago (1893). The M. Witmark Company, a powerful music publishing firm that had built its success publishing plantation songs, offered Harris ten thousand dollars for all rights to the song. Harris declined the offer, published the song himself, and was soon clearing around twenty-five thousand dollars a month. His success demonstrated that popular music could be a lucrative business and encouraged young entrepreneurs to set up their own publishing firms during the 1890s. These small-scale enterprises, many of which were wiped out during subsequent economic depressions, were the predecessors of the independent record labels that were to play so important a role in twentieth-century popular music.

"After the Ball" tells a tragic (if, from our viewpoint, rather unbelievable) story of mistaken identity, misplaced jealousy, and lost love. "After the Ball" is clearly related to the ballad tradition (see Chapter 1) in its employment of a series of verses, sung over a fixed melody, to tell a story with a beginning, middle, and end. As is the case in some ballads, each verse of "After the Ball" is followed by a **chorus**,[2] a contrasting section consisting of a fixed melody and lyric, repeated exactly each time around. Looked at as a whole, the large-scale structure of the piece thus consists of three main sections or **strophes**, each made up of a verse and a chorus.

Although its basic verse-and-chorus structure is ultimately derived from the ballad tradition, the degree of emphasis placed on the chorus in "After the Ball" positions it as a predecessor of twentieth-century popular songwriting techniques. The chorus announces the title of the song not once, but twice, helping

---

2. The chorus is also often called a refrain. To avoid possible confusion, we are reserving use of the term "refrain" in this book for Tin Pan Alley song forms in which the refrain constitutes a main, independent part of the piece. See the discussion of Tin Pan Alley song in Chapter 4.

to embed it in the listener's memory; it both foreshadows and summarizes the sentimental message of the song; and it is, in melodic terms, the catchiest part of the song, cleverly designed to lodge itself in the audience's consciousness. "After the Ball" draws upon the centuries-old storytelling techniques of Euro-American balladry, but it is also a perfect example of a pop song with a catchy "hook," crafted to hold a mass audience's attention and to generate millions of dollars in profit. In addition, "After the Ball" is a **waltz**, one of the most popular dance styles of the late nineteenth century. The song's mass appeal can only have been boosted by the fact that it was often included in the musical programs of ballroom dance orchestras.

LISTENING CHART   "AFTER THE BALL"

Music and lyrics by Charles K. Harris; published 1892

FORM	LYRICS	DESCRIPTIVE COMMENTS
Strophe 1		
Verse		
A	*A little maiden climbed an old man's knee,*	This is the opening **verse**,
	Begged for the story, "Do, Uncle, please.	designed to introduce the
A'	*Why are you single; why live alone?*	melody and chords and
	Have you no babies; have you no home?"	interest us in the story
B	*"I had a sweetheart, years, years ago;*	to follow.
	Where she is now, pet, you will soon know.	
A'	*List to the story, I'll tell it all,*	
	I believed her faithless, after the ball."	
Chorus		
C	*After the ball is over, after the break of morn—*	This is the **chorus (C)**, with new
	After the dancers' leaving; after the stars are gone;	chords and melody, and new
	Many a heart is aching, if you could read them all;	lyrics that begin and end with
	Many the hopes that have vanished after the ball.	the title words of the song.
Strophe 2		
Verse		
A	*"Bright lights were flashing in the grand ballroom,*	Back to the **A** melody, with new
	Softly the music, playing sweet tunes.	lyrics carrying the story forward.
A'	*There came my sweetheart, my love, my own—*	
	'I wish some water; leave me alone.'	
B	*When I returned, dear, there stood a man,*	
	Kissing my sweetheart as lovers can.	
A'	*Down fell the glass, pet, broken, that's all,*	
	Just as my heart was after the ball."	
Chorus		
C	*After the ball is over, after the break of morn—*	Another **chorus**; note that the
	After the dancers' leaving; after the stars are gone;	lyrics and music are repeated
	Many a heart is aching, if you could read them all;	exactly.
	Many the hopes that have vanished after the ball.	

Strophe 3		
Verse		
(as before)	*"Long years have passed, child, I've never wed,*	Back to the **A** music, with
	True to my lost love, though she is dead.	lyrics completing the story and
	She tried to tell me, tried to explain;	revealing the narrative twist.
	I would not listen, pleadings were vain.	
	One day a letter came from that man,	
	He was her brother, the letter ran.	
	That's why I'm lonely, no home at all;	
	I broke her heart, pet, after the ball."	
Chorus	*After the ball is over, after the break of morn—*	The final chorus **(C)**.
	After the dancers' leaving; after the stars are gone;	
	Many a heart is aching, if you could read them all;	
	Many the hopes that have vanished after the ball.	

THE RAGTIME CRAZE, 1896–1918

While songs like "After the Ball," derived from European musical traditions, dominated the popular mainstream of late nineteenth-century America, this same period also saw the intensification of African American musical influence, a trend best represented by **ragtime**. Ragtime music emerged in the 1880s, its popularity peaking in the decade after the turn of the century. In some regards the ragtime craze was a descendent of minstrelsy, in which white musicians used simplified elements of African American musical styles to spice up their performances. On the other hand, the ragtime style also represented a more intimate engagement with African American musical techniques and values, largely due to the increasing—if always unequal—involvement of black songwriters and performers in the music industry (see Box 2.1).

Although it is impossible to pinpoint the precise origins of ragtime, it is generally agreed that the word itself derives from the African American term "to rag," meaning to enliven a piece of music by shifting melodic accents onto the offbeats (a technique known as **syncopation**). This technique of playing "against the beat," when done competently, actually has the effect of intensifying the beat and creating rhythmic momentum. It has been suggested that the basic patterns of ragtime music were transferred from the banjo, a stringed instrument developed by slave musicians from African prototypes during the early colonial period. Ragtime was also influenced by Latin American rhythms such as the Cuban *habanera* (see Chapter 1) and by marching band music, which contributed the regular "oom-pah" bass so common in ragtime pieces. During the height of its popularity, from the late 1890s until the end of World War I, ragtime music was played by every imaginable type of ensemble: dance bands, brass bands, country string bands, symphony orchestras, banjo and mandolin ensembles, and, in the so-called classic ragtime style, by solo pianists.

The first piece of sheet music to bear the term "rag" was the unfortunately titled "All Coons Look Alike to Me," composed by the African American songwriter Ernest Hogan and published (complete with racist caricatures on the cover) in 1886. The so-called coon song, popular among white audiences from the 1890s until World

Box 2.1 Scott Joplin and "Maple Leaf Rag"

The best-known composer of ragtime music was an African American composer and pianist named <u>Scott Joplin,</u> born in Texas in 1868. He began to play piano around the town of Texarkana during his teens and received instruction in classical music theory from a German teacher. His first regular job as a pianist was in a cafe in St. Louis. Like other black pianists of the time, Joplin developed a "ragging" piano style, improvising around the themes of popular songs and marches in a syncopated style. In 1893 he attended the World's Columbian Exposition in Chicago, where he heard influential black ragtime pianists such as Tom Turpin and "Plunk" Henry (and may well have also heard John Philip Sousa's band performing "After the Ball"). While in Chicago he widened his knowledge of ragtime style and started a brass band. The following year, Joplin moved to Sedalia, Missouri, where he was to write most of his famous compositions. Between 1895 and 1915 Joplin composed many of the classics of the ragtime repertoire and helped to popularize the style through his piano arrangements, published as sheet music. Joplin's rags were also widely heard on player pianos. These elaborate mechanical devices were activated by piano rolls—spools of paper with punched holes that controlled the movement of the piano's keys.

Scott Joplin's first successful piece was "Maple Leaf Rag" (1898), named after the Maple Leaf social club in Sedalia, where he often played. The piece was published in 1899 and became a huge hit, spreading Joplin's fame to Europe and beyond. Other ragtime piano pieces had been published earlier—ironically, the first was "Mississippi Rag" by the white songwriter and bandleader William Krell (1897). But it was "Maple Leaf" that started a nationwide craze for syncopated music. An example of the piece, performed by Joplin himself, was recorded in 1911 on a piano roll (included on *The Smithsonian Collection of Classic Jazz*).

The form and style of "Maple Leaf Rag" are typical of "classic" ragtime. The piece is carefully composed, and Joplin plays it more or less exactly as written. "Maple Leaf" consists of a succession of four distinct themes, presented in the order AABBACCDD. This type of form is common in marches

Scott Joplin c. 1911. Frank Driggs Collection.

and shows the interrelationship of the two genres. The right hand (treble) part plays **syncopated** ("offbeat" or "staggered") rhythms against the regular bass part played by the left hand. This is a typical feature of piano ragtime style. The bass rhythm is derived from marching band music and a popular ballroom dance called the two-step. Most of the rhythmic interest comes from the interplay of the two hands. Although the writing down of these patterns tended to neaten things up, the African principle of pitting rhythms against one another was preserved in piano ragtime. Many jazz pianists took Joplin's composition and brought it back into oral tradition, treating it as the basis for extended, rhythmically complex improvisations (listen, for example to Ferdinand "Jelly Roll" Morton's version of "Maple Leaf Rag," also on *The Smithsonian Collection of Classic Jazz*).

War I, was usually accompanied by a simplified version of the syncopated rhythms of ragtime piano music. Most of these songs continued the older tradition of using a dialect purporting to be typical of black Americans' speech. "Coon songs," regarded as comic by white audiences, helped to promulgate the stereotypes established in the minstrel show during one of the worst periods of racism in American history (see the conclusion to this chapter).

Other ragtime-influenced songs were less derogatory in content, although they also owed less to the style developed by Joplin and other black pianists than to the popular craze for march songs by composers such as George M. Cohan (1878–1942), author of "You're a Grand Old Flag" (1907). A few of these tunes can still be heard today, including "A Hot Time in the Old Town Tonight" (Theodore Metz, 1896) and "Bill Bailey, Won't You Please Come Home?" (H. Cannon, 1902).

The growing market for ragtime songs at the turn of the century suggests a continuation of the white fascination with African American music first evinced in minstrelsy. In general, Tin Pan Alley composers simply added syncopated rhythms and ersatz black dialects to spice up otherwise bland popular tunes. The idea, then as now, was to create songs novel enough to stimulate the audience's interest but not so radical that they required a great deal of work on the listener's part. Just as the songs performed by blackface minstrels were largely European in style, most popular ragtime songs were vigorous march-style songs with a few "irregular" rhythms added for effect.

Racial imagery—the black "other" evoked in music and dialect and visually portrayed on the covers of sheet music—became complexly intertwined with social class and generational identity. Morality plays about the degeneracy of poor whites—say, the descent of a young woman into drug addiction and prostitution—often used ragtime (and association with blacks in general) as an index of depravity. Logically enough, some young whites appear to have associated with ragtime as a means of rebelling against the cultural conservatism of their parents and other authority figures, a pattern that became even more prominent during the so-called jazz age of the 1920s and the rock 'n' roll era of the 1950s. Ragtime is an interesting example of the complex crosscurrents of American musical history: rooted in the mastery of European musical forms by talented black musicians, the style circulated across boundaries of race, class, region, and generation and was put to different uses by various communities.

THE RISE OF THE PHONOGRAPH

The phonograph was invented in 1877 by Thomas Alva Edison and, at around the same time, by a French inventor named Charles Cros. These early machines transformed the energy of sound waves into physical impressions on a foil- or wax-coated cylinder, which could then be used to reproduce the original sounds. In 1887 Emile Berliner developed the flat gramophone disc, which was more durable, cheaper to produce, and easier to store than wax cylinders. In the 1890s the first "nickelodeons"—machines that played the latest hits for a nickel—were set up in public places. (These machines later became known as "jukeboxes.") By the turn of the century the American market in phonograph discs was firmly dominated by two companies, Columbia Records (formed in 1887) and the Victor Talking Machine Company (1901). In 1902 the twelve-inch shellac disc was introduced. Played at a standard speed of 78 r.p.m. (revolutions per minute), these discs could hold up to four minutes of music. In 1904 the double-sided disc was introduced. This was the standard type of record issued for sale in the United States until $33\frac{1}{3}$ r.p.m. long-playing discs and 45 r.p.m. singles were introduced in the late 1940s (see Chapter 7).

The first phonographs were largely regarded as toys and mnemonic devices, useful for preserving the voices of family members and presidents, but not for the commercial distribution of music. The dramatic commercial possibilities of sound recording were first revealed by the famous singer Enrico Caruso (1873–1921), who recorded a series of opera arias in London in 1902. The American rights to these recordings were bought by the Victor Company, who released the discs in 1904, after Caruso's American debut. The discs sold very well, indicating the popular appeal of classical music in the United States. Immediately following Caruso's death in 1921, Victor sold more than two million dollars' worth of his discs. (This established the notion of "death sales," a strategy that we can see repeated in the music industry's postmortem promotion of records by Hank Williams, Janis Joplin, Jimi Hendrix, Jim Morrison, and Kurt Cobain.)

Hit records in the years preceding World War I fall into two broad thematic categories. The unsettling effects of change—immigration, social and geographical mobility, and technological innovation—encouraged the continuing popularity of sentimental songs, including both nineteenth-century compositions like "Old Folks at Home" (1851) and "After the Ball" (1892) and newly composed nostalgic songs such as "In the Good Old Summer Time" (1902) and "Down by the Old Mill Stream" (1910). At the same time there was a strong interest in syncopated ragtime songs such as "Bill Bailey, Won't You Please Come Home?" (1902) and "Alexander's Ragtime Band" (1911), which represented the progressive, stimulating side of change. These two cultural themes—reverence for home, family, and the "good old days" versus the celebration of novelty and excitement—continue to figure prominently in American popular music today. Interestingly, some of the bestselling early recordings were not musical performances at all, but comic monologues such as "The Preacher and the Bear" (1905) and "laughing records"—basically three minutes of contagious guffawing.

The purchase of a phonograph for the home parlor was a symbol of upward mobility. There is evidence, however, that not everyone was wholly pleased with this change in the soundscape of domestic life. In 1904 a New York immigrant newspaper called the *Daily Forward* published an article entitled "The Victrola Season Has Begun" (Victrola was a brand name that had become virtually synonymous with "phonograph"):

> God sent us the Victrola, and you can't get away from it, unless you run to the park. As if we didn't have enough problems with cockroaches and children practicing the piano next door. . . . It's everywhere, this Victrola: in the tenements, the restaurants, the ice-cream parlors, the candy stores. You lock your door at night and are safe from burglars, but not from the Victrola. (Howe 1976, p. 127)

Despite such misgivings, the popularity of phonographs increased steadily before World War I. It has been estimated that by 1904 one out of every twenty-two households in the United States had a phonograph. By 1909 over twenty-six million discs and cylinders were being produced every year, and the modern record industry was well under way. (The discs were initially regarded as an inducement to buy the fancy furniture that enclosed the record player, and companies such as Victor and Columbia made both the "software" discs and the "hardware" to play them.)

The introduction of the phonograph in the late nineteenth century gave rise to a set of important philosophical and aesthetic issues that continue to inspire debate up to the present day. The process of mechanical recording introduced a phenomenon that has been termed *schizophonia,* the splitting of sounds from their original sources (Schafer 1977, p. 90). From this perspective, sound recording introduces a gap between the original context and meanings of music—its connections to community life and individual identity, for example—and its existence as sound, a purely acoustic phenomenon that can be reproduced and consumed by a huge audience. This development is decried by some contemporary critics as leading to the dehumanization of music. Others have argued that it was precisely this split between musical sound and live musical performance that enabled the phonograph to disseminate music to millions of people in America and around the world, spreading some styles far beyond their communities of origin. From this viewpoint,

A fashionable young lady listens, transfixed, to a phonograph in this 1908 photograph. Courtesy Library of Congress.

recorded music has become a medium by which people who will never meet face to face communicate with one another over wide geographical and cultural distances, and thus an important basis for the creation (and constant reinvention) of a distinctively American culture. Whatever one's position on these matters, there can be no denying that the introduction of the phonograph during the late nineteenth century was a epochal step in the development of popular music.

The period around the turn of the century was one of deep and pervasive change in American society. In 1890 fewer than one out of four Americans lived in communities with a population over twenty-five hundred; by 1920 more than half lived in urban areas. The transcontinental railroad system was nearly completed, the automobile began to replace the horse and buggy, and the first manned flight took place (1903). These new forms of transportation were in fact favorite themes for songwriters, who penned such immortal items as "In My Merry Oldsmobile" (Bryan/Edwards, 1905). The Spanish-American War (1898) expanded America's imperial designs and created a general feeling of optimism. Industrialization and good economic conditions were the twin motors for a rapid expansion of the American middle class, which was mostly white, northern, and urban. Apart from a brief economic downturn in 1907, the era of good feeling lasted until World War I.

This optimism did not penetrate far into black America, for the period around the turn of the century was one of the most difficult in history for American blacks. The Supreme Court's *Plessy v. Ferguson* decision (1896) confirmed the legality of racial segregation, and harsh "Jim Crow" laws were imposed throughout the South, where most of the descendants of Africans still lived. In 1900 alone 107 lynchings of blacks by white mobs were reported. "Coon songs" with offensive lyrics—written, ironically, by both white and black composers—were being published, often set to ragtime music. By this time the pattern that began with minstrelsy had been reinforced: the adoption of African American music by whites—often in the watered-down form of mildly syncopated dance music—was coupled with the vigorous rejection of blacks as people.

By the 1910s many basic elements of the modern music business were firmly in place: a pattern of fierce competition between publishing companies; mass promotion of songs, spread across several different media (newspapers, the theater, department stores, mail order catalogs); a highly asymmetrical ratio between hit songs and duds; and the dominance of a limited set of musical forms and lyrical themes. As we shall see in the next three chapters, the 1920s and 1930s gave rise to a number of important shifts in the production and consumption of popular music, including the supplanting of sheet music by phonograph discs, the rise of network radio and sound film, and the increasing influence of African American genres such as jazz and the blues. Yet all of these new developments played themselves out within institutional and musical frameworks that had already been established by the beginning of the twentieth century.

CHAPTER THREE

"CATCHING AS THE SMALL-POX"
Social Dance and Jazz, 1917–1935

This chapter and the next two focus on the 1920s and early 1930s, a pivotal period in the history of American popular music. From World War I through the prosperity of the "Roaring Twenties" and into the depths of the Great Depression, mass media, the music business, and popular musical taste underwent a series of important changes. Although the popular songs and dance music of the so-called Jazz Age may sound old-fashioned to us now, these shifts in popular taste and the production and consumption of music established basic patterns that continue to affect us today.

World War I—regarded at the time as "the war to end all wars"—was a watershed event in the cultural history of the United States. The war reinforced American influence overseas, stimulated and reorganized the national economy, and demonstrated the horrifying as well as liberating possibilities of modern technology. The ready availability of jobs and development of the national transportation system during and after the war encouraged migration from the country to the city, and from South to North. Immigrants from central and eastern Europe continued to add to the cultural heterogeneity of the big cities, as they had during the first decade of the twentieth century.

The 1920s was a crucial period in the development of American popular culture. For the first time, millions of families owned a car, the quintessential symbol of independence and mobility. Telephones, which had previously been the exclusive right of the wealthy, now appeared in middle-class homes. Phonographs, radio, Hollywood films, and tabloid newspapers began to create a unified national popular culture, and a new generation of celebrity performers emerged, their faces and voices familiar to the inhabitants of cities, towns, and hamlets coast to coast. It was during this period that the modern American entertainment industry began to take shape.

The 1920s was also a period of mass law-breaking and social conflict. Modern organized crime rose to new heights during this period, partly in response to the possibilities for illegal profits offered by the Eighteenth Amendment to the Constitution of the United States (in effect 1919–33), which prohibited the sale and transportation of alcohol. The Ku Klux Klan and other racist, anti-immigrant groups flourished during the 1920s and received a boost from the Great Depression, which threw millions of Americans out of work and exacerbated frictions between ethnic groups. Although African American traditions increasingly and directly influenced the popular culture of white America, the boundaries of racial segregation remained rigid.

During the 1920s unprecedented profit levels in the music business led to a bolstering of the centers of influence established at the end of the nineteenth century, especially the big music publishing firms and record companies in New York City. Organizations were set up to control the flow of profits from mass-reproduced music. The phonograph was introduced into millions of American homes, and advances in recording technology encouraged the development of new performance styles. Radio networks broadcast the latest songs and artists coast to coast, allowing people separated by thousands of miles to hear the same music simultaneously. The world of vaudeville entertainment went into a gradual decline, only to be supplanted in New York City's prestigious theater district, Broadway, by big musicals—extravaganzas featuring the songs of great Tin Pan Alley composers such as Irving Berlin, George Gershwin, and Richard Rodgers. Hollywood films with synchronized sound—the "talkies"—became an important medium for promoting songs and "star" entertainers, and Los Angeles began to compete with New York City as a center of the national entertainment industry. Increasingly, the mass media shaped the daily experience of Americans, not only in the big cities, but also in towns and small rural communities throughout the country.

TECHNOLOGY AND THE MUSIC BUSINESS

During the 1920s and 1930s the production and consumption of popular music was deeply influenced by new technologies, including radio and sound film, and by new institutions, designed to protect the rights of composers and music publishers. While the Great Depression severely affected the phonograph and film industries, it helped to boost the popularity of radio, which provided consumers with a cheaper way to hear a variety of music, recorded and live. The music industry became increasingly centralized during this period, and organizations were established to control profits accrued from the performance of popular music in Hollywood films and national radio broadcasts.

The *record industry* underwent a period of rapid expansion after World War I. This was followed by a precipitous decline, caused in part by the introduction of radio, and later exacerbated by the Great Depression. One important shift was the industry's increasing reliance on phonograph records, rather than sheet music, as the main means of promoting songs and artists. The year 1919 saw the first hit song to be popularized in recorded form before it was released as sheet music. This song was "Mary," composed by George Stoddard and performed by Joseph C. Smith's Orchestra (one of the most popular dance bands of the time). The record, released by the Victor Company, sold a phenomenal 300,000 copies in three months and brought the composer $15,000 in royalties. Later that same year, Victor released the first phonograph record to sell a million copies. It was a fox-trot arrangement of the song "Dardenella," written by an African American composer named Johnny S. Black and performed by the Selvin Novelty Orchestra, a popular New York dance band. The term "novelty" was commonly used as a sales gimmick in those days. Selvin's version of the song "Dardanella"—in which an Arab sheik professes his love for a woman and offers to add her to his harem—featured banjos and a slithering saxophone, sounds sufficiently unusual at this time to be regarded as "Oriental" effects. The sales standard for hit records was raised again the following year, when a recording of the songs "Whispering" and "The Japanese Sandman" (Oriental exotica again!), performed by Paul Whiteman and His Ambassador Orchestra, sold two million copies worldwide.

By the early 1920s nearly one hundred million records were being pressed each year in the United States. Records were no longer a by-product of the manufacture of phonographs, and record companies no longer waited until sheet music sales of a given song had been exhausted before releasing a version of the song on record. And by the mid-1920s an important threshold had been crossed: total national sales of phonograph discs surpassed those of sheet music for the first time.

In 1925 *electric recording*, using a new device called the *microphone,* replaced the older system of acoustic recording, in which performers had to project into a huge megaphone. While electric recording is regarded as a more "high fidelity" technology than acoustic recording, its introduction also allowed recording engineers greater latitude in manipulating musical sounds to produce certain effects (for example, inducing a feeling of intimacy between the singer and his or her listener). The development of the electric microphone allowed engineers to isolate and amplify particular sounds, including that of an individual human voice. As a result, a new manner of singing emerged, one that would have a significant impact on subsequent developments in American popular music. This intimate, gentle style, called *crooning*, was developed by a new generation of performers. Crooners such as Bing Crosby were the first modern superstars, their public images carefully honed and promoted across various mass media.

The major competition for phonograph record companies came from a new medium, the *radio network*. Radio had started out as a hobby for amateurs. In 1906 the first radio program in the United States—consisting of two musical selections and a poem—was broadcast from an experimental station in Massachusetts. After World War I the relaxation of military restrictions on broadcasting encouraged the growth of radio. In 1920 the first three commercial radio stations in the United States were established: KDKA in Pittsburgh, WWJ in Detroit, and WJZ in Newark, New Jersey. Once it took root, commercial radio grew by leaps and bounds—by 1922, 564 stations had been licensed.

The idea of network radio was born in 1922, when telephone lines were used to transmit a running account of a football game from Chicago to New York. In 1926 the first nationwide commercial radio network—the National Broadcasting Company (NBC)—was established. Three other networks—the Columbia Broadcasting System (CBS), the Mutual Broadcasting System, and the American Broadcasting Company (ABC)—soon followed. By 1927 there were over one thousand radio stations in the United States.

Popular music was an important staple of commercial radio from its inception in the early 1920s. Stations carried live broadcasts of dance bands and singers, and the establishment of the national networks allowed the listener in Chicago or San Francisco to hear celebrities live from New York. The first music stars created by radio were the Happiness Boys (Ernie Hare and Billy Jones), who began presenting their vaudeville-style act over WJZ in 1921. Increasingly, radio broadcasters went to the scene of musical performances, rather than bringing the performers into the studio. The first such "remote" broadcast, in 1921, featured a ballroom dance orchestra performing at the Hotel Pennsylvania in New York City.

The 1930s saw the further expansion of music broadcasting. Superstar crooners such as Rudy Vallee, Bing Crosby, and Russ Colombo competed for popularity on the air, sometimes engaging in well-publicized feuds. Sponsors—including cigarette, automobile, soap, and laxative companies—competed for access to the top shows and stars. The establishment of programs such as *Make Believe Ballroom* (1932) propelled *disc jockeys*—who played records and provided entertaining patter, sometimes actually impersonating absent bandleaders—into an important position. Disc jockeys helped to demonstrate the commercial potential of radio by promoting the sponsor's products over the air.

Radio had a tremendous impact on the musical experience and social habits of Americans. During the Great Depression people who could not afford to buy a phonograph and discs were sometimes able to purchase a radio receiver and thereby

Live radio broadcast at station WJZ, 1926. Courtesy Library of Congress.

enjoy a wide range of programming. Radio linked the smallest towns to the biggest cities and provided a source of excitement for working people. It became the most important medium for promoting songs and artists and for using music to sell other products.

Sound film, introduced in 1927, soon became an important means for the dissemination of popular music. The first film to exploit sound successfully was *The Jazz Singer* (1927), based on a successful Broadway play and starring Al Jolson, a vaudeville superstar of the 1910s and 1920s (see Box 4.3, p. 74). *The Jazz Singer*, the story of a Jewish cantor's son who becomes a success singing "jazz" songs in blackface, grossed the unprecedented sum of three million dollars. Much of the film was silent, but sound was introduced at critical points, especially when Jolson sang several songs that had already been popularized on the vaudeville stage (such as "Toot Toot Tootsie" and "My Mammy"). The projectionist was provided with a set of single-sided 33$\frac{1}{3}$ r.p.m. discs that contained the entire soundtrack of the film. He would mark certain points on the discs with colored crayon in order to allow precise synchronization of the film image with the music. (This technique is still employed today by hip-hop DJs, who use multiple turntables to create the "beats" for rap performances.)

The first "all talking, all singing, all dancing" film musical, *The Broadway Melody*, was released by MGM in 1929. The film won an Oscar in 1930 for best picture of the year, helping to establish musical cinema as a legitimate form. Within the period of a few years, the major Hollywood studios had produced over one hundred musical films.

Beginning in 1929 the Great Depression wiped out smaller studios and consolidated control in the hands of the major studios. In the period leading up to World War II, film became an increasingly important venue for popular music, challenging Broadway musical comedies and vaudeville shows. By the 1930s many of the biggest Tin Pan Alley song-publishing firms had been bought up by Hollywood film companies.

Licensing and copyright agencies were set up to control the flow of profits from the sale and broadcast of popular music. *ASCAP* (the American Society of Composers, Authors, and Publishers) was founded in 1914 in an attempt to force all business establishments that featured live music to pay fees ("royalties") for the public use of music. Until then copyright protection covered only the purchase and mechanical reproduction of published compositions; composers, lyricists, and publishers received no compensation from live performance of their music. After a series of legal battles, eventually reaching the Supreme Court, ASCAP won its case (1917), and all hotels, theaters, dance halls, cabarets, and restaurants were required to purchase a license from ASCAP before they could play music written or published by a member of the organization. Similar rulings were later handed down regarding radio stations and motion picture studios. By the 1920s almost all leading publishing houses and composers belonged to ASCAP, and by the mid-1930s some ten million dollars in licensing fees was being paid annually.

In the period between the two world wars the music industry exerted firm control over the production and promotion of popular music. The big recording and publishing companies couldn't really predict hit songs (any more than they can today), but they did limit the public's exposure to music outside the commercial mainstream. Apart from Tin Pan Alley songs (see Chapter 4) and the music of ballroom dance bands (see Chapter 6), the only other major forms of music available on phonograph discs were classical music, "race" and "hillbilly" records (see Chapter 5), and a variety of ethnic recordings, all of which were promoted to limited audiences. There was no serious competition for the big record companies, music publishers, and film studios, and the industry had an interest in making sure that things remained that way.

"FREAK DANCES": TURKEY TROT AND TANGO

Around the beginning of the twentieth century, several fundamental changes took place in American social dancing, closely paralleling shifts in popular music. Most important was the intensified influence of African American dance, which had begun, quite indirectly, with the cakewalk dance of nineteenth-century minstrelsy. Starting around 1910 the craze for orchestrated versions of ragtime songs (see Chapter 2) gave rise to a succession of fads loosely based on black styles, including the Texas Tommy, the turkey trot, the bunny hug, the grizzly bear, the Boston dip, the one-step, and, most popular of all, the fox-trot. Many of these ragtime dances appear to have developed initially in clubs and dance halls in cities such as San Francisco, Chicago, and Memphis, where they were observed by vaudeville entertainers who incorporated them into their acts. Professional dance teachers transmitted simplified versions of the steps to the public, and it was in this form that most ragtime dances made their way into the ballroom setting.

By World War I a variety of ensembles were responding to public demand for the new styles of syncopated dance music. Although these groups varied in regard to both instrumentation and size, the typical cabaret dance band included a violin (the lead melodic instrument), two or more brass instruments, two or more reed instruments, and a "rhythm section" made up of piano, banjo or guitar, and drums, sometimes augmented by a string bass or tuba. At the Grand Balls of the nineteenth century, dance orchestras played music in strictly prearranged sequences or "programs," but early twentieth-century dance bands began to make decisions on the spot, playing certain numbers in response to audience requests. A typical dance orchestra would have on hand arrangements in a variety of musical styles, designed to accompany new dances such as the fox-trot and tango, as well as the occasional nostalgic waltz. The popular songs of Tin Pan Alley, arranged for a singer with dance band accompaniment, or in a strictly instrumental setting, became a major portion of the dance music repertoire during this period. Responding to this emerging market, music publishers began to produce band arrangements of popular songs, complete with parts for individual instruments. This practice allowed dance bands across the country to perform the latest hit songs for local audiences.

The years around World War I saw the rise of hundreds of dance halls and cabarets in cities across America, set up to cash in on the succession of dance crazes that were sweeping the country. In big cities, restaurants and hotels built dance floors and hired live bands to entertain their customers. The cabaret—a term that by the mid-1910s had come to signify any establishment offering food, drinks, floor shows, and dancing—became both a laboratory for new dance steps and a major source of employment for musicians.

Dances such as the turkey trot represented a departure from the relatively restrained movements that had previously dominated social dancing among the white middle and upper classes. A newspaper article entitled "The Turkey Trot, Grizzly Bear and Other Naughty Diversions," published in 1912, included this description of the turkey trot:

> Starting as if in the good old-fashioned Two-Step, the dancers suddenly let go hands, the man slipping behind his fair companion, there is a little step and a hop, something like a turkey might be expected to do, then a fresh grip around the waist of the young lady, the man snuggles up ever so closely behind her and they hop, skip and jump and half run along. (Malnig 1992, p. 6)

While this may seem tame by today's standards, ragtime dances were regarded in some quarters as an outright threat to public morality. Mechanical devices called "bumpers" were sometimes inserted between the bodies of dancers to keep them separated by a respectable distance. The United Neighborhood Guild of Brooklyn went so far as to outlaw the turkey trot, the bunny hug, and other "shoulder-rocking, feet-dragging freak dances" within borough limits. As might be expected, the same moral authorities that disapproved of the new dance steps also took exception to the social contexts in which they were performed. Big-city cabarets were singled out for disapprobation, particularly after the prohibition of alcohol consumption in 1919, when they became associated with illicit activities such as drinking, gambling, and prostitution. Despite, or more likely because of these associations, the "racy" cabaret atmosphere was increasingly emulated at dances held by fraternal organizations, social clubs, and ethnic associations in towns and cities across the country. Newspapers of the time report the invasion of high society balls by young people, who would secure a corner of the dance floor to perform the fox-trot.

Ragtime dancing and syncopated music went hand in hand. Popular African American bandleaders such as W. C. Handy, Wilbur Sweatman, Ford Dabney, and James Reese Europe (see below) composed ragtime arrangements specifically for the ballroom, and the most popular white orchestras of the day followed suit, including such numbers in their repertoire. Phonograph recordings of ragtime-influenced dance bands from the 1910s and early 1920s sound quite dated today—they are typically rather rigid in rhythm and involve little or no improvisation. However, for most white Americans, who had little experience dancing to syncopated music, ragtime pieces apparently created a slightly disorienting or dizzying sensation. Descriptions of the time stress the titillating effect of offbeat rhythms, sometimes likening them to a pinch of pepper used to spice up an otherwise bland soup or stew. Of course, it is important to remember that the dancers' prior experience and cultural values conditioned these attributions of "spiciness." It seems likely that many African Americans would have found the mildly syncopated music performed by the most successful dance orchestras of the era neither stimulating nor scandalous.

Another stimulus for the general loosening up of American ballroom dancing was the *tango*, which developed during the late nineteenth century in Buenos Aires, Argentina. The tango, a blend of European ballroom dance music, the Cuban habanera, Italian light opera, and the ballads of the Argentine *gauchos* (cowboys), was introduced to New York City in 1910 by Maurice Mouvet, who performed the dance in a popular cabaret. The tango did not achieve mass popularity, however, until it appeared in a Broadway revue entitled *The Sunshine Girl* (1913), featuring the husband-and-wife dance team of Irene and Vernon Castle (see below). The Castles' performances of the tango and the turkey trot—actually rather staid versions of the original dances—created an immediate sensation and virtually eliminated the waltz from the musical comedy stage. The daring associations of the tango were reinforced by the rise of the so-called tango tea, an afternoon event in which society women took dance lessons (and sometimes formed romantic liaisons) with young male instructors. (Contemporary reports suggest that alcohol, not tea, was most commonly consumed at these events!) The tango craze soon gave rise to other dance superstars, the most famous of whom was Rudolph Valentino, a dance teacher and gigolo who went on to become one of the great stars of silent film. Often cast in the stereotypical roles of the passionate Latin lover or fierce sheik, Valentino boosted the tango's popularity when he performed it in his first starring role, in the film *The Four Horsemen of the Apocalypse* (1921).

One of the main distinguishing features of the tango—and of the ragtime dances with which it was often alternated in an evening's dancing—was a bent-knee posture, quite different from the upright, straight-legged posture of earlier ballroom dances. This posture—common to many African-influenced dance traditions in the Americas—had the effect of freeing up the dancers' hips and upper body; and this mobility, combined with the intimacy of contact between the male and female partner, was largely responsible for the morally daring aura that was attached to the tango. The Americanized tango popularized by Vernon and Irene Castle was a somewhat antiseptic version of the original, featuring a "promenade" in which the couple would embrace cheek to cheek and, with arms extended and knees bent, take long strides across the floor. As Irene Castle put it in her autobiography, "If Vernon had ever looked into my eyes with smoldering passion during the tango, we would have both burst out laughing" (Castle, Duncan, and Duncan 1980, p. 87).

The passionate associations of the tango were evoked musically by an insistent four-beat pulse, dramatic changes in volume, and sudden starts and stops. The typical instrumentation of a 1920s tango orchestra included a bandoneon (a kind of accordion), violin, bass, and piano. Performed onstage and in ballrooms and dance schools, and disseminated to a mass audience on phonograph records and silent films, the tango brought a new energy and intensity to American popular dance and the music that accompanied it.

JAMES REESE EUROPE AND THE CASTLES

Vernon and Irene Castle—arguably the biggest media superstars of the years around World War I—seem unlikely candidates for the role of popular culture revolutionaries. Vernon Blyth was an Englishman who stumbled into American show business almost by accident, while Irene, born in New Rochelle, New York, had been rejected as a stage dancer for being too "awkward." Yet from 1912, when they debuted in New York City, until 1918, when Vernon was killed in a military airplane accident, the Castles did more than anyone to change the course of social dancing in America. They attracted millions of middle-class Americans into ballroom classes, expanded the stylistic range of popular dance, and established an image of mastery, charisma, and romance that later bore fruit in the work of dance teams such as Fred Astaire and Ginger Rogers (who played the Castles in the biographical film of 1939). Patronized by the wealthy elites of New York City, the Castles democratized ballroom dance, bringing the elegance and excitement of the latest styles within the reach of millions of Americans.

Vernon was responsible for the couple's choreography and for breaking complex dance movements down into manageable sequences ("figures") that could be learned easily by nonprofessionals. Thus, while the tango was reputed to have 160 different figures, Vernon asserted that knowledge of six basic movements was sufficient for the "average ballroom Tango." In a sense this process paralleled what publishers of sheet music had already done for decades in the realm of music—that is, producing simplified versions of songs for performance by people with little formal musical training. More importantly, Vernon Castle suggested that students "could do the Figures as they occur to you," in essence freeing dancers (especially the men) to create their own combinations of movements on the dance floor. This was a real departure from the practices of nineteenth-century ballroom dancing and an important source of the Castles' appeal—you could imitate their grace and virtuosity while (to a limited degree) doing your own thing on the dance floor.

The Castles' spectacular, though brief, reign as arbiters of popular taste relied in large part upon a savvy marketing campaign, masterminded by a New York City socialite named Elizabeth Marbury. She wrote the laudatory introduction to the Castles' popular dance instruction manual, *Modern Dancing,* introduced them to the upper echelons of New York society, franchised their name and photographic image, and made sure that they took advantage of mass media such as newspapers and silent film. By the mid-1910s the Castles were being featured at such eponymous venues as Castle Park (at Coney Island), Castles-by-the-Sea (on Long Beach), and Castles-in-the-Air (on the roof of a theater in Manhattan), and their names appeared on clothing, phonograph records, books, and magazines. The promotional campaign for the Castles was a clear predecessor of the sort of cross-merchandising that is now commonplace in American show business and professional sports.

Vernon and Irene Castle in action. Frank Driggs Collection.

Another key element in the Castles' success was their decision to hire a brilliant young African American musician as their musical director. <u>James Reese Europe</u> (1880–1919) was born into a middle-class family in Mobile, Alabama. In 1889 the family moved to Washington, D.C., where young Jim Europe took violin and music theory lessons with the assistant director of the U.S. Marine Corps Band. Moving to New York City at the age of twenty-two, Europe found that there were few opportunities for even the most highly skilled black musicians. He gradually developed a reputation as an accomplished pianist and conductor, playing ragtime piano in cabarets and acting as musical director for several all-black vaudeville revues. In 1910 Europe founded the Clef Club, which functioned as a social club, booking agency, and trade union for African American musicians in New York City. (The main musicians' union, the American Federation of Musicians, did not admit blacks.) He booked musicians into dance halls and ballrooms and staged concerts at Carnegie Hall with a 125-piece orchestra. These concerts attracted the attention of elite patrons and resulted in invitations to perform at private parties in New York, London, and Paris.

In 1913 Irene and Vernon Castle attended a private society party in New York City, where they danced to Europe's Clef Club Orchestra. Although they had already achieved some notoriety as dancers, the Castles were generally limited to dancing with whatever music the orchestra hired for a particular occasion could provide. These bands were not able to provide the syncopated music required for the Castles' adaptations of ragtime dances, and Vernon realized immediately that Europe's band would be perfect for the job. From 1913 until 1918 Jim Europe composed music for all of the Castles' "new" dance steps and provided musicians for their live engagements. Although the instrumentation of Europe's Society Orchestra varied somewhat depending on context, a typical line-up included strings (violins, cello, and string bass), horns (cornet, clarinet, saxophone, trombone, and baritone horn), banjos, and drum set. Contemporary observers, black and white, emphasized the Europe band's superior ability to perform syncopated ragtime and tango arrangements and frequently remarked on the distinctiveness of their rhythmic approach and ensemble timbre. For many of Europe's high-society patrons this music was an exciting, exotic, yet familiar brew.

LISTENING TO   "CASTLE HOUSE RAG" (1914)

In 1913 Europe's Society Orchestra became the first black group to sign a contract with a record company. A series of recordings made by the Victor Company in 1914 includes the Society Orchestra's rendition of "Castle House Rag." While the sound quality of this recording is primitive by today's standards, it nonetheless gives us a sense of the style of Europe's band and some of its musical influences, including ragtime and marching band music. This is a relatively large version of the Society Orchestra, featuring violins, cellos, banjos, brass and wind instruments, and percussion (snare drum, cymbals, and orchestral bells). The musical form of "Castle House Rag" is typical of ragtime style (e.g., Scott Joplin's "Maple Leaf Rag"), with a series of themes arranged into a larger structure. In this case the structure is a bit more complicated: AABBACCDEEF. Each measure is two beats long.

Introduction (4 measures)	Violins foreshadow the syncopated melody of section A, while piano plays descending chords. Section ends with cymbal crash.
A (16 measures)	Violins and piano play syncopated melody; snare drum plays marchlike pattern that reinforces syncopations in the melody.
A (16 measures)	REPEAT
B (16 measures)	New melody. Section begins with dramatic effect, like a Sousa march—cymbal crashes, special (diminished) chords add to the dramatic effect. Second half of section is more ragtime-like.
B (16 measures)	REPEAT
A (16 measures)	BACK TO A
Transition (4 measures)	
C (32 measures)	Drums drop out. Violins carry melody. Stoptime effect featuring bells. This section is relatively quiet, gentle.
C (32 measures)	REPEAT
D (16 measures)	Drums come back in, and the energy increases. The violins and trumpets introduce a new syncopated ragtime theme.
E (16 measures)	Band plays collective improvisation on ragtime theme, led by cornet (Cricket Smith) and drums (Buddy Gilmore).
E (16 measures)	REPEAT
F (16 measures)	The intensity peaks! Drum solo, with other instruments playing stoptime. Ends with "shave and a haircut, two bits" figure.

While his career as a popular dance musician skyrocketed, Jim Europe continued to devote a great deal of energy to establishing a black symphony orchestra that would specialize in performing the works of African American composers. These activities were interrupted in 1916, when Jim Europe enlisted in the Fifteenth Infantry Regiment of the New York National Guard, an all-black outfit. He was soon asked by his commander to form a military band. Since the best musicians in New York were reluctant to leave their regular jobs, Europe traveled to Puerto Rico to recruit players. Forbidden by U.S. Army regulations from fighting alongside white soldiers in World War I, Europe's outfit (now the 369th Infantry Regiment) was transferred to the French Army, which had already accepted African troops.

Europe's company—popularly known as the "Hell Fighters"—proved to be highly effective in combat and were the first Allied regiment to cross the Rhine

River at the end of the war. The Hell Fighters Band played several concerts in Paris, creating a sensation and establishing the long-standing French enthusiasm for jazz. Returning to the United States in 1919, wearing the French government's *Croix de Guerre*, Europe took the Hell Fighters on a successful concert tour and began to lay plans for the next stage of his career. The Hell Fighters made a number of recordings for Pathé, a French company with a studio in New York. The future seemed bright for Jim Europe. But on May 9, 1919, he was stabbed by one of his band members after an argument and died that night. James Reese Europe, the most influential and popular African American musician of the early twentieth century, was buried with honors at Arlington Cemetery.

THE JAZZ CRAZE

Until World War I, the major influence on syncopated dance band music was ragtime. The next stage in the "African Americanization" of ballroom dance music was the so-called jazz craze, which began during World War I and continued through the 1920s.[1] Jazz—sometimes called "jass" or "hot music"—emerged in New Orleans, Louisiana, around 1900. New Orleans's position as a gateway between the United States and the Caribbean, its complexly stratified population—including culturally distinct white, Creole, and Negro communities—and its strong residues of colonial French culture, encouraged the formation of a hybrid musical culture unlike that in any other American city.

There has been a good deal of argument about the origins of jazz. The term "jazz" itself carried multiple meanings in New Orleans, including strictly musical references ("speeding up" or "intensifying") and a variety of sexual associations. Jazz music emerged from the confluence of New Orleans's diverse musical traditions, including ragtime, marching bands, the rhythms used in Mardi Gras and funerary processions, French and Italian opera, Caribbean and Mexican music (referred to by early jazz musicians as "the Latin tinge"), Tin Pan Alley songs, and African American song traditions, both sacred (the spirituals) and secular (the blues).

What were the earliest jazz bands like? The nineteenth-century dance music repertoire in New Orleans, as elsewhere, was dominated by the Grand Ball tradition, with its predetermined programs of polkas, mazurkas, schottisches, and quadrilles (see Chapter 2). Dance bands of the period typically included some combination of violin, guitar, mandolin, and string bass, and sometimes a wind instrument (clarinet or cornet). A number of sources suggest that "hot" or "ratty" ragtime-based music was being performed in New Orleans by the 1890s, largely as an accompaniment for dancing. This sort of music was played at dance halls or honkytonks such as the Pig Ankle and the Funky Butt, located in the city's tenderloin district. These often rowdy contexts for social dancing encouraged the addition of instruments such as the drum set, cornet or trumpet, trombone, and clarinet, which could project over the noise of a boisterous crowd. These wind and percussion in-

---

1. In this chapter we are primarily concerned with jazz as a form of popular music, rather than with the internal evolution of jazz as an art form. Many books may be used as an introduction to the history of jazz; one useful example is Mark Gridley's *Jazz Styles: History and Analysis*.

struments were also used in the large "official" bands connected with public institutions and the more informal neighborhood bands that performed in the streets during Mardi Gras.

JAZZ BECOMES POPULAR MUSIC: THE ORIGINAL DIXIELAND JAZZ BAND

Although jazz developed in New Orleans, the first recordings of the new music were made in New York City and Chicago. (This makes perfect sense when you consider that there were no recording studios in the South at that time.) The first recording to bear the designation "jass" was made in New York in 1917. It featured a white group from New Orleans called the Original Dixieland Jazz Band (ODJB). The leader of the group, cornet player Nick LaRocca (1889–1961), had started playing "hot music" with other white musicians as a teenager. The ODJB had already played for two years in Chicago before coming to New York to take up a steady engagement at Reisenweber's Restaurant in Manhattan. Within a few weeks the ODJB created a major sensation in New York City, attracting large crowds and quickly landing a recording contract with Victor Records. Their recording of "Livery Stable Blues" and "Dixieland Jass Band One-Step" was released in March 1917, and within a few weeks it had sparked a national fad for jazz music. The Original Dixieland Jazz Band's biggest hit was their 1918 recording of "Tiger Rag," composed by LaRocca. "Tiger Rag" will serve as our introduction to certain basic features of early jazz.

Like most New Orleans jazz bands, ODJB consisted of a "front line" of three wind instruments—cornet, clarinet, and trombone—and a "rhythm section." In this recording the rhythm section consists of piano and a "trap set," including snare drum, tom-tom, cymbals, and woodblock. (In live performance many bands also included a guitar or banjo and a string bass or tuba. Bass instruments are often left out of early recordings because of the tendency for low frequencies to make the needle of the acoustic recording machine jump.) Each instrument in this ensemble has a specific role. The cornet typically carries the main melody, with some embellishments; the clarinet weaves an active countermelody in and around the cornet part; and the trombone plays either a simple countermelody or the bass notes of the chords (sometimes using the "tailgate" technique of sliding or smearing from one note to the next). This style is sometimes referred to as "collective improvisation," since the players all simultaneously embellish their parts with personal touches. This music may also be called "polyphonic" ("many-sound") jazz, since in the earliest recordings all of the musicians tend to play together more or less continuously.

Another striking feature of this performance is the prevalence of syncopation. In our discussion of ragtime music, we noted that syncopation involves the accenting of offbeats and the creation of rhythms that pull against the main pulse of the music. In this piece the cornet player relies heavily on a particular syncopated rhythm pattern. Each main beat is subdivided into two smaller beats of equal length, and the accents tend to coincide with the main beats:

1		2		3		4		1		2		3		4	
X	x	X	x	X	x	X	x	X	x	X	x	X	x	X	x

In "Tiger Rag" the cornet player frequently groups these smaller beats into groups of three by accenting every third beat, like this:

1			2			3			4			1			2			3			4
X	x	x	**X**	x	x	**X**	x	x	**X**	x	x	**X**	x	x	**X**

Note that some of the accents fall between the main beats—this is syncopation. As an exercise you might try tapping the syncopated accents while a friend taps the main pulses.

How might this recording have struck the ear of an average white middle-class listener in 1918, someone accustomed to a diet of ballroom dance music and Tin Pan Alley songs? To begin with, the sheer energy of "Tiger Rag" must have been striking (exciting or repellant, depending on one's taste). The record starts abruptly, with all the players going full tilt, as though the needle has been dropped in the middle of an ongoing performance. The energy level remains high throughout, peaking at the end in a particularly intense "shout chorus" (the classic "Hold That Tiger!" routine). This impression of unbridled intensity was an important part of the ODJB's appeal to an audience hungry for novelty and excitement (and perhaps parallel to the effect of early rock 'n' roll records on some listeners).

Like most rags, "Tiger Rag" consists of a series of musical phrases of regular length, presented one after the other and varied to hold the listener's interest. Unlike most popular music of the time, there is no strongly identifiable melody throughout much of the performance. This means that the listener's attention is focused on other aspects of the music, including the ensemble interaction, the variations played by individual instruments, and the rhythmic drive of the performance. The use of musical tricks such as "stoptime" sequences (in which the band stops abruptly for a few beats and one instrument takes a brief solo) and unusual instrumental techniques (the glides and slides played by the trombone and clarinet) must only have increased the sense of novelty.

There is considerable controversy about the relationship of the music played by the ODJB on the first phonograph recordings designated as jazz to the style played by African American musicians in New Orleans. This controversy has been heated by the fact that the ODJB were white musicians who played, and helped to commercialize, a form of music pioneered by African American musicians. Nick LaRocca did not help matters with his patently false claim that white musicians in New Orleans had invented jazz.

While there is not room here to provide a comparative analysis of early jazz recordings, the interested listener might try juxtaposing the ODJB's "Tiger Rag" with the 1923 recording of "Dippermouth Blues" by King Oliver's Creole Jazz Band, one of the first recordings of black musicians from New Orleans (on *The Smithsonian Collection of Classic Jazz*). While the two ensembles are similar in structure (the Creole Jazz Band is a bit larger, with two cornet players and a banjo in the rhythm section), several differences stand out immediately between their approaches to the music. King Oliver's recording, although just as energetic as ODJB's, has a more relaxed and flowing rhythmic feeling, with the syncopations smoother and less jerky. Improvisation plays a more prominent role in the Creole Jazz Band; much of the musical material in ODJB recordings was prearranged and committed to memory. (While they played by ear, comparison of different takes of the same pieces by the ODJB indicate that a great deal of their "spontaneity" was preplanned).

To be fair, the differences between these recordings may have more to do with

King Oliver's Creole Jazz Band in a pose that clearly references the "wilder," "novelty" aspects of African American jazz as it was perceived in the 1920s. (Compare to the more staid photographs of Paul Whiteman's band, p. 57, and of Louis Armstrong's Hot Five, p. 95.) Frank Driggs Collection.

the five-year gap between them than with any firm distinction between white and black jazz styles. It has been suggested that the ODJB's recordings are rooted in the past—a tradition of semi-improvised ragtime ensemble playing, common to white, Creole, and black musicians in turn-of-the-century New Orleans—while the Creole Jazz Band recordings, featuring the brilliant young cornet player Louis Armstrong, point toward the future of jazz.

DANCE MUSIC IN THE "JAZZ AGE"

The recordings of the Original Dixieland Jazz Band helped to spark an era in American popular culture that is commonly referred to as the "Jazz Age." Although jazz music was initially regarded by the music industry as a passing fad or novelty, its impact on the popular music mainstream represented an important cultural shift. A new subculture emerged from the white upper and middle classes, symbolized by the "jazz babies" or "flappers" (emancipated young women with short skirts and bobbed hair) and "jazzbos" or "sheiks" (young men whose cool yet sensual comportment was modeled on the film star Rudolph Valentino). This movement involved a blend of elements from high culture—the novels of F. Scott Fitzgerald, the paintings of Pablo Picasso, the plays of Eugene O'Neill—and from popular culture, particularly styles of music, dance, and speech modeled on black American prototypes. The idea of the jazz age was promoted by the mass media, especially the burgeoning Hollywood film industry.

Following on the heels of the ragtime fad, the jazz craze represented the intensification of African American influence on the musical tastes and buying habits of white Americans. This process did provide expanded opportunities for some black musicians, including the songwriting team of <u>Noble Sissle</u> (1899–1975) and <u>Eubie Blake</u> (1883–1983), who had begun their career with James Reese Europe's orchestra in 1916. In 1921 Sissle and Blake launched the first successful all-black Broadway musical, *Shuffle Along*. This show, which included jazz-influenced songs such as "I'm Just Wild about Harry," was innovative in a number of regards. It was one of the first shows to portray romantic relationships between black characters with-

Noble Sissle and **Eubie Blake.** Frank Driggs Collection.

out resorting to degrading stereotypes, and it even included a "serious" love duet entitled "Love Will Find a Way." (It is reported that the promoters of *Shuffle Along* sat near the stage door the first night, fearing that violence would break out when the song was premiered!) The seating arrangements were also innovative—for the first time, blacks, usually restricted to the balconies of theaters, could also sit in sections previously reserved for whites. The "Jazz Age" was also an era of racial inequality, however, in which the first successful sound film, *The Jazz Singer*, featured a white vaudevillian performer singing in blackface. African American musicians still had to adapt to white stereotypes. For example, the orchestra of *Shuffle Along*—comprising sophisticated and fully literate musicians—had to memorize their parts so they could appear to be playing by ear. "White people didn't believe that black people could read music," Blake later explained. "They wanted to think that our ability was just natural talent" (Morgan and Barlow 1992, p. 113).

While the jazz craze did increase opportunities for some black musicians, the world of dance orchestras remained strictly segregated. The most successful black dance bands of the 1920s—McKinney's Cotton Pickers and the Luis Russell, Bennie Moten, Duke Ellington, and Fletcher Henderson orchestras—were able to extend their appeal across racial boundaries. Although the record companies began in the mid-1920s to establish special segregated catalogs for "race music" (see Chapter 5), the most popular black dance bands were listed in the mainstream popular catalogs as well. African American musicians appeared with increasing frequency in fancy downtown cabarets and hotel ballrooms (although they could enter these places only as employees, not customers). During the late 1920s white jazz fans began to frequent nightclubs in African American neighborhoods. In New York's Harlem and the South Side of Chicago, these "black and tan" cabarets offered their predominantly white clientele an exotic array of jazz music, floor shows with scantily clad dancers, fancy drinks, and images of Africa and the Orient. Performing at Harlem's famous Cotton Club, the great jazz pianist and composer Duke Ellington developed a style that he called "jungle music," featuring dense textures and dark, growling timbres. (In later, more politically correct times, Ellington bemusedly referred to his early style as "rain forest music"!) As in earlier periods, African American musicians had to work through the stereotypes of blackness prevalent in white society. Nonetheless, there is no denying that the 1920s saw an expansion of opportunities for black musicians in the cosmopolitan centers of the North.

It will come as no surprise that the most economically successful dance bands of the 1920s and 1930s were led and staffed by white musicians. Many bands maintained a "book" of written arrangements representing various styles of music—jazz numbers, Tin Pan Alley songs, and even the occasional waltz. As dozens of bands sprang up to feed the social dance craze, increasing competition encouraged bandleaders to focus on attracting a particular segment of the audience. (This tendency was reinforced after 1929, when the Great Depression cut into the market for live and recorded music.) Many bands tended to specialize in one of three main categories, "hot," "sweet," and "Latin." The hot bands, including the Coon-Sanders Nighthawks, the Jean Goldkette Orchestra, and the Casa Loma Orchestra, specialized in syncopated jazz arrangements. These bands were particularly popular at college dances. Sweet bands like Guy Lombardo and His Royal Canadians played romantic and nostalgic music. Although Lombardo's band was ridiculed by jazz fans for its "cornball" or "Mickey Mouse" style, the Canadians went on to sell over one hundred million records. (The great jazz trumpeter Louis Armstrong praised the band for its warm sound and high standards of musicianship. For his part, Lombardo claimed that black audiences loved his music, as long as he didn't try to play *their* music!) "Charmaine!" was released by Columbia Records in 1927 and was the first of Lombardo's twenty-six Number One hits, dominating the charts for seven weeks. This recording is a good example of the sweet dance band style, with a light beat that seems almost to float above the ground. The fact that "Charmaine!" is a waltz song with a sentimental lyric must only have added to its nostalgic effect.

Latin bands such as Don Azpiazú and his Havana Casino Orchestra and Xavier Cugat's Waldorf Astoria Orchestra played music to accompany ballroom adaptations of South American and Caribbean dances. Azpiazú's arrangement of the *rumba* piece "El Manicero"/"The Peanut Vendor," composed by the Cuban pianist Moises Simon and released by Victor in 1930, reignited a national fascination with Latin American music and ballroom dance steps. The recording opens with a rhythm called the *clave*, played on two wooden pegs that are also called *claves*. This rhythmic pattern is ultimately derived from West African music, and variants of it are found in a number of traditions of the Americas, including the Cuban rumba, the Brazilian bossa nova, and even in the "shave and a haircut, two bits" rhythm of 1950s rock 'n' roller Bo Diddley.

Once your ear has located the *clave* pattern, listen for the relationships among the other instruments, including reeds, trumpets, and trombones as well as percussion instruments such as bongo drums and maracas. As in much African-derived music, the pattern played by each individual instrument is carefully arranged to interlock with all of the others, creating a complex ensemble texture from the combination of fairly simple individual parts. On top of this rhythmic infrastructure, the solo trumpet comes and goes, interweaving with the voice of the singer, who imitates the cries of a street vendor selling hot peanuts (*Mani* . . .). Although the Victor Company delayed the record's release, fearing that its complex rhythms and imitation of the cries of Havana street vendors might be too strange for American ears, "El Manicero" was a smash hit. Within a year Azpiazú's band had embarked on a nationwide tour, and millions of Americans were taking ballroom dance classes to learn a simplified version of the Cuban rumba. "El Manicero" paved the way for later developments in Latin music, including the success of mainstream bands like the Desi Arnaz Orchestra (which performed "El Manicero" on one episode of the *I Love Lucy* show), and the rise of salsa music in the 1960s.

"THE KING OF JAZZ"

By far the most successful dance band of the 1920s was the Ambassador Orchestra, led by Paul Whiteman (1890–1967). Even now it is hard to comprehend the scale of Whiteman's commercial success, which in some regards has not been equaled by any musician since. Like James Reese Europe before him, Whiteman was both a fine musician and an astute businessman. However, his role in the history of jazz is ambiguous. On the one hand, his assumption of the title "King of Jazz" was clearly a public relations ploy, part of an attempt to promote a watered-down, "safe" version of jazz to the public. Whiteman's claim that he had "made an honest woman out of jazz" only threw fuel on the fire, for it seemed to some to imply that African

Paul Whiteman and His Orchestra, 1928. Frank Driggs Collection.

American music needed uplifting by white musicians. On the other hand, Whiteman did make some important contributions to jazz, widening the market for jazz-based dance music (and paving the way for the Swing Era), hiring brilliant young jazz players and arrangers, and establishing a level of professionalism that was widely imitated by dance bands on both sides of the color line. He also defended jazz against its moral critics (whom he called "jazz-klanners") and carried on aspects of Jim Europe's vision of a symphonic version of jazz. (The 1924 debut of George Gershwin's *Rhapsody in Blue* featured Whiteman's band.)

Born in Denver, Colorado, Paul Whiteman began studying music at the age of seven and joined the Denver Symphony Orchestra as a violist at seventeen. He initially encountered syncopated dance music in San Francisco, before World War I. Soon thereafter he formed a seven-piece dance band, which played around San Francisco until 1916, when he enlisted in the navy. During the war he directed a forty-piece concert band, where he was able to work out some of the basic principles of his approach to "symphonic jazz." After the war his band played at a hotel in Los Angeles, becoming a favorite of Hollywood film stars, and in 1919 moved to Atlantic City, New Jersey. Having begun a long engagement at the Ambassador Hotel, Whiteman took his band into the Victor studios for the first time. This session produced the instrumental versions of "Whispering" and "The Japanese Sandman," which, as we have already noted, set a new sales record.

"Whispering" contained the musical seeds of Whiteman's future successes. The arrangement is played at a medium tempo, with a straightforward, bouncy fox-trot rhythm, appropriate for ballroom dancing in the style popularized by Irene and Vernon Castle. After a brief introduction (actually the B section of the song), the main melody is introduced on the cornet and violin. The second time through the melody is picked up by the Swanee whistle (slide whistle), a novelty that apparently played an important part in selling the record. (After Whiteman's hit recording, it became almost unthinkable to perform "Whispering" without at least one chorus of whistling.) In the last chorus, the lead instruments take a somewhat looser, more syncopated approach to the melody, although the spontaneity is kept within careful limits. Hints of jazz influence in "Whispering" include a strummed banjo that stresses the offbeats, a bit of syncopation in the cornet and trombone parts, and especially in the last chorus, some mildly energetic woodblock playing by the drummer, vaguely reminiscent of the Original Dixieland Jazz Band.

This mixture of syncopation and careful arrangement, rhythmic pep and gentility, was to be the core of Whiteman's symphonic jazz. As the record quickly sold out of stores nationwide, the Victor Company realized that it had a gold mine on its hands. Whiteman's first record not only challenged the sales of reigning recording stars such as John Philip Sousa and Enrico Caruso but also surpassed the success of the Original Dixieland Jazz Band. There is even evidence that the Victor Company urged the ODJB to adopt Whiteman's "sweeter" approach to syncopated dance music on its last recordings.

"Whispering" was the first of an amazing string of hit records. Between 1920 and 1934 the Whiteman band had 28 Number One records, and 150 records ranking among the Top 10, a feat unmatched by any other recording artist in the entire history of American popular music. The Ambassador Orchestra, which comprised only ten players in 1920, had expanded to nineteen by the end of the decade (five brass instruments, five reed instruments, four violins, and a five-piece rhythm section). In 1927 Whiteman began to hire some of the leading white jazz musicians of the time, including the brilliant cornetist Bix Beiderbecke and the Dorsey brothers (Jimmy and Tommy), who would later achieve success as bandleaders in the Swing Era (see Chapter 6). At concerts and dances he used a small "band-within-a-band," made up of the best jazz musicians in his orchestra, to play "hot" music. Whiteman hired pioneering dance band arrangers—Ferde Grofé and Bill Challis—to craft his band's "book" (library of music), and he helped to promote jazz-influenced crooners such as Bing Crosby. Like the Castles, Whiteman franchised his music and his image. (A good-humored, portly man with a pencil-thin moustache, Whiteman embodied the good times and cheer of the years before the Great Depression.) By 1930 there were eleven official Paul Whiteman bands playing official Paul Whiteman arrangements in New York City, seventeen P.W. bands on the road, and forty others established in hotels and dance halls around the country. The "King of Jazz" had become an industry.

Whiteman's autobiography, entitled simply *Jazz*, gives us some insight into the attitudes and experiences that shaped his career. Early on in the book he describes an epochal event in his life, when a fellow classical musician took him to a dance hall in San Francisco:

> We ambled at length into a mad house. Men and women were whirling and twirling feverishly there. Sometimes they snapped their fingers and yelled loud enough to drown the music—if music it was. My whole body began to sit up and take notice. It was like coming out of the blackness into bright light. My blues faded when treated to the Georgia blues that some trombonist was wailing about. My head was dizzy, but my feet seemed to understand that tune. They began to pat wildly. I wanted to whoop. I wanted to dance. I wanted to sing. I did them all. Raucous? Yes. Crude—undoubtedly. Unmusical—sure as you live. But rhythmic, catching as the small-pox and spirit-lifting. That was jazz then. I liked it, though it puzzled me. Even then it seemed to me to have vitality, sincerity and truth in it. In spite of its uncouthness, it was trying to say something peculiarly American, just as an uneducated man struggles ungrammatically to express a true and original idea. (Whiteman and McBride 1974, p. 33)

Although Whiteman meant this as a defense of the inherent value of jazz—he considered himself a "jazz missionary"—this excerpt also illustrates a less laudable set of attitudes common among white Americans in the 1920s and 1930s. Jazz music, and African American culture more generally, were defined either negatively ("raucous," "crude") or by the absence of certain criteria of civilization (couthness, musicality, grammaticality). The references to "fever" and "small-pox" suggest that the point of contact between black and white culture—a "smoked-hazed, beer-fumed room"—was regarded as a zone of potential contagion. Whiteman's description of his jazz epiphany was couched in terms of a set of values common to millions of white Americans during the 1920s (and shared to some degree by many members of the African American middle class).

Whiteman begins his book by identifying African music and the slave trade as origin points of jazz: "Jazz came to America three hundred years ago in chains." But African Americans are as absent from the rest of his story as they were from his orchestra. Whiteman demonstrates the hybrid nature of his music by referring to the cultural diversity of his musicians: Italians, Irishmen, Scots, Norwegians, and Germans! This whitewashed image of what Whiteman called "America's melting pot" is even more strikingly presented in the 1930 sound film *The King of Jazz*, in which Whiteman appears as a magician stirring a bubbling cauldron, into which all of the ingredients of jazz are thrown, one after the other. We are shown English ballads, Scottish bagpipes, an Irish jig, an Austrian waltz, Italian opera, Spanish flamenco, even Russian balalaikas, but there is no evidence at all of the ethnic groups most responsible for the creation of jazz (African Americans) and for its inclusion in popular song, theater, and film (Jewish immigrants). These striking absences give us a glimpse of the limits of white middle-class perceptions of American culture during the 1920s.

While it is easy to regard the music labeled as jazz by the recording industry as a watered-down version of the improvised "hot" music pioneered by musicians in New Orleans, it is important not to underestimate the progressive impact that this music had in some sectors of American society. Throughout the 1920s and 1930s religious and political authorities fiercely criticized the influence of jazz music on

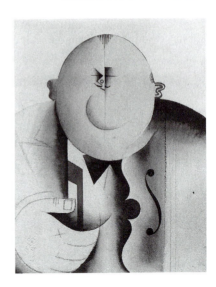

Caricature of **Paul Whiteman** by Miguel Covarrubias, c. 1924. Whiteman is shown holding sheet music, and a viola (Whiteman's first instrument) is encompassed within the image. Courtesy Library of Congress.

white youth. Jazz was widely associated with feeble-mindedness, crime, and immorality, and explicitly linked with immigration and interracial sex as primary causes of national degeneration. A survey of articles published in the *New York Times*—generally regarded as a paragon of responsible journalism—reveals a pattern of association between jazz, social dancing, and various forms of "deviance," including alcohol consumption, indiscriminate sex, effeminacy, suicide, bestiality, insanity, and indigestion. In a particularly imaginative elaboration on these themes, quoted in the *Times* in 1934, a religious authority asserted that "jazz was borrowed from Central Africa by a gang of wealthy international Bolshevists from America, their aim being to strike at Christian civilization throughout the world." (The frequency of references to Africa, and to "savagery," "cannibalism," and "cave men" in these moralistic criticisms of jazz, suggests that their primary motivation was really a fear that musical mixing between blacks and whites might encourage interracial miscegenation and thus compromise the social privileges enjoyed by whites.)

What factors contributed to the tremendous impact of jazz on mainstream popular music? First, the new music from New Orleans arrived at just the right moment to feed into the craze for syncopated dance music that had already swept the nation. It is clear that the white audience for such music initially regarded jazz basically as an updated form of ragtime, and many of the most popular early jazz band recordings feature music that is basically indistinguishable from ragtime. There is abundant evidence that jazz was from the beginning positioned in the music business as a kind of novelty music, or, as Duke Ellington once put it, a form of musical "stunt." Early recordings of jazz-influenced popular music often included raucous effects such as barnyard animal noises, and advertisements for popular jazz bands featured wacky poses, silly hats, and carnival-like attractions. (The African American bandleader Wilbur Sweatman was advertised for his ability to play three clarinets at the same time!) From the point of view of many in its white audience, jazz was heady, daring, humorous, and slightly dangerous, a way to experience black culture without proximity to black people.

In addition, the potential audience for jazz was expanded as a result of the great South-to-North migration that started during World War I. Seeking employment in the factories built during the war and in other businesses that sprang up in the economic boom years before the Great Depression, millions of southerners pulled up roots and moved to Chicago, Detroit, and New York. This population provided a ready-made support system for jazz musicians, particularly in neighborhoods dominated by African Americans (the South Side of Chicago, New York's Harlem). As we have already noted, more and more whites began to visit nightspots in black neighborhoods, creating a web of interactions that, though always unequal, did support jazz musicians.

———————

Jazz music was the anthem for the first well-defined youth culture to emerge from white America. Rebelling against the horrors of mechanized warfare and the strait-laced morality of the nineteenth century, millions of college-age Americans adopted jazz as a way to mark their difference from their parents' generation. Admittedly, the ability of youth to indulge in the sorts of up-to-date pastimes portrayed in Hollywood films and novels such as Fitzgerald's *The Great Gatsby* was strongly affected by their position in society—after all, not everyone could afford luxury automobiles, champagne, and top-flight dance orchestras. However, jazz's attraction as a symbol of sensuality, freedom, and fun does appear to have transcended the boundaries of region, ethnicity, and class, creating a precedent for phenomena such as the Swing Era (see Chapter 6), rhythm & blues (see Chapter 7), and rock 'n' roll (see Chapter 8). In the next chapter, we turn to the rise of the Tin Pan Alley tradition of popular song, which was to dominate the mainstream of popular taste for over half a century.

CHAPTER FOUR

"I GOT RHYTHM"

The Golden Age of Tin Pan Alley Song

During the 1920s and 1930s certain characteristic musical structures and styles of performance dominated popular song. Professional tunesmiths, working within a set of forms inherited from nineteenth-century popular music and influenced by the craze for ragtime and jazz music, wrote some of the most influential and commercially successful songs of the period. The lure of fame and financial success on a previously unknown scale attracted composers and lyricists with diverse skills and backgrounds. Irving Berlin (1888–1989) grew up poor in the Jewish ghetto of New York City, began his career as a singing waiter and achieved his first success writing ragtime-influenced popular songs (see Box 4.1). Richard Rodgers (1902–79), who produced many of the finest songs of the period in collaboration with lyricists Lorenz Hart and Oscar Hammerstein II, was the college-educated son of a doctor and a pianist. Cole Porter (1891–1964) was born into a wealthy family in Indiana and studied classical music at elite institutions such as Yale, Harvard, and the Schola Cantorum in Paris. And George Gershwin (1898–1937), the son of an immigrant leatherworker, was the songwriter who did the most to bridge the gulf between art music and popular music; he studied European classical music but also spent a great deal of time listening to jazz musicians in New York City (see Box 4.4, p. 81). The songs written by these men and a few others represent an achievement in terms of both quality and quantity that appears extraordinary to this day. The Tin Pan Alley composers produced many *standards,* songs that remain an essential part of the repertoire of today's jazz musicians and pop singers.

Jewish immigrants, particularly from central and eastern Europe, played a central role in the music business during the early twentieth century, as composers,

Two great Tin Pan Alley composers, posed formally (**Irving Berlin**) and less formally (**Cole Porter**). Frank Driggs Collection.

lyricists, performers, publishers, and promoters. The rise of anti-Semitism in eastern Europe during the 1880s encouraged the emigration of millions of Jews. Few of the first wave of immigrants were literate in English, and many had little experience of big-city life. By 1910 Jews made up more than a quarter of the population of New York City. Young entrepreneurs from the burgeoning neighborhoods of the East Side had secured a foothold in a variety of businesses, including the entertainment industry. Some of the hundreds of Jewish performers who worked the vaudeville circuit went on to become major celebrities on Broadway and in Hollywood: Al Jolson, Sophie Tucker, George Jessel, Jack Benny, George Burns, and Milton Berle.

The life stories of these performers suggest a couple of reasons for the high proportion of Jewish involvement in the entertainment industry. Lower-class immigrants, denied the possibility of upward mobility for centuries, poured their ambition into music, dance, and comedy, perfecting their skills on the streets of New York before gaining a foothold in vaudeville. By the turn of the century many of the biggest theatrical booking agencies were managed by Jews, and young performers did not face the degree of anti-Semitism present in other established businesses. And for the aspiring songwriters—Irving Berlin, Jerome Kern, George Gershwin, and others—the music business offered a kind of rough-and-tumble justice: if you could write songs that made money for the music publishers, you were a success.

Box 4.1 Irving Berlin (1888–1989)

Irving Berlin (born Israel Baline) is generally recognized as the most productive, varied, and creative of the Tin Pan Alley songwriters. His professional songwriting career started before World War I and continued into the 1960s. It has been said that Berlin often composed from three to seven songs a week; in 1969 the catalog of Irving Berlin compositions still available in print included 899 songs. His most famous songs include "Alexander's Ragtime Band," "Blue Skies," "Cheek to Cheek," "There's No Business Like Show Business," "White Christmas," and "God Bless America."

Like many Tin Pan Alley composers, Berlin was a European immigrant. He was born in Temun, Russia, in 1888, and his family fled the anti-Jewish pogrom there in 1892. Settling in New York City's Lower East Side, a haven for displaced Jews, the Balines began their life in America in desperate poverty. Young Israel was on the streets by eight, selling newspapers, and at fourteen he left home for good. He worked as a guide for a blind street musician, as a saloon pianist, and as a singing waiter. Like many other Tin Pan Alley tunesmiths, Berlin began his career as a song plugger—as a teenager he was paid five dollars a week by the songwriter Harry von Tilzer to join in "spontaneously" from the audience when von Tilzer's songs were performed at music halls.

The song that first brought Berlin mass acclaim was "Alexander's Ragtime Band," published in 1911. It actually had little to do with ragtime as performed by the great black ragtime pianists of the day, but it sold 1.5 million copies almost immediately. After World War I Berlin set up his own publishing company and founded a theater for the production of his own shows.

Like other Tin Pan Alley composers, Berlin wrote songs for the Broadway stage and for the new medium of sound film (he wrote music for eighteen films). An Irving Berlin song, "Blue Skies," was performed by Al Jolson in the first talkie, *The Jazz Singer*. The first motion picture featuring an entire score written by Berlin was the Marx Brothers debut movie, *The Cocoanuts*, produced in 1929. The 1942 film *Holiday Inn* introduced one of Berlin's must successful songs, "White Christmas," and music for the 1946 Broadway musical *Annie Get Your Gun*, composed by Berlin, probably included more hit songs than any other show ("They Say It's Wonderful," "The Girl That I Marry," "Doin' What Comes Naturally," and "There's No Business Like Show Business," among others). Berlin was the most prolific and consistent of Tin Pan Alley composers, with an active songwriting career spanning almost sixty years.

TIN PAN ALLEY SONG FORM

During the 1920s and 1930s this new generation of composers and lyricists explored the possibilities of song forms inherited from the nineteenth century, including the AABA structure of "Jeanie with the Light Brown Hair" and the verse-and-chorus form of "After the Ball" (see Chapter 2). Let's take a quick look at the most common form for Tin Pan Alley songs, which, in effect, fused these two to produce a **verse-refrain** form, with an AABA refrain. This schematic structure, in the hands of the more inventive composers, allowed for all sorts of interesting variations.

- First, the **verse.** The verse usually sets up a dramatic context or emotional tone. Although verses were the most important part of nineteenth-century popular songs, they were regarded as mere introductions by the 1920s, and today the verses of Tin Pan Alley songs are infrequently performed.
- Then, the **refrain**, the part that is usually considered "the song" today. It is usually made up of four sections of equal length, in the pattern:

$$A \quad A \quad B \quad A$$

  - The A section presents the main melody, the basic pattern of the lyrics, and a set of chord changes to support them.
  - The music of the A section is then repeated with new lyrics; often some slight melodic changes will be introduced, making this A', i.e., a variation of A.
  - The B section, or "**bridge**," is then introduced. The bridge presents new material—a new melody, chord changes, and lyrics.
  - Finally, the A melody and chord changes are repeated with new lyrics (and sometimes with further melodic alterations or with an addition called a "tag," producing an A", a second variation of A), and we're back at the "top" of the song.

Such song forms became the basis of listening habits; in those days, just as today, audiences were conditioned to hearing particular musical forms. A listener familiar with the AABA form would probably approach a new song (or a new recording of an old song) with the expectation that the A section should at some point be followed by a contrasting section with different chords, words, and melody (the bridge), and that the performance was likely to end with the A section heard again. Composers, singers, and **arrangers**—the individuals who bore responsibility for creating a musical environment (including choice of key, tempo, instrumental accompaniment, and so on) that would match a given singer's vocal strengths to a particular song—became adept at fulfilling these expectations while introducing just enough unexpected variation to keep the listener's attention. The attractiveness of a popular song, and of its rendering on a particular recording, had much to do with achieving a balance between predictability and novelty. Although a lot of mediocre music was produced by Tin Pan Alley composers, the best songwriters were able to work creatively within the structural limitations of standard popular song forms.

WHAT WERE TIN PAN ALLEY SONGS ABOUT?

Tin Pan Alley songs did not, by and large, deal directly with the troubling issues of the 1920s and 1930s: racism, massive unemployment, and the rise of fascism in central and eastern Europe. Only a few songs written by Tin Pan Alley composers even mention the Great Depression, during which some historians estimate that 60 percent of Americans were unemployed. The Tin Pan Alley song "Brother Can You

Box 4.2 Tin Pan Alley and Broadway

The close proximity of the music publishers on Tin Pan Alley to the stages of Broadway was not merely a happy accident of Manhattan Island geography. There was a long-standing and mutually beneficial relationship between the songs and the shows, and this relationship was never more fruitful than in the 1920s and 1930s—the so-called Golden Age of Tin Pan Alley song. Tin Pan Alley at this time offered a seemingly endless supply of fine new songs, written by a new generation of exceptionally talented composers and lyricists for contemporary audiences; Broadway's musical shows presented songs to new crowds receptive to contemporary entertainment on a daily basis. In strictly economic terms, then, Tin Pan Alley supplied a product for which Broadway had a demand, and Broadway in turn offered an outstanding show-case for that product: an abundance of exposure necessary if the product was to maximize its appeal to consumers.

Many songs became successful without being heard in shows, of course. But the nature of Broadway's musical shows in the period just following World War I was such that it was a relatively simple matter to incorporate Tin Pan Alley songs of many kinds into them. Revues, which featured se-quences of diverse skits, songs, dances, and performers—shows that were ob-vious successors to vaudeville, with such titles as "Follies" and "Scandals"—remained popular with audiences of the time. Many different writers could contribute songs to a single show of this type, and new songs could be in-troduced (or substituted for others that had worn out their welcome) to freshen things up if the show had a long run. And although musical shows with in-tegrated story lines and with scores composed by a single person (or by a composer/lyricist team) were also attracting audiences, the emphasis placed on plot and characterization in the vast majority of these productions was de-cidedly secondary to the emphasis placed on good songs and dancing. This meant, in effect, that the shows generally revolved around the musical num-bers, rather than vice versa. In these types of shows, consequently, it was also not a complicated matter to interpolate new songs or to make substitutions. It is indicative that Berlin, Porter, the Gershwin brothers, Rodgers and Hart, and other prominent songwriters of this period all wrote the scores to Broad-way shows—*many* shows—during the 1920s and 1930s. But with very few ex-ceptions, it is their *songs* that are remembered and that continue to live today, not the shows from which they came.

With the tremendous success of the musical *Show Boat* (1927, with score by Jerome Kern and lyrics by Oscar Hammerstein II), a new chapter opened in the history of the Broadway theater. *Show Boat* was, for its time, a musical show of unprecedented seriousness and depth; it addressed racial issues and presented a complex plot in which characters were allowed to experience gen-uine sorrow as well as joy. There was an attempt in *Show Boat* to tie the songs more obviously to specific characters and situations. Songs from the musical became popular, but they were known as songs from *Show Boat*. The trend to-ward musicals in which plot, character, and musical numbers are conceived

> as a highly integrated whole followed a winding path but was clearly in the ascendancy by the 1940s; the partnership of Oscar Hammerstein II with Richard Rodgers, beginning in 1943 with *Oklahoma!*, marks the triumph of this conception. With that triumph, the intimate ties between Tin Pan Alley and Broadway were clearly becoming frayed—although songs from Broadway musicals could still become chart hits. When rock 'n' roll took over the pop charts in the later 1950s, any close relationship between Broadway music and mainstream pop essentially dissolved. Not until 1968, with *Hair*, did Broadway have a musical that employed elements of rock style, and even though songs from *Hair* did become pop hits, such a phenomenon remains to this day the exception rather than the rule.

Spare a Dime?" (1932) stands almost alone in its serious treatment of poverty. In general, popular songs and the musical plays and films in which they appeared were designed to help people escape the pressures of daily life.

Both the lyrical content of Tin Pan Alley songs and their typical mode of performance were linked to the prominence of *privacy* and *romance* as cultural ideals. For many centuries the notion of a right to privacy was largely restricted to economic, intellectual, and religious elites. The development of middle-class culture in America during the late nineteenth and early twentieth centuries depended in large part on the adoption of elite manners and tastes, within the limits imposed by one's income. Middle-class aspirations were focused on the ownership of a home; the cozy parlor with its piano and mass-reproduced artworks, a center for family activities and for courtship, was a primary symbol of the homeowner's control over domestic space. This move toward privatization—which has culminated in the development of aural cloisters such as the portable CD player and the hermetically sealed automobile—is reflected in embryonic form in the content and style of popular songs of the 1920s and 1930s.

The ideal of romantic love, a theme inherited from European song and poetic traditions, is also reflected in the lyrical content and performance style of Tin Pan Alley songs. Unlike the old European ballads—in which the action of characters was often narrated from a vantage point outside the singer's own experience—the first-person lyrics characteristic of Tin Pan Alley songs (suggested in such song titles as "What'll I Do?," "Why Do I Love You?," "I Get a Kick Out of You," and "Somebody Loves Me") allowed the listener to identify his or her personal experience more directly with that of the singer. This first-person mode of address was reminiscent of elite poetic forms such as the sonnet, but Tin Pan Alley songwriters by and large avoided the flowery language of the Shakespearean ode, opting instead for a more down-to-earth manner of speech (songs like "Jeepers Creepers, Where'd You Get Those Peepers" took a vernacular approach to describing the loved one's physical charms, while the floweriness of Elizabethan love poems was expressly satirized in a song like "Thou Swell," written in 1927 by Rodgers and Hart for their Broadway musical *A Connecticut Yankee*). The idea that any working stiff could experience the bliss of romantic love—and, after a period of courtship, settle down and buy a home (his metaphoric "castle")—was widely disseminated by the mass media. Similarly, "torch songs"—songs that described the heartbreak of separation or of a romance gone sour—provided a ready-made outlet for the fear and uncertainty that many people experienced during the Great Depression.

The development of a singing style called *crooning* reinforced these links between popular music and personal experience. Listening to the early recordings of vaudeville performers such as Eddie Cantor or Al Jolson, whose exaggerated styles were developed for performances in large theaters, one feels that one is being "sung at" (sometimes even "shouted at"). A Bing Crosby or Fred Astaire recording, made after the introduction of the electric microphone in the mid-1920s, is an altogether different sort of musical experience, a *private* experience. The singer's silky, gentle, nuanced voice invites you to share the most intimate of confidences; it speaks to you alone. Sometimes, the listener imaginatively *enters* the voice of the singer, and a kind of psychological fusion occurs between two individuals who will never actually meet face to face.

The lyrical content and performance style of Tin Pan Alley songs thus reflected the efforts of professional composers to tap into the aspirations of an expanding and ethnically mixed but predominantly white middle class. These songs were also popular among other audiences, however, including the large numbers of southern whites and African Americans who migrated to urban centers during the 1920s and 1930s. This suggests that the images of romantic love and domestic bliss evoked by these songs, and the urbane sophistication of the superstar crooners who sang them on phonograph records and radio and in Hollywood films, exerted an appeal that crossed boundaries of race, region, and class. As we shall see in Chapter 5, many early blues and "hillbilly" musicians were influenced by the forms of Tin Pan Alley songs and by the manner in which they were performed.

Conversely, because Tin Pan Alley songs were closely linked to white middle-class identity, it is easy to overlook the influence that black music and musicians exerted on the composition of such songs. The turn of the century saw the increasing influence of African American traditions, especially ragtime, on the style and sensibility of mainstream popular music. This trend continued into the 1920s and 1930s with the popularity of songs and dance music influenced by **blues** and jazz. Although the mildly syncopated music that white audiences called jazz often bore little resemblance to the music that had developed in New Orleans, the so-called Jazz Age was nonetheless an important stage in the "Africanization" of American popular music and dance.

LISTENING AND ANALYSIS "MY BLUE HEAVEN"

Gene Austin's interpretation of the George Whiting–Walter Donaldson song "My Blue Heaven," released by the Victor Company in 1927, was the bestselling record of its era. (Not until Bing Crosby recorded "White Christmas" in 1942 did any record sell more copies.) Austin was one of the first *crooners*, singers who mastered the electric microphone after its introduction in 1925. He was a tremendously popular performer in the late 1920s: it is estimated that his recordings for Victor sold eighty-six million copies, an incredible number at the time.

A careful listening to "My Blue Heaven" will reveal many features that are typical of the Tin Pan Alley music of its period. We will also point out some features that might account for the unique success of this recording. The following description refers directly to the material found on the accompanying listening chart for "My Blue Heaven."

Basic Description

The record begins with a brief instrumental introduction. This serves to identify the tune of the **refrain,** so that anybody who had heard a previous performance of "My Blue Heaven" could immediately recognize the song from the outset. We could use a modern term and say that this instrumental introduction functions as a kind of **hook**.

Next, the voice enters and sings its own introduction. The lyrics and music here serve to set the scene for the main part of the song. This portion is the **verse**. Images of evening and homecoming in the words establish the peaceful physical setting and the gentle emotional tone of the song. Once the verse is finished, neither its words nor its music are heard again; we are fully prepared for the important business at hand.

The remainder of the record presents the **refrain** of "My Blue Heaven." This is where the most memorable tune and the most important words are found. As may be seen in the chart, the refrain is heard here a total of three times in succession. This assures that it will be quite familiar to the listener after only a single playing of the record.

Form

The *two-part verse-refrain form* is typical of Tin Pan Alley songs. "My Blue Heaven" is also typical insofar as its verse is shorter than its refrain. Although the verse-refrain form evolved out of the verse-chorus structure of strophic songs like "After the Ball," verses, by this time, usually assumed merely an introductory character and tended to have less verbal and musical interest than refrains. The lesser importance of Tin Pan Alley verses is reflected by the fact that they were often omitted altogether in recordings and other performances—or were occasionally played by the instruments alone as introductions to, or interludes in, the vocal part. There is no one typical form for a verse. In "My Blue Heaven," the verse has two clear sections, both of equal length and with nearly identical music.

The refrain of "My Blue Heaven" falls into four sections, which produce the typical AABA design. (This formal design was already present in nineteenth-century songs; see the earlier discussion of "Jeanie with the Light Brown Hair" in Chapter 2.) The first, second, and fourth sections have identical music and similar lyric construction, and all end with the crucial words of the title, "my blue heaven." The third section provides needed variety by presenting different music and a different rhythmic and rhyme arrangement in the lyrics; this is the **bridge** (sometimes called the **release**). There is a satisfying balance of repetition and contrast in this design, which helps explain why AABA forms were favored by the composers of Tin Pan Alley songs.

Why was "My Blue Heaven" so phenomenally successful? There is no single right answer, of course, but we can conjecture that its success was due both to the nature of song itself, as written by Whiting and Donaldson, and to the sound of Gene Austin's particular recording of it.

The Song

The lyrics of "My Blue Heaven" were written to appeal to the deepest aspirations of the Tin Pan Alley listening public. With just a few well-chosen images of benign nature ("when whippoorwills call") and domestic serenity ("a smiling face, a fireplace"), the lyrics present a familiar and comfortable version of the American dream: one's own home and family, offering a peaceful refuge from the pressures of the world outside. The picture—deliberately—is both sketchy enough, and suggestive enough, to appeal to a multitude of persons.

A nice poetic touch in the lyrics occurs in the bridge section of the refrain, where the earlier bird imagery is linked to human domesticity through the metaphor of the "nest." Note also the gentle pun as the "nest" is "nestled." Such poetic touches added to the sense of "classiness" exuded by many Tin Pan Alley songs, a sophistication that doubtless appealed to many in their intended audience.

However, it is probably the music of the refrain that accounts, more than anything else, for the appeal of "My Blue Heaven." It is that mysterious and distinctive phenomenon: a great tune—once heard, it is remembered, and remembered with affection. Particularly in the A sections, which begin with gentle upward curves of melody and fall to a satisfying sense of rest with the long notes on "my blue heaven," there is a feeling of inevitability both in the shape of the tune itself and in its perfect matching with the sense and the sound of the lyrics.

The Recording

Everything on Gene Austin's record of "My Blue Heaven" reinforces the feeling of quiet intimacy and tranquillity that characterizes the song's melody and lyrics. It may be this impressive mating of song and performance that contributed to the record's popularity.

The choice of a solo cello (discreetly accompanied by piano) to play the instrumental introduction was an inspired one. It set the record apart immediately from the norm of its time; much more typical would have been the choice of a dance band or orchestra. The solo instrument immediately establishes the desired tone of special intimacy. Also, the association of the cello with "high-class" symphonic and chamber music conveys an implied sophistication that obviously struck a chord with the record's intended audience. Like the poetic effects in the lyrics discussed previously, the choice of instrument may be seen as gently flattering the record buyer's taste and cultural aspirations (or pretensions). Cello and piano remain the chief instruments heard throughout this uninterruptedly soft and gentle record.

The accompaniment needs to be kept unobtrusive, for Austin's vocal itself scarcely rises above a tuneful whisper. This vocal is the perfect example of crooning. Austin's vocal performance would not have filled any but a small room, but the electric microphone picks up every detail of his delivery for the record without his ever having to exaggerate or stress anything. Crooning was still quite new in 1927, so apart from being intimate and therefore highly appropriate for this song, it was also felt at the time to be excitingly novel—and probably sexy in an understated way.

In the first half of the third presentation of the refrain, the melody is whistled in a warbling style reminiscent of the song of the whippoorwill (the whistler is Robert MacGimsey, famed for his ability to whistle two or three notes at the same time). Austin weaves his voice in and around the whistled melody, singing soft nonsense syllables. In places he speaks some of the words, creating the sense that he is talking directly to the listener. These techniques offer variety and also underline the atmosphere of intimacy and informality. At the very end, Austin effects a sense of conclusion by having his voice rise, instead of fall, on the concluding notes of the refrain.

LISTENING CHART "MY BLUE HEAVEN"

Music by Walter Donaldson, lyrics by George Whiting; published 1924; as performed by Gene Austin; recorded 1927

FORM		LYRICS	DESCRIPTIVE COMMENTS
[Instrumental intro]			Solo cello introduces the main melody of the refrain as a **"hook."**
Verse:		*Day is ending . . .*	Voice enters.
		Night shades falling . . .	Melody of the second half of the verse slightly varies that of the first half: their endings differ.
Refrain:	A	*When whippoorwill calls* . . .*	This is the main tune of the song.
	A	*I turn to the right . . .*	
	B	*A smiling face . . .*	The B section is the **bridge.**
	A	*Just Molly and me . . .*	
Refrain:	A		Cello takes over the melody; voice in background.
	A		
	B	*A smiling face . . .*	Voice dominates again.
	A	*Just Molly . . .*	
Refrain:	A		Whistled "bird sounds" represent the whippoorwills.
	A		
	B	*A smiling face . . .*	Voice dominates again.
	A	*Just Molly . . .*	Voice goes up, instead of down, at the end to mark the conclusion.

*In the published sheet music, the lyrics read, "When whippoorwills call . . ."

LISTENING AND ANALYSIS "APRIL SHOWERS"

A brief discussion of another popular song from this era will afford us a broader overview of Tin Pan Alley songwriting and performance styles. Al Jolson's hit record of the Buddy DeSylva–Louis Silvers song "April Showers," recorded in 1921, reveals the sound and style of the premicrophone period as exemplified by one of the most compelling and popular singers of the entire Tin Pan Alley era. "April Showers" was so successful, and so identified with Jolson, that he recorded it several times during his career; listening to his recording from 1932 illuminates further aspects of his distinctive approach to performance.

Basic Description

Like "My Blue Heaven," this song is a slow, sentimental ballad with a verse-refrain structure. And, as shown in the listening chart, Al Jolson's recordings of "April Showers" are patterned almost exactly like the Gene Austin recording of "My Blue Heaven": instrumental introduction, sung verse, sung refrain, repetition of the refrain. (In "April Showers" the refrain is heard twice, rather than three times.)

But the effect of "April Showers" on the listener is totally different from that of "My Blue Heaven," due to the special impact of Al Jolson's style. Where with Austin everything is quiet and intimate, Jolson's dominating, bigger-than-life approach turns this gentle song into a grand statement. The opposite approaches were the result, to some extent, of differences in the two singers' personalities and vocal abilities; but their approaches were also decisively influenced by technology—or, in Jolson's case, by the lack of it.

Jolson first made his reputation as a stage entertainer, in a period before electronic amplification was possible (see Box 4.3). Consequently, his voice and gestures were cultivated to fill a large space without assistance. This made him an ideal recording artist for the pre-1925 period, before the electric microphone came into use as an aid to small voices and intimate interpretations. His 1921 "April Showers" demonstrates the dominating character of his voice and interpretive style; despite the primitive technology, all of the song's lyrics and all of Jolson's musical gestures come across clearly and strongly on this recording. By 1932, of course, modern electric technology was available. But Jolson not only stood by the style that first brought him success, he also—if anything—emphasized and enlarged it. His 1932 "April Showers" is yet more dramatic and "theatrical" than his version of 1921, as if Jolson consciously set out to reaffirm his roots and to distance himself from the crooning style being cultivated by the younger generation of recording artists.

Form

As in "My Blue Heaven," the primary interest of "April Showers" lies in its refrain. This refrain can also be divided into four sections, showing a pattern of repetition and contrast. Here, however, the pattern is ABA'C, rather than the more common AABA. (The ABAC pattern is probably the second most common form for a refrain in a Tin Pan Alley song.)

The first and third sections of the refrain in "April Showers" begin in a musically identical fashion, but the third section continues with a slight alteration of the earlier melody and with a change in the accompanying chords (see the listening chart). The B and C sections are of equal length but are musically different; the C section brings the melody and chord structures to a satisfying sense of conclusion.

The Song

"April Showers" is similar to "My Blue Heaven," and to many other Tin Pan Alley songs, in its employment of genteel nature imagery. Here the imagery is not put in the service of a love song but illustrates some homespun philosophy with which all listeners were doubtless familiar: "every cloud has a silver lining." The words of the verse clearly establish that the ensuing nature

Al Jolson, as a cantor's son in the movie *The Jazz Singer* (1927), sings Irving Berlin's "Blue Skies" to his obviously delighted screen mother, while his screen father is clearly less than enchanted with this "jazz" music. Frank Driggs Collection.

Box 4.3 Al Jolson: A Vaudevillian Pop Star

Al Jolson (1886–1950) billed himself as "The World's Greatest Entertainer." He was the most popular performer of his generation, and his career overlapped the era of vaudeville stage performance and the rise of new media in the 1920s.

Born in Russia in 1886, Jolson migrated to the United States at the age of seven and grew up in a Jewish immigrant enclave in New York City. He began touring with a circus and a minstrel troupe at age thirteen, rose to success as a singer of "coon" songs in blackface, and made his Broadway debut in 1911. An advertisement that appeared in the music trade journal *Billboard* in 1907 touted Jolson as the "Blackfaced Comedian with the Operatic Voice. Never Idle." Jolson's energetic stage performances were in fact a major source of his popularity—it is said that he had trouble making his first studio recording because he couldn't force himself to stand still in front of the megaphone (the cone-shaped acoustic amplifier that preceded the electric microphone). Jolson was one of the first performers to use a "runway" that extended from the stage out into the audience (a technique now common in large pop, rock, and country music concerts).

In 1927 Jolson starred in *The Jazz Singer*. The following year, he appeared in *The Singing Fool*, one of the most successful early Hollywood sound films. His career went into a slump during the late 1930s, but was revived after World War II by the film *The Al Jolson Story* (1946), in which a younger actor played the lead role and Jolson supplied the vocals.

Many aspects of Jolson's style were derived from the nineteenth-century traditions of minstrelsy and vaudeville—he performed in blackface, spoke and sang (often a mixture of the two) in a loud "stage voice," and used exaggerated gestures appropriate for the large theaters in which he had learned his craft. Jolson was probably the first superstar to use fully the possibilities of all the new media available to him (which is what *made* him a superstar), and as such may be regarded as the ancestor of contemporary pop stars.

descriptions of the refrain are to be interpreted metaphorically, as representative of the sequence of life's moods, with the assurance that unhappiness will give way to better times.

Musically, "April Showers" possesses a memorable refrain in which the melody leaps repeatedly upward. This illustrates, in a sense, the sky-borne images of the words: rain showers, clouds, a bluebird. It also gives the tune a consistently uplifting feeling, which complements the underlying optimistic attitude the words seek to convey. Such a melody makes a perfect vehicle for a charismatic, big-voiced entertainer like Al Jolson; it is not surprising that his first (1921) recording of "April Showers" put his indelible stamp on the song, which remained associated with him for the rest of his career.

The Recordings

Al Jolson totally dominates "April Showers" from the moment of his entrance.[1] His exaggerated diction, his tendency to slow down and elongate the notes at the ends of phrases, his frequent swellings in loudness—all these characteristics make for a highly theatrical performance. (One can readily picture the gestures that probably accompanied his live performances of the song.) Nothing could be more "stagy" than Jolson's spoken portion of the 1932 recording; it makes for an amusing comparison with Gene Austin's occasional understated speaking in "My Blue Heaven."

In the 1921 recording Jolson is accompanied by an orchestra that plays an elaborate and decorative accompaniment suitable to the flowery sentiments of the song. The orchestral introduction of this version presents a melodic phrase from the song's refrain, providing an identifying **hook** (similar to that which opens "My Blue Heaven"). The same hook is repeated to conclude the song, resulting in an agreeable sense of overall symmetry. By 1932 the song was so well known that such a hook was unnecessary. Thus the brief introduction played by the dance band accompanying Jolson in the 1932 "April Showers" does not present any music from the verse or the refrain. Its function is purely anticipatory, as some ascending, billowy "cloud" music settles down gently to prepare the singer's entrance. There is also no concluding instrumental passage in this later recording.

In his 1921 recording Jolson simply sings through the refrain twice. Some attempt to make the repetition a varied, and intensified, experience is evidenced by such touches as the singer's more exaggerated treatment of the word "violets" at the end of the B section, and by his extended lingering on the word "song" within the concluding C section. In the later (1932) version, Jolson breaks into rhythmic speech during the repetition of the refrain, considerably heightening the impact of the performance as a whole and giving the record an overall feeling of steadily building intensification. Paradoxically, by returning to his old theater techniques, Jolson created a new version of "April Showers," reinvigorating his own standard tune—and giving his fans, many of whom doubtless already owned his 1921 recording, a reason to buy this later version. (A contemporary analogy is the creation of *remixes* of popular tunes, where a new version of a hit song is created through reengineering the recorded material.) One might well wonder whether the particular intensity of the 1932 "April Showers," with its firm admonition to see life's brighter side, wasn't also deliberately tailored to suit the anxious national mood of this depression-era year, a mood considerably altered from that of the prosperous 1920s.

It would be understandable if a modern listener's initial reaction to Jolson's recordings was to find them excessively mannered and impossibly old-fashioned.

---

1. Jolson's 1932 version of "April Showers" is obviously patterned after his original 1921 recording, which was the big hit. The observations here are relevant to both versions, unless reference is made directly to one or the other.

LISTENING CHART "APRIL SHOWERS"

Music by Louis Silvers, lyrics by Buddy DeSylva; published 1921; as performed by Al Jolson, recorded 1921

FORM		LYRICS	DESCRIPTIVE COMMENTS
	[Instrumental introduction]		Orchestra plays a "hook" phrase from the end of the refrain melody.
Verse:		*Life is not a highway . . .*	Voice enters.
Refrain:	A	*Though April showers . . .*	The main tune begins with a series of leaping gestures.
	B	*And if it's raining . . .*	
	A'	*And where you see clouds . . .*	Begins just like the first A section, changing at the end.
	C	*So keep on looking . . .*	New music brings the refrain to a conclusion.
Refrain:	A		Voice repeats the refrain, with slight variations added for the sake of interest and intensification.
	B		
	A'		
	C		
	[Instrumental conclusion]		Orchestra repeats the "hook" from the introduction.

LISTENING CHART "APRIL SHOWERS"

Music by Louis Silvers, lyrics by Buddy DeSylva; published 1921; as performed by Al Jolson, recorded 1932

FORM		LYRICS	DESCRIPTIVE COMMENTS
	[Instrumental introduction]		Band "sets the scene" with appropriate music.
Verse:		*Life is not a highway . . .*	Voice enters.
Refrain:	A	*Though April showers . . .*	The main tune begins with a series of leaping gestures.
	B	*And if it's raining . . .*	
	A'	*And where you see clouds . . .*	Begins just like the first A section, changing at the end.
	C	*So keep on looking . . .*	New music brings the refrain to a conclusion.
Refrain:	A		Voice alternates speaking the lyrics (in a highly theatrical style) and singing them, while the band plays the refrain melody.
	B		
	A'		
	C		

But Jolson's influence on the style of American popular entertainment cannot be underestimated. An emphasis on theatricality, on the *performer* and the *performance* as well as on the song—or even more than on the song—clearly has endured in the work of such disparate later entertainers as Elvis Presley, Tina Turner, Michael Jackson, Madonna, and Metallica.

LISTENING TO   BING CROSBY: "HOW DEEP IS THE OCEAN?"

Lyrics and music by Irving Berlin; recorded 1932

This recording of another Tin Pan Alley standard offers a fine example of Bing Crosby's style. Like Gene Austin, Crosby (1904–77) was a crooner, by far the most popular representative of the style. (Sales of his records have been estimated at more than 300 million.) However, a comparison of Crosby's performance here with that of Gene Austin in "My Blue Heaven" will immediately reveal Crosby's greater range and expressivity. Without ever losing the sense of intimacy essential to crooning—and to the interpretation of this deeply personal song—Crosby, unlike Austin, constantly varies his *dynamics* (relative softness and loudness) within individual phrases: becoming gradually louder to gently press certain questions ("How far would I travel . . . ?"), softening to color the pathos of "And if I ever lost you." Crosby doesn't hesitate to make the ending of this performance a relatively emphatic high point, turning the final questions in effect into a strong declaration of love; the singer projects certainty that his queries have no real, measurable answers. Other distinctive characteristics of Crosby's style are his use of delicate vocal ornaments to emphasize certain words (listen to the expressive quavers in "How many <u>times</u> a day do I think of <u>you</u>?"—and in many other places), and the general rhythmic freedom of his performance in terms of the singer's willingness to place words just ahead of, or just behind, the beat (which is especially noticeable in the repetition of the refrain, where the accompanying orchestra provides a steady rhythmic pulse throughout).

Irving Berlin's song, written for the film *Face the Music*, has a clear verse-refrain structure. The verse is short, consisting simply of four phrases, each one a question. The emphasis on questions continues into the refrain, of course, which falls musically into the ABAC type of pattern that we have seen before in "April Showers." One interesting technical feature is the way that the refrain moves from a beginning in a **minor** key to an ending in a different **major** key—a feature of another famous Berlin song, "Blue Skies"—while the verse presents this pattern in reverse. The constant use of questions (every single line in the song except for "I'll tell you no lie" is a question), which alternate from the personal ("How much do I love you?") to the metaphoric ("How deep is the ocean?") and back, makes this song both intimate and intense, and ultimately unique. Its lasting appeal to performers and audiences is no surprise.

WHAT MAKES A SONG A "STANDARD"?

If popular songs endure at all, they endure most commonly as nostalgia. Precisely because they capture the flavor of their times so tellingly, most popular songs sound unavoidably representative of their particular era. For the most part, it is difficult to imagine modern-day performances of old pop songs in anything but a nostalgic context.

Some popular songs, however, possess a continuing appeal that surpasses nostalgia. Since the nineteenth century, certain of Stephen Foster's songs have been performed so frequently that they may be said to belong to a stable core repertoire of American popular song. For a song to achieve such a status was relatively uncommon before the Tin Pan Alley era. But the period of the 1920s and 1930s yielded a sizable body of *standards*, songs that have remained in active circulation for more than seven decades. "My Blue Heaven," "April Showers," and "How Deep Is the Ocean?" are all examples of Tin Pan Alley ballads that have become standards.

Bing Crosby on the radio. Courtesy Library of Congress.

Let us now examine another standard from this era, in an attempt to illustrate another type of Tin Pan Alley song and to understand some of the factors that might account for its enduring appeal. The George and Ira Gershwin standard "I Got Rhythm" illustrates the impact of African American musical styles on Tin Pan Alley composition. George Gershwin's intense interest in jazz—he knew many of the prominent black bandleaders of the time and often heard them perform—left its mark on "I Got Rhythm," a song that combines structural elegance with rhythmic vitality.

"I Got Rhythm" was first introduced in the stage show *Girl Crazy* by twenty-one-year-old Ethel Merman in 1930 and became an instant sensation. The song was quickly recorded by many artists. Its enduring appeal is already suggested by the fact that Merman sensed a market for it as late as 1947, when she made the recording we will examine. This performance essentially recaptures the style and arrangement of 1930. That such a treatment did not produce a record that sounded significantly dated in

George Gershwin at the piano, with (left to right) DuBose Heyward (author of the novel *Porgy*) and Ira Gershwin (his brother's favorite lyricist): the trio that created the great American opera *Porgy and Bess*. Frank Driggs Collection.

1947—and that still has an immediate appeal more than fifty years later, for that matter—is indicative of the popularity and the stature of this song.

LISTENING AND ANALYSIS "I GOT RHYTHM"

Basic Description

"I Got Rhythm" introduces us to an uptempo Tin Pan Alley song. Such songs, of which there were many, often did not differ essentially from the slow ballads in form. As may be seen in the listening chart, "I Got Rhythm" follows the verse-refrain structure, and its refrain is in a typical AABA' form. The musical style of uptempo Tin Pan Alley songs is often very different from that seen in the ballads, however, because it is in the uptempo numbers that influences from African American music are most obvious. In particular, the refrain of "I Got Rhythm," with its consistent **syncopation,** conveys a jazz-influenced flavor that is unlike anything we have heard in the previous Tin Pan Alley examples.

In terms of performance style, an uptempo Tin Pan Alley song might naturally lend itself to a larger-scaled, more intensely rhythmic style than that exemplified, say, by Gene Austin's crooning in "My Blue Heaven." Ethel Merman's model is clearly more along the lines of Al Jolson and other premicrophone-era performers. (This is not surprising, since the song was introduced in a stage musical, where the practice of miking performers became common only in the second half of the century.) Merman was, in fact, a famous "belter" of songs, whose ability to fill an entire theater with her vocal presence became legendary, and she represents the continuing importance of this performance tradition through the 1930s and 1940s and beyond.

What were the uptempo Tin Pan Alley songs about? There were uptempo love songs, of course. The faster pacing also lent itself to novelty songs, such as "Yes, We Have No Bananas" from the late 1920s or "The Music Goes 'Round and Around" from the 1930s. One of the immediately distinguishing characteristics of "I Got Rhythm" is its resistance to such categorization. It is sort of a love song ("I got my man"), but this aspect seems almost an afterthought; and its rhythmic drive is certainly novel, but the song is in no sense a jest. Most essentially, perhaps, the song seems to be about the pleasures of music itself: "I got rhythm, I got music" are among the most famous words ever to come out of Tin Pan Alley.

Form

In seeking to understand the distinction of a song like "I Got Rhythm," an examination of form certainly helps. Surprisingly, what is most formally distinctive about the song is not its refrain but the length and complexity of its *verse*—and the rich relationship that verse establishes with the ensuing refrain. Unlike many Tin Pan Alley standards, in which the verse carries little weight, a great deal is lost when the verse to "I Got Rhythm" is omitted in a performance.

Gershwin's verse is nearly as long as his refrain, and it possesses its own in-

Box 4.4 George Gershwin (1898–1937)

The career and achievements of George Gershwin are unique. At the time of his tragically early death at the age of thirty-eight (from a brain tumor), he was already world famous, and to this day he remains probably the most widely known of American composers. Alone among his many distinguished Tin Pan Alley contemporaries, Gershwin sought and achieved success in the world of concert music (*Rhapsody in Blue*, *An American in Paris*) as well as popular music.

Ironically, it was Gershwin's acquaintance with the popular bandleader Paul Whiteman (see Chapter 3) that brought about his successful entry into the "classical" sphere. Whiteman commissioned *Rhapsody in Blue* from Gershwin for a 1924 concert, ambitiously titled "An Experiment in Modern Music," in which Whiteman and his band—now called an "orchestra"—set out to demonstrate the evolution of American popular music from "primitive" to more "sophisticated" forms. While virtually all the other music performed by the Whiteman ensemble on this occasion has been forgotten, the *Rhapsody in Blue* quickly achieved national and international success as an engaging example of new and distinctively American music.

Both Gershwin's popular songs and his "classical" works demonstrate a sophisticated incorporation of stylistic devices derived from African American sources—such as syncopated rhythms and **blue notes** (see Chapter 5)—that far surpasses the rather superficial use of such devices in most other white American music of the time. Gershwin's greatest composition, *Porgy and Bess* (1935), which he called an "American folk opera," represents his most thoroughgoing synthesis of European classical, mainstream popular, and African American stylistic influences—a synthesis that remains his own but that also celebrates the wide diversity of American culture.

tricate internal form (see the listening chart). In contrast to many Tin Pan Alley verses, it is notably tuneful itself and could *almost* serve as a refrain; in fact, it seems to be proceeding like an AA'BA refrain form, but it never completes itself. Instead of presenting a final A, Gershwin leaves the verse hanging open and proceeds right into the song's refrain—which then presents its own, completed AABA' form, in effect providing closure on two different levels. Structural sophistication of this order is the mark of an unusually gifted composer and of an unusually fine song.

All listeners will notice the striking difference in musical character between the verse and the refrain, accentuated in Ethel Merman's recording by the slower, flexible tempo of the verse and its more delicate orchestral accompaniment. The verse is rhythmically straightforward, offering scarcely a hint of the syncopation that will become a constant feature of the refrain. As a technical note, we may also observe that the verse and the refrain differ both in key and in mode, the verse being in a **minor** key, which moves at the start of the refrain to a **major** key higher than the original minor key.

Obviously, everything both in Gershwin's composition and in this performance of it is calculated to assure that the verse of "I Got Rhythm" will set up and complement the refrain. This fundamental contrast between the two main sections of the song also perfectly reflects the meaning and structure of the lyrics: the verse essentially poses a question (in effect, "why am I so happy?"), which is answered by the refrain. In tandem, they produce a whole of remarkable variety and richness.

The Song

Ira Gershwin's many fine song lyrics run a gamut from the highly sophisticated to the disarmingly straightforward. The play of rhythm and rhyme in the words to a song like "Embraceable You" (to be discussed next) is breathtaking, to mention just one example. On the other hand, the lyrics of "I Got Rhythm" flow so naturally and effortlessly that one is unconscious of any artistry at all—and yet this effect is precisely the result of great creativity. One clever feature is the presence of questions in the words of both the verse and the refrain, for clearly different purposes. The questions in the verse are real questions, while the refrain's repeated question ("Who could ask for anything more?") is obviously rhetorical, a reflection of the singer's feeling that all important questions have actually been answered.

Many aspects of the music in "I Got Rhythm" have already been mentioned. The celebrated refrain, like its lyrics, has the effect of simplicity itself. It is certainly and obsessively *about* rhythm, as the four-note rhythmic pattern first introduced—appropriately enough—on the words "I got rhythm" is applied over and over to changing words and changing note patterns. In much African American music a pattern that is repeated to create rhythmic momentum is called a **riff,** and it is likely that Gershwin derived the main musical *motive,* or compositional idea, of his song from jazz-influenced dance band music, where riffs are a common stylistic device. In "I Got Rhythm" every four-syllable phrase of text is set to this same rhythmic pattern ("I got rhythm," "I got music," "I got my man," and so on; in the bridge, "Old Man Trouble," "I don't mind him," and so forth). The pattern loses one note on the three-syllable line that ends the bridge, "'Round my door," but the only really significant break from this rhythmic obsession comes on the closing lines of the A sections, "Who could ask for anything more?"

How is it that these repeated rhythms engender excitement rather than monotony? There are several reasons. Like the riffs used in black dance band music of the time, the syncopated "I Got Rhythm" pattern is inherently exciting, since it begins off the beat and only the third of its four notes actually falls with the beat. This technique of "playing off the beat," commonly used in African American music, actually serves to intensify the listener's experience of the regular pulses that underlie the music. Furthermore, Gershwin assures that the melodic shapes paired with this rhythm sometimes ascend, sometimes descend, and sometimes, as in the bridge, emphasize repeated pitches. The sense of rhythmic release on the "Who could ask for anything more?" lines is especially marked, since the new rhythmic pattern here is much more aligned with the beat than the prevailing four-note one.

The refrain of "I Got Rhythm" is also associated with a characteristic pattern of chord changes. We mention this only because the chord sequence has become so widely used in jazz improvisation that it is referred to as "rhythm changes," after the title of this song. This is a further reflection of the song's enormous popularity and influence.

LISTENING CHART "I GOT RHYTHM"

Music by George Gershwin, lyrics by Ira Gershwin; published 1930; as performed by Ethel Merman; recorded 1947

FORM		LYRICS	DESCRIPTIVE COMMENTS
[Instrumental intro]			Assertive rhythms and sound of full orchestra anticipate the feeling of the refrain.
Verse:	**a**	*Days can be sunny . . . .*	Voice enters; slower, flexible tempo; soft accompaniment.
	a'	*Birds in the tree . . .*	Begins just like the preceding **a** section, changing at the end.
	b¹	*I'm chipper all the day . . .*	The **b** section is the same length as either **a** section but subdivides readily into two
	b²	*How do I get that way? . . .*	parallel parts that begin the same and end differently, thus mimicking the two preceding **a** sections. The formal effect of **b** is similar to that of a bridge.
[Orchestra picks up tempo and volume, leading into:]			
Refrain:	**A**	*I got rhythm . . .*	**Refrain** enters with completely new music, introducing the four-note rhythmic *motive*.
	A	*I got daisies . . .*	
	B	*Old Man Trouble . . .*	Melody changes for the **bridge,** but the rhythmic motive persists.
	A'	*I got starlight . . .*	Melody is extended and altered at the end, to effect a conclusion and accommodate repetition of the line "Who could ask for anything more?"
Refrain:	**A**		Voice holds high note, returning to words and tune only for "Who could ask . . . "; orchestra plays the melody in a big, "jazzy" style.
	A		High note again.
	B	*Old Man Trouble . . .*	Voice sings the bridge, adding spontaneous variants in words and melody.
	A'		High note again; voice goes up instead of down at the end to produce a big conclusion, set off by the slowing of tempo prior to the final high note.

The Recording

This exuberant song is ideally suited to Ethel Merman's full-throttle approach, and she holds nothing back. The slowing of tempo just before the refrain begins, and again just before the end of the record, is a theatrical device of obvious and proven effectiveness. In the repetition of the refrain, Merman's long-held high notes create a sense of climax rather than of rehashing—and also avoid the risk of rhythmic monotony that might arise from too many additional literal repetitions of the four-note rhythmic pattern. (An attentive listener will notice that, even in the first presentation of the refrain, Merman introduces some spontaneous small variations in this prevailing rhythmic pattern. This is a performer's privilege, of course, and in this case a natural result of having performed the song for over fifteen years.) Merman's move to a high note at the very end, in place of the expected conclusion of the melody, also allows the performance to end literally at a high point.

LISTENING TO "EMBRACEABLE YOU"

Nat "King" Cole's 1943 recording of the George and Ira Gershwin song "Embraceable You," published in 1930, illustrates the flexibility and creative possibilities of the best Tin Pan Alley songs. (For a discussion of Cole's career see Chapter 7.) The song is performed by a trio consisting of Cole, who accompanies his singing on piano, Oscar Moore on guitar, and Johnny Miller on string bass. As is often the case in both pop and jazz performances of Tin Pan Alley songs, Cole does not perform the introductory verse. After a brief instrumental introduction, we move straight into the refrain, which has an ABAC form (like "April Showers").

Gershwin's gift for crafting songs that seem to flow naturally from phrase to phrase is evident here. The A section is divided into two similar phrases. The first ("Embrace me, My sweet embraceable you") waits a beat before beginning with three rising notes ("Embrace me") that are followed by an extension of the same pattern ("my sweet embraceable you"). The second half of A ("Embrace me, You irreplaceable you") has the same melodic shape as the first, but begins on the highest pitch of the previous phrase. This ties the two halves of the A section together, creating a feeling of unity.

The B section ("Just one look at you—my heart grows tipsy in me; You and you alone bring out the gypsy in me") is also constructed of two related phrases, although in this case the second phrase begins lower in pitch than the first (a nice contrast with the A phrases). The music for A then returns with new lyrics ("I love all The many charms about you; Above all, I want my arms about you"), and the song culminates in the C phrase ("Don't be a naughty baby, Come to papa—come to papa—do! My sweet embraceable you").

The trio's accompaniment is sparse enough to let the beauty of Gershwin's melody, clothed in Cole's rich baritone voice, shine through. Cole's vocal treatment of the melody is relatively straightforward, although he introduces personal touches at various points, including some **blue notes** (see Chapter 5), shifts in the tone color of long vowels (e.g., the vowel sound in "you"), and subtle rhythmic variations on Gershwin's written melody. The ABAC form is played twice through. The first time Cole sings the whole song. The second time a guitar solo replaces the voice in the A and B sections, followed by a piano solo for the next A section, which ends with a descending pattern (harmonized by the guitar). The performance concludes with a vocal presentation of the C section. The overall form of the performance is thus

Vocal	A	B	A	C
Instruments	A	B	A	
	[guitar]		[piano]	
Vocal				C

By applying his own sensibilities as a skilled jazz pianist, Cole was able to create a recording that showcases both the song and the performers. Interested readers might want to compare other renditions of "Embraceable You"—a good place to start would be to listen to Charlie Parker's interpretations of the song, two of which are included in *The Smithsonian Collection of Classic Jazz*.

Popular song both reflected and helped to shape the profound changes in American society during the 1920s and 1930s: the intermixing of high and low cultures, the adoption of new technologies and expansion of corporate capitalism, the increasingly intimate interaction of white and black cultures during a period of virulent racism, and the emergence of a truly national popular culture. These songs no longer dominate popular taste as they used to. Nonetheless, they continue to be rediscovered by new generations of musicians and listeners. Tin Pan Alley and the singing style known as crooning were important (if often unrecognized) influences on rhythm & blues and rock 'n' roll during the 1950s and 1960s. Many Tin Pan Alley songs are still used by contemporary jazz musicians as a basis for improvising. Current pop stars still perform them—for example, Elvis Costello's recording of "My Funny Valentine" (composed by Richard Rodgers and Lorenz Hart), Willie Nelson's version of "Blue Skies" (Irving Berlin), Bono's duet with Frank Sinatra on "I've Got You under My Skin" (Cole Porter), and the Smashing Pumpkins' revival of "My Blue Heaven" in 1996. In the early 1990s the veteran crooner Tony Bennett appeared on MTV's *Unplugged* series, finding a new audience among fans of "alternative" music, who valued the combination of emotional intensity and sophistication in Bennett's style and in many of the old standard songs themselves.

In Chapters 3 and 4 we examined two key developments in the history of popular music of the 1920s and 1930s—the influence of jazz on popular taste and the rise of the Tin Pan Alley song tradition. Now we turn our attention to music that at the time existed only on the margins of the popular music marketplace. Genres such as the blues and so-called hillbilly music (later known as country music) grew out of southern folk music traditions, were shaped by the migration of millions of southerners from the country to the city, and eventually came to exert a profound influence on the development of American popular music.

CHAPTER FIVE

"ST. LOUIS BLUES"

Race Records and Hillbilly Music

As we have seen, many of the bestselling songs of the 1920s and 1930s were produced by professional tunesmiths who worked for a small number of music publishing firms, all situated within an area of Manhattan less than one square mile in extent (the musical equivalent of Wall Street). Although some composers and lyricists were able to work creatively within the constraints of a narrow range of song forms (including the AABA and ABAC forms analyzed in the last chapter), powerful institutions at the center of the music industry—including the recording and publishing companies, Hollywood, Broadway, and ASCAP—were more interested in guaranteeing profits than in encouraging musical diversity or experimentation.

Despite the essential conservatism of the music industry, it was during the years between World War I and World War II (1918–40) that companies targeted some specific new audiences and, in the process, recorded and disseminated types of music—particularly genres derived from the folk traditions of the American South—that had previously been ignored. This process of musical diversification was encouraged by the migration of millions of people from rural communities to cities such as New York, Chicago, Detroit, Atlanta, and Nashville in the years following World War I. These migrants constituted an audience for music that reflected their rural origins and for new, distinctively urban styles of music derived from the older oral traditions. The prevailing economic conditions also encouraged companies to seek out secondary markets. In 1921 the American record industry sold over one hundred million discs for the first time. This peak was followed by a decline in the demand for phonographs and discs, due in part to the expansion of commercial radio, which provided people with a cheaper means of access to a variety of programming. However, throughout the 1920s the market for performers working in idioms related to southern folk traditions continued to grow, countering the overall trend.

The terms *race* and *hillbilly* were used by the American music industry from the early 1920s until the late 1940s to classify and advertise southern music. "Race records" were recordings of performances by African American musicians produced mainly for sale to African American listeners. "Hillbilly" or "old-time" music, on the other hand, was performed by, and mainly intended for sale to, southern whites. The record companies who released this material—including small independent labels and the large record companies of the time—usually advertised it in racially segregated catalogs and brochures. Although there were some exceptions, the music industry in general reflected patterns of segregation more widespread in American society. Paradoxically, as we shall see, these records were also one of the main means by which music flowed across the boundaries of race.

Although a clear distinction was drawn between race music and hillbilly music—each of which comprised dozens of specific styles—the two had a number of important features in common. Both bodies of music originated mainly in the American South and were rooted in long-standing folk music traditions. As they entered the mass marketplace, both blended these older rural musical styles with aspects of national popular culture, including the minstrel show, vaudeville, and the musical forms, poetic themes, and performance styles of Tin Pan Alley pop. Race music and hillbilly music both grew out of the music industry's efforts to develop alternative markets during a national decline in record sales and were disseminated across the country by new media—including electric recording, radio, and sound film—and by the process of urban migration, which affected the lives of millions of rural Americans during the 1920s and 1930s. And both bodies of music provided the basis for forms of popular music that emerged after World War II (rhythm & blues, country and western, and rock 'n' roll), extending their appeal across regional and, in the end, international boundaries.

RACE RECORDS

Although the Victor Company had released records by the Dinwiddie Colored Quartet as early as 1903 ("genuine Jubilee and Camp Meeting Shouts sung as only negroes can sing them"), recorded performances by African American artists in the first two decades of the twentieth century were basically in the Tin Pan Alley mold, including ragtime- and jazz-tinged dance music and "coon songs" aimed mainly at the white market. It was not until the 1920s that the idea of recording material closer to African American folk traditions, and the associated idea of selling it to an African American *audience,* took hold in the record business.

The music industry's discovery of black music (and southern music in general) can be traced to a set of recordings made in 1920, featuring the black vaudeville performer <u>Mamie Smith</u> (1883–1946). Perry Bradford, a successful black songwriter and music store owner, brought Smith to the attention of the Okeh Record Company and suggested that she replace Sophie Tucker—a popular Jewish American vaudeville star who specialized in "Negro songs"—in a recording session. A record that featured Smith performing two of Bradford's songs was released in July 1920, and although Okeh made no special effort to promote it, sales were unexpectedly high. Smith reentered the studio two months later and recorded "Crazy Blues," backed with the song "It's Right Here for You (If You Don't Get It . . . 'Tain't No

Fault of Mine)." Okeh advertised "Crazy Blues" in black communities and sold an astounding seventy-five thousand copies within one month (at that time, five thousand sales of a given recording allowed a record company to recoup its production costs, meaning that any further record sales were almost all profit). Mamie Smith's records were soon available at music stores, drugstores, furniture stores, and other outlets in northern and midwestern cities, and throughout the Deep South.

The promotional catchphrase "race music" was first applied by Ralph Peer (1892–1960), a Missouri-born talent scout for Okeh Records who had worked as an assistant on Mamie Smith's first recording sessions. Although it might sound derogatory today, the term "race" was used in a positive sense in urban African American communities during the 1920s and was an early example of black nationalism; an individual who wanted to express pride in his heritage might refer to himself as "a race man." The term was soon picked up by other companies and was also widely used by the black press. The performances released on race records included a variety of musical styles—**blues,** jazz, gospel choirs, vocal quartets, string bands, and jug-and-washboard bands—as well as verbal performances such as sermons, stories, and comic routines. Not all recordings featuring African American artists were automatically classified as race records. For example, recordings by black dance orchestras or jazz bands with a substantial white audience—including James Reese Europe's Clef Club Orchestra—were listed in the mainstream pop record catalogs (see Chapter 3). A few records by African American artists even found their way into the hillbilly catalogs.

The emergence of race records set a pattern that has been repeated many times in the history of American popular music, in which talented entrepreneurs, often connected with small, independent record labels, take the lead in exploring and promoting music outside the commercial mainstream. Okeh Records, under the direction of Ralph Peer, was the first label to send mobile recording units into the South, seeking out and recording local talent. Traveling in a car with recording equipment and a team of two engineers, Peer recorded in Atlanta, Memphis, New Orleans, Dallas, and other cities and towns in the South. Paramount Records, the second company to enter the race music market, began in 1922 as a subsidiary of the Wisconsin Chair Company. Although this may seem like a strange sideline for a furniture company, the combination in fact made perfect sense: the company made phonographs and the wooden cabinetry that enclosed them, and the software side of the business (production and sale of discs) reinforced the hardware side (production and sale of phonographs). Helped by the business acumen and community connections of J. Mayo Williams, one of a handful of African American men influential in the management side of the record business, Paramount became one of the most important race record labels. Its records were sold by traveling salesmen and shop owners throughout the country, and a thriving mail-order service allowed the company to cultivate a substantial rural audience.

The large record companies took several years to catch on to the new trend: Columbia Records started its successful race series in 1923, and Vocalion/Brunswick Records entered the field in 1926, while the relatively conservative Victor Company—which had heard and rejected Mamie Smith in 1920—waited until 1927. We will see this same process—in which small independent record labels develop new musical trends and markets, while the big record companies wait several years before moving in to capitalize on the new markets—repeated in the 1950s with rock 'n' roll, in the 1970s with reggae and punk, in the 1980s with rap music, and in the 1990s with alternative rock.

The 1920s also saw the emergence of African American–owned record companies. The first of these was Black Swan, founded in 1921 in New York by Harry Pace, a former partner of the bandleader and songwriter W. C. Handy (see Box 5.1). In announcing the new company, Pace stated that it intended to meet "a legitimate and growing demand" among the twelve million people of African descent in the United States. Bandleader Fletcher Henderson—later to be the inspiration for the big-band swing style of the 1930s and 1940s (see Chapter 6)—was the label's musical director. Black Swan managed to buy its own pressing plant and eventually expanded its catalog to include hillbilly and operatic, as well as race, records. The range of businesses that sold race records is indicated by this announcement, placed by Black Swan in black newspapers in 1923:

> We Want Live Agents Everywhere! Music stores, drug stores, furniture dealers, news stands, cigar stores, manicuring and hairdressing parlors, delicatessen shops and all other places of business catering to retail trade.

By 1927 a total of some five hundred race records were being issued every year. Throughout the 1920s African Americans bought as many as ten million blues and gospel recordings a year, almost one per person, an astonishingly high figure when compared with the mainstream record market, especially considering that many black people lived in poverty. Although detailed information on the consumption of recorded music by African Americans during this period is sketchy, it seems clear that even in the most isolated communities, the phonograph was an important part of everyday life. A survey of rural communities in Alabama in 1930 found that 13 percent of Negro families—most of them living in grinding poverty—owned phonographs, bought on installment plans from local merchants. Many young people in these communities thus grew up with the sound of a phonograph as part of their everyday experience. Migrants from rural communities who had relocated to urban centers returned periodically, bringing with them the latest hit records and creating a continual flow of musical styles and tastes between city and country.

It is clear that the music business did not create race music or its intended audience out of thin air. It would be more accurate to say that the basis for an African American audience already existed and the companies, hungry for new markets, moved to exploit (and in some cases to shape) this sense of a distinctive black identity. This process in turn helped to create a truly national African American musical culture—for the first time, people living in New York City, Gary (Indiana), Jackson (Mississippi), and Los Angeles could hear the same phonograph records at around the same time. It was during this period that the first generation of national black music stars emerged, including Bessie Smith, Blind Lemon Jefferson, and Robert Johnson.

CLASSIC BLUES

One of the most influential kinds of music disseminated on race records was the **blues,** a musical genre that emerged in black communities of the Deep South—especially the region from the Mississippi Delta to East Texas—sometime around the end of the nineteenth century. In the beginning, the influence of this tradition on the American pop mainstream was quite indirect, taking the form of professionally composed "blues songs," filtered through the sensibilities of Tin Pan Alley and vaudeville, and shaped by the commercial needs of the music industry. In 1914 Prince's Orchestra, the studio ensemble that provided backing for many of Al Jolson's early recordings, released the first in a series of "blues" dance arrangements, numbers in a fox-trot style that bore little if any resemblance to the music played in southern black communities but that were nonetheless an important aspect of African American influence on mainstream popular dance (see Chapter 3). The first vocal performance labeled "blues"—"Nigger Blues," composed in 1912 and recorded in 1916—featured George O'Connor, a white attorney and lobbyist from Washington, D.C. As its offensive title suggests, this was actually a ragtime-influenced "coon song" in blues form (see below). (O'Connor, an amateur minstrel, performed his blackface routines at the White House for every president from McKinley to Truman.)

In this context, it is perhaps understandable that the first blues records by African American singers—including Mamie Smith's "Crazy Blues"—were not the country

---

Box 5.1 "Father of the Blues": W. C. Handy

The most influential of the classic blues composers was William Christopher Handy, born in Alabama in 1873. The son of a conservative pastor who forbade him from playing guitar (an instrument often associated with the devil, as well as with the lower classes), Handy instead channeled his musical talents into playing the cornet. He went on to receive a college degree and became a schoolteacher. To augment his income, Handy also worked as a freelance musician, taking the job of bandmaster for a minstrel troupe and eventually forming his own dance band. In 1908 Handy cofounded the first African American–owned music publishing house (his partner was Harry Pace, who would later go on to found Black Swan Records).

For a period of some twenty-five years Handy toured the South, where he became acquainted with forms of music not allowed into his house during his boyhood. As we shall see, Handy's blues actually owed much to Tin Pan Alley song forms but also drew substantially on African American folk traditions. W. C. Handy's first sheet music hit was "Memphis Blues" (1912), composed as a campaign song for Boss Crump, the famously crooked mayor of Memphis, Tennessee. His biggest hit was the song "St. Louis Blues" (1914), which went on to become one of the most frequently recorded American songs of all time. To capitalize on his success, Handy moved to New York City, where his dance band made a number of recordings and attracted a large, racially mixed audience. Regarded by many white Americans as the originator of the blues, Handy christened himself "father of the blues" and wrote a fascinating autobiography about his career. W. C. Handy died in 1958, the same year that Nat "King" Cole played him in a film adaptation of the autobiography.

Bessie Smith at the Apollo Theatre (Harlem, New York City), 1936. Frank Driggs Collection.

blues performed by sharecroppers and laborers in the Mississippi Delta and East Texas, but blues songs (sometimes called *classic blues*) written by professional song-writers eager to cash in on the national fascination with "authentic Negro music." Some of the most prominent composers of these Tin Pan Alley–style blues songs were middle-class African American men, who also led popular dance orchestras and composed ragtime songs (a genre that overlapped with blues songs). In many cases these songwriters viewed the folk traditions of the Deep South from a dis-tance and thus came to the blues as partial outsiders.

Classic blues songs were performed by high-class nightclub singers such as Al-berta Hunter (1895–1984), billed as the "Marian Anderson of the Blues," and Ethel Waters (1896–1977), who entertained the growing African American middle class in New York, Chicago, and other northern cities, and by singers who performed in a somewhat rougher style, including Gertrude "Ma" Rainey (1886–1939), popularly known as the "Mother of the Blues," and Bessie Smith (1894–1937), the "Empress of the Blues." Unlike their more refined middle-class counterparts, Rainey and Smith had developed their singing styles in the rough-and-tumble black vaudeville and tent shows that crisscrossed the country in the early decades of the century. Their early recordings, released during the height of the so-called blues craze (1920–26), sold well among both whites and blacks and signaled the emergence of a style of performance more directly and deeply informed by African American musical tra-ditions than either nineteenth-century minstrelsy or the ragtime-tinged pop songs of the early twentieth century.

LISTENING AND ANALYSIS "ST. LOUIS BLUES"

Bessie Smith's 1925 version of "St. Louis Blues" was the kind of recording that introduced much of white America—and a large section of black America—to the blues. It was typical insofar as it represented a hybrid approach both to blues composition and to blues performance. W. C. Handy's "St. Louis Blues" and Bessie Smith's interpretation of it are both some distance removed from what might today be regarded as the most "authentic," or at least the most roots-conscious, type of blues, namely, the "down-home" rural blues represented by composer/performers such as Charley Patton, Blind Lemon Jefferson, and Robert Johnson (all of whom we shall meet shortly). But as we have already seen, it was often the very process of musical hybridization that enabled marginal music to begin crossing over into the mainstream of American popular music.

Bessie Smith, along with other black singers who toured and performed in northern urban centers, adapted her repertoire and performing to suit the tastes of her audiences and came to represent the style called, paradoxically perhaps, classic blues. It was the unprecedented success of the classic blues singers and records that eventually prompted interest in the roots of the blues and led to the later recording of rural southern practitioners of the form. Bessie Smith's 1925 recording of "St. Louis Blues" was an early crossover hit, selling well among whites as well as blacks. Although there were no official industry charts for hit records at the time, it has been estimated that Smith's "St. Louis Blues" must have reached the equivalent of Number Three on the mainstream pop charts. Even more remarkable is the fact that Bessie Smith's first Columbia recording, of "Down Hearted Blues," was the bestselling record in America for four weeks in 1923. Smith's ability to attract an audience that crossed the color line during the 1920s has been credited with single-handedly saving Columbia Records from bankruptcy during that period.

"St. Louis Blues" will also serve as our introduction to the blues. As might be expected, it is more regular and predictable in its use of blues materials than typical rural examples of the form. W. C. Handy, a middle-class African American composer (see Box 5.1), combined elements borrowed from the country blues (see below) with structural elements borrowed from Tin Pan Alley in "St. Louis Blues." And the formal clarity of Handy's composition is respected by Bessie Smith and her accompanists, even as they use the song's structure as a springboard for subtle improvisations.

Basic Description

"St. Louis Blues" is a longer and more complex song than we have encountered heretofore, a result of composer Handy's fusion of blues with Tin Pan Alley elements. Hence, Bessie Smith's performance presents the song just one time through, without any repetitions; this is all she has time for in a record that nevertheless runs over three minutes in duration. The song's lyrics depict a representative blues subject and mood in their lament over love gone wrong and their projection of a desire to escape the scene of unhappiness. The slow tempo of this performance helps to accentuate the feeling of despair—notice especially the moaning quality of Smith's drawn-out vowel sounds.

Smith is accompanied on this record by reed organ and cornet. The organ is somewhat unusual; a more common choice would have been piano, but the less rhythmically emphatic organ certainly reinforces the singer's projection of hopeless lassitude. The cornet player is jazz great Louis Armstrong (see Box 5.2). Notice how Armstrong's cornet replies to each sung phrase, engaging in *call and response* with Smith in a manner that is typical of much African American music. Call and response is a common feature of blues and jazz performances of all types and periods.

Form

As may be seen in the listening chart, the form of "St. Louis Blues" is based on the AABA model commonly seen in Tin Pan Alley songs. In this instance, the final section is really a C, having a new melody but relating to the earlier A sections by virtue of its identical length and its use of the same basic progression of chords. These A and C sections are representative of *twelve-bar blues*, a formal concept so important in the history of American popular music that it demands our attention here. In Box 5.3 we explain some of the musical elements that make up twelve-bar blues.

The Song

"St. Louis Blues" begins as if it might be a kind of **strophic** folk blues, with two opening presentations of a typical twelve-bar blues format in both lyrics and musical structure. As we shall see, examples of southern rural blues often adhere to this format throughout. A major factor in the impact and complexity of Handy's song is that it sets us up for a repetitive structure and then deviates brilliantly and expressively from our expectations. The A music never returns, and instead we hear a succession of two new sections, B and C, after which the song concludes. (Handy might well have derived the inspiration for the form of "St. Louis Blues" from ragtime music, which often minimized large-scale elements of return or dispensed with them entirely.)

When the lyrics turn from a tone of general lament to the specifics of place and situation with the mention of the "St. Louis woman," the typical blues music of the A sections gives way to a B section of contrasting form and character, and striking length. In one sense, B functions like a bridge, insofar as it separates opening and closing sections based on the twelve-bar blues. But unlike almost all bridges in Tin Pan Alley songs, this B music presents an independent and memorable tune with its own distinctive structure (a-b-a-b; see the listening chart), and it is in fact longer than any other individual section of the song. It is the central core of the song, virtually a song-within-a-song, rather than a transition in any sense; the B tune is arguably the one people most remember and most identify with "St. Louis Blues." And this is only fitting in music to accompany lyrics that identify the villain of the piece and describe her allure.

The music of the B section, with its more graceful, insinuating rhythm (along with its change to a **minor** key from the prevailing **major**) hints strongly at Latin

Box 5.2 Louis Armstrong (1901–1971)

The career of the cornetist and singer Louis Armstrong (a.k.a. "Satchmo," "Satchelmouth") challenges the distinction that is sometimes drawn between the artistic and commercial sides of jazz music. In addition to establishing certain core features of jazz—particularly its rhythmic drive or swing and its emphasis on solo instrumental virtuosity—Armstrong also profoundly influenced the development of mainstream popular singing during the 1920s and 1930s.

The outlines of Armstrong's early life are well known. He was born into poverty in the slums of New Orleans in August 1901 and had his first encounter with the cornet in the band of a Colored Waif's Home at the age of twelve. Armstrong emerged as an influential musician on the local scene in the years following World War I, and subsequently migrated to Chicago to join the band of his mentor King (Joe) Oliver, playing on what are regarded by many critics and historians as the first real jazz records (1923). In 1924 Armstrong joined Fletcher Henderson's band in New York City, pushing the band in the direction of a hotter, more improvisatory style that helped to create the synthesis of jazz and ballroom dance music that would later be called swing (see Chapter 6). By the 1930s Armstrong was the best-known black musician in the world, as a result of his recordings and film and radio appearances. Between 1927 and 1939 Armstrong placed fifty-five singles in the Top 20, including his biggest hit, "All of Me," which was the bestselling record in America for two weeks in 1932.

Although none of the leading jazz-influenced crooners of the 1930s—including the reigning pop superstar Bing Crosby—were able to directly appropriate Armstrong's rough, gravelly tone color, or his rhythmic drive, or his gift for vocal improvisation (a technique referred to by jazz musicians as "scatting"), all were profoundly influenced by Armstrong's treatment of popular songs. His approach was shaped by the aesthetics of early New Orleans jazz, in which the cornet or trumpet player usually held the responsibility of stating the melody of the song being played. Throughout his career Armstrong often spoke of the importance of maintaining a balance between improvisation (or "routining," as he sometimes called it) and straightforward treatment of the melody. "Ain't no sense in playing a hundred notes if one will do," Armstrong is reported to have said on his seventieth birthday. In addition, Armstrong infused all of his vocal performances with his own warm and ebullient personality, making his approach a precursor to the highly personalized treatments of songs typical of later genres such as rhythm & blues and rock 'n' roll. Armstrong himself claimed that if it hadn't been for jazz, there would never have been rock 'n' roll.

Louis Armstrong's professional longevity was astounding. Although his popularity waned somewhat during the swing era and the 1950s, in 1964 Armstrong became the oldest musician ever to score a Number One hit with his version of "Hello Dolly!" (from the Broadway musical of the same name), the first single ever to push a Beatles record off the top of the charts. And in 1988, some sixty-five years after his first groundbreaking recordings with King Joe Oliver, Louis Armstrong once again broke into the Top 40 with a rendition of "What a Wonderful World." (Originally released in 1967, the song's reappearance on the charts was catalyzed by its inclusion in the soundtrack for the film *Good Morning, Vietnam*, starring Robin Williams. When this, his last hit record appeared, Armstrong had been dead for nearly seventeen years!) In 1990 Louis Armstrong was posthumously inducted into the Rock 'n' Roll Hall of Fame, a fitting tribute to the continuing influence of the man who Bing Crosby claimed was "the beginning and the end of American music."

Louis Armstrong's Hot Five, one of the most celebrated jazz ensembles of all time, photographed in Chicago in 1926 (left to right: Armstrong, Johnny St. Cyr, Johnny Dodds, Kid Ory, Lillian Hardin Armstrong). Frank Driggs Collection.

Box 5.3 Technical Note: Twelve-Bar Blues

A *bar*, or *measure*, is simply a rhythmic unit of music, consisting of one accented beat followed by one or more unaccented beats. *Beats* are equal measures of musical time; when you tap your foot or your finger to a tune, you are sensing and measuring its beats. Most popular music with which Americans are familiar is organized in bars of two, three, or four beats, following one right after another in regular patterns. For example:

MARCH: **One**, two; **One**, two; **One**, two; etc.

     ↑   ↑   ↑

   [accent]

(In the march, each rhythmic unit of **One**, two, is a *bar*.)

WALTZ: **One**, two, three; **One**, two, three; **One**, two, three; etc.

     ↑   ↑   ↑

   [accent]

(In the waltz, each rhythmic unit of **One**, two, three, is a *bar*.)

BLUES: **One**, two, three, four; **One**, two, three, four; **One**, two, three, four; etc.

     ↑   ↑   ↑

   [accent]

(In the blues, each rhythmic unit of **One**, two, three, four, is a *bar*.)

It is the pattern of accented and unaccented beats that creates the characteristic rhythmic organization that we associate with specific types of music. Marches are typically "in two," to accord with the regular motion of two feet; waltzes are invariably written with three-beat bars; most blues and jazz—and most Tin Pan Alley music of either ballad or uptempo type, for that matter—have four-beat bars.

Twelve-bar blues refers to a particular arrangement of four-beat bars. The bars are themselves grouped in fours, and each group of four bars corresponds to a unit—a line, a phrase—in the lyrics and is also associated with characteristic chord changes. (In an instrumental blues, it is the recurring pattern of chord changes by itself that creates the form.) This is easy to hear in the initial A section of "St. Louis Blues." Let us consider the lyrics first. In following the chart below, rely on the organ for rhythmic orientation, as it clearly articulates each beat:

Beats:	*1*	2	3	4	*1*	2	3	4	*1*	2	3	4	*1*	2	3	4
Bars:	1				2				3				4			
Lyrics:	I hate to see				the evenin' sun				go down. [cornet response . . . . . .]							

Beats:	*1*	2	*3*	4	*1*	2	3	4	*1*	2	3	4	*1*	2	3	4
Bars:	5				6				7				8			
Lyrics:	I hate to see				the evenin' sun				go down. [cornet response . . . .]							

Beats:	*1*	2	3	4	*1*	2	3	4	*1*	2	3	4	*1*	2	3	4
Bars:	9				10				11				12			
Lyrics:	It makes me think I'm				on my last				go-round. [cornet response . . . . . .]							

The three-line poetic stanza, in which the second line is a repetition of the first, is extremely common in twelve-bar blues and is an obvious clue to its presence. The same pattern is present in the lyrics of the second stanza, the second A section of "St. Louis Blues":

Feelin' tomorrow like I feel today,
Feelin' tomorrow like I feel today,
I'll pack my grip and make my getaway.

The issue of harmony in the twelve-bar blues is obviously a complex one, since the progression of chords, even in examples of classic blues, is by no means absolutely systematic or consistent. Still, the twelve-bar blues does tend to be marked by specific chord changes at particular points in the pattern. The thing to remember is that the chord changes need not be limited only to these typical ones; a given performance may add further changes at other points. If we call our starting chord the "home" chord (musicians would call it the **tonic**), this chart shows the most important, typical points of change in the twelve-bar blues pattern:

Bars: 1   2   3   4
Chords: ↑ **"Home"** . . . .

Bars: 5   6   7   8
Chords: ↑ **Change 1**   ↑ **"Home"**

Bars: 9   10   11   12
Chords: ↑ **Change 2**   ↑ **"Home"**

Note that the chords at "changes" 1 and 2 are different from one another; thus there are three essential chords that define the skeleton of the musical structure. (Musicians call the chord at bar 5 the *subdominant* and the chord at bar 9 the *dominant*.) Although there are additional chord changes, this basic skeleton is clearly in evidence in the two A sections of "St. Louis Blues," and it is good listening practice to try to pick it out. This same chord skeleton is present in the twelve-bar C section that concludes the song, even though the vocal melody paired with it is different. This is why C is also a twelve-bar blues, even though its pattern of lyrics is different also, presenting three different lines in the stanza instead of having a repeated line.

American dance music, suggesting aspects of both the habanera and the tango. This evokes at once the exotic and cosmopolitan nature of the "St. Louis woman," with music obviously far removed from the unpretentious, more down-home flavor of the twelve-bar blues sections that portray the jilted singer and her feelings. Precisely at the time Handy published "St. Louis Blues," ballroom dance stars like Vernon and Irene Castle were making the tango the new definition of urban sophistication and sexiness in dance (see Chapter 3).

As already noted, the C section once again presents a twelve-bar blues structure, providing return on one level while offering yet further variety with its new melody line and lyrics. Handy himself said of "St. Louis Blues," "here, as in most of my other blues, three distinct musical strains are carried as a means of avoiding the monotony that always resulted in the three-line folk blues." While we may well disagree with the statement that strophic folk blues are inevitably monotonous, and while we may appreciate that Handy may well have made such a statement primarily to distance himself—as a middle-class, educated, urban black man—from poor, uneducated, rural members of his race, the remarkable richness of "St. Louis Blues" is indisputable. This piece, which synthesizes aspects of European American music (Tin Pan Alley song form), African American music (twelve-bar blues), and Latin American music (habanera and tango dance rhythms), is as representative as any we could name of the achievements of twentieth-century American popular song.

The Recording

W. C. Handy's published sheet music for "St. Louis Blues" presents a composition using "blue" melodic inflections and rhythmic syncopations to a degree unusual for its time. In notating his song, Handy still needed to balance his interest in evoking effects of pitch and rhythm that originated in African American folk tradition against the inherent limitations of a European-based system of musical notation. Bessie Smith's performance of "St. Louis Blues" adds yet another layer of complexity to Handy's already rich synthesis. Although Smith was by no means a rural blues singer herself, she approached the song as one intimately familiar and comfortable with many of the varied oral traditions of African American music, and consequently her performance treated Handy's composition with considerable—but never inappropriate—freedom.

Handy's published composition contains many written **blue notes**: "bent" or "flattened" tones lying outside traditional European-based scale structures, tones that reflect particular African American melodic characteristics. Blue notes probably reflect the long-range influence of African scales (and have to be notated as "altered" flat notes in European-based musical notation). In addition to Handy's written blue notes, Bessie Smith adds *additional* blue notes of her own to her performance, intensifying the African American flavor yet further. The effect of blue notes is profoundly expressive and easy to hear, as blue notes in the melody generally clash poignantly with notes in the underlying chord. To help you locate and appreciate their effect, we will use the first A section of the recording as a source of examples. Below are the lyrics for this section. The particular words and syllables on which Smith sings the most prominent blue notes are marked with asterisks—single asterisks for those blue notes she takes from Handy's own notation, and double asterisks for those she has added on her own to enhance the performance:

```
            **        *
I hate to see the eve-nin' sun go down.
    **    **      **      *
I hate to see the eve-nin' sun go down.
    **        **     *  *  *
It makes me think I'm on my last go-round.
```

Handy's written composition also calls for a great deal of rhythmic **syncopation,** rhythms that play "off" or "against" or "between" the main beats that define the meter of the piece. In fact, Smith's performance goes even farther in playing around the main pulse established by the accompaniment. (For a visual representation of this effect, see the rhythmic diagram of the first A section in Box 5.3.) Louis Armstrong's improvised cornet responses to Smith's vocal phrases are perfectly aligned with the singer's own stylistic approach; like Smith, Armstrong continually incorporates blue notes and syncopation into his melody lines. Without ever upstaging the singer, he maintains and underlines the pervading feeling of intense melancholy. But notice also how no two of his responses are ever precisely the same.

A further analysis of this performance would necessitate detailed comparisons between Handy's sheet music and the auditory data of the recording; this would become quite academic and is obviously beyond the scope of this book. The miraculous thing is that all the intertwined and overlapping complexities that went into the making of this recording resulted in nothing remotely academic in effect: the performance comes across as immediate, direct, sincere, and emotionally devastating.

LISTENING CHART "ST. LOUIS BLUES"

Music and lyrics by W. C. Handy; published 1914; as performed by Bessie Smith, accompanied by Louis Armstrong, cornet, and Fred Longshaw, reed organ; recorded 1925

FORM	LYRICS	DESCRIPTIVE COMMENTS
A	*I hate to see . . .*	Twelve-bar blues, with *call and response* between voice and cornet.
A	*Feelin' tomorrow . . .*	
B: a	*St. Louis woman . . .*	The B section has its own distinctive melody and internal form; call and response continues.
b	*Pulls my man around . . .*	
a	*Wasn't for powder . . .*	
b	*The man I love . . .*	
C	*I got them St. Louis blues . . .*	The C section returns to the twelve-bar blues format, but with a new melody; call and response continues to the end.

The recordings of Bessie Smith and other classic blues singers were an important part of the process by which African American musical styles and musicians shaped the taste of the predominantly white mass audience during the 1920s and 1930s. But it would be a mistake to think that the mainstream popularity of these records means that they were not equally popular in black communities. In her autobiography, the great gospel singer Mahalia Jackson wrote about the classic blues recordings she heard as a child in New Orleans during the 1920s:

Everybody was buying phonographs—the kind you wound up on the side by hand— just the way people have television sets today—and everybody had records of all the Negro blues singers—Bessie Smith . . . Ma Rainey . . . Mamie Smith . . . all the rest. The famous white singers like [Enrico] Caruso—you might hear them when you went by a white folks' house, but in a colored house you heard blues. You couldn't help but hear blues—all through the thin partitions of the houses—through the open windows—up and down the street in the colored neighborhoods—everybody played it real loud. (Jackson and Wylie 1966, p. 29)

Although American cities, towns, and villages were still segregated along racial lines, recordings like Bessie Smith's version of "St. Louis Blues" created a kind of bridge or middle zone between black and white communities of taste. As we shall see, this middle zone proved to be fertile ground for the growth of distinctively American styles of popular music.

THE COUNTRY BLUES

What was the initial inspiration for the twelve-bar sections and blue notes of popular songs like "Crazy Blues" and "St. Louis Blues"? In his autobiography, W. C. Handy described an encounter with what he called "the weirdest music I had ever heard" at a train station in the Mississippi Delta in the year 1903:

A lean, loose-jointed Negro had commenced plunking a guitar beside me while I slept. His clothes were rags; his feet peeped out of his shoes. His face had on it some of the sadness of the ages. As he played, he pressed a knife on the strings of the guitar in a manner popularized by Hawaiian guitarists who used steel bars. The effect was unforgettable. His song, too, struck me instantly.

"Goin' where the Southern cross' the Dog"

The singer repeated the line three times, accompanying himself on the guitar with the weirdest music I had ever heard. The tune stayed in my mind. When the singer paused, I leaned over and asked him what the words meant. He rolled his eyes, showing a trace of mild amusement. Perhaps I should have known, but he didn't mind explaining. At Moorhead the eastbound and the westbound met and crossed the north and southbound trains four times a day. This fellow was going where the Southern cross' the Dog, and he didn't care who knew it. He was simply singing about Moorhead as he waited. (Handy 1941, p. 78)

The music Handy heard that day was the *country blues* (also referred to as "rural," "down-home," or "folk" blues). Although country blues had existed for decades before the first vaudevillian blues songs appeared on record, rural musicians who played in a style closer to the roots of the tradition were not recorded by phonograph record companies until the mid-1920s. Most scholars agree that the folk blues first emerged in the Mississippi Delta, a region of fertile land that stretches some two hundred miles along the river, from Memphis, Tennessee, in the north to Vicksburg, Mississippi, in the south. In the nineteenth century the delta had been the site of some of the most intensive cotton farming in the Deep South, and home to one of the largest populations of slaves in North America. After the Civil War many former slaves were relegated to the position of tenant farmers, or sharecroppers, still tied to the land owned by white farmers, and living in conditions of extreme poverty. Some men were compelled to work on the levees, a huge system of earthworks that protected the fertile delta farmlands from flooding. To escape this exploitative system and gain some measure of freedom, others took to the road, working on the railways and riverboats.

The blues was the music of this impoverished black work force, and it provided a dynamic, flexible framework for publicly recounting aspects of their experience. The earliest blues appear to have been influenced by various types of African American folk music that already existed in the late nineteenth century. These included "jump-ups," songs based on short repeated phrases and often used as accompaniment for dancing; African American story-songs such as "Frankie and Johnny" and "John Henry," that show influences from the English ballad tradition; work songs, rhythmic songs used to accompany and coordinate agricultural labor; and field hollers or "arhoolies," stylized cries sometimes used to communicate across the fields.

As we saw in the analysis of "St. Louis Blues," the basic features of classic blues form are (1) a twelve-bar structure made up of three phrases of four bars each, with (2) a basic three-chord pattern and (3) a three-line AAB text. In fact, the rural blues that provided the inspiration for classic blues songs displayed a much wider range of forms. There are eight-bar and sixteen-bar country blues; a rural blues singer may drop or add a couple of beats in order to better express himself, resulting in $11\frac{1}{2}$- or $12\frac{1}{2}$-bar forms; some blues use more than three chords, while others are based on a repeated rhythmic-melodic pattern (a **riff**) and do not really use chords at all. In addition, there were distinctive regional styles of blues, based in the Mississippi Delta, in the Piedmont region of the Carolinas and Virginia, in East Texas, and in other parts of the South.

In order to understand the evolution of musical forms such as the blues it is important to consider how songs are produced and how they are disseminated from one person or group to another. In the early twentieth century the country blues was an entirely oral tradition, in which versions of a song were passed down from generation to generation, learned by ear and carried in memory. Because the blues was essentially a personal form of music making, individual musicians could construct their own versions of existing songs or assemble new songs from parts of others. The Tin Pan Alley way of making music, on the other hand, depended on writing songs down in a standardized form. In addition, the music industry's reliance on sheet music as a means of distributing music to the public meant that songs often had to be simplified in order to allow customers without specialized musical training to perform them at home. Thus the neat and tidy form of classic blues songs is in part a by-product of the process of musical notation, which tends to create a standardized and authoritative version of any particular popular song.

The process of recording, which began to affect the blues tradition in the 1920s, was another means of transmission that shaped the evolution of the blues. To take one example, Bessie Smith's 1925 recording of "St. Louis Blues," with its slow tempo and personal expressive touches, became a kind of model on which other performers based their versions. During the early 1920s many blues musicians in the South, having heard the classic blues recordings of Bessie Smith, Ma Rainey, and other vaudeville-influenced singers, added the songs to their repertoires. Later in the 1920s, when rural blues artists began to be recorded, certain melodies, lines of text, and styles of performance were spread on phonograph records, helping not only to create a nationwide audience for the blues but also to establish shared ideals of an authentic "deep blues" sound. These cases show how sound recording—a process rooted in urbanization and industrialization—can become part of the process of oral tradition.

CHARLEY PATTON AND "TOM RUSHEN BLUES" (1929)

One of the earliest known pioneers of the Mississippi Delta blues style was Charley Patton (ca. 1881–1934). Patton, the son of sharecroppers, was a charismatic figure whose performance techniques included rapping on the body of his guitar and throwing it into the air. His powerful rasping voice, strong danceable rhythms, and broad range of styles made him ideal for Saturday night dances and all-day picnics.

Patton's reputation and ability to secure work were boosted by his work as a recording artist. Between 1929, when he was "discovered" by Henry Speir, a white record store owner from Jackson, Mississippi, who served as a talent scout for Paramount and other companies, and 1934, the year he died, Patton recorded nearly seventy songs. His recorded repertoire included not only blues but also African American ballads, ragtime, Tin Pan Alley hits, and even church songs (which he recorded under a pseudonym, Elder J. J. Hadley). Charley Patton's recordings are the best evidence we have of a first-generation bluesman apart from the Texan Blind Lemon Jefferson, whose work is discussed later in this chapter.

The popularity of blues performers and blues recordings in rural black communities throughout the South stemmed from the genre's ability to explore the shared concerns of African Americans through the details of personal experience, often presented in striking poetic images. Unlike European-derived ballads, in which a story is usually presented in narrative fashion—that is, in a linear sequence recounting the actual order of events—blues songs are more frequently like a series of evocative snapshots, assembled around a theme or set of themes: lost love, sexual desire, work, violence, loneliness.

Charley Patton's "Tom Rushen Blues," recorded by Paramount Records in 1929, has a twelve-bar form, three chords, and an AAB text (with a few minor variations, typical of rural blues performances). Patton sings in the rough, heavy voice typical of Delta blues, and his emphatic approach to guitar playing is also representative of the style. The lyrics recount an actual event from Patton's life; Tom Rushen is a sheriff who arrested him for public drunkenness. The story is loosely organized, with the names of two other characters appearing briefly and general observations about life interspersed in between reported events.

Laid down last night, hopin' I would have my peace
I laid down last night, hopin' I would have my peace
But when I woke up, Tom Rushen was shakin' me

When you get in trouble, it's no use to screamin' and cryin'
When you gets in trouble, it's no use to screamin' and cryin'
Tom Rushen will take you back to the prison house flyin'

It was late one night, Holloway was gone to bed
It was late one night, Holloway was gone to bed
But Mr. Day brought whiskey taken from under Holloway's head

Awww it's boozey-booze now, Lord, to cure these blues
It takes boozey-booze Lord to cure these blues
But each day seem like years in the jailhouse where there is no booze

I got up this mornin', Tom Day was standin' 'round
I got up this mornin', Tom Day was standin' 'round
If he lose his office now he's runnin' from town to town

Let me tell you folkses just how he treated me
I'm gonna tell you folkses just how he treated me
Aw he caught me yellin', I was drunk as I could be

The basic outlines of this story are not hard to follow: a drunk Charley Patton is rudely awakened by Sheriff Rushen, who unceremoniously carts him off to jail, where he spends the night. But a closer examination reveals additional layers to this text, encoded meanings that any listener in the know—that is, anyone familiar with the conditions of everyday life in small-town Mississippi during the 1920s—would be able to extract.

The use of encoded, or hidden, meaning in the blues has its roots in many earlier genres of African American music. The songs of slaves could embody secret messages that were impossible to state directly in the presence of the masters or overseers; a famous example is the folk song "Follow the Drinking Gourd," which described symbolically certain landmarks on the Underground Railroad, a path runaway slaves could follow to the North and freedom. (The "drinking gourd" was code for the Big Dipper asterism, which could be used in the night sky to locate the North Star and thus to lead the runaway in the right direction.) Work songs or prison songs might contain encoded messages about bosses or wardens that would lead to punishment if stated outright. The presence of encoded meanings was a great source of the blues' power and influence; we will meet this phenomenon at many other points in our survey of American popular music.

In "Tom Rushen Blues" Patton does not attack the institutionalized racism of the times in explicit terms. Nonetheless, it is obvious that several people in the story, including the jail guard and Judge Day, have been imbibing whiskey, and that Patton, the only black man in the story, is also the only one to pay a penalty for drinking. The critique of white privilege in "Tom Rushen," as in many other rural blues, is conveyed within an ironic framework. In the next-to-last stanza, the incarcerated bluesman slyly reveals that Judge Tom Day is concerned with losing an upcoming election and thus is being forced to wander "from town to town," much in the manner of an itinerant blues musician. This humorous way of dealing with serious issues—despair (the blues), alcoholism, and at a deeper level, racism and small-town politics—is typical of many blues lyrics. Patton manages to poke fun at everyone, including himself; in the last line, he simultaneously protests his arrest and admits his culpability ("I'm gonna tell you folkses just how he treated me; Aw he caught me yellin', I was drunk as I could be").

This combination of dysphoria and humor, earthiness and philosophy, typifies the best country blues. As in the romantic songs of Tin Pan Alley, we view the world through the window of another person's experience. Unlike the romantic pop song tradition, however, the blues provides a gritty, realistic engagement with everyday life, offering metaphoric revenge and a mordant sense of humor as the best available antidotes to oppression.

BLIND LEMON JEFFERSON: THE FIRST COUNTRY BLUES STAR

Although the genre appears to have originated in the Mississippi Delta, the first recording star of the country blues was the Texan <u>Blind Lemon Jefferson</u> (1897–1929). Born blind, Jefferson was living the typical life of a traveling street musician by the age of fourteen: wandering from place to place, performing for whoever would listen, living on handouts and the hospitality of friends, while hoping for steadier engagements that could bring in more income. His first records were released in 1926, after an enthusiastic market for blues had been established by more modern artists, and Jefferson's songs were advertised even then as "real old-fashioned blues by a real old-fashioned blues singer." Like Charley Patton, Jefferson recorded popular ragtime numbers as well as blues, and recorded church songs under a pseudonym, the Reverend L. J. Bates. However, Jefferson's East Texas style differs from Patton's Mississippi Delta blues in a number of ways: the vocal quality is generally more nasal and clearer, and the guitar accompaniments are sparser in texture and less rhythmically steady, generally subordinated to the vocal performance. Jefferson often used his guitar as an extension of his voice rather than as an accompaniment to it; he frequently played single-string passages on his guitar to answer a vocal line (another example of call-and-response technique).

Blind Lemon Jefferson.
Frank Driggs Collection.

Listening to a record like Jefferson's "That Black Snake Moan," recorded by Paramount Records in 1926, it is easy to grasp why music like this would have struck a middle-class black musician like W. C. Handy—not to mention the white advertising copywriter for Paramount Records!—as "weird." Jefferson's voice has a moaning quality, sliding among pitches and sometimes sounding closer to speaking than singing. The moaning quality is accentuated by the textless vocalizations, such as "aay," or "mmm," with which Jefferson punctuates the beginnings of many phrases in the song. The melodic character of the vocal part is restricted essentially to brief, repeated ideas; each of the six three-line stanzas (see the text below) is set essentially to the same music, and all the repeated lines of text are set to the same repeated music. These features are probably what led W. C. Handy to refer to the country blues as "monotonous."

Furthermore, there is little feeling of chord progression in "That Black Snake Moan," as the guitar part is characterized more by single-note playing than by the strumming of chords. And the rhythmic feeling of the piece is unpredictable throughout, with individual phrases lasting shorter or longer than expected, according to the performer's pleasure. (The suspicion that Jefferson never played this song exactly the same way twice is validated by the existence of another, quite different recording of "That Black Snake Moan" made by the singer not too long after the one under discussion.) Indeed, as Jefferson is the only performer here, he is not even obligated to keep a steady beat going, since he does not have to keep time with anybody else. While some parts of the song seem to have a clearly marked pulse, others do not, and it is frustrating to try to tap your foot regularly to this record. What establishes this song as a blues is the form of the text and the presence of blue notes in the melody—not the more formalized chordal and rhythmic patterns found in classic blues performances.

If we listen closely to what Jefferson actually *does* with his seemingly restricted materials, we may come to appreciate an expressive intensity in his work that could leave Tin Pan Alley records sounding impoverished by comparison. The variety in vocal timbre and rhythmic approach that Jefferson brings to each successive stanza of his song is remarkable. The repetitive textual and melodic structures are nothing more than a skeleton on which Jefferson builds a largely improvised performance of risky, and striking, immediacy. One can actually feel the pain of the bedbug bite in the third stanza, and the weariness in the singer's heart as he asks his lover in the fifth stanza, "What's the matter now?"

Of course, lyrics like these demand a completely different approach from those of Tin Pan Alley song. It is instructive to compare the lovers' relationship in "That Black Snake Moan" to the idealized middle-class one articulated in the lyrics to "My Blue Heaven," recorded in New York City the next year (see Chapter 4). There is a blunt realism in Jefferson's words, with their description of poverty and erotic desire. Whereas the "I" who hurries to "my blue heaven" is a kind of generic figure—is it the singer, the listener, the listener's spouse, or an imaginary lover?—there is no question that the person whose life is described in "That Black Snake Moan" is literally the singer himself; when he asks his "baby" for fifty cents, she addresses him by name: "Lemon, ain't a dime in the yard."

The sexual image around which the song is organized—the snake as phallic symbol—is typical of blues lyrics. Sexual puns and the theme of erotic love were an important part of the appeal of blues and other race records—Jefferson's series of "Black Snake Moan" recordings were his bestselling records, and blues musicians like Bo Carter made a living from double-entendre songs such as "Let Me Roll Your Lemon," "Pin in Your Cushion," and "My Pencil Won't Write No More." The sexual content of blues songs was, of course, also a source of middle-class outrage. The frankness of sexual discourse in rural African American culture, not atypical of farming communities where the facts of life are observed daily, ran counter to the social mores of "respectable" society and of the religious establishment, white and black.

The lyrics of "That Black Snake Moan" are even farther from the tradition of narrative storytelling in Anglo-American ballads than the lyrics of Charley Patton's "Tom Rushen Blues." There is no precise chronological ordering of events here, and certain stanzas could be placed in a different position without affecting our overall understanding of what transpires. Obviously a sexual encounter is being described; apart from that, it is not clear where or when certain exchanges of dialogue actually take place, nor is it important to know. The singer is obviously addressing his woman at times, but other lines seem to be addressed to an outside listener, or quite possibly to the singer himself. This nonlinear approach to storytelling actually relates these lyrics to certain long-standing and sophisticated oral traditions in West Africa, wherein the roots of this approach certainly lie. By learning about varied aspects of an occurrence, the people involved in it, and their surroundings, we gain an overall feeling for what happened. Using relatively few, carefully chosen words overall, Blind Lemon Jefferson manages to convey to us a distinct sense of himself, his environment, his sexual partner, the nature of their interaction, and the way they both feel about that interaction. As we have already suggested, this is a very different way of communicating human experience than that typically deployed in mainstream Tin Pan Alley songs of the 1920s and 1930s.

Aay, ain't got no mama now.
Aay, ain't got no mama now.
She told me late last night, "You don't need no mama no how."

Mmm, black snake crawlin' in my room.
Mmm, black snake crawlin' in my room.
And some pretty mama had better come an' get this black snake soon.

Oow, that must be the bedbug—baby, a chinch [another small insect] *can't bite that hard.*
Oow, that must be the bedbug—honey, a chinch can't bite that hard.
Ask my sugar for fifty cents, she say, "Lemon, ain't a dime in the yard."

Mama, that's all right, mama, that's all right for you.
Mama, that's all right, mama, that's all right for you.
Mama, that's all right, most any ol' way you do.

Mmm, what's the matter now?
Mmm, what's the matter now?
Tell me what's the matter. "I don't like no black snake no how."

Mmm, wonder where my black snake gone?
Mmm, wonder where is the black snake gone?
Black snake, mama, done run my darlin' home.

Blind Lemon Jefferson, like many other race record artists, was denied any share of the profits generated by his hit records, and in the end he died destitute. Jefferson was buried in an unmarked grave in Texas, where a grave marker was finally dedicated by his fans in 1967. A sermon by the Chicago preacher Reverend Emmett Dickinson entitled "Death of Blind Lemon," released by Paramount Records in 1930, gives some indication of his importance in the African American community:

Let us pause for a moment
And look at the life of our beloved Blind Lemon Jefferson who was born blind.
It is in many respects like that of our Lord, Jesus Christ.
Like Him, unto the age of thirty he was unknown,
And also like Him in a short space of a little over three years
His name and his works were known in every house.

ROBERT JOHNSON: STANDING AT THE CROSSROAD

If the recordings of Charley Patton and Blind Lemon Jefferson put us in touch with the roots of the blues, those of Robert Johnson (1911–38) seem to point almost spookily toward the future. Indeed, no country blues artist had a greater influence on later generations of blues and rock musicians than Johnson. His work was especially revered by the British guitarist Keith Richards of the Rolling Stones, and by Eric Clapton, whose band Cream released a celebrated cover of Johnson's "Cross Road Blues" in 1968. Eventually, Johnson's posthumous reputation was such that when his complete output was reissued on compact discs in 1990, the set quickly became a surprise million-seller.

Robert Johnson's brief life is shrouded in mystery and legend, much like the history of the blues itself; it is the stuff of which myths are made. Little is known of his early years. His guitar playing was so remarkable and idiosyncratic that stories circulated claiming Johnson had sold his soul to the devil in order to play that way; when performing for an audience, he apparently turned in such a position as to conceal his hands so that nobody could see what he was doing to produce his sounds. Only eleven records (twenty-two songs) by Johnson were released during his lifetime. Yet by late 1938 his fame had spread sufficiently that the American music talent scout and promoter John Hammond sought him out to appear with major African American folk and jazz artists in a "Spirituals to Swing" concert in New York City's celebrated Carnegie Hall—only to discover that Johnson had very recently died, apparently a victim of poisoning by a jealous husband.

Johnson's music, like Charley Patton's, is representative of Mississippi Delta blues, a much heavier, more emphatic style than the Texas blues of Blind Lemon Jefferson. "Cross Road Blues," recorded by Okeh Records in 1936, serves as a fine example of Johnson's artistry. Johnson's guitar here is forcefully rhythmic, and while the song as a whole exhibits the freedom of phrasing also seen in "That Black Snake

Robert Johnson studio portrait. Hooks Bros., Memphis, 1935. © 1989 Delta Haze Corporation. All Rights Reserved. Used by Permission.

Moan," there is a much stronger feeling of regular pulse throughout "Cross Road Blues." Unlike Jefferson, Johnson uses the guitar principally as a chordal instrument, and his aggressive, rapid strumming of chords gives his work a flavor that anticipates the electric guitar styles of rock music. This modern feeling is abetted by the wide range of timbres Johnson obtains from his acoustic guitar; note his effective alternations of high-pitched, strained chordal sounds with low-pitched, fuller chordal sounds. He also makes use of the *bottleneck* technique, common among Mississippi Delta blues guitarists. To achieve this effect, the guitarist slips the sawed-off neck of a glass bottle over a finger on his left hand, which allows him to produce smooth glides between individual pitches. In the hands of a great guitarist like Johnson, the bottleneck technique can even be used to imitate the sound of the human voice. Johnson's creative use of guitar timbres is mirrored in his singing, which also veers eerily from high to low, from strained to gruff colors, as if depicting through sound itself the desperation expressed in the words of the song. The expressive intensity of the performance is given shape by the form of the blues, which is heard in the basic chord sequences as well as in the poetic structure of the piece.

Although the lyrics of "Cross Road Blues" are not encoded in a typical way, they are certainly personal. Just where the "crossroad" is, what its special significance might be for the singer, and whether it even refers to a specific place at all or functions just as a metaphor—these are all unknowable mysteries. (The image probably represents a continuity with West African mythologies, in which the crossroad figures as a place of uncertainty, danger, and opportunity, and as a symbol of destiny.) Even in 1936 the name Willie Brown in the last stanza would have been recognized only by those who really knew their country blues (he was a mentor of Johnson's). In terms of narrative technique, "Cross Road Blues" hardly tells a story at all. Like some of the greatest lyric poetry, it uses words to evoke an emotional and spiritual condition, in this instance a condition of harrowing darkness and despair.

I went to the crossroad, fell down on my knees,
I went to the crossroad, fell down on my knees,
Asked the Lord above, "Have mercy, save poor Bob, if you please."

Mmm, standin' at the crossroad, I tried to flag a ride.
Mmm, standin' at the crossroad, I tried to flag a ride.
Didn't nobody seem to know me, everybody pass me by.

Mmm, the sun goin' down, boy, dark gon' catch me here.
Mmm, the sun goin' down, boy, dark gon' catch me here.
I haven't got no lovin' sweet woman that love and feel my care.

You can run, you can run, tell my friend-boy Willie Brown
You can run, you can run, tell my friend-boy Willie Brown
Lord, that I'm standin' at the crossroad, babe, I believe I'm sinkin' down.

EARLY COUNTRY MUSIC: HILLBILLY RECORDS

"Hillbilly music," later rechristened "country and western music" or simply "country music," developed mainly out of the folk songs, ballads, and dance music of immigrants from the British Isles. It would be a mistake, however, to regard early country music recordings as examples of a pure and untouched rural culture. By the end of World War I even the most isolated rural community had felt the influence of urban institutions, tastes, and technologies. The first southern musicians to be commercially recorded grew up under the influence of minstrelsy, vaudeville, circuses, and the medicine show—a traveling spectacle complete with glib-talking "doctors" hawking dubious bottled potions and musicians ranging from Swiss yodelers and Hawaiian guitar bands to country fiddlers. The first generation of hillbilly recording artists was also familiar with the sentimental songs of Tin Pan Alley, and this material became an important part of the country music repertoire, alongside the older Anglo-American ballads and square dance tunes.

Interestingly, it was the race record market, established in the early 1920s, that led to the first country music recordings. The first commercially successful hillbilly record, featuring a north Georgia musician named Fiddlin' John Carson, was made by Okeh Records in 1923 during a recording expedition to Atlanta. This field trip, led by Ralph Peer and a local record store owner named Polk Brockman, was actually aimed at locating new material for the race record market. As Ralph Peer later recalled:

Brockman began scouting around but to my amazement he didn't know of any Negro talent. . . . Finally there was this deal where he wanted me to record a singer from a local church. This fellow had quite a good reputation and occasionally worked on the radio. So we set a date with this fellow but his father was ill in some other town and he just couldn't make the date. So to take up my time, my distributor brought in Fiddlin' John Carson. He said Fiddlin' John had been on the radio station and he's got quite a following. He's really not a good singer, but let's see what he's got. So the beginning of the hillbilly [recording industry] was just this effort to take up some time. . . . I can't claim that there was any genius connected with it—not on my part, not on his part. (Porterfield 1979, p. 93)

Peer apparently had no inkling of the commercial potential of Carson's fiddle playing and singing on songs such as "The Little Old Log Cabin in the Lane" and "The Old Hen Cackled and the Rooster's Going to Crow," which Peer later described as "pluperfect awful." Polk Brockman, having a better sense of the local music scene, ordered five hundred copies of the disc for circulation in the Atlanta area. These sold out within a month, without any attempt to promote or advertise them, and Peer realized that the sales indicated an audience for country music among rural southerners and recent migrants to the city. Although this realization may have been a bolt from the blue for Peer and his northern recording company colleagues, the way had in fact been well prepared: Carson had already spent some forty years touring the South and building a reputation as a championship fiddler, and his fame had recently been reinforced by a series of appearances on radio station WSB in Atlanta.

The new medium of radio was in fact crucial to the rapid growth of the hillbilly music market. In 1920 the first commercial radio station in the United States (KDKA in Pittsburgh) began broadcasting, and by 1922 there were more than five hundred stations nationwide, including eighty-nine in the South. Many farmers and working class people who could not afford to buy new phonograph records were able to purchase a radio on a monthly installment plan and thereby gain access to a wide range of programming. That early radio played a large role in popularizing hillbilly music, and a practically nonexistent role in promoting race music, is not difficult to explain. Most radios, and all radio stations, were owned by whites. There simply were no black disc jockeys until the late 1930s, when Jack Cooper started his race music show in Chicago. This meant that radio played almost no role in popularizing race music, which was much more dependent on the phonograph (and correspondingly suffered more when radio began to eat away at record sales in the 1920s and 1930s).

The first station to feature country artists on a regular basis was WSB in Atlanta, which began broadcasting in 1922. In 1923 WBAP in Fort Worth, Texas, aired the first hour-long radio show featuring country music, an innovation soon copied by WLS in Chicago (*National Barn Dance*) and WSM in Nashville (the famous *Grand Ole Opry*). The "barn dance" format, the predecessor of televised country music shows (a relatively late but famous example is *Hee-Haw*) typically featured a variety of musical performers as well as comedians specializing in cornball humor that relied on stereotypes of rural "hicks," "rubes," and "rednecks." The musical performers on barn dance shows included string bands (featuring some combination of fiddle, guitar, banjo, and mandolin), solo and duet singers (performing in a wide range of vocal styles and often accompanying themselves on stringed instruments or piano), white gospel ("Sacred Harp") singers, Hawaiian guitar bands, harmonica players, saw players, whistlers, and yodelers. (One country music radio veteran has remarked that the first country music radio shows exploited "anybody who could sing, whistle, play a musical instrument, or even breathe heavy"!) Radio did more than any other medium to popularize hillbilly music, both among southerners and a wider audience.

Most hillbilly musicians of the 1920s and 1930s did not start out as full-time professional musicians. The country music historian Bill C. Malone has noted that the majority worked as textile mill workers, coal miners, farmers, railroad men, cowboys, carpenters, wagoners, painters, common laborers, barbers, and even an occasional lawyer, doctor, or preacher. One important exception to this rule was Vernon Dalhart (1883–1948), a Texas-born former light-opera singer who recorded the first big country music hit. Dalhart's recording career, which had begun in 1916, had started to wane, and he talked the Victor Company into letting him record a hillbilly number, in an effort to cash in on the genre's growing popularity. In 1924 Dalhart recorded two songs: "Wreck of the Old 97," a ballad about a train crash in Virginia, and "The Prisoner's Song," a sentimental amalgam of preexisting song fragments best known for the line "If I had the wings of an angel, over these prison walls I would fly." Although Dalhart's tenor voice bore unmistakable traces of his experience as a singer of sentimental songs and light classics, he adopted a southern dialect and performed in a plaintive manner that country music fans found appealing. This was the first big hillbilly hit, a million-seller that contributed to the success of the fledgling country music industry, made Vernon Dalhart a major star, and helped to ease the Victor Company's financial woes. From 1924 on, Vernon Dalhart recorded only hillbilly songs, and he did more to popularize early country music than any performer except the "Singing Brakeman," Jimmie Rodgers, whom we shall meet shortly.

It is instructive to compare Dalhart's early success in the hillbilly field to the classic blues recordings of Mamie Smith and Bessie Smith. Each represents a process of hybridization between southern folk music and Tin Pan Alley pop. These singers all stand at some distance from the rural origins evoked by their songs, yet are able to perform in a style respectful of those origins. Finally, recordings such as "St. Louis Blues" and "The Prisoner's Song" are early examples of a phenomenon that will become more important as we move on through the history of American popular music: the crossover hit, that is, a record that moves from its origins in a local culture or marginal market to garner a larger and more diverse audience via the mass media.

PIONEERS OF COUNTRY MUSIC: THE CARTER FAMILY AND JIMMIE RODGERS

Country music has always really been about the relationship between the country and the city, home and migration, the past and the present. This is not surprising if we consider the main audience for this music during the 1920s: rural people whose way of life was being radically transformed by the mechanization of agriculture and changes in the American economy, and migrants who left home behind to find jobs and establish new lives in the city. Early country music records provide us with a stereoscopic image of tradition in a period of rapid change: on the one hand, ballads and love songs, images of the good old days, family, hearth and home; and on

The Carter Family: Sara, A. P., and Maybelle, in 1932. Frank Driggs Collection.

the other, tales of broken love, distance from loved ones, and restless movement
from town to town. These two images are perhaps best personified by two of the
most popular acts of early country music, the Carter Family and Jimmie Rodgers.
The Carters and Rodgers were both "discovered" by Ralph Peer at a recording session in Bristol, Tennessee, in August 1927. Their fame boosted by hit records and
radio appearances, both acts exerted a profound influence on successive generations of country and western musicians.

The Carter Family, born in the isolated foothills of the Clinch Mountains of Virginia, are regarded as one of the most important groups in the history of country
music. The leader of the trio was A. P. "Doc" Carter (1891–1960), who collected and
arranged the folk songs that formed the inspiration for much of the group's repertoire; he also sang bass. His wife, Sara (1899–1979), sang most of the lead vocal parts
and played autoharp or guitar. Sister-in-law Maybelle (1909–78) sang harmony,
played steel guitar and autoharp, and developed an influential guitar style, which
involved playing the melody on the bass strings while brushing the upper strings
on the offbeats for rhythm. Their repertoire included adaptations of old songs from
the Anglo-American folk music tradition; old hymns from the Sacred Harp tradition; and sentimental songs reminiscent of turn-of-the-century Tin Pan Alley hits.
As Bill Malone puts it, "theirs was a music that might borrow from other forms,
but would move away from its roots only reluctantly" (Malone 1985, p. 65). Between 1927 and 1941 the Carters made over three hundred recordings for a half-

dozen companies. Their most popular songs include "Wildwood Flower," "Wabash Cannon Ball," "Keep on the Sunny Side," and "Can the Circle Be Unbroken," all of which are still performed by country musicians today. Rehearsing at home, they crafted traditional materials into three-minute gems designed for the 78 r.p.m. phonograph discs of the time.

The Carter Family were not professional musicians when their recording career started in 1927—as Sara put it when she was asked what they did after the Bristol session, "Why, we went home and planted the corn." The Carters' image, borne out in radio appearances and interviews, was one of quiet conservatism; their stage shows were simple and straightforward, and they generally avoided the vaudeville circuit and promotional tours. Despite their image of being firmly rooted in the rural past, however, the Carters' approach to working with folk music sources set a pattern that would shape the country music business for years to come. Doc Carter went on periodic song-collecting trips, gathering material from both black and white musicians and reworking it to suit the Carters' vocal and instrumental format. At the urging of Ralph Peer, Doc copyrighted all of the songs that the Carters recorded, whether or not he had actually composed them himself. Of course, the line between original compositions and folk songs is a blurry one, since most composition is consciously or unconsciously based on preexisting material, and any folk song is bound to exist in multiple variants, shaped by the tastes and values of particular performers. Ralph Peer published all of the songs through his own Southern Music Company and split the profits fifty-fifty with Doc.

Jimmie Rodgers, in a photograph he signed for the Carter Family in 1931. Frank Driggs Collection.

If the Carter Family's public image and musical repertoire evoked the country church and the family fireside, <u>Jimmie Rodgers</u> (1897–1933) was the quintessential rambler, a footloose man who carried home in his heart but drank deeply of the changing world around him. He was the most versatile, progressive, and widely influential of all the early country recording artists. The ex-railroad brakeman from Meridian, Mississippi, celebrated the allure of the open road and chronicled the lives of men who forsook the benefits of a settled existence: ramblers, hobos, gamblers, convicts, cowboys, railway men, and feckless lovers. Rodgers's devil-may-care personality and his early death from tuberculosis contributed to his charismatic mystique, a sort of white parallel to the black bluesman Robert Johnson. He was early country music's biggest recording star, and his influence can be seen in the public images of Hank Williams, Waylon Jennings, Willie Nelson, and almost every contemporary male country music star.

THE RECORDINGS OF JIMMIE RODGERS

One major reason for Rodgers's success was his receptivity to African American influences, complemented by his ability to reflect those influences in original compositions and performances that proved appealing to a substantial white audience. In a highly successful series of recordings called "blue yodels," he adapted the poetic and musical forms of the blues, and aspects of blues performance styles, to his own purposes. The first such record, called simply "Blue Yodel" (also known by its opening words, "T for Texas"), was a million-seller; its appearance high on the pop charts in 1928 indicated that its appeal was not limited to a rural audience but had "crossed over" to the mainstream urban audience as well. Some of the later records in this series were provided with specific names (such as "Blue Yodel No. 8 [Muleskinner Blues]" or "Anniversary Blue Yodel," the seventh in the series and another pop hit), while others went just by homely numerical titles (such as "Blue Yodel No. 11"), but all were informed by Rodgers's distinctive approach to what can only be called "white man's blues."

Rodgers's blue yodeling was a "high, lonesome sound" (to use a phrase that has come to be generally associated with white rural music), analogous in certain ways to the textless moans and howls heard in blues recordings by rural black artists, and serving much the same purpose: to underline the intensity and depth of the singer's feelings. Rodgers used this vocal effect on a large number of his recordings, not just those with "blue yodel" in their titles. As for the actual "Blue Yodel" recordings, taken as a group they demonstrate a significant diversity in formal approach, lyric content, and instrumentation. Some of the lyrics conceal encoded sexual messages:

> I believe to my soul, somebody's been riding my mule.
> I believe to my soul, somebody's been riding my mule.
> 'Cause every time I want to ride, she acts such a doggone fool.

"Blue Yodel No. 11" is particularly close to rural black models. Here Rodgers sings a loosely connected series of stanzas that suggest the familiar poetic and musical patternings of twelve-bar blues. The song has a highly personal tone—a not uncommon characteristic in Rodgers's blue yodels. Rodgers's performance of this song conveys a sense of freedom through unpredictable phrasing and of course through the yodels that occur between stanzas. These characteristics parallel the techniques of the black bluesmen we have studied. But there are obvious stylistic differences as well. Rodgers uses the guitar strictly as accompaniment, making no attempt to set up any kind of melodic response (as with Blind Lemon Jefferson) or rhythmic counterpoint (as with Robert Johnson) to his vocal. With its simple and repetitive figures, the guitar part also creates a greater sense of chordal and rhythmic regularity than tends to be present in performances by rural black artists. (Even on those infrequent occasions when Rodgers offers a substantial guitar solo, as he does in "Blue Yodel No. 8 [Muleskinner Blues]," it is clear that he is in no sense a guitar virtuoso like Jefferson or Johnson—nor did he aspire to be.) Furthermore, notwithstanding his occasional evocation of blue notes and the sliding effects in his yodels, Rodgers's vocal melodies stay much closer overall to European American scale structures than do the blues melodies of African American performers. This, of course, is unsurprising; what is remarkable is the extent to which Rodgers *did* manage to assimilate elements from black music successfully into his style.

If "Blue Yodel No. 11" has as its subject a typical lover's complaint, "Blue Yodel No. 8 [Muleskinner Blues]" may be regarded as Rodgers's adaptation of the African American field holler, a work song meant to ease the pain and tedium of physical labor. "Muleskinner Blues" uses the typical chord progressions of twelve-bar blues, here accompanying three-phrase stanzas in which the third phrase is an extensive yodel rather than a texted statement. (This recording is included in the Smithsonian's *Classic Country Music* collection.)

Perhaps Rodgers's most enduringly popular record was "Waiting for a Train," released by Okeh Records in 1928. It is a hobo song with a dark mood, reinforced by Rodgers's lonesome yodel. Certainly no record demonstrates his forward-looking versatility more thoroughly. Instead of the typical solo guitar accompaniment, an ensemble consisting of steel guitar, cornet, clarinet, and string bass joins the standard guitar in backing up Rodgers's vocal. The steel guitar is a particularly progressive touch here, and it makes the record sound remarkably modern in comparison to many others of its time; actually it was not until the mid-1930s that the sound of a steel guitar became commonplace in country bands and indelibly identified with the country sound (see Chapter 6). On the other hand, the cornet and clarinet clearly evoke the small jazz ensembles of the late 1920s and link "Waiting for a Train" to the wider spheres of mainstream dance and pop music. The unusual instrumentation gives the record an almost jaunty character at times, effectively counterbalancing the downbeat aspects of Rodgers's lyrics and underlining the resilience of the hobo who at least possesses the will to survive and the wisdom to appreciate "the moon and stars up above."

Although "Waiting for a Train" was recorded over a year before the stock market crash of October 1929, its lyrics seem to look forward as well: to the Great Depression, when countless rural Americans lost their homes and farms and had to live by luck and by their wits, like the protagonist in Rodgers's song. The myth of the *outcast*—the resourceful, lone wanderer—presented so effectively in "Waiting for a Train" has proven to be a potent force in country music up to the present time; the songs and the public personas of Merle Haggard and Willie Nelson, for example, would be unthinkable without it. Yet, with all his progressive qualities, Rodgers

Box 5.4 Southern Gospel Music, Black and White

"Gospel Ship," recorded by the Carter Family in 1935, and "The Sun Didn't Shine," recorded by the Golden Gate Quartet in 1941, exemplify the general importance of sacred music in southern culture and the popularity of commercial recordings of this music. They also introduce us to some of the significant differences between white and black styles of gospel music.

As we have seen, the Carter Family was the first prominent "group" act in country music. Much rural music was heard and nurtured in informal family settings, of course; the unprecedented popularity of the Carter Family as recording and performing artists opened the gates for a succession of family-based acts that is continuing to this day. (Well-known examples from country music include the Blue Sky Boys, the Everly Brothers, the group Alabama, and the Judds.) In the musical culture of a family like the Carters, there was no firm separation between secular and religious music, and they recorded both types extensively. Their gospel recordings typically present their own unpretentious arrangements of old folk hymns; two of the most enduringly famous examples are "Can the Circle Be Unbroken" and "Gospel Ship." The Carters' performance style on such records is an utterly straightforward, unadorned one, whose plainness was seen by the performers, and by sympathetic listeners, as indicative of the humility and devotion that marked authentic religious faith. This aesthetic of plainness was a longstanding feature of the culture of Protestant immigrants from Britain and Ireland.

In African American communities, religious music has tended to be centered more exclusively in the church. Rural black churches made extensive use of music, and this encouraged the development of a distinctive style for African American gospel music and led to the emergence of talented performers in the style. The great black gospel groups like the Golden Gate Quartet were not family acts but typically comprised unrelated individuals who came together through a common interest in, and talent for, singing religious music—often in a local church (or school) choir. Black gospel music thus developed an independent identity—separate from white religious traditions, obviously, but separate also to a certain extent from other musical traditions in the black community itself. Black gospel artists were expected to perform sacred music only, not to indulge in "dirty" music like the blues. This explicit division between religious and secular music remained an important characteristic of African American culture for a considerable time; a major sign of change came in the 1960s, when "soul music" emerged as a new term applied to secular music that consciously incorporated stylistic elements from black gospel.

In contrast to the restrained white gospel music exemplified by the Carter Family, black gospel music tended to favor extroversion and an intense expressivity; this music can be highly ornate, and it emphasizes the personal and ecstatic aspects of religious experience. These characteristics are clearly evident in the Golden Gate Quartet's performance of "The Sun Didn't Shine," with its remarkable displays of vocal virtuosity and rhythmic intricacy. Of particular interest in this performance is the extended, seemingly improvised, virtually textless buildup to the final chorus. Here the background voices assume the sound and role of insistent percussion instruments (portraying "the hammer . . . heard in Jerusalem's streets"), while the lead vocalist, Henry Owens, hums and moans in a sacred transformation of blues techniques, immersed in his contemplation of the Crucifixion.

Especially when it is juxtaposed with the brilliance of "The Sun Didn't Shine," the homely simplicity of the Carter Family's "Gospel Ship" might strain the appreciative faculties of today's sophisticated, largely urban audience for popular music. We could call attention to the unique dark vocal timbre of lead singer Sara Carter; her voice and the way she uses it call immediate attention to the significance of the words she is singing. And we could cite the firm, clean guitar style of Maybelle Carter, whose "Carter Family lick"—her technique of playing melody on the lower strings of the guitar while strumming higher-pitched chords above it—became one of the most widely imitated guitar sounds in country music. But it might be more to the point simply to quote the final verse of "Gospel Ship" as sung by Sara Carter. These words doubtless expressed the feelings of many "hillbillies" of abiding religious faith who had to endure the scorn of "sophisticated," "higher-class" people:

> If you are ashamed of me, you ought not to be.
> Guess you'd better have a care:
> If too much fault you find, you will sure be left behind
> While I'm sailing through the air.

remained grounded in tradition. He based "Waiting for a Train" on an old folk song. Reflecting meaningfully on the past while pointing toward the future, "Waiting for a Train" encompasses a duality that is characteristic of much of the finest southern music, white and black.

"Waiting for a Train" is based on a **strophic** form, but Rodgers employs a number of strategies to avoid monotony. He freely varies the basic melody as he goes along—a technique common in music based on oral traditions, as we have already observed in our examples of rural African American blues. (A particularly expressive example of this is the way he bends the melody upward to portray "the moon and *stars* up above.") In addition, Rodgers achieves a large-scale structural shaping by varying the close of every third strophe to produce a firm **cadence,** while allowing the other strophes to end inconclusively. The cadences are reinforced with a blue yodel, which adds yet another element to the already rich stylistic amalgam. The two groups of three strophes are separated by an instrumental interlude, thus giving the record as a whole a firm and convincing overall form.

Additional facets of Rodgers's extensive contribution to southern music may be illuminated by a quick look at the tender love song "Dreaming with Tears in My Eyes," recorded in 1933. While this was a newly composed song (by Rodgers and Waldo L. O'Neal), it also looks to the past: its prominent triple meter clearly recalls the waltz songs of the late nineteenth century. However, if its rhythm reminds us of a song like "After the Ball" (see Chapter 2), its homespun and delicate lyrics have little in common with the melodrama and wild coincidences of that earlier pop hit:

> *My heart is longing for you, dear, I cared for you more than you knew.*
> *Though you have broken each promise, and yesterday's dreams are untrue,*
> *Alone I'll be yearning tomorrow, when sunshine brings mem'ries of you.*
> *My sunshine will turn into sorrow, as I dream of the love we once knew.*

These lyrics provide a wonderful example of humble, virtually invisible artistry. With their abundant open vowel sounds, they "sing" beautifully, and the triple meter of the music is already explicit in the natural rhythms of the words. Rodgers's melodic line gently rises and falls with the inflections one would use in speaking these lines. While the components that make up "Dreaming with Tears in My Eyes"—words, rhythm, melody, and chords—might seem simple to the point of cliché if considered separately, their synthesis produces an elusive kind of art that achieves an effect of remarkable directness, intimacy, and poignant honesty.

Waltz songs remained popular in country music throughout the twentieth century. And they are frequently songs of sentiment, like "Dreaming with Tears in My Eyes," using straightforward materials and aspiring to the kind of natural yet artful expression achieved so memorably in Rodgers's song. But this is not easy to achieve. Rodgers left country music a rich and enduring, but challenging, legacy when he died of tuberculosis eight days after recording "Dreaming with Tears in My Eyes."

POPULAR MUSIC AND THE GREAT DEPRESSION

The Great Depression (1929–ca. 1939), which threw millions of Americans out of work, had a major impact on the music industry. In 1927, 106 million phonograph discs were sold nationwide; by 1932 sales had plummeted to only 6 million. Many small record companies—including those that had pioneered in the fields of race and hillbilly music—were wiped out overnight. Large companies such as Columbia and Victor were forced to reorganize and consolidate. Most people simply did not have the spare income to spend on records, despite the introduction of discs that cost as little as ten cents apiece, and network radio became even more influential as a result.

The race record market was crushed by the economic downturn, which hit African American consumers particularly hard. During the early 1930s the first black-owned music-publishing and film-producing companies were also wiped out. Increasingly, record companies relied on established artists and cut back on the field expeditions that had characterized the early years of the race record business. The most successful African American musicians of the depression era were those whose records were featured in the mainstream record catalogs, particularly jazz-oriented dance orchestras, discussed in some detail in the next chapter.

Hillbilly record sales were also affected by the depression, although not as severely as race records. However, although sales declined in absolute numbers, hillbilly music actually increased its share of the overall market during the economic downturn. In 1930, as the depression consolidated its stranglehold on millions of families, rural and urban, hillbilly records accounted for fully 25 percent of the total American market. Paradoxically, despite the general downturn in sales, it was during the depression that the country music business was really established, with the biggest stars signing lucrative advertising contracts and appearing on radio and in Hollywood movies. In 1933 Billy Hill's recording of "The Last Roundup"—a romantic cowboy song—was a huge hit, selling one hundred thousand copies, crossing over to the pop charts, and helping to establish the "western" music market. Hill's success also set the scene for popular cowboy singers such as Gene Autry and Roy Rogers, discussed in the next chapter.

Given that popular music of the early twentieth century tended to scrupulously avoid any mention of social problems, how, if at all, did the terrible impact of the Great Depression on the lives of Americans make itself felt in popular music? During the 1930s, while Tin Pan Alley and Hollywood provided vivid fantasies of life among the elite, some hillbilly and blues singers injected a note of social realism into popular music. They chronicled the suffering of the homeless and unemployed:

Woody Guthrie (reading the *HoBo News*) relaxes in New York's Central Park with fellow folksinger Burl Ives before a radio appearance, 1940. Courtesy Library of Congress.

the Dust Bowl farmers whose way of life was threatened by ecological, as well as economic, disaster; and the textile and mine workers of the South, whose attempts to unionize were resisted—sometimes violently—by big business. Examples of songs that dealt with the depression include the rare down-to-earth Tin Pan Alley song "Brother, Can You Spare a Dime?" (a Number One hit for crooners Bing Crosby and Rudy Vallee in 1932); hillbilly star Uncle Dave Macon's "All In Down and Out Blues," which argued that "Wall Street's propositions were not all roses"; and Casey Bill Weldon's "WPA Blues," which described a government demolition crew destroying dilapidated housing still occupied by African American families.

One of the musicians most closely associated with the plight of American workers during the Great Depression was Woodrow Wilson "Woody" Guthrie. Born in Oklahoma in 1912, Guthrie began his career as a hillbilly singer, performing the songs of the Carter Family and Jimmie Rodgers. With his father dead and his mother committed to an asylum, Guthrie quit school at sixteen and spent years wandering throughout the Southwest. In the late 1930s he migrated to California as part of the stream of impoverished "Okies" described in John Steinbeck's novel *The Grapes of Wrath*. These experiences turned Guthrie toward composing songs that were more overtly political in nature, including "This Land Is Your Land," "Talking Dust Bowl Blues," and "Ludlow Massacre." After 1940 he was known primarily as a protest singer—his political orientation summarized by a sign on his guitar that read, "This Machine Kills Fascists"—and was a direct influence on later urban folk musicians such as the Weavers (see Chapter 7) and Bob Dylan (see Chapter 10).

―――――――――――――

While the Great Depression marked the end of an important period in the development of American popular music, it was also an important time of transition. From around 1935 through World War II, as the national economy began to recover, the music business expanded and underwent certain important transformations. Musical styles and cultural themes that had first emerged in clear form after World War I were updated by a new generation of performers. These musicians, in adapting to new social and historical circumstances, elaborated the long-standing conversation between northern and southern, urban and rural, and white and black musical traditions, and created a style of dance music (and a cultural movement) called swing.

CHAPTER SIX

"IN THE MOOD"

The Swing Era, 1935–1945

Despite the commercial hoopla associated with the Jazz Age, we have seen that the influence of jazz on mainstream popular music was really rather indirect during the 1920s and early 1930s (recall our discussion of Paul Whiteman, the "King of Jazz," in Chapter 3). Some historians of popular music argue that the early years of the Great Depression (1929–35) were in fact marked by a shift in mainstream popular taste away from "hot" syncopated dance music and toward a "sweeter" style of ballroom music, more in keeping with the subdued mood of the times. Beginning in 1935, however, a new style of jazz-inspired music called *swing*, initially developed in the late 1920s by black dance bands in New York, Chicago, and Kansas City, transformed American popular music. (As of this writing, the music of the Swing Era is experiencing a revival, complete with youth-oriented television advertisements featuring big-band music and acrobatic "lindy hop" dancers.)

The word "swing" (like "jazz," " blues," and "rock 'n' roll") derives from African American English. First used as a verb for the fluid, "rocking" rhythmic momentum created by well-played music, the term was used by extension to refer to an emotional state characterized by a sense of freedom, vitality, and enjoyment. References to "swing" and "swinging" are common in the titles and lyrics of jazz records made during the 1920s and early 1930s.[1] However, it was the music industry that, around 1935, began to use "swing" as a proper noun, the name of a defined musical genre. (When the music business gets involved in promoting a style of music, it typically adopts colloquial terms that are verbs or adjectives and turns

---

1. For example, Duke Ellington's well-known composition "It Don't Mean a Thing if It Ain't Got That Swing" was first recorded in 1932.

them into nouns—that is, into *things*, marketable objects that can be promoted, sold, and bought by a mass audience.)

Between 1935 and 1945 hundreds of large dance orchestras—the best-known of them directed by celebrity bandleaders such as Benny Goodman, Tommy Dorsey, Duke Ellington, Count Basie, and Glenn Miller—dominated the national hit parade. These *big bands* appeared nightly on radio, their performances transmitted coast to coast from hotels and ballrooms in the big cities. Their music was featured on *jukeboxes,* coin-operated record players installed in nightclubs and restaurants. Many of the bands crisscrossed the country in busses, playing for dances and concerts at local dance halls, theaters, and colleges. The big bands were essentially a big-city phenomenon, a symbol of sophistication and up-to-dateness, and their occasional tour appearances in small towns generated a great deal of excitement. (In this sense the big bands played a role similar to traveling minstrel and vaudeville shows, which had largely died out by the late 1930s.)

Swing music was part of a broader cultural and aesthetic movement that included dance styles, modes of dress, and even architecture. Gradually supplanting the intimate cabarets of the 1920s, huge ballrooms, designed to cater to a larger and more diverse audience, sprang up during the 1930s. These new dance halls were constructed in keeping with the taste of the times, complete with streamlined modern designs of chrome, steel, and glass, evoking the power and forward momentum of airplanes and diesel trains. Photographs of dance bands taken during the big-band era also indicate a shift in visual presentation, from the publicity shots of 1920s "syncopated orchestras," in which musicians mugged and struck unusual poses, to the sleek, sophisticated, and erudite image of swing bands and bandleaders, adorned in fine suits and scholarly eyeglasses.

Swing music also played an important economic role. Record sales in the United States had plummeted from the 1921 high of $106 million in retail sales to only $6 million in 1933 (a decline of over 90 percent). By the late 1930s, largely as a result of the popularity of swing, the record industry had begun to recover: between 1935 and 1945 well over half of the records that sold more than a million copies were made by big dance bands. It is no exaggeration to state that swing music pulled the American music industry out of the Great Depression.

SWING MUSIC AND AMERICAN CULTURE

Swing music provides us with a window onto the cultural values and social changes of the New Deal era.[2] The basic ethos of swing music was one of unfettered enjoyment, "swinging," "having a ball." (This "let's party" attitude was doubtless encouraged by the repeal of Prohibition in 1933.) Like the voting bloc that elected Franklin D. Roosevelt to four terms in office, the audience for swing spanned the social boundaries that separated ethnic groups, natives and immigrants, southerners and northerners, city dwellers and country folk, the working class, the expand-

---

2. The New Deal was an ambitious set of public programs put into place by the administration of Franklin D. Roosevelt and designed to pull the country out of the economic depression of the early 1930s.

ing middle class, and progressive members of the educated elite. Democratic in spirit, swing music was actually quite regimented in performance—planned and written down in advance by professional arrangers, and often read note-by-note by musicians, with relatively little room for individual improvisation. This highly structured way of making music—a shift from the ideal of collective improvisation that had characterized early New Orleans jazz—has been correlated by some scholars with the increasing bureaucratization of American life during the New Deal era, including the growth of government institutions, labor unions, and big business.

If this connection between music and society seems a bit far-fetched—after all, many dance bands of the 1920s also played from written arrangements and improvised little—it certainly cannot be denied that the big-band era saw the growth of bureaucracy in the music industry. The swing craze was controlled and, at least in part, manufactured by large New York–based *booking agencies*, corporations formed to represent professional musicians and promote their music. The largest of these was MCA (Music Corporation of America), which, after barely surviving the depression, rose to become the dominant booking agency for big dance bands. MCA and other agencies served as liaisons between the bands, radio networks, and commercial advertisers. (Most successful bands had a set of official sponsors, including tobacco, beer, and automobile companies.) The agencies also managed the bafflingly complex logistics of nationwide tours. In 1937, when total profits from the swing music industry reached $80 million, $15 million went to the booking agencies. It is perhaps no wonder that MCA—cold, efficient, and businesslike—was viewed with a mixture of appreciation and distrust by musicians, who called the corporation the "Star Spangled Octopus." (These large booking agencies continue to play an important—some would say oppressive—role in the music business today.)

During the swing era network radio was the most important means of promoting popular music. A big band simply could not hope to achieve any significant level of popularity without constant radio exposure. Swing bands appeared live on remote broadcasts from dance halls and hotels, as well as on regularly scheduled studio-based programs. Interestingly, some of the most desirable places for a swing band to perform were hotels and ballrooms where they might actually expect to lose money. These venues were important because they had a "wire"—a connection to a local radio station—which allowed them to be used for live broadcasting. (The most famous of these "remote" venues was the Pennsylvania Hotel in New York City, which played an important role in launching the careers of Benny Goodman, Tommy Dorsey, Glenn Miller, and other top bandleaders.)

The 1930s also saw the appearance of radio shows featuring phonograph records rather than live performances. The most famous of these were the *Make Believe Ballroom* shows, broadcast from New York and Los Angeles. These shows featured *disc jockeys*, radio personalities who spun records and attempted to create the ambience of a live broadcast from a hotel. The first Top 10 radio show was *Your Hit Parade*, sponsored by Lucky Strike Cigarettes. Introduced in 1935, the show began with the following announcement:

> Your Hit Parade! We don't pick 'em, we just play 'em. From North, South, East and West, we check the songs you dance to . . . the sales of the records that you buy . . . and the sheet music you play. And then, knowing your preferences, we bring you the top hits of the week!

The announcement of top hit songs began with a dramatic drum roll and ended with the performance of "the top song in the country, Number One on Your Lucky Strike Hit Parade." This show, one of the most popular of the radio era, is the ancestor of the Top 40 shows of the rock 'n' roll era and MTV's music video countdown. (Very few radio stations featured African American disc jockeys during the swing era. The first well-known black **DJ** was Jack Cooper, who began broadcasting in Chicago in the late 1930s. There were few others until after World War II.)

As is often the case with popular music, swing was put to all sorts of political uses. Some left-wing activists saw swing music as a utopian embodiment of racial democracy and the common interests of working people. Other leftists regarded it with suspicion, seeing its mass popularity and the fervor of its fans as possible precursors of totalitarianism. Conservative commentators decried swing as an outgrowth and intensification of the moral decline marked by the ragtime and jazz crazes of the 1910s and 1920s. One prominent psychiatrist blamed a wave of sex crimes on the music, while another played Tommy Dorsey records for monkeys and gorillas, reporting that the former enjoyed swing, while the latter—being largely terrestrial, not arboreal primates—did not. Religious authorities were generally not thrilled with the new music or the often acrobatic styles of dance that it accompanied, called "jitterbugging" (see below). In 1938 Archbishop Beckman of New York went so far as to argue that "we permit, if not endorse, by our criminal indifference, 'jam sessions,' 'jitter-bugs,' and cannibalistic rhythm orgies to occupy a place in our social scheme of things, wooing our youth along the primrose path to hell!" (*The New York Times*, Oct. 26, 1938, p. 20).

These criticisms of swing—with their references to sexual deviance, animals, and cannibalism—echo the racist tone of attacks on syncopated dance music during the 1920s, which we discussed back in Chapter 3. American society remained segregated along racial lines, even as the country spent hundreds of thousands of lives and billions of dollars fighting World War II. (It is ironic that the while the war was ostensibly an attempt to save the free world from the racism of the Nazis, the U.S. Army itself remained largely segregated.) On the other hand, personal relationships and the exchange of stylistic influences between black and white musicians had on the whole become more direct and intimate. Although ballrooms remained segregated in certain parts of the country, photographs of big-band concerts and dances during the late 1930s and the war years provide evidence that big-city swing audiences were also decidedly mixed in racial terms. Some of the most popular white swing bands met with success at Negro venues such as Harlem's Apollo Theater, while the most successful African American dance bands always counted substantial numbers of white fans among their audiences.

The influence of black English on the speech of white youth also became more direct during this period. Terms such as "cool," "hip," "with it," and "in the groove" evoked a particular attitude or stance toward life—aware, sensually attuned, and in control of the situation—that has its roots in a distinctive African American aesthetic of personal comportment. (Linguists have traced the etymology of the term "hepcat" to "hipikat," a term used by the Wolof people of Senegal to describe a person who is particularly finely attuned to his surroundings, literally a person with his "eyes wide open." Many words in American English—including "jazz"—appear to have roots in African languages.)

The dance styles that paralleled swing music provide further evidence of the increasing centrality of black styles and sensibilities in American popular culture. Beginning in the late 1920s, dancers at the Savoy Ballroom in New York City—located on Harlem's "main stem," Lenox Avenue—began to develop a style called the lindy hop, named in honor of Charles Lindbergh's solo transatlantic flight (1927). The lindy differed from the popular jazz dance styles of the early 1920s—the bunny hug, turkey trot, and fox-trot—in several important ways. While the older dances emphasized bouncy, up-and-down movements, the lindy was smoother, with more fluid horizontal movements. In addition, the lindy provided greater scope for improvisation, including the "breakaway," a moment when dancers would part company and dance solo, exhibiting their skill. (The Savoy Ballroom had a special section of the dance floor, called the "Cat's Corner," set aside for these displays.) Gradually, this virtuosic element of the lindy became more prominent, including judolike "airsteps," in which the man would spin his partner, slide her between his arched legs, flip her over his back, and so on. The clothing worn by dancers matched the streamlined and somewhat formal aesthetic of the new ballrooms: expensive (or at least expensive-looking) jackets, ties, and loose trousers for the men, billowing skirts and silk blouses for the women. (Loose clothes were not only "hip" in appearance but also perfectly suited for the acrobatic moves of the lindy hop.)

It is impossible to discuss the development of swing music, the lindy hop, or the clothing and speech styles with which they were associated without some reference to New York's Harlem and its famous nightclubs and dance halls, including the Savoy Ballroom, the Cotton Club, and the Apollo Theater. Originally populated by European immigrant groups, Harlem was by the late 1920s home to a substantial, well-educated, and relatively prosperous black middle class. Much of the attention of scholars has focused on the "high art" aspects of the "New Negro" movement, later called the Harlem Renaissance, exemplified by the poetry of Langston Hughes and the paintings of Aaron Douglas. However, the cultural energy and creativity of black New York was also expressed through popular cultural forms, both in live performance and over the mass media. It could be argued that Harlem was the portal through which black styles and sensibilities entered American mass culture from the 1920s through the 1940s.

Although the creative impulses of the Harlem Renaissance came mainly from the black middle class, "black and tan" nightclubs like the Cotton Club were generally owned and operated by Italian and Jewish mobsters. The Cotton Club's audiences were predominantly white, including people with a genuine interest in jazz music and other aspects of cosmopolitan black culture, and others who came to Harlem in search of something akin to an exotic tourist experience (a practice called "slumming"). The most successful dance orchestras at the Cotton Club—led by Duke Ellington and Cab Calloway—provided musical accompaniment for stage acts featuring scantily clad "brown beauties," men in ape costumes, and jungle scenery. This scene—with black performers presenting caricatures of themselves to white consumers—is in some ways reminiscent of nineteenth-century minstrelsy. However, the steady income provided by the well-known Harlem nightclubs and dance halls provided many black musicians with an opportunity to develop successful careers in music.

On the one hand, it can be argued that the swing era—a period in which black people often attended concerts by white dance bands, and whites began to study and imitate black culture with greater passion and in greater numbers than ever before—did represent a step forward in cultural communication across racial boundaries. At the same time, we must recognize that this was not a relationship of full equality. Only a handful of dance bands were racially integrated (Benny Goodman was a pioneer in this regard), and even the most popular of black dance bands faced serious economic and social disadvantages vis-à-vis their white competitors. Between 1935 and 1945 the four most popular big bands led by white musicians—the Tommy Dorsey, Benny Goodman, Glenn Miller, and Jimmy Dorsey Orchestras—racked up a total of 292 Top 10 records, of which 65 were Number One hits. By way of contrast, the four most popular black swing orchestras—led by Duke Ellington, Count Basie, Jimmy Lunceford, and Chick Webb—scored only 32 Top 10 hits, 3 of which made it to Number One on the charts. While these figures may reflect broad differences in the economic status of black and white Americans, they were also shaped by the black musicians' difficulty in getting equal airtime on the radio, and in having their records included among the selections on the coin-operated jukeboxes that sprang up in thousands of restaurants and nightclubs across the country during this period.

Finally, although swing is regarded today as nostalgic music, it is important to remember that its core audience initially consisted of college-age adults and teenagers. Avid young dancers called "jitterbugs" studied the recordings of their favorite bands, spent hours perfecting dance steps, formed fan clubs, bought fan magazines, and sometimes trailed their favorite bands from town to town. (As you might expect, the swing craze was regarded with suspicion by many parents, who continued to patronize the older-style "sweet" bands led by musicians like Guy Lombardo.) In general, the big bands brought a youthful energy back to American popular music. At its best, swing was an exciting, brash, vital music, inspired by black aesthetics and consonant with the growing optimism of a nation emerging from a devastating economic depression. Although most of the big bands vanished from the scene after World War II, the musical and cultural influence of swing continued to be strongly felt in postwar rhythm & blues and country and western music (see Chapter 7), and eventually, in rock 'n' roll (see Chapter 8).

LISTENING AND ANALYSIS   FLETCHER HENDERSON'S "WRAPPIN' IT UP"

There are a number of differences between swing and the jazz-tinged syncopated dance music that had preceded it in the 1910s and 1920s (Chapter 3). These can best be illustrated by listening to the band widely credited with inspiring the rise of swing, Fletcher Henderson (1898–1952) and His Orchestra. On their 1934 recording of "Wrappin' It Up," the Henderson band is considerably larger than most syncopated dance bands of the 1920s, which typically included only eight or nine musicians. By contrast, Henderson's big band comprises five brass instruments (three trumpets and two trombones), four reed instruments (saxophones and clarinets) and a rhythm section consisting of piano, bass, drums, and guitar, a total of thirteen musicians. This expansion of the dance band was correlated with the development of an ensemble sound that was smoother, fuller sounding, and in structural terms, simpler than the polyphonic, collectively improvised style of New Orleans jazz. To be sure, the influence of the rich orchestral textures developed by James Reese Europe and Paul Whiteman is evident in many big-band recordings of the swing era. However, big band arrangers used the expanded instrumental resources of their ensembles in a manner different from most syncopated orchestras of the 1920s.

One of the signal features of swing music is an often thoroughgoing application of the call-and-response technique central to African American musical traditions such as gospel music and the blues. Beginning in the late 1920s, black dance band arrangers began to apply this principle to ensemble writing, treating the brass and reed instruments as separate sections and setting them off against one another. This basic approach—in which "conversations" were set up between parts of a band—was later adopted by white bands.

In addition, there was a change in the rhythmic organization or "feel" of the music. Rather than the "boom-chick," two-beat rhythms of much syncopated dance band music of the 1920s—correlated with the erect postures and largely up-and-down movements of the fox-trot and other popular dances—the rhythmic feeling of swing music is more continuous and flowing. This effect is created by having the bass player play on all four beats in a measure, rather than just the first and third beats, a technique referred to by jazz musicians as "walking" the bass. The drummer adds to this effect by playing all four beats with his bass drum pedal (a technique called "four on the floor") and playing a regular tapping pattern on his largest cymbal (a "ride" cymbal). In some bands, the guitarist would also play chords on every beat. In addition to this steady pulse, a good swinging groove depended on accents on the offbeats, that, is the second and fourth beats of each four-beat measure. These offbeat accents might be supplied by the rhythm section or by the horn arrangements. This combination of a steady, fluid pulse with an accent or "push" on every other beat creates the basic conditions for swinging.

Of course, there are many subtleties to creating a swing feeling in music, including seemingly tiny adjustments in the relationships among instruments in the rhythm section, and between the rhythm section as a whole and the reed and brass sections. If this all seems a bit abstract, simply play the Original Dixieland Jazz Band's 1918 recording of "Tiger Rag" back to back with Fletcher Henderson's 1934 recording of "Wrappin' It Up," and you'll get a more direct sense of the musical qualities we are attempting to describe here. "Tiger Rag" does have intensity, a bouncy rhythmic feeling, and lots of syncopations, but it doesn't swing. "Wrappin' It Up," on the other hand, has all of the characteristics we have described: a big, full, smooth ensemble texture; lots of call-and-response patterns between the brass and reeds; and a steady, flowing groove, with the bass, drums, and guitar playing on all four beats, while giving a slight push to beats 2 and 4.

Big-band arrangements commonly drew upon musical structures that should by now be familiar to us: the twelve-bar blues form and the thirty-two-bar Tin Pan Alley song form. Fletcher Henderson's "Wrappin' It Up" falls into the latter category: its basic structure is ABAC, each section being eight measures in length (and each measure, as is typical of swing music, being four beats in length). It should be fairly easy to hear the basic structure of the arrangement, since the beats are emphasized by the rhythm section.

"Wrappin' It Up" begins with an eight-measure introduction, in which the call-and-response relationship between the reeds and brass is established from the first moment. In the first measure the brass play a syncopated figure, which is answered in the second measure by the reeds. Measures 3 and 4 repeat this exchange. In the next two measures (5 and 6) the brass and reeds exchange even shorter figures (two beats in length), and everyone joins together in the last two bars (measures 7 and 8), launching us into the main body of the arrangement. The rest of the "chart" presents the thirty-two-bar ABAC form four times with all sorts of interesting variations, including adding an extra measure on the first and third times through the form (see listening chart). Working with a few basic musical ideas and techniques, Henderson holds our interest, alternating call-and-response patterns between the brass and reeds with **soli** scoring, musical passages in which a group of instruments play a melody together, often in harmony. (In swing arrangements, these *soli* passages often sound like improvised solos that have been written down for multiple instruments.) There are also three improvised solos, over various types of backgrounds played by the other instruments. Fletcher Henderson's "Wrappin' It Up" is a great example not only of the rhythmic flow and texture of swing music but also of the balance between simplicity and complexity that characterizes the best big-band arranging.

The listening chart outlines the basic structure of the arrangement. Don't worry if you can't follow all the details in the arrangement right away—you might begin by listening all the way through a few times, to see if you can keep track of the beats, measures, and larger form (ABAC). Then go back and listen for the individual sections, solos, use of call and response, *soli* sections, and so on.

LISTENING CHART   *"WRAPPIN' IT UP"*

Composed and arranged by Fletcher Henderson; as performed by Fletcher Henderson and his Orchestra; recorded 1934

FORM	DESCRIPTIVE COMMENTS
Intro (8 measures)	Bars 1–4: Brass and reeds play call-and-response figures (each one measure in length).
	Bars 5–8: Brass and reeds play shorter call-and-response figures, then join forces to launch us into the main body of the arrangement.
A (8)	Reeds play main theme, punctuated by brief brass responses.
B (8)	Reeds and brass play call-and-response patterns.
A (8)	*Soli* section, with brass and reeds playing melody together in harmony.
C (8 + 1)	*Soli* section concludes (an extra measure is added).

A (8)	Saxophone solo, supported by soft brass chords.
B (8)	Saxophone solo, supported by soft brass chords.
A (8)	Saxophone solo, supported by soft brass chords.
C (8)	Saxophone solo, supported by soft brass chords.
A (8)	Trumpet solo with reed *soli* backgrounds.
B (8)	Rapid call and response between brass and reeds.
A (8)	Trumpet solo with reed *soli* backgrounds.
C (8 + 1)	Trumpet solo with reed *soli* backgrounds (an extra measure is added).
A (8)	Call and response between brass and reeds.
B (8)	Clarinet solo, supported by soft brass chords in background.
A (8)	Reed *soli* (harmonized melody).
C (8)	Whole band *soli*—soft sustained piano note at end.

BENNY GOODMAN: THE KING OF SWING

Many genres of popular music are accompanied by stories describing a "founding moment," that is, an attention-grabbing performance or recording that establishes a musical era and brings a new audience into being. For the swing era that mythic event occurred in the summer of 1935, when a dance band led by a young jazz clarinetist named Benny Goodman (1909–86) embarked upon a tour of California. Goodman was born in Chicago, the son of working-class eastern European Jewish immigrants. He made his first records under his own name in 1927 and worked as a freelance musician during the depression years. Benny Goodman's career was boosted by John Hammond (1910–87), an influential jazz enthusiast and promoter who also helped Bessie Smith, Billie Holiday, Count Basie, and (much later) Aretha Franklin, Bob Dylan, and Bruce Springsteen receive recording contracts with Columbia Records, where he worked as an **A&R** (artists and repertoire) man. Hammond arranged Goodman's first recording dates with Columbia and pushed the band in the direction of the more strongly jazz-influenced music played by most black dance bands.

In 1934 the Goodman band got its first big break. The National Biscuit Company was promoting its new Ritz cracker and decided to sponsor a national radio program called *Let's Dance.* This show featured three bands, representing the three main dance music styles of the time: a sweet band, a Latin band, and Goodman's band, playing hot syncopated music. Under constant prodding from John Hammond, Goodman soon hired more jazz musicians. He also purchased a group of Fletcher Henderson's arrangements, which became the center of the Goodman band's collection of charts. Goodman was not only a skillful jazz improviser but also an astute businessman and a strict disciplinarian, insisting that his musicians play their parts with perfect precision. (His laser beam stare and readiness to fire miscreants were legendary among jazz musicians.) Benny Goodman brought to

Benny Goodman
with drummer **Gene Krupa,** in 1938.
Courtesy Library of Congress.

Henderson's arrangements a kind of neatness, smoothness, and control—a sound that appealed to the predominantly white, middle-class audience who were the main target of record companies and radio sponsors—without losing the swing feeling of the music.

Although initial audience reaction was not enthusiastic, the band went on a grueling cross-country tour of one-nighters, ending up in California. The tour had not been a great success: audiences did not warm to the hot arrangements that the band wanted to play, instead insisting that they play only sweet numbers. (The tour bottomed out in Denver, where dancers actually asked the band to give them their money back.) When they finally arrived at the famous Palomar Ballroom in Hollywood, relieved that the tour was almost over, the Goodman band was astounded to find lines of fans extending all the way around the block. Apparently their popularity had been built up by network radio appearances, though not in the way you might expect. The Goodman band had always played last on the New York–based show *Let's Dance,* not appearing until after midnight, when many in the audience had already gone to bed. But on the West Coast, where they were heard earlier in the evening, they had begun to build a long-distance following among teenagers and young adults who loved the swinging approach that Goodman had borrowed from Fletcher Henderson.

This, then, was the birth of swing, a national cultural phenomenon of unprecedented proportions, created on the one hand by the intensified impact of black musical styles and aesthetic values on popular dance music, and on the other by the intervention of the mass media. Other white dance band musicians—including Jimmy and Tommy Dorsey, Glenn Miller, and Artie Shaw—saw a golden opportunity, and dozens of swing bands sprang up overnight. (By the late 1930s *Metronome* magazine listed three hundred bands nationwide, and this was only scratching the surface!) As we have seen, swing became an industry, with the bands, radio networks, Hollywood studios, and corporate advertisers continually promoting one another, generating tens of millions of dollars in annual profits and pulling the recording industry out of its depression-era slump.

In a seeming echo of the hype surrounding Paul Whiteman's public image, the press crowned Benny Goodman the "King of Swing." However, there are several big differences between the so-called kings of jazz and swing. While Whiteman remained a classical musician all his life, Goodman was in fact a fine (if often underrated) improviser who studied jazz closely. While Whiteman's band played syncopated ballroom dance music in a style that borrowed its name from jazz, Goodman's really was a jazz band, performing music closely modeled on the innovations of African American musicians, composers, and arrangers. And while Paul Whiteman's dance orchestras of the 1920s never included musicians of color, Goodman was the first prominent white bandleader to hire black players, beginning with the pianist Teddy Wilson in 1936 and followed by the brilliant young electric guitarist Charlie Christian, vibraphonist Lionel Hampton, and trumpeter Cootie Williams.

It is clear that Benny Goodman owed a key element of his success to the adoption of a style innovated by Fletcher Henderson and other African American musicians. It is also evident that Goodman's success was determined not solely by his musicianship and business savvy but also by the relatively privileged access that he and other white musicians enjoyed to radio airplay, recording contracts, and corporate backing. However, it is not fair—as has sometimes been done—to imply that Goodman was himself a racist. His decision to hire black musicians led to the integration of other prominent big bands, including those led by Artie Shaw (whose band included the singer Billie Holiday) and the drummer Gene Krupa. On the one hand, the integration of formerly all-white big bands meant better pay and wider exposure for some African American musicians. On the other, integration made things even more difficult for all-black dance bands, who—like the Negro Leagues during the desegregation of baseball in the late 1940s—saw some of their most promising talent, and a portion of their audience, drained away.

LISTENING AND ANALYSIS "TAKING A CHANCE ON LOVE"

The Goodman band's 1940 recording of "Taking a Chance on Love," which reached Number One on the hit parade chart published in the influential trade journal *Billboard* in 1943, provides us with a good example of their popular approach. The arrangement is by Fletcher Henderson, who had by this time become a regular member of the Goodman band. Henderson makes use of the basic techniques of swing arranging, including call and response between reeds and brass and *soli* sections with a melody played in harmony. "Taking a Chance on Love" also illustrates a common aspect of the repertoire of big bands, that is, orchestrated versions of popular Tin Pan Alley songs. Composed by the Tin Pan Alley songwriter Vernon Duke (with lyrics by John Latouche and Ted Fetter), the song was popularized in a Broadway musical (and subsequent Hollywood film) called *Cabin in the Sky*.

This recording illustrates a dimension of big-band swing performances that we have not yet mentioned: the inclusion of a male or female crooner, featured on selected arrangements that were interspersed among the purely instrumental numbers. Today we are used to the idea that singers, rather than nonsinging instrumentalists, are generally the biggest stars in pop music. During the heyday of the big bands, however, it was the bandleader's name and not the singer's that appeared on the record label. On this recording the singer is Helen Forrest (1918–99), whose name is little known today, although she was in her time regarded as one of the greatest of the big-band crooners. Her warm, fluid voice and clarity of phrasing were much admired by musicians, and she eventually worked with three of the most prominent bands of the swing era (Goodman, Artie Shaw, and Harry James).

The form of the song "Taking a Chance on Love" is the familiar thirty-two-bar AABA song structure. Henderson's arrangement includes an interesting instrumental introduction, twenty-four measures in length. The introduction opens with a five-bar section, with the brass playing a melodic line and the reeds responding. Then the band plays two iterations of the A section of the song, with the brass carrying the melody in the first four measures (interrupted by responses from the reed section) and handing it off to Benny Goodman's solo clarinet in the second four measures. The second of these A sections is short-changed by one measure, shifting instead into a four-measure phrase played by the reeds, which moves us into the vocal section of the arrangement. The form of the introduction is thus 5 + 8 + 7 + 4 = 24 measures, a somewhat unusual structure that, reflecting Henderson's mastery of the art of big-band arrangement, sounds completely natural.

Once we get into the vocal section, it is easier to follow the form (it no doubt helps to have someone singing the melody and lyrics!). The vocal follows the AABA structure of the song, with Helen Forrest's voice supported by various combinations of reeds and brass. Forrest sings the song through once (AABA), and then the band takes over with another rendition of the song, with a saxophone solo on the B section (the bridge), and a brief tag to conclude the recording.

LISTENING CHART "TAKING A CHANCE ON LOVE"

Composed by Vernon Duke, lyrics by John Latouche and Ted Fetter; arranged by Fletcher Henderson; as performed by Benny Goodman and His Orchestra; recorded 1940

FORM	DESCRIPTIVE COMMENTS
Intro (24 measures)	
Opening section (5 measures)	Bars 1–3: Brass and reeds play call and response. Bars 4–5: Reeds play *soli* phrase.
A (8)	Bars 1–4: Muted brass play melody of the song, reeds respond. Bars 5–8: Solo clarinet plays melody, reeds respond.
A (7)	Bars 1–6: Muted brass play melody, reeds respond. Bar 7: Brass and reeds play melody together.
Linking section (4 measures)	Reeds play *soli* phrase, answered by brass, and leading us into the vocal section.
Vocal (32 measures)	
A (8)	Vocal ("Here I go . . . "), with saxophone backgrounds.
A (8)	Vocal ("Here I slide . . . "), with saxophone backgrounds.
B (8)	Vocal ("I thought . . . "), with brass backgrounds.
A (8)	Vocal ("Things are mending . . . "), with saxophone backgrounds.
Instrumental (32 measures)	
A (8)	Brass begin melody, solo clarinet takes over (saxophone backgrounds throughout).
A (8)	Brass begin melody, solo clarinet takes over (saxophone backgrounds throughout).
B (8)	Saxophone solo, punctuated by brass.
A (8)	Brass begin melody, solo clarinet takes over (saxophone backgrounds throughout).
Tag	Brass play melody, reeds play final chord.

LISTENING TO **THE MILLS BROTHERS' "PAPER DOLL"**

Although the dance bands dominated the charts between 1935 and 1945, the best-selling record of the swing era—leaving aside Bing Crosby's 1942 recording of "White Christmas," a perennial holiday bestseller—featured an unaccompanied performance by an African American vocal harmony group, the Mills Brothers.

The American vocal harmony group tradition includes many streams, white and black, sacred and secular, rural and urban. Some of the earliest commercial recordings—made in the 1890s and 1900s—featured performances by professional vocal quartets, singing Stephen Foster songs, Tin Pan Alley hits, and ragtime numbers. During the early twentieth century "jubilee" groups, usually male vocal quartets, became popular in black churches, and many of these appeared on race records. (The Golden Gate Quartet, discussed in Chapter 5, was part of this tradition.) The 1920s and 1930s also saw the rise of a new generation of popular vocal groups, trios and quartets who included hot syncopated songs in their repertoires. (Many of the biggest pop singers of the Jazz Age in fact began their careers singing with such groups: for example, Bing Crosby's first appearances with the Paul Whiteman Orchestra were as a member of a vocal trio called the Rhythm Boys.)

During the swing era vocal harmony groups such as the Boswell Sisters, the Andrews Sisters, the Ink Spots, and the Mills Brothers remained popular. While the Andrews Sisters are more widely remembered today—thanks in part to their wartime recording of "Boogie Woogie Bugle Boy," revived by the pop singer Bette Midler in the 1970s—the Mills Brothers were the most successful and longest-lived of these swing era vocal groups. Unlike many "brother" and "sister" groups, the original Mills Brothers really were siblings. Born in Ohio, Herbert (1912–89), Harry (1913–1982), Donald (b. 1915), and John Mills Jr. (1911–35) perfected a secular version of the African American jubilee quartet tradition in the late 1920s. Their smooth, jazz-influenced style appealed to a broad audience, and they were one of the first black musical groups to be broadcast on network radio and to score commercial success in the mainstream pop music market. (One key to their success was the brothers' ability to mimic the sound of various musical instruments. Their 1931 recording of the Original Dixieland Jazz Band's "Tiger Rag," one of the bestselling records of that year, featured an imitation of a New Orleans–style jazz band.) In 1935 John, the group's bass singer and guitarist, died and was replaced by his father, John Sr. With seventy hit records spread over almost four decades, the Mills Brothers were the most popular vocal harmony group of the twentieth century. Their recordings had a huge impact on vocal harmony ("doo-wop") groups of the rock 'n' roll era, and as far afield as South Africa, where a 1950s vocal group actually called itself the African Mills Brothers.

"Paper Doll," the Mills Brothers' biggest hit, was recorded in 1942 and became a chart success in 1943. The record sold six million copies—an unprecedented figure—and stayed on the pop charts for thirty-six weeks, twelve of them at Number One. The phenomenal success of "Paper Doll" is partly attributable to a recording ban, which barred instrumental musicians from making records for a period during the war and thereby cleared the field for vocal groups (see Box 6.1). But this cannot account for the record's singular appeal, which was due mainly to the Mills Brothers' polished performance, a sophisticated vocal arrangement of an old Tin Pan Alley love song, which in other hands might have seemed hopelessly old-fashioned to swing era listeners. The song was composed in 1915 by the African American songwriter Johnny S. Black.

"Paper Doll" expresses the anxieties of a young man who has decided to fashion an inanimate lover—a paper cut-out of a woman—in order to protect himself from the treachery of "real live girls." The mildly misogynist tone of the lyric—which places blame for the narrator's problems on the putative fickle-mindedness of young women—makes an interesting contrast with the Victorian high-mindedness of "After the Ball" (1892; see Chapter 2), in which the male narrator's suspicions of infidelity on the part of his female partner are proved unfounded. From our viewpoint the song may seem almost a parody of itself—

just another day in the life of a nerd—but ragtime-era listeners apparently interpreted it as a straightforward expression of heartache.

GUITAR INTRODUCTION
"Slow" Section (Refrain)

I'm gonna buy . . .	A (16 measures)
	[Slow, sentimental style, in a two-beat rhythm]
When I come home . . .	B (16 measures)

"Fast Section" ("Double-time" Feel)

I guess I had a million dolls . . .	VERSE—Part one (16 measures)
	[Note "walking bass," typical of swing music]
I'll tell you boys . . .	VERSE—Part two (16 measures)
	REFRAIN
I'm gonna buy . . .	A (16 measures)
When I come home . . .	B (16 measures)

Let's fast-forward to 1942 and the Decca Record Company's studios in New York City, where the Mills Brothers reharmonize, rearrange, and breathe new life into the thirty-year old song. (They apparently spent only fifteen minutes in the studio to record the song, which was not expected to be a huge hit.) The only instrumental accompaniment is a guitar, which plays a brief introduction. The brothers sing through the refrain in a two-beat rhythm, with the bass notes landing on beats 1 and 3 and the lead voice supported by rich, dreamy vocal harmonies. Then they abruptly switch gears, introducing the verse and then singing the refrain in a four-beat rhythm typical of swing music. (Although the music seems to be going by twice as fast, if you count along you will discover that the phrases of the song are going by at the same speed. For example, although the second refrain feels as though it's moving by twice as fast as the first, the words are really moving at the same speed. This technique, in which the bass part is doubled in speed, is called "double-time feel.") This rethinking of the presentation of the song's form offers a good example of what we might call the "arranger's art." The brothers alternate vocal techniques, sometimes singing in close harmony—rather like a saxophone *soli* section in a big-band arrangement—sometimes in unison, and occasionally allowing the lead voice to go it alone. The cheerful, lively approach of the latter part of the arrangement puts the lyrics into an entirely new context and suggests that the Mills Brothers knew that the swing era audience would have had a hard time taking the song seriously if it were presented in a "straight" sentimental fashion.

BIG BAND BLUES: BASIE, ELLINGTON, AND MILLER

Although big bands relied heavily on arrangements of popular Tin Pan Alley songs, the blues—with its twelve-bar structure, three-chord pattern, blue notes, and call-

and-response patterns—also remained a mainstay of swing music. In this section, we will take a brief look at three arrangements—"One O'Clock Jump," "Ko-Ko," and "In the Mood"—that reflect the quite varied approaches to the blues taken by popular bands of the swing era.

Of all the big bands, the one most closely associated with the blues tradition was led by the jazz pianist William "Count" Basie (1904–84). Basie, born in New Jersey, gained much of his early experience as a player and bandleader in Kansas City, Missouri. In the 1920s Kansas City was in many ways still a frontier town, with a famously crooked mayor ("Boss" Pendergast) whose administration tacitly encouraged the development of a lively (and, during Prohibition, largely illegal) nightclub scene. Many of the greatest jazz musicians honed their improvisational skills in "K.C.," at competitive all-night jam sessions or cutting sessions. These Olympian contests provided a chance for budding virtuosos to test their musical skills and endurance against one another.

During the 1920s and early 1930s black dance bands in Kansas City had developed their own distinctive approach to playing hot dance music. *Territory bands* such as the Bennie Moten Orchestra and Andy Kirk's Blue Devils toured the southwest-

Count Basie. Courtesy Library of Congress.

ern United States, developing a hard-swinging, powerful style with lots of room for improvised solos. The Kansas City style was more closely linked to the country blues tradition than the style of the New York bands, and it relied more heavily upon **riffs** (repeated patterns). Few of the jazz musicians in Kansas City had the formal music education of East Coast musicians like Fletcher Henderson. As a consequence, they often played with a looser, less precise feeling, and relied heavily on "head charts," arrangements that evolved during jam sessions and were written down only later, almost as an afterthought. In rhythmic terms, the Kansas City bands tended to swing more intensely and with greater abandon than the East Coast dance bands.

One important influence on the rhythmic conception of the K.C. bands was the *boogie-woogie* blues piano tradition, which sprang up during the early twentieth century in the "southwest territory" states of Texas, Arkansas, Missouri, and Oklahoma and became a popular fad during the big-band era. The style developed in the environment of the barrelhouses, rowdy nightspots patronized by the men who worked in the lumber and turpentine camps of the area. Solo pianists, a cheap and readily available form of entertainment, responded to the rowdy environment of the barrelhouses by developing a powerful style that could be heard over the crowd noise. In boogie-woogie performances the pianist typically plays a repeated pattern (or riff) with his left hand, down in the low range of the piano, while improvising **polyrhythmic** patterns in his right hand. The greatest boogie-woogie piano players—men like Pete Johnson, Albert Ammons, Meade Lux Lewis, and Pine Top Smith—were said to have "a left hand like God," an admiring reference to the volume, steadiness, and authority of their bass patterns. Big-band musicians from Kansas City were strongly influenced by the boogie-woogie style, especially its rhythmic drive and heavy reliance on riffs. (During the war boogie-woogie became a national fad, spawning a series of hit records—"Boogie Woogie," "Boogie Woogie Bugle Boy," and even "The Booglie Wooglie Piggy." The genre was later to exert a strong influence on rock 'n' roll, via the influence of "southwestern" musicians such as Big Joe Turner and Jerry Lee Lewis.)

In 1936 John Hammond, who had recently helped start Benny Goodman's career, heard Count Basie's band on a late-night shortwave radio show in Chicago. "I just happened to tune in to an experimental radio station at the very top of the dial, just beyond the last station on the regular AM wavelength," he later recalled. Excited by the band's loose but energetic sound, Hammond worked to sign Basie on with MCA and to secure engagements in Chicago and New York City. Although the band's rough-hewn style did not catch on immediately, Hammond was able to get Basie a recording contract with Decca, a new record company interested in capitalizing on the swing craze. Basie's recollection of the contract he signed with Decca is a good example of the disadvantageous position that black musicians were in at that time vis-à-vis the music industry.

> Without realizing what I was doing, I had agreed to record twelve records a year for $750 a year outright, no royalties! I didn't know anything about royalties. John [Hammond] couldn't believe it. He couldn't get us out of that contract, but he was able to get Decca to raise the musicians' pay. . . . I guess I just had to learn some things the hard way. (Basie and Murray 1995, p. 167)

"One O'Clock Jump," recorded by Decca in 1937, was the Count Basie Orchestra's theme song. It is an excellent example of the Kansas City bands' relaxed but energetic rhythmic approach, their emphasis on jazz improvisation, and their reliance on informal and flexible head arrangements. In structural terms, this recording of "One O'Clock Jump" consists of ten choruses of twelve-bar blues. The basic arranging technique involves heavy use of riffs and call-and-response patterns—divided between the brass and reeds—and a succession of improvised jazz solos. The closest thing to a melody, in the sense that the term would be used in the Tin Pan Alley songwriting tradition, does not appear until the next-to-last chorus. Listening to it, one has the feeling that the band could probably go on all night, as long as there were soloists waiting in line to play.

The recording begins with an eight-bar piano boogie-woogie introduction and two improvised twelve-bar blues choruses by Basie, his piano supported gently but energetically by the rest of the rhythm section (Jo Jones on drums, Walter Page on bass, and Freddie Green on guitar). Then there is a key change, the band enters, and we hear a series of solos, on saxophone, trombone, saxophone again, and trumpet, each supported by background riffs. (Although this section seems largely improvised, it is worth noting that the order of solos alternates between reeds and brass, and that each reed instrument is supported by brass, and vice versa).

After these solos, Basie plays another chorus in his famous (and elegant) "two-fingered" style, and then the entire band comes in. The final three choruses of riffs are what identify "One O' Clock Jump" for swing fans and musicians alike. This is an important point, for while riffs were one of several important techniques for East Coast arrangers such as Fletcher Henderson, here the basic identity of the piece lies in its riffs, continually tossed back and forth between the brass and reeds. In a piece like this, the horns seem almost to become part of the rhythm section—their function is less to play a melody than to help propel the music along with greater and greater intensity.

Our second example of a Swing arrangement based on the blues form is "Ko-Ko," recorded in 1940 by the Duke Ellington Orchestra. Edward Kennedy "Duke" Ellington (1899–1974) is widely regarded as one of the most important American musicians of the twentieth century. Although both men shared an African American heritage, Ellington's background was quite different from Bill Basie's. Born in Washington, D.C., the son of a navy blueprint maker, Ellington came from a middle-class background and received formal musical training at a young age. As a kid he hung around the bars and pool halls where ragtime pianists played, and he formed his first dance band while still in high school. This band, the Washingtonians, began playing syncopated dance music in New York in the early 1920s. In 1923 an expanded and improved version of the band debuted at a Broadway nightspot called the Kentucky Club. Three years later, Ellington's band was heard by a song publisher and promoter named Irving Mills, who arranged a recording contract for them. In 1927 Mills was able to secure them a regular engagement at the Cotton Club, where the band often had to accompany "exotic" revues and Ellington developed a style that he called "jungle music," characterized by dense textures, unusual harmonies, and muted, growling sounds in the brass. While this style reinforced the stereotypes of black culture that many of the white patrons of the Cotton Club came to see and hear, it also provided Ellington with the basis for a unique approach to arranging for the big band.

While he had the same basic musical resources at hand as other big band arrangers, Ellington was an experimenter. He devised unusual musical forms, com-

Duke Ellington and his band at the Hurricane Club in New York City, 1943, photographed by Gordon Parks. Courtesy Library of Congress.

bined instruments in unusual ways, and created complex, distinctive tone colors. (Ellington's experiments were aided by the remarkable stability of his band, some of whose members worked with him for over fifty years. He grew to know the individual players' strengths and weaknesses and often wrote parts specifically for particular musicians.) Despite some big hits like "I Let a Song Go Out of My Heart" (Number One, 1938), Ellington's idiosyncratic approach meant that his band enjoyed less commercial success than more mainstream-sounding dance orchestras.

"Ko-Ko" is in formal terms a twelve-bar blues, with an eight-measure introductory section. However, the relationship of Ellington's arrangement to the blues tradition (see Chapter 5) goes well beyond its structural attributes. It could be argued that "Ko-Ko" is in fact an attempt to evoke the *feeling* of the blues through the application of sophisticated musical techniques. Certainly, the overall mood of this piece is not the happy, upbeat emotion typical of much swing music. The ensemble sound is dark and thickly textured, an approach hearkening back to the jungle-music style of Ellington's early years at the Cotton Club. Throughout much of the piece the trombones and trumpets have sound-altering devices called mutes inserted into the bells of the instruments, a technique that creates subdued, murky timbres quite different from the loud, bright sound usually associated with brass instruments.

Although Ellington makes use of the usual call-and-response techniques of big-band writing, he complicates things by combining instruments in unusual ways, by splitting the instruments into more than two groups, or by having some of them play a complicated melody softly in the background. In particular, "Ko-Ko" spotlights the lower-pitched instruments such as baritone saxophone, trombones, and string bass, which are usually assigned an accompanying role in swing music. (This recording even includes a bass solo, rare in any kind of popular music.) In addition, there is no "melody" here, in the sense of a catchy tune designed to lodge itself in the listener's memory. Ellington's melodic lines were often designed to be played on instruments rather than sung, and this is especially true of "Ko-Ko." Although one might ask whether a piece of music as far from the stylistic mainstream as "Ko-Ko" is really popular music, Ellington's recording, widely regarded by jazz scholars and musicians as one of his masterpieces, did make it onto the pop charts, reaching Number Twenty-five for one week in 1940. And it is certainly a successful attempt to evoke the emotional feeling of the blues, as well as a use of its formal structure.

LISTENING AND ANALYSIS "IN THE MOOD"

Our third and final example of a big-band arrangement making use of the blues form is the Glenn Miller Orchestra's 1939 recording of "In the Mood," which held the Number One position on the charts for twelve weeks. From 1939 until 1942 the Miller Orchestra was the most popular dance band in the world, breaking records for record sales and concert attendance. Glenn Miller (1904–44) worked as a trombonist on numerous recordings before launching his own band in 1937. Like other bandleaders, his popularity was boosted by live radio broadcasts from hotels and dance halls. Miller developed a peppy, clean-sounding style that appealed to small-town midwestern people as well as to the big-city, East and West Coast constituency that had previously sustained swing music. In terms of sheer popular success, the Miller band marked the apex of the swing era, racking up twenty-three Number One recordings in a little under four years.

"In the Mood" is probably the best-known swing recording, and its structure is easy to follow. Like the classic blues of W. C. Handy, "In the Mood" alternates the twelve-bar blues form with a bridge phrase reminiscent of Tin Pan Alley songs. (This bridge is eight bars long in "In the Mood.") The main riff—that is, the featured saxophone part by which most people remember the recording—had been around for quite a while before Miller got hold of it. (Fletcher Henderson had used it in an arrangement as early as 1930.) Miller's contribution was to position this venerable riff as the centerpiece of an uncluttered arrangement, constructed from simple building blocks and varied in ingenious ways to hold the listener's interest. A particularly famous aspect of "In the Mood" is its "trick" ending, with the band getting quieter and quieter (and the arranger adding and subtracting a few measures here and there, so you're not quite sure when they will move to the next section) and then exploding into a big finish.

Although it lacks the energetic momentum and bravado of Count Basie's "One O'Clock Jump," or the textural and harmonic complexity of Duke Ellington's "Ko-Ko," "In the Mood" was one of the most commercially successful applications of the blues form in the history of American popular music. Jazz critics have tended to make fun of Miller's music, considering it shallow and unadventurous, both a reminder of the sweet music of Paul Whiteman's band and a harbinger of the schmaltzy mainstream pop music of the 1950s. Nonetheless, there is no denying his tremendous success as a popular musician, and it is worth taking a moment to consider the basis of his music's attraction for millions of Americans.

One of the most obvious qualities of "In the Mood"—and other Miller hits such as "Chattanooga Choo-Choo," "Tuxedo Junction," and "A String of Pearls"—is its predictability. After the first time you have heard "In the Mood," its trick ending can never again come as a surprise. Rather, the pleasure comes from anticipating and then reexperiencing something one already knows by heart. The pleasures of "In the Mood" are those neither of passion nor inventiveness; rather, they are the pleasures of the familiar, the comfortable, the expected. And if we take a moment to imagine ourselves living in a country about to enter a global war, a conflagration that was to bring tragedy to every com-

LISTENING CHART   "IN THE MOOD"

Composed by Joe Garland and Andy Razaf; arranged by Glenn Miller; as performed by Glenn Miller and His Orchestra; recorded 1939

FORM	DESCRIPTIVE COMMENTS
Intro (8 measures)	Bars 1–4: Saxophones play syncopated "fanfare" figure. Bars 5–8: Brass take over main melody.
A (12-bar blues)	Saxophones play the main riff, with brass responses (two-measure phrases).
A (12)	Repeat.
B (8-bar phrase)	Saxophones play a different riff, brass answer (two-bar phrases); last two bars everyone together, with crescendo to push us into the next phrase.
B (8)	Repeat.
B (8)	Two saxophones take turns soloing (two-bar phrases); brass play last two bars.
B (8)	Repeat.
Connecting phrase (4)	Brass for two bars, then brass and reeds together (rhythm section stops for first two bars, comes back in for second two).
B (8)	Trumpet solo, with saxophone and trombone riff accompaniment.
B (8)	Repeat.
Connecting phrase (2)	Whole band.
A (12 + 2)	The main riff returns; in the saxophones, with trombones playing a sustained low note in response. An extra two-bar phrase is added, for suspense.
A (12 + 2)	Same music, but quieter.
A (12)	Same music, even quieter (listen for cowbell in background, very softly).
A (12 + 6)	Same music, coming back two measures before you expect it, *loud*!!! At the end of this section there is another musical trick—the chorus is extended by an additional six bars, delaying and intensifying the final resolution to the tonic chord.

munity in the United States, it is perhaps easier to understand the importance of such qualities.

Today we view World War II from afar, through black-and-white photographs or old movies about the heroism of soldiers. This sense of distance makes it hard for us to imagine what it was actually like for people on the "home front," living with the knowledge that an officer might show up at their door at any moment to report the death of a loved one. To be sure, "In the Mood," like most big hits of the swing era, was escapist in content and outlook. But people sometimes need a means of escape, however temporary, from the anxieties of life. This has all along been one of the most important functions of popular music: in times of great stress or tragedy, it simply helps people to carry on.

COUNTRY MUSIC IN THE SWING ERA: ROY ACUFF, SINGING COWBOYS, AND WESTERN SWING

Although the big bands dominated the pop charts, the appeal of so-called hillbilly performers and their music, based in Anglo-American folk traditions, continued to grow between 1935 and 1945. Uprooted by the Great Depression, the mechanization of agriculture, and ecological catastrophes such as the Dust Bowl drought of the late 1930s, millions of white southerners migrated in search of industrial employment, forming enclaves in urban centers such as Nashville, Atlanta, Detroit, Chicago, Cincinnati, St. Louis, and Los Angeles. This mass population movement created a new urban audience for hillbilly music, a genre referred to by its increasingly cosmopolitan listeners, and eventually by the music industry, as country and western music, or simply country music.

At the same time, the appeal of country music also appears to have spread among many people who were not born in the South. During the late 1930s listeners throughout the country were exposed to country music on the radio, including the far-reaching fifty-thousand watt stations located just across the border in Mexico, and in North American cities such as Fort Worth, Texas (WBAP), Chicago (WLS), and Nashville, Tennessee (WSM). By the end of World War II there were over six hundred hillbilly radio programs on the air nationwide. Many people who looked down their noses at country music, making fun of the singers' nasal voices, "hick" dialects, and conservative cultural values, still listened to shows such as WSM's *Grand Ole Opry*, and many found their musical tastes shaped by the experience.

A number of other factors contributed to the expansion of country music during the War. The formation of *BMI* (see Box 6.1) provided opportunities for country songwriters to publish their compositions and to receive royalties. The American Federation of Musicians' recording ban, which kept members out of the studios, created more recording opportunities for hillbilly musicians, most of whom were not allowed to join the union. New record companies such as Capitol Records, based in Los Angeles, achieved success in part because of their large rosters of country recording artists. A number of small *independent record labels* (*"indies"*) specializing in hillbilly music also sprang up during the war, particularly in towns such as Nashville, Cincinnati, and Los Angeles, with their large populations of southern migrants. After the recording ban ended, major companies began to pay more attention to country music, and popular mainstream artists such as Bing Crosby and the Andrews Sisters released bestselling versions of country songs. By the close of the war, the American music industry had awakened to the commercial potential of country music, which by some estimates provided nearly a third of its total revenues.

The war helped to expand the audience for country music, not only by stimulating rural-urban migration on the home front, but also by bringing millions of servicemen from the North and Midwest into more intimate contact with their southern-born counterparts. While coresidence did not automatically confer musical brotherhood, many Americans who had previously paid little or no attention to hillbilly music began to develop a taste for it. Over the Armed Forces radio network, on "V-discs" ("Victory discs") produced by the U.S. government for servicemen, and at USO concerts designed to boost the morale of the troops, music rooted in the old traditions of the American South played an important role in the daily lives of servicemen and had a profound and lasting impact on their musical sensibilities.

Themes of sentimentality, morality, and patriotism, already prominent in hillbilly recordings of the 1920s, played an important role in country music's popularity during the war. Prominent country music stars composed and recorded songs such as "Smoke on the Water," "Gold Star in the Window," "Cowards over Pearl Harbor," and "Hitler's Last Letter to Hirohito," targeted at servicemen and the families they had left behind. One survey of American soldiers in Europe actually found that the GIs preferred hillbilly musician Roy Acuff to the big-band crooner Frank Sinatra by a substantial margin. Attacking a marine position on Okinawa, a Japanese *banzai* charge reportedly used a battle cry designed as the ultimate insult to Americans: "To hell with Roosevelt, to hell with Babe Ruth, to hell with Roy Acuff"!

The object of this epithet was Roy Claxton Acuff (1903–92), the most popular hillbilly singer of the swing era. Like many other country music performers, Acuff began his career with a traveling medicine show and in 1935 formed his own band, the Crazy Tennesseans. In 1938 he joined the regular cast of WSM's *Grand Ole Opry* and soon became its biggest star. Acuff performed in a style that was self-consciously rooted in southern folk music. He sang old-timey songs in a sincere, unaffected style with a pronounced southern twang, and his band used instruments derived from the southern string band tradition, including the fiddle, banjo, and guitar. In general, Acuff was a traditionalist, accepting only those innovations that fit within the framework of musical traditions he had learned growing up in Tennessee.

Acuff's initial rise to fame was in large part due to the popularity of two songs that are still closely associated with him, "Wabash Cannon Ball" and "Great Speckled Bird." The latter song—widely regarded as the national anthem of country and western music—was Acuff's first hit record. Recorded in Chicago in 1936, Acuff's rendition of "Great Speckled Bird" crossed over to the mainstream pop charts, reaching Number Thirteen on the *Billboard* Hit Parade in 1938. Following in the tradition of gospel-derived performance established by the Carter Family and other early country music performers (see Chapter 5), the lyric—composed by a southern preacher—portrays the church as an embattled group of individuals. The

Box 6.1 ASCAP, the AFM, and the Decline of the Big Bands

The swing era lasted almost exactly a decade, ending almost as suddenly as it had begun. By the close of 1946 many of the top dance bands in the country had either broken up or formed smaller, more economical units, including the band that started the swing craze, the Benny Goodman Orchestra. There is evidence that mainstream popular taste had already begun to shift during the war, away from the brassy exuberance of the big bands, toward lushly orchestrated, sentimental recordings by popular crooners. However, the sudden decline of the big bands involved changes in the music business as well as shifts in popular musical taste.

Some swing bandleaders had joined the armed forces, leading dance bands made up of enlisted men. These bands toured Europe and the Pacific, playing for the Allied troops. A number of well-known musicians were killed in the war, including Glenn Miller, whose plane went down over the English Channel in 1944.

On the home front, the music business was affected by shortages in gas and vehicles, which made it difficult for the bands to travel to engagements; by the limits on the supply of shellac for pressing phonograph records; by restrictions on ownership of radio receiving and broadcasting equipment; and by the imposition of a 20 percent entertainment tax and a midnight curfew (called a "brownout"), both of which discouraged people from going out to hear live music.

The situation of the big bands was also adversely affected by a series of struggles among powerful institutions in the music business, including the record companies, the radio networks, music-licensing agencies, and the musicians' union. To begin with, the four big radio networks—NBC, CBS, ABC, and Mutual—were engaged in a bitter feud with ASCAP, the American Society of Composers, Authors, and Publishers, which had grown tremendously since its founding in 1914. By 1939 ASCAP had licensed around 90 percent of Tin Pan Alley songs. ASCAP had already been working for a number of years to ensure that its members—the composers and music-publishing companies—received royalties from the radio industry for the broadcast of their songs. As profits from network radio broadcasts rose—partly stimulated by the big-band craze—ASCAP turned up the legal pressure on the networks to turn over a larger portion of their revenues.

In 1940 the radio networks counterattacked and formed a rival licensing agency, *Broadcast Music, Incorporated (BMI)*, specifically designed to challenge ASCAP's monopoly. While BMI was not initially expected to survive for long, its "open door" policy allowed songwriters working outside Tin Pan Alley to claim royalties from the use of their songs on the broadcast media. This gave a boost to musicians working in the idioms of country and western and rhythm & blues, genres that had largely been ignored by ASCAP, and which rose in economic importance during and after the war.

In 1941 the struggle between ASCAP and the radio networks came to a head, and ASCAP called a strike, withdrawing the rights to broadcast any material composed by their members. This wiped out overnight a lion's share of the big-band repertoire, which, as we have seen, relied heavily on arrangements of popular Tin Pan Alley songs. The quality of songs produced by BMI-licensed composers was at first not equal to that of the top ASCAP songwriters (Irving Berlin, the Gershwins, Cole Porter, Rodgers and Hart, and so on). The bands, unable to play either their most popular arrangements or their theme songs on the air, had to quickly assemble a replacement repertoire free of ASCAP songs. Big-band arrangers were sometimes forced to turn to older materials, including classical music themes and nineteenth-century popular songs such as "Jeanie with the Light Brown Hair," "London Bridge Is Falling Down," and "My Old Kentucky Home." The battle between ASCAP and radio reached ridiculous extremes. For example, jazz musicians have traditionally often quoted bits of popular song melodies when playing improvised solos. During 1941 ASCAP began to take note of melodic phrases from licensed songs appearing in the solos of swing musicians and to charge for their use. This meant that all "improvised" solos had to be written out and approved by the radio networks before they could be played on the air.

To further complicate matters, on August 2, 1942, the musicians' union (the *American Federation of Musicians*) called a strike against the recording companies. James Caesar Petrillo, president of the AFM, claimed that the union's members—including the musicians in all of the top dance bands—were not being properly compensated for their performances. In particular, he wanted the recording companies to make sure that musicians received a share of royalties when their records were played on radio broadcasts and coin-operated jukeboxes, which now numbered some four hundred thousand nationwide. While many musicians disagreed with Petrillo's decision—they recognized better than he the importance of recording and broadcast media to the future of their profession—he stuck to his guns, and for more than a year no major record company made any records with instrumentalists. Recording had already been curtailed by the wartime shellac shortage, and record companies chose to focus on vocal performances, including star crooners backed by choirs. (At that time the union did not consider singers to be "musicians" and thus did not allow them to join.) In 1943 Decca and Capitol Records—both new companies—signed a new contract with the union and were able to resume recording instrumental music. The biggest companies, Columbia and Victor, however, did not agree to the AFM's demands until 1944. By that time the swing bands had been dealt a severe blow, and within a year or two many of the professional dance band musicians whom Petrillo had claimed he was protecting were thrown out of work. This, along with other developments, created the conditions for the postwar success of other styles of music, including country and western and rhythm & blues (see Chapter 7).

Roy Acuff (with fiddle). Courtesy Library of Congress

speckled bird is a metaphor for the church, a sign of God's Word (as inscribed in the Bible), and a vehicle for the salvation of the faithful:

What a beautiful thought I am thinking
Concerning a Great Speckled Bird
Remember her name is recorded
On the pages of God's holy word

With all the other birds flocking 'round her
She is so despised by the squad
The Great Speckled Bird is the Bible
Representing the great Church of God. . . .

When He cometh descending from Heaven
On the clouds as he writes in His Word
I'll be joyfully carried to meet Him
On the wings of that Great Speckled Bird

This lyric is based on Jeremiah 12:9, "Mine heritage is unto me as a speckled bird, the birds round about are against her." The huge commercial success of Acuff's recording of "Great Speckled Bird"—and the song's subsequent incorporation into the services of many Pentecostal Holiness churches—was in large part due to the song's religious theme. During a time of profound change, in which millions of families were uprooted from a rural way of life, the church became a touchstone of moral and cultural continuity.

The traditional ethos of "Great Speckled Bird"—one source of its great appeal to southern-born listeners—is reinforced by Acuff's straightforward, unadorned vocal performance, and by the form of the song, derived from the **strophic** pattern of

Anglo-American ballad singing. (In this case the sixteen-bar strophe is performed a total of five times.) The melody of "Great Speckled Bird" is also quite similar to that of "I'm Thinking Tonight of My Blue Eyes," a song popularized by the Carter Family, and its familiarity to many of Acuff's listeners may account in part for its success.

Although his reputation rested upon a folksy, down-home approach, Acuff was not averse to using technological innovations that fit within the framework of the southern string band tradition. His recording of "Great Speckled Bird" features a new version of the standard six-string guitar called the Dobro, which used a round metal plate (a resonator) to amplify the sound of the strings. On this recording the blunt edge of a steel knife is used to play melodic patterns on the Dobro, allowing the player to glide between pitches, interweaving with the singer's voice. (This technique, pioneered by Hawai'ian and African American guitarists in the early twentieth century, is called "bottleneck guitar.") Acuff was a shrewd businessman—in 1942 he responded to wartime changes in the music industry by cofounding a music publishing company, Acuff-Rose, which went on to make millions of dollars from the expanding postwar market for country songs.

Another important development of the late 1930s and 1940s was the rise of the *singing cowboy*. The heroic image of the old cowhand, popularized after World War I in cheap dime novels, published collections of cowboy songs, and the movies of silent film stars such as Tom Mix, was adopted by many country musicians during the depression years as a substitute for the often-denigrated image of the hillbilly. Like the South, the Wild West has long been a place in the imagination, a repository of images and stories that Americans tell themselves about their history, their traditions, and character. However, images of the South in American popular culture, whether positive or negative in tone, typically evoke tradition, religious morality, and the past, while the West is popularly associated with movement, independence, and the future. From the 1930s through the 1950s, as country musicians sought to reach a wider audience, the term "western" became a substitute for "hillbilly." Many country singers, whatever their place of birth, wore cowboy hats and shirts, and adopted nicknames such as "Tex," "Slim," "Hank," or "the Lone Cowboy." (Today the cowboy image is still evident in the public image of country singers such as Garth Brooks.)

The first successful singing cowboy was <u>Gene Autry</u> (1907–98), born in Texas. In the early 1930s Autry's musical career received a boost from regular appearances on the *National Barn Dance*, broadcast nationwide from the Chicago radio station WLS. Autry's early performances actually included few cowboy songs: he was a hillbilly singer, known for his imitations of Jimmie Rodgers. The big shift came in 1934, when Autry moved to Hollywood and got a bit part in a cowboy movie. In a series of over ninety movies for various film companies—including a number of popular serials, the cinematic ancestors of today's weekly television series—Autry institutionalized the image of the singing cowboy, a heroic figure as adept with his voice and six strings as with a six-shooter.

In his filmed performances and popular recordings, Autry developed a style designed to reach out to a broader audience, with a less pronounced regional accent, a deep baritone voice, and a touch of the crooner's smoothness. Like Roy Acuff, but to an even greater degree, Autry was able to score crossover hits in the pop as well as the hillbilly market, and he paved the way for other western recording artists, including Roy Rogers, Patsy Montana, Tex Ritter, and the Sons of the Pioneers. In spreading his own fame, Gene Autry helped to bring country music to a much wider and more diverse audience—including the millions of fans of cowboy movies—and to establish the "western" component of country and western music. (By the 1940s some prominent black popular musicians were making cowboy films, though none of these referred to the very real tradition of nineteenth-century African American cowboys.)

The increasing professionalism of country music, and the close links between western themes in popular music and Hollywood films, are particularly evident in the recordings of the vocal group Sons of the Pioneers. This group had originated as a vocal trio in 1933, at the instigation of Len Slye (1911–98), who later left the group and became a film and television star under the name Roy Rogers. The Sons of the Pioneers sang in many cowboy movies and represented the cosmopolitan end of western music. They specialized in sophisticated vocal harmonies, influenced to some degree by the Mills Brothers, and were known for writing their own songs, including "Tumbling Tumbleweeds," "At the Rainbow's End," and "Cool Water," all composed by group member Bob Nolan.

"Cool Water," recorded in 1941, was a bestseller in the country music market and reached Number Twenty-five on the pop charts. It features the vocal trio's smooth, carefully rehearsed harmonies and the lead singing of Bob Nolan, backed by guitar, fiddle, and bass. The recording opens with the guitar and fiddle, playing the basic "hook" of the song (*"cool, clear water"*). The song's structure is strophic, with a series of verses, each consisting of a solo line sung by Nolan and a response from the trio, and a repeated chorus, sung in unison by the three men.

Verse 1
solo: All day I've faced a barren waste without the taste of water
trio: Cool water
solo: Old Dan and I with throats burned dry and souls that cry for water
trio: Cool clear water

Chorus
Keep a'movin,' Dan, don't you listen to him, Dan, he's a devil not a man, and he spreads the burning sand with water
Dan, can you see that big green tree where the water's runnin' free and it's waitin' there for me and you?

Verse 2
solo: The nights are cool and I'm a fool, each star's a pool of water
trio: Cool water
solo: But with the dawn I'll wake and yawn and carry on to water
trio: Cool, clear water

Chorus

Verse 3
solo: The shadows sway and seem to say, "Tonight we'll pray for water"
trio: Cool water
solo: And way up there He'll hear our prayer and show us where there's water
trio: Cool, clear water

Chorus
solo falsetto voice: Cool, clear water . . .

The mise-en-scène of this recording would have been familiar to most listeners, a cliché straight from the Hollywood cinema: two cursed souls (a man and his horse?), crawling through the desert's "barren waste," and praying for water to quench their terrible thirst. The impact of the song's lyric lies in its use of the first-person voice, and in its verbal imagery, which impressionistically conveys the singer's experience: dehydrated to the point of madness, he hears the voices of swaying shadows and sees the night stars as pools of water. In the verses the singer seems to rest and take stock of his situation. In the chorus—sung by all three men in unison, with an insistent, almost marchlike rhythm—he strives to keep moving forward through the "burning sand," only to collapse into a hallucinatory fantasy, the mirage of a big green tree. Throughout the recording the voices and the fiddle drift lazily from pitch to pitch, fluctuating precariously in energy, and the dreamlike quality of the recording is underpinned by the obsessive repetition, in falsetto, of the single word, "water." It is this distant, tantalizing, almost ghostly voice that gives us a sense of the desert's unforgiving vastness, the man's helplessness, and his stubborn hope for salvation. More than half a century after its release, "Cool Water" remains a remarkable example of musical craftsmanship, in which the skills of songwriting, arrangement, and studio recording are brought together with imagery derived from Hollywood films to create something that is more than just a song. In less than three minutes, the Sons of the Pioneers manage not only to tell us a story but also to show us a movie.

Another important part of the "western" element in country music during the big-band era was *western swing*, a concatenation of country fiddle music, blues, boogie-woogie, and swing music. The genre developed in Texas and accordingly reflected that state's diverse musical traditions, including cowboy songs, German and Czech polkas, and Texas-Mexican (Tejano) genres such as *corridos* (narrative ballads in Spanish), *conjunto acordeon* ("accordion band" music), and *mariachi* ("marriage") music, played by ensembles consisting of violins, guitars, and two or more trumpets. (A market for Mexican and Tejano recordings had started in the late 1920s, as record companies sought to create Latin American parallels to the race and hillbilly record business.)

The seminal figure in the national popularization of western swing was Bob Wills (1905–75), a fiddler from East Texas whose musical career ran from the 1920s through the 1960s. Raised in a family of fiddle players, Wills played with several dance bands in the Southwest before forming his own group, The Texas Playboys, in 1934. During the late 1930s the band established itself in Tulsa, Oklahoma, making daily radio appearances, playing nightly in a local ballroom, and going on tours of the "southwest territories." (This geographical area—Oklahoma, Arkansas, Kansas, and Texas—was also home to the boogie-woogie piano blues and the bigband tradition of Count Basie and other black "territory bands," both of which exerted an influence on western swing.) In 1943, after being discharged from the army, Bob Wills relocated to California. There he opened his own nightclub and attracted huge audiences, composed in part of migrants from the southwest territories who were already familiar with his music. The Texas Playboys' style became so popular in California that even mainstream swing bands were asked by dancers to add western swing–style numbers to their repertoires.

The heart of the Texas Playboys' style was southern string band music, and many of Wills's most popular arrangements were based on old fiddle tunes and other types of dance songs that he had learned as a young man. To this traditional

Bob Wills and His Texas Playboys. Frank Driggs Collection.

core he added elements from big-band swing, including call-and response riffs, and instruments such as trumpets, saxophones, and the drum set. This balance between traditionalism and innovation was the key to Wills's ability to build a large and diverse audience, one that overlapped the division between mainstream pop and country music.

Bob Wills's success was also based on his ability to hire and retain first-rate musicians, many of them versed in blues and jazz as well as hillbilly and cowboy music. Among the best remembered of these were the guitarist Leon McAuliffe, responsible for making the electronically amplified steel guitar a permanent part of country and western music, and vocalist Tommy Duncan, whose stylistic flexibility and warm baritone voice were an important part of the band's sound. During the Texas Playboys' performances Bob Wills acted as impresario, cracking jokes, calling out musicians' nicknames, and giving out enthusiastic cries and whoops of encouragement.

The Texas Playboys' biggest hit was their recording of "New San Antonio Rose," which was a country bestseller, and reached Number Eleven on the pop charts in 1940. (Bing Crosby recorded his own version of the song in 1941, reaching Number Seven on the pop charts and suggesting once again the crossover potential of country music, if not always of the original performers themselves.) The structure of the song is the AABA thirty-two-bar form, familiar to us from Tin Pan Alley song, and the performance exemplifies the unique blend of stylistic elements achieved by Wills. The sixteen-piece ensemble combines a string band (fiddle, banjo, and three guitars, including McAuliffe's electrified steel guitar) with a big band (piano, string bass, drums, two trumpets, and six saxophones).

After a brief introduction that sounds as though it could have been taken straight out of a Benny Goodman arrangement, the trumpets and saxophones play the A section of "New San Antonio Rose" twice, while the rhythm section maintains a bouncy dance rhythm. We then move into the vocal section of the arrangement, sung by Tommy Duncan (*Deep within my heart . . .*). The vocal takes us through the entire thirty-two-bar AABA structure of the song, Duncan's singing supported with soft harmonies in the brass and reeds and occasionally interrupted by Wills's trademark vocal interjections. This is followed by a trumpet duet, playing the B section in the style of a Mexican mariachi band, and the arrangement concludes with a saxophone *soli* statement of the A section.

Although western swing bands did not dominate the country charts after World War II, the style exerted a permanent influence on country music, particularly in the introduction of amplified steel guitar and drum set, the incorporation of African American and Latin American musical influences, and the emphasis placed in live performances on improvised instrumental solos (called "takeoffs"). Western swing has been revived from time to time—the most notable example being the group Asleep at the Wheel, who had a number of hit records during the 1970s and 1980s—and Bob Wills is today widely regarded as one of the pioneers of modern country and western music.

The swing era represented the peak of jazz's influence on popular music. After World War II many jazz musicians moved in other directions, less concerned with record sales than with artistic achievement and instrumental virtuosity. The singers who had appeared with big bands became even bigger celebrities in their own right, overshadowing bandleaders who had formerly enjoyed the spotlight. Another branch of swing music—christened "rhythm & blues" by the record industry—maintained its function as social dance music and came to dominate musical taste in African American communities during the postwar era. At the same time, so-called hillbilly music continued its move to the city and accounted for an increasing share of the market. In the next chapter we will examine these postwar developments, precursors of the rise of rock 'n' roll.

CHAPTER SEVEN

"CHOO CHOO CH' BOOGIE"
The Postwar Era, 1946–1954

Many pop music historians portray the years between the decline of the big bands (1946) and the rise of rock 'n' roll (1955) as a period of musical stagnation or, at best, gestation. In fact, it could be argued that the postwar decade was one of the most interesting, complex, and dynamic eras in the history of American popular music. The entertainment industry grew rapidly after the war, and in 1947 record companies achieved retail sales of over $214 million, finally surpassing the previous peak, established back in 1921 (more than a quarter of a century earlier!). This growth was supported by the booming postwar economy, and by a corresponding increase in the disposable income of many American families.

In particular, record companies began for the first time to target young people, many of whom had more pocket money to spend on records than ever before. During World War II the demand for workers in military-related industries meant that many teenagers took on adult responsibilities, working for wages while continuing to attend high school. The idea that teenagers had the right to earn a salary of their own led after the war to the widespread practice of a weekly allowance in return for doing the household chores. Many young adults spent a considerable portion of their income on films, jukeboxes, and records. A survey of record retailers conducted in 1949 estimated that people under twenty-one constituted fully one-third of the total record-buying population of the United States, a great increase from previous eras. Although the music produced by the largest record companies was still mainly aimed at an older audience, the increasing importance of a new marketing category—the teenager—was a harbinger of the rock 'n' roll era (see Chapter 8).

Many of the hit records of the late 1940s and early 1950s were romantic songs, performed by crooners with orchestral backing. The sentimentality of these songs can be gleaned from their titles: "Prisoner of Love" and "(I Love You) For Sentimental Reasons" (1946), "My Darling, My Darling" and "You're Breaking My Heart" (1949), "Cold, Cold Heart" and "Cry" (1951), "No Other Love" and "You You You" (1953), all Number One pop hits. Big-band swing was also supplanted by the romantic "light music" of Jackie Gleason, Percy Faith, and Mantovani and His Orchestra. These recordings typically featured string orchestras or choruses, with an occasional light touch of the exotic—maracas, castanets, a harpsichord, or a vaguely Latin rhythm. (These "easy listening" records soon became a mainstay of Muzak, a corporation that had since the late 1930s supplied businesses with recorded music, designed to subliminally encourage worker productivity.) Romantic vocal and orchestral recordings were interspersed on the hit charts with catchy, light-hearted novelty songs, including Number One hits such as "Woody Woodpecker" (Kay Kyser, 1948), "The Thing" (Phil Harris, 1950), "I Saw Mommy Kissing Santa Claus" (Jimmy Boyd, 1952), and "The Doggie in the Window" (Patti Page, 1953).

The roots of this musical conservatism are not difficult to pinpoint. Although there was a brief depression just after the war (see discussion of "Choo Choo Ch' Boogie" below), the national economy expanded rapidly during the postwar decade, fueled by the lifting of wartime restrictions on the production of consumer goods, the increased availability of jobs in the industrial and service sectors of the economy, and the G.I. Bill, which provided educational and job opportunities for returning servicemen. After the uncertainty and personal sacrifice of the war years, many people simply wanted to settle down, raise a family, and focus on building their own futures. For millions of Americans who had served in the armed forces, or come to the city in search of work during the war, or whose immigrant parents and grandparents had fled poverty earlier in the century, this represented the first opportunity to buy a home and to fulfill the ideals of domestic tranquillity and privacy evoked so tenderly two decades earlier in Gene Austin's 1927 recording of "My Blue Heaven" (see Chapter 4). If we also take into account the underlying uncertainties and tensions of the postwar era—including the threat of nuclear war and Cold War conflicts in Europe and Asia—it makes perfect sense that many new members of the American middle class preferred popular music that focused on private emotions and helped to create a comforting sound environment in the home.

The economics of the music industry also played a role in this conservative trend, and in the uneven quality of much mainstream pop music produced during this period. It is during the postwar decade that we see clearly for the first time a phenomenon that has helped to shape the development of popular music in the United States ever since—a constant tug-of-war between, on the one hand, the music business's efforts to predict (and therefore perchance control) the public's consumption of music, and on the other hand, the periodic eruption of new musical fads, usually based in youth culture. In general, the center of the music business—like many other sectors of corporate America—became increasingly routinized after the war. Music was now a product, sold in units, and listeners were consumers.

The idea of *Top 40 radio programming*—another attempt to control the uncertainty of the marketplace—was developed in the early 1950s by Todd Storz, a disc jockey in Omaha, Nebraska. Storz observed teenagers dropping coins in jukeboxes and noticed that they tended to play certain songs repeatedly. He applied this idea to radio programming, selecting a list of forty top hits, which he played over and over. The idea spread quickly, and within a few years many AM stations were playing the same set of songs. The ability of radio stations to control the public's exposure to new recordings led to a practice called **payola,** in which record companies paid **DJs** to put their records into "heavy rotation." By the mid-1950s this profitable practice had come under legal scrutiny, ending the careers of some prominent record executives and disc jockeys.

If the late 1940s and early 1950s were generally profitable for the music business—publishing firms, licensing agencies, record corporations, and radio networks—it was also a period of uncertainty. The executives who ran these powerful institutions, and who were therefore in charge of deciding how much and what sorts of music would be recorded and broadcast, were mainly veterans of an earlier era. Many of these men looked down their noses at the idea of producing music for a teenage audience, and this limited their ability to spot and exploit new trends.

At the same time, the increasingly rapid turnover of hit songs on the radio and jukebox meant that record companies started producing many more records than the public was willing to buy. In general, the big record companies competed by saturating the market with records, sometimes sending as many as one hundred thousand copies of a new record out to stores, with a guarantee that they could return all of the discs they didn't sell. This is clearly not a sound business strategy, and it adversely affected the overall quality of pop music during the early 1950s— one record company executive referred to the technique of market saturation as "throwing a lot of shit at the wall to see if anything sticks" (Clarke 1995, p. 311).

In general, the major record companies of the period—RCA Victor, Columbia, Decca, and the new Los Angeles–based company, Capitol Records—experienced considerable growth. However, it was during the postwar era that musical genres regarded as marginal by the industry came to influence even more strongly the musical taste of middle-class white Americans. As we saw in the last chapter, country and western music had expanded its audience during the war, and this trend continued through the early 1950s. The market for black popular music, rechristened rhythm & blues, also expanded as a result of postwar prosperity—the income of the average black family had tripled during the war—and a growing (though still small) white audience, whose musical conversion had been prepared by the swing era. The market was supported by a new generation of independent record labels, such as Chess (Chicago), Aladdin (Los Angeles), Atlantic (New York), King (Cincinnati), Sun (Memphis), and Duke/Peacock (Houston). In addition, a new licensing agency (BMI) and publishing houses were eager to work with songwriters outside the Tin Pan Alley mainstream. As a result, with the increased access to the airwaves (including the new medium of television), country music and rhythm & blues experienced a golden age.

In retrospect, the music business of the late 1940s and early 1950s could be envisioned as a Jurassic scenario, in which huge, slow, powerful carnivores ruled the roost, but only in continual competition with lighter, smaller, faster beasts. These little omnivores—"indie" record labels, renegade radio DJs, talented musicians who had for various reasons been excluded from the wellsprings of profit, and entrepreneurs and hustlers of all stripes—shared a double advantage over the big boys. First, they were musically omnivorous, feeding on styles outside the mainstream of popular music; and second, they were more keenly attuned to changes in the environment, particularly the increasing importance of the teenage market for popular music. Although many of the little guys did get eaten, in the long run it was precisely these adaptive qualities that allowed them to play an indispensable role in the development of American poplar music.

POPULAR MUSIC AND TECHNOLOGY IN THE POSTWAR ERA

During the decade following World War II the music industry was affected by the introduction of new technologies for the reproduction and transmission of musical sound and visual images. *Magnetic tape recording,* developed by the Germans and the Japanese during the 1930s, offered a number of advantages over the established means of recording music. In the recording studio, tape was better able to capture the full range of musical sounds than the older process of recording directly onto "master" phonograph discs. In addition, tape recording allowed musicians to rerecord over the unsatisfactory parts of previous performances and to add layers of sound to a recording (a process called "overdubbing"). The best-known innovator in this field was the guitarist/inventor <u>Les Paul</u> (1915–97), who designed his own eight-track tape recorder and began in 1948 to release a series of popular recordings featuring his own playing, overdubbed to sound like an ensemble of six or more guitars.

By the late 1940s recording studios were using audiotape, rather than "transcription discs," to produce most recordings, and some artists (notably Bing Crosby) had begun to use tape to prerecord their appearances on radio. In 1948 the Ampex Corporation, backed by Crosby, introduced its first tape recorder, a machine that soon became a mainstay of the recording industry. The year 1949 saw the introduction of a two-track recorder, which could record simultaneous inputs from two microphones and thus produce stereo effects. While tape recorders were not initially successful as a home consumer item, the advantages of magnetic recording were felt immediately in the music industry.

The postwar era also saw a fierce competition over new disc technologies, known as the "Battle of the Speeds." In 1948 Columbia Records introduced the twelve-inch long-playing disc. Spinning at a speed of $33\frac{1}{3}$ revolutions per minute (r.p.m.), the LP could accommodate more than twenty minutes of music on each side, a great improvement over the three- to four-minute limitation of 78 r.p.m. discs. In addition, the LP was made of vinyl, a material at once more durable and less noisy than the shellac used to make 78s. In introducing the new discs at a Columbia Records board meeting, an executive put a fifteen-inch stack of LPs next to an eight-*foot* stack of 78s containing the same amount of music, in order to convince shareholders and the press to back the new technology. Interestingly, although the long-playing disc opened the possibility of longer uninterrupted recordings—a great advantage for fans of classical music and Broadway musicals—most pop music LPs were "albums" of three-minute performances. This suggests that what from the engineering point of view had seemed to be a technological restriction—the three-minute limit of 78 r.p.m. phonograph records—had long since become a musical habit. To this day, many pop music recordings are no longer than four minutes in length.

In 1949, responding to Columbia's innovation, the RCA Victor Corporation introduced yet another new disc format, the seven-inch 45 r.p.m. single. The "45," actually close to the old 78 r.p.m. discs in overall recording time, required a special mechanical record changer that fit the large hole at the center of the disc. However,

45s had at least one decided advantage from the consumer's viewpoint. Using a record changer, the listener could load a stack of singles, thus preprogramming a series of favorite recordings, each of which would begin less than fifteen seconds after the end of the previous record. This meant that consumers could focus their spending power on their favorite recordings, rather than buying a prepackaged series of songs by a single artist on an LP. Building on the basic principles of the jukebox, the marketing of 45s pointed the way forward to today's digital technologies, which allow consumers to program specific tracks in any order they choose.

In the end, the battle of the speeds was resolved by a technological compromise, in which turntables were set up to accommodate all three existing formats (78, 45, and $33\frac{1}{3}$ r.p.m.). LPs continued to serve as a medium for albums of pop songs and longer musical works such as Broadway cast recordings, while the 45 became the favored medium for distributing hit singles.

Radio broadcasting was also affected by technological change in the postwar period. In addition to the older AM (amplitude modulation) broadcasting technology that had dominated the field since the early 1920s, the postwar period saw the rapid growth of FM (frequency modulation) broadcasting. FM radio, which used higher frequencies than AM, had better sound quality and was not as easily subject to electrical disturbances such as lightning. (By the late 1950s FM was also being used for stereo broadcasting.) The first commercial FM broadcast took place in 1939, and by 1949 around seven hundred FM stations were operating in the United States, along with well over one thousand AM stations.

Of all of the new electronic technologies of the postwar era, television exerted the most profound influence on American culture. The development of television broadcasting, foreseen by science fiction writers of the nineteenth century, started in earnest in the 1920s. At the 1939 New York World's Fair RCA introduced its first fully electronic television system to the public. (At that time a television set cost $660, more than half the price of a new automobile!) During the war production of television was interrupted, but in the postwar years, with the economy booming and cheaper sets available, the new medium took off. In 1946 it was estimated that Americans owned six thousand television sets; this figure shot up to three million in 1948, then twelve million in 1951. For better or worse, by the early 1950s television had become the central focus of leisure time in millions of Americans households.

Television's massive success rested on its ability to fuse the forms and functions of previous media, including radio, the record player, and cinema. Like Hollywood film, television was a multiple medium, combining sound and moving images. Like radios and record players, the TV set could be brought into the family parlor (now called a "living room") and incorporated into the daily round of domestic life. TV quickly became the main outlet for corporate advertising, and by 1952 the four big networks—NBC, CBS, ABC, and Dumont—began to turn significant profits. TV broadcasters used a great deal of recorded and live music, and the postwar era saw the eruption of complex legal disputes over fees to be paid for use of songs on the air (a recapitulation of the battles between radio and the music business during the 1930s and 1940s). On the one hand, there can be no doubt that the new medium was perceived by the record industry as a threat. (In 1949 retail sales of records fell drastically, while sales of television sets increased by some 400 percent!) However, by the mid-1950s, television had become the most important medium for launching new performers and recordings, and established stars such as Perry Como, Nat

"King" Cole, Tommy Dorsey, and Jackie Gleason hosted their own weekly variety shows.

RISE OF THE BIG SINGERS

By 1946 the main focus of popular attention had shifted away from celebrity instrumentalist/bandleaders such as Benny Goodman, Count Basie, and Glenn Miller, toward a new generation of crooners. Many of the top singers of the late 1940s and early 1950s—including Frank Sinatra, Perry Como, Nat "King" Cole, Frankie Laine, Peggy Lee, and Rosemary Clooney—had started their careers during the swing era. In the early 1950s these pop stars had been joined by a younger generation of vocalists, who specialized in sentimental ballads, novelty numbers—cheerful, disposable songs that often resembled advertising jingles—and crooner-style cover versions of country and western and rhythm & blues hits. These vocalists were promoted to the expanding teenage audience.

The musicians' union recording ban of 1942–44—which had banned instrumentalists from recording but did not apply to even the most musically gifted vocalists—encouraged a number of big band singers to begin recording under their own names, sometimes with choral accompaniment. Those singers with the most entrepreneurial savvy, or the best business agents, were able to parlay this opportunity into long-lasting success. In addition, the music industry's mastery of cross-media promotion—on radio, films, and television—reached new heights. Following in the footsteps of Bing Crosby, many of the biggest singing stars of the postwar era also became film stars (for example, Frank Sinatra and Doris Day) or hosted their own television shows (Perry Como and Nat "King" Cole).

Frank (Francis Albert) Sinatra (1915–98) was one of the first big-band singers to take advantage of changes in the music business. Born into a working-class Italian family in Hoboken, New Jersey, Sinatra attracted public attention in 1935 when he appeared as a member of a vocal quartet on a popular radio show called *Major Bowes' Amateur Hour*. From 1937 to 1939 he worked as a singing waiter at the Rustic Cabin, a nightclub in New Jersey. (Although the job paid little, Sinatra wisely kept it because the place was wired for radio broadcasts.) In 1939 the bandleader Harry James hired him, and later that same year he joined the Tommy Dorsey Orchestra.

In 1942 Sinatra convinced the Victor Company to let him make a solo recording—against Tommy Dorsey's wishes—and soon thereafter bought out his contract with the Dorsey band. A series of appearances on the national radio show *Your Hit Parade* helped him build a national following, particularly among younger listeners. During the AFM strike Sinatra continued to work in the studio, performing with choral accompaniment on several hit records. The magnitude of Sinatra's celebrity became clear for the first time in December 1942, when he appeared at the Paramount Theater in New York City with the Benny Goodman Orchestra. Goodman, introducing Sinatra, suddenly found himself confronted with thousands of screaming young women. (The startled bandleader—himself no stranger to celebrity—is reported to have blurted out, "What the f— is *that?*")

Promoted on radio, at the movies, and in the press (including biographical comic books aimed at high school–age females), Sinatra's popularity soared, culminating

Waiting for Frankie outside, and celebrating his presence inside. Frank Driggs Collection.

in the first documented example of modern pop hysteria, the so-called Columbus Day Riot of 1944. The occasion was a return engagement at the Paramount Theater by Sinatra and the Goodman band, and thirty thousand fans—including thousands of teenage girls, called "bobby soxers"—showed up to claim tickets. The Paramount could seat only thirty-six hundred people, and many fans refused to leave after the first show, triggering a riot among fans lined up outside the theater. In a sense, Sinatra was the direct predecessor of the teen idols of the rock 'n' roll era, and of the Beatles after them. Falling into a "Sinatrance," young women cried, screamed, and tore their hair. They followed the singer everywhere, fighting for pieces of his clothing and treating his used cigarette butts as sacred objects. The press and public bestowed nicknames on Sinatra: he was *Swoonatra*, *The Sultan of Swoon*, or, simply, *The Voice*.

Oddly handsome, with a triangular head, golf-ball Adam's apple, and jug-handle ears, Sinatra projected a combination of confidence and vulnerability. Asked to explain his early popularity, Sinatra later conjectured that he represented to those at home all the local boys that were gone, drafted into the war. It is also undeniable that Frank Sinatra's early success lay partly in his keen business sense, his access to media exposure, and his sheer stamina. (In 1946 he did as many as forty-five shows a week, singing eighty to one hundred songs a day!) And he was also a highly skilled singer and talented interpreter of popular songs, respected by the musicians with whom he worked.

Sinatra's approach to singing took shape in response to his early hero, Bing Crosby. In a 1965 article Sinatra wrote:

When I started singing in the mid-1930s everybody was trying to copy the Crosby style—the casual kind of raspy sound in the throat. Bing was on top, and a bunch of us . . . were trying to break in. It occurred to me that maybe the world didn't need another Crosby. I decided to experiment a little and come up with something different. What I finally hit on was more the bel canto Italian school of singing.[1] . . . That meant I had to stay in better shape because I had to sing more. It was more difficult than Crosby's style, much more difficult. (Pleasants 1974, p. 189)

Sinatra's combination of Crosby's crooning style with the bel canto technique of Italian opera was further enriched by other influences. In addition to female jazz and cabaret singers such as Billie Holiday and Mabel Mercer, Sinatra talked about the influence of instrumental soloists on his vocal approach:

The thing that influenced me the most was the way that Tommy [Dorsey] played his trombone. He would take a musical phrase and play it all the way through without breathing, for eight, ten, maybe sixteen bars. How in the hell did he do it? Why couldn't a singer do that, too? Fascinated, I began to listen to other soloists. I bought every Jascha Heifetz record I could find, and listened to him play the violin hour after hour. His constant bowing, where you never heard a break, carried the melody line straight on through, just like Dorsey's trombone. It was my idea to make my voice work in the same way as a trombone or violin—not sounding like them, but "playing" the voice like those instruments. (Pleasants 1974, p. 192)

In performance, these various stylistic influences combined with Sinatra's mastery of the microphone, which he regarded as an extension of his vocal instrument. While Bing and other early crooners seemed to be *overheard* by the microphone, Sinatra and others of his generation *played* it, subtly shifting it to achieve certain tone qualities, accentuate melodic passages or lyric phrases, and avoid the "popping" of consonants. Perhaps it was this approach to his craft—that of an instrumental musician—that helped him avoid the lachrymose sentimentality of many crooners of the postwar era. Although Sinatra's popularity took a nosedive in the early 1950s—largely as a result of well-publicized difficulties in his personal life—his success in later years (see Chapter 8) was in no small part due to the connection his audience perceived between his voice and his personality, each involving a delicate balance between emotionalism and rationality, deep feeling and technical control.

LISTENING AND ANALYSIS "NANCY (WITH THE LAUGHING FACE)"

Frank Sinatra's 1945 recording of "Nancy (With the Laughing Face)," which peaked at Number Ten on the *Billboard* charts, gives us an example of the singer's style just at the dawn of the postwar era. One big change from his recordings of the swing era is immediately apparent: string instruments dominate the instrumental accompaniment for Sinatra's singing. The song, which has a conventional thirty-two-bar AABA form, was cowritten by the Tin Pan Alley veteran Jimmy Van Heusen and television and film comedian Phil Silvers in honor of the birth of Sinatra's daughter, Nancy. (Part of the song's appeal for audiences lay in the fact that its lyric could be interpreted on more than one level.)

---

1. *Bel canto*, a technique used by opera singers, emphasizes breath control, a fluid and relaxed voice, and the use of subtle variations in pitch and rhythmic phrasing for dramatic effect.

Frank Sinatra: the "Sultan of Swoon" in the 1940s, the ultimate cool "saloon singer" in the 1950s. Frank Driggs Collection.

The brief orchestral introduction begins with four bars of **waltz** rhythm (three beats per bar), then shifts into the four-beat meter of the song. As Sinatra's voice enters (*"If I don't . . . "*), the orchestra slows down, creating a sense of anticipation. (This stretching of the tempo for expressive purposes is called *tempo rubato,* an Italian phrase that literally means "stolen time.") Sinatra sings straight through the song's AABA form, backed by the orchestra, which includes strings, brass, and a harp. (The tempo is quite slow, so you will have to count carefully to follow the form.) He stretches the time slightly in several places to create drama—another example of *tempo rubato*. The orchestra then takes over again for five measures, and Sinatra sings a final A section, followed by an orchestral **coda** (a concluding section).

Sinatra's voice is relaxed and unforced, with warmth and a slight vibrato, and his hard-earned ability to sing long uninterrupted passages allows him to connect the phrases of the song into one smooth contour. In this, as in all of his best recordings, Sinatra conveys the central emotion of a song to his listeners while at the same time maintaining a certain distance, an ability to keep the feeling of the moment in perspective. The arrangement complements Sinatra's voice beautifully, and the subtle tempo changes, the prominence of the harp (associated in the popular imagination with angels), and the brief references to waltz time at the beginning and end all contribute to the romantic atmosphere of the recording.

LISTENING CHART   "NANCY (WITH THE LAUGHING FACE)"

Music and lyrics by Jimmy Van Heusen and Phil Silvers; as performed by Frank Sinatra with the Alex Stordahl Orchestra; recorded 1945

FORM	LYRIC	DESCRIPTIVE COMMENTS
Orchestral introduction		8 measures: 4 measures of triple (waltz) time plus 4 measures of 4-beat time *Strings playing in tempo rubato*
A	*If I don't . . .*	8 measures *Strings and harp*
A	*She takes . . .*	8 measures *Muted trumpets (hint of big band sound)*
B	*Have you ever . . .*	8 measures *The tempo slows down for dramatic effect*
A	*I swear . . .*	8 measures
Orchestral interlude		5 measures *(tempo rubato)*
A	*Keep Betty . . .*	8 measures
Orchestral tag (coda)		8 measures *(tempo rubato)* Music closely related to the introduction

While few postwar crooners were able to match Frank Sinatra's artistry or longevity, this does not mean that there was no serious competition. Despite the very small number of African American artists on the pop music charts of the early 1950s, it could be argued that the greatest postwar crooner—in both musical and commercial terms—was a black musician, Nat "King" Cole (1917–65). Nathaniel Coles was born in Montgomery, Alabama, and his family moved to the South Side of Chicago when he was only four years old. His father was pastor of a Baptist church, and young Nat was playing organ and singing in the choir by the age of twelve. He made his first recording in 1936, in the Solid Swingers, a jazz band led by his brother Eddie Cole. Nat Cole, a brilliant piano improviser, exerted a strong influence on later jazz pianists such as Oscar Peterson and Bill Evans. He moved from Chicago to Los Angeles in 1937 and formed his own group, the King Cole Trio. (This is the group we heard at the end of Chapter 4, performing George Gershwin's "Embraceable You.")

Nat "King" Cole was by far the most successful black recording artist of the postwar era, placing a total of fourteen recordings in the Top 10 pop charts between 1946 and 1954. Along with the Mills Brothers and Louis Jordan, Cole was one of the first African American musicians to cross over regularly to the predominantly white pop charts. Although he continued to record a range of material—including jazz performances with the King Cole Trio—Cole's biggest commercial successes were sentimental ballads, accompanied by elaborate orchestral arrangements: "(I Love You) For Sentimental Reasons" (1946); "Nature Boy" (1948); "Unforgettable" (1950); his biggest hit, "Mona Lisa" (1950), which sold over five million copies; and "Too Young" (1951), perhaps the first teenage love ballad.

Nat "King" Cole performs in a nightclub, 1954. Courtesy Library of Congress.

Given the racial prejudice prevalent in the American music industry, and in society as a whole, Nat "King" Cole's professional success was truly remarkable, comparable to the baseball career of Jackie Robinson, who became the first black player in the major leagues in 1947. Promoted by Capitol Records as a "sepia Sinatra," Cole was the first black musician to host his own weekly radio series (1948–49) and the first to have a network television show (1956–57). He recorded hundreds of songs for Capitol Records, helping to keep the new Los Angeles–based company afloat during its early years. Nat "King" Cole entered a field dominated exclusively by white artists and bested all but the most popular of them in both artistic and commercial terms. And unlike many pop crooners of the time, Cole thought of himself first and foremost as a musician, a musician who sang because his public wanted him to sing. In response to jazz critics who lambasted him for his success as a pop crooner, Cole noted that critics weren't the ones who bought records: "They get 'em free."

LISTENING TO NAT "KING" COLE'S "NATURE BOY"

"Nature Boy" was the first record to present Nat "King" Cole's voice with full orchestral accompaniment, and it is also one of his most interesting pop recordings. Released in 1948, Cole's record held the Number One position on the *Billboard* pop charts for eight weeks. "Nature Boy" was composed by Eden Ahbez (1908–95), whose creative frame of reference was about as far from the professional songwriting business as can be imagined. Ahbez can best be described as a proto-hippie, a long-haired, bearded vegetarian who lived in the hills and deserts around Los Angeles with only a sleeping bag, a bicycle, and a juice squeezer. "Nature Boy," which Ahbez claimed was inspired by his studies of yoga and Eastern religions, was originally part of a suite of songs called the *Gospel of Nature.* Although the mystical message of "Nature Boy" may in fact be related to Ahbez's studies of Asian philosophy, musicologists have noted that the melody of the song is similar to that of a Yiddish folk song called "Schweig Mein Hartz" ("Be Still, My Heart"). (Popular Jewish music had long provided inspiration for the melodic "orientalisms" in Tin Pan Alley songs.)

"Nature Boy" is a good example of the importance of the **arranger** in certain kinds of popular music. As we have seen, the arranger is a musician who takes a song—a melody, with words and a few basic harmonies—and fashions it into a finished musical product. The multitude of choices made by an arranger—what key, what tempo, which instruments to use, and so on—are crucial elements both in the overall sound of a recording and in the success of the artists and record companies who pay for his services. We have already discussed the importance of arrangements in big-band music; in many cases the arrangers hired by a bandleader were the most important factor in shaping the band's distinctive sound. After the war, as studio recording became more elaborate and technologically refined, the role of the arranger became even more important.

Frank DeVol's arrangement of "Nature Boy" is an example of the difference an arranger can make. The song itself is quite brief, and its ABAB' structure, made up of eight-bar sections, appears rather mundane at first glance. "Nature Boy" does have a few distinguishing musical features. Its opening melodic phrase begins with an ear-catching upward leap, followed by a descent ("There *was* a boy. . . ."), a pattern that reappears several times in the course of the song. The song is in a **minor** key, infrequent in mainstream popular music but common in Jewish music, and associated in the popular imagination with sadness, longing, and exotic images of the Orient. It is the orchestral arrangement, however, that makes this record work, along with Cole's honeyed baritone voice. In providing a dramatic musical context for Ahbez's vision of a mysterious boy who arrives one day with a utopian message for humankind, DeVol reached deeply into his professional bag of tricks.

The first moments, before Cole's voice enters, are complex and carefully crafted. We first hear a lonely French horn, playing a melodic phrase that foreshadows that of the song itself (*"There was a boy . . ."*). The strings enter soon afterward, and for a moment it is hard to find the basic pulse of the music. (This is an extreme example of *tempo rubato,* a technique discussed above in connection with Sinatra.) In this swirl of sound a flute and an oboe play tag, tossing melodic phrases back and forth. None of these choices are arbitrary: the French horn and flute have long been used in orchestral music to evoke the countryside, and the oboe is a stereotyped signifier of "Eastern" music. Suddenly the orchestra begins to play in a steadier tempo, and we move into the vocal part of the arrangement.

Unlike Frank Sinatra, who sought to connect the notes of a melody in a continuous stream of breath, Cole treats each note as a somewhat distinct entity, often leaving just a bit of space in between. (It has been suggested that this approach may have been influenced by Cole's long experience with the piano, an instrument that, unlike the violin or trombone, cannot glide between pitches.) This singing technique seems particularly appropriate in the case of "Nature Boy," where Cole has to make the most out of a very few words. Notice also how he explores and savors the tone color of certain vowels, particularly evident here on words such as "boy" or "love." The intimacy of Cole's baritone voice, and his unique ability to caress the lyric of a song, allow him to draw the maximum effect from each word of the text.

As we begin the song the orchestra seems almost to breathe along with Cole, pausing slightly after each of the first two lines (*"There was a boy . . ."* [the flute plays birdsong-like phrases], *"A very strange enchanted boy . . ."* [more birdsong]), then speeding up slightly (*"They say he wandered very far, very far . . ."*), and slowing toward the end of the phrase (*"Over land and sea . . ."*). Here we pause, building anticipation slightly, and then begin to breathe again: *"A little shy . . ."* [the oboe takes over, adding its exotic flavor] *"And sad of eye . . ."* [more oboe] *"But very wise . . ."* [strings cascade upward, then downward, like water] *"Was he . . ."* [flute and oboe together]. This structure then repeats itself with new lyrics, and with many of the same arranging techniques applied. However, just before we reach the last two lines of the lyric—the punch line of the song, if you will—the orchestra grabs our attention with a more emotional swirl of sound, like leaves blowing into a whirlpool and then settling. And as the fateful lines are delivered, the orchestra gets out of the way almost entirely, leaving Cole's voice and piano fully exposed.

At this point—two-thirds of the way through the recording—DeVol hands the melody to Cole's piano, with light support from the orchestra. Things move along somewhat predictably until, suddenly, a violinist seems to stride in from the wings, playing an ardent passage reminiscent of Hollywood interpretations of Gypsy music. And, as the tempo slows down and the orchestra once again moves out of the way, Cole drives the last two lines home again, just to make sure we get the point: "The greatest thing you'll ever learn is just to love and be loved in return." The end of the recording brings back the flute birdsong and the exotic oboe, and we "fade to black." (The studio fadeout, still a novelty in the late 1940s, was an effect made much easier to produce with the advent of magnetic tape recording.) Whatever one feels about the ultimate value of Eden Ahbez's message, there can be no doubting the formidable technique at work here, both in Cole's vocal performance and in DeVol's evocative orchestral setting.

URBAN FOLK MUSIC: THE WEAVERS

During the early 1950s a new genre of popular music, called "urban folk," showed up on the pop charts. This genre combined a number of seemingly contradictory tendencies. It was inspired by rural folk music, yet performed by urban intellectuals. It drew inspiration from the populist protest songs of Woody Guthrie (see Chapter 5), yet was used by the record industry to generate millions of dollars in profits. Many urban folk recordings were seemingly harmless singalongs, designed to invite audience participation. Yet, only a few years after the initial burst of public interest in this music, some of its best-known practitioners were being persecuted for their political beliefs. And the record industry really didn't know what to do with urban folk music. Was it "folk music"? Or "country and western"? Or perhaps "novelty music"?

The first urban folk group to achieve commercial success was the Weavers, a quartet led by singer, banjo player, and political activist Pete Seeger (b. 1919). The Weavers, formed in 1948, grew out of an earlier group called the Almanac Singers, which had included Seeger and Guthrie. With a repertoire based on American and international folk songs, the Weavers performed at union rallies, college concerts, and urban coffeehouses. The group was "discovered" at a New York City nightclub by Gordon Jenkins, managing director of Decca Records, and between 1950 and 1954 they placed eleven records in the Top 40. It is difficult to gauge what impact the Weavers might have had on pop music had they been allowed to sustain their early success. Three members of the group, including Seeger, were accused of being Communists during the early 1950s.[2] (Their main accuser later admitted that

---

2. In the environment of the Cold War there was an upsurge of anticommunist sentiment in the United States. This led to hearings in the House of Representatives by the so-called Un-American Activities Committee, in which many people were targeted for alleged subversive activities and intentions. In the entertainment business, many careers were temporarily derailed or totally destroyed by this process.

he had fabricated the charges and went to prison for perjury.) Decca Records, unwilling to withstand the heat, dropped their contract, and the Weavers never again appeared on the pop music charts. Seeger, however, continued to play a leading role as a champion of folk music and a populist activist; he has been called "America's tuning fork."

The Weavers' singalong version of "Goodnight Irene," composed by the Mississippi-born musician Huddie Ledbetter (a.k.a. Leadbelly, 1889–1949), was the most successful of their recordings, reaching the Number One position on the pop charts in 1950. The strophic form of the song is clearly related to the folk ballad tradition, with a series of verses, and a recurring chorus (*Irene goodnight, Irene goodnight . . .*). Of course, this is not folk music in any strict sense. On "Goodnight Irene," as on their other hit records of the early 1950s ("Tzena, Tzena, Tzena," "So Long (It's Been Good to Know Ya)," "On Top of Old Smoky," and "Wimoweh"), the Weavers were accompanied by the orchestral arrangements of Gordon Jenkins, who also worked with Frank Sinatra, Nat "King" Cole, and other pop stars. Despite their folksy informality—listen closely to "Goodnight Irene" and you may even hear one of the Weavers coughing in the background during one of the refrains, a glitch that would certainly have been edited out of most pop recordings—"Goodnight Irene" and the Weavers' other hits are *pop* records, through and through. They helped to define a niche in the popular market for folk-based popular music, including the later work of the Kingston Trio (see Chapter 8), Peter, Paul, and Mary, and Bob Dylan (see Chapter 10). In addition, the Weavers' use of international materials—including Israeli, Cuban, and South African songs—make them the first world beat artists, a category of popular music that would not emerge in defined form for another thirty years (see Chapter 14).

SOUTHERN MUSIC IN THE POSTWAR ERA

After World War II the market for forms of popular music rooted in the traditions of the American South reemerged with new vigor. The old categories "race music" and "hillbilly music" underwent a series of name changes, reflecting shifts in social attitudes and in the music industry's perception of the economic potential of southern music. In 1942 *Billboard* began for the first time to list these records, subsuming them under the single category "Western and Race," a hybrid designation that was soon changed to "American Folk Records." In 1949 *Billboard* began using the terms "Rhythm & Blues" and "Country and Western" as more dignified and up-to-date replacements for "Race" and "Hillbilly," respectively.

During the late 1930s and 1940s millions of people had migrated from the rural South in search of employment in defense-related industries. Cities such as Chicago, Detroit, Pittsburgh, New York, Washington, D.C., Nashville, Atlanta, and Los Angeles were all home to large populations of transplanted southerners, whose musical tastes were doubly shaped not only by their experience of rural traditions but also by the desire to forge new, urbanized identities (and thereby distance themselves from the stereotyped image of the "hick" or "rube"). This migrant population greatly expanded the target audience for southern-derived music, providing a steady source of support for the urban honky-tonks, juke joints, and lounges where country and western and rhythm & blues groups played.

Leadbelly, the composer of "Goodnight Irene," and **the Weavers** (Pete Seeger, Lee Hays, Fred Hellerman, Ronnie Gilbert). Courtesy Library of Congress.

Radio also played a crucial role in the popularization of these types of music. There was a substantial increase in the number of radio stations catering specially to transplanted southerners, some capable of saturating the entire country's airwaves, others low-wattage affairs with a broadcasting radius of only a few miles. The country music radio business was positively booming in the late 1940s and early 1950s, with new shows modeled on Nashville's *Grand Ole Opry* coming on the air in all of America's major cities and on hundreds of small stations that sprouted in rural areas. During the war a number of white disc jockeys began to mix black popular music in with their usual diet of pop records, and 1949 saw the inauguration of the first radio station dedicated exclusively to playing music for a black audience—WDIA in Memphis, Tennessee, featuring the popular blues musician and disk jockey B. B. King. (Although this station catered to a predominantly black audience in the Mississippi Delta area, it was in fact owned by white businessmen.) In 1953 a nationwide survey in *Billboard* reported that pop music accounted for an average of 31 hours a week of radio programming, with country music occupying $11\frac{1}{2}$ hours, and R&B $2\frac{1}{2}$. (The rest of the time was taken up with news, sports, comedy, and drama.) While these figures may not seem impressive at first glance, the fact that country music was being heard more than an hour a day on average, and that R&B recordings were getting any airplay at all on mainstream pop radio stations, is an indication of the expanding audiences for these styles.

The jukebox business—which had expanded greatly during and just after the war—also played an important role in promoting country and western and rhythm & blues records. In addition, the Movieola—a type of jukebox that played short musical films or "soundies" on demand and was thus an ancestor of today's music videos—also played a part in popularizing southern-based musicians. The AFM recording ban of 1942–44 and the rise of BMI (described at the end of Chapter 6) provided many southern-born musicians with new opportunities for recording. Because many of these performers did not belong to the musicians' union, the ban on studio recording did not apply to them, and they were free to continue making records. Similarly, the success of BMI at licensing southern-born songwriters was based on ASCAP's long-standing refusal to admit these musicians as members. In the end, the combined prejudice of these mainstream music institutions against rural, southern, and black musicians backfired. Finally, the success of country and western and rhythm & blues music (and other nonmainstream styles such as the polka and Mexican-American music) was indebted to the reemergence, during and just after the war, of dozens of small independent record labels. As in the 1920s, this new generation of "indies" was made possible by a strong national economy and by the activity of small-scale entrepreneurs, eager to create new market niches, develop specialized audiences, and exploit areas of America's musical map that the major companies did not perceive as significant. These small record companies played an important role in country music and, as we shall see, almost completely dominated the R&B field.

RHYTHM & BLUES

Although *Billboard* adopted a new designation in 1949 for what had formerly been called "race records," in some ways the commercial logic underlying the category hadn't really changed much since the 1920s and 1930s. Like the older term, "rhythm

& blues" described music performed almost exclusively by black artists, and produced in the main (at least at first) for sale to African American audiences.

R&B, as the genre came to be known, was a loose cluster of styles, rooted in southern folk traditions and shaped by the experience of returning military personnel and hundreds of thousands of black Americans who had migrated to urban centers such as New York, Chicago, Detroit, and Los Angeles during and just after the war. The top R&B recordings of the late 1940s and early 1950s included swing-influenced "jump bands," Tin Pan Alley–style love songs performed by crooners, various styles of urban blues, and gospel-influenced vocal harmony groups.

The reappearance of small independent record labels during and just after the war provided an outlet for performers who were ignored by major record companies such as Columbia, RCA Victor, and Capitol. The development of portable tape recorders made record producers and studio owners out of entrepreneurs who could not previously have afforded the equipment necessary to produce master recordings. Each company was centered on one or two individuals, who located talent, oversaw the recording process, and handled publicity, distribution, and a variety of other tasks. These label owners worked the system in as many ways as time, energy, and ingenuity allowed. They paid radio DJs **payola** to promote their records on the handful of stations that played black music. They visited nightclubs to find new talent, hustled copies of their records to local record store owners, and occasionally attempted to interest a major label in a particular recording or artist with crossover potential.

Most "indie" label owners worked a particular piece of musical and geographical territory. However, they also had dreams of the huge financial success that would accrue to the label that found a way to cross R&B records over to the pop music charts. The middle-class white audience for this music, and the big record companies' and radio networks' interest in it, were growing—but the competition was fiercer than ever. By 1951 there were over one hundred independent labels slugging it out for a piece of the R&B market, and few of them lasted more than a few months.

Indie owners often put their names down for composer credits on songs they recorded and thereby often earned more royalties from a given song than the actual composer. (This was a long-standing practice in the music business—for example, Ralph Peer was listed as co-composer of a number of hillbilly songs, and Irving Mills, Duke Ellington's manager, was listed as co-composer of some of Ellington's most popular songs.) In the postwar era the importance of composers' credits was based on the fact that artists and record companies often tried to cash in on the potential popularity of a recording by creating their own (sometimes almost indistinguishable) versions of it. Although the most famous examples of this practice involve white musicians (and major record companies) exploiting songs first recorded by black artists (and independent record companies), the profit motive led to a variety of interactions, including pop versions of hillbilly songs and black versions of Tin Pan Alley songs. In general, this practice—called *covering* a song or making a *cover version*—was crucial to the increasing crossover success of black music (and, to a lesser degree, black musicians) during the 1950s. (We shall examine this process more closely in Chapter 8.)

Jump blues, the first commercially successful category of rhythm & blues, flourished during and just after World War II. During the war, as shortages made it more difficult to maintain a lucrative touring schedule, the leaders of some big bands were forced to downsize. They formed smaller combos, generally made up of a rhythm section (bass, piano, drums, and sometimes guitar) and one or more horn players. These *jump bands* specialized in hard-swinging, boogie-woogie–based party music, spiced with humorous lyrics and wild stage performances.

The most successful and influential jump band was the Tympany Five, led by Louis Jordan (1908–75), an Arkansas-born saxophone player and singer who began making recordings for Decca Records in 1939. Jordan was tremendously popular with black listeners and, like Nat "King" Cole, was able to build an extensive white audience during and after the war. But Jordan himself regarded Cole as being in "another field"—the pop field. Although Cole enjoyed greater financial success, in the end Jordan had a bigger impact on the future of popular music, inspiring a number of the first rock 'n' roll artists (see Chapter 8). As the rock 'n' roll pioneer Chuck Berry put it, "I identify myself with Louis Jordan more than any other artist" (Shaw 1986, p. 64). James Brown, the godfather of soul music, was once asked if Louis Jordan had been an influence on him: "He was *everything*," Brown replied (Chilton 1994, p. 126).

Jordan's first big hit, "G.I. Jive," reached Number One on *Billboard*'s "Harlem Hit Parade," as the R&B chart was labeled in the earlier 1940s, held the top spot on the pop music charts for two weeks, and sold over a million copies. From 1945 through 1948 Jordan, working with a white record producer named Milt Gabler (b. 1911), recorded a string of crossover hits, including "Caldonia" (Number One R&B, Number Eleven pop in 1945), "Stone Cold Dead in the Market" (an adaptation of a calypso from Trinidad, which reached Number One R&B and Number Seven pop in 1946), and "Ain't Nobody Here but Us Chickens" (Number One R&B, Number Six pop in 1946). The popularity of the Tympany Five was reinforced by a series of films featuring the band. These short musical features were rented to individual movie theaters and shown as a promotional device a few days before the band was due to hit town. (Louis Jordan was a gifted comedian, as well as a musician, and many of the films had a decidedly wacky tone. One was a musical parody of Western movies, with Jordan in full cowboy gear, astride a horse with his sax slung across his back.) Jordan's films, like his records, were popular in white as well as black movie theaters, even in the Deep South. However, the fact that his music appealed to an interracial audience should not lead us to assume that Jordan's career was not affected by racism. An article published in 1944 described what was to become a standard practice for booking popular black musicians:

> Due to the Louis Jordan band's popularity with both white and colored audiences, promoters in larger cities are booking the quintet for two evenings, one to play a white dance and the other a colored dance. (Chilton 1994, p. 107)

As R&B artists like Jordan began to attract a more diverse audience, the separation between white and black fans was maintained in various ways. Sometimes white R&B fans sat in the balcony of a segregated theater or dance hall, watching the black dancers below in order to pick up the latest steps. At other times a rope was stretched across the middle of the dance floor to "maintain order." Then, as at other times, the circulation of popular music across racial boundaries did not necessarily signify an amelioration of racism in everyday life.

Louis Jordan and His Tympany Five, 1946. Frank Driggs Collection.

LISTENING AND ANALYSIS "CHOO CHOO CH' BOOGIE"

"Choo Choo Ch' Boogie," Louis Jordan's biggest hit, exemplifies key elements of the jump blues style of R&B. Released in 1946 by Decca Records, the song topped the R&B charts for an amazing eighteen weeks, reached Number Seven on *Billboard*'s pop hit list, and sold over two million copies. "Choo Choo Ch' Boogie" was cowritten by Milt Gabler, Jordan's producer, and two country and western musicians who worked at a radio station in New York City. The title of the song draws a parallel between the motion of a railroad train—a metaphor of mobility and change long established in both country music and the blues—and the rocking rhythm of boogie-woogie music. Boogie-woogie, which had experienced a craze during the swing era, provided an important link between rhythm & blues and country music during the postwar period, a connection that was to prove important in the formation of rock 'n' roll.

"Choo Choo Ch' Boogie" consists of a series of verses in twelve-bar blues form, alternated with an eight-bar chorus, a structure that combines elements of African American music and Tin Pan Alley song. (We have encountered this compositional strategy before, in W. C. Handy's song "St. Louis Blues"; see Chapter 5.) The song's lyric describes a situation that would have been familiar to many Americans, particularly to ex-GIs returning to the United States during the postwar economic downturn of 1946, when jobs were temporarily scarce and the future seemed uncertain. The song brings back a character from the Great Depression era, the poor but honest hobo, hopping freight trains and traveling from city to city in search of work. The protagonist arrives home, weary of riding in the back of an army truck, and heads for the railroad station. His initial optimism is tempered as he searches the employment notices in the newspaper and realizes that he does not have the technical skills for the few positions that are open. (The history of encoded lyrics in African American popular music—discussed in Chapter 5 in connection with the rural blues—suggests that African American listeners may have interpreted the line "the only job that's open needs a man with a knack" as a comment on the employment practices of the many businesses that favored white over black veterans.) Despite his misfortune, however, our hero remains cheerful, and the lyric ends with an idyllic description of life in a shack by the railroad track.

The arrangement—devised by Gabler and Jordan—opens with a twelve-bar instrumental introduction in which the horns (a trumpet and two saxophones) imitate the sound of a train whistle, while the rhythm section (piano, bass, and drums) establishes a medium-tempo boogie-woogie rhythm. (This infectious four-beat dance rhythm, common in Jordan's recordings, is sometimes called a "shuffle.") The rest of the arrangement follows a clear blueprint, alternating the song's two basic building blocks, twelve-bar verse and eight-bar chorus. After the introduction the form should be easy to follow: first a verse, sung by Jordan and backed by riffs in the horn section; then a chorus, also sung by Jordan; followed by a twelve-bar boogie-woogie piano solo. The whole structure is then repeated (with a twenty-bar saxophone solo instead of a piano solo). The record concludes with a ten-bar instrumental tag, comprising an eight-bar chorus and an extra two bars at the very end.

LISTENING CHART   "CHOO CHOO CH' BOOGIE"

Music and lyrics by Milt Gabler, Denver Darling, and Vaughan Horton; as performed by Louis Jordan's Tympany Five; recorded 1946

FORM LYRICS	DESCRIPTIVE COMMENTS
Instrumental intro	**12 bars (4 + 8)** During the first four bars, the horns imitate the sound of a train whistle

Verse 1	Headin' for the station with a pack on my back	**12 bars**
	I'm tired of transportation in the back of a hack	
	I love to hear the rhythm of a clickety-clack	
	And hear the lonesome whistle, see the smoke from the stack	
	And pal around with democratic fellows named Mac	
	So take me right back to the track, Jack.	
Chorus	Choo choo, choo choo, ch' boogie	**8 bars**
	Woo woo, woo woo, ch' boogie	
	Choo choo, choo choo, ch' boogie	
	Take me right back to the track, Jack.	
Piano solo		**12 bars**
Verse 2	You reach your destination, but alas and alack	**12 bars**
	You need some compensation to get back in the black	
	You take a morning paper from the top of the stack	
	And read the situation from the front to the back	
	The only job that's open needs a man with a knack	
	So put it right back in the rack, Jack.	
Chorus		**8 bars**
Saxophone solo		**20 bars (12-bar blues + 8-bar chorus)**
Verse 3	Gonna settle down by the railroad track	**12 bars**
	And live the life of Riley in a beaten-down shack	
	So when I hear a whistle I can peep through the crack	
	And watch the train a-rollin', when it's ballin' the jack	
	Why, I just love the rhythm of the clickety-clack	
	So take me right back to the track, Jack.	
Chorus		**8 bars**
Instrumental tag		**10 bars (8-bar chorus + 2-bar extension)**

If jump bands represented the hot end of the R&B spectrum, the cool end was dominated by a blend of blues and pop singing sometimes called the *blues crooner* style. The roots of this urbane approach to the blues reached back to a series of race recordings made in the late 1920s and 1930s by pianist <u>Leroy Carr</u> (1905–35) and guitarist <u>Scrapper Blackwell</u> (1903–62). Carr, born in Indianapolis, Indiana, developed a smooth, laid-back approach to blues singing that contrasted sharply with the rough-edged rural blues recordings of Charley Patton and Blind Lemon Jefferson, and he attracted a national black audience. The late 1930s jazz recordings of the King Cole Trio, with its instrumentation of piano, bass, and guitar, were a more immediate influence on postwar blues crooners, although Cole's later recordings took him out of the category of R&B, strictly defined, and into the field of pop music.

In 1944 a black GI from Nashville, Tennessee, named <u>Cecil Gant</u> (1913–51) walked up to the stage at a war bond rally in Los Angeles and asked if he could play a few songs on the piano. The crowd loved him, and Private Gant, the "G.I. Sing-sation," was soon signed by a new independent record label called Gilt-Edge. Later that year Gant recorded a love song called "I Wonder," sung in a gentle, slightly nasal, bluesy style, and accompanied only by his own piano playing. "I Wonder" reached the Number One position on *Billboard*'s "Harlem Hit Parade" and also attracted attention from some white listeners. Unfortunately, Gant was never able to repeat the success of his first hit, although he made dozens of recordings for various independent record labels.

The most successful blues crooner of the late 1940s and early 1950s was a soft-spoken Texas-born pianist and singer named <u>Charles Brown</u> (b. 1922). Brown, who had studied classical piano as a child, graduated from college in 1942 at the age of twenty. He moved to Los Angeles in 1943 and joined Johnny Moore's Three Blazers, a small combo that played pop songs for all-white parties in Hollywood and a more blues-oriented repertoire in the black nightclubs along L.A.'s Central Avenue. His smooth, sensitive, somewhat forlorn vocal style (sometimes called "cocktail blues") attracted attention, and he began to develop a national reputation with the release of "Drifting Blues," one of the top-selling R&B records of 1945 and 1946. In 1948 Brown left to form his own quartet and had a Number One R&B hit the following year with "Trouble Blues." Over the next three years he recorded ten Top 10 hits for Aladdin Records—one of the dozens of independent labels popping up in Los Angeles at the time—and became one of the most popular R&B singers nationwide. A handsome, dapper, gracious man, Brown projected an image of ease and sophistication. His repertoire—which included blues, pop songs, and semiclassical numbers such as the *Warsaw Concerto*—suggested a man in touch with his roots but not constrained by them. Brown was never able to break through to the pop charts—Columbia Records offered him a solo contract in 1947, but he turned it down out of loyalty to his bandmates. But he was rediscovered by a new generation of R&B fans in the 1980s and went on to develop a successful international touring career, culminating in a Grammy nomination.

"Black Night," one of Charles Brown's most successful recordings, held the Number One position on the R&B charts for fourteen weeks in 1951. The fact that "Black Night" did not show up on the pop charts can in part be attributed to the record's dark mood, slow tempo, and somber lyrics:

> *Nobody cares about me, ain't even got a friend*
> *Baby's gone an' left me, when will my troubles end?*
> *Black night is falling, oh how I hate to be alone*
> *I keep crying for my baby, but now another day is gone.*
>
> *I've got no one to talk with, to tell my troubles to*
> *Don't even know I'm living since I lost you*
> *Black night is falling, oh how I hate to be alone*
> *I keep crying for my baby, but now another day is gone.*
>
> *My mother has her troubles, my father has his, too*
> *My brother's in Korea, and I don't know just what to do*
> *Black night, black night is falling, oh how I hate to be alone*
> *I keep crying for my baby, but now another day is gone.*

In formal terms, "Black Night" is a twelve-bar blues, although the very slow tempo can make it hard to hear the overall structure of the song at first. It also exemplifies the continuing importance of the blues in black popular music, not only as a musical form, but also an emotional state and a perspective on the world. This is a truly haunting recording, with Brown's subdued voice, accompanied by the sparse textures, blue notes, and dirgelike tempo of the rhythm section and the mournful tenor saxophone of Maxwell Davis. The lyric conveys a deep anxiety about the future and a fear of loneliness, evoked by the coming of night. Advertisements for the record in black newspapers and magazines typically suggested that the record would make listeners forget their own troubles; but this song also spoke volumes to a people weary of deferred promises. After 1952 Brown's blues ballad style became less popular, as the urban black audience's taste shifted toward more hard-edged singers, perhaps reflecting the growth of active resistance to racial segregation.

A very different urban blues tradition of the postwar era, *Chicago electric blues*, derived more directly from the Mississippi Delta tradition of Charley Patton and Robert Johnson. Chicago was the terminus of the Illinois Central railroad line, which ran up through the Midwest from the Mississippi Delta. Although Chicago's black neighborhoods were well established before World War II, they grew particularly rapidly during the 1940s, as millions of rural migrants came north in search of employment in the city's industrial plants, railroad shops, and slaughterhouses. The South Side's nightclubs were the center of a lively black music scene that rivaled New York's Harlem and L.A.'s Central Avenue. The musical taste of black Chicagoans, many of them recent migrants from the Deep South, tended toward rougher, grittier styles, closely linked to African American folk traditions but also reflective of their new, urban orientation.

Chicago electric blues was a response to these demands. On the one hand, it could be argued that the rural blues tradition had almost completely died out as a commercial phenomenon by the time of World War II, as the urbanizing black audience sought out more cosmopolitan forms of entertainment. From this point of view, the mid-1930s recordings of Robert Johnson (Chapter 5) represent the final flowering of the Delta blues. (Unlike white southerners, who tended to regard older forms of music with nostalgia, blacks had every reason to want to forget their rural past.)

However, the old Delta blues style didn't really die out—rather, it emerged in a reinvigorated, electronically amplified form. The career of <u>Muddy Waters (McKinley Morganfield)</u> (1915–83) exemplifies these developments. Waters was "discovered" in the Mississippi Delta by the folk music scholars John and Alan Lomax, who recorded him in the late 1930s for the Library of Congress. (Waters apparently had some difficulty in getting copies of these recordings, but when he did they were played on jukeboxes in the delta and became regional hits.) In 1943 he moved to Chicago and found work in a paper mill, while continuing to work as a musician at nightclubs and parties. In response to the noisy crowds, and to the demand for dance music, Waters soon switched from the acoustic to the electric guitar (1944) and eventually expanded his group to include a second electric guitar, piano, bass, amplified harmonica ("blues harp"), and drum set. During the late 1940s and early 1950s he was the most popular blues musician in Chicago, with a sizeable following among black listeners nationwide.

Waters's approach to the blues is different from that of blues crooners like Charles Brown and represents direct continuities with the tradition of Charley Patton and Robert Johnson. Like many of the great Mississippi guitarists, Waters was a master of bottleneck slide guitar technique. He used his guitar to create a rock-steady, churning rhythm, interspersed with blues licks, which were counterpoised with his voice in a kind of musical conversation. The electric guitar, which could be used to create dense, buzzing tone colors (by using **distortion**) and long sustained notes that sounded like screaming or crying (by employing **feedback**), was the perfect tool for extending the Mississippi blues guitar tradition. Waters's singing style—rough, growling, moaning, and intensely emotional—was also rooted in the Delta blues. And the songs he sang were based on themes long central to the tradition: on the one hand, loneliness, frustration, and misfortune ("I Feel Like Going Home" and "Still a Fool"), and on the other, independence and sexual braggadocio ("Just Make Love to Me" and "Mannish Boy").

"Hoochie Coochie Man," composed by <u>Willie Dixon</u> (1915–92), Chess Records' house songwriter, bass player, producer, and arranger, is perhaps the best example of the latter theme. The song was Waters's biggest hit for Chess Records, reaching Number Three on the R&B charts in 1954. (Although none of Waters's recordings crossed over to the pop charts, his music was later to play an important role in inspiring rock musicians such as Eric Clapton and the Rolling Stones—who adopted their name from one of his songs.) This recording typifies Chicago urban blues, with its loud volume and dense textures, its buzzing, growling tone colors, and its insistent beat. "Hoochie Coochie Man" is also an example of a common variation on the blues form, a sixteen-bar blues. The first eight bars of the song feature a technique called "stop time," in which the beat is suspended in order to focus attention on the singer's voice. (In essence, this is equivalent to the first four bars of a twelve-bar blues, made twice as long by application of the stoptime technique.) Then the regular pulse is reestablished, and the last eight bars are played. Because the lyric of the stoptime section changes each time (like a verse), while the words in the second eight-bar section are repeated (like a chorus), the song combines the blues form with a strophic verse-chorus structure.

The lyric of "Hoochie Coochie Man" is essentially an extended boast, related to the African American tradition of "toasts," fantastic narratives emphasizing the performer's personal power, sexual prowess, and ability to outwit authority.

> *I got a black cat bone, I got a mojo too*
> *I got a Johnnie Conkaroo, I'm gonna mess wit' you*
> *I'm gonna make you girls lead me by my hand*
> *Then the world'll know I'm a hoochie-coochie man*

The song draws a direct link between the personal power of the singer (quintessentially expressed through sex) and the southern folk tradition of *mojo*, a system of magical charms and medicines, including the black cat bone and John the Conquerer root. This image of supernatural power applied in the service of personal goals was ultimately derived from the cultures of West Africa, and it tapped a common reservoir of experience among Waters's listeners, many of whom were not many years removed from the folk culture of the rural South. In essence, the lyric of "Hoochie Coochie Man" is an argument for the continuing relevance of deep traditional knowledge in the new urban setting, and it is easy to see why this would have been an attractive message for recent urban migrants.

Another important thread in the tapestry of postwar rhythm & blues was *vocal harmony groups*. (Although this tradition is today sometimes called "doo-wop," the earliest performers did not use this term.) In previous chapters we have come across variants of the African American vocal harmony tradition, both sacred (the Golden Gate Quartet) and secular (the Mills Brothers). During the postwar era this tradition moved into the R&B market, as young singers trained in the black church began to record secular material. Many of these vocal groups were made up of high school kids from the black neighborhoods of cities such as New York and Washington, D.C., and interviews with the singers indicate that these groups served a number of functions: a means of musical expression, an alternative or adjunct to urban gangs, and a route to popularity. Few members of these groups initially saw singing as a way to make a living; this perception changed rapidly after the first vocal R&B groups achieved commercial success.

The vocal harmony group most responsible for moving away from the pop-oriented sound of the Mills Brothers and creating a new, harder-edged sound more closely linked to black gospel music, was the Dominoes, led by vocal coach Billy Ward, a strict disciplinarian and savvy entrepreneur. In 1950 Ward started rehearsing with a number of his most promising students and a seventeen-year old tenor singer named Clyde McPhatter (1932–72), whom he hired away from a gospel group. The Dominoes' first big hit was "Sixty Minute Man," recorded in New York City and released by the independent label Federal Records in 1951. A large part of the song's popularity was due to its lyric, which catalogued the singer's lovemaking technique in some detail:

> *There'll be fifteen minutes of kissin',*
> *Till you holler please don't stop*
> (GROUP: *Don't stop!*)
> *There'll be fifteen minutes of teasin'*
> *Fifteen minutes of pleasin'*
> *And fifteen minutes of blowin' my top!*

The combination of a naughty lyric, rocking dance rhythm, and bass lead vocal caught the attention of the R&B audience, and "Sixty Minute Man" monopolized the Number One spot on the R&B charts for fourteen weeks during the summer of 1951. It was also one of the first vocal-group R&B records to cross over to the pop charts, where it reached the Number Seventeen position—doubtless without the assistance of AM pop radio.

But it was the Dominoes' next big hit, "Have Mercy Baby," that pushed vocal-group R&B firmly in the direction of a harder-edged, more explicitly emotional sound. Recorded in Cincinnati, Ohio, and released by Federal Records in 1952, "Have Mercy Baby" was the first record to combine the twelve-bar blues form and the driving beat of dance-oriented rhythm & blues with the intensely emotional flavor of black gospel singing. The song's commercial success (Number One R&B for ten weeks in 1952) was in large part due to the passionate performance of the Dominoes' lead tenor, Clyde McPhatter, the former gospel singer from North Carolina. McPhatter, the son of a Baptist preacher and a church organist, was like many other R&B musicians insofar as the black church played a major role in shaping his musical sensibility. While in formal terms "Have Mercy Baby" is a twelve-bar blues, it is essentially a gospel performance dressed up in R&B clothing. With a few changes in the lyrics—perhaps substituting the word "Lord" for "baby"—McPhatter's performance would have been perfectly at home in a black Baptist church anywhere in America. The sheer intensity of McPhatter's plea for redemption—you can actually hear him weeping during the fadeout ending—spoke directly to the core audience for R&B, many of whom had grown up within the African American gospel music tradition.

To be sure, this mixing of church music with popular music was controversial in some quarters, and McPhatter and later gospel-based R&B singers faced occasional opposition from some church leaders. But in retrospect the postwar confluence of the sacred and secular aspects of black music, and its commercial exploitation by the music business, seem almost inevitable. Although it did not appear on the pop music charts, "Have Mercy Baby" attracted an audience among many white teenagers, who were drawn by its rocking beat and emotional directness. In addition, the Dominoes were featured on some of the earliest rock 'n' roll tours, which typically attracted a racially mixed audience. Although McPhatter soon left the Dominoes to form a new group called the Drifters, the impact of his rendition of "Have Mercy Baby" was profound and lasting—the record is a direct predecessor of the soul music movement of the 1960s, and of the recordings of Ray Charles, James Brown, and Aretha Franklin.

WOMEN IN R&B: RUTH BROWN AND BIG MAMA THORNTON

Like many other genres of popular music, rhythm & blues played an important role as a stylized medium for enacting sexual politics. This was particularly important during the postwar period, as black families came under the disintegrating pressures of social change and individuals sought to cope with the sometimes alienating experience of urban life. We have already seen several portrayals of male identity in R&B, including Charles Brown's dejected lover and Muddy Waters's magically charged mojo man. Here we want to examine briefly images of male-female relationships in the work of two influential female R&B singers, Ruth Brown and Willie Mae "Big Mama" Thornton.

Ruth Brown (b. 1928), also known as "Miss Rhythm," was born in Virginia. As a child she participated in two streams of the black church tradition, the AME (African Methodist Episcopal) and Baptist denominations. In musical terms, the Methodist services she attended were relatively restrained, with the accompaniment of a piano and big church organ, while the Baptist ceremonies, held in a rough-hewn country church, were often ecstatically emotional and featured only hand clapping and tambourine as accompaniment. Both of these streams can be detected in Brown's later work, which ranged from crooner-style ballads to jump band blues songs.

Although her parents initially resisted the idea of her singing outside the church, Brown began her professional career at the age of sixteen, and in 1949 signed with the new independent label Atlantic Records. Chart figures suggest that Ruth Brown was the most popular black female vocalist in America between 1951 and 1954, and it is said that she almost single-handedly kept Atlantic Records alive during its precarious early years. The song with which Ruth Brown was most closely associated was "Mama, He Treats Your Daughter Mean," which held the Number One position on the R&B charts for five weeks in 1953 and reached as high as Number Twenty-three on the pop charts. Brown, the daughter of a respectable, churchgoing family, did not feel comfortable with the song at first:

> That tune, I didn't want to do. I thought, when I first heard it, "That's the silliest mess I have ever heard." At that time, I wasn't having too much of a problem [with men], so I felt like, "What is she talking about, Mama he treats your daughter mean. . . . Mama, the man is lazy, almost drives me crazy." I wasn't dealing with that kind of a lifestyle, so it didn't make sense to me. (Deffaa 1996, p. 35)

According to Brown, the song was recorded quickly, without much rehearsal, and its crossover success on the R&B and pop charts came as something of a surprise. The form of "Mama, He Treats Your Daughter Mean" is another example of the blending of blues and Tin Pan Alley–derived forms. The song's A section (*Mama, he treats your daughter mean . . .*) is a sixteen-bar blues. (Unlike Willie Dixon's "Hoochie Coochie Man," the twelve-bar form here is expanded by adding four extra bars in the middle of the song; rather than the a-a-b text form typical of twelve-bar blues, the lyric follows an a-a-a-b pattern.) The B section (*Mama, he treats me badly . . .*) is also sixteen bars in length. The band plays the song at a medium tempo, with the horns (saxophones and trumpets) riffing behind the singer. Certain characteristics of Brown's vocal style are clearly evident on this record, including a warm, somewhat husky tone, a strong rhythmic feeling, and the little upward squeals she places at the ends of words such as "mama," "man," and "understand." This fits the somewhat complaining tone of the song, in which a young woman turns to her to her mother for help in dealing with a good-for-nothing lover. One of the most memorable features of the recording—and a link to the church music of Brown's youth—is the solo tambourine, which starts the record and continues throughout.

Brown was paid less than seventy dollars for recording the song, in addition to a promised royalty of 5 percent of sales. As was often the case in the R&B business, she received few of her royalties, since the cost of studio time, hiring musicians, and the songwriters' royalties were charged to her account. One of the biggest stars of the postwar era, Brown ended up leaving the music business entirely for a decade and working as a domestic servant in order to raise her children. She was rediscovered in the 1970s and worked to publicize the plight of older rhythm & blues artists who had been denied their share of profits by record companies. In the 1980s she appeared in the Broadway show *Black and Blue* and won a Tony Award in 1989.

Big Mama Thornton (1926–84), born in Montgomery, Alabama, was the daughter of a Baptist minister. She began her professional career as a singer, drummer, harmonica player, and comic on the black vaudeville circuit and later settled in Houston, Texas, working as a singer in black nightclubs. Her imposing physique and sometimes malevolent personality helped to ensure her survival in the rough-and-tumble world of con artists and gangsters. One producer and songwriter who worked with Big Mama described her in vivid terms (in the liner notes to the 1992 MCA release *Big Mama Thornton: Hound Dog/The Peacock Recordings*):

> In rehearsal she'd fool around, pick up one of those old microphones with a heavy, steel base with one hand and turn it upside down with the base in the air and sing like that. She was a powerful, powerful woman. She had a few scars, looked like knife scars on her face, and she had a very beautiful smile. But most of the time she looked pretty salty.

In the early 1950s Thornton arrived in Los Angeles and began working with Johnny Otis (Veliotes), a Greek-American drummer, promoter, bandleader, and nightclub owner who lived in the black community and was a major force in the R&B scene. Looking for material for Big Mama to record, Otis decided to consult two white college kids who had been pestering him to use some of the songs they had written. After hearing Thornton's powerful singing, Jerry Leiber and Mike Stoller ran home and composed a song that they felt suited her style: "Hound Dog." The combination of Leiber and Stoller's humorous country-tinged lyric, Johnny Otis's drumming, and Thornton's powerful, raspy singing produced one of the top-selling R&B records of 1953: Number One for seven weeks. (This was the first hit written and produced by the team of Leiber and Stoller, who were to become a major force in early rock 'n' roll music; see Chapter 8.)

Of course, most people today know "Hound Dog" through Elvis Presley's version of the song, recorded by RCA Victor in 1956. If you are familiar only with Presley's version, then the original recording may come as something of a revelation. From the very first phrase (*You . . . ain't . . . nothin' . . . but a houn' dog . . .*) Thornton lays claim to the song, and to our attention. Her deep, raspy, commanding voice, reprimanding a ne'er-do-well lover, projects a stark image of female power rarely if ever expressed in popular music of the 1950s. The bluntness of the lyric is reinforced by the musical accompaniment, which includes a bluesy Delta-style electric guitar, a simple drum part played mainly on the tom-toms, and hand clapping on beats 2 and 4. The tempo is relaxed, and the performance is energetic but loose. The basic form of the song is a twelve-bar blues, but the band adds a few extra beats here and there, in response to Thornton's phrasing, another feature that links this urban recording to the country blues. The final touch, with the all-male band howling and barking in response to Big Mama's commands, reinforces not only the humor of the record but also its feeling of informality, the sense that these are not distant pop stars but people you could get to know and maybe even party with.

Although both records are intended to create a humorous effect, the defiant attitude of "Hound Dog" does make an interesting comparison with the complaining tone of "Mama, He Treats Your Daughter Mean," a quality that Ruth Brown herself apparently did not find particularly appealing. Both songs were composed by men and sung by women; and both implicitly rely on the "offstage" presence of a male persona, a lazy, deceitful jerk. But the similarities between the two songs and performances end there. "Hound Dog" was designed specifically to fit Thornton's strong, rough-hewn persona. "Mama," written by professional tunesmiths with no particular singer in mind, presents the image of a female narrator unable to deal with the male problem in her life. One woman expresses her frustration with cute little squeals, the other growls her anger. One gossips, the other threatens to inflict physical harm. One—we might imagine—is a somewhat spoiled middle-class teenager, the other an older woman from a working-class background. Of course, these are stylized images, exaggerated for dramatic effect; but it is their very exaggeration that allows them to convey popular conceptions of sexuality and gender identity in a particular place and time. (One male singer, Rufus Thomas, responded to Thornton's "Hound Dog" with a song entitled "Bear Cat." This was an example of a trend popular in the R&B market at the time—the "answer" record, which put new lyrics to the melody of a hit song in an attempt to ride the original's coattails; see the discussion of "It Wasn't God Who Made Honky-Tonk Angels" later in this chapter.)

COUNTRY AND WESTERN MUSIC

Country and western, the industry's new name for what used to be called hillbilly music, mushroomed in popularity after World War II. Although the South remained a lucrative area for touring performers, the wartime migration of millions of white

Box 7.1 The Prince of Wails: Johnnie Ray

In the early 1950s the former big-band crooners were joined by a younger generation of pop singers. As the record industry began explicitly to target the newly affluent teenage audience, these young singers were cultivated by the record companies, who created their public images and promoted their recordings on radio and television. Of all the new singers who came up during this period, the most memorable (and in some ways the most interesting) was Johnnie Ray (1927–90). Partially deaf since childhood—the result of an accident suffered during a Boy Scout expedition—Ray rose nevertheless to become one of the biggest international pop stars of the early 1950s. Crowned the "Prince of Wails" and parodied as the "Guy with the Rubber Face and the Squirt Gun Eyes," Ray created an idiosyncratic style based partly in African American modes of performance, and in so doing paved the way for the rock 'n' roll stars of the later 1950s.

During the late 1940s Johnnie Ray spent several years performing in nightclubs in Detroit, where he worked alongside black rhythm & blues performers, and was eventually "discovered" and signed to Okeh Records (the former race and hillbilly label, revived after the war by Columbia Records). During this period he developed a highly emotional performance style that involved sighing, sobbing, and stretching each syllable of a song out over as many melodic notes as possible (a practice called **melisma,** common in African American singing traditions). He was the first white pop performer to remove his microphone from its stand and go down into the audience, seeking direct contact. His stage act was dynamic: Ray writhed, wept, and fell to his knees. In 1952 *Billboard* described one of Ray's concerts as "a masterful display of showmanship that evoked a mass hysteria resembling a Holy Roller meeting. It was hard to say who screamed more—Ray or the customers."

Many older musicians and fans detested "Cry" (1951), Johnnie Ray's biggest hit, with a passion. (Television comedians of the early 1950s loved to lampoon Ray's tendency to burst into tears while performing, and Frank Sinatra apparently used his name as an expletive.) But Johnnie Ray's melodramatic, over-the-top approach appealed to the expanding white teenage audience for popular music. Interestingly, his records apparently also sold well in black communities. "Cry" reached Number One on both the pop and rhythm & blues hit parades. This means that Ray was the only white performer to reach the top of the black charts between 1946 and 1956, when Elvis Presley's "Hound Dog" reached Number One on both the pop and R&B charts. In this sense, Johnnie Ray was a crucial link between the crooners of the postwar era and the rock 'n' roll stars of the later 1950s.

southerners meant that huge and enthusiastic audiences for country and western music had also been established in the cities and towns of Pennsylvania, Ohio, Michigan, and California. The postwar era saw the rapid spread of country music programming on radio, and by 1949 over 650 radio stations were making live broadcasts of country performers. The continuing success of WSM's *Grand Ole Opry,* broadcast from Nashville, inspired a new generation of country music shows, including Shreveport's *Louisiana Hayride,* Dallas's *Saturday Night Shindig,* Boston's *Hayloft Jamboree,* and *Hometown Jamboree,* broadcast from Los Angeles. As in the R&B field, dozens of independent record labels specializing in country music sprang up after the war, and Nashville, Tennessee, and southern California began to assert themselves as centers for the production of country music. In 1950—when Capitol Records became the first major company to set up its country music operation in Nashville—it was estimated that country music accounted for fully one-third of all record sales nationwide.

As country music's core audience moved north, west, and upward into the urban middle class, the "mainstreaming" of country music continued apace. Pop artists such as Bing Crosby ("Sioux City Sue," Number Three pop in 1946) and Tony Bennett ("Cold, Cold Heart," Number One pop in 1951) had huge chart successes with their adaptations of country material. Since the 1920s the New York–based music industry had underestimated—and often seemed embarrassed by—the popularity of popular styles based in southern folk music. But by 1950, when a pop-style rendition of the country song "Tennessee Waltz" became the fastest-selling record in twenty-five years, the record company executives had no choice—country music was off the porch and sitting in the living room.

Patti Page (b. 1927 in Oklahoma) sold more records than any other female singer of the early 1950s. She had success with love songs ("All My Love," Number One pop in 1950) and novelty items like "The Doggie in the Window" (Number One pop in 1953), but her biggest hit was a recording of "The Tennessee Waltz." Page's version of the song—previously recorded by one of its writers, Grand Ole Opry star Pee Wee King—held the number one position on the pop charts for thirteen weeks, and eventually went on to sell more than six million copies. In some ways this was a recording that pointed back toward the nineteenth century—a sentimental **waltz** song packed with nostalgic references to the South. However, the popular appeal of this record was also apparently boosted by two technological innovations: the use of multi-track tape recording, which allowed Page to sing a duet with herself, and the fact that this was one of the first songs to be issued as a 45 r.p.m. single. "Tennessee Waltz" helped to make Mercury Records into a major label, spawned a rash of cover versions by other artists, and served notice that a pop-styled approach to country and western music could not only penetrate, but actually dominate, the mainstream.

In some ways, the range of country music styles during the postwar era resembles contemporaneous developments in rhythm & blues. There were *country crooners,* who specialized in a smooth, pop-oriented style; *bluegrass* musicians, who focused on the adaptation of traditional southern music in a package suitable to the times; and *honky-tonk* musicians, who performed in a hard-edged, electronically amplified style, and wrote songs about the trials and tribulations of migrants to the city and the gender roles and male/female relationships during a period of intense social change.

The rise of *country crooners* was not without precedent—in Chapter 5 we discussed Vernon Dalhart, the light opera singer who in 1924 scored a big commercial success with his recording of "The Prisoner's Song," a southern ballad sung in the pop style of the time. However, the stakes had risen considerably by the end of World War II, as southern-born country musicians watched pop stars reap huge profits covering country material. The later rise of *countrypolitan* music seems in retrospect an inevitable outcome of the growth of the country music industry and the mainstreaming of country music.

The most popular country crooner was <u>Eddy Arnold</u> (b. 1918), who not only dominated the country charts from 1947 to 1954 but also scored eleven Top 40 hits on the pop charts. Arnold began his career as a country singer on local radio shows in his native Tennessee and joined the cast of the *Grand Ole Opry* in the mid-1940s. In his early recordings, two key elements of his style are already evident: a smooth, warm baritone voice, and a propensity for sentimental songs. Eddy Arnold's transformation from country singer ("The Tennessee Plowboy") into country-tinged crooner parallels that of Nat "King" Cole, who moved from jazz toward pop stardom at around the same time. If Cole's breakthrough as a singer of romantic love songs was his 1946 recording of "(I Love You) For Sentimental Reasons" (Number One pop, Number Three R&B), Arnold's turning point came only a year later, with his recording of "Bouquet of Roses," which topped the country charts in 1947 and also crossed over into the pop market. The song itself, composed by Steve Nelson and Bob Hillard, combined the two-beat rhythm of country music with touches of Tin Pan Alley harmony and a sentimental lyric. More than the character of the song itself, however, the crossover success of this record was mainly due to its presentation, positioned midway between country and pop. In particular, Arnold's rich baritone voice had just a hint of rasp; his round pronunciation of vowels was colored with only the lightest touch of Tennessee dialect; and the orchestral accompaniment combined a typical country band of the period (electric guitars, electric bass, drum set, and piano) with a string orchestra. It is easy to understand why this record provided a bridge between country music and the mainstream pop music audience. Despite his eventual induction into the Country Music Hall of Fame, many tradition-oriented country fans still view Arnold as a sell-out, a country singer who turned his back on tradition. (This bears more than a passing resemblance to the criticism of Nat "King" Cole's pop recordings by jazz fans. For his part, Eddy Arnold has always maintained that he listened to all kinds of music and was unaware that music was divided into categories.)

While some musicians sought to move country music onto the mainstream pop charts, others reached back into the musical traditions of the American South, refurbishing old styles to fit new circumstances. While this "neotraditionalist" impulse took many forms, the most influential was probably the rise of *bluegrass music,* a style rooted in the venerable southern string band tradition. The pioneer of bluegrass music was <u>Bill Monroe</u> (1911–97), born in Kentucky. Monroe started playing music at a young age and was influenced by his uncle (a country fiddler) and by a black musician and railroad worker named Arnold Schulz, whose influence can be seen in the distinctive bluesy quality of Monroe's music. (As we saw in our discussions of Jimmie Rodgers and Bob Wills, the interaction between white and black styles has long been an important aspect of country music.) In 1935 Bill formed a duet with his brother, Charlie. The Monroe Brothers played throughout the southeastern United States, creating a sensation with their vocal harmonies and virtuoso fiddle and guitar playing. In 1938 Bill started his own group, the Blue Grass Boys, and the following year joined the cast of the *Grand Ole Opry*.

The Blue Grass Boys' recording of "It's Mighty Dark to Travel," recorded in Nashville in 1947, is a classic example of bluegrass, a blend of Anglo-American string band music, traditional singing of the Appalachian Mountains, and influences from black music, especially the blues. The instrumentation is typical of bluegrass groups: an acoustic quintet made up of fiddle, mandolin, banjo, guitar, and string bass. Unlike many postwar country bands, the Blue Grass Boys avoided amplified instruments, which added to the traditional feeling of the music.

The first seconds of "It's Mighty Dark to Travel" establish the virtuosity and high energy for which this group—and bluegrass music in general—is well known. The stringed instruments are all assigned well-defined roles within the ensemble: for example, Bill Monroe's mandolin plays short, "chop-style" chords on the second and fourth beats of each measure, driving the music along; Earl Scruggs's highly syncopated, three-finger technique on the banjo interlocks with the rhythm of the other instruments; and the string bass provides steady support, playing on the first and third beats of each measure. The vocal performance, with Bill Monroe's tenor voice in the lead, is closely related to the "high lonesome" style popularized first by the Carter Family and then by hillbilly duets such as the Blue Sky Boys and the Monroe Brothers. But bluegrass is at its core a music for instrumentalists, featuring sections of flashy solo improvisation ("breakaways") rooted in the tradition of country fiddle contests and reinforced by the influence of black music, including jazz. Although bluegrass never really dominated the country charts—Bill Monroe himself was never able to score a Number One country hit—its unique blend of traditionalism and innovation has continued to inspire country musicians.

A third major direction in postwar country and western music is represented by *honky-tonk music*—sometimes called "hard country" or "beer-drinking music"— a style that conveyed the sound and ethos of the roadside bar or juke joint. During the Great Depression the oil fields of Texas and Oklahoma provided a lucrative (and rare) source of steady, well-paid work, attracting thousands of men from the American southwest and farther afield. When Prohibition was repealed in 1933, the formerly illegal drinking establishments that serviced these men multiplied and became a major source of employment for country and western musicians. These honky-tonks, as the people who frequented them called them, provided relief from the daily pressures of work on the oilfields, in the form of drinking and dancing. (The practice of going from bar to bar on a Saturday night is still called "honky-tonking.") By the postwar period thousands of these rowdy nightspots were sprinkled across the American southwest and further afield, ranging from small, dimly lit dives to big, neon-lit roadhouses.

Country and western music, both recorded and performed live, was crucial to the profitability of honky-tonks. Many of them featured colorfully glowing (and loud) jukeboxes, the mechanical record players that had spread rapidly in popularity during and after World War II. In adjusting to the honky-tonk milieu, country musicians made a number of changes in their performance practice. First, many of the old-time songs about family and the church seemed out of place in the new setting. Musicians began to compose songs about aspects of life directly relevant to their patrons: family instability, the unpredictability of male-female relationships, the attractions and dangers of alcohol, and the importance of enjoying the present. When the rural past was referred to, it was usually through a veil of nostalgia and longing. Honky-tonk vocal styles were often directly emotional, making use of "cracks" in the voice and stylistic features from black music, such as **melisma** and **blue notes.** Like urban blues musicians such as Muddy Waters, country musicians adapted traditional instruments and playing techniques to the rowdy atmosphere of the juke joint. The typical instrumentation of a honky-tonk band included a fiddle, a steel guitar, a "takeoff" (lead) guitar, a string bass, and a piano. The guitars were electronically amplified, and the musicians played with a percussive, insistent beat (sometimes called "sock rhythm") well suited to dancing.

When today's musicians talk about playing "good old country music," they are most often referring to the postwar honky-tonk style rather than to the rural folk music of the South or the hillbilly recordings of the 1920s and 1930s. Honky-tonk stars such as Ernest Tubb, Hank Williams, Lefty Frizzell, Hank Snow, George Jones, and Webb Pierce dominated the country and western charts during the early and mid-1950s. Although their fortunes declined somewhat after the emergence of rock 'n' roll—especially a country-tinged variety of rock 'n' roll called **rockabilly** (see Chapter 8)—honky-tonk music remains the heart and soul of modern country music.

As you might expect, many of the pioneers of honky-tonk music were born in Texas. Ernest Tubb (1914–84) began his career in the 1930s as a disciple of Jimmie Rodgers, "the Singing Brakeman." By the 1940s he had developed into one of the first honky-tonk performers, singing in a deep baritone voice roughened by many years of singing in juke joints. Tubb was one of the first musicians to move toward a harder-edged country sound and to switch to amplified instruments, and he wrote some of the classic songs in the honky-tonk genre. His first big hit was "Walking the Floor over You" (released by Decca Records in 1941), which secured him a spot on the cast of the *Grand Ole Opry* and helped him to create a nationwide following. After the war Tubb recorded a series of honky-tonk classics, including "Slipping Around" (Number One country in 1949), often cited as the first country song to deal explicitly with marital infidelity.

Hank Thompson (b. 1925), a native of Waco, Texas, created a popular variation on honky-tonk music by mixing it with elements of western swing. Thompson, who began his career as "the Hired Hand," achieved his first success through his appearances on a Dallas radio show called *Cornbread Matinee*. In the late 1940s, after his discharge from the military service, he formed a band, the Brazos Valley Boys, and began performing in honky-tonks throughout the Southwest. His biggest hit was "The Wild Side of Life," which held the Number One position on the country charts for fifteen weeks in 1952. (The recording was made in Hollywood, a reflection of the burgeoning country music business in southern California.) The song, composed by William Warren and Arlie Carter, was based on Warren's personal experiences with a "honky-tonk angel" who found the "glamour of the gay nightlife" too hard to resist, and it reflects a major theme of postwar honky-tonk music: the dislocations of urban working-class life, and the transience of male-female relationships.

> You wouldn't read my letter if I wrote you
> You asked me not to call you on the phone
> But there's something I'm wanting to tell you
> So I wrote it in the words of this song
>
> I didn't know God made honky-tonk angels
> I might have known you'd never make a wife
> You gave up the only one that ever loved you
> And went back to the wild side of life

The glamour of the gay night-life has lured you
To the places where the wine and liquor flow
Where you wait to be anybody's baby
And forget the truest love you'll ever know

I didn't know God made honky-tonk angels
I might have known you'd never make a wife
You gave up the only one that ever loved you
And went back to the wild side of life.

The melody of this song might seem familiar—it was adopted from Roy Acuff's prewar hit "Great Speckled Bird," discussed in Chapter 6. Of course, the same melody had a long history before Acuff fashioned it into a popular song, and it provides more evidence of the strong historical continuities in country music, even during its periods of greatest change.

Although women were generally not able to adopt the footloose, hard-drinking persona of male stars like Lefty Frizzell and Hank Thompson, this does not mean that female singers were absent from the country charts of the early 1950s. In fact, it was during this period that the first female superstar of country music, Kitty Wells (b. 1918), rose to prominence. Born in Nashville, Tennessee, Muriel Dearson married a popular country entertainer named Johnny Wright and began appearing with him on the radio in 1938. (Her stage name was adopted from an old southern parlor song, "Sweet Kitty Wells.") Like that of most other postwar country stars, her reputation was spread by network radio, particularly a series of appearances on the

Kitty Wells. Frank Driggs Collection.

Louisiana Hayride show, second in popularity only to the *Grand Ole Opry*. Kitty Wells specialized in songs of love and betrayal, with titles like "Paying for That Back Street Affair" and "Whose Shoulder Will You Cry On," sung in a restrained, high-pitched, plaintive voice closely linked to the traditions of the Appalachian mountains. While her stage image was that of a sweet, dignified country housewife, Kitty Wells was able to articulate a distinctively female perspective on the themes of honky-tonk music, paving the way for later stars such as Patsy Cline, Loretta Lynn, and Dolly Parton. Her hit records and radio appearances also helped to establish Nashville as a new center of the country music business.

In 1952 Kitty Wells recorded her biggest hit, a pointed response to "The Wild Side of Life" entitled "It Wasn't God Who Made Honky-Tonk Angels." (It was also a part of a fad then sweeping the country and R&B markets, the "answer" record.) The song was a critique of the male domination of urban beer hall culture, where the unattached "honky-tonk angel" was regarded as both a lure and a threat. This "woman's song" was written by J. D. Miller, a commercially astute male composer. (The two examples of female perspectives in R&B music we examined earlier in this chapter—"Mama, He Treats Your Daughter Mean" and "Hound Dog"—were also written by male songwriters. It was rare at the time for women to succeed as professional songwriters in the fiercely competitive, male-centered popular music industry.) The song's narrator is a betrayed woman whose bitter memories of a formerly happy married life are evoked by hearing Thompson's voice on the jukebox:

> *As I sit here tonight, the jukebox playing*
> *The tune about the wild side of life*
> *As I listen to the words you are saying*
> *It brings memories when I was a trustful wife*
>
> *It wasn't God who made honky-tonk angels*
> *As you said in the words of your song*
> *Too many times married men think they're still single*
> *That has caused many a good girl to go wrong.*
>
> *It's a shame that all the blame is on us women*
> *It's not true that only you men feel the same*
> *From the start most every heart that's ever broken*
> *Was because there always was a man to blame*
>
> *It wasn't God who made honky-tonk angels*
> *As you said in the words of your song*
> *Too many times married men think they're still single*
> *That has caused many a good girl to go wrong.*

Wells's reserved, soulful style emphasizes the lyric content of the song, the melody and structure of which are modeled precisely on the original (and, in turn, upon "Great Speckled Bird."). "It Wasn't God Who Made Honky-Tonk Angels" was a historic recording, the first by a solo female performer to top the country and western charts. That the means of communication between the two singers is the jukebox, rather than a letter (the main medium for songs of heartbreak in an earlier era), suggests once again the central place of the jukebox, and of country music, in honky-tonk culture. This music functioned not only as entertainment but also as a repository for memory and emotion; it helped people to make sense of the sometimes radical changes they were undergoing.

HANK WILLIAMS

Hank Williams (1923–53) was the most significant single figure to emerge in country music during the immediate post–World War II period. Williams wrote and sang many songs in the course of his brief career that were enormously popular with country audiences at the time; between 1947 and 1953 he amassed an astounding thirty-six Top 10 records on the country charts, including such Number One hits as "Lovesick Blues," "Cold, Cold Heart," "Jambalaya (On the Bayou)," and "Your Cheatin' Heart." All of these Number One hits—along with many other Williams songs—have remained long-term country favorites and are established "standards" of their genre. In addition, his songs were successfully "covered" by contemporary mainstream pop artists, thus demonstrating the wide-ranging appeal of the new country material. "Cold, Cold Heart" helped launch the career of Tony Bennett when the young crooner scored a huge success with it in 1951 (Number One pop for six weeks).

Hank Williams reinvigorated for the postwar country audience the enduring myth of the hard-living, hard-loving rambler that had been established a generation earlier by Jimmie Rodgers (see Chapter 5). Although the details of Williams's life seem in retrospect to have custom-designed him for legendary status, it is important to realize that these *were* the actual facts of his life: born into crushing poverty in Alabama, this son of a sharecropper learned to make his way at an early age by performing on the street, learning a great deal from a black street singer named Rufe "Tee-Tot" Payne. By the time he was sixteen, Williams, now called "the Singing Kid," had his own local radio show; shortly thereafter he formed a band, the Drifting Cowboys, and began touring throughout Alabama. Enormous success came to Williams by the time he was in his midtwenties, but it did not come without its problems. By 1952 he was divorced, had been fired from the *Grand Ole Opry* (for numerous failures to appear), and was seriously dependent on alcohol and painkilling drugs. He was dead on New Year's Day 1953 at age twenty-nine, having suffered a heart attack in the back of his car while en route to a performance.

Williams affirmed the importance of religious traditions in country music by recording some gospel material. However, the fact that he recorded his sacred tunes under a pseudonym, rather than under his own name, ties him more closely to the practices of black secular singers than to those of most white artists. (Then again, his actual choice of pseudonym, "Luke the Drifter," links these records back to the rambler image projected by the bulk of Williams's secular work.)

A brief look at two of the most famous songs written and performed by Hank Williams will demonstrate his debts to country music traditions as well as the progressive elements in his music. "I'm So Lonesome I Could Cry" is a timeless lament that builds clearly on earlier models in both its words and its music, while "Hey, Good Lookin'" is an almost startling anticipation of the style that, in the later 1950s, would come to be called **rockabilly.**

 "I'm So Lonesome I Could Cry" evokes the flavor of "old-timey" country music with its waltzlike triple meter and its straightforward strophic structure. (Its basic mood and musical ambience are somewhat reminiscent of Jimmie Rodgers's

Hank Williams performs, while Chet Atkins—soon to be a hugely influential figure in country music himself, as a guitarist and producer—looks on admiringly. Ernie Newton is playing bass. Courtesy of Country Music Hall of Fame and Museum.

touching waltz-lament, "Dreaming with Tears in My Eyes"; see Chapter 5.) The lyrics too refer to traditional country images. The "wide open spaces" are called up with pictures of birds, of the moon going behind the clouds, and of the "silence of a falling star" that illuminates the sky, while the presence of the "midnight train . . . winding low" affirms Williams's ties to the spirits of the ramblers who came before him. Against the steady rhythmic backdrop of guitars and bass, the sound of the fiddle asserts Williams's kinship with earlier country music. On the other hand, the prominent steel guitar throughout helped create a sense of modernity for Williams's audience and assured that the essence of his music would be a feeling of utter immediacy—of a song for the here-and-now.

Like much of the finest rurally based music, black and white, "I'm So Lonesome I Could Cry" is structured to capitalize on the regional characteristics of the singer-composer's performance style. The abundance of sustained vowel sounds placed on the downbeats of measures, as in "Hear that lonesome whippoorwill," or "The silence of a falling star," draws out the characteristic twang of Williams's accent and lends a particular expressivity to the actual *sound* of the lyrics that underlines their dark emotional content. Williams's drawl also leads him naturally to delay somewhat the full force of those vowel sounds, so that he seems rhythmically behind the beat. Again, this beautifully reinforces the mournful essence of the song—as if it is a constant effort for the singer to rise to the high notes on those vowels (and this makes the fall in pitch that marks the end of every phrase in the song seem that much more inevitable, and that much sadder). When he approaches the end of the song, the almost-break in Williams's voice as he sings "and as I wonder where you are" is heartbreaking; there seems to be no separation between the singer and the song, or between the sound of his country voice and the meaning of its expression. It's no wonder Williams evoked such a response in the burgeoning country music audience after World War II.

Along with a few of Williams's other records, the jaunty "Hey, Good Lookin'" was actually something of a minor crossover hit for him (Number Twenty-nine pop, but Number One on the country chart—for eight weeks—in 1951). This should not seem surprising, given its danceable character and its pop-friendly thirty-two-bar AABA form borrowed from Tin Pan Alley models. With its prominent steel guitar and fiddle parts, not to mention the character of Williams's vocal, there's still no mistaking the record's basis in country music. What is most arresting here, however, is the specific targeting of a youthful audience. The lyrics address cars, dancing, and young romance, and the use of terms like "hot-rod Ford," "soda pop," "go steady," and "date book" create what would—about five years later—have been called a "teen-friendly" piece of material.

In a sense, "Hey, Good Lookin'" came a little too early, and Hank Williams of course died much too young. Had Williams been able to bring this same song, or something like it, to a savvy record producer in late 1955 or early 1956—to a producer aware of the noise being made by the young Elvis Presley or by Carl Perkins at the time—that cynical producer might have said something like this: "Hank, you've got something there. Please throw out those fiddles, though—too hillbilly. And replace the steel guitar with a regular electric guitar played R&B-style. Add some R&B-based drumming too, with strong backbeats. I think you'll have a hit rock 'n' roll record." And had Williams been interested, which is questionable, his name might well have been added to the **rockabilly** roster, perhaps even close to the top of it. As it is, Williams's early death leaves us pondering what might have been; but in any case, a song like "Hey, Good Lookin'" attests to the forward-looking character of his creativity.

The decade following World War II saw important changes in the popular music business, including the introduction of new technologies such as tape recording; the "covering" of rhythm & blues and country and western songs by mainstream pop artists; and the entertainment industry's increasingly sophisticated application of marketing techniques aimed increasingly at youth. All of these were preconditions for the rise of rock 'n' roll and the rapid transformation of American popular music that took place in the mid-1950s, the subject of our next chapter.

CHAPTER EIGHT

"ROCK AROUND THE CLOCK"
Rock 'n' Roll, 1954–1959

The advent of rock 'n' roll music in the mid-1950s brought enormous changes to American popular music, and eventually to world popular music—changes whose impact is still being felt today. Most significantly, styles that previously had remained on the margins of pop music from a marketing standpoint now began to infiltrate the center and eventually to dominate the center completely. Rhythm & blues and country music recordings were no longer necessarily directed to specialized and regionalized markets; they now began to be heard in significant numbers on mainstream pop radio, and many could be purchased in music stores nationwide that catered to the broadest general public.

The emergence of rock 'n' roll was surely an event of great significance in cultural terms. Because of its importance, we must be careful not to mythologize it or to endorse common misconceptions about it. In particular, the following issues demand our attention: first, rock 'n' roll was neither a "new" style of music, nor was it any single style of music; second, the era of rock 'n' roll does not mark the first time that music was written specifically to appeal to young people; third, rock 'n' roll is certainly not the first American music to bring black and white popular styles into close interaction. In fact, the designation "rock 'n' roll"—like "Tin Pan Alley," "hillbilly music," or "rhythm & blues"—was introduced as a commercial and marketing term, for the purpose of identifying a new target audience for musical products.

This new audience was dominated by those born into the so-called baby boom generation at the end of, and immediately following, World War II. It was a much younger audience than had ever before constituted a target market for music, and it was a large audience that shared some specific and important characteristics of group cultural identity. These were kids growing up in the 1950s, a period of relative economic stability and prosperity, but also a period marked by a self-conscious return to "normalcy" defined in socially and politically conservative ways, following the enormous destabilizing traumas of world war. In terms of the entertainment industry, this was the first generation to grow up with television as a readily available part of its culture; this powerful new mass medium proved a force of incalculable influence and offered another outlet for the instantaneous nationwide distribution of music.

Yet the 1950s was a period characterized by its own political and cultural traumas. Cold War tension between the United States and the Soviet Union fed an intense anticommunism in America that resulted in such controversial phenomena as congressional hearings concerning "un-American activities" and the blacklisting of many writers, musicians, and entertainment personalities who had been involved in suspect left-wing groups and actions in the 1930s, 1940s, and 1950s. During these years, children grew up amid fears induced by the introduction of atomic weapons and their further development by the American and Soviet—and eventually other—superpowers. Furthermore, new levels of racial awareness and tension in America emerged in the wake of the 1954 Supreme Court decision in the case of *Brown v. Board of Education,* which mandated the end of racial segregation in public schools.

Perhaps the most important factor of all for adolescents during the 1950s was simply their identification by the larger culture itself as a unique generational group, even as they were growing up. Thus they quickly developed a sense of self-identification as teenagers (this category was not necessarily limited to young people between the ages of thirteen and nineteen; many ten-, eleven-, and twelve-year-olds participated fully in "teen" culture). Naturally such a group, from a young age, had to have its own distinctive emblems of identity, including dance steps, fashions, ways of speaking, and music. The prosperity of the 1950s gave these young people an unprecedented collective purchasing power, as the allowances of millions of kids went toward leisure and entertainment products geared especially to this generation's tastes and sense of identity. What resulted was an increasingly volatile give-and-take between, on the one hand, products and trends that were prefabricated for teens by the adult commercial culture, and on the other hand, products and trends chosen and developed unpredictably by the members of the new generation themselves. Rock 'n' roll music was at the center of this give-and-take. It emerged as an unexpected musical choice by increasing numbers of young people in the early to mid-1950s; it then became a mass-market phenomenon exploited by the mainstream music industry in the later 1950s; and eventually it was to some extent reclaimed by these teenagers themselves in the 1960s as they grew old enough to make their own music and, increasingly, to assume some control of the production and marketing of it.

The term "rock 'n' roll" was probably first used for commercial and generational purposes by disc jockey Alan Freed (1922–65). In the early 1950s Freed discovered that increasing numbers of young white kids were listening to and requesting the rhythm & blues records he played on his *Moondog Show* nighttime program in Cleveland—records he then began to call "rock 'n' roll" records. Freed also promoted concert tours featuring black artists, playing to a young, racially mixed audience, and promoted them as "rock 'n' roll revues." The term "rock 'n' roll" itself was derived from the many references to "rockin'" and "rollin'" (sometimes separately, sometimes together) that may be found in rhythm & blues songs,

Teenagers study the offerings on a jukebox, 1957. Courtesy Library of Congress.

and on race records dating back at least to the late 1920s. Among the relevant recordings that would have been known to Freed and his audience were the late-1940s rhythm & blues hit "Good Rockin' Tonight" (recorded by a number of different artists after first becoming a hit for its composer, Roy Brown) and the huge 1951 hit by the Dominoes, "Sixty Minute Man" (which featured the lyric "I rock 'em, roll 'em, all night long, I'm a sixty-minute man"). "Rock" and "roll" are clearly associated in these and other songs with sexual implications, but like the similar original implications of the word "jazz," these implications faded as "rock 'n' roll" increasingly came to refer simply to a type of music.

In 1954 Freed moved to station WINS in the larger New York radio market, taking the phrase "rock 'n' roll" with him to identify both the music he played and his target audience. Freed continued to promote African American musicians, in the face of considerable resistance in the society as a whole to the idea of racial integration. In 1957 a TV show sponsored by Freed was canceled after the black teenage singer Frankie Lymon was shown dancing with a white girl. In 1958 Freed himself was arrested for anarchy and incitement to riot after a fight broke out at one of his rock 'n' roll concerts in Boston. In the early 1960s Freed was prosecuted for accepting **payola**—the illegal practice, common throughout the music industry, of paying bribes to radio disc jockeys in order to get certain artists' records played more frequently—while promoters like Dick Clark (who handled mainly white rock 'n' roll artists) escaped relatively unscathed. Freed was blackballed within the music business, and he died a few years later, a broken man.

Disc jockey **Alan Freed** in Cleveland. Courtesy Library of Congress.

Whatever his indiscretions, Alan Freed was clearly in the vanguard of an increasing number of disc jockeys, all over the country, who wished to capture the new, large audience of young radio listeners and potential record buyers, and who consequently embraced the term "rock 'n' roll" to refer to virtually any kind of music pitched to that audience. This included records that would previously have been marketed purely as rhythm & blues or as country and western, along with an expanding group of hybrid records that drew freely on multiple stylistic influences, including those associated with mainstream Tin Pan Alley–type music. Strange as it now seems, in the early heyday of rock 'n' roll Chuck Berry, Pat Boone, Fats Domino, Ricky Nelson, the Everly Brothers, and Elvis Presley were all lumped together as "rock 'n' roll singers"—meaning simply that they all had records being listened to and purchased by large numbers of teenagers. This was a period of remarkable heterogeneity on radio and on the record charts, as all of the above singers, along with the likes of Frank Sinatra and Patti Page, could be heard jostling each other on Top 40 radio stations and seen nudging each other on the pop charts. In the marketing confusion that resulted, rock 'n' roll records appeared on different, previously exclusive, charts simultaneously; early in 1956 Carl Perkins's "Blue Suede Shoes" and Elvis Presley's "Heartbreak Hotel" both made chart history by climbing to the upper reaches of the country and western, rhythm & blues, and pop charts all at the same time.

The purchase of rock 'n' roll records by kids in the 1950s proved a relatively safe and affordable way for kids to assert generational identity through rebellion against previous adult standards and restrictions of musical style and taste. (The original associations of the term "rock 'n' roll" with marginalized African American musical styles and with sexually risqué lyrics obviously didn't hurt the sense of rebellion at all, for those familiar with the associations—whether they were the kids themselves, or their parents!) Thus the experience of growing up with rock 'n' roll music became an early and defining characteristic of the baby boom generation. Rock 'n' roll records accompanied the boomers in their progress from preadolescence through their teenage years. It is consequently not surprising that this music increasingly and specifically catered to this age group, which by the late 1950s had its own distinctive culture (made possible by abundant leisure time and economic prosperity) and its associated rituals: school and vacation (represented in rock 'n' roll songs such as "School Day" and "Summertime Blues"), fashions ("Black Denim Trousers and Motorcycle Boots" and "Itsy Bitsy Teenie Weenie Yellow Polka-dot Bikini"), social dancing ("At the Hop" and "Save the Last Dance for Me"), and courtship ("Teen-Age Crush," "Puppy Love," "A Teenager in Love," and "Poor Little Fool"). Some rock 'n' roll songs—for example, "Roll over Beethoven" and "Rock and Roll Is Here to Stay"—self-consciously announced themselves as emblems of a new aesthetic and cultural order, dominated by the tastes and aspirations of youth.

It would not be an exaggeration to say that the 1950s essentially invented the teenager as a commercial and cultural entity, and that rock 'n' roll music, along with television and, to some extent, movies, played an essential role in this invention. Although popular music of all eras has reached out to young audiences with plentiful songs about love and courtship, the virtually exclusive emphasis on appeal to one particular, extremely young, generation is what most distinguishes the phenomenon of rock 'n' roll. It is thus not surprising that teenagers themselves were recruited, with increasing frequency, as performers to market this music, beginning with the popular group Frankie Lymon and the Teenagers (who scored their first and biggest hit "Why Do Fools Fall in Love?" early in 1956, when lead singer Lymon himself was only thirteen years old), and continuing in the following years with a string of "teen idols" like Ricky Nelson, Paul Anka, and Annette Funicello. (The popularity of both Nelson and Funicello was closely linked to television; the former was already well known to audiences as the younger son on *The Adventures of Ozzie and Harriet* show before he started making records, and the latter was prominently featured on *The Mickey Mouse Club*—a show obviously aimed at the baby boomer audience.) The association of rock 'n' roll with adolescence and adolescents was so complete that, in the 1960s, practitioners of the music who had grown out of their adolescent years, and who wanted to appeal to a maturing audience of their peers, rechristened their music simply *rock*.

For all this appropriate emphasis on the generational culture of rock 'n' roll, we should not ignore that the shift in musical marketing away from primarily racial and regional considerations (and their associated class-related aspects) toward primarily generational considerations had some unforeseen and extremely significant consequences that profoundly affected the American cultural landscape. There was a period in the later 1950s when much of the same popular music—rock 'n' roll records—would be played for dances at inner-city, primarily black, public schools, for parties at exclusive white suburban private schools, and for socials in rural settings catering to young people. This was a new kind of situation, especially in the society of the 1950s, which was in most respects polarized in terms of race, class, and region. In the preceding chapters of this book, we have seen how extensive the influences and interactions among supposedly exclusive groups of musicians (black and white, rural and urban, upper and lower class) have been throughout the history of American popular music. But rock 'n' roll music seemed to offer a bridge connecting supposedly exclusive *audiences*. If you were young in the 1950s, no matter where you lived, no matter what your race or class, rock 'n' roll was *your* music. An important, if ultimately fragile, potential of popular music to create new connections and relationships among audiences in a highly fragmented society was first glimpsed on a large scale in the period of rock 'n' roll.

COVER VERSIONS AND EARLY ROCK 'N' ROLL

One of the most important precedents for the rise of rock 'n' roll was a commercial and musical phenomenon known as the *cover version*. In the broadest sense, this term simply refers to the practice of recording a song that has previously been recorded by another artist or group. However, practitioners, merchants, and scholars of popular music have usually used the term in a more restricted sense, to refer to a version—sometimes an almost exact copy—of a previously recorded performance, often involving an adaptation of the original's style and sensibility, and usually aimed at cashing in on its success. Of course, the process of musical borrowing is no doubt as old as music itself. But this process takes on new significance when the element of financial profit is introduced, and when issues of social inequality are involved. In such contexts, the influence of one tradition, style, or performer on another can also be seen as a kind of musical appropriation, and borrowing becomes something more akin to stealing.

In Chapters 6 and 7 we noted a number of instances of cover versions, including Benny Goodman's "slicked-up" renditions of arrangements previously recorded by Fletcher Henderson's band, and Bing Crosby's and Patti Page's pop versions of country and western songs. The practice of covering often worked in both directions, and country and rhythm & blues musicians sometimes recorded their own stylized renditions of Tin Pan Alley songs that had previously been popularized by pop crooners. However, the most notorious examples—and those most important for understanding the rise of rock 'n' roll in the mid-1950s—involved white performers covering the work of African American recording artists. This was a relationship not simply between individual musicians but also between competing institutions, since the underlying motivation for covering a recording typically involved the major record companies' attempt to capitalize on the musical discoveries of small independent record labels. The practice also represented a new stage in the evolution of white fascination with black music, a theme that we have followed from the beginning of this book.

To better our understanding of this phenomenon, let's look at specific examples of cover versions. In 1947 a black singer and pianist named Paula Watson recorded a song called "A Little Bird Told Me" for the independent label Supreme. Watson's version of the song, released in 1948, reached Number Two on the R&B charts and made an impact on the pop charts, peaking at Number Six. This early crossover hit attracted the attention of Decca Records, which immediately issued a cover version of the song performed by a white singer named Evelyn Knight. Knight's version of the song reached Number One on the pop charts, in large part owing to the promotional power of Decca Records and the fact that white performers enjoyed privileged access to radio and television play.

The tiny Supreme label sued Decca Records, claiming that its copyright to the original had been infringed. In this case the crux of the matter was not the song per se—its author, Harvey Brooks, collected composer's royalties from both record companies. Rather, Supreme claimed that Decca had stolen aspects of the original recording, including its arrangement, texture, and vocal style. Although Evelyn Knight had indeed copied Paula Watson's singing precisely—to the degree that it fooled musical experts brought in as witnesses—the judge ultimately decided in favor of the larger company, ruling that musical arrangements were not copyrighted property and therefore not under legal protection. This decision affirmed the legal principle that the song (published in the form of sheet music) was a copyrightable form of intellectual property, but that individual interpretations or arrangements of a given song could not be protected under the law. This meant the continuation of an older conception of music's legal status—focused on the written document—in an era when recordings, rather than sheet music, had become the dominant means of transmission. (Today, in the era of digital sampling, these questions continue to loom large in court cases concerning the ownership of popular music. In certain instances, specific aspects of a recorded performance have been deemed protectable by copyright. See Chapter 14.)

The "Little Bird Told Me" decision opened the floodgates for cover versions during the 1950s, for better or worse. Now let's take a closer look at three more examples of cover versions, each of which gives us a different perspective on the complex musical, economic, and social forces that converged to create rock 'n' roll in the mid-1950s.

Cover Version 1: "Shake, Rattle, and Roll"

Original version performed by Big Joe Turner (Number One R&B, Number Twenty-two pop, 1954); cover version performed by Bill Haley and the Comets (Number Seven pop, 1954)

Perhaps the most famous example of a mid-1950s cover version is the song "Shake, Rattle, and Roll," composed in 1954 by Jesse Stone, the black producer and talent scout for Atlantic Records. (The song was actually published under the pseudonym Charles Calhoun.) "Shake, Rattle, and Roll" is a twelve-bar blues, with an a-a-b text scheme and a repeated section that functions like a chorus (*Shake, rattle, and roll . . .*). The original recording of the song, released by Atlantic in 1954, is in the jump blues R&B style. It features <u>Big Joe Turner</u> (1911–85), a forty-three-year old vocalist who had begun his career as a singing bartender in the depression-era nightclubs of Kansas City and had sung with various big bands during the swing era. Turner was one of Atlantic's early stars, and his recording of "Shake, Rattle, and Roll" not only held the Number One position on the R&B charts but also crossed over to the pop charts, where it reached Number Twenty-two.

This crossover hit soon caught the attention of executives at Decca Records and of a former country and western bandleader named Bill Haley (see Box 8.1). Later in 1954 Bill Haley and the Comets recorded a rendition of "Shake, Rattle, and Roll" that was clearly indebted to Turner's original but also departed from it in significant ways. While the Atlantic recording features a band made up of veteran jazz musicians, playing a medium-tempo shuffle rhythm, the Haley recording emphasizes guitars rather than saxophones and has a rhythmic feeling more akin to western swing than jump blues R&B. One of the most obvious differences between the two versions lies in the song's text. The original lyric, as written by Jesse Stone and embellished by Big Joe Turner, is full of fairly obvious sexual references:

> *Well, you wear those dresses, the sun come shinin' through*
> *Well, you wear those dresses, the sun come shinin' through*
> *I cain' believe my eyes, all that mess belong to you*
>
> *I'm like a one-eyed cat, peepin' in a seafood store*
> *I'm like a one-eyed cat, peepin' in a seafood store*
> *Well I can look at you, tell you ain' no child no more*

Presumably because these lyrics would have proved too wild for AM radio and offended many in the predominantly white pop music audience, Haley sang a bowdlerized (censored) version of the song:

> *Wearin' those dresses, your hair done up so nice*
> *Wearin' those dresses, your hair done up so nice*
> *You look so warm, but your heart is cold as ice.*
>
> *I'm like a one-eyed cat, peepin' in a seafood store,*
> *I'm like a one-eyed cat, peepin' in a seafood store*
> *I can look at you, tell you don't love me no more*

That the "one-eyed cat, peepin' in a seafood store" line survived the censor's blade is surprising, since it is a fairly obvious double-entendre reference to the male and female sexual organs. The person charged with rewriting the lyric may have been a bit too square to catch the sexual reference, a fact that must have delighted those who knew the original version.

The other major difference between Turner's and Haley's versions of "Shake, Rattle, and Roll" is the level of profit generated by the two recordings. In fact, this is not the most egregious example of a white band and major record company reaping profits from a song originally recorded by black musicians for an independent label, since both versions appeared on the pop charts, and each sold over a million copies. There are crucial differences between the two, however. While Big Joe Turner's version crossed over to the pop chart (and the expanding white teenage audience for black popular music), the majority of Atlantic's sales was nonetheless focused in the black community. Haley's version reached Number Seven on the pop chart but did not appear on the R&B charts at all, indicating that black audiences preferred Turner's jump band–style approach to the country-tinged style of the Comets. While Haley built on his early hit success, going on to become the first "king" of rock 'n' roll music, Turner was never again able to score a Top 40 pop hit or a Number One R&B hit. Atlantic sought to promote the middle-aged blues shouter to the teen audience for rock 'n' roll, but his time had passed. Turner himself claimed that "rock 'n' roll" was just another name for the same music he had always sung, but that he got "knocked down" in the traffic of a newly crowded scene.

The two versions of "Shake, Rattle, and Roll" represent a pivot point between early 1950s R&B and later 1950s rock 'n' roll. And they are also a junction at which two popular musicians crossed paths—Big Joe Turner on his way down, and Bill Haley on his way up.

Cover Version 2: "Sh-Boom"

Original version composed and performed by the Chords (Number Two R&B, Number Five pop, 1954); cover version performed by the Crew Cuts (Number One pop for nine weeks, 1954)

"Sh-Boom" is one of the most famous cover versions of the early rock 'n' roll era. In fact, its original recording by the Chords is often cited as one of the very first rock 'n' roll records. Certainly the Chords' "Sh-Boom" is a prime example of the rhythm & blues black vocal group style and, as a Top 10 pop hit, was also one of the first records to demonstrate the huge appeal that style could have to a mass audience. It is particularly significant that the Chords managed to place their record near the top of the pop charts in spite of a massively successful cover version of the tune by the white group the Crew Cuts. The Crew Cuts' "Sh-Boom" was one of the two biggest pop hits of 1954 and thus offers a particularly instructive example of the "cover record" phenomenon. A splendid irony underlying all this is the fact that the Chords' original "Sh-Boom" was in fact on the "flip" side of their own cover version (for the R&B market) of white pop singer Patti Page's hit "Cross over the Bridge"! If some discerning listeners and some enterprising disc jockeys hadn't turned the Chords' record over and enthused over the apparent throwaway number on the B-side, you wouldn't be reading this right now.

The Chords' "Sh-Boom" also illustrates how the presence of unexpected elements in the arrangement and performance of a rather ordinary tune can help create an extraordinary and original pop record. Essentially, the song is a standard AABA love ballad whose sentimental lyrics and stereotypical chord changes would suggest, on paper, either a slow rhythm & blues ballad or some grist for a latter-day pop crooner's mill. However, the Chords made the striking decision to treat the song as an uptempo number and to add some novel touches that were appropriate to an uptempo record but that also made this one really stand out. Among these novel touches on the Chords' recording (see the outline below) are: an **a cappella** vocal introduction; the incorporation of brief passages of **scat singing,** borrowed from jazz, at strategic points in the performance; a long and sizzling instrumental break, in the form of a saxophone solo—accompanied by the vocal group's rhythmic "doo-wop" nonsense syllables in the background—right in the middle of the record; and an unexpected ending on the term "sh-boom" itself, intoned by the group on an especially rich chord. This record anticipates the kind of unexpected syntheses from different musical styles that would come to characterize the most inventive rock 'n' roll records. For example, the sax solo would have been typical of an uptempo urban blues or dance-oriented R&B recording, but would probably not have been expected in a record with love ballad lyrics, while "doo-wop" vocal sounds—expected in R&B love ballads—were not typically paired with hot instrumental solos. The association made in the record between jazz-related scat vocal solos and the nonsense syllables of vocal group doo-wop, while logical, was also quite original.

There are novel touches in the Crew Cuts' recording as well, which help account for its great popular success. As shown in the outline below, this version begins with scat singing. In the middle of the record, instead of a saxophone solo, there are two brief sections of group nonsense-syllable singing—each of which is punctuated by an isolated, loud, and humorous kettledrum stroke. Toward the end of the recording there are not one but *two* "false" conclusions. Arguably, all these effects tend to push this version into the category of a full-fledged novelty record (whereas the Chords' version comes across as an uptempo R&B record with some novel aspects).

In terms of singing style, the Crew Cuts are crooners. The alternation between phrases where a solo voice takes the lead and phrases that are sung by the full group produces some agreeable variety in their arrangement, but there is really no difference in vocal coloration between the solo and the group; that is to say, the group passages are, in effect, "crooning times four." In contrast, the Chords' vocal arrangement is typical of a rhythm & blues approach insofar as it exploits differences in vocal timbre among the group's members, as well as the opposition between solo and group singing. This is heard most clearly in the B section (bridge) of the Chords' version, where the lead is taken by a solo bass voice that presents a strong contrast to the sound of the lead tenor heard in the first two A sections. Of course, the Chords' general approach throughout is rougher in sound than that of the Crew Cuts, underlining the much more aggressive rhythmic feeling of their recording as a whole. And the overriding difference between the Chords' and the Crew Cuts' recordings of "Sh-Boom" has to do precisely with that rhythmic feeling: simply put, the former swings hard and the latter does not.

OUTLINE: THE CHORDS' "SH-BOOM"	OUTLINE: THE CREW CUTS' "SH-BOOM"
Introduction (full group a cappella, then band enters)	**Introduction (scat singing)**

A ("Life could . . . "; tenor lead)
  (Scat singing interlude)
A ("Life could . . . "; tenor lead)
B ("Every time . . . "; bass lead)
A ("Life could . . . "; full group)
  (Scat singing interlude)
Sax Solo (with group "doo-wop" sounds in
  background; this is the length of two
  A sections)
A (full group; same words as first A section)
  (Scat singing interlude, leading to
  sudden ending with the full group)

A (tenor lead)
A (tenor lead)
B (tenor lead, then full group)
A (tenor lead)
Group "nonsense" singing (two sections,
  each the length of an A section,
  punctuated by kettledrum strokes)
B (full group)
A (full group, then tenor lead; same words
  as first A section)
  (Scat singing interlude, leading to
  first "false" ending, then to:)
A (full group, then tenor lead; same words
  as the second A section)
  ("False" fadeout leads to sudden loud
  conclusion with the full group)

Original version composed and performed by Junior Parker (no chart appearance, 1953); cover version performed by Elvis Presley (Number Eleven country and western, 1955)

Cover Version 3: "Mystery Train"

The biggest star of the rock 'n' roll era—and arguably of the entire history of American popular music—was Elvis Presley (1935–77). Presley was born in Tupelo, Mississippi, the only child of a poor family, and his musical taste was shaped at a young age by the white gospel music he heard at church, by radio broadcasts of country music and rhythm & blues, and by the popular crooners of the postwar era, especially Dean Martin. (At the age of eight Presley won a talent contest at a Mississippi county fair, singing an old country song called "Old Shep.") As a teenager he moved to Memphis, took a job as a truck driver, and nurtured his ambition to become a singing film star.

In 1954 Presley came to the attention of Sam Phillips, the owner of Sun Records, a small independent label in Memphis, Tennessee, that specialized in country and rhythm & blues recordings and had scored a few regional hits. Phillips teamed Presley with two musicians from a local country band called the Starlite Wranglers, Scotty Moore (b. 1931) on electric guitar and Bill Black (1926–65) on string bass. Presley made a series of recordings with an R&B cover version on one side and a country song on the other. In essence, Sam Phillips was fishing with Elvis as bait, trying to see if he could develop a single artist who could sell to both white and black audiences. In his early live appearances, Elvis was billed as "the King of Country Bop," an attempt to indicate his idiosyncratic combination of black and white influences. The last record that Elvis made with Sam Phillips—just before he signed with RCA Victor and went on to become a national celebrity—was a cover version of an R&B song called "Mystery Train," and it is this recording that we want to examine in some detail.

In 1953 Herman ("Little Junior") Parker (1927–71), a singer, songwriter, and harmonica player who was achieving some success with his rhythm & blues band Little Junior's Blue Flames, had recorded a tune called "Mystery Train" for Sam Phillips's Sun label. The song received little attention at the time of its release, but at some point the young Elvis Presley must have noticed it, for he recorded "Mystery Train" early in 1955—also for Sun Record Company. Examining these two versions of "Mystery Train" will assist us in understanding the developing synergy between rhythm & blues and country music that led to the phenomenon called rock 'n' roll. It will also serve to underline the essential role of small independent record labels in disseminating "marginal" music and thus in contributing to this synergy. And it will help trace the origins of Elvis Presley's unique style, illuminating what Sam Phillips (who worked extensively with both black and white artists during the heyday of Sun Record Company) had in mind when he made his oft-quoted, oft-paraphrased observation that if he could find a white man with "the Negro sound and the Negro feel," then he could become a millionaire.

"Mystery Train" as a composition is credited to Parker and Phillips, and it is a strophic twelve-bar blues structure, at least in its original version (with one harmonic irregularity: some strophes begin on the subdominant chord rather than on the **tonic,** so that the first two four-bar phrases of these particular strophes are harmonically identical). Both Parker's original performance and Presley's cover version are individually fine recordings. What is most remarkable, however, is how *different* they are from one another. Although Presley obviously learned a great deal from listening to Parker, and to dozens of other fine rhythm & blues artists, Presley's "Mystery Train" is arguably less a traditional cover than a reconceptualization of the song—a reconceptualization that reflects both Presley's distinctive self-awareness as a performer and his emerging (if probably implicit) ideas regarding his listening audience and how to engage it.

Junior Parker's original "Mystery Train" is a darkly evocative record with obvious roots both in rural blues and in rhythm & blues traditions. The train was a favorite subject and image for country blues singers, and the spare, nonlinear lyrics in Parker's song are clearly aligned with country blues traditions; this train is certainly "mysterious." In the first strophe, the "long black train," with its "sixteen coaches" taking the singer's "baby" away, paints a funereal picture. By the time we reach the third and final strophe, the train is bringing "baby" back to the singer, and the mood has brightened. But that brightening is darkened by the certainty already communicated in the second strophe: the train that took her away will "do it again." Parker's "Mystery Train" articulates a pessimistic worldview characteristic of the blues by asserting that the singer may triumph over adversity, but only temporarily—that is to say, life is a cycle of misfortunes offering, at best, periodic relief, but no permanent reprieve. (Two out of the three strophes portray "baby"'s departure, while only one depicts her anticipated return.)

Parker's band constitutes a fairly typical rhythm & blues lineup for its time: electric guitar, acoustic bass, piano, drums, and saxophone. The "chugging" rhythm conveys a perfect sense of the train's steady, inexorable momentum. The saxophone is confined basically to long, low notes that evoke the train's whistle, while an additional atmospheric touch is added at the end of the recording, with a vocal imitation of the sound of the train's brakes as it finally comes to a stop (an event marked by the concluding guitar chord and the cessation of the "chugging" rhythm).

Elvis Presley's "Mystery Train," recorded when the "hillbilly cat" was barely twenty years old, conveys a breathless sense of intensity, excitement, and even enthusiasm (listen to Presley's spontaneous-sounding, triumphant "whoop" at the end of the recording!) that makes for a totally different experience from that offered by Parker's rendition. The much faster tempo of the Presley record is of course a decisive factor, but it is only the most obvious of many reasons that may be cited for the essential transformation "Mystery Train" undergoes here. There is little, if any, attempt at naturalistic evocation of the train by Presley's band, which consists simply of electric guitar, acoustic guitar, acoustic bass, and drums. One might hear a trainlike rhythm in the pattern of the drumsticks, but the speed of the recording encourages one to imagine a roller coaster rather than a train (especially by 1955 standards). In fact, unlike Parker's record, Presley's version focuses on the singer rather than the train. Parker's protagonist seems ultimately at the mercy of the train, which has taken away his "baby" and will do so again, even if it occasionally brings her back. But Presley's vocal portrays a confident protagonist who projects control over his own future.

Presley's version presents significant alterations of Parker's original in the internal structuring of both the words and the music. In the lyrics to the second strophe, Presley makes a crucial substitution, asserting that while the train took his "baby," "*it never will again*"! As if to emphasize this essential change, Presley repeats this second strophe, with its altered lyrics, at the end of his record, so that now there are a total of four strophes, three of which look toward the return of his "baby," while only one (the first one) emphasizes her departure. That departure now becomes a one-time occurrence, as the song assumes a linear narrative shape that it did not have in Parker's original version. Even more importantly, this revision of the lyrics expresses and underlines the singer's feeling of control over the situation—definitely not an attitude traditionally associated with the blues. (It would be hard to imagine Parker asserting that the train will never take his lover away again.) In Parker's "Mystery Train," the instrumental break occurs between the second and third strophes, emphasizing, and allowing the listener to ponder, the singer's assertion that the train is going to take his "baby" again; arguably, this structural arrangement colors significantly our entire perception of the song. In Presley's version, by contrast, the instrumental break occurs after the third strophe, leaving the singer's words "she's mine, all mine" resonating in the listener's ears.

While Parker's "Mystery Train" follows the standard format of twelve-bar blues in the rhythmic arrangement of all its phrases and strophes, Presley's version is highly irregular by comparison. Many of the phrases in Presley's "Mystery Train" are longer than they "should" be; if we attempted to notate his performance in terms of a twelve-bar blues paradigm, we would find ourselves constantly having to add "half-bar" extensions (two extra beats) to many phrases. While there seems to be a general pattern formed by these extensions throughout the first three strophes, Presley breaks free of even this suggested pattern in his final strophe, extending one of the phrases yet further than before, while constricting another. (One of the truly remarkable things about this "Mystery Train" is that Presley's band was able to follow the apparent spontaneity, and consequent unpredictability, of his phrasing—especially given the breakneck speed of the performance.) Clearly, this singer is constrained by nothing; the rhythmic freedom of the music itself is reflective of his apparently limitless confidence.

With all these differences, we still should not ignore Presley's obvious debts to the blues and rhythm & blues traditions represented by Parker's original composition and recording. It is not difficult to hear strong aspects of what Sam Phillips called "the Negro sound and the Negro feel" in Presley's performance: in particular, the strong regional accent and the frequency of **blue notes** and of sliding between pitches. These characteristics are, of course, points of intersection between black blues and white country traditions. What is important is to understand how Presley emphasized these common elements to form a style that sounded significantly "blacker" (particularly to white audiences) than that of virtually any other white singer who had emerged in the post–World War II era. (Presley also incorporated some vocal effects more specifically associated with white traditions—especially the kind of rapid stuttering, "hiccuping" effect heard in lines like "comin' dow-*how*n the li-*hi*ne" or "she's mine, a-*hall* mine.") Even the kind of rhythmic freedom that we have observed in Presley's "Mystery Train" reflects practices common in African American music, although one would have to go back to rural blues recordings to find anything comparably irregular, as most rhythm & blues records were tied to the kind of regularity in phrasing that was usually expected in music designed to be suitable for dancing.

This observation brings us to our final point. In sum, Elvis Presley's "Mystery Train" is unique in our experience of cover records thus far because it is more aggressive and "raw" than the original on which it was modeled. But the freedom and rawness of Presley's version is not primarily in the service of a vision that seeks to return us to the original flavor and context of rural blues—far from it. Rather, Presley's "Mystery Train" is the expression of a young white singer who is looking with optimism toward an essentially unbounded future, flush with new possibilities for stylistic synthesis that would help assure both intensely satisfying personal expression and an unprecedented degree of popular success. Unlike Parker's "Mystery Train," which is the expression of a man working knowledgeably within a tradition that both defines and confines the outlines of his music, and of his worldview, Presley's "Mystery Train" offers a totally new kind of ride, a ride without

The young **Elvis Presley** in action, 1956. Courtesy Library of Congress.

preconceived limits or conditions. No wonder so many other young singers, and a remarkably large young audience, wanted to climb aboard!

THE ROCK 'N' ROLL BUSINESS

To comprehend the emergence of rock 'n' roll as a musical genre and a commercial category, it is important that we gain some understanding of the economics of the music business in the mid-1950s. The overall vitality of the American economy after World War II helped push the entertainment industry's profits to new levels. Sales of record players and radios expanded significantly after the war. Total annual record sales in the United States rose from $191 million in 1951 to $514 million in 1959.

This expansion was accompanied by a gradual diversification of mainstream popular taste, and by the reemergence of independent ("indie") record companies, whose predecessors had been wiped out twenty years before by the Great Depression. Most of these smaller companies—established by entrepreneurs in New York and Los Angeles, and in secondary centers such as Chicago, Cincinnati, Nashville, Memphis, and New Orleans—specialized in rhythm & blues and country and western recordings, which had begun to attract a national mass audience. This process was viewed with a mixture of interest and alarm by the directors of the "majors" (large record companies such as RCA Victor, Capitol, Mercury, Columbia, MGM, and Decca), which still specialized mainly in the music of Tin Pan Alley, performed by crooners. A few of the majors—for example, Decca, which had already made millions from the sale of R&B and country records—did manage to produce some early rock 'n' roll hits. Other large record companies took a couple of years to react to the emergence of rock 'n' roll. RCA Victor, for example, scored a Number One hit in 1956 with Kay Starr's rendition of "Rock and Roll Waltz" (a song that described a teenager watching her parents try to dance to the new music, accompanied by music more akin to a ballroom waltz than to rock 'n' roll). But RCA also signed the **rockabilly** singer Elvis Presley and set to work transforming him into a Hollywood matinee idol and rock 'n' roll's first bonafide superstar.

The sales charts published in industry periodicals like *Billboard* and *Cashbox* during the 1950s chronicle changes in popular taste, the role of the indies in channeling previously marginal types of music into the pop mainstream, and the emergence of a new teenage market. The charts also reveal a complex pattern of competition among musical styles. As an example, let's have a look at the *Billboard* charts for July 9, 1955, when Bill Haley and the Comets' "Rock around the Clock" became the first rock 'n' roll hit to reach the Number One position on the "Best Sellers in Stores" chart (see Box 8.1). This event is cited by rock historians as a revolutionary event, the beginning of a new era in American popular culture. However, two very different recordings, reminiscent of earlier styles of popular music, held the Number One positions on the jukebox and radio airplay charts on July 9—the Latin American ballroom dance hit "Cherry Pink and Apple Blossom White," by Perez Prado and His Orchestra, and "Learning the Blues," performed by the former big-band crooner Frank Sinatra with the accompaniment of Nelson Riddle and His Orchestra. And lest we assume that this contrast in styles represented a titanic struggle between small and large record companies, it should be noted that all three of the above records were released by majors (Decca, RCA Victor, and Capitol, respectively).

The record that pushed "Rock around the Clock" out of the Number One position two months later was "The Yellow Rose of Texas" (a nineteenth-century minstrel song), performed in a deliberately old-fashioned singalong style by the Mitch Miller Singers. Miller was the powerful director of the **A&R** (artists and repertoire) department at Columbia Records, and in that role had helped to establish the careers of pop crooners such as Doris Day, Tony Bennett, and Frankie Laine. He was also an arch-enemy of rock 'n' roll music and of its increasing influence on AM radio programming, which he derided as being geared to "the eight- to fourteen-year-olds, to the pre-shave crowd that make up twelve percent of the country's population and zero percent of its buying power" (Clarke 1995, p. 410). It is not hard to understand Miller's anger over the domination of radio by Top 40 playlists—predetermined lists of records by a limited number of artists, often backed up by bribes from record company officials to radio station personnel. One could see the free-form FM broadcasts of the late 1960s (Chapter 10) and the rise of alternative stations in the 1980s and 1990s as similar reactions against the playlist concept. But his refusal to recognize the teenage market was nothing if not short-sighted. A 1958 survey of the purchasing patterns of the nineteen million teenagers in the United States showed that they spent a total of nine million dollars a year and strongly influenced their parents' choices of everything from toothpaste and canned food to automobiles and phonographs. And, of course, they bought millions and millions of records.

Bill Haley and the Comets shake up a crowd at the Sports Arena, Hershey, Pennsylvania, 1956. Courtesy Library of Congress.

Box 8.1 Bill Haley and "Rock around the Clock" (1955) *1st King of Rock + Roll*

<u>Bill Haley</u> (1925–81) would seem an unlikely candidate for the first big rock 'n' roll star, but in the early 1950s this leader of various obscure western swing groups was seeking a style that would capture the enthusiasm of the growing audience of young listeners and dancers, and he accurately sensed which way the wind was blowing. He dropped his cowboy image, changed the name of his accompanying group from the Saddlemen to the Comets, and in 1953 wrote and recorded a song, "Crazy, Man, Crazy," that offered a reasonable emulation of dance-oriented black rhythm & blues music. The record, released by a small indie label, rose as high as Number Twelve on the pop charts. In 1954 the Comets were signed by Decca Records, where they worked in the studio with A&R man Milt Gabler. Gabler, who had produced a series of hit records with Louis Jordan and His Tympany Five (see Chapter 7), helped to push Haley's style further in the direction of jump band rhythm & blues—"I'd sing Jordan riffs to the group that would be picked up by the electric guitars and tenor sax," he later said.

As we have already mentioned, Bill Haley and the Comets recorded commercially successful cover versions of rhythm & blues hits in the mid-1950s, notably "Shake, Rattle, and Roll" (Number Seven, 1954) and "See You Later, Alligator" (Number Six, 1956). But they attained their unique status in pop music history when their record of "Rock around the Clock" became, in 1955, the first rock 'n' roll record to be a Number One pop hit. It stayed in the top spot for eight consecutive weeks during the summer of 1955 and eventually sold over twenty-two million copies worldwide.

"Rock around the Clock," written by Max C. Freedman and Jimmy DeKnight, was actually recorded in 1954 and was not a big hit when first released. But then the record was prominently featured in the opening credits of the 1955 movie *Blackboard Jungle*, which dealt with inner-city teenagers and juvenile delinquency, and "Rock around the Clock" quickly achieved massive popularity—and forged an enduring link that has connected teenagers, rock 'n' roll, and movies ever since. Bill Haley's claim to have "invented" rock 'n' roll deserves as little credibility as Paul Whiteman's claim a generation earlier to be the "King of Jazz." But, like Whiteman, Haley proved to be an important <u>popularizer of previously marginalized musical sounds and ideas,</u> and he paved the way for the widespread acceptance of many more creative artists working with rock 'n' roll.

"Rock around the Clock" demonstrated the unprecedented success that a white group with a country background could achieve playing a twelve-bar blues song driven by the sounds of electric guitar, bass, and drums. It proved a portent of the enormous changes that were about to overtake American popular music and opened the floodgates for artists like Elvis Presley, Carl Perkins, and Buddy Holly. "Rock around the Clock" also helped prepare a receptive mass audience for the sounds of rhythm & blues, and for black artists building on the rhythm & blues tradition. While the song was still at the top of the pop chart in 1955, Chuck Berry's trailblazing "Maybellene" made its appearance on the same chart, and before long was itself in the Top 10.

Box 8.2 The Electric Guitar

It is almost impossible to conjure up a mental image of Chuck Berry—or Buddy Holly, or Jimi Hendrix—without an electric guitar in his hands. Certainly, one of rock 'n' roll's most significant effects on popular music was its elevation of the electric guitar to the position of centrality that the instrument still enjoys in most genres of popular music today. The development of the electric guitar is a good example of the complex relationship between technological developments and changing musical styles. Up through the end of World War II, the guitar was found mainly in popular music that originated in the South (blues and hillbilly music), and in various "exotic" genres (Hawai'ian and Latin American guitar records were quite popular in the 1920s and 1930s). Because of its low volume, the acoustic guitar was difficult to use in large dance bands and equally difficult to record. Engineers began to experiment with electronically amplified guitars in the 1920s, and in 1931 the Electro String Instrument Company (better known as Rickenbacker) introduced the first commercially produced electric guitars. Laid across the player's knees like the steel or Hawai'ian guitars used in country music and blues, these instruments were called "frying pans" because of their distinctive round bodies and long necks. By the mid-1930s the Gibson Company had introduced a hollow-body guitar with a new type of pickup—a magnetic plate or coil attached to the body of the guitar, which converts the physical vibrations of its strings into patterns of electric energy. This pickup later became known as the Charlie Christian pickup, after the young African American guitarist from Texas (1916–42) who introduced the guitar into Benny Goodman's band and helped to pioneer the modern jazz style called *bebop*. Despite Christian's innovations with the Goodman band, few of the big swing bands introduced the instrument, and none allowed it to play a prominent role.

The *solid-body electric guitar* was developed after World War II and was first used in rhythm & blues, blues, and country bands—the country musician Merle Travis (1917–83) had one designed for him as early as 1946, and blues musicians such as T-Bone Walker (1910–75) and Muddy Waters were also recording with electric guitars by the late 1940s. The first commercially produced solid-body electric guitar was the Fender Broadcaster (soon renamed the Telecaster), brainchild of Leo Fender and George Fullerton. This model, released in 1948, featured two electronic pickups, knobs to control volume and tone (timbre), and a switch that allowed the two pickups to be used alone or together, allowing the player to create a palette of different sounds. In 1954 Fender released the Stratocaster, the first guitar with three pickups, and the first with a "whammy bar" or "vibrato bar," a metal rod attached to the guitar's bridge that allowed the player to bend pitches with his right as well as his left hand. Fender's most successful competitor, the Gibson Company, released a solid body guitar in 1952, christening it the Les Paul in honor of the popular guitarist who helped to popularize the new instrument and the use of multiple track tape recording. The first widely popular electric bass guitar, the Fender Precision Bass, was introduced in 1951.

What is it about electric guitars that makes them such an object of fascination—sometimes bordering on fetishism—for musicians and fans alike? Like any kind of influential technology—say, the automobile or the phonograph—the meaning of the guitar is a complex matter. To begin with, the instrument came into the popular mainstream with a somewhat dubious reputation, perhaps a carryover from the medieval European association of stringed instruments with the Devil, and associated with the music of marginalized regions (the South, Latin America) and people (sailors and railway men, sharecroppers and hobos, blacks, Latinos, and poor southern whites). A lot of the put-downs aimed at young rock 'n' rollers by the mainstream music press of the 1950s ridiculed the guitar, suggesting that it was an instrument that anyone could play (if you believe *that*, we suggest that you take a few guitar lessons!). The electric guitar became a symbol of the energetic diversity that was elbowing its way into the mainstream of American popular music during this period. This feeling of excess and invasion was reinforced by the development of portable tube amplifiers, which, if pushed hard enough, could provide a dense, sizzling, and very loud sound, eventually augmented by special effects devices such as wah-wah pedals and "fuzz boxes," and perfectly designed to drive parents and other authority figures nuts. In addition, the suitability of the guitar for use as a phallic symbol—a formerly male practice more recently appropriated by female rockers—has added to the instrument's aura of danger and excitement.

LISTENING AND ANALYSIS   "MAYBELLENE"

Basic Description

Charles Edward Anderson ("Chuck") Berry (b. 1926) burst precipitously onto the pop music scene with his first record, "Maybellene." It was a novel synthesis that did not sound precisely like anything before it, and it introduced listeners to an already fully formed style of songwriting, singing, and guitar playing that would exercise a primal influence on virtually all the rock 'n' roll to follow.

Berry was born in California but grew up in St. Louis, where he absorbed blues and rhythm & blues styles. He was one of the first black musicians to consciously forge his own version of these styles for appeal to the mass market—and he was certainly the most successful of his generation in this effort. Like many other black musicians, Berry also knew country music, and he found that his performances of country songs in clubs appealed strongly to the white members of his audience. He put this knowledge and experience to good use: "Maybellene" was distantly modeled on a country number called "Ida Red." Nevertheless, the primary elements of "Maybellene" trace their roots clearly to rhythm & blues: the thick, buzzing timbre of Berry's electric guitar (see Box 8.2); the blue notes and slides in both voice and guitar; the socking backbeat of the drum; and the form, derived from twelve-bar blues structures.

Chuck Berry in 1959.
Courtesy Library of Congress.

What, then, made "Maybellene" sound so startlingly new? The explosive tempo, for one thing; while swing bands occasionally may have played for dancing at a tempo like this, no vocal-based rhythm & blues had ever gone at this pace, because it's exceptionally hard to articulate words, and have time to breathe, when trying to sing at this tempo. But Berry pulls it off, articulating the words with clarity and remarkable force. This brings up another essential aspect of the record's novelty and appeal, which is the lyrics themselves. The lyrics to "Maybellene" provide an original and clever description of a lovers' quarrel in the form of a car chase, complete with a punning invented verb form (*motorvatin'*), humorous details ("Rain water blowin'" under the automobile hood, which is "doin' my motor good"), and a breathless ending in which the singer catches Maybellene in her Cadillac at the top of a hill—an ending that still leaves listeners room to imagine a wide range of sequels. And what could reach out to a young audience more effectively than a story featuring both cars and sex appeal?

In addition, we shouldn't miss the implied class distinction the lyrics make between Maybellene, in her top-of-the-line Cadillac Coupe de Ville, and the narrator, in his more humble, middle-class, but eminently functional "V-8 Ford." As he chases and finally catches the Cadillac (and Maybellene), there is a sense of the underdog's triumphing in the race, and the boastful claim of the first verse, that nothing could outrun his V-8 Ford, is vindicated. (Cars have long been an important status symbol in American culture, and African American culture is certainly no exception to this. A song recorded by Bessie Smith in 1928, a generation before "Maybellene," called "Put It Right Here (Or Keep It Out There)," described the singer's deadbeat lover as follows: "Once he was like a Cadillac, now he's like an old worn-out Ford." The concern with cars persists into contemporary rap music; an early example of this is "Sucker M.C.'s," a 1983 hit by Run-D.M.C.).

All the basic ingredients that would inform a string of successive, successful Chuck Berry records are present in "Maybellene." These elements became his trademarks: an arresting instrumental introduction for unaccompanied electric guitar; relentless intensity produced by a very fast tempo and a very loud volume level; formal and stylistic elements strongly related to earlier rhythm & blues music; and witty lyrics, clearly enunciated and designed to appeal to the lifestyle and aspirations of his young audience.

Form

The form of "Maybellene" is clearly based on the twelve-bar blues. The **chorus** ("Maybellene, why can't you be true?") adheres to the traditional twelve-bar structure in every respect: three four-bar phrases, standard chord pattern, even the three-line poetic arrangement where the second line is a repetition of the first. But the **verses,** while twelve bars long, completely suppress chord changes, remaining on the "home" (or **tonic**) chord throughout while the voice delivers rapid-fire lyrics using brief, repetitive patterns of notes (see listening chart). Ironically, by eliminating chord changes and restricting melodic interest in the verses, Berry turns what could have been a static, purely strophic form into something more dynamic. Instead of a string of standard twelve-bar blues stanzas, we hear an alternating verse-chorus structure that allows Berry to tell his story, and to build his record, in a more exciting way.

The stripped-down music of the verses focuses all attention on their lyrics—which is appropriate, as it is the verses that relate the ongoing progress of the car chase. Their repetitive melodic formulas allow Berry to concentrate on articulating the densely packed words; the continuous verbal activity more than compensates for the lack of musical variety. Actually, the verses build enormous tension, so that when the choruses at last bring some chord changes—basic as they are—there is a feeling of release and expansion. The pace of the lyrics also slows down momentarily for the choruses, which reinforces this effect of expansion and allows Berry to lean expressively on the crucial name "Maybel*lene*." Yet, while the choruses provide variety and release, they create tension of another sort, as they postpone the continuation of the story being told in the verses. This same effect is created on a larger scale by the instrumental break before the final verse: variety and release on the one hand (and an opportunity for Berry to showcase his considerable guitar chops), along with a real sense of racing along down the highway, but tension and postponement of the story's climax on the other.

The manipulation of a limited set of musical materials to achieve maximal results of variety, novelty, and excitement is the essence of effective rock 'n' roll. "Maybellene" is an outstanding case in point. The formal issues discussed above may seem either obvious or all but lost in the pure visceral intensity of the record, but the seamlessness of Chuck Berry's artistry should not blind us to the man's brilliance. Above all, "Maybellene" is a beautifully formed record, building inexorably from start to finish, where everything is made to count, without a single word or note wasted.

The Song/The Recording

In Chuck Berry's "Maybellene," the song *is* the recording. When people think of or cite "Maybellene," they are referring to Berry's original recording of it—the ultimate, and really the only important, source material. The culture of rock 'n' roll centered to an unprecedented extent on records: records played on the radio, records played at dances, records purchased for home listening. Studio recordings thus increasingly came to represent the original, primary documents of the music, often preceding and generally taking precedence over any live performances of the material. Baby boomers went to hear rock 'n' roll stars perform the hits they already knew from the records they heard and bought; on the nationally broadcast television program *American Bandstand,* singers came without accompanying bands and lip-synched their songs while the records played in the background. The issuing of sheet music was becoming an afterthought, an ancillary to the recording. In many future discussions, consequently, we will be discussing the song and the recording as one, rather than as separate entities.

The record opens arrestingly with the sound of Berry's hollow-body electric guitar playing a bluesy lick that literally sizzles with sonic energy. The impact of "Maybellene" is in no small part due to the infectious rhythmic groove and texture established by Berry and a gifted group of sidemen, including the great blues composer and bassist Willie Dixon, an integral part of Muddy Waters's recordings for Chess Records (see Chapter 7); Jerome Green, whose maracas were central to the Bo Diddley sound; and pianist Johnny Johnson, who may well have played a role in the creation of Berry's songs. Some credit for the overall sound of the recording must also go to Phil and Leonard Chess, who in their years of recording Chicago blues musicians such as Muddy Waters and Howlin' Wolf had learned how to stay out of the way of a good recording. They sometimes offered advice but never tried to radically alter a musician's style for commercial effect.

Amid the numerous elements borrowed from rhythm & blues and urban blues, we may hear in "Maybellene" a prominent, very regular, and *un*syncopated bass line, alternating between two notes on beats 1 and 3 of each bar. The rhythmic feel of this bass line is stylistically much more suggestive of country music than of anything found typically in rhythm & blues, and its presence here points to Berry's knowledge of country music and to what Berry himself has identified as the country origins of "Maybellene." As we shall see repeatedly, rock 'n' roll music is often based on a synthesis of widely diverse stylistic elements.

LISTENING CHART "MAYBELLENE"

Music and lyrics by Chuck Berry (also credited to disc jockeys Russel Fratto and Alan Freed);[1] as performed by Chuck Berry and His Combo; recorded 1955

FORM	LYRICS	DESCRIPTIVE COMMENTS
Instrumental intro		Solo electric guitar "hook" establishes characteristic sound (suggesting auto horns) and tempo.
Chorus	*Maybellene . . .*	Twelve-bar blues.
Verse 1	*As I was . . .*	Twelve bars, without any chord changes; very fast pacing of lyrics.
Chorus	*Maybellene . . .*	As before.
Verse 2	*The Cadillac . . .*	As in verse 1.
Chorus	*Maybellene . . .*	As before.
Instrumental break		Two successive twelve-bar sections.
Chorus	*Maybellene . . .*	As before.
Verse 3	*The motor . . .*	As in verse 1.
Chorus	*Maybellene . . .*	As before.
Instrumental coda		Fades out.

EARLY ROCK 'N' ROLL STARS ON THE R&B SIDE

We will represent the rhythm & blues–based side of rock 'n' roll with the three most prominent African Americans to be identified with the new music. Of the three, Chuck Berry was the songwriter/performer who most obviously addressed his songs to teenage America (white and black) in the 1950s; Little Richard was the cultivator of a deliberately outrageous performance style that appealed on the basis of its strangeness, novelty, and sexual ambiguity; and Fats Domino's work most directly embodied the continuity of rhythm & blues with rock 'n' roll. As might be expected from this description, Domino was the earliest of the three to become an established performer (although he was slightly younger than Berry)—he cut his first rhythm & blues hit, "The Fat Man," in 1949 at the age of twenty-one. But all three crossed over to the

---

1. In the early years of rock 'n' roll, the record market was fluid and unpredictable, and agents, promoters, distributors, and disc jockeys were often given (or would take) songwriting credits in exchange for the "favor" of pushing particular artists or records. There was nothing new in this practice; it just became much more widespread. In any case, it is doubtful that Fratto and Freed had anything substantial to do with the creation of "Maybellene," although they certainly helped it to be heard and to become popular.

pop charts and mainstream success within the first few months following the massive success of Bill Haley's "Rock around the Clock" (see Box 8.1).

Chuck Berry

After the success of "Maybellene," Chuck Berry went on to write and record other excellent rock 'n' roll songs that became more and more explicit celebrations of American teenage culture and its music. "Roll Over Beethoven" (1956) praises rhythm & blues at the expense of classical music. "School Day" (Number Eight pop, Number One R&B in 1957) describes drudgery relieved by an after-school trip to the "juke joint," at which point the record becomes literally an advertisement for itself and an anthem for the music it represents: "Hail! Hail! Rock 'n' roll! Deliver me from the days of old!" "Rock and Roll Music" (Number Eight pop, Number Six R&B, also in 1957) articulates the virtues of its subject, as opposed to the limitations of "modern jazz" or a "symphony." "Sweet Little Sixteen" (Number Two pop, Number One R&B in 1958) wittily describes the young collector of "famed autographs," coping with growing up ("tight dresses and lipstick"), for whom a rock 'n' roll show becomes—in her mind, at least—a national party where all the "cats" want to dance with her.

Berry's consummate statement on rock 'n' roll mythology is doubtless "Johnny B. Goode" (Number Eight pop, Number Five R&B in 1958). Here he relates the story of a "country boy" who "never learned to read or write so well" but who "could play a guitar just like a-ringin' a bell." (Berry's autobiography states that the "country boy" was originally a "colored boy," but Berry opted to make his tale colorblind, recognizing the diversity of his audience and the potential universality of his myth.) The boy's mother predicts his coming success as a bandleader with his "name in lights, saying 'Johnny B. Goode tonight' "—as one of pop music's greatest verbal puns embodies the dream of every teenager with a guitar and a wish to succeed as a rock 'n' roller (with parental approval and appreciation, no less)!

It cannot be known how many careers in music were inspired or encouraged by "Johnny B. Goode," but a list of pop musicians who have been obviously and singularly influenced by Chuck Berry would read like a who's who of rock stars from the 1960s and beyond. He is probably the only musician of his generation to be inescapably influential on three different, and essential, fronts: as a brilliantly clever and articulate lyricist and songwriter; as a fine rock 'n' roll vocal stylist; and as a pioneering electric guitarist. The mass adulation belonged to Elvis Presley, but the greatest influence on musicians unquestionably was made by Berry.

Little Richard

The centrality of records to the culture of rock 'n' roll didn't negate the significance of live performances. Indeed, live performances disseminated via the new mass medium of television, or on the movie screen, assumed a new importance for performers of rock 'n' roll music, and individual artists and vocal groups sought to cultivate visual characteristics or mannerisms that would set them apart from others and encourage listeners to remember them—and to go out and buy their records. Chuck Berry had his famous "duck walk" as a stage device. But no performer in the early years of rock 'n' roll was as visually flamboyant as Little Richard.

Richard Wayne Penniman ("Little Richard") (b. 1932) spent several lackluster years as a journeyman rhythm & blues performer before hitting the pop charts early

Little Richard in 1957. Frank Driggs Collection.

in 1956 with his wild performance of the nonsensical song "Tutti-Frutti." Based on the twelve-bar blues, "Tutti-Frutti" alternated nonsense choruses ("Tutti-frutti, au rutti, a-wop-bop-a-loom-op a-lop-bam-boom!"—and variants thereof) with non-specific but obviously leering verses ("I got a gal named Sue, she knows just what to do"), all delivered by Little Richard in an uninhibited shouting style complete with falsetto whoops and accompanied with a pounding band led by Little Richard's equally uninhibited piano. In retrospect, it seems surprising that records like "Tutti-Frutti" and its even more successful—and more obviously salacious—follow-up, "Long Tall Sally" (see listening chart, p. 224) got played on mainstream radio at all. It must have been assumed by programmers that Little Richard was a novelty act and that therefore nobody would pay attention to, or understand, the words of his songs. But teenage listeners in the 1950s certainly understood that Little Richard embodied the new spirit of rock 'n' roll music in the most extroverted, outrageous, and original way.

Any doubts on the matter would surely have been resolved by seeing Little Richard's performances in any of the three rock 'n' roll movies in which he appeared during the two years of his greatest popular success, 1956–57: *Don't Knock the Rock, The Girl Can't Help It,* and *Mister Rock 'n' Roll.* Heavily made up, with his hair in an enormous pompadour, rolling his eyes, playing the piano while standing and gyrating wildly, Little Richard epitomized the abandon celebrated in rock 'n' roll lyrics and music. (Although new to his audiences, Richard's appearance and approach to performance had clear antecedents, going back to vaudeville and minstrelsy.) Both the sound of his recordings and the visual characteristics of his performances made Little Richard an exceptionally strong influence on later performers; the white rockabilly singer-pianist Jerry Lee Lewis was inestimably in his debt, and in the 1960s the English Beatles and the American Creedence Clearwater Revival—along with many other bands—played music whose roots could readily be traced back to Little Richard. Moreover, the lingering (and carefully crafted) ambiguity of Little Richard's sexual identity—available evidence suggests that he might best have been classified in the early days as an omnivore—paved the way for the image of performers such as David Bowie, Elton John, and Prince.

Our representative example of Little Richard's music is "Long Tall Sally" (see the listening chart). Like most of Little Richard's songs, this one is built on the twelve-bar blues. Like Chuck Berry and other artists who came out of rhythm & blues to seek pop stardom, Little Richard adapted the twelve-bar blues structure so as to reflect the more traditionally pop-friendly format of verse-chorus. Here, the first four bars of each blues stanza are set to changing words—**verses**—while the remaining eight bars, with unchanging words, function as a repeated **chorus.** This simple but surprisingly effective formal arrangement is reflected in both identical and varied ways in many rock 'n' roll songs of the period; for examples of variations on this structure, see the listening charts for Elvis Presley's "Don't Be Cruel" and for the Coasters' "Charlie Brown."

Fats Domino

Antoine "Fats" Domino (b. 1928), a singer, pianist, and songwriter, had been an established presence on the rhythm & blues charts for several years by the time he scored his first large-scale pop breakthrough with "Ain't It a Shame" in 1955 (Number Ten pop, Number One R&B). In this case, mainstream success was simply the result of the market's catching up with Domino; there is no significant stylistic difference between his earlier rhythm & blues hits and his rock 'n' roll bestsellers like "I'm in Love Again" and "I'm Walkin'." Domino himself remarked that he was always playing the same music, that they called it "rhythm & blues" first and "rock 'n' roll" later, and that it made no difference to him—although it surely did make a difference to him when the rock 'n' roll market catapulted his record sales into the millions and eventually made him the second biggest-selling recording artist of the 1950s, right behind Elvis Presley.

Domino was born in New Orleans and grew up bathed in the rich and diverse musical traditions of that city. His distinctive regional style best exemplifies the strong connections between rock 'n' roll and earlier pop music. Jazz, especially boogie-woogie (see Chapter 6), was a strong early influence on him, along with the rhythm & blues piano style of Professor Longhair (1918–80; real name Henry Roeland Byrd) and the jump band style of trumpeter Dave Bartholomew's ensemble. Bartholomew became Domino's arranger, producer, and songwriting partner, and their collaboration produced a remarkable string of consistently fine and successful records. Their "New Orleans" sound was also widely admired and imitated among musicians; Domino played piano on hit records by other artists, and Little Richard recorded in New Orleans to use the city's distinctive sidemen and thus try to capture some of the city's rock 'n' roll magic. (Little Richard's "Long Tall Sally" is modeled directly on Domino's "Ain't It a Shame," both in formal layout and musical arrangement.)

Given his strong links to tradition, it is not surprising that Fats Domino recorded a number of standards—in contradistinction to artists like Chuck Berry and Little

Fats Domino and his band, in a scene from the 1958 movie *The Big Beat*. Courtesy Library of Congress.

Richard, who concentrated on novel songs and styles to appeal to their new audience. In fact, Domino's 1956 remake of "Blueberry Hill" proved to be his most popular record, reaching the Number Two position on the pop charts and topping the R&B charts. "Blueberry Hill" was a Tin Pan Alley tune that had originally been a big hit in 1940 for the Glenn Miller Orchestra (with vocal by Ray Eberle). Domino preserved his own rhythm & blues–based style when performing "Blueberry Hill" and other standards, however, thus bringing a new kind of musical hybrid to mass-market attention, and with this phenomenon a new and important musical bridge was crossed. We might say that, rather than crossing over himself, Domino made the music cross over to him. Smooth Tin Pan Alley–style crooning and uninflected urban diction were replaced by Domino's rhythmically accented, full-throated singing in his characteristic New Orleans accent, and it certainly wasn't the sound of a sweet band backing him or shaping his own piano accompaniment. Another pop success for Domino was his rocking uptempo version of "My Blue Heaven," which makes a striking and amusing contrast to Gene Austin's original recording (see Chapter 4).

Fats Domino, Little Richard, and Chuck Berry all achieved their successes recording on independent labels, thus demonstrating the great importance of the indies to the popularization of rock 'n' roll. Domino recorded for Imperial, a Los Angeles–based concern headed by Lew Chudd, that also issued records by the important rhythm & blues electric guitar stylist Aaron "T-Bone" Walker. Little Richard was an artist for Specialty Records, Art Rupe's Hollywood label, that had on its

Box 8.3 Tin Pan Alley Lives! The Standard in the Age of Rock 'n' Roll

The advent of rock 'n' roll is often viewed as the death of Tin Pan Alley. It is easy to see why this would seem to be so. Country- and rhythm & blues–based musical styles were moving to the center of the pop world from the peripheries, and Tin Pan Alley music was the mainstream music of the generation that the baby boomers were rebelling against: it was their parents' music. However, the Tin Pan Alley style proved versatile enough to survive, and even to flourish, in a number of different guises during the early years of rock 'n' roll.

Fats Domino was not the only rock 'n' roller to successfully adapt standard songs to a rhythm & blues–based style. The procedure was a stock in trade of many black vocal groups; the Platters virtually made a career of it, scoring Number One hits with "My Prayer" (1956), "Twilight Time" (1958), and "Smoke Gets in Your Eyes" (1959). These were all Tin Pan Alley tunes, dressed up with strong backbeats and a commanding, extroverted lead vocal, that were accepted by young listeners as rock 'n' roll ballads. From the country side, Elvis Presley included Tin Pan Alley standards in his performing repertoire from the beginning of his career with Sun Records, and in 1959 the country artist Carl Mann achieved a pop hit with his rockabilly version of "Mona Lisa," a song that had been a huge success in 1950 for Nat "King" Cole as a Tin Pan Alley–style ballad.

Furthermore, new songs in the old Tin Pan Alley style could be found on the pop charts even in the late 1950s, right along with the new rock 'n' roll hits. In what might seem one of the unlikeliest musical success stories of the era, the young singer Johnny Mathis (born 1935, the same year as Elvis Presley) began a career in 1957 as a latter-day crooner with gentle pop ballads like "It's Not for Me to Say" and "Chances Are," and soon found himself a best-selling recording artist who appealed as much to the rock 'n' roll generation as he did to their parents. Mathis's widespread acceptance makes one hesitate to call his approach anachronistic and demonstrates again the fluidity of pop music styles and trends during this period.

Perhaps the most remarkable manifestation of Tin Pan Alley endurance may be found in the career and recordings of Frank Sinatra during the 1950s. Sinatra's status as *the* pop icon of the 1940s (see Chapter 7) seemed well on the wane in the opening years of the new decade; his records were no longer selling well, and by 1952 Columbia had allowed his contract to lapse. Reluctantly picked up by Capitol Records, Sinatra turned to the adult audience and to the new medium of the long-playing record album to reinvent himself, and he spectacularly revived his career. This involved a rethinking of the standard Tin Pan Alley repertoire, along with some novel ideas about the possibilities inherent in the pop album format.

Working with distinguished arranger/conductors like Billy May and Nelson Riddle, Sinatra conceived fresh interpretations of standards that renovated these old songs and, in some cases, brought new and unexpected meanings to them. One of the most famous examples of this is Sinatra's 1956 recording of

"I've Got You under My Skin," a Cole Porter standard from the 1930s. The song most readily suggests a mood of acquiescence—of giving in to the condition of being obsessed by, and possessed by, another. But Sinatra's interpretation brings a novel and occasionally aggressive intensity to the song, as if the singer is surprised and even somewhat at war with his own newly discovered sense of vulnerability. This version uncovers new layers of richness and potential in a song that other singers and listeners might just have taken for granted in the 1950s, and Sinatra managed to do this with many of the standards he recorded during this decade. Furthermore, Sinatra presented these standards not as single records but in groups, in albums that were designed by him and his arranger/conductors as complete and integrated listening experiences, as opposed to essentially random collections of single songs. For example, "I've Got You under My Skin" was on the album *Songs for Swingin' Lovers*, where Sinatra's distinctive interpretation of Cole Porter's standard clearly meshed with the active, worldly implications of the album's theme. Among other Sinatra albums from this period that present standards in thematically unified groups are *In the Wee Small Hours* (1955, a collection of world-weary "saloon" songs) and *Come Dance with Me* (1959). Although the term did not come into common use until the mid-1960s, it is arguable that Sinatra's are the first real *concept albums* (see Chapter 10). Like the songs within them, these albums have themselves become "standards" of pop excellence and innovation.

Spurred by his new success as an album artist, Sinatra also sought out good new material in the Tin Pan Alley mold to reestablish a strong presence on the pop singles charts. Many of these songs came from movies—a medium through which Sinatra also reinvigorated his career in the 1950s, by appearing successfully as a dramatic actor in nonmusical films, in addition to starring in musicals. One of Sinatra's major hits of this period, "Love and Marriage," which he introduced in 1955 on a television production of the Thornton Wilder play *Our Town*, found new life—and a new audience—as the theme song for another television show in the 1980s, the long-running comedy *Married with Children*. By this time, Sinatra, in his seventies, was himself the longest-running superstar in the history of American popular music.

---

roster such rhythm & blues stars as Percy Mayfield, Lloyd Price, and Guitar Slim, along with important African American gospel groups and soloists. Berry's records were issued on Chess, the Chicago label of the Chess brothers Leonard and Phil, that also served as home for an impressive list of blues-based artists like Muddy Waters, Howlin' Wolf, and Willie Dixon, along with other rock 'n' rollers like Bo Diddley and the Moonglows.

EARLY ROCK 'N' ROLL STARS ON THE COUNTRY SIDE

Elvis Presley

The biggest rock 'n' roll star to come from the country side of the music world was of course Elvis Presley. Presley's early career with the independent label Sun

Records was briefly considered in the previous discussion of "Mystery Train." When RCA Victor bought out Presley's contract from Sun in late 1955, at the then-extravagant price of thirty-five thousand dollars, this mainstream major label set about consciously trying to turn the "hillbilly cat" into a mainstream performer without compromising the strength of his appeal to teenagers. In this they were assisted by two major players. First, there was Presley's manager, Colonel Thomas Parker, who saw to it that Presley was seen repeatedly on television variety shows and in a series of romantic Hollywood films. Second was RCA's Nashville **producer** Chet Atkins, who saw to it that Presley's records for the label were made pop-friendly, according to Atkins's standards. (In the 1960s Atkins became the producer most credited with developing the "Nashville Sound" of pop-oriented country music; see Chapter 10.) They succeeded beyond anyone's expectations. Although Presley's television performances were denounced by authorities as vulgar because of the singer's hip-shaking gyrations, the shows were attended by hordes of screaming young fans and were admired on the screen by millions of young viewers. And Presley's records racked up astronomical sales as he dominated the top of the pop charts steadily from 1956 on into the early 1960s, quickly establishing himself as the biggest-selling solo artist of rock 'n' roll, and then as the biggest-selling solo recording artist of *any* period and style—a title he still holds at the beginning of the twenty-first century!

Presley's biggest hit, "Don't Be Cruel," topped the charts for eleven weeks in the late summer and fall of 1956, eventually yielding pride of place to another Presley record, "Love Me Tender." "Don't Be Cruel" is based on the twelve-bar blues (see the listening chart below). Presley's vocal is heavy with blues-derived and country inflections; we hear a striking regional accent, and the occasional "hiccuping" effect ("baby, it's just you I'm *a*-thinkin' of") is one associated particularly with rockabilly singers like Presley, Gene Vincent, and Buddy Holly. The strong backbeat throughout evokes rhythm & blues, while the repeated electric guitar figure at the opening is reminiscent of rhythmic ideas favored by western swing bands (and ultimately derived from boogie-woogie). Imposed on all these diverse and intense stylistic elements is a wash of electronic **reverb**—an attempt by the engineers at RCA's Nashville studios to emulate the distinctive (and decidedly low-tech) "slap-back" echo sound of Presley's previous recordings on Sun Records. There is also the sweetening sound of the backing vocal group, the Jordanaires, whose precise "bop, bop"s and crooning "aah"s and "ooo"s are doubly rooted in white gospel music and in the most genteel, established, mainstream pop style. Whether this odd amalgam is deemed to work as a source of stylistic enrichment, or whether listening to Presley and the Jordanaires together on this record seems like listening to the Chords and the Crew Cuts *simultaneously* performing "Sh-Boom" (see the preceding discussion of cover versions) will obviously be a matter of personal taste. It can never be known how much the Jordanaires added, or if they added at all, to the appeal of this and many other records Presley made with them for RCA. But the commercial success of these records was unprecedented, and their mixture of styles was yet another indication of the extent to which the traditional barriers in pop music were falling down. (Major labels often tended to sweeten recordings by rock 'n' roll singers for the mass market, while the indies went for a rawer, more basic sound. For example, many of

Frank Sinatra and **Elvis Presley** on television together in 1960: it looks like the young "idol" is trying to teach the older "idol" some new moves. Frank Driggs Collection.

Jackie Wilson's rhythm & blues–based recordings for the Brunswick label—a subsidiary of the major Decca—featured elaborately arranged backing choruses and orchestral arrangements.)

On the other side of "Don't Be Cruel" was Presley's version of "Hound Dog," a song that had been a major rhythm & blues hit in 1953 for Big Mama Thornton. Comparing Presley's cover of "Hound Dog" for RCA with the earlier cover he did for Sun of the rhythm & blues tune "Mystery Train" sheds further light on the shaping of Elvis's image for mainstream consumption. Whereas his rockabilly "Mystery Train" is noticeably faster, looser, and wilder than Junior Parker's original, his "Hound Dog" has lost some of its teeth—so to speak—as a result of the bowdlerization of the original words. Big Mama Thornton's version is full of sexual innuendo, making it clear that the term "hound dog" is being used metaphorically, not literally ("daddy, I know you ain't no real cool cat"; "you can wag your tail, but I ain't gonna feed you no more"; see the discussion in Chapter 7). Such sexual implications are gone in Presley's rendition, which seems to be literally about a pathetic mutt who is "cryin' all the time" and "ain't never caught a rabbit." With the lyrics cleaned up in this way for mass consumption, the undeniable passion of Presley's performance seems a bit over the top for the subject matter, turning the record into a kind of novelty song. But this certainly didn't bother the singer's audience, most of whom could not have been familiar with Thornton's original anyway; "Hound Dog" proved just about as popular as "Don't Be Cruel" itself.

Presley's extraordinary popularity established rock 'n' roll as an unprecedented mass-market phenomenon. His reputation as a performer and recording artist endured up to his death in 1977 at the age of forty-two—and continues beyond the grave; Graceland, his home in Memphis, Tennessee, is now a public museum dedicated to his memory and it is visited by upwards of 600,000 people annually. Presley gave strong performances and made fine records at many points throughout his career, and he starred in many movies. But it cannot be denied that Elvis Presley's principal importance as a musical influence and innovator—like that of Chuck Berry, Little Richard, and Fats Domino—rests upon his achievements during the early years of rock 'n' roll. In 1956 Presley cut a handful of records that literally changed the world for himself and for those around him, and the unbridled exuberance of his live performances at that time were the model for every white kid who wanted to move mountains by strumming a guitar, shaking his hips, and lifting his voice.

Buddy Holly

Buddy Holly (Charles Hardin Holley) (1936–59) offered an image virtually the opposite of Presley's intense, aggressive, suggestively sexual stage persona. Here was a clean-cut, lanky, bespectacled young man—obviously nobody's idea of a matinee idol—but one who certainly knew his way around a guitar and a recording studio. The Texas-born Holly began his career with country music but soon fell under the influence of Presley's musical style and success and formed a rock 'n' roll band, the Crickets.

Holly's first record in his new style, "That'll Be the Day," rose to Number One on the pop charts in late 1957 and established his characteristic and highly influential sound. "That'll Be the Day" combined elements of country, rhythm & blues, and mainstream pop in the kind of synthesis that typified rock 'n' roll in a general sense, but which nevertheless projected a distinctive approach and sensibility. Holly's vocal style, full of country twang and hiccups, along with expressive **blue notes,** projected that mixture of toughness and vulnerability that forms the essence of both fine country singing and fine blues singing. The Crickets' instrumental lineup of two electric guitars (lead and rhythm), electric bass, and drums provided

Buddy Holly. Frank Driggs Collection.

an intense support for Holly's voice, and during instrumental breaks, Holly's lead guitar playing was active, riff-based, and hard-edged in a way that reflected the influence of Chuck Berry. "That'll Be the Day" is structured like a typical pop song, alternating verses and choruses of eight bars each; but when it comes time to provide an instrumental break, the Crickets play a twelve-bar blues pattern. This works, because important aspects of both vocal and instrumental style throughout the record are based on blues- and rhythm & blues–derived elements. On some later records, like "Oh, Boy!" and "Peggy Sue," Holly used a twelve-bar blues structure for the song itself.

Buddy Holly's career was tragically cut short when he was twenty-two by a plane crash that also claimed the lives of two other prominent rock 'n' roll personalities: the promising seventeen-year-old Chicano singer and songwriter Ritchie Valens, and the Big Bopper (J. P. Richardson), who had achieved success with novelty records. A measure of Holly's importance for later pop music may be seen in the fact that the Beatles modeled their insect-based name, their four-piece instrumental lineup, and aspects of their vocal style on the Crickets—and through the Beatles, of course, the influence passed on to innumerable bands. Holly was also, like Chuck Berry, an important rock 'n' roll songwriter; in addition to the songs already mentioned, he wrote and recorded "Everyday," "Not Fade Away," "Rave On," and others, which became increasingly popular in the years after his death and were covered by rock bands. Furthermore, Holly's work with arrangements and studio effects looked forward to some of the recording techniques of the 1960s. He frequently used *double-tracking* on his recordings—a technique in which two nearly identical versions of the same vocal or instrumental part are recorded on top of one another, foregrounding that part so that it seems to come right out of the speaker at the listener—and some of his last records used orchestral strings.

LISTENING COMPARISON OF TWO BLUES-BASED ROCK 'N' ROLL SONGS: "LONG TALL SALLY" AND "DON'T BE CRUEL"

LISTENING CHART "LONG TALL SALLY"

Music and lyrics credited to Enotris Johnson, Richard Penniman, and Robert Blackwell; as performed by Little Richard and unidentified band; recorded 1956

FORM	LYRICS	DESCRIPTIVE COMMENTS
Verse 1	*Gonna tell Aunt Mary . . .*	Underlying rhythmic and chord structure is that of the twelve-bar blues, with the first four bars constituting the verse and the final eight bars the chorus; loud,
Chorus	*Oh, baby . . .*	flamboyant vocal style throughout.
Verse 2	*Well, Long Tall Sally . . .*	Twelve-bar blues pattern persists throughout the song.
Chorus	*Oh, baby . . .*	
Verse 3	*Well, I saw Uncle John . . .*	
Chorus	*Oh, baby . . .*	
Instrumental break		Two twelve-bar blues sections; intense saxophone solo reflects the mood of the vocal.
Repetition of verse 2 + chorus, then verse 3 + chorus		
Conclusion	*We're gonna have some fun tonight . . .*	Extended choruslike section; twelve-bar blues structure.

LISTENING CHART "DON'T BE CRUEL"

Music and lyrics by Otis Blackwell and Elvis Presley;[2] as performed by Elvis Presley, vocal and guitar, with the Jordanaires and backing instrumentalists; recorded 1956

FORM	LYRICS	DESCRIPTIVE COMMENTS
Instrumental intro		Repetitive guitar hook, strong backbeat (four bars long)
Verse 1	*If you know . . .*	Twelve-bar blues structure, arranged to suggest a verse-chorus pattern, with the first eight bars constituting the verse and
Chorus	*Don't be cruel . . .*	the final four bars the chorus.

[2]Presley, though not generally known as a songwriter, was credited as coauthor of a handful of his early hits for RCA.

Verse 2	*Baby, if I made you mad . . .*	Twelve-bar blues structure, with an extension added (six bars in length) to the chorus.
Chorus + extension	*Don't be cruel . . .* *I don't want . . .*	
Verse 3	*Don't stop a-thinkin' of me . . .*	Twelve-bar blues, plus extension (as before).
Chorus + extension	*Don't be cruel . . .* *Why should we . . .*	
Verse 4	*Let's walk up . . .*	Twelve-bar blues, plus extension (as before).
Chorus + extension	*Don't be cruel . . .* *I don't want . . .*	
Concluding chorus +	*Don't be cruel . . .*	
Additional extension	*Don't be cruel . . .* *I don't want . . .*	

SONGWRITERS AND PRODUCERS OF EARLY ROCK 'N' ROLL

The relatively clear lines of division between songwriters and performers that characterized the world of mainstream pop music up to around 1955 no longer held up in the early years of rock 'n' roll's mainstream success. This is because the roots of rock 'n' roll lie with rhythm & blues and country music, areas of activity where, as we have seen, performers often wrote their own songs and, conversely, songwriters frequently performed and recorded their own works. Of the five early rock 'n' roll stars we have discussed in detail, only Elvis Presley did not regularly write his own material. This diminishing importance of the independent songwriter represented another major shift brought about by the rock 'n' roll revolution. In time, it came to be expected that performers would be the composers of their own songs, and this led to a correspondingly stronger identification of artists with specific material. Here lie the origins of the mystique of the pop music personality as a creative artist, rather than as merely an interpreter—a mystique that came into its own in the later 1960s.

None of this meant that important nonperforming songwriters ceased to exist, of course. As we shall see in the next chapter, the early 1960s actually brought a renewed emphasis on songwriting as an independent craft, prior to the heyday of songwriting bands like the Beatles and songwriter-performers like Bob Dylan. And with the increasing importance of the recording itself as the basic document of rock 'n' roll music, another behind-the-scenes job grew steadily in importance in the later 1950s and the early 1960s: that of the record **producer.** Producers could be responsible for many things, from booking time in the recording studio, to hiring backup singers and instrumentalists, to assisting with the engineering process. Essentially, though, the producer was responsible for the characteristic *sound* of the finished record, and the best producers left as strong a sense of individual personality on their products as did the recording artists themselves. When the producer and the songwriter were the same person (or persons), his or her importance and influence could be powerful indeed.

This was the case with the most innovative songwriting/producing team of the early rock 'n' roll years, <u>Jerry Leiber</u> and <u>Mike Stoller</u> (both born 1933). Leiber and Stoller were not recording artists, but they were already writing rhythm & blues songs when they were teenagers. Eventually they wrote and produced many hits for Elvis Presley, and they did the same for one of the most popular vocal groups of this period, the Coasters. (They also produced and did occasional writing for the Drifters, and the elaborately produced orchestral sound of these records in the early 1960s was possibly even more influential than Leiber and Stoller's previous records had been in the later 1950s.) The team constructed what they called "playlets" for the Coasters, scenes from teenage life of the 1950s distilled into brilliantly funny rock 'n' roll records. Like many by Chuck Berry, the Coasters' hits were specifically about, and for, their intended audience. An examination of "Charlie Brown" will enable us to appreciate in detail this targeting of the teenage audience, along with the vocal artistry of the Coasters and the behind-the-scenes writing and production artistry of Leiber and Stoller.

LISTENING AND ANALYSIS   "CHARLIE BROWN"

Basic Description

"Charlie Brown" presents an indelible portrait of a ubiquitous figure, the class clown. Although such a song topic would probably not have occurred to anyone prior to the 1950s, it certainly made an effective choice at a point when, for the first time ever, the biggest market of potential record buyers consisted of schoolkids: the junior high schoolers and high schoolers, even elementary schoolers, each of whom probably knew a "Charlie Brown" in at least one of his or her classes. The specific time period and culture of the 1950s is evoked through a sparing but telling use of then-current slang terms like "cool" and "daddy-o."

From the first arresting vocal hook, "Fee fee, fie fie, fo fo, fum," the record brims with unrelenting high energy. Like Chuck Berry, the Coasters were adept at delivering a dense, cleverly worded text very clearly at a fast tempo. The intensity of the Coasters' vocal style owes much to rhythm & blues, although certain comic effects—like the low bass voice repeatedly asking, "Why's everybody always pickin' on me?" and asking, "Who, me?" in the bridge—suggest roots going back to vaudeville routines. (The low bass voice was also a staple element of rhythm & blues group singing style; see the discussion of the Chords' "Sh-Boom" previously in this chapter.) Highly effective are the contrasts between passages that are essentially vocal solos, with occasional, minimal contributions by the rhythm instruments (at the start of each A section—see the listening chart), and the following passages where the full band offers a steady accompaniment and the saxophone engages in call-and-response with the vocal group.

Form

"Charlie Brown" combines aspects of two different formal designs we have seen in previous musical examples. The song reveals its mainstream pop roots in its

Box 8.4 The Kingston Trio: Folk Music in the Age of Rock 'n' Roll

One of the later hits of the 1950s was "Tom Dooley," an adaptation of an old ballad song, at once a throwback to an earlier era and a harbinger of important currents in American popular music of the 1960s. Even as the taste of most young people was attracted to the electrified sounds of rock 'n' roll, the urban folk-pop tradition that had been pioneered by the Weavers in the early 1950s (see Chapter 7) continued to expand its appeal. The most popular of the folk groups was the Kingston Trio, composed of Dave Guard, Nick Reynolds, and Bob Shane. Formed in 1957, the group was named after the capital of Jamaica—a gesture in the direction of the Caribbean calypso-pop hits of Harry Belafonte and other folk singers of the mid-1950s. The group featured smooth, pop-style performances of folk songs and accompanied themselves on acoustic instruments (guitar, banjo, and string bass). In a sense the Kingston Trio—three bright, smiling, well-scrubbed young white men in collegiate sweaters—represented a neatened-up and depoliticized version of the Weavers. Operating in a middle zone between the abandon of Elvis Presley and the nostalgia of Frank Sinatra, they were able to appeal to many younger listeners while not scaring Mom and Dad.

While their music may have lacked the creativity and social engagement of the Weavers or later folk artists such as Bob Dylan, the Kingston Trio were responsible for keeping public interest in folk music alive through the late 1950s and early 1960s. In addition, their hit records represent a new trend in the record business, the hit LP. While only two of their single releases made it into the Top 10, the Kingston Trio dominated the sales of 33$\frac{1}{3}$ r.p.m. LP albums. They had five Number One albums on the pop charts between 1958 and 1960; fifteen Top 10 albums between 1958 and 1963; and four of their LPs stayed on the *Billboard* charts for over two years, an astonishing feat.

The Kingston Trio's only Number One hit single was their adaptation of "Tom Dula," a nineteenth-century American ballad about an innocent man hanged to death for allegedly murdering his girlfriend. The trio's adaptation of this old song, "Tom Dooley," reached Number One on the pop charts in 1958, sold more than three million copies, and was the most popular song on their debut LP, *The Kingston Trio*, which stayed on the Billboard album charts for over three and a half years. (The song even inspired a movie, *The Legend of Tom Dooley*.) The form of "Tom Dooley" should be familiar to you by now—it is a **strophic ballad,** with a series of verses telling a story and a chorus that comes back between the verses. There is a strange contrast between the grim tale told by the lyrics—that of an innocent man waiting to be hung—and the cheerful, upbeat tone of the trio's performance. When they sing, "Hang down your head, Tom Dooley, poor boy, you're bound to die" they almost sound happy about it. While the contrast between the content and style in this recording may strike you as a bit odd, this approach was an important element of the Kingston Trio's huge success in the late 1950s and early 1960s—they were optimistic, enthusiastic, and not given to deep philosophical exploration or political experimentation, just nice boys, and fun to sing along with in the bargain.

overall AABA structure. But the A sections are twelve-bar blues stanzas, which would not of course be typical of a Tin Pan Alley tune; furthermore, each A section divides the twelve bars into a little verse-chorus structure of the type we have seen in "Long Tall Sally" and "Don't Be Cruel." The most direct kinship is with "Long Tall Sally": four bars of verse, followed by eight bars of chorus. The kinship is that much more marked because of an additional similarity between the two; in both "Charlie Brown" and "Long Tall Sally" the twelve-bar blues stanzas start off with vocal solos, and a continuous full accompaniment does not join in until the chorus portions at the fifth bar of the structure. The B section, in contrast, is eight bars in length, providing a harmonic and rhythmic **release** from the succession of blues structures.

LISTENING CHART   "CHARLIE BROWN"

Music and lyrics by Jerry Leiber and Mike Stoller; as performed by the Coasters with accompanying band (King Curtis, sax solo); recorded 1958

FORM	LYRICS	DESCRIPTIVE COMMENTS
A (verse)	*Fee, fee, fie, fie, fo, fo, fum,* *I smell smoke in the auditorium!*	Twelve-bar blues stanza, divided into a four-bar verse (vocal solo) and an eight-
(chorus)	*Charlie Brown, Charlie Brown,* *He's a clown, that Charlie Brown.* *He's gonna get caught, just you wait* *and see.* *"Why's everybody always pickin' on me?"*	bar chorus with full accompaniment and call and response between the voices and the saxophone.
A (verse)	*That's him on his knees, I know that's him,* *Yellin' "seven come eleven" down in* *the boys' gym.*	As before.
(chorus) B	*Charlie Brown . . .* *Who's always writing on the wall?* *Who's always goofin' in the hall?* *Who's always throwing spitballs?* *Guess who? ("Who, me?") Yeah, you!*	Bridge section.
A (verse)	*Who walks in the classroom cool* *and slow?* *Who calls the English teacher "Daddy-o"?*	As before.
(chorus)	*Charlie Brown . . .*	
Instrumental break		Twelve-bar blues stanza, constructed exactly like the A sections, but with the voices absent and the saxophone freely improvising over the rhythmic and chordal structure; blue notes are noticeable in the sax solo.
Repetition of final A section		
Instrumental fade-out		

The Song/The Recording

As songwriters, Leiber and Stoller always had an interest in mixing—even scrambling—elements derived from rhythm & blues music, which they knew well and loved, with elements derived from mainstream pop. This interest is evident in the form of "Charlie Brown" itself, as we have discussed, but it may also be seen in certain details. For example, the twelve-bar blues stanzas in the song are noticeably *lacking* in blue notes; Leiber and Stoller wrote a simple pop-oriented melody and just directed the bass singer to speak his solo line. But as producers, Leiber and Stoller brought in King Curtis, a Texas-born rhythm & blues saxophonist, to play on the record. In his twelve-bar instrumental break Curtis emphasized blue notes, jumping in front of and behind the beat in a syncopated manner evocative of stuttering (this style, as much indebted to country hoedown music as to R&B, was also used successfully by the country and western saxophonist Boots Randolph). Curtis's "yackety sax" sound links the Coasters' record to both rhythm & blues and country music, and creates a humorous, goofy effect perfectly suited to the comic tale of Charlie Brown.

Apart from the sparkling clarity of the recording, there is only one prominent production effect in "Charlie Brown": the artificially high voices in the bridge on "Yeah, you!" This effect was produced by playing a tape of normal voices at double speed, a device that was popular on novelty records at this time. Here we see the modest beginnings of the kind of artificial studio effects that would be found on more and more records as producers took increasing advantage of increasingly sophisticated recording studios and techniques.

The rise of rock 'n' roll in the mid-1950s transformed the landscape of American popular music, further cementing the popularity of southern-derived styles ultimately derived from the blues and country music, and transforming the teenager into both a marketing concept and a cultural icon. The dominance of youth culture—and of the music industry's sometimes clumsy attempts to interpret and shape it—was to become even more predominant during the following decade, as rock 'n' roll gave way to rock. In the next two chapters we will follow this story in some detail, from the emergence of a new generation of American teen pop stars and the onset of the so-called British Invasion through the rise of soul music and the musical experimentalism of the late 1960s counterculture.

CHAPTER NINE

"GOOD VIBRATIONS"

American Pop and the British Invasion, 1960s

Few eras in American history have been as disruptive, controversial, and violent as the decade of the 1960s. The Civil Rights Movement, the Vietnam War, and the assassinations of President John F. Kennedy and the Reverend Martin Luther King Jr. are events that still inspire impassioned debate among both historians and everyday citizens at the beginning of the twenty-first century. But one claim about the decade that could scarcely be contested is this: popular music played a role of unprecedented centrality and importance in defining the character and spirit of the 1960s. This is because the baby boom generation played a vital role in the essential political and cultural events of this period—and the boomers were a generation identified, by themselves and by others, and to a remarkable degree, with their own popular music: rock 'n' roll. As rock 'n' roll developed and changed with the times, eventually becoming "rock," it came increasingly to serve as an outlet for expression of the hopes and fears of a generation coming to terms with American politics, the racial climate in the country, and a controversial war in Southeast Asia.

The decade surely began innocently enough, however. In fact, the Number One song in the country at the turn of the decade—as the innovative, rockin' 1950s gave way to the revolutionary, rockin' 1960s—was an acoustic, deliberately old-fashioned cowboy ballad, "El Paso," written and performed by the country singer Marty Robbins. This historically inconvenient fact is worth pausing over, for a number of reasons. It reminds us of the extent to which popular views of history inevitably entail simplification and the neatening out of the complex and disorderly details that form much of the substance of life and culture in any period and place. It also reveals once again how diverse and unpredictable the pop music market remained, in 1960 and beyond. Furthermore, the popularity of "El Paso" attests to the pull that country music—and not just rockabilly!—continued to exert on mainstream pop at this time. This is important, because the significant contributions of country music to mainstream American pop of the 1950s and 1960s tend to be largely underestimated and undervalued by most historians and critics. The sudden reemergence of country music as a major market force in the late 1980s and the 1990s came as a surprise only to those who had been ignoring the full picture for a long time; country has surely gained commercial strength recently, but it has never been absent from the pop scene since the beginnings of hillbilly recordings in the 1920s.

THE EARLY 1960s: DANCE MUSIC AND "TEENAGE SYMPHONIES"

The early 1960s are often described as a lackluster period in the development of American popular music: a time of relative stasis between the excitement of the early rock 'n' roll years and the coming of the Beatles to America in 1964. But at least three important trends emerged in the early 1960s. A new kind of social dancing developed, inspired by "The Twist" and a spate of other dance-oriented records, that gave rock 'n' roll music for the first time a new and distinctive set of movements and social customs to accompany it. Members of the first generation to grow up with rock 'n' roll began to assume positions of shaping power in the music industry as writers and producers, as the Tin Pan Alley system was reinvented for the new music and its new audiences at the Brill Building in New York, at Gold Star Studios in Los Angeles, and at the Motown headquarters in Detroit. And new stylistic possibilities (and cultural contexts) for rock 'n' roll began to emerge out of California, spearheaded by the Beach Boys, whose leader, Brian Wilson, established a model for many to follow by being an innovative performer, writer, and producer all rolled into one.

The Twist

"The Twist" began its popular career inauspiciously, as the B-side of a 1959 single by the veteran rhythm & blues group Hank Ballard and the Midnighters. Ballard was convinced that he had written a smash hit with "The Twist," a teen-oriented rock 'n' roll song using a twelve-bar blues structure; it celebrated a simple, hip-swiveling dance step that was gaining some popularity among young African Americans. But the decision makers at Ballard's indie label, King, didn't agree and promoted the other side of the record, a perfectly fine but more old-fashioned rhythm & blues ballad called "Teardrops on Your Letter." This tune peaked at Number Eighty-nine on *Billboard*'s "Hot 100" chart (although both sides of the record enjoyed popularity among rhythm & blues fans) and promptly disappeared from view—along with, one would have assumed, "The Twist." However, the dance named in Ballard's song continued its still somewhat obscure existence.

Meanwhile, somebody must have paid serious attention to that flip side of "Teardrops on Your Letter," somebody with connections at another indie label, Parkway. Since Parkway was based in Philadelphia, its artists had particularly easy access to *American Bandstand,* the teen-oriented, nationally broadcast television show that originated in the same city. *American Bandstand* was all about dancing: rock 'n' roll records were played, and the camera showed the teenagers in the studio dancing to them. It was the perfect venue for promoting a new dance record, and a new dance, to the broad rock 'n' roll audience.

Parkway recording artist <u>Chubby Checker</u> was himself all of eighteen when he cut a cover of Hank Ballard's "The Twist" in 1960. (His real name was Ernest Evans; his stage name had in fact been suggested by the wife of *American Bandstand* host Dick Clark, based on Evans's resemblance to a young Fats Domino.) This record was heavily promoted, and this time around Ballard's conviction about the song proved justified: it reached the Number One position on the charts. Checker's version adhered so closely to the vocal inflections and the arrangement of the original that Ballard (when interviewed for the 1993 documentary movie *Twist*) claimed he mistook it for his own record the first time he heard it on the radio!

Even more than the song, the dance itself caught the imagination of young people nationwide as they had the opportunity to observe it on *American Bandstand*. (In fact, Ballard's original recording also entered the pop charts at this time, swept there by the wave of enthusiasm engendered by the dance.) The twist was essentially an individual, noncontact dance without any real steps. Although it was generally done by a boy-and-girl couple facing one another, there was no inherent reason why it had to be restricted to this format; it could at least hypothetically be performed by any number of people, including one, in any dance floor pattern, in any gender combination. The twist was not the first noncontact, free-form dance to emerge in the history of American social dancing, but its enormous popularity signaled a sea change in the entire culture of popular dance. Against all apparent odds, it turned out to be much more than a passing novelty.

Soon adults of all ages and classes and races were doing the twist, along with the teenagers. In turn, the popularity and wide social acceptance of this free-form dancing brought rock 'n' roll music to a significantly broader audience than ever before: it was no longer just music for teenagers but an accepted fact of American social life. Clubs called *discotheques,* dedicated to the twist and other free-form dances that followed in its wake—the pony, the mashed potatoes, the monkey, and countless others—sprang up all over; one of the most famous, New York's Peppermint Lounge, gave its name to one of the biggest hits of early 1962, "Peppermint Twist," recorded by the club's house band, Joey Dee and the Starliters. Less than a year after it completed its first chart run, Chubby Checker's "The Twist" was back on the Hot 100 for another go-round and reached Number One a second time. (This feat has been accomplished by only two records in the history of the pop charts; that the other one is Bing Crosby's "White Christmas" gives some indication of the extraordinary level of popularity of both the twist as a dance and "The Twist" as a record.) Live rock 'n' roll shows began to include female "go-go" dancers along with the singing acts; in the later 1960s these dancers also began to be featured, with or without their clothes, in clubs where recorded rock music was played.

The free-form dances that have accompanied, and in some cases inspired, so much of American popular music from the 1960s to the present thus all find their point of origin in the twist. The discotheques of the 1960s were the ancestors of the discos of the 1970s, and the spirit of bodily freedom represented by those institutions persisted in the mosh pits and related venues of the 1990s and beyond. Rock 'n' roll had found a social body language that matched the novelty of the music and the feeling of liberation that it celebrated.

It should come as no surprise that, in the wake of "The Twist," many other popular songs of the early 1960s were dance-oriented. To cite only a few represen-

In 1961 *everybody* did the twist! Teenagers on *American Bandstand*; **Chubby Checker** (center), with country singer **Conway Twitty** (left) and *American Bandstand* host **Dick Clark.** Courtesy Library of Congress.

tative examples: Chubby Checker recorded "Let's Twist Again" in 1961; teenager Dee Dee Sharp cut a duet with Chubby Checker, "Slow Twistin'," as well as "Mashed Potato Time" (both 1962) and "Do the Bird" (1963); songwriter Carole King tapped her babysitter, sixteen-year-old Little Eva (Eva Narcissus Boyd), to record her song "The Loco-Motion" in 1962; and the Motown group the Miracles sang about "Mickey's Monkey" (1963). (As we will see, the later disco craze of the 1970s inspired an analogous flood of dance-oriented songs—see Chapter 12. Popular music designed specifically for dancing remained popular through the 1980s into the 1990s; at the time of this writing, "dance" is treated by the music trade magazines as a separate and substantial genre of American and world pop music.) For the most part, the dance songs of the 1960s, like their later counterparts, were catchy and functional and tended to break no new ground musically or lyrically—which may account, at least somewhat, for the poor reputation of this period in many histories of American pop. Simple verse-chorus formats predominated. But if the songs were not in themselves novel or important, the new dance culture to which they contributed certainly was. And a few of these songs have retained the affection of a large public for a surprisingly long time: Chubby Checker joined with the rap group Fat Boys in a successful revival of "The Twist" (subtitled "Yo, Twist!") in 1988, and "The Loco-Motion" was a Number One song for the hard-rock group Grand Funk in 1974 and for the Australian singer Kylie Minogue in 1988.

Phil Spector

As we have seen, many teenagers achieved success as recording artists in the early years of rock 'n' roll. At the age of seventeen, Phil Spector (b. 1940) had a Number One record as a member of a vocal group, the Teddy Bears, whose hit song "To Know Him Is to Love Him" was also composed and produced by Spector. (The multitalented young man also played guitar and piano on the record, which was the first one he ever made!) It may initially seem surprising, then, that Spector elected not to follow the path of songwriting performers like Chuck Berry and Buddy Holly. Instead he emulated Jerry Leiber and Mike Stoller (see Chapter 7), with whom he apprenticed, and by the early 1960s Spector had established himself as a songwriter-producer, working behind the scenes of rock 'n' roll rather than in

Phil Spector in 1965. Library of Congress.

its spotlights. But Spector must have sensed where the real emerging power was in this young music business: with the people who actually shaped the sounds of the records. The wisdom of his decision is reflected in the fact that his name today is probably better known, and certainly more widely revered among pop musicians, than that of Chubby Checker, Little Eva, and any number of young performers active in the early 1960s.

By the time he was twenty-one years old, Spector was in charge of his own independent label, Philles Records, and he brought a new depth of meaning to the phrase "in charge." Working with personally selected songwriters (and often serving as a collaborator in their writing) and with hand-picked vocalists, instrumentalists, arrangers, and engineers, he supervised every aspect of a record's sound. Spector's level of involvement, and his obsession with detail, became legendary; as a result a Philles record has a distinctive kind of sonority, tied more closely to Spector's personal talents and vision than to the contributions of any other songwriters, or of the technicians, or even of the actual performers. That is to say, more than records by the Crystals or the Ronettes, these are "Phil Spector records." It is indicative that Spector is, at the time of this writing, the only American pop music producer to have had a CD box set issued under his own name; in fact, if you want to hear the hits of the Crystals or the Ronettes, you need to buy *Phil Spector: Back to Mono (1958–1969)*, a set of four compact discs issued in 1991.

The characteristic Philles sound was at once remarkably dense and remarkably clear, and it became known as the "wall of sound." Spector achieved this effect by having multiple instruments—pianos, guitars, and so forth—doubling each individual part in the arrangement, and by using a huge amount of echo, while carefully controlling the overall balance of the record so that the vocals were pushed clearly to the front. The thick texture and the presence of strings on these records led them to be called "teenage symphonies." A perfect example is "Be My Baby," to be discussed in detail shortly. However, Spector explored many different types of sound textures on his recordings, and a record like "Uptown," also discussed below, has a decidedly different and more intimate—while no less impressive—impact.

Philles Records helped establish a new and important model for the production and marketing of pop records. Many indie companies, mimicking the practice of major labels with earlier styles of pop music, rushed as many records as they could into the rock 'n' roll market, often without much thought for quality control, hoping for the occasional hit. In contrast, as would be expected from the description provided above, Phil Spector turned out an exceptionally small number of records, about twenty in a two-year period, an astoundingly large percentage of which were hits. Of course, the increasingly high profile of record producers through the later 1960s and up to the present (one need only recall the importance of George Martin's work with the Beatles) is a direct outgrowth of Spector's contribution and notoriety; a 1965 essay by the noted writer Tom Wolfe dubbed the then-twenty-four-year-old millionaire "the first tycoon of teen." And when today's bands labor painstakingly for a year or more over the studio production of a disc, they are demonstrating, knowingly or not, Spector's legacy at work.

It is also significant that Spector's own preferred recording venue was Gold Star Studios in Los Angeles; this was an early indication of the coming shift away from New York as the dominant power center of the pop music industry. The studio musicians with whom Spector worked regularly at Gold Star Studios came to be known as the "wrecking crew"; individually and collectively they made essential contributions to a remarkable number of hit records from the 1960s on. Among the best known of these musicians are Hal Blaine, drummer; Carol Kaye, bassist; and Jack Nitzsche, arranger and percussionist.

Phil Spector preferred to work with vocal groups over individual artists (although he did do some work with soloists), and his output as producer helped assure, as a result both of its own quality and of its influence, that the early 1960s were a golden age for rock 'n' roll vocal groups. Spector's predilection for vocal groups—shared by many songwriters and producers at the time—was probably due to a couple of factors. The groups offered great potential for intricate and varied vocal textures, of course. But the groups also had a kind of anonymity, as far as the listening public was concerned: they had no star leaders known by name, and their personnel could be reduced, augmented, or otherwise altered at the will of the producer. The increased power of the producer in this situation was most likely the critical issue here. Cultural historians would also attach significance to the fact that the producers of vocal group rock 'n' roll in this period tended to be, like Phil Spector, male and white, while a large proportion of the most popular vocal groups were female (the so-called *girl groups*), and of these, a significant number were composed exclusively of African Americans. In effect, the increased specialization and resulting hierarchical arrangement of power and influence that occurred in an operation like Philles Records restored a Tin Pan Alley–like model to the creation and marketing of some of the most successful rock 'n' roll. The parallel even extends to the fact that a large number of the most important songwriters and producers of this period, including Spector himself, were Jews born in New York.

To list the songwriters with whom Spector worked is to list some of the most prodigious talents of the early 1960s, including the teams of Carole King and Gerry Goffin, Barry Mann and Cynthia Weil, and Jeff Barry and Ellie Greenwich. For these and many other aspiring songwriters of the time, New York's *Brill Building* (at 1619 Broadway) served as a base of operations, where they worked in little cubicles with pianos, all packed tightly together, turning out songs for large numbers of artists and (mostly indie) labels. Producers and label executives were constantly in attendance or close at hand, and the Brill Building became quite literally rock 'n' roll's vertical Tin Pan Alley. The successful songwriters were often working with a number of different artists, producers, and labels at the same time, and consequently could hope to have several hits on the charts simultaneously; the regular work at a stable location and the promise of considerable royalty income made this type of work seem both more reliable and more potentially lucrative than that of performers. (Some of the Brill Building songwriters did perform occasionally on records, playing instruments, providing background vocals, and sometimes even doing a lead vocal, but this was not a regular thing. In the early 1960s the only one of this group to have a name as a recording artist was Neil Sedaka, who generally performed his own material; Carole King's performing career took off much later.)

Like Phil Spector, a large proportion of the Brill Building songwriters tailored their output toward vocal groups, and many of the resulting records remain classics of their period. The Drifters performed "Save the Last Dance for Me" by Doc Pomus and Mort Shuman (Number One, 1960), "Up on the Roof" by Goffin and King (Number Five, 1963), and "On Broadway" by Mann and Weil and Leiber and

Songwriters at work in New York City's Brill Building: **Barry Mann, Cynthia Weil,** and **Carole King**. Frank Driggs Collection.

Stoller (Number Nine, 1963); the Shirelles—one of the first successful girl groups—recorded "Will You Love Me Tomorrow?" by Goffin and King (Number One, 1961); the Dixie Cups sang "Chapel of Love" by Barry and Greenwich and Spector (Number One, 1964); and the list could go on and on. Talented hopefuls flocked to the Brill Building. In addition to those already mentioned, Neil Diamond also got his start as a writer there before becoming a superstar singer-songwriter in the late 1960s and 1970s.

Phil Spector retired from steady writing and production work in 1966. But he has periodically resurfaced to work on special projects that attract his interest. The best-known of these involved the Beatles; he worked on the last album released by the group, *Let It Be* (1970), and then assisted individual members with solo albums in the early 1970s.

LISTENING TO TWO PHIL SPECTOR PRODUCTIONS

"Be My Baby," composed by Phil Spector, Ellie Greenwich, and Jeff Barry, performed by the Ronettes (Number Two, 1963); "Uptown," composed by Barry Mann and Cynthia Weil, performed by the Crystals (Number Thirteen, 1962)

"Be My Baby" was one of the biggest hits among the many produced by Spector, and it remains a favorite to this day on oldies radio. With its employment of a full orchestral string section, pianos, an array of rhythm instruments, and a background chorus behind the lead vocal, it is an opulent "teenage symphony" and a fine illustration of Spector's "wall of sound" at full tilt. It is certainly the arrangement and production that gives this record its individual and enduring character. As a composition, the song itself is a simple if effective vehicle, expressing the most basic romantic sentiments in a straightforward verse-chorus framework. But the listener is hooked from the first, as an aggressive, distinctive rhythmic pattern on the solo drum gives the record its beat from the get-go and draws us immediately into the song. (Notice also the spectacular effect achieved by the surprise recurrence of this drum introduction just before the final repetitions of the song's chorus; this sudden crack in the wall of sound has an explosive impact!)

"Uptown" is an earlier, very different Philles record (one of the first to be issued) that serves well to illustrate another aspect of Spector's production talents. "Uptown" is a song quite unlike "Be My Baby," and Spector appropriately provided it with a highly individual arrangement and production. Although "Uptown" uses orchestral strings and percussion effects in as sophisticated a manner as "Be My Baby," the earlier song conveys a much more open, spacious feeling, as if illustrating in sound the relief experienced by the protagonist when he leaves work each evening and goes uptown.

"Uptown" deals with class inequalities and economic injustice; the fact that it does this gently makes it no less remarkable for 1962, when pop songs on such subjects were virtually nonexistent. (These subjects would have been regarded as appropriate for urban folk music at this time, but not for the pop market; see Chapter 10.) The hero of the song works downtown, where he "don't get no breaks," and it is only when he comes uptown in the evening to his lover's "tenement," where they "don't have to pay much rent," that he can feel like a "king" with the world "at his feet." The contrast between downtown and uptown is captured in the music as well. The downtown sections are in a **minor** key (also unusual for this period), while the uptown sections move to a **major** key. Note also the striking effect of the flexible tempo of the opening section on the record, which helps establish the unusual atmosphere and functions as a kind of atypical hook, by setting up a high degree of anticipation in the listener. The suspense is relieved when a steady tempo is established at the first occurrence of the word "uptown."

Spector recorded "Uptown" in New York. Given his own New York background, which he shared with the songwriters Mann and Weil, it is hard to escape the conviction that "Uptown" is indeed about New York, where uptown and downtown Manhattan exemplify the economic and class distinctions depicted in the lyrics. Furthermore, given the many "Spanish"-sounding features of this recording, one suspects that the specific uptown location is probably New York's Spanish Harlem, a largely Puerto Rican enclave that had gained pop music notoriety just a year before the release of "Uptown" through a song actually called "Spanish Harlem"—a Top 10 hit for Ben E. King that was cowritten by Phil Spector himself.

Several factors contribute to the general Latin feeling of "Uptown." (Like so much pop music, "Uptown" is concerned with the general evocation of an "exotic" locale, not with any kind of ethnomusicological accuracy. The "exotic" stylistic effects in "Uptown" are actually not specifically characteristic of Puerto Rican music at all.) The ornate guitar figures heard as accompaniment to the opening verse are obviously reminiscent of flamenco guitar style. The prominent use of castanets (also present in "Be My Baby," but just as part of the wall of sound, not as a specifically evocative presence) for percussion, and the general rhythmic feeling of Latin American dance throughout the record (aspects of *baion* rhythm in the accompaniment, and aspects of Cuban *bolero* rhythm in the song's melody) also contribute strongly to the exotic coloration of "Uptown." We dwell on this because "Uptown" has to serve as the basic example here of an important trend—the incorporation of Latin American elements into the fabric of 1960s rock 'n' roll. The trend is also clearly evident in "Spanish Harlem" and in many records of the early 1960s by the Drifters (the most famous of which is "Save the Last Dance for Me").

Berry Gordy and Motown

Meanwhile, in Detroit, Berry Gordy Jr. (b. 1929) was creating his own songwriting/producing/marketing organization along lines directly analogous to Philles Records. But Motown (named after the "Motor town" or "Motor city"—i.e., Detroit, the automobile production capital of America) came to be a success story that surpassed even that of Philles; more importantly, it came to be the most stunning success story in the entire history of African American businesses in this country. Motown was not the first black-owned record company by a long shot (see the discussion of Black Swan in Chapter 5). The intensity and duration of its commercial success (and it is still an important market presence at the time of this writing) may be attributed to the distinctive dual thrust of Gordy's vision.

First of all, he was determined to keep all of the creative *and* financial aspects of the business under African American control—which effectively meant under *his* control. This worked because Gordy had an uncanny ability to surround himself with first-rate musical talent in all areas of the record-making process, and to maintain the loyalty of his musicians for substantial periods of time. It also worked, of course, because Gordy had a shrewd head for business as well as for music, and this leads us to the second element of his visionary plan. Unlike the music of earlier black-owned record companies, Motown's music was not directed primarily at black audiences. Gordy unapologetically sought to make an African American pop music addressed to the widest possible listening public. The only segregation Gordy permitted his product was geared to age; like rock 'n' roll itself, Motown's music was designed to cut across divisions of race, region, and class, but it definitely was—as the label itself proclaimed—"the sound of young America."

It is almost as if Gordy launched his enterprise as a kind of counteroffensive against the expropriation of African American music and the exploitation of African

American musicians that had been as much a part of the early history of rock 'n' roll as it had been of other periods in the development of American popular music. And the unique genius of Gordy—and of his entire Motown organization—was the ability to create a black music aimed right at the commercial mainstream that somehow never evoked the feeling, or provoked the charge, of having sold out. With remarkably few exceptions, Motown recordings avoided direct evocations of earlier rhythm & blues forms and styles; twelve-bar blues patterns are strikingly rare, as are the typical devices of doo-wop or anything suggestive of the 1950s sounds of Chuck Berry, Fats Domino, or Little Richard. Yet a generalized blues or gospel manner remained a defining characteristic of Motown's performers; sometimes it could be very subtle, as is often the case with William "Smokey" Robinson, and sometimes much more overt, as is the case with Martha Reeves. And this manner proved sufficient to give a definite African American slant to the pop-structured, pop-flavored songs that were characteristic of Motown.

Like Phil Spector, Berry Gordy Jr. started his career as a songwriter (he cowrote a number of pop and rhythm & blues hits performed by Jackie Wilson in the late 1950s), although unlike Spector he did not perform on records. Motown, which began its operations in 1959 but at first grew very slowly, was reaching its commercial peak just at the point when Spector folded Philles in 1966. The Motown model was strikingly similar to that employed by Philles: tight quality control on all levels of creation and production, and the concentration on a small number of records to yield a high proportion of hits. It is impossible to determine direct influence, one way or the other, between the Philles and Motown organizations; it seems to be a case of two remarkable talents having similar ideas, and similar success, at around the same time. However, Gordy's organization was noticeably larger in its scope and ambition than Spector's.

From the beginning, Gordy planned a group of labels rather than just one: records under the Motown, Tamla, Gordy, and Soul names were all issued from his Detroit headquarters, and each label boasted its own roster of hitmakers. Furthermore, whereas Spector was essentially interested only in the records themselves, Gordy specifically chose and developed his recording artists to be charismatic and sophisticated live performers, complete with characteristic modes of dress and distinctive stage choreography—not to mention strict codes of conduct on and off stage that apparently were enforced quite vigorously. There were complaints about the iron hand with which Gordy ruled his roost, just as there were complaints about Spector's passion for control. But there can be no doubt that Gordy's active encouragement of his artists to be more than just recording acts made it possible for both individuals and groups from the organization to develop long-term careers. It is no accident that groups like the Supremes and the Temptations are significantly better known to a wide public than are the Crystals or the Ronettes—or that individuals like Smokey Robinson and Diana Ross were able to win the kind of name recognition that enabled them eventually to branch off from the groups with which they initially were associated (the Miracles and the Supremes, respectively) and to forge hugely successful solo careers.

The Motown records of the early 1960s exemplify the rock 'n' roll trends of their time. Among the biggest of Motown's early hits were "Please Mr. Postman" by the Marvelettes (Number One, 1961), a quintessential girl group record, and "Do You Love Me" by the Contours (Number Three, 1962), a hard-driving dance record that linked success in romance to the ability to perform currently popular dance steps, such as the twist and the mashed potatoes. (The Contours' "Do You Love Me" found renewed chart success in 1988, on the strength of its prominent employment on the soundtrack of the movie *Dirty Dancing,* which is set in the early 1960s.) By the mid-1960s a more complex, occasionally lush sound came to characterize Motown's productions. Surely the Temptations' "My Girl" (see the "Listening To" section) is as much a "teenage symphony" as any of Phil Spector's most elaborate offerings. Just like Spector, however, Motown never lost touch with a danceable beat, and although the Supremes' "You Can't Hurry Love" (see the "Listening To" section) has a much more sophisticated sound and arrangement than "Please Mr. Postman" from five years earlier, both records share an irresistible **groove.** Gordy's touch seemed never to falter, and his organization steadily increased its share of the hit record market throughout the 1960s; in the year 1970 alone, Motown and its affiliated labels placed sixteen records in the Top 10 and scored seven Number One records (out of the year's total of twenty-one Number One songs)!

Motown's headquarters in Detroit (which Gordy named "Hitsville, USA") served as a magnet for a spectacular array of talented individuals, some of whom did session work or even office work until they finally managed to get the attention of Gordy. Among performers, Gordy—like so many other producers—tended to favor vocal groups, although he did have important solo acts from early on, such as Marvin Gaye, Mary Wells, and Stevie Wonder, and did eventually wean some solo performers from the groups that they fronted. Important Motown groups not yet mentioned include Martha (Reeves) and the Vandellas, Junior Walker and the All Stars, the Four Tops, Gladys Knight and the Pips, and the Jackson Five; the last-named group made their first record for Motown in 1969, when lead singer Michael was all of eleven years old, and their string of hits for the label helped assure Motown's fortunes well into the 1970s. Gordy's organization was also blessed with remarkable songwriting and production talent, and Gordy would often have his teams of songwriting producers compete for the privilege of working with particular hot recording acts. Among the most famous of these Motown writing/production teams were (Eddie) Holland–(Lamont) Dozier–(Brian) Holland, Norman Whitfield and Barrett Strong, and Nickolas Ashford and Valerie Simpson. Smokey Robinson was unusual among the earlier Motown artists in being both a performer and a songwriter/producer; he furnished material not just to his own group, the Miracles, but also to Mary Wells, the Marvelettes, and the Temptations. Later on, in the 1970s, Marvin Gaye and Stevie Wonder also took on writing and production responsibilities for their own records.

Finally, but certainly not least in importance, Motown had a sterling house band, the so-called Funk Brothers, in every sense a match for Phil Spector's Wrecking Crew in assuring that the highest level of instrumental musicianship was always present to back up and inspire the vocal performers. Bass player James Jamerson, drummer Benny Benjamin, and keyboardist Earl Van Dyke were among the most important contributors to the Motown sound.

In 1971 Berry Gordy moved the Motown headquarters to Los Angeles, at last joining the "westward migration" that had been playing an important role in American pop music, and in American culture generally, since the early 1960s. We now turn our attention specifically to California, to surf music, and to Brian Wilson—who did more than any other single person to make California the new focus of America's rock 'n' roll mythology.

LISTENING TO **THE MOTOWN SOUND**

"My Girl," composed and produced by Smokey Robinson and Ronald White, performed by the Temptations (Number One, 1965); "You Can't Hurry Love," composed by Holland-Dozier-Holland, produced by Brian Holland and Lamont Dozier, performed by the Supremes (Number One, 1966)

"My Girl" is a moderate-tempo love ballad. As a composition, it is a song of sweetly conventional romantic sentiment in a straightforward verse-chorus form. But as a recording, it is lifted emphatically beyond the ordinary by virtue of the Temptations' thoroughly engaging performance and by virtue of Motown's spectacular production values.

From the outset, the arrangement hooks the listener: a repeating solo bass motive establishes the beat, over which a lead guitar enters with a memorable melodic figure. (Both of these instrumental hooks are also used later on in the recording, so that they are firmly fixed in the listener's mind after one hearing of the song.) Then the drums and lead voice enter, followed subtly by background vocals; by the time the first chorus is reached, brass instruments are present in the accompaniment, to which are then added orchestral strings. The cumulative layering of sounds gives a sense of steadily increasing passion and intensity to the song, as the singer's words metaphorically detail his feelings for his "girl." The second verse brings new brass fanfares in response to the lead vocalist's calls. There is a sumptuous instrumental interlude before the third (last) verse, dominated by the strings, which play a new melodic figure over the song's characteristic chord progressions. Then, as a final intensifying gesture, a dramatic upward key change takes place just before the concluding verse and chorus.

If "My Girl" showcases the brilliance of Motown's arranging and producing staff, "You Can't Hurry Love" demonstrates that Motown's writers could also come up with clever, innovatively structured pop songs. The listening outline below conveys the intricacies of this Holland-Dozier-Holland composition, although the most casual hearing of the record will affirm that—as with so much of the finest pop music—catchiness was absolutely not sacrificed to the cause of sophistication.

The opening A section of "You Can't Hurry Love" is extremely short, just half the length of each of the ensuing B and C sections. The function of this A is at first unclear, both because of its brevity (is it a kind of introduction? or is it a very short verse?) and because of its similarity to the music of B; the basic chord progressions underlying both A and B are virtually identical, even though their vocal melodies differ. C brings a striking chord change and another change of melody, which might initially suggest a kind of bridge section. But when A fails to return after C, and instead B and C alternate with one another, we seem to be in an unorthodox verse-chorus type of situation, in which we hear the first verse (C) after the chorus (B), and in which the words of the chorus aren't always exactly the same. Just when a pattern seems to have been established, A unexpectedly returns with a vengeance. Instead of proceeding right to B, it is played

The Supremes (Diana Ross is on the right). Frank Driggs Collection.

twice through, creating a composite section that is now as long as B or C. Then, in the most clever formal maneuver of all in this already complex song, an ambiguous section is inserted, as the composers take advantage of the chord progression shared by A and B; with minimal melodic activity from the voice, which keeps "waitin'," we can't tell for sure which of the two sections we're actually hearing! The instruments tease us briefly here by playing the melodic motive associated with B, "you can't hurry love." But the voice holds back until we're at the top of the chord progression again, at which point it finally begins a proper, full repetition of B, toward the end of which the record fades out.

All this play with form would be just so much intellectual busywork if it didn't reflect on the meaning of the song. "You Can't Hurry Love" is a song about the importance of waiting. Formally, the song keeps us guessing—waiting for clarification of the functional relationships among the different sections. When the A section at last returns, it keeps us waiting extensively for B and its restatement of the song's essential message. On the level of detail, notice also in the second and third B sections how the lead vocalist avoids or postpones singing the words "you can't hurry love," again forcing the listener to wait. This makes the final B that much more of a release of tension, as it behaves in an expected manner at last.

Like all the great Motown hits, "You Can't Hurry Love" submerges its many subtleties beneath an irresistible pop-friendly surface. Maybe this is why you don't tend to find it, or other Motown records, the subject of discussion when matters turn toward innovative aspects of 1960s music. Still, any list of the significant music of this period that omits a record like "You Can't Hurry Love" is surely missing something important.

LISTENING OUTLINE: "YOU CAN'T HURRY LOVE"

Form	Lyrics
Instrumental intro	
A	I need love . . .
B: b	You can't hurry love . . .
b	You can't hurry love . . .
C	But how many heartaches . . .
B: b	(You can't hurry love—) no . . .
b	How long must I wait? . . .
C	No, I can't bear . . .
B: b	(You can't hurry love—) no . . .
b	You can't hurry love . . .
Brief instrumental break	
A	No, love, love don't come easy . . .
A	for that soft voice . . .
A or B?	I keep waitin' . . .
B: b	You can't hurry love . . .
b	You can't hurry love . . .

Brian Wilson and the Beach Boys

Brian Wilson (b. 1942) formed the Beach Boys with his two brothers, a cousin, and a friend in Hawthorne, California, in 1961. The band was achieving national chart hits within a year and thrived right through the period of the "British Invasion" to become not only the bestselling American group of the 1960s but probably the most nationally and internationally celebrated American rock group ever—and certainly the one with the longest history of chart success. (They scored a Number One hit as late as 1988, with "Kokomo.") As songwriter, arranger, producer, and performer, Brian Wilson was the guiding spirit of the Beach Boys during the first decade of the group's existence, when their artistic and commercial importance and influence were at a peak. Wilson's clear, and stated, model was Phil Spector, and Wilson worked regularly in the Los Angeles recording studios with many of the same musicians who graced Spector's productions. Unlike Spector, however, Wilson was always an essential performing presence on the records he wrote, arranged, and produced for the Beach Boys. Even after he stopped touring with the group in 1964, the sound of Wilson's clear, intense falsetto remained a defining element of the Beach Boys' studio recordings.

By participating significantly in the creation of beautifully produced "teenage symphonies" featuring vocal groups, Wilson and the Beach Boys obviously contributed to one of the central trends of the early 1960s. But if we wish to understand why their importance and influence went well beyond this, we have to look at even broader issues.

If we were to conceptualize a defining model for the career of a self-sustaining, trend-setting rock group of the 1960s, it would look something like this:

- Start out by demonstrating a mastery of the basic early rock 'n' roll ballad and uptempo styles
- Create original material based on, and extending, those styles
- Eventually branch out totally beyond the traditional forms, sounds, and lyric content of rock 'n' roll to create something truly different and unique

The Beach Boys, with Brian Wilson in the car, leaning back. Capitol Records.

The reference point that most people would use for constructing a model like this would probably, and understandably, be the career of the Beatles—the shape of their career is surely encapsulated in the description above—or possibly one of the other "British Invasion" groups. But the group that first established this model, and did so with outstanding success, was the Beach Boys. The Beach Boys were in fact a clear, and stated, model for the Beatles, especially during the remarkably productive and innovative years (for both groups) of 1965–67.

In a sense, Brian Wilson was the first self-conscious second-generation rock 'n' roller. By this we mean two things. First, that Wilson explicitly acknowledged his reliance on, and reverence for, his predecessors in the rock 'n' roll field—by covering, and quoting from, their records. Second, that at the same time, Wilson carved out distinctive new ground—by deliberately moving the lyrics, and eventually the music, of his own songs beyond the territory carved out by his predecessors, into novel areas that were of particular meaning to him, to his time, and to his place in America. (The Beatles, the Rolling Stones, and other bands were also self-conscious second-generation rock 'n' rollers in this sense, but it is important to realize that Brian Wilson was, in all essential respects, the first fully realized representative of this type of pop musician.)

Brian Wilson's place in America was, of course, southern California, and that land of sun and surf was celebrated in song after song by the Beach Boys. These songs enshrined Wilson's somewhat mythical version of California indelibly in the consciousness of young Americans—to such an extent that still, for legions of pop music fans, merely the titles are sufficient to summon an entire state of mind: "Surfin' Safari," "Surfer Girl," "The Warmth of the Sun," "California Girls," and so forth. Wilson's vision was appealingly inclusive, even as it remained place-specific; "I wish they all could be California girls," he sang. (One also thinks of the opening lines of "Surfin' USA": "If everybody had an ocean, across the USA, then everybody'd be surfin' like Californ-i-ay.") Cars retained their importance to status and young romance in Wilson's California mythology, the models suitably modernized and spruced up to serve the new time and place, as in "409," "Little Deuce Coupe," "Little Honda," and other songs.

A few examples may suffice to trace Wilson's journey from imitation, through emulation, to innovation. The Beach Boys' first Top 10 hit, the famous "Surfin' USA" (Number Three, 1963), simply borrows the music of Chuck Berry's 1958 hit "Sweet Little Sixteen" as a setting for Brian Wilson's paean to California's—and America's—new beach craze. While the words are all new, they also embody an indirect homage to Berry's original lyrics, insofar as Wilson adopts Berry's idea of national celebration while changing its mode of expression from dancing to surfing. The many listeners who knew "Sweet Little Sixteen" encountered in "Surfin' USA" an unusual hybrid: musically a cover record that shortened and simplified the form of Chuck Berry's original, lyrically a tribute to the spirit of Berry that reworked and updated his approach to writing rock 'n' roll anthems to suit the requirements of a new time and place. The B-side of "Surfin' USA," "Shut Down," was a substantial hit as well. In "Shut Down," Wilson employed an established rock 'n' roll song form, the AABA pattern in which the A sections are twelve-bar blues structures (see the discussion of "Charlie Brown" in Chapter 8), to tell the story of a drag race between two high-powered automobiles. Needless to say, it is the singer's car that wins!

The Beach Boys' next hit, "Surfer Girl" (Number Seven, 1963), reinvigorated the sound and spirit of the doo-wop ballad by infusing it with California beach content. "Fun, Fun, Fun," the group's first hit of 1964, evoked Chuck Berry again, in an initially overt but ultimately more subtle way. The solo guitar introduction cops its twelve-bar blues licks directly from Berry's "Roll Over Beethoven" and "Johnny B. Goode." But after paying its respects (or its dues?) to Berry in this way, the main body of the song pursues an original path. It's a strophic form, with newly composed music and words, whose sixteen-bar strophes have nothing to do with the structure of the blues—but everything to do with what Brian Wilson learned from Chuck Berry about how to write and perform rock 'n' roll anthems. That is to say, after acknowledging Berry by quoting his signature manner of beginning a record, Wilson surprises his listeners and proceeds to pay his mentor the best possible tribute: not by copying him, but by revealing how well his lessons have been absorbed. "Fun, Fun, Fun" turns imitation into emulation. With its rapid-fire, clearly articulated lyrics, that manage to compress a remarkable number of deeply resonant references to youth culture (fancy cars, car radios, fast driving, hamburger stands, schoolwork, parents, the pursuit of romance and—naturally—fun) into two minutes' time, and its eminently catchy and danceable music, "Fun, Fun, Fun" is the kind of song Chuck Berry might have written had he been born sixteen years later, in southern California. (In the song "Do You Remember?"—an album track from the Beach Boys' *All Summer Long* [1964]— Berry is mentioned as "the greatest" of the early rock 'n' rollers to whom Brian Wilson pays tribute.)

By mid-1964 Wilson had moved past obvious emulation into a period of aggressive experimentation with his inherited styles and forms. "I Get Around," the Beach Boys' first Number One record, turns the uptempo rock 'n' roll anthem into a thoroughly individual kind of expression; the song's adventurous chord changes and quirky phrase structure take it well beyond the boundaries of 1950s rock 'n' roll, without ever sacrificing the immediate appeal and accessibility so essential to the genre. On the other hand, an album track like "The Warmth of the Sun" (from *Shut Down, Volume 2*, released in 1964), while clearly a descendent of the doo-wop ballad in sound, rhythm, and vocal texture, presents lyrics that probe the dissolution of young romance in a newly poignant and personal way, set to music that so enlarges the melodic and harmonic boundaries of the style that one quickly forgets the song's antecedents and focuses instead on its remarkable individuality. While it is questionable whether a song like "Warmth of the Sun" would have been successful as a single, it is unquestionable that songs like this were heard and appreciated, both by listeners and by those involved in the making of pop music, and thus contributed significantly to the evolution of musical style. We can also see here the beginnings of a significant trend: namely, the increasing importance of album tracks, and eventually of albums themselves, in the development of adventurous popular music. Rock 'n' roll was on its way to becoming rock.

By 1965 Brian Wilson was achieving international acclaim as a composer and recording studio wizard who produced brilliant singles and albums, and the Beach Boys were being viewed as the most serious creative and commercial threat—in America *and* in England—to the dominance of the Beatles, whose American triumph in 1964 had turned the entire world of pop music upside down. Let us now catch

Box 9.1 Other "Surf Music"

The Beach Boys were not the only representatives of a distinctive "California sound" in the early 1960s. The popular duo Jan (Berry) and Dean (Torrence) worked with Brian Wilson and the Beach Boys on a number of mutual projects; Wilson in fact cowrote Jan and Dean's biggest hit, "Surf City" (Number One, 1963). In addition, a highly influential style of guitar-dominated instrumental rock 'n' roll was pioneered in southern California, principally by Dick Dale (b. 1937), who performed with his band, the Del-Tones. Dale employed a solid-body guitar, a high-wattage Fender amplifier, and lots of **reverb** to achieve the "wet" sound of what came to be known as "surf guitar." A characteristic device was Dale's rapid, descending **tremolo**—borrowed by a group called the Chantays to open their recording of what became the most famous surf instrumental, "Pipeline" (the title is a surfing term for the curl of a wave before it breaks). Sustained national recognition eluded Dick Dale in the 1960s, but it finally became his in the 1990s, when his recording of "Misirlou," from 1962, was used as opening music for the hit film *Pulp Fiction*. The most successful instrumental group associated with surf rock was, paradoxically, a Seattle-based ensemble, the Ventures, who adopted aspects of the style after it became popular in California.

up with the Beatles, whose music in its turn was providing Brian Wilson, and many, many others, with creative stimulation and challenges.

THE BEATLES, THE BRITISH INVASION, AND THE AMERICAN RESPONSE

By the time the Beatles had their first Number One record in America, "I Want to Hold Your Hand," which topped the charts at the beginning of February 1964, they were established stars in Great Britain and were widely known throughout Europe. Already in 1963, spurred by the mass adulation surrounding the group across the Atlantic that had come to be known as "Beatlemania," some small American indie companies had licensed Beatles recordings for stateside release—but the group's British hits did not catch on here at first.

Much ink has been spilled over conjectures regarding the timing of the Beatles' remarkable success on American shores. Many historians of pop culture point to the impact of the assassination of President John F. Kennedy on November 22, 1963, claiming that as a new year began, young people were hungry for a change in the prevailing national mood of solemnity, and that the Beatles provided just the ticket in the form of something novel, "exotic," uplifting, and fun. This seems a convenient but facile explanation. A more practical, if also more cynical, one might be that the Beatles really "hit" in America only when a major label, Capitol (the American label officially linked to the Beatles' British label, EMI), launched a major promotional campaign behind the first Beatles single they chose to release here, "I Want to Hold Your Hand," and its accompanying album, *Meet the Beatles*. But outpourings of mass enthusiasm for entertainers were nothing new in the America of 1964; one thinks of the manias for Frank Sinatra in the 1940s and for Elvis Presley in the 1950s. Arguably the chief common element in these and other related phenomena in the entertainment business is their unpredictability.

Still, although America has retained a cultural fascination with things British throughout its history, American Beatlemania does represent the first time this degree of adulation was bestowed on non-native pop musicians. America had been exporting its popular music to Great Britain, to Europe, and increasingly throughout the industrialized world with enormous success for a long time, but the impact of the Beatles in this country marked the significant beginning of an aggressively reciprocal process. Of course, the reciprocities involved here are deep and complex. As we have seen, American popular music, especially that of the twentieth century, is built on a complex amalgam of influences that may be traced to a variety of world sources. And the most direct, formative influences on the music of the Beatles themselves—and of countless other British bands of the 1960s—were those of 1950s American rock 'n' roll.

One immediate result of the Beatles' popularity in America was to unleash a flood of recordings by British bands on the American market, an astoundingly large number of which were successful. Although the impact of many of these "British Invasion" bands was short-lived, other groups have retained substantial, long-term importance in the pop culture of this country; one thinks particularly of the Rolling Stones, the Who, and the Kinks. Another immediate result was the formation—or adaptation—of American groups to mimic distinctive aspects of "British" style, which of course included fashion (particularly Beatles-style, "mop-top" haircuts) and pseudo-English accents along with the musical characteristics that were supposed to evoke the Beatles or their countrymen. An extreme example of the effect of the British Invasion may be found in the career of the Walker Brothers, an American group that actually went to England in 1964 to record. They became popular in England and achieved some American hits—after being marketed here as a British Invasion band! (They weren't really brothers either!)

The close interconnections between American and British pop music that were established in the wake of the Beatles' stateside success continue to this day; among the most successful artists on the American charts in the 1990s were British acts like Eric Clapton, Elton John, Sting, and the group Oasis. Even more significantly, the British Invasion was the first of many developments that may be seen as indicative of an accelerating receptivity in America to *overt* pop music influences from all over the world. The Beatles themselves modeled such receptivity in their own embrace of influences from Indian music—first heard as a surface element in their employment of an Indian instrument, the *sitar,* in "Norwegian Wood" (a track from the album *Rubber Soul*, 1965), and later heard as a more profound influence on both the sound and structure of "Within You without You" from *Sgt. Pepper's Lonely Hearts Club Band* (1967; see the discussion of this album in Chapter 10). At present, "world music" is important enough in the culture of American pop to represent a distinctive marketing category, a category responsible for the sale in this country of increasing numbers of albums from international sources. And the mingling of

The Beatles in an open rehearsal for their first television appearance in the United States, February 1964. Left to right: Paul McCartney, George Harrison (both also shown on the monitor), Ringo Starr, John Lennon. Courtesy Library of Congress.

American and world popular musics, with all their attendant reciprocal influences, continues to accelerate.

This may seem a rather elaborate heritage to trace ultimately to one group, a group that had an American chart run of just over six years before they announced their disbandment. But the remarkable thing about the Beatles is that they proved truly worthy of the early adulation heaped upon them: up to the end of their career as a group, they continued to evolve in new and unexpected directions and to challenge themselves and their wide audience. They altered the character of pop music profoundly and bequeathed to popular culture a remarkably rich, and complex, inheritance.

We can trace the evolution of the Beatles by using the model advanced for describing the career of the Beach Boys. They started out as a performing band

Box 9.2 Other British Invasion Bands

It was not only the Beatles' immense popularity but also the wide-ranging and eclectic character of their musical output that made their influence on American pop so great. No other 1960s band—British or American—had the range or reach of the Beatles. The other British Invasion acts that did make a long-term impact in America started as the Beatles did: with firm roots in American rhythm & blues and rock 'n' roll. But the Rolling Stones, the Animals, the Who, the Kinks, and Eric Clapton all remained closer to these roots, on the whole, during their careers than did the Beatles. Indeed, it was just at the point that the Beatles became a studio band and began producing music that was essentially uncategorizable, like "Eleanor Rigby" and many of the songs on the album *Sgt. Pepper's Lonely Hearts Club Band* (see Chapter 10), that the Rolling Stones—who to this day play international live tours—began to call themselves the "World's Greatest Rock 'n' Roll Band." Regardless of one's feelings about that claim, there is no doubt that, of all the British Invasion acts other than the Beatles, the Rolling Stones have had the greatest cumulative influence in America.

The Rolling Stones excelled in presenting covers and original songs of an intense, gritty, and often dark character. They cultivated an image as "bad boys," in deliberate contrast to the friendly public image projected by the Beatles. Perhaps their most famous hit record is "(I Can't Get No) Satisfaction" (Number One, 1965, composed by band members Mick Jagger and Keith Richards); with its memorable buzzing guitar "hook," its unrelenting beat, and its unabashedly self-oriented and ultimately sexual lyrics, the song perfectly exemplifies the distinctive low-down, hard-rocking essence both of the Rolling Stones themselves and of their music. The Rolling Stones experimented occasionally in the later 1960s with unusual instrumentation and unconventional forms, as did virtually every other major British and American group—one had, after all, to keep up with the Beatles in some sense. But while a record like "As Tears Go By" (Number Six, 1966) is undeniably affecting and effective, its gently somber atmosphere and employment of orchestral strings render it a highly atypical Stones opus. The ultimate importance of the Rolling Stones lies in the power and longevity with which they kept, and continue to keep, the spirit of basic rock 'n' roll alive. (As late as 1986, the group achieved a Top 10 hit with "Harlem Shuffle," their faithful remake of a neglected American rhythm & blues hit from 1964 by Bob and Earl.)

It is obviously impossible to do justice in this book to the Rolling Stones or to many other important British acts of the 1960s and beyond—although we will return to the Stones for a while in Chapter 11. Although the importance of these artists to the stylistic development of American pop may not be extensive, their presence on the American and world pop music landscape has been, and continues to be, a formidable one.

modeled on Buddy Holly's group, the Crickets (see Chapter 8); after some initial shifts in personnel, the Beatles achieved a stable lineup by 1962 consisting of John Lennon and George Harrison (lead and rhythm guitars and vocals), Paul McCartney (bass and vocals), and Ringo Starr (drums and occasional vocals). During their extended apprenticeship period, the Beatles played at clubs in their home town of Liverpool and elsewhere—most famously in Hamburg, Germany—performing an imitative repertoire that centered on covers of songs by the American rock 'n' roll artists they most admired, such as Chuck Berry, Little Richard, Carl Perkins, and naturally Buddy Holly. (The country/rock 'n' roll duo the Everly Brothers also exercised a significant influence on the Beatles' group singing style.) Several such covers found their way onto early Beatles albums, once their manager Brian Epstein managed, after much difficulty, to get them a recording contract (in 1962). A few of these cover recordings were also eventually chart hits for the Beatles in America, among them "Matchbox," a Carl Perkins tune (Number Seventeen, 1964) and the Beatles' best-known cover record, "Twist and Shout" (Number Two, 1964), a rhythm & blues dance number composed by Phil Medley and Bert Russell that the Beatles doubtless learned from the 1962 hit recording by the Isley Brothers.

"Twist and Shout" was on the Beatles' first album, *Please Please Me,* released in Great Britain in 1963. By the time of this recording the Beatles were entering a period of emulation by writing some of their own songs; *Please Please Me* contains six covers and eight original selections. The Beatles' chief songwriters were Lennon and McCartney, who, at least at first, worked as a team, but eventually Harrison began to contribute songs as well, and by the end of the Beatles' career even Starr had emerged occasionally as a songwriter. This brings up an important point. Unlike the Beach Boys in the 1960s, whose creative center was unquestionably found in one member of the group, the Beatles throughout their prime years were a kind of multiple-threat team. The many creative and performing abilities shared among the four Beatles allowed the group to achieve a wonderful collective synergy, a whole both greater than and different from the sum of its parts. (The after-the-fact proof of this statement may be seen in the four contrasting solo careers the individual members of the group had after the Beatles broke up in 1970.) The Beatles were also blessed with a sympathetic and encouraging producer in George Martin. Martin was sometimes called "the fifth Beatle" in acknowledgment of his increasingly essential role in the recording studio in the later 1960s, as the Beatles came to attempt more and more sophisticated arrangements and electronic engineering effects on their recordings.

Four representative songs will serve well to chart the Beatles' career as songwriting performers from 1962 to 1966, the year that they quit touring, gave up live performance, and went on to become the world's first famous studio rock band. These four songs demonstrate their development from emulators to innovators; the final phase of their career will be discussed in the next chapter. From very early on, the Beatles' original songs showed considerable individuality and creativity in dealing with the inherited materials of rock 'n' roll. By 1965, with the appropriately titled "Yesterday," they were revealing an ability to emulate Tin Pan Alley as well as American rockers. And with "Eleanor Rigby" in 1966, the Beatles achieved a song that was—and is—truly "beyond category," a song that helped certify their new status as not only the most popular band in the history of rock 'n' roll but also the most innovative one.

LISTENING TO FOUR SONGS BY THE BEATLES, 1962–1966

"Please Please Me" was recorded in late 1962. It was the Beatles' first Top 10 hit in Britain and was one of the songs unsuccessfully released in America in 1963. But indie label Vee-Jay rereleased the single when "I Want to Hold Your Hand" began its rapid ascent on the American charts in early 1964, and before long "Please Please Me" was up in the Top 3 along with "I Want to Hold Your Hand" and another Beatles hit, "She Loves You," which had also initially been released in this country in 1963. (During a now-famous week in early April 1964 the Beatles achieved the unprecedented and still unique feat of having all of the top five records on the American charts for the week—an index of the intensity of American Beatlemania at the time.)

"Please Please Me," a fine example of the early Beatles' songwriting and performing, is a straightforward uptempo love song in a typical AABA form. The group sings and plays it crisply, energetically, and efficiently—once through the song, and it's over, in just two minutes' time.

Still, individualistic features in the song already point to the creative energy at work in the group. The lyrics contain some clever internal rhymes, as when "com*plainin*" is rhymed with "*rain in* [my heart]" at the beginning of the B section. The title itself plays with the word "please," using it both as verb and adverb. Effective rhymes and wordplay would become two trademarks of the Beatles' songwriting.

Musically, as shown in the listening chart, the A sections have their own distinctive internal form that proves a source of considerable interest. First there are two identical phrases (*a, a*) to set the poetic couplets that open these sections. These *a* phrases have a basically descending melodic motion over minimal chord changes. In the rather unexpected third phrase, *b,* where the text consists simply of the repeated words "Come on, come on," the music becomes the focus of interest, with continuous chord changes and a steadily ascending melodic line depicting the intensity that underlies the unchanging lyrics. With the final phrase, *c,* a melodic high point is reached as the lyrics arrive at the words of the song's title, "Please please me," after which the melody descends once again and the harmony presents a conclusive **cadence**. The musical form of the A sections, a-a-b-c, also delineates the rhyme scheme in the four-line stanzas of the lyrics.

"A Hard Day's Night," a Number One hit in 1964, was the title song from the Beatles' first movie. It shares a few surface characteristics with "Please Please Me." The name of the song once again demonstrates wordplay, in characterizing the work experience of those who do their "hard day's work" at night—like members of a rock band. The overall form of the song is once again AABA. But the considerably more subtle and elaborate playing with formal characteristics and expectations clearly demonstrates the increasing sophistication of

LISTENING CHART "PLEASE PLEASE ME" (1962)

Written by John Lennon and Paul McCartney; performed by the Beatles

FORM	LYRICS	DESCRIPTIVE COMMENTS
Instrumental intro		As a hook, the lead guitar and harmonica play the melody of the first two phrases of A.
A: a	*Last night . . .*	
a	*I know . . .*	Same melody line, new words.
b	*Come on . . .*	Note steady chord changes, ascending melody.
c	*Please please me . . .*	High point of melody comes on words of the title.
A: a	*You don't . . .*	Same music as before, with new words for
a	*Why do I . . .*	the first two lines of the stanza.
b	*Come on . . .*	
c	*Please please me . . .*	
B: d	*I don't . . .*	Bridge section; new music.
d'	*I do . . .*	Note change and extension at the end of this phrase, leading back to the final A.
A	*Last night . . . (etc.)*	Exact repetition of the opening A, with brief extension at the end.

the Beatles' songwriting. And while the performance of the song is fully as energetic and engaging as that of "Please Please Me," some novel touches reveal the group's increasing attention to details of sound and arrangement.

In a sense, "A Hard Day's Night" may be heard as the Beatles' updating of the subject matter of "My Blue Heaven" (see Chapter 4): the delights of returning home to a rewarding domestic relationship. (It is not at all unthinkable that the Beatles knew "My Blue Heaven," especially since Fats Domino had revived it and made it a hit again, in rock 'n' roll style of course, in 1956. Domino was very popular in Britain, and the Beatles eventually created an implicit tribute to his New Orleans style by writing and recording "Lady Madonna" in 1968. Domino appreciated the compliment and returned it by recording the song himself the same year.) Musically, "A Hard Day's Night" is clearly modeled on those AABA song forms in which the A sections are twelve-bar blues stanzas. But while the A sections are indeed twelve bars in length, have three four-bar phrases, and incorporate **blue notes,** they are not exactly traditional twelve-bar blues structures. In the lyrics, the Beatles begin by making a reference to the standard a-a-b poetic stanza found in many blues, by having the second line begin with the same words as the first (see listening chart). But that second line ends with different words, and the following A stanza features three completely independent lines. In the music of these A sections, the Beatles do not follow the traditional chord structure of twelve-bar blues. There are chords used in addition to the traditional three (**tonic,** subdominant, and dominant—see the discussion of twelve-bar blues in Chapter 5), and the traditional chords do not always occur in the expected places. In particular, the usual chord change at the start of the second phrase

LISTENING CHART "A HARD DAY'S NIGHT" (1964)

Written by John Lennon and Paul McCartney; performed by the Beatles

FORM	LYRICS	DESCRIPTIVE COMMENTS
Introductory guitar chord, then pause		Dissonance followed by open space creates anticipatory tension.
A	*It's been a hard day's night . . .* *It's been a hard day's night . . .* *But when I get home to you . . .*	Music and lyrics of A sections are modeled on twelve-bar blues patterns but introduce significant variations.
A	*You know I work all day . . .* *And it's worth it . . .* *So why on earth should I moan . . .*	Same music, new lyrics.
B	*When I'm home . . .*	Bridge section; new music, consisting of two similar phrases.
A	*It's been a hard day's night . . .*	Exact repetition of the first A section.
A	[Instrumental interlude] *So why on earth should I moan . . .*	Guitar solo for the first eight bars, then voices return for the last phrase (four bars) of the section.
B	*When I'm home . . .*	As before.
A	*It's been a hard day's night . . .*	As before.
Instrumental coda		Fades out.

(the move to the subdominant chord) is postponed to the start of the third and final phrase of the twelve-bar section. This yields an interesting result: although the lyrics to the A sections do not conform to the a-a-b pattern, the *musical* phrases do.

These musical alterations are not merely technical details, for they serve the meaning of the lyrics. It is the third line in each of the A stanzas that describes the trip home from work and the actual reuniting with the loved one. Thus it is entirely appropriate that the harmony should wait until this point to make its own anticipated move. (The harmony does return to the **tonic** at the expected point—in the eleventh bar—as the singer settles down with his lover at home and feels "all right," or "okay.")

Lastly, we may mention three aspects of the song's arrangement. The song begins literally with a bang: a loud, isolated guitar chord whose unexpected harsh **dissonance** is permitted to ring in the air before the song actually gets going. This is the most effective and efficient of hooks, and it also perfectly prepares the tense feelings described in the opening words of the song. Notice also the unique guitar **timbre** employed for the instrumental solo in the middle of the record, which allows this solo on the twelve-string guitar to stand out from the many other guitar sounds heard elsewhere throughout the performance. The very end brings an unexpected instrumental **coda,** as a solo guitar gently strums a repeating figure that fades out. The abrupt cessation of drums and accompanying chords underlines the relaxed character of this ending, which creates an effective counterbalance to the song's unnerving opening and surely signifies the final lifting of tension after the "hard day's night" and the settling in to the delights of being home.

"Yesterday," which reached the Number One position on the pop charts in 1965, may be the Beatles song with the most wide-ranging and enduring popularity; certainly it has been the one most performed by other artists, and its appeal cuts across generational and stylistic divides. The song comes across with a remarkable directness and simplicity, so natural in its verbal and melodic expression that it seems hardly to have been consciously composed. But, as we know from many previous examples of fine popular music, such an effect is difficult to achieve and almost invariably conceals much art.

As a composition, "Yesterday" obviously evokes Tin Pan Alley models. Musically, it employs a standard AABA form. Its lyrics approach the time-honored theme of broken romance in a gentle, general, and straightforward manner, such that virtually anyone could understand and empathize, and virtually nobody could take offense. (One aspect of the song's appeal is that the feelings involved are utterly clear, whereas the specific situation remains vague enough to stimulate the imagination of many different listeners: "Why she had to go I don't know, she wouldn't say.") But the song may assert its kinship with Tin Pan Alley most tellingly in its emphasis on a distinctive and expressive melodic line, a line that fits the words beautifully. The melody is accompanied by equally expressive harmonies, which explore a wider range of chords than was typical for rock music at this time. The moderate tempo, and the general avoidance of any intense rhythmic effects, also distance "Yesterday" from the rock mainstream and edge it closer in spirit to Tin Pan Alley.

The Beatles' recording of "Yesterday" underlines the song's unexpected character in every way. The use of a solo voice throughout, the similarity of Paul McCartney's lyrical and unaffected style of delivery to Tin Pan Alley–style crooning, the choice of acoustic (rather than electric) guitar, the employment of orchestral string instruments to augment the accompaniment, the lack of any drums or percussion instruments, the prevailingly soft dynamic level—all these elements set the record apart from others of its time, including other records by the Beatles, as if to emphasize that this song is a deliberate venture into new musical territory. While anyone who had been listening carefully to the Beatles knew by 1965 that they were capable of writing beautifully melodic love ballads (such as "And I Love Her" and "If I Fell," both from the Beatles' 1964 movie *A Hard Day's Night*), "Yesterday" was designed to—and did—make listeners really sit up and take notice. Maybe the Beatles were more than just a good old rock 'n' roll band, or even more than a good new rock band. Maybe they were just something else entirely.

As you listen to "Yesterday," try to notice some of the artistry that went in to the creation and performance of this famous song. Each of the A sections begins with an isolated, essential word that serves as a decisive hook into the story (see listening chart); these single opening words are set to foreshortened musical phrases (one bar in length, as opposed to the standard two bars) that func-

LISTENING CHART "YESTERDAY" (1965)

Written by John Lennon and Paul McCartney; performed by the Beatles (actually Paul McCartney, vocal solo, accompanied by guitar and string ensemble)

FORM	LYRICS	DESCRIPTIVE COMMENTS
Brief intro: acoustic guitar vamp		
A	*Yesterday . . .*	Guitar accompaniment continues.
A	*Suddenly . . .*	String ensemble joins the guitar; fuller sound.
B	*Why she had to go . . .*	Bridge section; new music, consisting of two
	I said something wrong . . .	similar phrases.
A	*Yesterday . . .*	

Repetition of B and final A sections, followed by brief coda, in which the voice hums the closing melodic phrase of A accompanied by the strings.

tion equally as focusing hooks. The ascending gestures in the melody always depict the receding past ("all my troubles seemed so far away," "I'm not half the man I used to be," and so forth), while the immediately following descending gestures always bring us back down to earth in the present ("Now it looks as though they're here to stay," "There's a shadow hanging over me," etc.). The lyrics to the bridge section reveal again the Beatles' adeptness at internal rhyming: "I said something *wrong,* now I *long* for yesterday." And the final word in the bridge, "yesterday," links this B section effectively to the final A, which begins with the same word. In terms of the arrangement, we can admire how withholding the entrance of the orchestral strings until the second A section makes their arrival a wonderfully rich, intense surprise that goes splendidly with the word "suddenly."

"Eleanor Rigby," a Number Eleven pop hit in 1966, was not quite the smash hit the preceding three songs were. Actually, it was issued as the B-side of "Yellow Submarine," a novelty number that went to the Number Two position on the charts; it is a tribute to the impact of "Eleanor Rigby" that it made the charts at all, let alone that it reached nearly as high as the Top 10.

"Eleanor Rigby" is a startling song right from the outset. Without any preparation, the voices enter with a high, loud cry of "Ah," accompanied by an active string ensemble (violins, violas, and cellos). Orchestral strings are traditionally associated with lyrical music—an association exemplified by a song like "Yesterday"—but here they are confined to steady, repeated chords and brief rhythmic figures, assuming functions much like those of the rhythm guitar and drums in a more typical rock configuration. The harmony is equally dislocating. The song opens on a big **major** chord, but after the initial vocal phrase it settles onto an unexpected **minor** chord. These two chords alternate throughout the song, and they are in fact the only two chords used. The restriction of the chordal vocabulary (which beautifully suits the story of repression told by the song), the

oscillation between two chords that do not share a traditional harmonic relationship, and the fact that it is the second, minor chord (rather than the opening
major chord) that proves to be the central focus (or **tonic**) of the song as a whole,
are all factors contributing strongly to the unique atmosphere of "Eleanor Rigby."

The subject matter of the song, loneliness, is not in itself an unusual one in
pop music, but "Eleanor Rigby" looks at loneliness and the lack of human connection from a uniquely philosophical, even spiritual, viewpoint rather than from
a romantic viewpoint. Eleanor Rigby and Father McKenzie, introduced in two separate verses of the song, remain isolated from one another—and from other people—in their lives. And even in death! Only Father McKenzie is even aware of
Eleanor's passing; they "meet" in the third and final verse only in a graveyard
that finalizes their nonrelationship, and the "good" Father can only wipe dirt from
his hands as he walks away from the site of Eleanor's burial. As the lyrics say,
so succinctly and eloquently, "No one was saved." This is somber stuff indeed,
and it is to the Beatles' credit that the song conveys its despairing message
in an efficient and utterly unsentimental way, which of course maximizes the
effect.

Apart from the striking introduction, the form of the song suggests that of
the traditional folk **ballad,** with verses that tell a developing story alternating with
a repeated chorus (see the listening chart). By the mid-1960s the urban folk revival had already been in full swing for years (see Chapter 10), so it was not surprising to see the Beatles laying claim to the folk ballad form as they continued
to expand their musical horizons. What was, and remains, surprising is their
unique take on this tradition. The ballad form was conventionally used as a means
of telling a large-scale, dramatic, often tragic story. (See the adaptation of ballad form in the sentimentally tragic "After the Ball," discussed in Chapter 2.) And
many of the urban folk performers, such as Bob Dylan, adapted the form in their
original songs to serve the same kind of dramatic purpose. In "Eleanor Rigby,"
on the other hand, *nothing* happens in the lives of the protagonists. And that,
the Beatles tell us, is the source of this tragedy.

The bowed strings take over the role of a strumming guitar in the "ballad"
of "Eleanor Rigby," paradoxically giving the song a much harder edge. As you
listen, notice the slight variations in the string parts from verse to verse and even
in the repetitions of the chorus; they help maintain interest in the emerging story.

A few more musical details deserve mention here. The phrase structure of
the verses is distinctive: a long initial phrase (of four bars): "Eleanor Rigby picks
up the rice in a church where a wedding has been," is answered by a very short
(one-bar) phrase: "Lives in a dream." The consistent, atypical, extreme asym-
metry of these paired phrases gives the song an unquiet quality of continual incompletion—especially since the shorter phrases are left to hang melodically at
a relatively high point, without any conventional feeling of resolution. This is a
perfect musical illustration of the incompleteness that characterizes the lives being described. (In a sense, this kind of phrase structure is the reverse of that used
in "Yesterday," where the opening phrase of each section is foreshortened while
the ensuing phrases blossom out to traditional lengths.) Also, in the chorus, no-

LISTENING CHART   "ELEANOR RIGBY" (1966)

Written by John Lennon and Paul McCartney; performed by the Beatles, with accompanying string ensemble

FORM		LYRICS	DESCRIPTIVE COMMENTS
Introduction		*Ah, look at all . . .*	Voices and strings enter at once.
		Ah, look at all . . .	Exact repetition.
Verse 1:	**a**	*Eleanor Rigby . . .*	Solo voice, accompanied by strings marking
		Lives in a dream.	each beat with a chord; unusual phrase structure
	a	*Waits at the window . . .*	creates a striking effect.
		Who is it for?	
Chorus:	**b**	*All the lonely people . . .*	
	b'	*All the lonely people . . .*	Second phrase of chorus changes the melody to go higher than the first phrase.
Verse 2:	**a**	*Father McKenzie . . .*	As before.
		No one comes near.	
	a	*Look at him working . . .*	
		What does he care?	
Chorus:	**b**	*All the lonely people . . .*	
	b'	*All the lonely people . . .*	
Introduction recurs		*Ah, look at all . . .*	As before.
		Ah, look at all . . .	
Verse 3:	**a**	*Eleanor Rigby . . .*	As before.
		Nobody came.	
	a	*Father McKenzie . . .*	
		No one was saved.	
Chorus:	**b**	*All the lonely people . . .*	As a conclusion, the melody and lyrics of the
	b'	*All the lonely people . . .*	Introduction are sung in counterpoint against the melody and lyrics of the chorus, then strings bring the song to an abrupt ending.

tice how the second phrase goes higher than the first, making the question it asks ("Where do they all belong?") even more intense and insistent.

Finally, the Beatles find extremely imaginative uses for their introductory material later on in the song, demonstrating again their originality and mastery of form. Just at the point when two successive verse-chorus sections have us convinced that we are listening to a straightforward **strophic** form, the introduction is unexpectedly brought back. The renewed cry of "Ah, look at all the lonely people!" underlines the song's theme and helps set off the crucial third verse. Then, at the very end, the final chorus is rendered climactic rather than simply repetitive because the introduction's words and melody are sung simultaneously with it in **counterpoint**. This brings the song full circle; there is nothing left to say, and the strings bring "Eleanor Rigby" to a quick, brusque conclusion.

The Beatles and their music have been discussed in such detail in this book simply because the impact of their popularity and originality on American popular music has been incalculable; the group was *the* central fact of American pop culture in the 1960s. Brian Wilson viewed them as his principal rivals in the creation of innovative pop music, and even Motown's Temptations acknowledged, in their own hit song "Ball of Confusion," that "the Beatles' new record's a gas"! Thus the Beatles are an essential part of the history of American pop; or, put another way, with the arrival of the Beatles on our shores and on our charts, the history of American pop becomes unavoidably international.

Meanwhile, Back in California . . .

While the other Beach Boys were out on tour, Brian Wilson was preparing his response and challenge to the Beatles, whose late 1965 album *Rubber Soul* had particularly inspired him, in the form of an elaborately produced and strikingly unconventional album called *Pet Sounds*. Less a work of rock 'n' roll than a nearly symphonic cycle of songs, *Pet Sounds* charts a progression from youthful optimism ("Wouldn't It Be Nice" and "You Still Believe in Me") to philosophical and emotional disillusionment ("I Just Wasn't Made for These Times" and "Caroline, No"). Released in mid-1966, *Pet Sounds* was arguably rock's first *concept album*—that is, an album conceived as an integrated whole, with interrelated songs arranged in a deliberate sequence. (The listening sequence was easier to mandate, obviously, in the days of long-playing records with two numbered sides, played on phonographs without remote controls, than in today's world of single-sided compact discs whose contents listeners may readily program, and edit, for themselves by pushing a few buttons.) *Pet Sounds* was a modest seller compared to some other Beach Boys albums, but it had an enormous impact on musicians who heard it. With its display of diverse and unusual instrumentation, including orchestral wind instruments as well as strings; its virtuosic vocal arrangements, showcasing the songs' advanced harmonies; and its occasional formal experiments, exemplified by the AA'BCC' form of the remarkable instrumental "Let's Go Away for Awhile," the album was state-of-the-art pop music in every sense, designed to push at the boundaries of what had been considered possible. Its historical importance is certified by Paul McCartney's affirmation that *Pet Sounds* was the single greatest influence on the Beatles' landmark 1967 album *Sgt. Pepper's Lonely Hearts Club Band* (see next chapter).

Wilson furthered his experimentation with the late 1966 single "Good Vibrations," which reached Number One on the charts and has remained probably the Beach Boys' most famous song (see the "Listening and Analysis" section). By this time, Wilson was also at work on an album to be called *Smile*. Eagerly anticipated for many months, *Smile* was never finished, and the collapse of what was evidently a strikingly novel and ambitious project—even by Wilson's exceptionally high standards—marked the onset of a decline in his productivity and achievement from which he has never really recovered. The material from the *Smile* sessions that has occasionally surfaced, on later albums and CD compilations by the Beach Boys, hint at how unprecedented and stunning the album might well have been if Wilson had managed to complete it; listen, for example, to the song "Surf's Up," from the 1971 album of the same name.

LISTENING AND ANALYSIS "GOOD VIBRATIONS"

Basic Description

"Good Vibrations" may well be the most thoroughly innovative single from the singular decade of the 1960s. Virtually every aspect of the record is unusual, from the vocal arrangement to the instrumentation, from the chordal vocabulary to the overall form. Beginning with a gentle, unaccompanied sigh in a high solo voice right at the outset (which might be an anticipation of the opening word, "I," but could also be just the sighing sound "ah"), "Good Vibrations" establishes a unique world of sounds, textures, and feelings.

Probably the only remotely conventional thing about the song is its lyrics, with their admiring references to the beloved's "colorful clothes," hair, perfume, smile, and eyes. But there is something otherworldly about the lyrics as well—at least when they claim, "I don't know where, but she sends me there," or when they refer to "a blossom world," not to mention the "good vibrations" themselves. Notice also the extensive periods on the recording where lyrics are of secondary importance, or of no importance at all: the C section, the following instrumental transition, and the concluding "variations on B" section (see listening chart). These are in no sense secondary or unimportant portions of the record itself; it is just that here *sound* becomes more significant than *sense* (literally speaking)—or better, here the sound *becomes* the sense of the song. The sound is the way in which Wilson musically communicates the sensuous experience that is the essential subject matter of "Good Vibrations."

Form

There is no name for the form of "Good Vibrations"; it is as individual and distinctive as everything else about this recording. The best way to follow it is with the listening chart. The formal freedom is that much more effective because Wilson sets the listener up at first to expect a straightforward, predictable verse-chorus form with his initial ABAB pattern—since the lyrics to A change but those to B remain the same—and then goes on to present the unexpected. The C section could seem at first like a bridge, but instead of any return to A we get totally new material in D. In fact, the A music never returns at all, which is probably the second most surprising thing about this formal structure. The most surprising thing is that Wilson somehow manages to make this unconventional form work so effectively.

It works because of subtle interconnections that are established among the different musical sections. The C section has overlapping vocal textures that are reminiscent of the vocal textures in B sections, even though the specific music and the words are different. In the unexpected D section, the organ and percussion accompaniment maintains a kinship with the A sections, which also prominently feature those instruments. In addition, the clear presence of the words "good vibrations" in the D section provides a textual link between it and the preceding B sections, and also ties D to the concluding section, which we are calling "variations on B."

This final section requires a few comments. Its relationship with the earlier B sections is textually and musically obvious, but it is also clear that this is not a literal repetition, nor is it the kind of slight modification that would mandate a B′ label. Rather, Wilson is taking verbal, musical, and textural ideas from his B material and arranging them in new ways to create a section that sounds evolutionary rather than stable. We could borrow a term from classical music and call this a kind of "development" of the ideas; "development" is a term rarely if ever needed to describe formal sections of popular songs, but then most popular songs do not behave like "Good Vibrations." (Wilson employs one particularly sophisticated music device here. At the beginning of the "variations on B" he plays the characteristic chord progression of the earlier B sections, but in *reverse* order, starting on the final chord and ending on the opening chord. This allows him to proceed by then taking the opening chord again and playing the chords in the original order—but with new, textless vocal parts. The material is constantly in flux.) Remarkably, the song fades out while immersed in this development section, never having returned to its point of origin or to any other stable reference point. In a way, this is a perfect ending for a record so thoroughly liberated from traditional formal constraints.

The Song/The Recording

As a composition, "Good Vibrations" boasts memorable melodic hooks and a wide and colorful palette of chords. Both the high opening minor-key melody of the A section (which first ascends, and then descends) and the major-key bass line "I'm pickin' up good vibrations" of the B section (which first descends, and then ascends) are instantly memorable tunes—and beautifully contrasting ones. Consequently, they serve as effective landmarks for the listener who is journeying for the first time through this complex musical landscape. The D section offers a new but equally memorable melody. Some details of the harmony are indicated on the listening chart, for those who may wish to follow them.

The instrumentation of "Good Vibrations" is perhaps the most unusual ever employed on a hit record. Organ, flutes, solo cello, and colorful percussion instruments are all in evidence, clearly differentiating the sound of this recording from anything commonly associated with rock 'n' roll. But the ultimate exotic touch is provided by the *theremin*—the whirring, sirenlike, other-worldly instrument that appropriately illustrates the "good vibrations" in the B sections. (There is some question about whether the recording actually employed a theremin or a somewhat different instrument that sounds very much like one. But such questions are not of great significance to listeners; the exotic effect is certainly achieved!) Notice how Wilson also uses the voices of the Beach Boys as an additional choir of sound colors, pitting solo against group sounds, high voices against low, and so forth. Some prominent details of both the instrumental and vocal parts are indicated in the descriptive comments on the listening chart.

"Good Vibrations" was an extremely costly recording to produce, in terms of both time and money. Wilson tried out many different instrumental and vocal arrangements and a number of different formal schemes, committing hours and hours of rehearsal time to tape before he finally settled on the version we can hear today on record—which is actually a composite of several tapes made at various times. Thus, "Good Vibrations," which Brian Wilson called his "pocket symphony," is an important milestone in the developing history of rock production, as well as a landmark hit record of the 1960s.

LISTENING CHART *"GOOD VIBRATIONS"*

Music by Brian Wilson; lyrics by Mike Love; produced by Brian Wilson; as performed by the Beach Boys with instrumental accompaniment; recorded 1966

FORM	LYRICS	DESCRIPTIVE COMMENTS
A	*I love the colorful clothes . . .*	High solo voice, with delicate, high-range accompaniment of organ, flutes, and eventually percussion; minor key.
B	*I'm pickin' up good vibrations . . .*	Bass voice enters, accompanied by cello, theremin, and percussion, then rest of group comes in with overlapping vocal parts; major key.
A	*Close my eyes, she's somehow closer now . . .*	As before.
B	*I'm pickin' up good vibrations . . .*	As before; formal structure up to to this point suggests verse-chorus form.
C	[soft humming at first, then more vocal activity, then:] *I don't know where, but she sends me there . . .*	Steadily building tension; no stable key.
Brief instrumental transition: organ and percussion		New key established (major).
D	*Gotta keep those lovin' good vibrations happenin' with her.*	Solo voice, then group, with organ accompaniment; the line of text repeats, then fades out while organ finishes the section.
Transition	[*Aah!*]	
Variations on B	*I'm pickin' up good vibrations . . .*	Full group texture, with overlapping vocal parts; major key; then voices drop out, leaving cello and theremin, which are joined by percussion before fading out; no stable key.

By the mid-1960s the transition from rock'n' roll to rock music was well under way, under the influence of performers such as the Beach Boys, the Beatles, and Bob Dylan. In the following chapter we will follow American popular music into the culturally and politically turbulent period of the late 1960s, tracing the development of country and western, soul music, and the urban folk movement; the rise of psychedelia and the counterculture; and the diversification of rock—now positioned at the center of the popular mainstream—into dozens of subcategories and specialized audiences.

CHAPTER TEN

"PAPA'S GOT A BRAND NEW BAG"

Country, Soul, Urban Folk, and the Rise of Rock, 1960s

In Chapter 8 we stressed the integration of country- and rhythm & blues–based styles into the mix that came to be known as rock 'n' roll. Rhythm & blues was an obvious influence on virtually all the music discussed in Chapter 9. While the country influences on 1960s rock 'n' roll were far less obvious, they remained present as well. In particular, the Beatles' close harmony singing owed not a little to the model of the Everly Brothers—and thus to the whole history of country's "high lonesome" duet and group sounds. One of the Beatles' chart-making cover recordings was of "Act Naturally"; issued on the B-side of "Yesterday," the song had originally been a Number One hit on the country charts in 1963 for Buck Owens.

However, this mentioning of the country charts brings us to the fact that the pre–rock 'n' roll distinctions among genres and audiences did not simply collapse after 1955, although the situation was much more fluid than it had been. One still finds much significantly popular music that did *not* cross over into the mainstream during the late 1950s and 1960s, even though eclectic influences were everywhere present on the pop charts. Artists and records that appealed to select or regional audiences were much less likely to find their way onto the pop charts than those that managed to cut across such distinctions. Listeners to pop- and rock-oriented radio stations in New York City or Detroit could probably have gone through the whole decade of the 1960s totally unaware of performers like Buck Owens or Merle Haggard. Yet these performers—along with many others who would not have been heard on those urban radio stations, such as George Jones, Sonny James, Webb Pierce, Kitty Wells, and Loretta Lynn—were the bread and butter of country stations in the southern and western parts of the United States during this same period. Thus we have the striking anomaly that, among all the artists just mentioned, only one achieved a national Top 40 pop hit during the entire decade, and he did so only once: Buck Owens's "I've Got a Tiger by the Tail" got up to Number Twenty-five in 1965. Yet the same record occupied the Number One spot on *Billboard*'s country charts for five weeks, and was just one of *twenty-one* Number One country songs for Owens during the decade. Sonny James had twelve Number One country hits during this same period, Merle Haggard had seven, and the list could go on.

But the anomalies don't end there. Those same listeners in New York or Detroit might in turn have heard rhythm & blues–oriented music on their radios that, while popular locally, failed to make much of a dent in the national pop charts. Although Motown's records had no trouble crossing over—they were, as we have seen, designed to do so—a record like Freddie Scott's "Are You Lonely for Me," issued on the small Shout label, could hold the Number One spot on *Billboard*'s R&B chart for four weeks in 1967, while climbing no higher than Number Thirty-nine (and then for one week only) on the pop chart.

Just how much weight should be given to all this chart data is, of course, a justifiable question. But regardless of the actual numbers, it seems clear that such data does reflect some clear and persistent divisions among markets and audiences for popular music, divisions that had at least something to do with racial and ethnic factors, geographical location, and distance from major urban centers. The especially large differences between the country and the pop charts for much of the 1960s might have resulted, to a certain extent, from some inherent bias on the part of the data collectors toward the large radio stations and record retailers centered in the big cities of the North.[1] But these differences also reflected the authentic, and increasingly wide, gulf between the lingeringly rural cultures of the South and Southwest and the urban cultures that dominated much of the North. (The feeling of separateness that characterized much of the country audience was articulated memorably in Merle Haggard's controversial 1969 recording "Okie from Muskogee"—a critique of the late 1960s **counterculture** that may or may not have been made with deeply serious intent—that rose to Number One country, Number Forty-one pop.) In spite of all this, country music did have a much wider impact on the pop music of the 1960s than is generally acknowledged.

Many of the younger country artists at this time, while not directly embracing the rockabilly styles of Elvis Presley or Buddy Holly, wanted to update the sound of their honky-tonk roots. Starting with a basis in the ballad style of Hank Williams— taking, we might say, a song like "I'm So Lonesome I Could Cry" instead of "Hey, Good Lookin'" as their point of orientation (see the discussion of Hank Williams in Chapter 7)—they opted for a newly sophisticated approach to the vocal presentation and instrumental arrangement of country music, a highly influential approach that came to be known as *countrypolitan*, a fusion of "country" and "cosmopolitan." Nashville was at the center of this development, and the style was also often called

---

1. Such a bias would also help explain the relatively much greater congruence between the R&B and pop charts during this time, as R&B is a largely urban (albeit not exclusively northern) music. The R&B and pop charts were getting close enough to each other that *Billboard,* over-optimistically, briefly dropped the separate R&B charts for a little over a year, from late 1963 to early 1965; then the R&B charts resumed their appearance. Significantly, when *Billboard* changed its methods of gathering data in the early 1990s, relying on electronically generated data of actual record sales and radio play instead of accepting reports from selected outlets, the presence of country records on the pop charts increased dramatically.

the "Nashville sound." Among its most important manifestations were the recordings of Patsy Cline.

PATSY CLINE AND THE NASHVILLE SOUND

Patsy Cline (1932–63) began her career as a hit maker in 1957 with her recording of
"Walkin' after Midnight," which was indicative of her future achievements and importance insofar as it was successful on both the country (Number Two) and the
pop charts (Number Twelve). Such crossover success from country to pop was of
course not uncommon in the fluid record market of 1957. But it was noteworthy
when Cline achieved even greater crossover success in 1961, at a time of vastly increasing segregation between the country and pop markets. Her two big hits of that
year, "I Fall to Pieces," which reached Number One country and Number Twelve
pop, and "Crazy" (Number Two country, Number Nine pop) reflected a particular
kind of sensibility: they were ballads of broad appeal, in no sense "teen" records,
performed by Cline in a manner that, while sophisticated in phrasing and articula-
tion, had sufficient hints of rural and bluesy inflections to show where her roots
lay. The crooning background voices gave these records a pop sheen, while the
high-register piano remained evocative of the honky-tonk origins of this type of
music. Cline continued to be a significant presence on both country and pop charts
until her premature death in a plane crash in early 1963.

Other recordings of the early 1960s that demonstrated the crossover appeal of
the Nashville sound were those of Jim Reeves and Floyd Cramer. A ballad like
Reeves's "He'll Have to Go" (Number Two pop, Number One country—for fourteen weeks!—in 1960) demonstrates a similar mixture of elements to those that made
Cline's records so successful; Reeves possessed a fine, full, deep baritone voice that
was particularly well suited for mainstream pop appeal. Floyd Cramer was a
Nashville session pianist who combined his honky-tonk-derived style with orchestral strings to produce the huge instrumental hit "Last Date" (Number Two pop,
Number Eleven country, 1960).

The impact of the Nashville sound on 1960s pop is clear if we consider certain
records by artists not primarily identified with country music. Connie Francis and
Brenda Lee, the two most popular female vocalists of the early 1960s, depended
mainly on the young rock 'n' roll audience for their reputation and record sales,
and both certainly made uptempo records obviously addressed to the new teenage
audience (such as Francis's 1962 hit "Vacation" and Lee's 1960 smash "Sweet
Nothin's"). But Connie Francis's two biggest hits, "Everybody's Somebody's Fool"
and "My Heart Has a Mind of Its Own"—both of which made it to Number One
on the pop charts in 1960—betray a significant Nashville sound influence, and
Brenda Lee's own biggest hit, the 1960 Number One "I'm Sorry," shows that influence even more transparently. Indeed, "I'm Sorry," with its strings and crooning chorus backing Lee's mournful and blues-inflected vocal performance, features
a type of sound that has been prominent on the country charts for much of the latter part of the twentieth century. These mainstream pop hits by Francis and Lee
may well have paved the way for Patsy Cline's crossover successes in 1961.

The records made by rock 'n' roller Elvis Presley from 1960 on (after he returned
from a tour of duty in the army) reflected an increasingly eclectic set of influences,

but the Nashville sound is especially prominent among them. Good illustrations of this would be his 1961 hit "Can't Help Falling in Love" and his 1965 recording of "Crying in the Chapel," originally a country hit in 1953.

It might seem initially surprising that the Nashville sound's influence extended into rhythm & blues in the early 1960s, but given the constant interchanges between white and black musicians throughout the history of American popular music, this really shouldn't strike us as unexpected. Two hits by Solomon Burke, "Just Out of Reach (Of My Two Open Arms)" (Number Twenty-four pop, Number Seven R&B, 1961), and "Cry to Me" (Number Forty-four pop, Number Five R&B, 1962) sound for all the world like country records performed by a black vocalist, and a large number of similar-sounding records were made in the wake of their success, by Burke and by other artists associated with rhythm & blues. By the later 1960s the career of Charley Pride—an African American who set out to appeal principally to the country audience—was in full swing; by 1983 Pride had racked up an astonishing twenty-nine Number One country hits (none of which even dented the rhythm & blues charts), thus illustrating once again how color-blind music and its audiences really can be some of the time.

But the most remarkable and unexpected synthesis of country with rhythm & blues elements was probably achieved by Ray Charles. Charles's achievement looms so large in the annals of American popular music that we must stop here to consider his career in some detail.

RAY CHARLES AND SOUL MUSIC

Ray Charles (born Ray Charles Robinson in 1930) was a constant presence on the rhythm & blues charts during the 1950s, but major crossover success eluded him until 1959, which is why we have not grouped him with early African American rock 'n' roll stars like Chuck Berry, Little Richard, and Fats Domino. In any case, Charles was never interested in being typecast as a rock 'n' roller, and he never consciously addressed his recordings to the teen market—or to any obviously delimited market, for that matter. Characteristically, as soon as he established himself as a mass-market artist with the stunning blues-based and gospel-drenched "What'd I Say" (Number Six pop, Number One R&B, 1959), he immediately sought new worlds to conquer; his next record was a highly individual cover of Hank Snow's 1950 hit "I'm Movin' On," one of the biggest country records of all time. Within a year, Charles had achieved his first Number One pop hit with his version of the old Tin Pan Alley standard "Georgia on My Mind" (by Stuart Gorrell and Hoagy Carmichael), which also made it to Number Three on the rhythm & blues chart. But Charles's most astounding success was with his version of country artist Don Gibson's "I Can't Stop Loving You," which brought Charles's unique take on country music to the top spot on *both* the pop and rhythm & blues charts (five weeks Number One pop, ten weeks Number One R&B) in 1962 and gave him the biggest hit record of that entire year.

Ray Charles was certainly not the first artist to assay many different genres of American popular music, and he was of course only one of many to achieve remarkable crossover success. What is it then that makes his career so distinctive, that has made him such a universally admired pop musician—by audiences, critics, and

Ray Charles in 1960. Courtesy Library of Congress.

other musicians—that the appellation "genius" has clung to his name for decades, as if he had been born to the title?

Part of it is the astounding range of talents Charles has cultivated. He is a fine songwriter, having written many of his early rhythm & blues hits, including classics of the genre like "I've Got a Woman" and "Hallelujah I Love Her So." He is a highly skilled arranger, as well as an exceptionally fine keyboard player who is fluent in jazz as well as mainstream pop idioms. And above all he is an outstanding vocalist, with a timbre so distinctive as to be instantly recognizable and an expressive intensity that, once heard, is difficult to forget. But this still is not the whole story. Charles's most characteristic recordings are not only distinguished, individual statements but also unique and encompassing statements about American popular music *style.*

After an apprenticeship period, during which he emulated the pop-friendly vocal and instrumental approach of Nat "King" Cole and the King Cole Trio (see Chapters 4 and 7), Ray Charles established a style that immediately expressed his interest in synthesis. Charles's first Number One rhythm & blues recording, "I've Got a Woman" (recorded in 1954), is an obviously secular song based on gospel models, performed by Charles in a manner clearly related to gospel vocal stylings. Although black gospel music had been a long-term influence on aspects of secular "race" records and rhythm & blues (see Chapters 5 and 7), arguably nobody before Charles had brought the sacred and secular idioms into such a direct and intimate relationship; by the time of "Hallelujah I Love Her So" (Number Five R&B, 1956) he was expressing the connection in the song's very title! Needless to say, some people were scandalized by this. The final portion of "What'd I Say," in which Charles shouts and groans in call and response with a female chorus to produce music that simultaneously evokes a wild Southern Baptist service and the sounds of a very earthly sexual ecstasy, was banned on many radio stations in spite of the record's status as a national hit.

Although the term "soul music" would not enter the common vocabulary until the later 1960s, it is clearly soul music that Ray Charles was pioneering in his gospel-blues synthesis of the 1950s. He is now widely acknowledged as the first important soul artist, and his work proved an incalculable influence on James Brown, Aretha Franklin, Curtis Mayfield, Otis Redding, Sly Stone, and innumerable others. When Charles went on to record Tin Pan Alley and country material in the 1960s, far from leaving his soul stylings behind, he brought them along to help him forge new, wider-ranging, and arguably even braver combinations of styles.

When Charles recorded "Georgia on My Mind," he did not attempt to turn the Tin Pan Alley standard into a rhythm & blues song (the way Fats Domino did with "My Blue Heaven"). Neither did he remake himself into a crooner (the way Elvis Presley often did when performing mainstream pop-oriented material). Rather than using the jump band group that had backed him on most of his earlier records—and then perhaps adding some superficial sweetening with strings and crooning background chorus—Charles wholeheartedly embraced the Tin Pan Alley heritage of the song and presided over a sumptuous arrangement of it, with orchestral strings and accompanying chorus, that virtually outdid Tin Pan Alley itself in its elaborateness and unrestrained sentiment. But against this smooth and beautifully performed backdrop (Charles always insisted on the highest musical standards from all personnel involved in his performances), Charles sang "Georgia on My Mind" as if he were performing a deeply personal blues. While the original words, melody, and phrasing of the song were clearly conveyed, Charles employed an intense and sometimes rough-edged vocal timbre, used constant syncopation, and selectively added shakes, moans, and other improvised touches ("*I said-a*, Georgia") to reflect what was at this point his natural, individual vocal approach, rooted in gospel and blues. And he occasionally provided jazz-based fills in his piano part between vocal phrases, to evoke call and response within his own performance, while the backing chorus echoed his words at strategic intervals, producing call and response between them and Charles himself.

The result of all this was an extraordinary and unprecedented juxtaposition and dialogue of styles within a single recording. And as the description above indicates, this was no haphazard jumble of different elements; it came across as expressive and utterly purposeful. In effect, Ray Charles did more than reinterpret "Georgia on My Mind"; he virtually reinvented the song for a new generation of listeners and left his mark on the song permanently. It seems only appropriate that in 1979 his recording was named "the official song of the state of Georgia."

In 1962 Charles cast his stylistic net still wider, producing a concept album, *Modern Sounds in Country and Western Music,* that stands as a milestone in the history of American popular music. When Charles first announced to his record company that he wanted to do an album of country songs, the project was derisively labeled "Ray's folly"; it was thought that he would lose his audience. Charles is not a man to be crossed, however, and he persevered, with the result of course that he enlarged his audience even further—and beyond anyone's expectations. By this point, Charles was aggressively and creativity playing with stylistic mixtures, and the album essentially redrew the map of American popular music, both appealing to and challenging fans of radically different genres.

Every song on *Modern Sounds in Country and Western Music* was transformed from its origins into something rich and strange. The Everly Brothers' "Bye, Bye, Love" and Hank Williams's "Hey, Good Lookin'" became big-band shouts to book-end the album, while other songs received orchestral treatments worthy of the best Tin Pan Alley arrangements—or of Charles's "Georgia on My Mind." It's hard to think of any major aspect of American pop that isn't represented, or at least implied, somewhere on this amazingly generous record, which weaves a tapestry of stylistic and historical associations, reaching across space, time, and race to build radically new bridges. The enormously popular "I Can't Stop Loving You" merges aspects of country, Tin Pan Alley, gospel, and blues, and even (as in "Georgia") a hint of jazz piano. Here Charles engages in stylistic call and response with the large background chorus, personalizing the lyrics that they sing in smooth massed harmony. The deliberateness of this dialogue is clearly revealed toward the end of the record by Charles's seemingly offhand, but illuminating, aside to the chorus: "Sing the song, children" (a remark that also confirms, as if there could be any doubt, exactly who's in charge here).

Although Ray Charles's many country-oriented records of the 1960s did extremely well on both the pop and rhythm & blues charts, they did not register on the country charts of the time. Perhaps Charles's genre-bending approach was a bit too exotic for the typical country music fan at the time. Still, these records were heard and deeply appreciated by many country musicians. We can take the word of no less an authority than Willie Nelson, who is quoted in the booklet accompanying the Ray Charles box set *Genius & Soul*: "With his recording of 'I Can't Stop Loving You,' Ray Charles did more for country music than any other artist." Charles finally did crack the country charts in the 1980s with some of his later efforts in the genre.

Ray Charles has remained active into the twenty-first century, performing and recording in all the many genres (and mixed styles) of which he is a seasoned master. In summarizing an astounding career that steadfastly resists summarizing, we might paraphrase what Jerome Kern reportedly said about Irving Berlin: this man has no "place" in American music; he *is* American music! Or perhaps we can leave the last word to Charles himself (as quoted by Quincy Jones in the booklet accompanying *Genius & Soul*): "It's all music, man. We can play it all."

JAMES BROWN AND ARETHA FRANKLIN

Among many significant artists whose names became linked with the concept of "soul music" in the 1960s, James Brown and Aretha Franklin may be selected as representative. Like Ray Charles, Brown and Franklin are exceptionally popular performers with multidecade careers; in fact, *Joel Whitburn's Top R&B Singles, 1942–1995* lists Brown and Franklin as the top two rhythm & blues artists of this entire time period. Both Brown (known as "Soul Brother Number One") and Franklin (known as "Lady Soul") brought experience with gospel singing to bear upon their performances of secular material. In so doing, they each developed an intense, flamboyant, gritty, and highly individual approach to the singing of pop music, and their approaches represented distinctive analogues to the "soul" style of Ray Charles.

James Brown

If Charles employed "soul" as an avenue of approach to the most diverse kinds of material, James Brown (b. 1933) revealed different tendencies virtually from the beginning. His first record, "Please, Please, Please" (Number Five R&B, 1956), which Brown wrote himself, is indicative: while the song is in the general format of a strophic 1950s R&B ballad, Brown's vocal clings obsessively to repetitions of individual words (the title "please," or even a simple "I") so that sometimes the activity of an entire strophe will center around the syncopated, violently accented reiterations of a single syllable. The result is startling and hypnotic. Like a secular version of a transfixed preacher, Brown shows himself willing to leave the traditional notions of verbal grammar, and even meaning, behind, in an effort to convey a heightened emotional condition through the effective employment of rhythm and vocal timbre, animating repetitive ideas. Later on, Brown would leave the structures of 1950s R&B far behind and eventually would abandon chord changes entirely in many of his pieces. By the later 1960s a characteristic Brown tune like "There Was a Time" (Number Three R&B, Number Thirty-six pop, 1968) offered music focused almost exclusively on the play of rhythm and timbre, in the instrumental

James Brown in action, 1964. Courtesy Library of Congress.

parts as well as in the vocal. While the singer does tell a story in this song, the vocal melody is little more than informal reiterations of a small number of brief, formulaic pitch shapes; the harmony is completely static, with the instrumental parts reduced to repeating riffs or held chords. But this description does the song scant justice—when performed by Brown and his band, its effect is mesmerizing. James Brown's fully developed version of soul is a music of exquisitely focused intensity, devoted to demonstrating the truth of the saying "less is more."

In the politically charged "Say It Loud—I'm Black and I'm Proud," which reached Number One on the R&B and Number Ten on the pop charts in 1968, Brown pares his vocal down to highly rhythmic speech, backed once again by a harmonically static but rhythmically active accompaniment. Although the term would not be in use for at least a decade, "Say It Loud—I'm Black and I'm Proud" is for all intents and purposes a *rap* number, a striking anticipation of important black music to come (both in its musical style and in its emphasis on the black experience as subject matter) and a telling illustration of Brown's pivotal role in the history of pop culture generally. In the wake of the urban folk movement of the early 1960s and the subsequent folk rock (which we will discuss below), in which white singers presented themselves as spokespeople for the political and social concerns of their generation, Brown led black musicians in assuming a comparable role for the black community, especially in the time of enormous unrest and political instability that followed the assassination of the Reverend Martin Luther King Jr. in 1968. For his constructive contributions to the politics of his time, Brown was publicly honored by both Vice President Hubert Humphrey and President Lyndon Johnson. Thus soul musicians came to be seen not merely as entertainers but as essential contributors to—and articulators of—African American life and experience, and this was the view not only of the black community but also of the national political leadership.

From the late 1960s through the disco music of the 1970s, from the beginnings of rap on through the flowering of hip-hop in the 1990s, no other single musician has proven to be as influential on the sound and style of black music as James Brown. His repetitive, riff-based instrumental style, which elevated rhythm far above harmony as the primary source of interest, provided the foundation on which most of the dance-oriented music of this entire period has been based. His records are **sampled** by hip-hop artists more than those of any other musician—which is not surprising, given his achievement as a pioneer of rap style.

Brown's focus on rhythm and timbre, and in particular the complex, interlocking **polyrhythms** present in many of his songs, have been cited as demonstrating his strong conceptual links with African music styles. Certainly, the minimizing or elimination of chord changes and the consequent deemphasis on harmony makes Brown's music seem, both in conception and in actual sound, a lot less "Western" in orientation than a good deal of the African American music that preceded it. On the one hand, this quality in Brown's work resonated with many aspects of African American culture in the late 1960s and the 1970s, when there was a marked concern with the awareness of African "roots." On the other hand, one could argue that the acceptance and wide influence of the "non-Western" aspects of Brown's music helped provide a foundation for the recent explosion of interest in world musics of many sorts, which has been such a significant and distinguishing characteristic of the cultural scene in the 1980s and 1990s.

One additional and fascinating aspect of Brown's work is the relationship it suggests to the "minimalist" music by avant-garde "art music" composers, such as Philip Glass and Steve Reich, that was developing simultaneously if independently in the late 1960s in New York. This was also music based on repetitive rhythmic patterns with a deemphasis on traditional harmonic movement. There is no issue of direct influence here, one way or the other. But it could be argued that only old cultural habits and snobbery have kept James Brown out of discussions of minimalism in scholarly forums and journals.

As influential as his recordings were and are, Brown is above all an artist who exults and excels in live performance, where his acrobatic physicality and remarkable personal charisma add great excitement to the vocal improvisations he can spin over the ever tight accompaniment of his band. A typical Brown show ends with the singer on his knees, evoking once again the intensity of the gospel preacher as he exhorts his "congregation," "Please, please, please"! Although he was not the first pop artist to release a "live" album, Brown's *Live at the Apollo,* recorded in concert at the famed Apollo Theater in Harlem in late 1962, proved an important pop breakthrough both for him and for the idea of the concert album, as it reached the Number Two position on the *Billboard* chart of bestselling albums in 1963 and remained on that chart for well over a year. In particular, the album allowed the listener to experience without interruption an example of one of Brown's remarkable extended "medleys," in which several of his songs would be strung directly together, without dropping a single beat, to produce a cumulative effect of steadily mounting excitement. Many pop artists since have released "live" albums—in fact, the "live" album has become virtually an expected event in the recording career of any artist with a significant following—but few have matched the sheer visceral thrill of James Brown's *Live at the Apollo.*

Aretha Franklin

Like Ray Charles and James Brown, <u>Aretha Franklin</u> (b. 1942) underwent a long period of "apprenticeship" before she achieved her definitive breakthrough as a pop star in 1967. After an unfocused and less than stellar career as a Columbia Records artist from 1960 to 1966, during which time she recorded a mixture of Tin Pan Alley standards and unremarkable rhythm & blues material, she went over to Atlantic Records. Atlantic, an indie label with a long history of R&B success, knew what to do with Franklin. Atlantic producers Ahmet Ertegun and Jerry Wexler encouraged her to record strong material well suited to her spectacular voice and engaged stellar and empathetic musicians to back her up (usually the Muscle Shoals Sound Rhythm Section, based in Alabama). The rest, as they say, is history. Beginning with "I Never Loved a Man (The Way I Love You)" (Number One R&B, Number Nine pop, 1967), Franklin produced an extraordinary and virtually uninterrupted stream of hit records over a five-year period that included thirteen million-sellers and thirteen Top 10 pop hits. Although the later 1970s and early 1980s witnessed a decline in Franklin's status as a top hit maker, she was never completely absent from the charts, and the mid-1980s brought her a resurgence of popularity, with hits like "Freeway of Love" (Number One R&B, Number Three pop, 1985) and a duet with George Michael, "I Knew You Were Waiting (For Me)" (Number One pop, Number Five R&B, 1987). As of 1994 Franklin was still a presence on the R&B charts and the pop album charts.

Aretha Franklin performs on television, 1967. Courtesy Library of Congress.

Unlike Ray Charles and James Brown, Franklin literally grew up with gospel music; her father was the Reverend C. L. Franklin, the pastor for a large Baptist congregation in Detroit and himself an acclaimed gospel singer. Aretha Franklin's first recordings were as a gospel singer, at the age of fourteen, and she occasionally returned to recording gospel music even in the midst of her career as a pop singer—most spectacularly with the live album *Amazing Grace* (1972), which was actually recorded in a church. *Amazing Grace* built on Franklin's established popularity to introduce legions of pop music fans to the power of gospel music. The album was a Top 10 bestseller and the most successful album of Franklin's entire career; it sold over two million copies.

What is most important about Aretha Franklin is the overwhelming power and intensity of her vocal delivery. Into a pop culture that had almost totally identified female singers with gentility, docility, and sentimentality, her voice blew huge gusts of revisionist fresh air. When she demanded "respect" (see the "Listening To" section), or exhorted her audience to "think about what you're trying to do to me" (in the hit recording "Think" of 1968, which she cowrote), the strength of her interpretations arguably moved her songs beyond the traditional realm of personal intimate relationships and into the larger political and social spheres. Especially in the context of the late 1960s, with the civil rights and black power movements at their heights, and the movement for women's empowerment undergoing its initial stirrings, it was difficult *not* to hear large-scale ramifications in the records of this extraordinary African American woman. Although Aretha Franklin did not become an overtly political figure in the way that James Brown did, it may be claimed that she nevertheless made strong political and social statements just through the very character of her performances.

Directly tied to this issue is the fact that Franklin was not only a vocal interpreter on her records but also—like Charles and Brown—a major player in many aspects of their sound and production. She wrote or cowrote a significant portion of her repertoire (this involvement goes back to her early days at Columbia). In addition, Franklin is a powerful keyboard player; her piano is heard to great advantage on many of her recordings. And she also provided vocal arrangements, which were colored by the call and response of the gospel traditions in which she was raised.

In other words, Franklin not only symbolized female empowerment in the sound of her records but also actualized female empowerment in the process of making them. By the time she recorded a tune called "Sisters Are Doin' It for Themselves" (with Eurythmics) in 1985, she was, in effect, telling a story that had been personally true of her for a long time. But in the 1960s female empowerment was something quite new and important in the history of pop music. And neither its novelty nor its importance was lost on the rising generation of female singer-songwriters, such as Laura Nyro, Joni Mitchell, and Carole King, whose ascent to prominence began directly in the wake of Aretha Franklin's conquest of the pop charts.

LISTENING TO   TWO CLASSICS OF SOUL MUSIC

"Papa's Got a Brand New Bag," composed by James Brown, performed by James Brown and the Famous Flames (Number Eight pop, Number One R&B, 1965); "Respect," composed by Otis Redding, performed by Aretha Franklin (Number One pop, Number One R&B, 1967)

Both of these recordings exemplify the intense vocal performance and use of call-and-response technique characteristic of soul music. In Brown's case, the call and response takes place between his solo vocal and the instrumental accompaniment, while on Franklin's recording a female singing group provides the responses to her lead vocal. Each of the records under discussion was career-defining for its respective artist. "Papa's Got a Brand New Bag" was Brown's first Top 10 pop hit and the biggest R&B hit of his entire career, while "Respect" was for Franklin both her first Number One pop hit and the biggest R&B hit of *her* entire career.

"Papa's Got a Brand New Bag" is an excellent representative example for James Brown, as it is a record that, in a sense, looks both forward and back in his career. In terms of its form, the song uses the time-tested twelve-bar blues pattern as its basis, breaking up the pattern after two strophes with an eight-bar bridge section (a device we have also seen before, the roots of which go back to "St. Louis Blues") before continuing with further blues-based stanzas. In terms of subject matter, the song's lyrics obviously recall the dance-oriented rock 'n' roll songs of the early 1960s, as the singer praises "Papa's"—presumably Brown's—ability to do the jerk, the fly, the monkey, the mashed potatoes, the twist (naturally), and even the "boomerang"; Brown's dancing was a legendary aspect of his live shows. However, the title tells us that "Papa's Got a Brand *New* Bag," and even if the song itself looks toward the past in its form and its lyrics, Brown's actual recording sounds nothing like a typical blues-based R&B record of its time or a typical teen-oriented dance song. Instead, the record looks forward to the riff-dominated records by Brown and others that would virtually define dance-oriented soul music in the later 1960s and the 1970s.

The critical factor here is the repeating instrumental riff, which embodies a kind of call-and-response pattern, as two strong, short, rhythmic "stabs" on successive beats are answered by a four-note figure in the horn section of the band, landing on an accented final note (da-da-da-*dum*). This riff is used for all of the twelve-bar blues stanzas in "Papa's Got a Brand New Bag." The pitches change slightly to accommodate the chord change at the fifth bar of each stanza (see the discussion of twelve-bar blues in Chapter 5), but the really arresting event occurs at the tenth bar, where the instrumental accompaniment stops entirely for a few beats, creating a passage of what jazz musicians call "stoptime." This produces enormous tension, and after Brown completes his next vocal phrase, the lead guitar bursts back in with an aggressive pattern of rapidly strummed chords that prepares the return of the riff and of the rhythm section. Thus the listener's attention is directed away from the harmonic changes in the twelve-bar blues pattern and more toward events defined by *rhythm*: the presence or absence of the riff, and stoptime as opposed to rhythmic continuity. Even the sense of a separate bridge section is downplayed considerably on this recording, as the harmony remains fairly static throughout the bridge (whereas typically it would wander, and change, if anything, more rapidly than elsewhere), while a slightly different—but nonetheless clearly related—three-note horn riff is heard in every bar.

When listening to "Papa's Got a Brand New Bag," then, one experiences musical shaping created more emphatically by rhythmic patterns than by chord changes or melodic lines. In terms of the sound and the **groove** of the recording, we are here well on our way toward the minimizing or even elimination of chord changes that would characterize much of Brown's later work. It is this aspect of the record that is so arrestingly novel, and that represents such a significant discovery on Brown's part.

James Brown's "Papa's Got a Brand New Bag" is worthy of its title and of its enduring popularity. In 1965 it represented a enormous flying leap into the future of soul, a musical analogy to Brown's own daring acrobatic leaps onstage.

Merely by undertaking to record "Respect," Aretha Franklin took a daring step. The song had already been a significant hit for its composer, Otis Redding, in 1965 (Number Four R&B, Number Thirty-five pop); by covering it, Franklin was, in a sense, going head to head with one of the most impressive and powerful soul singers of the day—and on his home turf, so to speak, by taking on a song he had written for himself. But the implications of Franklin's cover extend well beyond this, because Redding's song is a demand for "respect" from one's lover, and by putting the song in a woman's voice Franklin radically shifts the sense of who is in control in the relationship. In her version, it is *she*—the woman—who has "what you want" and "what you need," not to mention "money" as well! And Franklin makes a telling change in the lyrics of the second strophe. In Redding's original, he acknowledges that his woman might do him wrong, yet it's all right with him so long as she only does so "while I'm gone." But Franklin tells her lover that "I ain't gonna do you wrong while you're gone" (presumably his doing *her* wrong is not even in question), but only "'cause I don't wanna." It could not be clearer just who is holding all the cards in Franklin's version!

Of course, none of Franklin's play with the gender issues implicit in "Respect" would have any effect if it weren't for the overwhelming power and assurance with which she delivers the song and makes it her own. Each strophe of the song builds effectively to the crucial word "respect," at which point the backing group joins in call and response with Franklin. But Franklin is also careful to structure her entire performance around a steadily building intensity, so that the listener hears something much more than a song with four identical strophes. By the time we reach the third strophe, she is improvising variants on the basic melody, and the call and response is varied as well ("just a, just a, just a, just a, just a, just a, just a, just a little bit"). After this a brief but completely unexpected instrumental break, with totally unexpected chords new to the song, raises the emotional temperature in preparation for the final strophe. The last time around, Franklin reaches her highest note yet in the song on "All I want you to *do* for me," and the backing group matches her new intensity with its own new response: "re-re-re-re-re-re-re-re-*spect.*" Then, instead of ending, this final strophe is extended with a stoptime solo for Franklin, after which the group responds with a shot heard 'round the world ("sock it to me, sock it to me, sock it to me . . .") and the record fades with Franklin and her backing singers trading shout for shout.

After the daring and achievement of this recording, Aretha Franklin never had to demand "respect," at least from musicians and audiences, again. It was hers wherever and whenever she brought her great and insightful gifts of song.

URBAN FOLK MUSIC IN THE 1960s: BOB DYLAN

Urban folk music continued to flourish during the early days of rock 'n' roll and into the 1960s. We have not been discussing it because, to a large extent, it followed an independent course through the early 1960s, remaining an acoustic guitar–based music aloof from the new styles and the large-scale changes that characterized much of the pop music of this time. In the early 1960s it was even fashionable for urban folk performers to look down their noses at rock 'n' roll as "unserious"; the dour liner notes to the hugely successful first album by Peter, Paul, and Mary (1962) exhorted readers, "No dancing, please!" But by 1967 electric instruments and drums had joined Peter, Paul, and Mary's acoustic guitars, and they were in the pop Top 10 singing (somewhat ironically, but with a firm bid for continuing relevance) "I Dig Rock and Roll Music"! The individual most responsible for this shift was not Peter or Paul or Mary, but the man who had written their biggest acoustic hit, "Blowin' in the Wind" (Number Two, 1963). He was also the man who, virtually single-handedly, dragged urban folk music—with some people kicking and screaming—into the modern era of rock. His name was Bob Dylan (b. 1941).

Dylan (born Robert Zimmerman) first established himself as an acoustic singer-songwriter in New York City's burgeoning urban folk scene. The early 1960s was a period of explosive growth for acoustic urban folk music. The baby boomers were reaching college age, demonstrating increasing cultural and political interests and awareness, and they represented an expanding audience both for traditionally based folk music and for newly composed "broadsides" on the issues of the day (such as the Cold War with the Soviet Union, the testing and stockpiling of nuclear arms, and racial bigotry). Encouragement and a sense of history were provided by elder statesmen of the urban folk scene, such as Pete Seeger and the Weavers, whose careers in turn were reinvigorated by the thawing of the political climate after the blacklisting days of the 1950s (see Chapter 7) and by the enthusiasm of younger folk performers and their audiences. By 1962 even the extremely popular Kingston Trio (see Box 8.4)—whose acoustic folk repertoire almost always stayed within the bounds of safe traditional material or the occasional novelty number—ventured to record Pete Seeger's poignant antiwar song "Where Have All the Flowers Gone," unexpectedly scoring a pop hit with it (Number Twenty-one). This attests to the increasing politicization of the urban folk movement and its audiences at this time; the success of "Where Have All the Flowers Gone" doubtless helped pave the way for that of "Blowin' in the Wind" the following year.

Bob Dylan's contemporaries in the urban folk scene included such gifted performers as Joan Baez and Judy Collins, and such talented songwriters as Tom Paxton and Phil Ochs. But Dylan stood out early for two basic reasons. First was the remarkable quality of his original songs, which reflected from the beginning a strong gift for poetic imagery and metaphor and a frequently searing intensity of feeling, sometimes moderated by a quirky sense of irony. (His interest in poetry was manifest in the choice of his new last name, borrowed from the Welsh poet Dylan Thomas.) Second was Dylan's own style of performance, which eschewed the deliberate and straightforward homeliness of the Weavers, the smooth and pop-friendly approach of the Kingston Trio and Peter, Paul, and Mary, and the lyrical beauty of Joan Baez and Judy Collins, in favor of a rough-hewn, occasionally aggressive vocal, guitar, and harmonica style that demonstrated strong affinities to rural models in blues and earlier country music. Dylan's performance style was sufficiently idiosyncratic in the context of the urban folk scene to keep him from being truly pop-marketable for years; his early songs were introduced to Top 40 audiences by other, smoother performers. Still, it may be claimed that Dylan's own performances serve the distinctive intensity of his songs more tellingly than the inevitably sweeter versions of other singers.

Bob Dylan the songwriter was introduced to many pop fans through Peter, Paul, and Mary's recording of his "Blowin' in the Wind," and to this day the song remains probably Dylan's best-known work. The opening strophe clearly reveals Dylan's gift for concise, evocative, and highly poetic lyric writing, the ability to suggest much with a few finely tuned images:

> How many roads must a man walk down
> Before you call him a man?
> Yes, 'n' how many seas must a white dove sail
> Before she sleeps in the sand?
> Yes, 'n' how many times must the cannon balls fly
> Before they're forever banned?
> The answer, my friend, is blowin' in the wind,
> The answer is blowin' in the wind.

The three successive questions build in specificity and intensity. The first question could imply many different things having to do with maturity and experience. The image of the "white dove" in the second question is one traditionally associated with the idea of peace. With the third question, the subject of war becomes inescapable, and it becomes clear that Dylan is asking, in three different ways, just what it will take, and how long it will take, before humankind develops the maturity to put a stop to wars. What makes the song so poignantly effective, though, is that Dylan leaves the answer—and even the issue of whether there *is* an answer—up to us, and in our hands: the phrase "The answer is blowin' in the wind" returns to the deliberate, thoroughgoing ambiguity of the opening question. This effectively sets up the two additional strophes of the song, which are similarly structured as three increasingly pointed questions followed by the same ambiguous answer. Dylan's avoidance of any specific political agenda in "Blowin' in the Wind" is typical of many of his best "protest songs" and is actually a source of strength, as it helps assure their continuing relevance despite changes in the political climate. In any case, the questions posed in "Blowin' in the Wind" surely—if unfortunately—ring with a resonance not limited by the time and place of the song's creation.

As is the case with many of the finest folk songs, whether traditional or newly composed, the melody of "Blowin' in the Wind" provides a simple, functional, and immediately memorable setting for the words. In this **strophic** form, notice how Dylan's melody makes each of the three questions hang unresolved; a final feeling of **cadence** in the melody is delayed until we reach the "answer" on the last word of each strophe.

It is illuminating to compare the Peter, Paul, and Mary recording of "Blowin' in the Wind" with Dylan's own performance as heard on his second album, *The Freewheelin' Bob Dylan* (1963). The folk trio performs the song with a touching sincerity and simplicity; the various questions posed in the lyrics are sung by different numbers and combinations of voices, at varying levels of intensity, while the "answer" is always provided by Mary's gentle solo sound. One might initially find Dylan's rendition monochromatic in comparison. But his syncopation of the melodic line— a performance approach utterly lacking in the Peter, Paul, and Mary interpretation—throws rhythmic weight on the most pointed words in the song (such as, in the opening stanza, "be*fore* they're *for*ever *banned*") and the resulting feeling of angularity, reinforced by the intense and unpretty timbre of Dylan's voice, arguably presses the listener to ponder the lyrics that much more seriously.

In addition to writing impressive topical songs like "Blowin' in the Wind," Dylan quickly distinguished himself as a composer of more intimate but highly original songs about human relationships. One hesitates to call a song like "Don't Think Twice, It's All Right" (also on *The Freewheelin' Bob Dylan,* and also a Top 10 single for Peter, Paul, and Mary—their followup hit to "Blowin' in the Wind") a "love song," however. Dylan himself is quoted in the liner notes to the *Freewheelin'* album concerning this song: "A lot of people make it a sort of a love song—slow and easygoing. [Was he thinking of a performance like Peter, Paul, and Mary's?] But it isn't a love song. It's a statement that maybe you can say to make yourself feel better." Dylan's gift for irony, to which we have previously referred, is exemplified memorably in the lyrics of "Don't Think Twice, It's All Right":

Box 10.1 Tin Pan Alley <u>Still</u> Lives!
Dionne Warwick and the Songs of
Burt Bacharach and Hal David

We have already seen how the Tin Pan Alley model for the creation and marketing of popular music was adopted for rock 'n' roll by 1960s organizations like Philles and Motown. And performers based in Tin Pan Alley traditions, both older (Frank Sinatra and Tony Bennett) and younger (Johnny Mathis), continued to command substantial audiences throughout the 1960s. However, arguably the most remarkable testament to the resilience of the Tin Pan Alley aesthetic in the 1960s was the extensive series of hit songs written for singer <u>Dionne Warwick</u> (b. 1940) by composer <u>Burt Bacharach</u> (b. 1928) and lyricist Hal David. In Warwick, the two songwriters found a distinctive young African American vocalist who, despite a training in gospel music that might have more typically prepared her for a career as an R&B–oriented performer, was willing to cultivate more of a crooning approach to performance that proved perfect for the convincing delivery of their work. (This is not to say that Warwick couldn't shout soulfully when needed, as any listener who has enjoyed the explosive endings of "Anyone Who Had a Heart" and "Promises, Promises" can affirm.)

The kinship of the Bacharach-David songs to Tin Pan Alley models is the result of a number of factors. David's lyrics are almost always intelligent and adult-oriented, and they can exhibit a cleverness of structure and rhyme that might remind one of Ira Gershwin or Cole Porter (as in "Do You Know the way to San Jose"). Bacharach's music generally owes little to rock in terms of direct influence; its emphasis is rather on melodic and harmonic sophistication of a nature that clearly links him to the tradition of someone like George Gershwin (as may be heard in songs like "Alfie" and "Promises, Promises," in particular). Yet Bacharach is not an imitator, and therein lies his importance and achievement. His use of **minor** keys—in songs like "Walk on By" and "The Look of Love"—is noteworthy, but perhaps most distinctive is Bacharach's way of incorporating highly original phrasing and rhythms into his songs. His novel rhythms are not those of rock, but are related rather to complexities of meter found more often in modernistic art music or in the jazz of a rhythmic innovator like Dave Brubeck than in pop song. (The chorus section of "I Say a Little Prayer" may serve as a good example of Bacharach's rhythmic gifts; a listener attempting to count out the patterns here will have a pleasantly dizzying experience!)

Every virtue of the Bacharach-David songs is emphasized in Dionne Warwick's elegant recordings of them, as Warwick is both melodically expressive and rhythmically precise, while articulating the lyrics with clarity and intensity. These recordings are among the glories of 1960s music. Although the Bacharach-David team provided excellent material to other artists as well ("What the World Needs Now Is Love," recorded by Jackie DeShannon, and "One Less Bell to Answer," performed by the Fifth Dimension, are two famous and outstanding examples), and although Dionne Warwick also found success with songs by other writers, a certain synergic magic was undeniably lost when the singer and the songwriters parted company early in the 1970s.

Still I wish there was somethin' you would do or say
To try and make me change my mind and stay.
We never did too much talkin' anyway,
But don't think twice, it's all right.

Clearly, this situation is not "all right" at all, and the blunt realism underlying Dylan's view of romantic relationships, as expressed in this song and in many others, sounded a refreshingly original note in a pop landscape where the typical treatment of relationships was still that reflected in a song like "Be My Baby," and where a relationship crisis might be represented by a date's inability to do the twist or the mashed potatoes. Dylan's own performance of "Don't Think Twice, It's All Right" does the song full justice by conveying a deep, underlying sense of personal injury.

We have been stressing the innovative character of Dylan's songwriting, but he maintained important ties with folk traditions as well. Many of his original compositions were modeled, implicitly or explicitly, on the musical and poetic content of preexisting folk material. For example, one of his most famous "protest" songs,

Bob Dylan as urban folkie (c. 1964) and as folk rocker (c. 1966). Courtesy Library of Congress.

"A Hard Rain's A-Gonna Fall," is clearly based on the old English ballad "Lord Randall"; both employ a strophic pattern, in which each strophe opens with a pair of questions addressed by a mother to her son, followed by the son's answer or answers, ending always with the same concluding line. Even the melodic lines of "Lord Randall" and "A Hard Rain's A-Gonna Fall" are distinctly similar. But Dylan is never merely a mimic, and "A Hard Rain's A-Gonna Fall" introduces a highly original structural device that has no parallel in "Lord Randall": its strophes are of widely varying lengths, depending on the number of times the third melodic phrase is repeated to changing words. (The son offers anywhere from five to twelve answers to the individual questions posed by his mother.) The concept of the "variable strophe," as we might call it, is found in a number of Dylan's finest songs, notably "Mr. Tambourine Man" and—as we shall see shortly—"Like a Rolling Stone."

The year 1965 was the pivotal one in Bob Dylan's career, the year in which he moved from being the most distinctive songwriter among American urban folk artists to being an epochal influence on the entirety of American popular culture. We may cite four major events that proved decisive in this extraordinary development, involving the release of an album, two hit singles (one by the Byrds and one by Dylan himself), and a live performance.

Early in 1965 Dylan released his fifth album, *Bringing It All Back Home,* in which acoustic numbers demonstrating Dylan's now-familiar style shared disc space with songs using electric guitar and drums. In addition to adumbrating a radical shift in Dylan's sound, the album featured several songs that carried Dylan's flair for intense and unusual poetic imagery into the realm of the surreal. One such song, "Mr. Tambourine Man," which was not one of those performed by Dylan in a rock-oriented style, was covered by the fledgling California rock group the Byrds; their truncated version of "Mr. Tambourine Man," adapted to fit the customary length for radio play, soared remarkably to Number One in June 1965, thus becoming the first landmark *folk-rock* hit. The Byrds' combination of Dylan's lyrics and melody with a musical accompaniment that included tambourine (naturally), drums, and their own trademark electric Rickenbacker twelve-string guitar sound was unique, memorable, and—obviously, if unexpectedly—marketable. The lesson was not lost on Dylan himself, who returned to the recording studio early in the summer with a rock band to cut his own breakthrough single, "Like a Rolling Stone." This six-minute, epic pop single, which made it to Number Two on the charts, certified that a sea change was taking place in American popular culture. (See the detailed discussion of this song below.) As if to affirm that there would be no turning back, Dylan then appeared at the famous Newport Folk Festival in late July with an electric band. Many folk purists were appalled by this assault on their home turf, and Dylan was booed off the stage (returning later to do an acoustic set). But he had the last laugh, of course, as it was not long before many urban folk artists had followed his lead into the electric wonderland of rock music.

From our latter-day vantage point, all the fuss about Dylan's "going electric" can seem quite silly. We have seen that the entire history of American popular music has been a story of influences, interactions, and syntheses among its various streams. The steadily increasing popularity of both urban folk music and rock 'n' roll in the early 1960s made it inevitable that these two supposedly independent styles would eventually interact with one another, and even fuse to some extent.

But the boost given to this fusion by the fact that the most individual and creative of the young urban folk artists, Bob Dylan, was the first to promote it—and to promote it aggressively and enthusiastically at that—cannot be underestimated.

From Dylan's own point of view, he was probably just following a model already well established by performers in the genres of blues and country music, genres to which his personal performing style had always demonstrated obvious ties. Rural blues artists like Muddy Waters and Howlin' Wolf had long ago made their way to the city and developed electric blues, just as country artists like Bob Wills and Hank Williams had developed the western swing and honky-tonk styles (see Chapter 7). And these newer blues- and country-based styles had themselves played an essential role in the 1950s synthesis that is called rock 'n' roll. Why, then, was there such a shock wave produced by the concept of Bob Dylan as a rock 'n' roll star?

It probably had to do with the differing cultural roles assigned by most people to urban folk music on the one hand and to rock 'n' roll on the other. Urban folk in the early 1960s was, as we have seen, an increasingly topical, political, socially conscious music. Even the singing of traditional folk songs often carried with it a subtext of political identification—with labor, with the poor, with minority groups and other peoples seen as oppressed, with a movement for international peace and understanding—depending on the nature and origins of the particular songs chosen. Thus the words were of paramount importance in urban folk music, and the acoustic guitar accompaniments enabled the words to be heard clearly. Besides, acoustic guitars were easily portable, readily accessible, and presented no elaborate barrier between performers and audiences. It was a relatively simple matter to bring an acoustic guitar along to a political meeting or demonstration, and to set it up and play it there when and if the occasion presented itself, which surely cannot be said of rock 'n' roll band equipment. And of course rock 'n' roll was identified—even, perhaps especially, by those who enjoyed it—as a "fun" music, a music to accompany dancing and other socializing, whose lyric content was by definition light, . amusing, sometimes clever, often generic, but virtually never serious.

By the mid-1960s changes within rock 'n' roll were already in the wind, as we have seen in previous discussions of music by the Beatles and the Beach Boys. But Bob Dylan's electric style and other manifestations of folk rock had the effect of an enormous injection of growth hormones into the pop music scene. Suddenly, it was all right—expected, even—for rock 'n' roll to be as "adult" as its baby boomer audience was now becoming itself, and rock 'n' roll abruptly grew up into rock. Pop records on serious subjects, with political and poetical lyrics, sprang up everywhere; before long, this impulse carried over into the making of ambitious concept albums, as we shall see. The later 1960s flowered into a period of intense and remarkable innovation and creativity in pop music. (Of course, the pressure to be adult and creative also inevitably led to the production of a lot of pretentious music as well.)

Dylan was, naturally, the main man to emulate. In the summer and fall of 1965 it seemed that almost everybody was either making cover records of Dylan songs or producing imitations of Dylan's songs and style. For example, both the Byrds and the pop singer Cher were on the charts during the summer with competing versions of Dylan's "All I Really Want to Do," and the first Number One pop hit of the fall was the politically charged, folk-rock "Eve of Destruction"—composed by the Los Angeles songwriter P. F. Sloan in an obviously Dylanesque style, complete with variable strophes, and sung in a gruff Dylanesque voice by Barry McGuire, who had been a member of the acoustic urban folk group the New Christy Minstrels.

Despite the popularity of "Like a Rolling Stone" and of a few singles that followed, Bob Dylan never really established himself as primarily a "singles artist." Rather, he was the first important representative of yet another pop phenomenon: the rock musician whose career was sustained essentially by albums. (Among many prominent figures who followed in these particular footsteps of Dylan, we could cite Frank Zappa, Joni Mitchell, Led Zeppelin, and the Grateful Dead.) Every single Bob Dylan album except his very first one has appeared on *Billboard* magazine's "Top Pop Albums" chart. Although his influence was at its peak in the 1960s—and one way to measure that peak is to remember that Dylan was the choice of the then-new *Rolling Stone* magazine for president of the United States in 1968!—Dylan has continued to be a widely admired and closely followed artist into the new century. Never content to be pigeonholed or to fall into a predictable role as elder statesman for any particular movement or musical style, Bob Dylan has over the course of his career produced a distinctive, heterogeneous, and erratic output of albums that, taken together, represent a singular testament to the spirit of pop music invention. Among these albums may be found examples of country rock (*Nashville Skyline*, 1969), what would later be termed Christian rock (*Slow Train Coming*, 1979), and even latter-day forays back into traditional acoustic folk material (*Good as I Been to You*, 1992)—along with many examples of the folk-rock approach that initially sealed his place in the pantheon of American music. As of this writing, Dylan is still touring and recording tirelessly, and challenging his audiences to guess what his next move might be.

LISTENING AND ANALYSIS "LIKE A ROLLING STONE"

Composed and performed by Bob Dylan (with unidentified instrumental accompaniment); recorded 1965

Basic Description

"Like a Rolling Stone" is one of a handful of watershed recordings in the history of American popular music. It effectively put an end to previous restrictions on length, subject matter, and poetic diction that had exercised a controlling influence on the creation of pop records. Although surely other recordings had mounted some challenges to these restrictions before Dylan cut "Like a Rolling Stone," no other pop record had attacked them so comprehensively or with such complete success. After the huge acceptance of "Like a Rolling Stone," literally nothing was the same again.

In discussing the impact of this recording, its sheer *sound* must not be neglected. "Like a Rolling Stone" has an overall timbre and a sonic density that were unique for its time, owing to the exceptional prominence of *two* keyboard instruments—organ and piano—that dominate the texture even more than the electric guitars, bass, and drums. And the distinctive sound of Dylan's vocal cuts aggressively through this thick instrumental texture like a knife. It is difficult to say which was more influential on the future sound of rock: the keyboard-dominated band, or Dylan's in-your-face vocal style, which was positioned on the cutting edge between rhythmic speech and pitched song.

The density of sound and the aggressiveness of the vocal style are clearly suited to this fierce song about a young woman's fall from a state of oblivious privilege into one of desperation. The lyrics range from the bluntest realism:

> *You've gone to the finest school—all right, Miss Lonely, but you know you*
> *only used to get . . .*
>   *juiced in it.*
> *Nobody's ever taught you how to live out on the street, and now you're gonna*
> *have to get . . .*
>   *used to it.*

to the kind of novel surrealistic imagery that Dylan was pioneering in many of his lyrics at this time:

> *You used to ride on a chrome horse with your diplomat,*
> *Who carried on his shoulder a Siamese cat.*

The chorus that concludes each strophe is typical of Dylan insofar as it provides no resolution or answers; instead, it hurls a defiant question at the song's protagonist—and at the listener:

> *How does it feel*
> *To be without a home*
> *Like a complete unknown,*
> *Like a rolling stone?*

Doubtless for many of those in Dylan's audience, reaching adulthood and venturing out on their own for the first time, this question possessed a profound and pointed relevance.

Form

"Like a Rolling Stone" reveals its antecedents in Dylan's acoustic folk style in a number of ways, the most obvious of which relate to form. Like "Blowin' in the Wind" and many of Dylan's other early compositions, "Like a Rolling Stone" falls into a strophic verse-chorus pattern (see the listening outline). But the strophes in "Like a Rolling Stone" are extremely long; it is as if every formal aspect present in "Blowin' in the Wind" has been enlarged to create an effect of great intensity and expansion. In the strophes of the earlier song, each verse consists of three questions, which are followed by the "answer" of the chorus. Each of the questions, as well as the "answer," is eight bars long; the result is a rather typical thirty-two bar formal unit. In "Like a Rolling Stone," however, the verse portions alone are forty bars in length. In the chorus portions, Dylan employs his "variable strophe" idea on a small scale but to considerable effect: the chorus in the first strophe is twenty bars long (five four-bar phrases), while in succeeding strophes the chorus expands to twenty-four bars in length (*six* four-bar phrases, the result of an additional repetition of a musical phrase, accompanying added words).

This formal expansion is necessary to accommodate the song's poetic content. The remarkable thing is that "Like a Rolling Stone" feels denser, not looser, than "Blowin' in the Wind"; compare a typical phrase in the lyrics of the latter:

> *How many roads must a man walk down*
> *Before you call him a man?*

with the opening phrase of the former:

> *Once upon a time you dressed so fine; you threw the bums a dime in your prime*
> *Didn't you?*

Obviously, the lyrics are packed more tightly in an eight-bar phrase of "Like a Rolling Stone" than they are in a comparable eight-bar phrase of "Blowin' in the Wind." The combination of greater verbal density (note the internal rhymes in the line quoted above, which are not atypical of "Like a Rolling Stone" and add considerably to the effect) with overall formal expansion creates an ongoing, coiled-spring intensity. This is the more marked because Dylan's choruses in "Like a Rolling Stone" don't even afford the listener the comfort of an ambiguous "answer"; they only ask questions. Poetically, "Like a Rolling Stone" takes the question-answer format of "Blowin' in the Wind" and in effect turns it on its head.

The Song/The Recording

In a strophic form, it is obviously the lyrics that must supply a sense of continuing development. Each succeeding strophe of "Like a Rolling Stone" widens its focus, as the alienation of the protagonist from her earlier realm of privilege becomes more and more marked and painful. The opening strophe basically describes the protagonist and her behavior. The second strophe mentions the school she used to attend; the third refers to "the jugglers and the clowns" who entertained her and the "diplomat" with whom she consorted. With the final strophe, we are given a wide-angle picture of "all the pretty people" who are "drinkin', thinkin' that they got it made"—a party at which the protagonist is no longer welcome.

Dylan's music serves its purpose of reinforcing the tension embodied in the content of the lyrics. We have already discussed this in terms of the overall sound of the recording. Notice also how every phrase in the verse portions ends with a sense of melodic incompletion, keeping the tension alive. This is another structural similarity to "Blowin' in the Wind." And, again as in the earlier song, a cadence is reached only in the chorus portions—although this arguably has an ironic effect in "Like a Rolling Stone," since the words offer no sense of completion whatsoever at these points. (Dylan's recording of "Like a Rolling Stone" fades out rather than actually concluding—like a typical rock 'n' roll song—while his "Blowin' in the Wind" comes to a formal ending, like a typical acoustic folk song.)

One further connection with acoustic folk traditions in the recording of "Like a Rolling Stone" lies in the fact that this record is, for all intents and purposes, simply a document of a live studio performance—with minimal, if any, editing or obvious "production" effects. Dylan has remained true to this kind of sound ideal throughout his recording career, eschewing the highly produced sound typical of so much 1960s (and later) rock.

At a duration of six minutes, "Like a Rolling Stone" was by far the longest 45 r.p.m. pop single ever released up to that time. Dylan's record company knew they were making history; the time "*6:00*" was emblazoned on the label in huge black numerals, demanding as much attention as the title of the song and the name of the artist! At first, some record stations pared the record down to conventional length by playing only the first two of the song's four strophes. But before long the complete single was being heard widely on national radio, and an important barrier in pop music had been broken. By the end of the 1960s, pop singles lasting over seven minutes had been made—the Beatles' "Hey Jude" (1968), the biggest chart hit of the entire decade, clocked in at seven minutes, eleven seconds.

LISTENING OUTLINE: "LIKE A ROLLING STONE"

Form	Lyrics
Strophe 1: *Verse*	*Once upon a time . . .*
Chorus	*How does it feel . . .*
Strophe 2: *Verse*	*You've gone to the finest school . . .*
Chorus [expanded]	*How does it feel . . .*
Strophe 3: *Verse*	*You never turned around to see the frowns on the jugglers and the clowns . . .*
Chorus [expanded]	*How does it feel . . .*
Strophe 4: *Verse*	*Princess on the steeple and all the pretty people . . .*
Chorus [expanded]	*How does it feel . . .*

THE COUNTERCULTURE AND PSYCHEDELIC ROCK

The explosive entrance of folk rock into the wide arena of American popular culture coincided, as we have seen, with the development of increasingly innovative approaches to rock 'n' roll itself (exemplified most forcefully in the work of the Beatles and the Beach Boys in 1965–66). Both of these phenomena were abetted, of course, by the maturation into early adulthood of the baby boomer audience, and by the maturation of many of those actually making the music. This was also a period of increasing political restlessness and ferment in the United States. America's engagement in the Vietnamese civil war was steadily escalating, while the civil rights movement was challenging the persistence of racial segregation and inequality everywhere on the home front. There were many who sensed a relationship between these two volatile political issues, linking what they viewed as external

Box 10.2 Simon and Garfunkel

Perhaps nothing illustrates the changes wrought by the phenomenon of folk rock so well as the story of Simon and Garfunkel's first hit record, "The Sounds of Silence." In early 1965 Paul Simon and Arthur Garfunkel were an urban folk duo with a fine acoustic album to their credit, *Wednesday Morning, 3 A.M.*, that was causing no excitement whatsoever in the marketplace. When folk rock hit the scene in midyear and Bob Dylan went electric, Simon and Garfunkel's producer, Tom Wilson—who was also the producer for Bob Dylan's records at the time—had a "bright idea." He took one of Simon's original compositions from the *Wednesday Morning* album, a highly poetic song about urban alienation called "The Sound of Silence," overdubbed a rock band accompaniment of electric guitars, bass, and drums onto the original recording, speeded it up very slightly, changed the title for some reason to "The Sounds of Silence," and released it as a single—all without Simon or Garfunkel's prior knowledge or permission! The duo found little to complain about, however, as they found themselves with a Number One pop hit on New Year's Day

Art Garfunkel (left) and **Paul Simon** in a recording studio, 1966. Courtesy Library of Congress.

1966. Needless to say, they never looked back. Simon and Garfunkel became one of the most enduringly popular acts ever to perform in a folk-rock style. Although the duo broke up in 1970 (they have occasionally reunited for special occasions), their songs and albums continue to be popular to this day.

We will meet Paul Simon again later on, as he is among the few singer-songwriters to come to prominence in the 1960s who arguably achieved his creative peak considerably later on. To say this is not to denigrate Simon's work with Simon and Garfunkel, which includes such memorable and varied songs as "A Hazy Shade of Winter," "America," and "Bridge over Troubled Water"; it is simply to claim that these earlier compositions would probably not lead one to suspect that Simon would eventually go on to produce such adventurous works of world music as *Graceland* and *The Rhythm of the Saints* (see Chapter 13).

---

colonialism—an inappropriate involvement with the affairs of a so-called Third World country—with internal colonialism—that is, the systematic oppression of minority peoples and cultures within the United States itself. This connection was made the more readily because of the large proportion of African American soldiers serving in the U.S. forces in Vietnam.

The youth audience for pop culture was directly implicated in the politics of the Vietnam War, as all young American men between the ages of eighteen and twenty-six were eligible to be drafted into the armed forces—and increasing numbers of them were drafted. Antiwar groups and organizations began to multiply, attracting large numbers of young—especially college-aged—men and women. In addition, a significant number of young people were involved in various ways with the many organizations, demonstrations, and legal initiatives that formed the civil rights movement.

In the later 1960s the meeting of the culture surrounding new rock music with the political and social discontents that largely defined the era resulted in a famous, if slippery, phenomenon: the emergence of what was called the **counterculture.** This was never the kind of systematic, highly organized movement that many liked to claim it was at the time (and later on). Although the mythic typical member of the counterculture was a young rock music fan who supported the civil rights movement and opposed the Vietnam War, it is important to remember that many older folks opposed the Vietnam War, and many of these probably had no special fondness for the new rock music; that many young rock music fans were apolitical, or even supporters of conservative political agendas; and that many of the same movements that promulgated utopian visions of a new, more just social order excluded most women and people of color from leadership positions. In other words, the notion of a counterculture, while it provides us with a convenient label for the more innovative, rebellious, and radical aspects of 1960s musical, political, and social culture taken all together, is inevitably a simplification, and unless we are careful, it may involve us in a number of dubious historical fictions. What is probably most significant here, for our purposes, is to note that rock music—the 1960s descendent of 1950s rock 'n' roll—was an essential part of the definition of the counterculture, which demonstrates once again the remarkable degree of identification between the baby boomer generation and the music they chose to make and hear.

Along with rock music and radical politics, the counterculture developed its own characteristic jargon, fads, and fashions: long hair for both women and men; beards; beads; "peasant," "eastern," and tie-dyed shirts; and blue jeans. The slang terms most often associated with hippies—"groovy," "far out," "stoned," and so on—were mainly derived from black English, a continuation of a historical pattern that goes back to nineteenth-century minstrelsy. In addition, the counterculture's fascination with "exotic" cultures—as reflected in the popularity of Indian classical music, Nehru jackets, and African dashikis—also has deep historical roots. At the same time, a distinctive openness and sense of freedom regarding sexual activity also emerged—encouraged to no small extent by the successful development and marketing of the first birth-control pills for women.

Many members of the counterculture were members of the American middle class, born into families that were predominantly white, Christian or Jewish, and financially solvent. It is thus understandable that the rebellious attitude of young people during the late 1960s—as during earlier periods—focused as much on a critique of the values and social habits of the middle-class family as they did on resistance to government policies or the operations of big industry. This critical attitude toward bourgeois values and attitudes was perhaps quintessentially embodied in the concept of communal living, regarded as an antidote to the psychological pathologies of the nuclear family. (Some prominent San Francisco rock bands, including the Grateful Dead, actually *were* communes.) These communitarian values were embodied in large, loosely bounded public events called "be-ins," which emphasized informal musical performance, spontaneity, and camaraderie. This communal, "let it all hang out" ethos spilled over into the large concert venues where rock music was typically played in the late 1960s, including San Francisco's Avalon Ballroom and the Fillmore West. The countercultural commitment to antiestablishment values included a variety of anarchist and libertarian philosophies. This commitment was correlated with a rejection of the romanticism of mainstream pop music, and a rejection of the commercial motivations of the big corporations that marketed pop music. (Ironically, some rock bands associated closely with the counterculture—including the Jefferson Airplane—had enough business savvy to secure lucrative contracts with major labels. Some of the biggest record corporations—for example, Columbia Records—actually promoted themselves as specializing in countercultural music.)

The issues surrounding free love—or liberated sexuality—in the 1960s have become so controversial and mythologized (especially in light of our more recent, ongoing crises with AIDS) that straightforward discussion of them is still nearly impossible. In fact, the sexual mores of the period had surprisingly little direct effect on the style or substance of pop music. Surely there was much intricate and newly poetic probing of the *emotional* nature of relationships in the song lyrics of the era, owing chiefly to the influence of Dylan and other folk rockers. But apart from isolated, and slightly later, examples (one could cite "Love the One You're With," a hit for both Stephen Stills and the Isley Brothers in 1971, or "The Pill," a 1975 recording by country star Loretta Lynn), the sexual revolution of the 1960s seems not to have been significantly documented in the music of the time. Of course, it could also be claimed that sexuality has been at least an implicit subject in most of the popular love songs of any period—we could go back to "My Blue Heaven," where "baby makes three" (see Chapter 4)—and that consequently there was little need to change the basic character of love song lyrics in the 1960s to accommodate a new generation. Presumably, everybody who needed to know knew what was being sung about when a singer pleaded "I want you," whether that singer was Elvis Presley in the culturally conservative 1950s ("I Want You, I Need You, I Love You," 1956) or Bob Dylan in the culturally radical 1960s ("I Want You," 1966).

Similarly, the contemporary dilemma of drug use in American society—including the abuse of drugs by very young people—makes it hard to provide a simple, unambiguous evaluation of the counterculture's relationship to intoxicants and recreational chemicals. The vulgar catchphrase was "sex, *drugs,* and rock and roll"; and instead of (or in addition to) the alcohol of their parents' generation many young people in the 1960s came to favor psychedelic substances, particularly marijuana and LSD (lysergic acid diethylamide, or "acid"). Unquestionably there was lots of drug use, both by musicians and by their audiences, in the later 1960s. Many recordings and concerts were experienced by "stoned" young people; at least some of those recordings and concerts were probably intended by the musicians to be experienced in that way; and some of the musicians involved made the music while stoned themselves. There is, for example, no possible dispute about the subject matter of a song with a title like "Don't Bogart That Joint." But when questioned about the Beatles' song "Lucy in the Sky with Diamonds," whose title and psychedelic imagery was widely assumed to be connected to LSD, John Lennon replied that the song had been inspired by a picture drawn by his four-year-old son that the little boy had himself called "Lucy in the sky with diamonds," and Lennon disclaimed any connection between the song and drugs. (Of course, one could choose to be skeptical about Lennon's statement as well; the point is that there is no absolute "truth" that can be determined here.) Certainly the flamboyant, colorful visual effects used on rock music posters and record jackets and in the light shows at rock concerts were to some degree modeled on the experience of tripping. In the end, however, it is not easy to determine to what degree the characteristic open-endedness of many rock music performances—including the hours-long musical explorations of bands like Jefferson Airplane and the Grateful Dead—is directly attributable to drug use.

In order to put the drug culture of the 1960s into perspective, it is necessary to remember a number of things. The use and abuse of alcohol, marijuana, cocaine, heroin, and other drugs has formed a part of the culture of musicians and their audiences in this country for a very long time. The pressures and doldrums of a performer's life have led many musicians to use stimulants, depressants, and intoxicants of various kinds, and unhealthy dependencies have naturally resulted all too frequently, prematurely snuffing out some of the brightest lights in America's musical history. (A partial list would include Charlie Parker, Hank Williams Sr., Elvis Presley, Janis Joplin, and Jimi Hendrix, among many others.) Furthermore, the venues in which pop music is heard live are most commonly those in which the legal—and sometimes illegal—consumption of intoxicants forms an essential aspect of the audience's "good time." In this connection, it is important to recall that during the era of Prohibition, 1919–33, the manufacture and sale of alcoholic beverages were illegal in the United States. Thus many adults who were nonplussed by younger people's consumption of illegal marijuana and LSD in the 1960s had doubtless themselves enjoyed the new pop music and jazz of the 1920s and early 1930s to the accompaniment, in speakeasy clubs or at home, of illegal bootleg liquor.

An appropriate perspective on the drug use of the 1960s would also take into account that many participants in the counterculture, including musicians and members of the rock audience, were not involved with drugs. Furthermore, along with the pleasure seekers who sought only to enjoy themselves and follow fashion while repeating the slogans of the time about "mind expansion" and "turning on," there were those who were quite seriously seeking alternatives to the prevailing American bourgeois lifestyle, who may have employed hallucinogens such as peyote, psilocybin mushrooms, and LSD carefully and sparingly as an aspect of spiritual exploration (in a manner akin to that found in certain nonwestern cultures—there was, for example, a good deal of interest in Indian culture among members of the counterculture, some of it superficial and trendy but some of it assuredly serious). In the end, it appears that the value of psychoactive substances depends on the context and manner of their use; and that the drug culture of the 1960s was, at various times, both an enabler and a destroyer of musical creativity. Interviews with rock musicians of the late 1960s—now in their fifties and sixties—are notable for their lack of nostalgia in relation to drug use.

It was, and is, easy to poke fun at stereotypical images of the counterculture. Frank Zappa, assuredly a participant in the counterculture (and reportedly a nondrug user), wrote a savagely satirical song in 1967 called "Who Needs the Peace Corps?" that targeted "phony hippies" and their "psychedelic dungeons." Yet the greatest virtue of the 1960s counterculture, for all its naïveté and excesses, may be that it gave birth to and encouraged some innovative and remarkable creative manifestations, among which are certainly the works of Zappa himself. We will now look at a few of these creative reflections of, and influences on, the "age of psychedelia."

SGT. PEPPER'S LONELY HEARTS CLUB BAND

Summer 1967 was the so-called Summer of Love, when many young participants in the newly self-aware counterculture were following the advice of a pop hit that told them to head for San Francisco (whose Haight-Ashbury district was already a legendary center of countercultural activity), wearing flowers in their hair. But the group celebrations called "love-ins" were not limited to San Francisco. In fact, a sense of participation in the counterculture was readily available that summer to anyone who had a phonograph and the spending money to purchase the Beatles' new album, *Sgt. Pepper's Lonely Hearts Club Band,* as revolutionary a work of pop musical art as had ever been made.

The countercultural ambience of *Sgt. Pepper* was obvious in a number of ways. The unprecedented and now-famous album cover, a wild collage of faces and figures surrounding the four Beatles dressed in full formal band regalia, pictured a number of people from many different time periods who were associated with aspects of the counterculture: Karl Marx, Oscar Wilde, Marlon Brando, James Dean, not to mention Bob Dylan. (The figure of a young girl off to the side was dressed in a sweater that read "Welcome the Rolling Stones"!) The song that opened the second side of the record, "Within You without You," was the most thoroughgoing of the Beatles' attempts to evoke the sound and spirit of Indian music; it featured Indian instruments (sitar and tabla, in lieu of guitars and Western drums), unusual meters and phrase structures, and deeply meditative, philosophical lyrics.

The lyrics to a number of other songs had what could easily be interpreted as drug references, for those so inclined. We have already mentioned "Lucy in the Sky with Diamonds," but among other examples well noted at the time were "A Little Help from My Friends," which features the repeated line "I get high with a little help from my friends," and the concluding song "A Day in the Life," which ends the album with the famous line "I'd love to turn you on." Furthermore, the record had many musical sounds and sound effects that could be—and were—interpreted as psychedelic in inspiration. Among the most celebrated of these were the electronically distorted voices in "Lucy in the Sky with Diamonds" and the chaotic orchestral sweep upward that occurs twice in "A Day in the Life."

Arguably more important than any specific countercultural references in *Sgt. Pepper* was the way in which the album was structured to invite its listeners' participation in an implied community. The record is a clearly and cleverly organized performance that reflects an awareness of, and actually addresses, its audience. The

The *Sgt. Pepper*–era **Beatles.** Frank Driggs Collection.

opening song, "Sgt. Pepper's Lonely Hearts Club Band," formally introduces the "show" to come and acknowledges the listener(s) with lines like "We hope you will enjoy the show," and "You're such a lovely audience, we'd love to take you home with us." This song is reprised, with different words ("We hope you have enjoyed the show") as the penultimate selection on the album, after which the "performance" ends and the performers return to "reality" with "A Day in the Life" ("I read the news today, oh boy"). Yet even in this final song, the continued presence of the listener(s) is acknowledged, at least implicitly, with the line "I'd love to turn you on."

The Beatles' brilliant conceit of *Sgt. Pepper* as a "performance" is evident even before the music begins: the opening sounds on the record are those of a restless audience. Audience sounds of laughter and applause are heard at schematic points in both the initial presentation and the reprise of the song "Sgt. Pepper's Lonely Hearts Club Band." Yet this is clearly not a recording of an actual live performance. Virtually every song on the album features a unique instrumental arrangement significantly different from that of the songs that precede and follow it—in other words, the songs are arranged to provide maximum variety and contrast on a record album, not as a practical sequence for a live performance situation. Even more obviously, the album is full of studio-produced effects, the most spectacular of which are the sound collage that actually overlaps the ending of "Good Morning Good Morning" with the reprise of "Sgt. Pepper's Lonely Hearts Club Band," and the explosively distorted final chord of "A Day in the Life," which very gradually fades out over a duration of about forty-five seconds. In the employment of these effects, and in many other aspects of the album, the hand of the producer George Martin is clearly evident.

There is a profound irony in the fact that the first album made by the Beatles after they decided to abandon live performing and assume an identity solely as a recording act is an album that, in effect, mimics and creatively reimagines the concept of performing before an audience. This irony would, of course, not be lost on Beatles fans, who were well aware of the group's highly publicized decision, and who had to wait longer for this album than for any previous one by the group. (More than nine months separated the release of *Sgt. Pepper* from that of the Beatles' immediately preceding album, *Revolver,* and that was a long time in those days.) But *Sgt. Pepper* in turn so widened and enriched the idea of what a rock album could be that, it could be argued, the gain at least somewhat balanced the loss of the Beatles as a touring group.

Rock 'n' roll had always communicated to its widest audience by means of records. *Sgt. Pepper* simply turned that established fact into a basis for brilliantly self-conscious artifice. When the Beatles sang "We'd love to take you home with us" in the opening song of the album, they must have done so with ironic recognition of the fact that it was actually their audience that takes *them* home—in the form of their records. As we have already attempted to show, everything about *Sgt. Pepper* is inclusionary; it posits the rock album as the creator of an audience community, a community for which that album also serves as a means of communication and identity. And in fact the album achieved unprecedented success in reaching a large community, even by the Beatles' standards: it sold eight million copies and remained on *Billboard*'s album charts for more than three years.

The most historically significant fact about *Sgt. Pepper* is the way in which it definitively redirected attention from the single-song recording to the record album as the focus of where important new pop music was being made. That *Sgt. Pepper* was conceived as a totality, rather than as a collection of single songs, is apparent in many ways, but most indicative perhaps was the unprecedented marketing decision not to release any of the songs on the album as singles. (The singles gap was filled by the Beatles' release of "All You Need Is Love" in the summer of 1967, a song that would only later be collected on an album.) *Sgt. Pepper* was not the first concept album, but it was the first album to present itself to the public as a complete and unified marketing package, with a distinctive and interrelated collection of parts, all of which were unavailable in any other form: not just the songs on the record itself, but also the cover art and the inside photograph of the Beatles in their band uniforms, the complete song lyrics printed on the back of the album jacket (a first, and a precedent-setting one), the extra page of "Sgt. Pepper cut-outs" supplied with the album, and even (with the earlier pressings) a unique inner sleeve to hold the record that was adorned with "psychedelic" swirls of pink and red coloring!

Sgt. Pepper did for the rock album what Dylan's "Like a Rolling Stone" had done for the rock single. It rewrote all the rules, and things were never the same again. Countless albums appearing in the wake of *Sgt. Pepper* imitated aspects of the Beatles' tour de force, from its cover art to its printed lyrics to its use of a musical reprise, but few could approach its real substance and achievement. To their credit, the Beatles themselves did not try to imitate it but went on to other things, continuing to produce innovative music on albums and singles until they disbanded early in 1970. As of the present writing, interest in the Beatles continues unabated; their three *Anthology* collections (on discs and videos) of previously unreleased material have all been recent best-sellers, and in 2000 a new compilation of their top-selling singles, entitled simply *1*, was released and proved extremely popular.

SAN FRANCISCO ROCK: JEFFERSON AIRPLANE, JANIS JOPLIN, AND THE GRATEFUL DEAD

During the late 1960s an "alternative" rock music scene, inspired in part by the Beatles' experimentalism, established itself in San Francisco. The city had already long been a center for artistic communities and subcultures, including the "beat" literary movement of the 1950s, a lively urban folk music scene, and a highly visible and vocal gay community. "Psychedelic rock," as the music played by San Francisco bands was sometimes called, encompassed a variety of styles and musical influences, including folk rock, blues, "hard rock," Latin music, and Indian classical music. In geographical terms, San Francisco's psychedelic music scene was focused on the Haight-Ashbury neighborhood, center of the hippie movement.

A number of musical entrepreneurs and institutions supported the growth of the San Francisco rock music scene. Tom Donahue, a local radio **DJ,** challenged the mainstream Top 40 AM pop music format on San Francisco's KYA and later pioneered a new, open-ended, and eclectic broadcasting format on FM station KMPX. (Donahue is the spiritual forefather of today's alternative FM formats, including many college stations.) The foremost promoter of the new rock bands—and the first to cash in on the music's popularity—was Bill Graham. Graham, a European immigrant who had worked as a taxi driver to support his business studies, began staging rock concerts in San Francisco in 1965. For one of his first rock concerts

Graham rented a skating rink, which he later renamed the Fillmore. The Fillmore—renamed the Fillmore West when Graham opened the Fillmore East in New York City—was a symbolic center of the counterculture, and psychedelic posters advertising its concerts are today worth thousands of dollars. Other individuals built professional careers out of the job of creating psychedelic atmosphere for rock concerts: Chet Helms, for example, was responsible for developing the multimedia aesthetic of light shows at the Fillmore and Avalon Ballroom.

Jefferson Airplane was the first nationally successful band to emerge out of the San Francisco psychedelic scene. Founded in 1965, the Airplane was originally a semiacoustic folk-rock band, performing blues and songs by Bob Dylan. Eventually they began to develop a louder, harder-edged style with a greater emphasis on open forms, instrumental improvisation, and visionary lyrics. Along with the Quicksilver Messenger Service and the Grateful Dead (see below), Jefferson Airplane was one of the original triumvirate of San Francisco "acid rock" bands, playing at the Matrix Club (center of the San Francisco alternative nightclub scene), larger concert venues such as the Avalon Ballroom and Fillmore, and at communal outdoor events such as happenings and be-ins. In late 1965 the Airplane received an unprecedented twenty-thousand-dollar advance from RCA, one of the largest and most powerful corporations in the world. (Despite the anticommercial rhetoric of the counterculture, this event was responsible for sparking off the formation of dozens of psychedelic bands in the Bay Area eager to cash in on the Airplane's success. Parallels to this seemingly paradoxical link between countercultural values and the good old profit motive may sometimes be observed in connection with today's "alternative" music movements.) The Airplane's 1967 LP *Surrealistic Pillow* sold over one million copies, reaching Number Three on the pop album charts and spawning two Top 10 singles. The biggest celebrity in the group was vocalist Grace Slick (b. 1939), who—along with Janis Joplin—was the most important female musician on the San Francisco scene.

Jefferson Airplane were introduced to a national audience by their recording of "Somebody to Love," which reached Number Five on the national pop charts in 1967. "Somebody to Love" exemplifies the acid rock approach, including a dense musical texture with plenty of volume and lots of electronic distortion. (The process of making hit singles encouraged the band to trim its normally extended, improvised performances down to a manageable—and AM radio–friendly—three minutes.) The song itself, which originated in an act of familial composition by Grace Slick, her husband, and her brother-in-law, exemplifies the tendency of late 1960s rock musicians to compose their own material. (Another paradox of the psychedelic rock movement was that it combined the urban folk musicians' emphasis on communal creativity with the influential rock-musician-as-artist ideology represented in the work of the Beatles, Bob Dylan, and Brian Wilson.)

Grace Slick's only serious competition as queen of the San Francisco rock scene came from Janis Joplin (1943–70), the most successful white blues singer of the 1960s. Born in Port Arthur, Texas, Joplin came to San Francisco in the mid-1960s and joined a band called Big Brother and the Holding Company. Their appearance at the Monterey Pop Festival in 1967 led to a contract with Columbia Records, eager to cash in on RCA's success with Jefferson Airplane, and on the growing national audience for acid rock. Big Brother's 1968 album *Cheap Thrills*—graced with a cover design by the underground comic book artist Robert Crumb—reached Number One on the pop charts and included a Number Twelve hit single (the song "Piece of My Heart," a cover version of a 1960s R&B hit by Erma Franklin).

Joplin's full-tilt singing style and directness of expression were inspired by blues singers such as Bessie Smith, and by the R&B recordings of Big Mama Thornton. (Joplin rediscovered Big Mama in the late 1960s and helped to revive her performing career.) She pushed her voice unmercifully, reportedly saying that she would prefer a short, exceptional career to a long career as an unexceptional performer. Although her growling, bluesy style made her an icon for the mainly white audience for rock music, Joplin was not a success with black audiences, and she never managed to cross over to the R&B charts.

One of Joplin's most moving performances is her rendition of the George and Ira Gershwin composition "Summertime," written in 1935 for the American folk opera *Porgy and Bess*. Although this recording was criticized for the less-than-polished accompaniment provided by Big Brother and the Holding Company, Joplin's performance is riveting. She squeezes every last drop of emotion out of the song, pushing her voice to the limit, and creating not only the rough, rasping tones expected of a blues singer but also multipitched sounds called "multiphonics." The impression one retains of Janis Joplin—an impression reinforced by listening to her

Janis Joplin performs with Big Brother and the Holding Company, 1968. Courtesy Library of Congress.

recordings—is actually that of a sweet, vulnerable person, whose tough exterior and heavy reliance on drugs functioned as defense mechanisms, and as armor against life's disappointments.

No survey of the 1960s San Francisco rock scene would be complete without mention of the Grateful Dead, a thoroughly idiosyncratic band—actually as much an experience or institution as a band in the usual sense—whose career spanned more than three decades. (Although it is often stated that the Grateful Dead were not a commercially successful band, eight of their LPs reached the Top 20, including 1987's *In the Dark,* which held the Number Nine position on *Billboard*'s album charts.) "The Dead," as they are known to their passionately devoted followers, grew out of a series of bands involving <u>Jerry Garcia</u> (1942–95), a guitarist, banjoist, and singer who had played in various urban folk groups during the early 1960s. This shifting collective of musicians gradually took firmer shape and in 1967 was christened the Grateful Dead (a phrase Garcia apparently ran across in an ancient Egyptian prayer book). The Dead helped to pioneer the transition from urban folk music to folk rock to acid rock, adopting electric instruments, living communally in the Haight-Ashbury district, and participating in public LSD parties ("acid tests") before the drug was outlawed. (These experiences were chronicled in Tom Wolfe's book *The Electric Kool-Aid Acid Test.*)

In musical terms, it is hard to classify the Grateful Dead's work. For one thing, their records do not for the most part do them justice. The Dead were the quintessential "live" rock band, specializing in long jams that wander through diverse musical styles and grooves and typically terminate in unexpected places. The influence of folk music—prominent on some of their early recordings—was usually just below the surface, and a patient listener may expect to hear a kind of "sketch-map" of American popular music—including folk, blues, R&B, and country music, as well as rock 'n' roll—with occasional gestures in the direction of African or Asian music. Their repertoire of songs was huge; in any given live performance, one might have heard diverse songs from different periods in the band's existence. (This means that each performance was also a unique musical version of the band's history, at least for those who had studied it.)

If the Grateful Dead were a unique musical institution, their devoted fans—"Deadheads"—were a social phenomenon unparalleled in the history of American popular music. Traveling incessantly in psychedelically decorated buses and vans, setting up camp in every town along the tour, and generally pursuing a peaceful mode of coexistence with local authorities, hardcore Deadheads literally lived for their band. While it has been pointed out that much of the satisfaction of this mobile/communal lifestyle has to do with the creation of a special social ethos, there can be no denying that the core source of appeal for serious Deadheads was the band's music. They taped the band's performances—were often *encouraged* to tape the band's performances, something quite unusual in the popular music business—and then circulated these tapes (called *bootlegs*), building up extensive lists that chronicle every concert the band ever played. There are now entire sites devoted to this purpose on the World Wide Web, with precise descriptions of the repertoires played at particular concerts and statistical breakdowns of the frequency of certain songs and certain sequences of songs. Although other popular musicians have certainly inspired adoration—Frank Sinatra, Elvis Presley, and the Beatles come immediately to mind—the devotion of Deadheads remains truly unique.

Box 10.3 "Cloud Nine": The Motown Response to Psychedelia

With its gaze always fixed firmly on the commercial mainstream, the Motown organization was never one that could directly be associated with the conception of a counterculture. But Motown was also "the sound of young America," and Berry Gordy Jr. was pop-savvy enough to realize that completely ignoring the influence of artists like Bob Dylan and the Beatles on the rock audience would relegate Motown's music to the dreaded realm of the irrelevant and unhip. Sure enough, the Supremes' "summer of love" hit in 1967, "Reflections," opened with the sounds of a strange, repeated electronic beep, followed by an explosion! After this tip of the hat to psychedelia, the record proceeded in a style basically identical to that of the Supremes' earlier efforts—except for the occasional recurrence of the strange beep.

A more thoroughgoing, serious attempt by Motown to respond to currents in the counterculture is represented by the late 1960s and early 1970s records of the Temptations. Producer Norman Whitfield, who was cowriting songs for the Temptations with Barrett Strong, actually caused some controversy within the Motown organization when he came up with "Cloud Nine" in late 1968. The "cloud nine" of the song, where "you can be what you want to be" and "you're a million miles from reality," is obviously a drug reference, but the context is far removed from that of blissful, mind-expanding psychedelia; the reality of the song is that of the urban slums, where people turn to drugs out of desperation. The gritty depiction of slum life in the lyrics of "Cloud Nine" related the song much more closely to the spirit of socially conscious urban folk rock than to the spirit usually associated with psychedelia. The sound of the record was also quite novel for Motown, with distorted electric guitars and echolike effects setting off a vocal arrangement that made a point of contrasting the varied vocal timbres and ranges represented among the members of the Temptations. In effect, "Cloud Nine" represented a new kind of hybrid for Motown, one that fused elements of the new rock and folk rock with the potent synthesis of pop and rhythm & blues that had always characterized its music. (A parallel may be drawn with the music being developed at this same time by the San Francisco–based interracial "psychedelic soul" group Sly and the Family Stone, which was attempting a similar kind of complex fusion. This group was headed by the African American songwriter/producer Sylvester Stewart.)

The success of "Cloud Nine" (Number Six pop, Number Two R&B) established the marketability of Whitfield's new approach and led, naturally enough, to other hit records by the Temptations along analogous lines, like "Run Away Child, Running Wild," "Psychedelic Shack," "Ball of Confusion (That's What The World Is Today)," and "Papa Was a Rollin' Stone." Other Motown acts also made their contributions to the organization's hipper image; 1970 brought Edwin Starr's protest song "War"—another Whitfield-Strong composition that reached Number One on the pop charts—and a record by the Supremes called "Stoned Love."

Jerry Garcia died in 1995—partly as a result of longtime drug and alcohol use—and the band has officially broken up, but the remaining members still assemble periodically to hit the road, with their huge entourage in tow. And although in the span of more than three decades the band placed only one single in the Top 40 ("Touch of Gray," a Number Nine pop hit in 1987), the thirty-odd albums recorded by the Grateful Dead continue, year by year, to sell hundreds of thousands of copies to one of the most loyal audiences in the history of American popular music.

GUITAR HEROES: HENDRIX AND CLAPTON

The 1960s saw the rise of a new generation of electric guitarists who functioned as culture heroes for their young fans. Their achievements were built on the shoulders of previous generations of electric guitar virtuosos—Les Paul, whose innovative tinkering with electronic technology inspired a new generation of amplifier tweakers; T-Bone Walker, who introduced the electric guitar to R&B music in the late 1940s; urban blues musicians such as Muddy Waters and B. B. King, whose raw sound and emotional directness inspired rock guitarists; and early masters of rock 'n' roll guitar, including Chuck Berry and Buddy Holly. Beginning in the mid-1960s, the new guitarists—including Jimi Hendrix, Eric Clapton, Jimmy Page, Jeff Beck, and the Beatles' George Harrison—took these influences and pushed them farther than ever before in terms of technique, sheer volume, and improvisational brilliance.

The Jimi Hendrix Experience. Frank Driggs Collection.

Jimi Hendrix (1942–70) was the most original, inventive, and influential guitarist of the rock era, and the most prominent African American rock musician of the late 1960s. His early experience as a guitarist was gained touring with rhythm & blues bands. In 1966 he moved to London, where, at the suggestion of the producer Chas Chandler, he joined up with two English musicians, bassist Noel Redding and drummer Mitch Mitchell, eventually forming a band called the Jimi Hendrix Experience. The Experience was first seen in America in 1967 at the Monterey Pop Festival, where Hendrix stunned the audience with his flamboyant performance style, which involved playing the guitar with his teeth and behind his back, stroking its neck along his microphone stand, pretending to make love to it, and setting it on fire with lighter fluid and praying to it. (This sort of guitar-focused showmanship, soon to become commonplace at rock concerts, was not unrelated to the wild stage antics of some rhythm & blues performers. Viewing the Hendrix segment of the documentary film *Monterey Pop,* it is clear that some people in the self-consciously hip and mainly middle-class white audience found themselves shocked and therefore delighted by Hendrix's boldness.)

Jimi Hendrix's creative employment of feedback, distortion, and sound-manipulating devices like the wah-wah pedal and fuzz box, coupled with his fondness for aggressive dissonance and incredibly loud volume—all of these characteristics represented important additions to the musical techniques and materials available to guitarists. Hendrix was a sound sculptor, who seemed at times to be consciously exploring the borderline between traditional conceptions of music and noise, a pursuit that links him in certain ways to composers exploring electronic sounds and media in the world of art music at around the same time. (One of the most famous examples of Hendrix's experimentation with electronically generated sound was his performance of the American national anthem at the Woodstock Festival in 1969. Between each phrase of the melody, Hendrix soared into an elaborate electronic fantasy, imitating "the rockets' red glare, the bombs bursting in air," and then landing precisely on the beginning of next phrase, like a virtuoso jazz musician. This was widely taken as an antiwar commentary, though Hendrix had himself served in the U.S. Army paratroopers.) All of these cited characteristics, along with any number of striking studio effects, may be heard on the first album by the Experience, *Are You Experienced?* (1967), and particularly on its famous opening cut, "Purple Haze."

In one limited sense, "Purple Haze" is a strophic song with clear roots in blues-based melodic figures, harmonies, and chord progressions. But to regard the extraordinary instrumental introduction, the guitar solo between the second and third strophes, and the violently distorted instrumental conclusion all as mere effects added to a strophic tune is really to miss the point. In fact, it could be argued that the strophic tune serves as a mere scaffolding for the instrumental passages; but at the least, the effects are equal in importance to the elements of the tune itself. The radical character and depth of Hendrix's contribution may be seen in the extent to which he requires us to readjust our thinking and terminology in the effort to describe appropriately what constitutes the real essence of his song. When we add in the impact of the lyrics, with their reference to "blowin' my mind" and lines like "'scuse me while I kiss the sky," it is easy to see why Hendrix became an iconic figure for the counterculture, as well as a role model for rock musicians.

It is emblematic of how far Hendrix had strayed from his rhythm & blues roots in music like "Purple Haze" that neither this song, nor any other released by Hendrix as a single, ever made a dent in the in the R&B charts. Hendrix was not a singles artist in any case, and his real kinship was with the new rock audience that viewed the record album as its essential source of musical enlightenment. In a sense, this made him a new kind of crossover artist. His audience rewarded him by elevating all of the five albums he designed for release in his all-too-brief lifetime into the Top 10.

We have noted that Hendrix's notoriety as a creative force first developed in England, and this was no accident. On the one hand, it was arguably difficult for an African American musician who neither fit into nor cared much about popular definitions of black musical style to find acceptance in the American popular music scene. And the way toward Hendrix's success in London was also paved by a thriving British pop culture scene, including boutiques, nightclubs, and youth movements such as the "mods"—who wore elaborate clothing reminiscent of centuries-old fashions and listened to American soul music—and the "rockers"—leather-jacketed rock 'n' roll fans. As we have seen, British youth seized upon American popular music with a passion during the 1960s, and an important part of this fascination was focused on the electric guitar.

Eric Clapton (b. 1945) was the most influential of the young British guitarists who emerged during the mid-1960s. Influenced by the blues recordings of Robert Johnson and B. B. King, he first attracted notice as a member of the Yardbirds, a band that had little pop success but served as a training ground for young guitarists, including Clapton, Jeff Beck, and Jimmy Page (later a member of Led Zeppelin). Clapton soon began to attract the adulation of young blues and R&B fans, largely as a result of his long, flowing blues-based guitar solos. (The most common graffiti slogan in mid-1960s London was "Clapton is God," an index of his popularity.) From 1966 to 1968 Clapton played in a band called Cream, featuring the drummer Ginger Baker and bassist Jack Bruce. Cream, the first in a line of rock "power trios" that formed during the late 1960s and early 1970s, exerted a major influence on early heavy metal music (see Chapter 11). Their performances were more akin to avant-garde jazz than to pop music, using "songs" as quickly discardable excuses for long, open-ended improvised solos. Cream took the United States by storm in the late 1960s, selling millions of LPs in the space of three years and placing two singles in the Top 10.

Although it is difficult to summarize the work of a musical improviser in a single recording, Cream's version of Robert Johnson's "Cross Road Blues," retitled "Crossroads," recorded live at the Fillmore West in San Francisco, does convey a sense of the power and passion of Eric Clapton's guitar playing. While this song represents the deep respect that many rock guitarists held for Robert Johnson, the 1936 and 1968 recordings are in many ways light-years apart. In stylistic terms, Cream's performance is more indebted to postwar urban blues and R&B than to the Delta blues. Johnson's complex guitar accompaniment has been reduced to a single powerful riff, played in unison by the electric guitar and bass guitar, and projected by a veritable wall of amplifiers. Clearly, the recordings of Robert Johnson were an inspiration and not a direct musical model for young guitarists like Clapton.

Still, there is at least one similarity between the musical challenges faced by the two master guitarists, playing some thirty years apart: both men's performances are highly exposed, Johnson playing solo and Clapton with only bass and drum set ac-

---

Box 10.4   Roots Rock: Creedence Clearwater Revival

In 1969, a year when the influence of the counterculture seemed to be at a new height—what with domestic political turmoil on the one hand, and the Woodstock music festival attracting nearly half a million fans on the other—the pop charts were ruled by Creedence Clearwater Revival. This seems initially like another of pop music's great historical ironies. Creedence was a deliberately old-fashioned rock 'n' roll band, consisting of two guitarists, a bass player, and a drummer, performing both original material and some old 1950s rock 'n' roll tunes in a musical style essentially untouched by the trappings of the psychedelic era: no exotic instruments, no unusual or extended guitar solos, no studio effects, no self-conscious experimentation with novel harmonies, rhythms, or song forms. Creedence was one of the all-time great singles bands, turning out a spate of incredibly catchy, uptempo two- to three-minute pop records that cut right through all the psychedelic haze and scored major hits for the group one after the other. Given these songs' lack of pretension, they were as effective as live performance vehicles as they were as pop recordings. In addition, the albums put out by Creedence were all huge sellers, despite—or perhaps we should say because of—the fact that they were essentially just old-fashioned collections of great singles.

Creedence Clearwater Revival restored to rock music a sense of its roots at precisely the point when the majority of important rock musicians seemed to be pushing the envelope of novel possibilities as far and as rapidly as they could. Creedence was in no sense a reactionary phenomenon, however; the group's choice of the word "revival" was an astute one. The many original songs in their repertoire, all written by lead singer and guitarist John Fogerty, possessed solid musical virtues, and several of them also reflected a decidedly up-to-date political awareness (such as "Bad Moon Rising" and "Fortunate Son") that nevertheless was not tied to any specific agenda (much like the kind of awareness found in Bob Dylan's lyrics). In fact, Creedence's best songs have arguably stood the test of time better than a lot of other music from the 1960s that might have seemed much more adventurous and relevant at the time.

Creedence Clearwater Revival was the first widely successful "roots" rock 'n' roll band. Perhaps owing to their extraordinary popularity, many other roots artists have appeared as rock has continued to evolve. But Creedence set the standard in this realm, and it is one that has yet to be approached by anyone else.

---

companiment. This has the effect of focusing attention on the guitarist and requiring that he play more or less constantly to keep the performance moving. Clapton's approach to this task involves not only the application of highly developed technical skills but also the use of electronic **feedback,** which allows him to sustain long notes and create flowing streams of shorter notes. The performance opens with Clapton singing a few stanzas of Johnson's song, then launching into an escalating series of improvised twelve-bar choruses. This is "busy" music, designed to show-case the virtuosity of the performers, and Baker and Bruce play constantly through-out, driving Clapton along to higher and higher emotional peaks. Although some rock critics regard Cream as an example of the self-indulgence and showiness of some late-1960s rock music, there can be no disputing that Clapton, Baker, and Bruce both upped the technical ante for rock musicians and paved the way for later guitar-focused bands. And they also helped to establish the importance of the con-cert as a venue for experiencing rock music—hardcore fans argued that unless you heard Clapton play live, you hadn't really heard him at all.

During the second half of the 1960s, the popular music favored by many young Americans took on a harder-edged, more emphatic tone. African American soul musicians reemphasized the gritty, down-to-earth side of rhythm & blues and made its political dimensions more explicit. And a new generation of musicians—raised on a diet of blues, R&B, urban folk music, and rock 'n' roll—helped to create rock, the loud, unruly, and increasingly profitable child of the music pioneered by Chuck Berry, Elvis Presley, and others in the 1950s.

In Chapter 11 we will follow rock music's transformation from an experimen-talist, countercultural movement into a profit-making center of the American en-tertainment industry. It was during the 1970s that the tension between commer-cialism and authenticity that characterizes rock music right up to the present day arose in a clear form. In addition, the 1970s saw the first appearance of rock 'n' roll nostalgia, a sign both that the baby boomers were aging and that rock music had begun to develop a sense of its own history.

CHAPTER ELEVEN

THE 1970s

Rock Music and the Popular Mainstream

One of the most pervasive stereotypes about the 1970s—famously captured in novelist Tom Wolfe's epithet, "The Me Decade"—has to do with a shift in the values of young adults, away from the communitarian, politically engaged ideals of the 1960s counterculture, toward more materialistic and conservative attitudes. While this generalization should be taken with a large grain of salt, it is undeniable that the early 1970s did see a kind of turning inward in American culture. The majority of Americans had grown weary of the military conflict in Vietnam, which drew to a close with the U.S. withdrawal from Saigon in 1975. Around the same time, popular attention was focused on domestic problems, including the oil crisis (1973) and economic inflation, which threatened the financial security of millions of Americans. If the assassination of President Kennedy in 1963 had robbed many Americans of a certain political idealism, the Watergate hearings—viewed by millions on television—and the subsequent resignation of President Nixon (1974) occasioned a growing cynicism about politics.

Meanwhile, the ideological polarization of the late 1960s continued unabated, and popular music remained a favorite target of conservative politicians and commentators, much as it had been during the jazz and rock 'n' roll "scares" of the 1920s and 1950s. It is interesting that in 1970, just as America was taking a conservative turn, hippie dress and slang, psychedelic imagery, and rock music had begun to enter the cultural mainstream of AM radio, network television, and Hollywood movies. (This suggests an analogy to the 1920s, when the "jazz age" was born in a period of strong political conservatism.) In the early 1970s the market for popular music became focused on two main categories of consumers: a new generation of teenagers, born in the late 1950s and early 1960s; and adults aged twenty-five to forty, who had grown up with rock 'n' roll and were looking for more mature (i.e., more conservative) material. Nostalgic fare such as the film *American Graffiti* (1973), the Broadway musical and film *Grease* (1972 and 1978, respectively), and the popular television series *Happy Days* used early rock 'n' roll—now nearly twenty years old—to evoke the so-called Golden Age of 1950s America, before the Kennedy assassination, the invasion of the Beatles, the rise of the counterculture, and the escalating social conflicts of the late 1960s.

If many Americans wished that the 1960s would just go away, others mourned the decade's passing. For rock fans, the end of the counterculture was poignantly symbolized by the deaths of Jimi Hendrix (1970), Janis Joplin (1970), and Jim Morrison of the Doors (1971), and by the breakup of the Beatles, who, more than any other group, inspired the triumphs (and excesses) of rock music. On December 31, 1970, Paul McCartney filed the legal brief that was to formally dissolve the business partnership of the Beatles. For many rock fans, the demise of the "Fab Four" was incontrovertible proof that the 1960s were dead and gone. But this certainly didn't mean that rock music itself was moribund. If in the late 1960s rock was the music of the counterculture, defined by its opposition to the mainstream of popular music, by the 1970s it had helped to redefine the popular mainstream, becoming the primary source of profit for an expanding and ever more centralized entertainment industry.

During the 1970s the music industry reached new heights of consolidation. Six huge corporations—Columbia/CBS, Warner Communications, RCA Victor, Capitol-EMI, MCA, and United Artists–MGM—were responsible for over 80 percent of record sales in the United States by the end of the decade. Total profits from the sale of recorded music reached new levels—two billion dollars in 1973 and four billion dollars in 1978—in part owing to the increasing popularity of prerecorded tapes. (The eight-track cartridge and cassette tape formats had initially been introduced during the mid-1960s, and their popularity expanded rapidly during the early 1970s. By 1975 sales of prerecorded tapes accounted for almost one-third of all music sales in the United States.)

However, the music industry had also become increasingly risky. During the 1970s the industry came to depend on a relatively small number of million-selling ("platinum") LPs to turn a profit. A small number of "multiplatinum" superstars—including Paul McCartney, Elton John, and Stevie Wonder—were able to negotiate multimillion-dollar contracts with the major record companies. Unable to compete in this high-end market, small independent labels of the sort that had pioneered rock 'n' roll in the 1950s accounted for only about one out of every ten records sold in the early 1970s. (The energy crisis of 1973 created a shortage of polyvinyl chloride, the petroleum-based substance from which tapes and discs were made, and this also helped to drive many small record companies out of business.) Yet, as we shall see in Chapter 12, the indies came back to exert an important musical influence in the second half of the decade, introducing new genres such as disco, punk rock, funk, and reggae.

Like other big businesses, the record industry was increasingly impelled to present more choices (or at least to create the impression of choice) for its customers. This imperative led to the emergence of dozens of specialized types of popular music—middle of the road (MOR), easy listening, adult contemporary, singer-songwriters, country pop, soft soul, urban contemporary, funk, disco, reggae, oldies, and lots of subgenres of rock music, including country rock, folk rock, soft rock, hard rock, pop rock, heavy metal, southern rock, jazz rock, blues rock, Latin rock, art rock, glam rock, punk rock, and so on—each with its own constellation of stars and target audience. Record stores were organized in more complex patterns, with dozens of distinct categories listed on the labels of record bins.

On the other hand, the Top 40 playlist format, based on nationally distributed, pretaped sequences of hit songs, increasingly dominated the AM radio airwaves, resulting in a diminished range of choices, at least for AM radio listeners. By the mid-1970s most AM radio stations relied heavily on professional programming consultants, who provided lists of records that had done well in various parts of the country. Throughout the decade, these radio playlists grew more and more restricted, making it difficult for bands without the backing of a major label to break into the Top 40.

While some hard rock or progressive rock bands were able to get singles onto Top 40 radio, the primary medium for broadcasting rock music was FM radio. During the 1970s the number of FM radio stations in the United States increased by almost a thousand, and the popularity of FM—with its capability for high-fidelity stereo broadcasting—surpassed that of AM radio. The eclectic free-form FM programming of the late 1960s—in which a **DJ** might follow a psychedelic rock record with a jazz or folk record—became restricted mainly to community- or college-based stations situated at the left end of the dial (where many such stations remain today). Seeking to boost their advertising revenues, many FM stations moved to a format called _AOR (album-oriented rock)_, aimed at young white males aged thirteen to twenty-five. The AOR format featured hard rock bands, such as Led Zeppelin and Deep Purple, and art rock bands like King Crimson; Emerson, Lake, and Palmer; and Pink Floyd. AOR generally excluded black artists, who were featured on a radio format called urban contemporary. (The only exceptions to this rule seem to have been Marvin Gaye, Stevie Wonder, and Sly and the Family Stone, whose music transcended the boundary between soul and rock.) While these changes led to greater economic efficiency, the definition of rock as white music, and the increasingly strict split between black and white popular music formats, reflected the general conservatism of the radio business and of the music industry as a whole.

A survey of _Billboard_ charts during the 1970s reveals a complex picture in which the various traditions discussed throughout this book—Tin Pan Alley, black popular music (now called "soul"), and country music—continued to intermingle with one another, as well as with rock music. The commercial mainstream, as defined mostly by AM radio, featured a variety of styles, each designed to reach a mass audience:

- _Pop rock_, an upbeat variety of rock music (represented by artists such as Elton John, Paul McCartney, Rod Stewart, Chicago, Peter Frampton)
- _Adult contemporary_, an extension of the old crooner tradition, with varying degrees of rock influence (Barbra Streisand, Neil Diamond, Roberta Flack, the Carpenters)
- _Singer-songwriters_, a cross between the urban folk music of Peter, Paul, and Mary and Bob Dylan and the commercial pop style of the Brill Building tunesmiths (Paul Simon, Carole King, James Taylor)[1]

---

1. Of course, performing artists can and did write their own material in all kinds of styles, but singer-songwriters were most frequently identified with the style indicated here.

- *Soft soul*, a slick variety of rhythm & blues, often with lush orchestral accompaniment (the O'Jays, the Spinners, Al Green, Barry White)
- *Country pop*, a style of soft rock, lightly tinged with country music influences (John Denver, Olivia Newton-John, Kenny Rogers)
- *Bubble gum*, cheerful songs aimed mainly at a preteen audience (the Jackson Five, the Osmonds)
- *Disco*, a new form of dance music in the late 1970s characterized by elaborate studio production and an insistent beat (Donna Summer, Chic, the Village People, the Bee Gees)

The 1970s also saw the beginnings of "oldies radio," which played hits of the 1950s and early 1960s. This is a further instance of the nostalgic tendencies that characterized the period—tendencies also symbolized by the renewed popularity of Elvis Presley, who scored more than twenty Top 40 hits during the 1970s, and of Chuck Berry, who charted his first Number One pop record in 1972, the double-entendre song "My Ding-a-Ling."

It is worth taking a moment to consider what these changes meant for African American musicians, who had, after all, provided much of the inspiration for new forms of popular music. By the mid-1970s older soul and R&B stars such as Aretha Franklin and James Brown, though still popular among black listeners, found it more difficult to penetrate the pop- and rock-dominated Top 40 charts. (However, both Franklin and Brown staged big comebacks during the 1980s.) Atlantic Records, a pioneer in the field of R&B and soul music, increasingly turned its attention to grooming and promoting white rock acts such as Led Zeppelin. Motown Records continued to score successes on Top 40 radio and the pop singles charts with artists such as Diana Ross (who left the Supremes to become a solo act in 1970), the "soul bubblegum" group Jackson Five, the Spinners, and Marvin Gaye. But Motown no longer enjoyed its former dominance of the crossover market.

Many of the black performers featured on the AM radio airwaves and Top 40 charts specialized in a smooth, romantic style called "soft soul," clearly indebted to the Motown sound of the early to mid-1960s. One of the most commercially successful forms of soul music during the 1970s was the so-called Philadelphia sound, produced by the team of Kenny Gamble and Leon Huff, and performed by groups such as the O'Jays ("Love Train") and Harold Melvin and the Blue Notes ("If You Don't Know Me by Now"). These groups had a great deal of crossover success in the 1970s, regularly scoring Top 10 hits on the pop charts and the soul (the equivalent of the old R&B) charts. In retrospect, it does seem that much 1970s soul music was less assertive in its lyrics and its rhythms than its 1960s counterpart, and some observers have suggested that this was a strategic counterreaction on the part of radio stations and record companies to the racial violence that had erupted on the streets of Watts, Detroit, and Newark during the late 1960s.

Watching today's cable television advertisements for collections of "classic seventies hits," one could come to the conclusion that rock music had by 1970 pushed the old Tin Pan Alley songwriting tradition off the map entirely. That would be inaccurate, however, for the first Number One single of the 1970s was a throwback to the Brill Building era of the early 1960s (see Chapter 9), a sprightly and thoroughly escapist pop song entitled "Raindrops Keep Fallin' on My Head," performed by former country singer B. J. Thomas. This record—which stayed on the charts for nearly six months, in no small part owing to its being featured in the soundtrack of a popular film, *Butch Cassidy and the Sundance Kid*—was composed by Hal David and Burt Bacharach, third-generation Tin Pan Alley songwriters (see Box 10.1), and the song was shopped around to various other singers (including Bob Dylan!) before Thomas was chosen to record it. (Interestingly, the song was a crossover hit, reaching Number Thirty-eight on the R&B charts in 1970, in a cover version by the black soul singer Barbara Mason.) Several Number One singles of the 1970s—such as Roberta Flack's "Killing Me Softly with His Song" (1973), Debby Boone's "You Light Up My Life" (1977), Barbra Streisand's film theme "The Way We Were" (1973), and her romantic duet with Neil Diamond on "You Don't Bring Me Flowers" (1978)—attest to the continuing popularity of an approach to composing and performing songs directly derived from the Tin Pan Alley tradition. While rock critics tend to regard most "soft rock" and "adult contemporary" as the musical equivalent of pond scum, there is no denying their mass popularity throughout the 1970s.

COUNTRY MUSIC AND THE POP MAINSTREAM

During the 1970s, country and western music—now generally just called "country"—became a huge business, reaching out to young and middle-class listeners while at the same time reinforcing its traditional southern and white working-class audience base. In 1974 the *Grand Ole Opry* moved from the run-down Nashville theater where it had been broadcasting since 1941 into a multimillion-dollar facility, complete with a 110-acre theme park called "Opryland." The national weekly magazines *Newsweek* and *Time* ran sympathetic cover stories on country stars Loretta Lynn and Merle Haggard; three country music shows were being featured on network television in the early 1970s (*The Glen Campbell Goodtime Hour, The Johnny Cash Show,* and *Hee-Haw*); and eventually Hollywood films such as *Nashville* (1975) and *Coal Miner's Daughter* (1980, a depiction of Loretta Lynn's life story) helped to broaden country's audience and to ameliorate long-standing stereotypes of country fans as "rednecks." The generally conservative mood of the country—reflected in Richard Nixon's landslide victory over George McGovern in the 1972 presidential election—helped to reinforce country's popularity among the American middle class.

The country-pop crossover of the 1970s—an updated version of the success enjoyed by Patti Page and Eddy Arnold during the 1950s (see Chapter 7)—was accomplished by a new generation of musicians, many of whom had developed their careers in the fields of pop, urban folk music, and rock 'n' roll. During the mid-1970s a number of records reached the Number One position on both the pop and country charts—Charlie Rich's ballad "The Most Beautiful Girl" (1973), John Denver's "Thank God I'm a Country Boy" (1975; see below), Glen Campbell's rendition of "Rhinestone Cowboy" (1975), and the truckers' anthem "Convoy," recorded by C. W. McCall in 1975 in the midst of nationwide fuel shortages and a Teamsters' Union strike. The last record helped to spread the popularity of citizens band (CB) radio, part of a more general "redneck chic" movement, in which millions of middle-class Americans adopted southern working-class cultural practices.

These "country pop" stars came from diverse musical and social backgrounds. Glen Campbell was born in Arkansas in 1936. He worked with western swing bands

Box 11.1 Hardcore Country: Merle Haggard and the Bakersfield Sound

During the 1970s, as country music became a multimillion dollar business dominated by various blends of country and pop music, some musicians returned to the straightforward, emotionally direct approach of postwar honky-tonk musicians like Hank Williams and Ernest Tubb (see Chapter 7). The "back to the basics" spirit of so-called hardcore country is perhaps best captured in the recordings of Merle Haggard, born near Bakersfield, California, in 1937. The son of migrants from Oklahoma (the "Okies," whose lives formed the basis for John Steinbeck's novel *The Grapes of Wrath*), Haggard wandered from place to place as a child, spending time in a series of juvenile homes and reform schools. When as a nineteen-year-old he began serving three years for burglary in San Quentin Prison, it did not appear that Merle Haggard had much of a future.

However, Haggard's talents as a musician and songwriter, and his newfound gift for being in the right place at the right time, eventually bailed him out. In the early 1960s, after his release, Haggard worked odd jobs around Bakersfield, playing at night in local honky-tonks. Bakersfield was at precisely this moment emerging as the center of a distinctive style of country music, an outgrowth of the rockabilly style of the 1950s (see Chapter 8). Defined by a spare, twangy sound, electric instrumentation, and a strong backbeat, the "Bakersfield sound" stood in direct opposition to the slick sound of much Nashville country music. Popularized by musicians like Haggard and Buck Owens, this was one of the most influential country genres of the late 1960s, reviving the spirit of postwar honky-tonk and setting the stage for subsequent movements such as country rock and outlaw country.

In 1965 Haggard scored a Top 10 country hit with the song "(My Friends Are Gonna Be) Strangers," which established the name for his band (the Strangers), and led to a recording contract with Capitol Records. In the late 1960s Haggard capitalized on his experience as a convict to write songs about life outside the law (e.g., "The Fugitive," a Number One country hit in 1967). An important aspect of Haggard's work as a songwriter is his commitment to chronicling the lives and attitudes of everyday people in gritty, realistic language. The central character of many Haggard songs is a white male worker, struggling to achieve the comfort and security of middle-class life. Hardworking, beer-drinking, patriotic, and politically conservative, this character's voice is perhaps most famously heard in Haggard's 1969 recording of his song "Okie from Muskogee," which reached Number One on the country charts and Number Forty-one on the pop charts and garnered him an invitation to Richard Nixon's White House:

> *We don't smoke marijuana in Muskogee*
> *We don't take our trips on LSD*
> *We don't burn our draft cards down on Main Street*
> *We like livin' right, and bein' free. . . .*

We don't make a party out of lovin'
We like holdin' hands and pitchin' woo
We don't let our hair grow long and shaggy
Like the hippies out in San Francisco do. . . .

We still wave Old Glory down at the courthouse,
In Muskogee, Oklahoma, USA.

Although this song alienated many liberal listeners who had previously lauded Merle Haggard as a "poet of the common man" and therefore expected him to share their own political sentiments, there is no denying that Haggard's songs reflected the real concerns and aspirations of millions of Americans, particularly migrants from the South who struggled to support their families through the shifting economic climate of the 1970s. Songs like "If We Make it through December" (Number One country, Number Twenty-eight pop in 1973) captured the real-life dilemmas of working-class Americans struggling to create secure lives for their families in a hostile world:

Got laid off down at the factory
And their timing's not the greatest in the world
Heaven knows I been working hard
Wanted Christmas to be right for Daddy's girl
I don't mean to hate December, it's meant to be the happy time of year
And my little girl don't understand why Daddy can't afford no Christmas
*   here.*

If we make it through December everything's gonna be all right, I know
It's the coldest time of year and I shiver when I see the falling snow . . .
If we make it through December we'll be fine.

in the Southwest as a teenager and moved to Los Angeles in 1958, where he developed a career as a studio session guitarist and vocalist. Starting in the late 1960s he had a string of crossover hits on the country and pop charts, including "Gentle on My Mind" (1967), "By the Time I Get to Phoenix" (1967), and "Wichita Lineman" (1968). In 1969 he began hosting his own network television series, and his genial, laid-back style helped to expand his national popularity. Charlie Rich, the "Silver Fox," was also born in Arkansas, in 1932. Rich was a talented jazz and blues pianist whose career started as part of the stable of rockabilly performers at Sam Phillips's Sun Records. By the 1960s he had switched to the pop-oriented country-politan style, and he scored a series of Number One crossover hits during the mid-1970s, winning the Country Music Association's award as Entertainer of the Year in 1974. At the following year's CMA awards ceremony, Rich announced the country-tinged pop singer John Denver as his successor for Entertainer of the Year and demonstrated his distaste by setting fire to the envelope. Denver was born John Henry Deutschendorf in New Mexico, in 1943. Denver's work will be discussed later in this chapter in connection with Top 40 music. Here it suffices simply to note that many in the traditional audience for country music despised Denver and his pop-oriented hit records even more than Charlie Rich did.

The dichotomy between pop performers who capitalized on the popularity of country music, on the one hand, and established country musicians who moved toward the pop mainstream, on the other, is well illustrated by the careers of two female recording stars of the 1970s: Olivia Newton-John and Dolly Parton. Newton-John was born in England in 1948 and grew up in Australia. During the mid-1970s she scored a series of Top 10 country pop crossover hits—"Let Me Be There," "If You Love Me (Let Me Know)," and "Have You Never Been Mellow"—and in 1974 won the Country Music Association's award for Female Singer of the Year. After the awards ceremony, a group of veteran country musicians met to form a new association—the Association of Country Entertainers—dedicated to resisting the perceived invasion of pop singers like Olivia Newton-John and John Denver, who were eager to capitalize on country's burgeoning popularity but ambivalent about identifying themselves too exclusively with the genre. The suspicions of hardcore country fans seemed justified when in the late 1970s Newton-John abandoned country music to jump on the oldies rock 'n' roll bandwagon, appearing in the film *Grease* and on its bestselling soundtrack album (1978). In fairness, however, it must be noted that pop opportunists such as Newton-John and Denver played a major role in widening the national audience for country music during the 1970s.

At about the same time that Newton-John was moving out of country music, Dolly Parton, an established country music star, was making her first major inroads into pop. Born in the hill country of Tennessee in 1946, Parton began her recording career at the age of eleven, moved to Nashville in 1964, and built her career with regular appearances on country music radio and television, including the *Grand Ole Opry*. Parton's flexible soprano voice, songwriting ability, and carefully crafted image as a cheerful sex symbol combined to gain her a loyal following among country fans. (Parton succeeded Olivia Newton-John as the CMA's Female Singer of the Year in 1975 and 1976, and later on, in the 1980s, was the first female country musician to host her own national television series.) Although she scored a series of Number One hits on the country charts during this period, it was not until the late 1970s that Parton was able to get a record into the Top 40 pop charts. (Her rendition of "Here You Come Again"—written by veteran Brill Building composers Barry Mann and Cynthia Weill—reached Number Three pop and Number One country in 1977.) Between them, Olivia Newton-John and Dolly Parton illustrate the extremes of the seventies country pop continuum—one a pop performer seeking to capitalize on the rising popularity of country music, and the other a country singer seeking to maintain her loyal following in that market while extending her appeal to a wider audience.

A 1970s JUKEBOX: SOME CHARACTERISTIC SOUNDS OF THE DECADE

Although the jukebox was in decline as an outlet for disseminating pop music in the 1970s, we are using the image of a jukebox here for our overview of six representative hit singles that, taken together, may be said to typify many aspects of the that decade's music. These six recordings differ widely in style, but they were all hugely popular—all were Number One singles—and thus can serve to demonstrate the diversity that was embraced by "mainstream pop" audiences during this period. All are records by artists who had multiple hit singles *and* hit albums during the 1970s. For all these artists, that decade was also the period of their maximum influence and popular success; all of them are still principally identified with the music that they recorded during this period.

Although some of these selections reflect the influence of the music of the 1960s, this influence tends to be felt in relatively subtle ways. None of these records are overtly novel or experimental in character, in the way that was characteristic of such representative 1960s artists as the Beatles or Bob Dylan. This conservatism typifies the nature of most mainstream pop in the 1970s, which tended to avoid the self-conscious tendency to "push the envelope" that is evident in much of the popular music from the preceding decade. In particular, we may observe that the six selections in our "1970s jukebox," regardless of their length, all display straightforward and readily accessible song forms. Except for the instrumental "Love's Theme," which is in the venerable AABA form, all the songs are clearly based on the simple and time-honored verse-chorus principle.

Yet the changes wrought by the 1960s have left unmistakable traces on this group of hits. With the sole exception of "Thank God I'm a Country Boy," these records reflect the move toward longer singles that became manifest during the second half of the 1960s: "It's Too Late," "Superstition," "Crocodile Rock," and "Love's Theme" are all well over three minutes in duration, and "Hotel California" exceeds six minutes of playing time. All of these songs were also featured cuts on top-selling albums by their respective artists—albums whose release was closely coordinated with that of the singles. Obviously, the singles were designed not only to be big sellers in their own right but also to call attention to the new albums from which they were drawn and to encourage the purchase of those albums. Thus the increasing prominence of the album over the single as a prime vehicle for marketing pop music performers—another trend that began in the 1960s—continued unabated throughout the 1970s. Finally, all of the artists represented here are closely identified with material that they wrote (or cowrote) themselves, primarily for their own performance; that is to say, like so many of the most representative individuals and groups from the 1960s, they are *singer-songwriters.* (Although John Denver's "Thank God I'm a Country Boy" is not his own composition, it is once again "the exception that proves the rule," as all of his other big hits were self-penned, and all of the other five songs showcased here were written or cowritten by the artists who perform them.)

"It's Too Late" (1971)

Performed by Carole King; written by Carole King and Toni Sterne

The career of <u>Carole King</u> in the 1970s illustrates, perhaps better than any other example could, the central prominence of singer-songwriters during this period. King had been an important songwriter for more than a decade (in the 1960s, she wrote many hits with Gerry Goffin, her husband at that time; see Chapter 9) but was virtually unknown as a performer until she released the album *Tapestry,* from which the single "It's Too Late" was drawn, in 1971. The astounding popularity of both the single and the album established Carole King as a major recording star. In the aftermath of King's success as a performer, relatively few songwriters were content to remain behind the scenes; it came to be expected that most pop songwriters would want to perform their own material and, conversely, that most pop singers would want to record material that they had written themselves. Just the same, few singer-songwriters at this time were able to achieve the degree of success won by King. "It's Too Late" held the Number One spot for five weeks, and even its flip side, "I Feel the Earth Move"—also a cut from *Tapestry*—proved popular in its own right and was frequently played on the radio. (Both songs remained long-term favorites of King's fans.) *Tapestry* itself was an unprecedented hit. It was the Number One album for fifteen weeks, remained on the charts for nearly six years, and sold in excess of ten million copies, more than any album by the Beatles.

Carole King was approaching the age of thirty when she recorded "It's Too Late." Clearly she was far from being the teenager who had written such songs as "Will You Love Me Tomorrow?" and "Take Good Care of My Baby" for a market consisting principally of other teenagers; King had matured, and her audience had matured along with her. "It's Too Late" is clearly an *adult* relationship song, written from the point of view of someone who has long left behind teenage crushes, insecurities, and desperate heartbreak. The singer describes the ending stage of a significant relationship with a feeling of sadness, but also with a mature philosophical acceptance that people can change and grow apart, and an understanding that this does not represent the end of the world for either of them.

The music of "It's Too Late" also reflects King's maturity. Her acoustic piano is the song's backbone, and it leads us through a sophisticated progression of relatively complex chords that portray a musical world far removed from the harmonic simplicity of early rock 'n' roll. When, toward the end of the substantial instrumental interlude preceding the final verse of the song, the saxophone enters to play a melody, the context evokes a kind of light jazz, rather than earlier rock. (The recording as a whole epitomizes the kind of sound that came to be known—fortunately or otherwise—as "soft rock.") Like the words of the song, the sound of its music was clearly geared toward an audience of maturing young adults. It is equally clear that the audience was out there and more than ready to appreciate a recording like this one.

"Superstition" (1972)

Performed and written by Stevie Wonder

Stevie Wonder was a highly successful singer and songwriter during his teenage years with Motown in the 1960s. But he established a new benchmark of achievement for a pop music figure in 1971 when, at the age of twenty-one, he negotiated a new contract with the Motown organization that guaranteed him full artistic control over all aspects of his music. As a master of all trades—singer, songwriter, multi-instrumentalist, arranger, and producer—Wonder was able to use this control to his utmost advantage, and he made all his subsequent recordings his *own* to a degree that has rarely been approached by other artists in the field. We can hear the results of this on an incredibly tight cut like "Superstition," on which Wonder plays most of the instruments (synchronizing the performance by *overdubbing* several tracks on the recording tape) to accompany his own singing of his own composition. "Superstition" was the first featured single from the album *Talking Book*, which also achieved tremendous popularity.

"Superstition" blends elements borrowed from different aspects of African American musical traditions and adds its own distinctive flavorings to the mix. The use of a repeated riff over an unchanging chord as the song's hook—a riff heard right from the outset, and which persists throughout all three verse sections of the song—obviously reflects the influence of James Brown's brand of late 1960s soul music (see Chapter 10). But Wonder gives this music his own inflection through his employment of the electric keyboard instrument called the *Clavinet*—a novelty at the time—to play the riff. (Throughout the early 1970s, Wonder was a pioneer in the use of new electronic instruments, including *synthesizers*, in pop music.) The chorus section ("When you believe . . .") introduces chord changes that are suggestive of blues influence; taken as a whole, the large verse-chorus unit of the song may be heard as an expanded variant of the twelve-bar blues in terms of both phrase structure and harmonic vocabulary. The persistence and flexibility of blues traditions in American popular music remains a source of wonder. The lyrics, however, take a thoroughly modern, sophisticated stand ("Superstition ain't the way"); in "Superstition," Stevie Wonder thus fused something old and something blue with the borrowed and the new to create an irresistible pop hit.

"Crocodile Rock" (1972)

Performed by Elton John; written by Elton John and Bernie Taupin

By the 1970s the "British invasion" of the 1960s had turned into a long-running "British occupation" of the American pop charts, as numerous artists from across the Atlantic achieved hit singles and albums in the United States on a regular basis. No artist illustrates this trend better than Elton John (Reginald Kenneth Dwight), named in Joel Whitburn's *Top Pop* books as "the #1 Pop artist of the 70s" in America. "Crocodile Rock," which was released late in 1972 and topped the charts in February 1973, was the first of six Number One hits for John during this decade. It was a featured single on his album *Don't Shoot Me I'm Only the Piano Player*, the second of seven consecutive million-selling Number One albums for John during this same period.

Like Carole King and Stevie Wonder, Elton John was a keyboard-playing singer-songwriter; the sound of John's piano is essential to the character of "Crocodile Rock," and to many of his other hits. Lyricist Bernie Taupin was John's songwriting partner not only for "Crocodile Rock" but for all of John's major hits of the 1970s.

"Crocodile Rock" reveals how thoroughly Elton John had assimilated the basic sounds and feelings of American rock 'n' roll while still being able to add his personal touch. The song capitalizes in a savvy way on the nostalgia that seemed to be sweeping the pop music landscape at the time of its release. In late 1972 Chuck Berry and Ricky Nelson were both back in the Top 10 for the first time in many years, while Elvis Presley was enjoying his biggest hit in a long time and the last Top 10 hit of his career ("Burning Love"). This was also the period when aging baby boomers began to flock to rock 'n' roll "revival" shows, in which artists from the 1950s and early 1960s (frequently including vocal groups with old names but lots of new faces) appeared to play their original, now "classic," hits. (Note the sly reference to the old Bill Haley hit "Rock around the Clock" in the opening verse of "Crocodile Rock.") Not insignificantly, just a year before "Crocodile Rock" hit Number One, the singer-songwriter Don McLean made an enormous impact with his own Number One hit "American Pie"—a record whose subject matter was nostalgia for the early years of rock 'n' roll and the conviction that something of great innocence and promise had been lost amid the tumult and violence that marked the end of the 1960s.

Like "American Pie," "Crocodile Rock" deals with nostalgia and the sense of loss, but in a much more lighthearted fashion. It seems to emphasize the happy memories ("I remember when rock was young, me and Susie had so much fun") over the unhappy present ("But the years went by and rock just died"); in fact, the second verse ends up affirming the persistence of remembered joy ("But they'll never kill the thrills we've got"), and the final verse is simply a return back to the first, "when rock was young." Musically, the flavor is clearly that of an upbeat teenage dance song, and even though there never actually was a famous rock 'n' roll dance called the "crocodile," the song may be deliberately evoking the memory of other "animal" dances, like the monkey. The chord progressions of "Crocodile Rock" obviously recall those of early rock 'n' roll songs without duplicating them exactly, and an element of novelty is added in the wordless part of the chorus with the kazoo-like sound of John's Farfisa organ.

No single record could be cited to represent an artist's entire career when the artist's musical output has been as substantial and as varied as that of Elton John.

Elton John receives an obviously unexpected hug from a grinning **Barry White** in California, c. 1975. James Fortune/Hulton Archive.

But "Crocodile Rock" can surely serve as a representation of John's characteristic good humor, and of the way in which he typically is able to link commercial smarts with musical intelligence.

"Love's Theme" (1973)

Performed by the Love Unlimited Orchestra, conducted by Barry White; written by Barry White

A dizzying upward sweep in the strings; the pulse kicks in, subtly at first, but becoming progressively stronger; and a downward lunge on the keyboard ushers in "Love's Theme," one of the biggest instrumental hits of the 1970s. The Love Unlimited Orchestra, a forty-piece studio ensemble, was the brainchild of Barry White, a multitalented African American singer, songwriter, arranger, conductor, and producer, who had already begun to have a string of solo vocal hits by the time that "Love's Theme" hit the Number One spot on the pop chart in February 1974. Originally formed to back the female trio Love Unlimited, which was yet another one of White's projects as a writer and producer, the Love Unlimited Orchestra also played on some of White's solo recordings, in addition to having hit instrumental records under its own name. ("Love's Theme" was featured on *Rhapsody in White,* the cleverly titled Top 10 album by the Love Unlimited Orchestra.)

The instrumental pop hit, which reached its pinnacle as a genre during the swing era (see Chapter 6), never totally died out during the early years of rock 'n' roll or during the emergence of rock in the 1960s. In fact, as we have seen, instrumental virtuosity on the electric guitar became one of the defining elements of late 1960s and 1970s rock. Still, "Love's Theme" represented a different kind of instrumental for the 1970s; guitar pyrotechnics play no part in the arrangement, although the use of the "scratch" guitar sound as a recurring percussive element throughout the recording does constitute a nod to the more advanced guitar styles of the period cultivated by artists such as Jimi Hendrix. Instead, the emphasis in "Love's Theme" is on two things: danceability on the one hand, and the sweet sound of string-dominated melody on the other. Its successful synthesis of these two elements, which might seem at first to be unlikely bedfellows, is one of the strikingly original—and very influential—aspects of this record.

The danceability of "Love's Theme" made it one of the earliest *disco*-styled hits (see Chapter 12), as it quickly became a favorite in dance clubs. This recording was the first in a long line of instrumental, or largely instrumental, disco records. These records followed the lead of "Love's Theme" insofar as they typically presented a similar combination of a strong beat with an elaborate arrangement featuring bowed string instruments; examples include the Number One hits "TSOP (The Sound of Philadelphia)" by MFSB (which topped the charts later in 1974), "The Hustle" by Van McCoy and the Soul City Symphony (1975), and "Fly, Robin, Fly" by Silver Convention (also 1975). In addition, the lush arrangement of "Love's Theme," featuring a melody designed to take full advantage of the way orchestral string instruments can hold long notes, links this instrumental in a general way to the sound of what was called "soft soul," a popular genre in the later 1960s and throughout the 1970s, exemplified by languid or midtempo love songs with similarly "romantic" arrangements. (Examples include recordings by the Delfonics, the Spinners, the Stylistics, and by Barry White himself as a solo vocalist.) In a sense, "Love's Theme" has it both ways; it's like a love ballad for instruments with a double-time dance beat. The steady, syncopated dance groove keeps the string sounds from spilling over into sentimentality, while the smooth string melody prevents the dance pulse from seeming overly mechanical or depersonalized.

While listening to "Love's Theme," it is a relatively simple matter to pick out the tune's basic AABA structure—yet another testament to the remarkable durability of this formal arrangement. Note how the bridge section (B) is slightly longer than the others, and how effective this extension of the bridge is, as we wait for the return of A.

Barry White is best known for his full, deep voice, which he could employ to great and seductive effect, not only in actually singing his love songs, but also in the spoken introductions he sometimes provided for them (as in his 1974 Number One solo hit, "Can't Get Enough of Your Love, Babe"). Still, the single biggest hit record with which White was associated remains "Love's Theme," and in terms of the long-range impact of its sound on the pop music market, it may also be his most influential recording. It is no accident that the lead-off cut on *The Disco Box*, a four-CD compilation of the dance-oriented music of the 1970s and early 1980s (issued by Rhino in 1999) is "Love's Theme."

"Thank God I'm a Country Boy" (1975)

Performed by John Denver; written by John Martin Sommers

Throughout the 1970s it was fashionable in certain hip circles to praise the virtues and alleged simplicity of rural life. Country-flavored rock was popular during this period, as is demonstrated by much of the recorded output of the Eagles (see below). Obviously a recording like John Denver's "Thank God I'm a Country Boy" partook of, and benefited from, this trend, even if John Denver himself was generally not regarded as being particularly hip by the standards of the day.

The late John Denver got his start in the 1960s in the urban folk movement (as a member of the Chad Mitchell Trio), and the sound of the acoustic guitar remained a prime element in many of the records he made as a solo artist in the 1970s. Several of his early hits, including his first two Top 10 records ("Take Me Home, Coun-

John Denver. Frank Driggs Collection.

try Roads" and "Rocky Mountain High," from 1971 and 1972 respectively) were "country" records more in terms of their subject matter than in terms of their actual musical style, which might best be described as an urban folk style flavored with some pop elements. By the time he achieved his third Number One hit with "Thank God I'm a Country Boy" in 1975, however, Denver was obviously going all-out to portray himself as a country artist musically as well. In this he was obviously successful, insofar as he was a significant presence on the country charts as well as on the pop charts in the mid-1970s—the only artist in our jukebox for whom this is true. (The Eagles scored an isolated hit on the country charts with their "Lyin' Eyes" in 1975; aside from this, only John Denver among our jukebox artists ever even made it into the country music Top 40.) This demonstrates that the strong sense of separation between the country and the mainstream pop charts that we noted as characteristic of the 1960s continued, in many ways, into the 1970s.

"Thank God I'm a Country Boy" is a cut taken from Denver's live album *An Evening with John Denver,* which documented his concert performances in Los Angeles during the summer of 1974. Although live albums were commonplace by this time, live singles were still relatively uncommon, but the sense of immediacy and spontaneity so essential to the character and appeal of this recording obviously results directly from the presence of an actual, enthusiastic concert audience. The opening, with Denver singing unaccompanied except for the rhythmic hand-clapping of his audience, captures something of the ambience of a real country dance party. The rural flavor of Denver's vocal of course adds to this impression; it should be noted that Denver came by this flavor naturally, having been raised in the South and the Southwest. When the instruments enter on the second verse of the song, the fiddle-led ensemble directly evokes the general sound and feeling of the old-time acoustic country string bands. The lyrics also make continual reference to the fiddle as a marker of country culture, and the second verse even mentions directly the classic country fiddle tune "Sally Goodin."

A cynic might call a recording like "Thank God I'm a Country Boy" an example of "country lite," and certainly there is no trace of hardship in the lyrics' description of "life on a farm," where things are "kinda laid back" and "life ain't nothin' but a funny, funny riddle"; the joyful music and singing also lie quite a distance from the "high lonesome" sound of much early country music and bluegrass music. Still, even if this record is regarded as the musical equivalent of a city dweller's Sunday drive into the country (and we should remember that it was recorded in Los Angeles), John Denver and his accompanying musicians make the drive an exhilarating one, and there is no trace of condescension either in their deliberate evocation of country style or in the singer's exuberant delivery of the song's message.

"Hotel California" (1976)

Performed by the Eagles; written by Don Felder, Don Henley, and Glenn Frey (all members of the Eagles)

California in the 1970s retained the central position in American popular culture that it had attained during the 1960s, and if the Beach Boys epitomized the culture of southern California in the earlier decade, then the Eagles were the group that most obviously inherited that distinction. Indeed, the close association of this Los Angeles–based group with the Golden State was so well established at the time of their peak popularity (1975–80) that it lent particular authority to their ambitious saga of "Hotel California"—the million-selling single from the extraordinarily successful album of the same name (which has sold in excess of fourteen million copies).

The Eagles serve as an excellent case in point to illustrate the accelerating ascendancy in importance of albums over singles during the 1970s. When the Eagles issued their first compilation of singles in album form, *Eagles/Their Greatest Hits, 1971–1975,* the album achieved sales far beyond those of all its hit singles taken together; it was, in fact, the first recording to be certified by the Recording Industry Association of America (RIAA) as a million-selling ("platinum") album, and it went on to sell more than twenty-six million copies.

Starting out in 1971 with feet firmly planted in what was called "country rock," the Eagles had moved from laid-back tunes like "Take It Easy" and "Peaceful Easy Feeling," and songs that evoked traditional Western imagery like "Desperado" and "Tequila Sunrise," to harder-hitting material like "One of These Nights" by 1975. "Hotel California" was the fourth of their five Number One singles, and it introduced a new, complex, poetic tone into the Eagles' work. Indeed, of all the selections in our 1970s jukebox, "Hotel California" sounds closest to an ambitious late-1960s record. This is due to several factors: its length, its minor-key harmonies, and its rather unusual overall shape (with extended guitar solos at the *end* of the record) all contribute to the effect, but surely it is the highly metaphoric lyrics that establish the most obvious kinship with the songwriting trends of the 1960s.

The tone of "Hotel California," however, is pure 1970s. The sense of loss and disillusionment that is treated so casually in "Crocodile Rock" here assumes a desperate, almost apocalyptic, character:

> *Her mind is Tiffany twisted. She got the Mercedes bends.*
> *She got a lot of pretty, pretty boys, that she calls friends.*
> *How they dance in the courtyard; sweet summer sweat.*
> *Some dance to remember; some dance to forget.*

When the visitor asks the hotel captain to bring up some wine, he is told, "We haven't had that spirit here since nineteen sixty-nine." Finally, as the last verse ends, the fleeing visitor is told by the "night man" at the door that "you can check out any time you like, but you can never leave." As if to illustrate all the implications of this memorable line, the song neither proceeds to the now-expected chorus ("Welcome to the Hotel California," whose pop-friendly major-key music assumes an increasingly ironic edge as the record progresses) nor fades out quickly. Instead, those words become the final words we hear, and the Eagles launch into lengthy guitar solos—over the chords of the verses, *not* those of the chorus—as if to underline our "stuck" situation and to eliminate anything that remotely suggests "welcoming." California, that sun-blessed beacon to the generation of "peace and love" in the 1960s, has here become a sinister trap for those who have no place left to go.

ROCK COMES OF AGE

During the 1970s rock music, the brash child of rock 'n' roll, diffused into every corner of the music industry. Influenced by the Beatles, Bob Dylan, Brian Wilson, and Jimi Hendrix, many progressive rock musicians had come to view themselves as Artists, and their recordings as works of Art. While this occasionally led to the production of self-indulgent dross, some musicians used the medium of the long-playing record album to create innovative and challenging work. At the same time, the music industry moved to co-opt the appeal of rock music, creating genres like "pop rock" and "soft rock," designed to appeal to the widest possible demographic and promoted on Top 40 radio and television. Musicians as diverse as Led Zeppelin; Stevie Wonder; Elton John; Carole King; Pink Floyd; Paul Simon; Neil Diamond; Crosby, Stills, and Nash; the Rolling Stones; Frank Zappa and the Mothers of Invention; and Santana were promoted by record companies under the general heading of rock music. Even Frank Sinatra, scarcely a rock musician, tried his hand at a Beatles song or two.

There were, however, some important exceptions to the general popular appeal of rock music. Record sales in black communities, as reflected in the *Billboard* soul charts during the 1970s, do not suggest much interest in rock music. (The Rolling Stones managed to get only one of their singles into *Billboard*'s soul Top 40 chart during the decade, and multiplatinum rock acts such as Led Zeppelin, Deep Purple, and Pink Floyd made no dent whatsoever.) While the Monterey and Woodstock rock festivals had featured performances by African American artists, the promise of rock music as a zone of interracial interaction seemed to have largely vanished by the early 1970s. Many of the white rock stars who had formed their styles through exposure to earlier styles of blues and R&B seemed to have little interest in contemporary black popular music of the 1970s. As one critic put it in 1971, "Black musicians are now implicitly regarded as precursors who, having taught the white men all they know, must gradually recede into the distance" (Morse 1971, p. 108).

While there was no clear successor to Jimi Hendrix in the decade following Woodstock—that is, no single artist who could champion the presence of black musicians in rock music—we can point to a number of interestingly diverse interactions between soul music and rock. Several prominent black musicians—Sly Stone, Stevie Wonder, Marvin Gaye, and George Clinton—were able to connect long-standing aspects of African American musical traditions with elements from rock, including the notion of the musician as an artistic mastermind and of the LP record album as a work of art. In addition to their intrinsic importance, the varied work of these musicians paved the way for later artists such as Prince and Michael Jackson.

Early rock festivals such as Monterey (1967) and Woodstock (1969), regarded as the climax of the 1960s counterculture, had by the early 1970s mutated into highly profitable mass-audience concerts, held in civic centers and sports arenas across the country. In 1973 the British hard rock group Led Zeppelin (see below) toured the United States, breaking the world record for live concert attendance set by the Beatles during their tours of the mid-1960s. A whole series of bands that sprang up in the early 1970s—Styx, Journey, Kansas, REO Speedwagon, ZZ Top, Rush, and others—tailored their performances to the concert context, touring the country with elaborate light shows, spectacular sets, and powerful amplification systems, transported in caravans of semi trucks. For most rock fans, the live concert was the peak of musical experience—you hadn't really heard Led Zeppelin, it was said, until you'd heard and seen them live (and spent a little money on a poster or T-shirt, imprinted with the band's image). Of course, the relationship between rock stars and their devotees at these concerts was anything but intimate. Nonetheless, the sheer enormity, the sound and spectacle of a rock concert, helped to create a visceral sensation of belonging to a larger community, a temporary city formed by fans.

In the 1960s recordings such as the Beach Boys' *Pet Sounds* (1966), the Beatles' *Sgt. Pepper's Lonely Hearts Club Band* (1967), and the Who's "rock opera" *Tommy* (1969) established the idea of the record album as a thematically and aesthetically unified work and not simply a collection of otherwise unrelated cuts. By the early 1970s the twelve-inch high-fidelity LP had become established as the primary medium for rock music.

What makes a rock album more than a mere collection of singles? Let's start with a basic fact about the medium, its capacity: a twelve-inch disc, played at $33\frac{1}{3}$ r.p.m., could accommodate more than forty minutes of music, over twenty minutes per side. In the 1950s and early 1960s little creative use was made of this additional real estate—most rock 'n' roll–era LPs consist of a few hit singles, interspersed with a lot of less carefully produced filler. During the second half of the 1960s rock musicians began to treat the time span of the LP as a total entity, a field of potentiality akin to a painter's canvas. They also began to put more effort into *all* of the songs on an album, and to think of creative ways to link songs together, creating an overall progression of peaks and valleys. (Of course, old habits die hard, and most progressive rock albums still used songs, each approximately three to six minutes in length, as basic building blocks.)

The development of studio technology also encouraged musicians to experiment with novel techniques. High-fidelity stereo sound, heard over good speakers or headphones, placed the listener in the middle of the music (and the music in the middle of the listener!) and allowed sound sources to be "moved around." The advent of 16-, 24-, and 32-track recording consoles and electronic sound devices allowed musicians—and the record producers and studio engineers with whom they worked—to create complex aural textures, and to construct a given track on an LP over a period of time, adding and subtracting (or "punching in" and "punching out") individual instruments and voices. Innovations in the electronic synthesis of sound led to instruments like the Melotron, which could imitate the sound of a string orchestra in the studio and at live performances.

The musical response to the opportunities provided by these technological changes varied widely. Some rock bands became famous for spending many months (and tons of money) in the studio to create a single rock "masterpiece." A few multitalented musicians, such as Stevie Wonder and Edgar Winter, took advantage of multitracking to play all of the instruments on a given track. Other musicians reacted against the dependence on studio technology, recording their albums the old-fashioned way, with little overdubbing. (As we shall see, when punk rock arose in the late 1970s as a reaction against the pretentiousness of studio-bound progressive rock, musicians insisted on doing recordings in one take to create the sense of a live performance experience.) Studio technology could even be used to create the impression that studio technology was not being used, as in many folk rock albums.

Although the idea of creating some sort of continuity between the individual tracks, and of creating an inclusive structure that could provide the listener with a sense of progression, was shared widely, rock musicians took a range of approaches to this problem. One way to get a sense of this range is to listen to a handful of classic rock LPs from the early 1970s.

Some rock albums are centered on a fictitious character whose identity is analogous to that of one or more musicians in the band. Perhaps the best-known example of this strategy is *The Rise and Fall of Ziggy Stardust and the Spiders from Mars*

(1972), the creation of "glam rock" pioneer <u>David Bowie</u>. (Glam—short for *glamour*—rock emphasized the elaborate, showy personal appearance and costuming of its practitioners.) In this case, the coherence of the album derives more from the imaginative and magnetic persona of the singer and his character than from the music itself. As Bowie put it, "I packaged a totally credible plastic rock star," an alien who comes to visit Earth and becomes first a superstar and finally a "Rock 'n' Roll Suicide," perishing under the weight of his own fame. Much of the LP's effect was connected with the striking image of Bowie playing the role of Ziggy, decked out in futuristic clothing and heavy facial makeup, a sensitive rocker, sexy in an androgynous, cosmic way. The *Ziggy Stardust* concert tour was a theatrical tour de force, with special lighting effects and spectacular costumes, and set the standard for later rock acts, ranging from "new wave" bands like the Talking Heads (see Chapter 12) to hard rockers like Kiss. Bowie's unique ability to create quasi-fictional stage personae, and to change them with every new album, was a precedent for the image manipulation of 1980s stars like Michael Jackson, Prince, and Madonna. (As of this writing, Bowie is planning to resurrect Ziggy in a project called *Ziggy Stardust 2002*, with new photographic, theatrical, cinematic, and multimedia material.)

Other successful rock albums were held together not by a central character or coherent plotline, but by an emotional, philosophical, or political theme. The album *Blue* (1971), composed and performed by the singer-songwriter <u>Joni Mitchell</u>, consists of a cycle of songs about the complexities of love. The album is carefully designed to create a strong emotional focus, which is in turn clearly related to the autobiography of the singer herself. In some ways *Blue* is a culmination of the tendency inherent in the folk rock and singer-songwriter genres toward self-revelation. Even the most optimistic songs on the album—"All I Want," "My Old Man," and "Carey"—have a bittersweet flavor. Some—such as "Little Green," about a child given up for adoption, and the concluding track "The Last Time I Saw Richard"—are delicate yet powerful testimonials to the shared human experience of emotional loss. The sound of the LP is spare and beautiful, focusing on Mitchell's voice and acoustic guitar. This is a case where studio technology is used to create a feeling of simplicity and immediacy.

Dark Side of the Moon (1973), an album by the British rock band Pink Floyd is based on the theme of madness and the things that drive us to it—time, work, money, war, and fear of death. The LP opens with the sound of a beating heart, then a ticking clock, a typewriter, a cash register, gunfire, and the voices of members of Pink Floyd's stage crew, discussing their own experiences with insanity. The album's feeling of unity has something to do with its languid, carefully measured pace—most of the songs are slow to midtempo—as well as its musical texture and mood. In terms of style, the progression moves from spacey, neo-psychedelic sound textures to jazz and blues-influenced songs and then back to psychedelia. The sound of the record, produced by Alan Parsons, is complex but clear, and interesting use is made of sound effects, as in the song "Money," with its sampled sounds of clinking coins and cash registers, treated as rhythmic accompaniment. (This achievement is particularly impressive when we recall that 1973 was before the advent of digital recording techniques.)

If there was ever an antidote to the notion that popular music must be cheerful and upbeat in order to be successful, *Dark Side of the Moon* is it. This meditation on insanity stayed on the *Billboard* Top LPs charts for over fourteen years, longer than any other LP in history, and sold twenty-five million copies worldwide. In recent years, various mythologies have grown up around *Dark Side of the Moon.* For example, it is claimed that the album can be synchronized with the 1939 film *The Wizard of Oz.* Many people maintain that if you start the album up after the MGM Lion's third roar there are some amazing synchronicities. (For example, the song "Brain Damage" begins playing just as the Scarecrow starts to sing "If I Only Had a Brain"). Whatever the merit of these claims, it is clear that Pink Floyd's *Dark Side of the Moon* continues to exert a powerful, if somewhat dark, fascination upon millions of rock fans.

A final example of the "theme album" is <u>Marvin Gaye</u>'s bestselling LP *What's Going On* (1971), which fused soul music and gospel influence with the political impetus of progressive rock. The basic unifying theme of this album is social justice. The title track, inspired by the return of Gaye's brother from Vietnam, is a plea for nonviolence, released during the peak of antiwar protests in the United States. Other songs focus on ecology, the welfare of children, and the suffering of poor people in America's urban centers. Gaye cowrote the songs and produced the album himself, supporting his voice—overdubbed to sound like an entire vocal group—with layers of percussion, strings, and horns. Once again, the producer's consideration of the overall sound texture of the album had a great deal to do with its aesthetic effect and commercial success.

Motown owner Berry Gordy initially didn't want to release *What's Going On,* thinking it had no commercial potential. This was a rare case of misjudgment on Gordy's part; the album reached Number Two on the LP charts and generated three Number One singles on the soul charts, all of which crossed over to the pop Top 10: the title song, "Mercy Mercy Me (The Ecology)," and "Inner City Blues (Make Me Wanna Holler)." Two other tracks, "Wholy Holy" and "Save the Children," inspired hit cover versions by Aretha Franklin and Diana Ross. But the significance of this album, and of Marvin Gaye's commitment to a socially responsible aesthetic vision, surpasses any measure of commercial success. Along with Stevie Wonder and Sly Stone, Marvin Gaye showed that soul and R&B albums could provide artistic coherence that transcended the three-minute single, managed to bridge the divide between AM Top 40, FM album-oriented radio, and the soul music market, and held open the possibility that popular music might still have something to do with social change, as well as money making and artistic self-expression.

A strategy that was fairly unusual in rock music was the adoption of elements of large-scale structure from European classical music. The live album *Pictures at an Exhibition* (1971), recorded by the art rock band Emerson, Lake, and Palmer, adopts its main themes and some of its structural elements from a suite of piano pieces by the Russian composer Modest Musorgsky (1839–81). This was a canny choice, since Musorgsky's composition—inspired by a walk through an art gallery—consists of a sequence of accessible, reasonably short, easily digestible "paintings," a parallel with the song format of much popular music. Some sections of the LP are reorchestrations of the original score (making prominent use of Keith Emerson's virtuosity on organ and synthesizer), while others are improvisations on the borrowed materials, and still others new songs by the band, musing on ideas in the music. The album concludes with "Nutrocker," a rock 'n' roll version of Tchaikovsky's *Nutcracker Suite.*

In the end, however, rock music is less centrally concerned with large-scale, architectural structures than with the immediate experience of musical texture, rhythmic momentum, and emotional intensity. Many of the most effective rock albums do not have an overarching structural logic, a story to tell, or a single organizing image, but rather find their unity in a visceral cohesion of musical style, texture, and attitude. *Exile on Main Street* (1972), now often cited as the best album ever recorded by the Rolling Stones, had decidedly mixed reviews when it first came out, because of its impenetrable sound and the inaudibility of its lyrics. Even the

Box 11.2 Album Art

If the rock LP was a container for music, it was also an art object in its own right. LP dust jackets often featured a printed version of the lyrics and a range of highly imaginative designs. Covers conveyed a lot, not only about a rock group's physical appearance, but also about their aesthetic aims and personality. Some showed concert photos of the artists at work; Jimi Hendrix's *Band of Gypsys* (1970) and Deep Purple's *Made in Japan* (1973) were bestselling examples. Others revealed some aspect of the musicians' private lives; the eponymous LP *Crosby Stills and Nash* (1969) has a cover photo of the three folk rock musicians lounging on an old sofa on the front porch of a house, while the inside of Marvin Gaye's *What's Going On* (1971) contains a photo collage of his family. The sexuality of rock stars was often emphasized, as on the Rolling Stones' quadruple-platinum LP *Sticky Fingers* (1971), which featured a close-up photograph of the crotch of Mick Jagger's blue jeans, complete with a working zipper! Other covers, particularly of hard rock and heavy metal albums, tapping into the sexual fantasies of the young male audience for rock music, featured scantily clad women in suggestive poses. Alternative models of sexuality also found their way onto album covers, the most notorious example being David Bowie's *Diamond Dogs* (1975), which featured an androgynous Bowie-canine creature with its genitals exposed. (The cover created a furor and was soon yanked from the shelves of record stores and replaced with a tamer alternative.)

Record companies often gave dust-jacket artists wide latitude to invent visual analogues to the music inside. The cover of *Brain Salad Surgery* (1973), a Top 10 LP by the art rock band Emerson, Lake, and Palmer, was designed by the Swiss artist H. R. Giger, who went on create the nightmarish creature in the film *Alien*. The Latin rock band Santana's second LP, *Abraxas* (1971), presented a colorful psychedelic rendering of the fusion of European and African cultural influences. Even reissues of oldies from the 1950s and 1960s were given imaginative treatments, as on the Drifters' *Greatest Recordings* album cover (1971), which took an old publicity photo and turned it into a psychedelic image. Finally, some album designs featured a minimalist approach, the prototypical example being *The Beatles* (1968), whose stark white cover earned it the nickname "the White Album."

cover art for the LP—a photographic collage of freaks and misfits—seemed designed to repel many in the Stones' loyal audience, who had followed the band since their early days as the slightly nasty counterpart of the Beatles. In *Exile on Main Street* we have an album—actually a double album, containing two LPs and eighteen songs—that is held together by its texture (dense, dark, guitar-based rock 'n' roll), its rough, unpolished studio sound (reminiscent on some tracks of Elvis Presley's early work with Sun Records), and its bad attitude (personified by the sneering, mumbling Mick Jagger). The material is strongly oriented toward the Stones' musical roots, as it consists mainly of blues-based rockers like "Rocks Off," "Shake Your Hips," and "Tumbling Dice," with a few examples of country and folk music influence ("Sweet Virginia" and "Sweet Black Angel").

    Exile on Main Street was recorded in the basement of guitarist Keith Richards's home in France—where the Stones were living in tax exile at the time—and Jagger's voice is purposefully buried in the mix, under the gritty guitars, bass, and drums, and the occasional horn section. (The producer Jimmy Miller was largely responsible for creating the LPs cohesive sound palette.) The overall impression is one of bleakness and desolation, a reflection of the Stones' state at the time. The band's abuse of drugs and alcohol was so intense that members of the band have since wondered aloud how they ever got the record made. *Exile on Main Street* is at once an apotheosis of the Stones' image as bad boys, and a tip of the hat to the influences that formed their style, including urban blues, soul, and country music.

LISTENING AND ANALYSIS "STAIRWAY TO HEAVEN" AND "OYE COMO VA"

To gain a better sense of the variety of rock music during the early 1970s, we are going to take a closer look at two tracks from highly successful albums: "Stairway to Heaven," from *Led Zeppelin IV* (1971); and "Oye Como Va," a Top 20 hit from Santana's quadruple-platinum album *Abraxas* (1970). These two examples will suffice to show the diversity of music that was produced, promoted, and consumed under the general label of rock music during this period. One was the granddaddy of heavy metal music, a bombastic fusion of guitar-driven rock 'n' roll, psychedelia, art rock, and folk music; and the other a fascinating amalgam of blues, jazz, rock, and Latin American popular music, a progenitor of the world beat movement of the 1980s and 1990s (see Chapter 14).

Led Zeppelin and Heavy Metal

By the early 1970s the British hard rock band Led Zeppelin, formed in London in 1968, was well on its way to becoming the most profitable and influential act in rock music. "Zep," as its fans called it, was made up of Jimmy Page, a brilliant guitarist who had honed his skills as Eric Clapton's successor in a pioneering British band called the Yardbirds; John Bonham, who established the thunderous sound of heavy metal drumming; John Paul Jones, who provided the band's solid bottom, doubling on electric bass and organ; and Robert Plant, whose agile high tenor voice established the norm for subsequent heavy metal singers. Zeppelin's sledgehammer style of guitar-focused rock music drew on various influences, including urban blues, San Francisco psychedelia, and the virtuoso guitar playing of Jimi Hendrix. Although Led Zeppelin is usually associated with the heavy textures and extremely loud volume of their hard rock repertoire, their recordings also included another important stream—an interest in folk music, particularly the traditions of the British Isles.

"Stairway to Heaven" is Led Zeppelin's most famous recording, and it reflects certain unique features of the band's musical approach, as well as its position vis-à-vis the commercial mainstream of pop music. To begin with, the song presents us with a fascinating marketing strategy, at first glance perverse, but actually quite brilliant. Although "Stairway to Heaven" was the most frequently requested song on FM radio during the 1970s, the eight-minute track was never released as a single. In other words, to own a copy of "Stairway to Heaven," you had to buy the album. Of course, that could prove difficult for the uninitiated consumer, since the band insisted on an album cover that bore neither the name of the album, nor the name of the band, nor the name of the record company. (Atlantic Records was horrified by this design, but the band held the master tapes for the album hostage, and the record company had no choice but to go along.) Driven in part by the popularity of "Stairway to Heaven," the LP *Led Zeppelin IV* reached the Number Two position on the *Billboard* Top LP charts and stayed on the charts for five years, eventually selling fourteen million copies.

"Stairway to Heaven" has been called the "anthem" of heavy metal music, a genre that developed out of hard rock in the 1970s and achieved mainstream success in the 1980s (see Chapter 13; other examples of early proto-metal bands include Deep Purple and Black Sabbath). What accounts for this recording's tremendous commercial success and its ability to ignite the imaginations and inspire the loyalty of millions of fans? To begin with, "Stairway" skillfully juxtaposes two dimensions of Led Zeppelin's musical persona—the bone-crushing rock band, known for inspiring riots and dismantling hotel rooms, and the folk music aficionados, steeped in a reverence for ancient English and Celtic mythology. While these two sensibilities might seem diametrically opposed, the twin musical threads of sonic aggression and acoustic intimacy run through the entire history of heavy metal. (Most heavy metal albums include at least one "ballad," a term that in this context usually implies the use of acoustic guitar.) For many fans in Zeppelin's predominantly young, male audience, the combination of rock physicality and folk mysticism in "Stairway to Heaven" created something akin to a sacred experience. The somewhat inscrutable song text, composed by singer Robert Plant during a rehearsal, was also an important source of the recording's attraction. Both Plant and Jimmy Page were at the time exploring the writings of the noted English mystic Aleister Crowley—into whose house Page eventually moved—and reading scholarly tomes like *Magic Arts in Celtic Britain*, which Plant later said influenced the lyrics for "Stairway." The text's

LISTENING CHART   "STAIRWAY TO HEAVEN"

Music and lyrics by Jimmy Page and Robert Plant; performed by Led Zeppelin; recorded 1971

FORM	LYRICS	DESCRIPTIVE COMMENTS
Section One (0:00)		
A (8 measures)	Instrumental	Six-string acoustic guitar; double-tracked recorder (flute) duet enters in measure 5; Slow tempo (72 beats per minute).
B (8)		Guitar and recorders continue.
A (8)	*There's a lady . . .* *When she gets there . . .*	Vocal enters.
B (4)	*Ooo . . .* *And she's buying . . .*	
A (8)	*There's a sign . . .* *In a tree . . .*	
A' (4)	Instrumental	Six-string guitar and recorders continue.
Section Two (2:14)		Twelve-string guitar, soft electric guitar, electric piano; intensity increases, tempo slightly faster (80 b.p.m.).
B (8)	*Oooo, It makes . . .* *Oooo, It makes . . .*	
A (8)	*There's a feeling . . .* *In my thoughts . . .*	
X (1)	Instrumental	One-measure linking section; electric guitar becomes more dominant.
B (8)	*Oooo, It makes . . .* *Oooo, really makes . . .*	Texture thickens, volume and tempo increase slightly.
A (8)	*And it's whispered . . .* *And a new day . . .*	
X (1)	Instrumental	Linking section.
B (8)		Slight crescendo, slight tempo increase. Drums enter at end, leading us into next section.
Section Three (4:19)		
C (8)	*If there's a bustle . . .* *Yes there are . . .*	New minor chord progression; electric guitar, twelve-string acoustic guitar, plus electric bass and drum set; tempo faster (84 b.p.m.).
X (1)	Instrumental	Linking section.
B (8)	*And it makes . . .*	
C (8)	*Your head . . .* *Dear lady . . .*	
X—(2)	Instrumental	Linking section, plus one measure pause.
D (8)		Instrumental fanfare using chords from C; Tempo speeds up, leading us into next section.

Guitar Solo (20)		Chord pattern continues; tempo faster (ca. 98 b.p.m.); multitracked guitar plays supporting pattern under solo (last 8 measures).
C (18)	*And as we . . . (4)* *There walks . . . (4)* *How everything . . . (4)* *The tune . . . (4)* *To be a rock . . . (2)*	
C (8)	Instrumental	Tempo slows down, intensity decreases.
B (3)	*And she's buying . . .*	Solo voice (rubato).

references to mythological beings—the May Queen and the Piper—and rural images—paths and roads, rings of smoke through the forest, a songbird by a brook, the whispering wind—helped to create a cumulative mood of mystery and enchantment.

Although the basic building blocks of "Stairway to Heaven" are straightforward four- and eight-bar phrases, the overall arrangement is quite complex in formal terms (see the listening chart). There are three main sections. Section One alternates two eight-measure phrases, which we are calling A and B. The basic form of Section One is ABABAA' (the last section being an abridged version of A). Section Two reverses the order of the phrases and inserts a brief one-measure linking phrase (which we are calling X). The form of Section Two is BAXBAXB. Section Three, which takes up almost half of the total eight minutes of recording time, introduces a new (though closely related) chord progression and melody, which we are calling C.[1] The first part of Section Three has the form CXBCX. After a one-measure pause, this is followed by an instrumental fanfare that propels us into Jimmy Page's guitar solo. Robert Plant's voice then reenters, and there is an extended vocal section, using the harmonies from phrase C. The arrangement concludes with an instrumental phrase, slowing down and becoming much quieter in the last two measures. The track concludes quietly, with Robert Plant repeating the key line of the text: *And she's buying a stairway to heaven*. The arrangement of "Stairway to Heaven" is constructed to create a continual escalation in density, volume, and speed. (The tempo increases from around 72 beats per minute at the opening of the recording to 84 beats per minute at the beginning of Section Three, and peaking at around 98 b.p.m. during the guitar solo. This substantial, though gradual, increase in speed is crucial to the overall impact of the recording.)

If "Stairway" seems complex in purely structural terms, this may be because the logic of its organization is fundamentally emotional and metaphoric. The recording can itself be seen as an analogue of the heavenly stairway, springing

---

1. Throughout "Stairway to Heaven," the harmonies circle around a set of closely related chords, including A minor, C major, and F major, giving the performance an additional sense of continuity.

from the rural, mythological past (symbolized by acoustic instruments), soaring on jet-powered wings of metal, and finally coming to rest on a high, peaceful plateau. Similarly, the outer cover of the original album juxtaposes the sepia image of a peasant with that of a modern skyscraper rising over the formerly rustic landscape. The inner jacket portrays a mysterious hooded figure standing atop an icy peak with a staff and a lantern, looking down at a bell-bottomed seeker of knowledge who struggles to reach the top. Also included inside the album's dust jacket are the lyrics to "Stairway to Heaven" and a set of mystical symbols, or runes, one of which inspired the informal name for the album, "zoso." In seeking to understand what a recording like "Stairway" meant to its fans, the analysis of musical form must be coupled with a consideration of its other expressive dimensions, including the song text and the graphic design of the album on which it appeared.

Santana: The Roots of Rock Multiculturalism

If rock was quintessentially defined for many listeners by white bands like Led Zeppelin, Pink Floyd, and the Rolling Stones, the San Francisco–based group Santana reveals a nascent trend within rock music toward multicultural engagement. The band was led by guitarist Carlos Santana (b. 1947, in Mexico), who began his musical career playing guitar in the nightspots of Tijuana. As a kid he was exposed to the sounds of rock 'n' roll, including the music of Mexican American musicians such as Ritchie Valens, whose version of the folk song "La Bamba" had broken into the *Billboard* Top 40 in early 1959. Santana moved to San Francisco at age fifteen, where he was exposed to other forms of music that were to play a profound part in shaping the style and sensibility of his music: jazz, particularly the experimental music of John Coltrane and Miles Davis; salsa, a New York–based style of Latin dance music strongly rooted in Afro-Cuban traditions; and in the late 1960s, San Francisco rock, including artists as diverse as Janis Joplin, Jimi Hendrix, and Sly and the Family Stone (see Chapter 10). Around 1968 Santana put together a group of middle- and working-class Latino, black, and white musicians from varied cultural backgrounds. The band's eponymous first album, *Santana*, released in 1969, reached Number Four on the Top LPs chart, in large part due to the band's spectacular performance in the film and soundtrack LP of *Woodstock*.

In 1970 Columbia Records released Santana's second LP, which firmly established both the band itself and a strong Latin American substream within rock music. *Abraxas* held the Number One position on the LP charts for six weeks, spent a total of eighty-eight weeks on the charts, and sold over four million copies in the United States alone. The album also produced two Top 40 singles: "Black Magic Woman" (Number Four pop in 1970), originally recorded by the English blues rock band Fleetwood Mac; and the infectious "Oye Como Va" (Number Thirteen pop, Number Thirty-two R&B in 1971), composed by New York Latin percussionist and dance music king Tito Puente. These two singles, which had a great deal to do with the success of the album, were shorter versions of the tracks found on the LP. (This was a typical strategy, given the duration of tracks on many rock LPs.) Tying blues, rock, and salsa together in one multicultural

Carlos Santana. Frank Driggs Collection.

package, *Abraxas* also featured less commercial tracks such as "Gypsy Queen" (composed by the jazz guitarist Gabor Szabo), and the impressionistic "Singing Winds, Crying Beasts."

We will take a closer look at the LP version of "Oye Como Va," since it allows the band to stretch out a bit and best illustrates certain features of Santana's style. To appreciate what goes into a recording like "Oye Como Va," we must consider not only the instrumentation—essentially a guitar-bass-keyboards-drums rock band plus Latin percussion—but also the recording's "mix," that is, the precise tonal quality, balancing, and positioning of sounds recorded on various tracks in the studio. (*Abraxas* was coproduced by the band and Fred Catero, whose straightforward approach to studio production can also be heard on early LPs of the jazz rock band Chicago.) Santana's instantly recognizable sound focused on the fluid lead guitar style of Carlos Santana and the churning grooves created by the drummer (Mike Shrieve), the bass player (Dave Brown), and two Latin percussionists (Jose Areas and Mike Carabello). The rhythmic complexity of "Oye Como Va"—essentially an electrified version of an Afro-Cuban dance rhythm—required that the recording be mixed to create a "clean" stereo image, so that the various instruments and interlocking rhythm patterns could be clearly heard. Listening over headphones or good speakers, you should be able to hear where the various instruments are positioned in the mix. The electric bass is in the middle, acting as the band's rhythmic anchor; the guitar and keyboards are placed slightly to the left and right of center, respectively, and thus kept out of each other's way; and the percussion instruments (including guiro, a ridged gourd scraped with a small stick; *timbales*, a set of two drums played with flexible sticks; *agogo*, a metal bell; and *congas*, hand-played drums) are positioned even farther out to the left and right.

The track opens with the electric bass and Hammond B-3 organ—one of the most characteristic sounds of 1970s rock music—playing the interlocking pattern that functions as the core of the groove throughout the recording. (In a salsa band, this two-measure pattern would be called the *tumbao*.) In the background we hear someone say "Sabor!" ("Flavor!") and at the end of the fourth measure the *timbales* and *agogo* enter, bringing in the rest of the instruments at the beginning of the fifth measure. At this point all of the interlocking repeated patterns—bass, organ, bell, scraper, and congas—have been established. The signature sound of Carlos Santana's guitar enters in the ninth measure, as he plays a two-measure melodic theme four times. This is followed by the first of four sections in which the whole band plays a single rhythmic and melodic pattern in unison (in the listening chart we call these sections B and B', respectively). Throughout the track, the rhythm functions as the heart of the music. As if to remind us of the importance of this deep connection with Afro-Latin tradition, all of the other layers are periodically stripped away, laying bare the pulsing heart of the music.

At the most general level, we can make a few observations about how the four minutes and seventeen seconds of "Oye Como Va" are organized. The whole arrangement is 136 measures in length; out of that total only 16 measures (about 12 percent of the total) is devoted to singing, which in this context seems almost a pretext for the instrumental music. In general, song lyrics are less important than the musical groove and texture in most of Santana's early recordings. (The lyric for this song consists of a short phrase in Spanish, repeated over and over, in which the singer boasts about the potency of his "groove" to a brown-skinned female dancer.)

Taking away the other obviously precomposed elements—the guitar melody (phrase A), unison figures played by the whole band (B, B', and the call-and-response figure after the first guitar solo), and the other interlude sections—we find that nearly half of the recording (66 measures) is devoted to improvised solos by the guitar and organ. The other elements of the arrangement—including the dramatic group crescendos that lead into the last two solos—seem designed to support improvisation. In essence, then, "Oye Como Va" is a vehicle for instrumental soloing, more like a jazz performance than a Top 40 pop song. (Of course, it is precisely the solos that Columbia Records chose to cut when they edited the track for AM radio airplay.) In particular, Carlos Santana's solos on "Oye Como Va" provide us with a good example of the work of a talented rock improviser. Rather than playing torrents of fast notes to show off his guitar technique (which was and remains considerable), Santana uses the electric guitar's ability to sustain notes for long periods of time to create long, flowing melodic lines that gradually rise in intensity, lifting the whole band with him. In live performance, of course, Santana and other instrumental soloists could stretch out for much more than four and a half minutes. If the soft side of rock often worked within the restricted time format imposed by Top 40 radio, progressive rock bands such as Santana, the Allman Brothers, and the Grateful Dead kept alive the notion of extended, open-ended performance, an important part of the legacy of the San Francisco rock scene of the late 1960s (see Chapter 10).

LISTENING CHART "OYE COMO VA"

Music and lyrics by Tito Puente; performed by Santana; recorded 1971

FORM	LYRICS	DESCRIPTIVE COMMENTS
Groove (8)	Instrumental	The basic *cha-cha* rhythm is established on organ, electric bass, and (from the fifth measure) percussion.
A (8)		The guitar states a two-measure melodic phrase four times (with minor embellishments).
B (4)		A unison figure, played by the whole band.
C (8)	*Oye como va . . .*	Vocals (two four-measure phrases)
B' (2)	Instrumental	The unison figure again (first half only).
Guitar Solo (20)		Extended solo by Carlos Santana.
Interlude (6)		Call-and-response exchange between guitar and band.
Groove (4)		Stripped down to the basics again.
Interlude (8)		Suddenly quieter; organ and guitar play chord pattern; gradual crescendo.
Organ solo (22)		
Groove (4)		One more time!
B' (2)		The unison figure again (first half only).
C (8)	*Oye como va . . .*	Vocals (two four-measure phrases)
Interlude (4)	Instrumental	Suddenly quieter, then crescendo.
Guitar solo (24)		Another solo by Carlos Santana.
B (4)		The unison figure again, functioning as a tag.

Although the 1970s are often portrayed as a time of corporate consolidation and conservatism in popular music, that was only one dimension of a more complex story. In the next chapter we will examine a number of developments that extend a pattern we have discerned in earlier periods: the continual refreshing of popular music by performers and styles situated at the margins of the commercial mainstream. In the creativity and energy of genres such as progressive country, reggae, punk, funk, and disco, we will find affirmation both of changes in the business of music and of deep continuities underlying the history of American popular music.

CHAPTER TWELVE

OUTSIDERS' MUSIC

Progressive Country, Reggae, Punk, Funk, and Disco, 1970s

Although the 1970s are often described as a period of stylistic conservatism and corporate consolidation in popular music, the decade also fostered music that did not fit neatly into the frameworks of Top 40 radio, album-oriented rock, or the Nashville sound. The genres we will be discussing in this chapter arose, for the most part, as a response to the conservatism of the music industry; the exception is reggae music, which came from completely outside the commercial mainstream of the American music industry. Each of these genres embodied in its own way the contradictions built into the popular music industry, and the complex processes by which the mainstream and the margins of popular music are continually redefined.

THE OUTLAWS: PROGRESSIVE COUNTRY MUSIC

During the late 1960s and early 1970s, mainstream country music was dominated by the slick Nashville sound, by the hardcore country of artists like Merle Haggard, and by various blends of country and pop promoted on AM Top 40 radio (see Chapter 11). But a new generation of country musicians at this time began to embrace the music and attitudes that had grown out of the 1960s counterculture. *Progressive country,* as this movement came to be known, was inspired by the honky-tonk and rockabilly amalgam of Bakersfield country music, the singer-songwriter genre (especially the work of Bob Dylan), and the country rock style of musicians like Gram Parsons, who was a member of the Byrds for a brief time in the late 1960s. In general, progressive country performers wrote songs that were more intellectual and liberal in outlook than their contemporaries and were more concerned with testing the limits of the country music tradition than with scoring hits. Many of the movement's key artists—including Willie Nelson, Kris Kristofferson, Tom T. Hall, and Townes Van Zandt—were not polished singers by conventional standards, yet they wrote distinctive, individualistic songs and had compelling voices. Such artists developed a sizable cult following, and progressive country began to inch its way into the mainstream, usually in the form of cover versions. Tom T. Hall's "Harper Valley PTA" was a Number One pop and country hit for Jeannie C. Riley as early as 1968, while Sammi Smith took Kris Kristofferson's "Help Me Make It through the Night" to the top of the country charts and into the pop Top 10 in 1971.

One of the most influential figures in the progressive country movement was Willie Nelson (born in Texas in 1933). Nelson had already developed a successful career as a professional songwriter when he left Nashville to return to Texas in 1971. (Nelson's song "Crazy" had been a Top 10 country and pop hit for Patsy Cline in 1961.) He settled in Austin, a university town and home to one of the most energetic and eclectic live music scenes in the country. At "cosmic cowboy" venues such as the Armadillo World Headquarters, and on Austin radio station KOKE-FM, a fusion of country music and countercultural sensibilities was already well under way. Nelson fit right in to the Austin scene, letting his hair and beard grow long and donning a headband, an earring, jogging shoes, and bluejeans (one of the few markers of cultural identity shared by rednecks, cowboys, and hippies!). Singing in an unpolished, almost conversational voice—an approach that had frustrated his attempts to gain success as a recording artist in Nashville—Willie Nelson bridged the gap between rock and country without losing touch with his honky-tonk roots. In the summer of 1971 he organized the first of a series of outdoor festivals that included older country musicians (e.g., Roy Acuff and Earl Scruggs) as well as younger musicians who were experimenting with a blend of country and rock music. These "picnics," closer in ethos to Woodstock than to the *Grand Ole Opry,* brought thousands of rock fans into the fold of country music and prepared the way for Nelson's ascendance as the preeminent male country music star of the 1980s.

Willie Nelson's initial rise to national fame came in the mid-1970s, through his association with a group of musicians collectively known as "the Outlaws." The centerpiece of the Outlaws was another Texas-born musician, Waylon Jennings (1937–2002). Jennings began his career as a musician and disk jockey and in 1958 joined Buddy Holly's rock 'n' roll group, the Crickets. In the early 1960s he set up shop at a nightclub in Phoenix, Arizona, where the clientele included businessmen, college students, and cowboys, a diverse audience that encouraged him to develop a broad repertoire. In 1965 he was signed by RCA Victor and relocated to Nashville. Although RCA producer Chet Atkins—who had remolded Elvis into a pop star in 1956—attempted to push him in the direction of the countrypolitan sound popular at the time, Jennings resisted these efforts, eventually winning substantial leeway in his choice of material. (His early 1970s LPs included Beatles songs such as "Norwegian Wood" and "You've Got to Hide Your Love Away.")

While he chose to remain close to the music industry in Nashville rather than return to Texas, Jennings cultivated an image as a rebel, and in 1972 recorded an album called *Ladies Love Outlaws.* On the cover he appeared in "bad guy" dress, complete with a black cowboy hat and a six-shooter. The commercial potential of the outlaw image was soon recognized by music publicists in Nashville, who lost

Box 12.1 A Country Concept Album: *Red-Headed Stranger* (1975)

One of the ideas that progressive country musicians adopted from rock music during the 1970s was that of the concept album. The central medium for the transmission of country music during the 1970s was still the individual song, and although some country LPs sold well, 45 r.p.m. singles remained the bread and butter of the industry. During the mid-1970s, however, progressive country musicians began to create albums unified around a single theme or dramatic character. Perhaps the best example of this trend is Willie Nelson's album *Red-Headed Stranger* (1975), which sold over two million copies and reached Number Twenty-eight on *Billboard*'s Top LPs chart. (*Billboard* had no separate LP charts for country or soul music, since these genres were assumed by definition to be singles-oriented.) *Red-Headed Stranger* included Nelson's first big crossover hit as a singer, rather than as a songwriter—"Blue Eyes Crying in the Rain," Number Twenty-one pop and Number One country—and established the notion of the country concept album.

Of course, the technique of telling stories through song had long been part of the Anglo-American ballad tradition, one of the main taproots of country music. In putting together *Red-Headed Stranger*, a meticulously crafted song cycle outlining the saga of a broken-hearted cowboy, Nelson stuck close to the traditional time limit of three minutes per song, alternating songs with shorter bits of material that established the narrative context (for example, dance music to give us the feeling of a turn-of-the-century saloon in Denver). The musical accompaniment—acoustic guitar, electric guitar, mandolin, piano, harmonica, electric bass, and drums—is strikingly spare and restrained, and some tracks use only acoustic guitar and piano (played by Nelson's sister). The jacket sleeve featured excerpts from the lyrics, accompanied by paintings of the red-headed stranger in the various scenarios portrayed by the songs.

The album opens with the song "Time of the Preacher":

It was a time of the preacher, when the story began
Of a choice of a lady, and the love of a man
How he loved her so dearly, he went out of his mind
When she left him for someone that she'd left behind

He cried like a baby, and he screamed like a panther in the middle of the
   night
And he saddled his pony, and he went for a ride
It was a time of the preacher, in the year of '01
Now the preaching is over, and the lesson's begun.

In the next song, only a minute and a half in length, Nelson adopts the first-person voice of the jilted cowboy, who discovers his wife's infidelity—"I couldn't believe it was true." This is followed by a reappearance of the "Time of the Preacher" song, which functions throughout the album as a thematic refrain, connecting the various songs. As the story unfolds, we observe the red-headed stranger tracking down his wife and her lover, shooting them dead in a tavern, and riding off on his black stallion. As in rock concept albums based on a dramatic character—say, *The Rise and Fall of Ziggy Stardust and the Spiders from Mars*—the line dividing the fictional persona in the song and the musician who sings the song is thin indeed. The album cover of *Red-Headed Stranger* portrays Nelson in cowboy dress, with a beard and long, ragged red-tinted hair, an image clearly intended to reinforce the longtime Nashville songwriter's public image as an outlaw musician.

no time turning it into a commercial term. The Outlaws were never a cohesive performing group: in fact, the label "outlaw country" was largely a product of the record industry's search for a way to capitalize on the overlap between audiences for rock and country music.

In 1976, after musicians such as Willie Nelson and Waylon Jennings had begun to receive substantial radio airplay, RCA Victor released a compilation of their early 1970s recordings entitled *Wanted: The Outlaws*. This LP included a mix of material, ranging from a version of the country music classic "T for Texas," first recorded under the title "Blue Yodel" by Jimmie Rodgers in 1927, to a cover of an Elvis Presley hit ("Suspicious Minds"), to Willie Nelson's humorous song "Me and Paul," in which the country singer compares his problems on the road to those of rock star Paul McCartney. The album was a huge success—it reached the Top 10 on *Billboard*'s Top LPs chart, soon became the first platinum country music LP, and eventually sold over two million copies. Though the Outlaws—like most "alternative"

Willie Nelson, looking very much the country outlaw. Frank Driggs Collection.

music movements—had a commercial dimension, they did represent a heartfelt re-bellion against the conservatism of the country music establishment. Their approach found common ground in the past and the future of country music, managed to challenge briefly country pop's hold on the charts in the mid-1970s, and paved the way for later alternative country artists such as k.d. lang, Dwight Yoakam, and Lyle Lovett.

The song "Pancho and Lefty," performed by its composer, <u>Townes Van Zandt</u> (born 1944 in Ft. Worth, Texas, died 1997), is an instructive example of the idio-syncratic sensibility of much progressive country. Van Zandt was a singer-song-writer who became a cult hero of the progressive country movement. Though Van Zandt never placed a record on the country Top 40 charts, his fifteen LPs became underground classics, and his songs were covered by prominent country musicians. (Willie Nelson and Merle Haggard took a version of "Pancho and Lefty" to the top of the country charts in 1983.)

Van Zandt's performance of "Pancho and Lefty," from his 1972 LP *The Late, Great Townes Van Zandt*, is typical of his work: a spare, unpolished vocal style, with guitar accompaniment that often uses more complex harmonies than are typical in country music. (The use of Mexican mariachi-style trumpets at some points in the arrangement evokes the story's location, near the Rio Grande River.) In structural terms, this song fits within the European-derived ballad tradition that we encoun-tered in our overview of early country music (see Chapter 5). More specifically, "Pancho and Lefty" evokes an old Spanish ballad tradition that took root in Mex-ico, where it developed into a genre known as the *corrido*. Typical *corridos* exhibit the familiar ballad form, a series of four-line stanzas that tell a story about famous heroes and villains, historical events, or tragic romances, sung to a repeated melody and interrupted at regular intervals by a chorus.

Since the very beginnings of recorded country music songwriters have drawn on the themes and images of the Anglo-American cowboy ballad and the Mexican *corrido* in singing their stories of the exploits of heroes and outlaws along the Rio Grande. In a manner typical of progressive country songwriters, however, Van Zandt manages to put some new twists into an old form. The tale of Pancho and Lefty begins with a four-line stanza that functions as a framing device, in which the singer seems to be addressing one of the characters in the story in a direct, second-person voice:

> *Livin' on the road my friend, was gonna keep you free and clean*
> *Now you wear your skin like iron, and your breath's as hard as kerosene.*
> *You weren't your mama's only boy, but her favorite one it seems*
> *She began to cry when you said good-bye, and sank into your dreams.*

Van Zandt then sinks into the typical third-person voice of the ballad singer, an ob-server recounting a sequence of events. In a series of carefully constructed stanzas he describes the outlaw team of Pancho and Lefty, the former a young Mexican bandit who dies at the beginning of the story, the latter his Anglo accomplice, who through a series of misfortunes ends up in a flophouse in Cleveland, Ohio, wast-ing away as an old man.

> *Well the poets tell how Pancho fell, and Lefty's living in a cheap hotel*
> *The desert's quiet and Cleveland's cold, so the story ends we're told*

Pancho needs your prayers it's true, but save a few for Lefty, too
He just did what he had to do, and now he's growing old.

This is not the usual fate of outlaw heroes in the ballad tradition, who typically either meet their end in a hail of bullets or, through sheer wits, manage to escape to fight another day. As Van Zandt moves through the song, it becomes increasingly apparent that Lefty isn't such a hero after all, a point driven home by the chorus which describes the "kindness" shown Lefty by the federal marshals (*Federales*) who were his natural enemies:

And all the Federales say they could have had him any day
They only let him hang around out of kindness, I suppose.

The chorus becomes the object of a subtle manipulation, in which just a few words are altered each time through. After we find out that Lefty has fled to Ohio, the chorus informs us that the *federales* claim to have purposefully allowed the pitiful sap to escape with his life, out of kindness. By the end of the song, the federal marshals too have aged, and the chorus takes on an ironic tone:

A few grey Federales say they could have had him any day
They only let him go so wrong out of kindness, I suppose.

In the end, the listener is left uncertain—did Lefty betray his Mexican partner, leaving him at the mercy of the federal marshals, or is the whole story simply the dream-like fantasy of a lonely old man, as the first stanza suggests?

Townes Van Zandt died prematurely at the age of fifty-two. However, his songs—which combine the straightforwardness of traditional country music with the poetic subtlety of singer-songwriters such as Bob Dylan—have inspired country and rock musicians ranging from Lyle Lovett to Neil Young.

"I SHOT THE SHERIFF": THE RISE OF REGGAE

Reggae—a potent mixture of Caribbean folk music and American rhythm & blues—was the first style of the rock era to originate in the so-called Third World. The popularity of reggae in America may be related both to earlier "exotic" music crazes—the Argentine tango and the Cuban rumba—and to the coming world beat movement of the 1980s and 1990s. Born in the impoverished shantytowns of Kingston, Jamaica, reggae first became popular in the United States in 1973, after the release of the Jamaican film *The Harder They Come* and its soundtrack album. (This is yet another example of the importance of film as a medium for promoting popular music, exemplified by the Hollywood musicals of the 1930s and rock 'n' roll films of the 1950s.) During the 1970s a handful of Jamaican musicians—notably Bob Marley and Jimmy Cliff—achieved a measure of commercial success in the United States, while numerous American and British rock musicians—including Eric Clapton, Paul Simon, the Police, and Elvis Costello—found inspiration (and profit) in the style. In addition, rap music of the 1980s was strongly influenced by Jamaican "dub," a branch of the reggae tradition in which verbal performances are improvised over prerecorded musical accompaniments.

Reggae music was itself a complex composite of influences, some of them from the United States. The history of reggae thus gives us an opportunity to examine not only the burgeoning interest of American musicians in "world music" but also the influence of American forms on local music elsewhere, a fascinating story that mainly lies outside the scope of this book. The roots of reggae lie in the Jamaican equivalent of country music, a genre called *mento*. Mento—a mixture of Jamaican folk songs, church hymns, sailor's shanties, and Cuban influences—arose in rural Jamaica during the late nineteenth century. By World War II, mento had lost its popularity among the thousands of young Jamaicans who were migrating to the capital city of Kingston. (Today's tourist resorts on Jamaica's north coast are among the last places where mento can be heard.) During the 1940s and early 1950s swing bands from the United States—including those of Benny Goodman, Count Basie, and Glenn Miller—became popular in the dance halls of Kingston. Jamaican musicians formed what they called "road bands," local swing bands that toured from town to town, playing public dances.

Starting in the 1950s American rhythm & blues—broadcast by powerful radio stations in Miami and New Orleans—became popular among youth in Kingston. Migrant Jamaican workers in Costa Rica, Panama, Cuba, and the United States brought back the hit recordings of American artists such as Louis Jordan and Fats Domino, and local entrepreneurs set up portable sound systems to play R&B records for dances and parties, driving the road bands out of business. In the 1960s a shortage of U.S. records encouraged some sound system operators to set up their own recording studios in Kingston. Some of these men—including Coxsone Dodd and Leslie Kong—became leading producers in the Jamaican popular music business.

During the 1960s a succession of new popular genres emerged out of the intersection of Jamaican folk music and American rhythm & blues. The first of these was *ska* (an onomatopoeic term derived from the style's typical sharp offbeat accents). The instrumentation of ska bands was derived from R&B, with a rhythm section of piano, bass, guitar, and drums and a horn section including some combination of brass instruments and saxophones. Ska music was usually played at fast tempos, with the bass playing a steady four-beat pattern and the piano, guitar, and drums emphasizing the backbeats. The singing on ska records was strongly influenced by R&B, ranging from rougher blues-influenced styles to romantic crooning. The biggest star of Jamaican ska was Don Drummond, a trombonist and leader of a band called the Skatalites. The Skatalites also worked as a studio band, backing many of the most popular singers of the time and exerting a substantial influence on the youth culture of Kingston, particularly when several members of the band joined the Rastafarian religious movement.

It is worth taking a moment here to discuss the Rastafarian movement, since it is such a prominent theme in reggae music. Rastafarianism was founded by Josiah Marcus Garvey (1887–1940), a Jamaican writer and political leader who inspired a "Back to Africa" repatriation movement among black Americans in the 1920s. Before leaving Jamaica for the United States in 1916, Garvey wrote, "Look to Africa for the crowning of a black king; he shall be the redeemer," a phrase that was taken quite literally as prophecy by Garvey's followers. In 1930, when Haile Selassie ("Power of the Trinity") was crowned king of the African nation of Ethiopia, preachers in Kingston saw this as confirmation of Garvey's prediction and proceeded to scrutinize the Old Testament in search of passages that supported the authenticity of Selassie's divinity. The Rastafarians' reinterpretation of the Bible focused on passages that dealt with slavery, salvation, and the apocalyptic consequences that would eventually be visited upon the oppressors (collectively referred to as Babylon). Rastafarianism became associated with a unique set of cultural practices, including special terminology (for example, "I-and-I" is substituted for "we"), the use of marijuana (*ganja*) as a sacramental herb, and the wearing of a distinctive hairstyle called "dreadlocks."

The Rastafarian movement spread rapidly, through an extensive network of neighborhood churches and informal prayer meetings, where music and dance were used to "give praise and thanks" (*satta amassanga*) and to "chant down Babylon." In the mountainous interior of Jamaica, where communities of escaped slaves called "maroons" had been living since the nineteenth century, Rastafarian songs and chants were mixed with an African-derived style of drumming called *burru*, creating a heavier, slower sound. This style in turn fed back into urban popular music, resulting around 1966 in an updated version of ska called *rock steady*. Rock steady was considerably slower in tempo than ska, reflecting the aforementioned influence of *burru* drumming, and some of its leading exponents—notably Alton Ellis, who had the first big rock steady hit in 1966—began to record songs with social and political content.

The main patrons of rock steady were the Rude Boys, a social category that included anyone against "the system": urban Rastas, thugs hired by competing political parties, and lower-class youth generally. An informal and unruly Jamaican youth movement, halfway between the Black Panthers and urban street gangs in the United States, Rude Boys increasingly came into conflict with the Jamaican police, and media coverage of their exploits helped to create the image of romantic outlaw heroes. The film that initiated reggae music's popularity in the United States, *The Harder They Come* (1972), was in fact a thinly disguised biography of one such ghetto hero (Vincent Martin, a.k.a. Rhygin', a Jamaican outlaw of the early 1960s). Bob Marley's song "I Shot the Sheriff" (see Box 12.2) is about a young man who is persecuted by the local sheriff and then accused of murdering both the sheriff and his deputy in cold blood.

Under the influence of Rastafarian religiosity and Rude Boy street politics, a new genre called reggae took shape in Kingston during the late 1960s. (The word "reggae" is derived from "raggay," a Kingston slang term meaning "raggedy, everyday stuff.") In musical terms reggae was a further extension of the evolution from ska to rock steady. In reggae music the tempo was slowed down even further, creating wide spaces between notes, allowing the music to breathe and emphasizing the polyrhythmic heritage of Afro-Jamaican traditions. Each instrument in a reggae band has its own carefully defined role to play. The heart of reggae music consists of "riddims," interlocking rhythmic patterns played by the guitar, bass, and drums. The guitar often plays short, choppy chords on the second and fourth beat of each measure, giving the music a bouncy, up-and-down feeling. The bass-drum combination is the irreducible core of a reggae band, sometimes called the "riddim pair." (The most famous of these are the brothers Aston and Carlton Barrett, who played in Bob Marley's band, and Sly Dunbar and Robbie Shakespeare, who have appeared on literally hundreds of reggae recordings, and on the LPs of rock artists such as Bob Dylan, Mick Jagger, and Peter Gabriel.) This musical mixture was further enlivened by the influence of contemporary black American popular music, particularly the soul recordings of James Brown and Aretha Franklin. Political messages were central to reggae music—while ska musicians of the early 1960s, like their American R&B counterparts, sang mainly about love and heartbreak, the most popular reggae artists focused their attention on issues such as social injustice and racism.

The film *The Harder They Come* featured reggae songs by a number of the most popular Jamaican musicians. The star of the film, and the vocalist on the title track of the soundtrack LP, was Jimmy Cliff (b. 1948). Like Ivan, the outlaw character he portrayed in the film, Cliff was only a teenager when he left the rural Jamaican town of St. James for the city of Kingston. Cliff arrived in Kingston in 1962 and made his first record within a year. Working with the producer Leslie Kong, he recorded a series of Jamaican Top 10 hits during the mid-1960s. While performing at the 1964 World's Fair in New York City, Cliff met Chris Blackwell of the English independent label Island Records, who convinced him to move to London. After working as a backup singer and scoring a few hits on the European charts, he returned to Jamaica in 1969 and recorded the song "Many Rivers to Cross," which inspired the director Perry Henzel to offer him the lead role in *The Harder They Come*. Although the film did not reach the mass audience commanded by many Hollywood movies, it did create a devoted audience for reggae music in the United States, particularly among young, college-educated adults, who were attracted by the rebellious spirit of the music and its associations with Rastafarianism and *ganja* smoking. (The film played for seven years straight at a movie theater in Boston, Massachusetts, sustained mainly by the enthusiasm of that city's large student population.)

Jimmy Cliff's 1972 recording of "The Harder They Come" exemplifies the reggae style of the early 1970s: a moderate tempo; strong guitar chords on the second and fourth beats of each measure; R&B-influenced singing; and a gritty lyric about the individual's struggle against oppression.

> *I keep on fighting for the things I want*
> *Though I know that when you're dead you can't*
> *But I'd rather be a free man in my grave*
> *Than living as a puppet or a slave*
>
> *So as sure as the sun will shine*
> *I'm gonna get my share now what is mine*
> *And then the harder they come, the harder they fall*
> *One and all*

Although Cliff was the first Jamaican musician to gain recognition in the United States, his contemporary Bob Marley (1945–81), leader of the Wailers, quickly surpassed Cliff in popularity. A national hero in his native Jamaica, Marley was reggae's most effective international ambassador. His songs of determination, rebellion, and faith, rooted in the Rastafarian belief system, found a worldwide audience that reached from America to Japan and from Europe to Africa. The son of a British naval officer who deserted his family when Bob was six years old, Marley migrated to Kingston from the rural parish of St. Ann at the age of fourteen. His early career reflects the economic precariousness of the music industry in a Third World country. After making a few singles for the Chinese-Jamaican producer Leslie Kong, Marley formed the Wailers in 1963 and signed with Coxsone Dodd's studios. Following a long period with little financial success (including a year of factory work

Bob Marley.
© S. I. N./Corbis.

for Marley in Wilmington, Delaware), the Wailers signed with the producer Lee Perry, who added Aston and Carlton Barrett, a masterful bassist-and-drummer "riddim pair."

In 1972 Chris Blackwell, who had launched Jimmy Cliff's international career, signed Bob Marley and the Wailers to Island Records and advanced them the money to record at their independent Tuff Gong studio in Jamaica. Marley's recognition abroad was boosted by the success of Eric Clapton's cover of "I Shot the Sheriff," from the Wailers' second LP for Island Records (see Box 12.2). The Wailers' first major concert in the United States took place in 1974 in Boston, where for a year and a half over a thousand young people a day had been viewing *The Harder They Come*. Between 1975 and 1980 Marley recorded six gold LPs for Island Records, including *Rastaman Vibration*, which reached Number Eight on the *Billboard* Top LPs charts in 1976. Wounded in a politically motivated assassination attempt in 1976,

Box 12.2   The Popularization of Reggae

Although the majority of American listeners became conscious of reggae as a distinctive musical style only in the mid to late 1970s, with the steadily increasing popularity in this country of Bob Marley and the Wailers, there are individual instances long before this of Jamaican music appearing on the American charts. In fact, among the many imported hits during the British Invasion year of 1964 was a ska-flavored recording by the Jamaican teenager Millie Small called "My Boy Lollipop," which climbed all the way up to Number Two on *Billboard*'s list of top singles. In 1968 Johnny Nash, an African American pop singer who established a recording studio in Jamaica, had a Top 5 hit with the reggae-influenced "Hold Me Tight," and 1969 saw the American success of two reggae records by Jamaican artists: "Israelites" by Desmond Dekker and the Aces (Number Nine pop), and "Wonderful World, Beautiful People," by Jimmy Cliff (Number Twenty-five pop).

Both Johnny Nash and Jimmy Cliff went on to bigger things in the early 1970s. Nash hit the Number One spot for four weeks in 1972 with another reggae-flavored tune, "I Can See Clearly Now." Nash wrote this song himself (as was also the case with "Hold Me Tight"), but he assured a sense of Jamaican authenticity by arranging for members of the Wailers to provide his instrumental support on the track. He then followed this up with a cover of Bob Marley's "Stir It Up" (Number Twelve pop, 1973). As for Jimmy Cliff, his starring role in the 1972 movie *The Harder They Come* introduced both him and the Jamaican music scene to a significant American audience previously unaware of both. (We might recall here the significance of another movie, *Blackboard Jungle*, in popularizing another music from the margins, rock 'n' roll, in 1955; see Chapter 8.) In a fine illustration of the reciprocal relationships that tend to characterize so much of pop music history, Cliff returned to the charts for the first time in many years, and hit the American Top 20 for the first time, in the early 1990s with nothing other than his own cover of Nash's "I Can See Clearly Now" (Number Eighteen pop, 1994), which was also featured in a movie, *Cool Runnings*.

Surely the best-known cover version of any reggae number is Eric Clapton's million-selling recording of Bob Marley's "I Shot the Sheriff," a Number One hit in 1974, which appears on Clapton's Number One album from the same year, *461 Ocean Boulevard*. Clapton's name on the label, along with his easygoing vocal delivery, doubtless helped to propel the single to the top of the charts; considered in terms of the song's lyrics and music, "I Shot the Sheriff" seems an unlikely 1970s hit. It is clearly a political song, but for anyone not thoroughly versed in contemporary Jamaican politics, its precise significance is difficult to grasp. This is an example of a "coded" lyric, reminiscent of the coded blues lyrics (see Chapter 5) that communicate something extra to members of a specific group who are attuned to its message. Furthermore, the music of the song is appropriately dark in color, with a predominance of minor chords.

It is instructive to compare Clapton's version with Bob Marley's own recording of "I Shot the Sheriff," which may be found on the 1973 album

Burnin' and on compilations issued after Marley's death in 1981. Marley's version sounds much more insistently rhythmic and intense than Clapton's. Actually, Marley's tempo is only a hairbreadth faster than Clapton's, but the greater prominence of both bass and percussion in Marley's recording emphasizes the distinctive "riddims" of Jamaican reggae and creates the illusion of a considerably faster performance. (The recording closes with just the bass guitar and drums—the heartbeat of reggae—played by the riddim pair of Aston and Carlton Barrett.) In addition, the high range of the Wailers' voices creates a strong element of urgency that is lacking in the Clapton recording. Marley and the Wailers add small but effective and apparently spontaneous variations in the vocal lines of the successive verses of the song, giving a sense of familiarity and freedom with the material that also has no real counterpart in the cover version. And there is of course no substitute for the Jamaican patois (a dialect of English with strong African influence) in Marley's original ("Ev'ry day the bucket a-go-a well; one day the bottom a-go drop out"). It is to Clapton's credit, however, that he doesn't even try to mimic Marley's rendition of a Jamaican proverb about the eventual triumph of the oppressed (he sings "Every day the bucket goes to the well, but one day the bottom will drop out").

In sum, Clapton made an effective 1970s pop single out of Marley's "I Shot the Sheriff" by smoothing out its sound. The traditional rock backbeat (emphasizing with the drums the second and fourth beats of the four-beat measures), clearly to be heard on Clapton's recording, ties it to the rock mainstream, while the basic rhythmic character of Marley's version is decidedly outside that mainstream (with all the beats much more evenly emphasized, and the syncopated patterns imposed over them brought strongly forward). It may seem ironic to find a hero of the 1960s counterculture like Eric Clapton cast in the role of mainstream popularizer for a new marginal music in the 1970s, but the history of American popular music is full of such ironies, as one decade's rebel becomes the next decade's establishment.

Marley died of cancer in 1981, at the age of thirty-six. His appeal and popularity, both in America and worldwide, has only grown in the years since his death: the 1984 LP compilation *Legend* has sold over eight million copies in the United States alone.

"PSYCHO KILLER": 1970s PUNK AND NEW WAVE

During the 1970s the first "alternative" movements emerged within rock music. While rock had begun as a vital part of the 1960s counterculture, by 1975 it had come perilously close to occupying the center of popular taste, a development that left some young musicians feeling that its rebellious, innovative potential had been squandered by pampered, pretentious rock stars and the major record companies that promoted them. The golden age of *punk rock*—a "back to basics" rebellion against the perceived artifice and pretension of corporate rock music—lasted from around 1975 to 1978, but both the musical genre and the sensibility with which it was associated continue to exert a strong influence today on alternative rock musicians. *New wave* music, which developed alongside punk rock, approached the critique of corporate rock in more self-consciously artistic and experimental terms. (The term "new wave" was soon picked up by record companies themselves, who began using it in the late 1970s to refer to pop-influenced performers such as Blondie). Although the initial energy of the punk and new wave scene was largely expended by the start of the 1980s, young musicians inspired by the raw energy and minimalism of this movement went on to create distinctive regional music scenes in Los Angeles; Minneapolis; Seattle; Athens, Georgia; and elsewhere.

Punk was as much a cultural style—an attitude defined by a rebellion against authority and a deliberate rejection of middle-class values—as it was a musical genre. The contrarian impulse of punk culture is evoked (and parodied) in the song "I'm against It," recorded by the Ramones in 1978.

> I don't like sex and drugs
> I don't like waterbugs
> I don't care about poverty
> All I care about is me
>
> I don't like playing Ping-Pong
> I don't like the Viet Cong
> I don't like Burger King
> I don't like anything
>
> Well I'm against it, I'm against it

In its automatic gainsaying of everything from sex and drugs to the Viet Cong and Burger King, this song evokes the motorcycle gang leader played by Marlon Brando in the archetypal teen rebellion film *The Wild One* (1954). When asked by a young woman, "What are you rebelling against?" the Brando character responds, "Whaddaya got?"

Punk was in fact both the apotheosis and the ultimate exploitation of rock 'n' roll as a symbol of rebellion, a tradition that began in the 1950s with white teenagers gleefully co-opting the energy and overt sexuality of black rhythm & blues to annoy their parents, and continued through the 1960s with songs like the Who's 1966 youth anthem "My Generation" ("Why don't you all just f-f-fade away?"). To many of its fans, punk rock represented a turn toward the authentic, risk-taking spirit of early rock 'n' roll and away from the pomposity and self-conscious artistry of album-oriented rock. On the other hand, like all alternative styles of popular music, punk rock was riven through with contradictions.

To begin with, if punk was explicitly against the standards of traditional commercial fashion, it was also a fashion system in its own right, with a very particular look: torn blue jeans, ripped stockings, outfits patched with ragged bits of contrasting materials, and perhaps a safety pin through the cheek. If some punk musicians framed their challenge to established authority in terms of progressive social values, others flirted with fascist imagery, attaching Nazi swastikas to their clothing and associating with the racist "skinhead" movement. Many in the punk movement—including musicians, fans, and those rock critics who championed the music—saw punk as a progressive response to the conservatism of the record in-dustry. Yet the nihilism of much punk rock—the music's basic "I don't give a f——" stance—posed a crucial question that still resonates in today's alternative rock mu-sic: is it possible to make music that is "authentic" or "real" while at the same time loudly proclaiming that you don't care about anything?

In musical terms, punk rock turned progressive rock—with its artistic aspira-tions and corporate backing—on its head. As the drummer for the Ramones, widely regarded as the first punk rock band, put it:

> We took the rock sound into a psychotic world and narrowed it down into a straight line of energy. In an era of progressive rock, with its complexities and counterpoints, we had a perspective of non-musicality and intelligence that took over from musi-cianship. (Laing 1985, p. 23)

Punk was a stripped-down and often purposefully "nonmusical" version of rock music, in some sense a return to the wildness of early rock 'n' roll stars like Jerry Lee Lewis and Little Richard, but with lyrics that stressed the ironic or dark di-mensions of human existence—drug addiction, despair, suicide, lust, and violence. As David Byrne, the leader of the new wave band Talking Heads, put it (on the PBS television series *Rock & Roll*):

> Punk . . . was more a kind of do-it-yourself, anyone-can-do-it attitude. If you only played two notes on the guitar, you could figure out a way to make a song out of that, and that's what it was all about.

Punk rock and its more commercial cousin, new wave, took shape in New York City during the mid-1970s. One of the predecessors of punk rock was an American musical institution called the *garage band*, typically a neighborhood operation, made up of young men who played mainly for themselves, their friends, and the occa-sional high school dance. A few of these local groups went on to enjoy some com-mercial success, including the Los Angeles–based Standells (whose "Dirty Water" was a Number Eleven pop hit in 1966); ? and the Mysterians, from the industrial town of Flint, Michigan (who took "96 Tears" to the top of the charts in the same year); and Portland, Oregon's Kingsmen, best known for their cover version of the 1950s R&B song "Louie, Louie" (Number Two pop in 1963). The rough-and-ready, do-it-yourself attitude of the garage bands—something akin to a rock 'n' roll–based folk music movement—paved the way for punk rock.

Three groups, none of them very successful in commercial terms, are frequently cited as ancestors of 1970s punk music, and of later genres such as new wave, hard-core, industrial, and alternative rock: the Velvet Underground, the Stooges, and the New York Dolls. The Velvet Underground, a New York group, was promoted by the pop art superstar Andy Warhol, who painted the famous cartoonlike image of a banana on the cover of their first LP. Their music was rough-edged and chaotic, extremely loud, and deliberately anticommercial, and the lyrics of their songs fo-cused on topics such as sexual deviancy, drug addiction, violence, and social alien-ation. The leaders of the Velvet Underground were singer and guitarist Lou Reed—who had worked previously as a pop songwriter in a Brill Building–style "music factory"—and John Cale, a viola player active in the avant-garde art music scene in New York, who introduced experimental musical elements into the mix, including electronic noise and recorded industrial sounds.

If the Velvet Underground represented the self-consciously experimentalist roots of 1970s new wave music, the Stooges, formed in Ann Arbor, Michigan, in 1967, were the working-class, motorcycle-riding, leather-jacketed ancestors of punk rock. The lead singer of the Stooges, Iggy Stooge (a.k.a. Iggy Pop, James Osterburg), was famous for his outrageous stage performances, which included flinging himself into the crowd, cutting himself with beer bottles, and rubbing himself with raw meat. Guitarist Ron Asheton has described the Stooges' approach:

> Usually we got up there and jammed one riff and built into an energy freak-out, until finally we'd broken a guitar, or one of my hands would be twice as big as the other and my guitar would be covered in blood. (Palmer 1995, p. 263)

The Stooges' eponymous first album (1969), produced by the Velvet Underground's John Cale, created a devoted if small national audience for the Stooges' demented "garage band" sound. A good example of the sensibility that underlay much of the Stooges' work—the depression of unemployed Michigan youth caught in the middle of a severe economic recession—is the song "1969," which evokes a world light-years distant from the utopianism of the hippie movement and the Woodstock festival, held that same summer:

The New York Dolls make a fashion statement. Frank Driggs Collection.

Well it's 1969 OK all across the USA
It's another year for me and you
Another year with nothing to do
Last year I was 21 I didn't have a lot of fun
And now I'm gonna be 22 I say oh my and a boo-hoo

Another year with nothing to do
It's 1969, 1969, 1969, 1969, 1969, baby

Another band that exerted a major influence on the musical and visual style of the punk rock movement was the New York Dolls, formed in New York City in 1971. Dressed in fishnet stockings, bright red lipstick, cellophane tutus, ostrich feathers, and army boots, the all-male Dolls were an American response to the English glam rock movement, typified by the reigning master of rock gender bending, David Bowie (see Chapter 11). Their professional career began inauspiciously—at a Christmas party in a seedy welfare hotel in Manhattan—but by late 1972 they had built a small and devoted following. Although the New York Dolls soon succumbed to drug and alcohol abuse, they did establish certain core features of punk antifashion and helped to create a new underground rock music scene in New York City.

The amateur energy of garage band rock'n' roll, the artsy nihilism of the Velvet Underground, the raw energy and abandon of the Stooges, and the antifashion of the New York Dolls converged in the mid-1970s in New York City's burgeoning club scene. The locus of this activity was a converted folk music club called CBGB & OMFUG ("Country, Bluegrass, Blues & Other Music for Urban Gourmandizers"), located in the run-down Bowery area of Manhattan. The first rock musician to perform regularly at CBGBs was Patti Smith (b. 1946), a New York–based poet, journalist, and singer who had been experimenting with combining the spoken word and rock accompaniment. In 1975 Smith began a stint at CBGBs, establishing a beachhead for punk and new wave bands, and signed a contract with Arista, a new label headed by Clive Davis, the former head of Columbia Records. (Her critically acclaimed album *Horses* reached Number Forty-seven on the *Billboard* charts in 1976.) Other influential groups who played at CBGBs during the mid-1970s included Television—whose lengthy instrumental improvisations were inspired by the Velvet Underground and avant-garde jazz saxophonist Albert Ayler—Blondie, and the Voidoids, featuring the alienated lyrics and howling voice of lead singer Richard Hell, one of the original members of Television.

The first bonafide punk rock band was the Ramones, formed in 1974 in New York City. The Ramones' high-speed, energetic, and extremely loud sound influenced English punk groups such as the Sex Pistols and the Clash and also became a blueprint for 1980s L.A. hardcore bands. Although they projected a street-tough image, all of the band's members were from middle-class families in the New York City borough of Queens. The band—not a family enterprise, despite their stage names—consisted of Jeffrey Hyman (a.k.a. Joey Ramone) on vocals; John Cummings (Johnny Ramone) on guitar; Douglas Colvin (Dee Dee Ramone) on bass; and Tom Erdelyi (Tommy Ramone) on drums. The band's first manager, Danny Fields, had previously worked with the Stooges and Lou Reed and thus had a good sense of the Ramones' potential audience.

Taking the stage in blue jeans and black leather jackets—a look calculated to evoke the sneering, rebellious ethos of 1950s rock 'n' rollers—the Ramones began playing regularly at CBGBs in 1975. By the end of the year they had secured a recording contract with Sire Records, an independent label that signed a number of early punk groups. Their eponymous debut album was recorded in 1976 for just over six thousand dollars, an incredibly small amount of money in an era of expensive and time-consuming studio sessions. The album gained some critical attention and managed to reach Number 111 on the *Billboard* album charts.

Later that year the Ramones staged a British Invasion in reverse. Their concerts in English cities, where their records had already created an underground sensation, were attended by future members of almost every important British punk band, including the Sex Pistols (see Box 12.3), the Clash, and the Damned. In 1977 the Ramones scored a U.K. Top 40 hit with the song "Sheena Is a Punk Rocker" (Number Eighty-one U.S.), which announced that the center of the rock 'n' roll universe had shifted from the beaches of southern California to the lower east side of Manhattan:

> *Well the kids are all hopped up and ready to go*
> *They're ready to go now*
> *They've got their surfboards*
> *And they're going to the discotheque au go go*

The Ramones: Johnny, Dee Dee, Tommy, and Joey. Frank Driggs Collection.

But she just couldn't stay
She had to break away
Well New York City really has it all
Oh yeah, oh yeah.

Sheena is a punk rocker, Sheena is a punk rocker, Sheena is a punk rocker now.

The Ramones' music reflected their origins as a garage band made up of neighborhood friends. As the guitarist Johnny Ramone phrased it in an interview with the popular music scholar Robert Palmer:

> I had bought my first guitar just prior to starting the Ramones. . . . It was all very new; we put records on, but we couldn't figure out how to play the songs, so we decided to start writing songs that were within our capabilities. (Palmer 1995, p. 274)

These songs had catchy, pop-inspired melodies, were played at extremely fast tempos, and generally lasted no more than two and a half minutes. (In live performances, the Ramones managed to squeeze twelve or thirteen songs into a half-hour set.) The band's raw, hard-edged sound was anchored by a steady barrage of notes, played on drums, bass, and guitar. Johnny Ramone rarely if ever took a guitar solo, but this makes sense when you consider the band's technical limitations and the aesthetic goal of the music—a rejection of the flashy virtuosity of progressive rock music, with its extended and sometimes self-indulgent solos.

The song "I Wanna Be Sedated," from the band's fourth album, *Road to Ruin* (1978), is a good example of the Ramones' style, and of their mordant—one is tempted to say twisted—sense of humor:

Twenty-twenty-twenty-four hours to go, I wanna be sedated
Nothin' to do and nowhere to go-o-o, I wanna be sedated
Just put me in a wheelchair, get me to the show
Hurry hurry hurry, before I gotta go
I can't control my fingers, I can't control my toes
Oh no no no no no

Ba-ba-bamp-ba ba-ba-ba-bamp-ba, I wanna be sedated
Ba-ba-bamp-ba ba-ba-ba-bamp-ba, I wanna be sedated

The song text's images of drug-induced insanity (and its putative antidote, drug-induced paralysis) are juxtaposed with a catchy pop melody and Beach Boys–like chorus, a combination that affirms Joey Ramone's early description of the band's style as "sick bubblegum music."

It is, in fact, hard to know how seriously to take the Ramones. Although they played alongside self-consciously "cutting-edge" bands like the Patti Smith Group and Television, the Ramones identified themselves as a band that was "able to just play and be song-oriented and sound great, people who play real rock 'n' roll." Nonetheless, some of their recordings did provide grim "news flashes" on the facts of life in many working-class and middle-class homes during a period of severe economic recession. The song "I Wanted Everything" (1978) is a kind of punk counterpart to Merle Haggard's hardcore country song "If We Make It through December" (1973, see Chapter 11), sung, however, by a dispossessed son rather than a struggling father. The stark realism of this tale of a good boy gone wrong is

Box 12.3 "The End of Rock 'n' Roll": The Sex Pistols

We have already mentioned the impression made by the Ramones on musicians in the United Kingdom, an "American Invasion" that began some twelve years after the Beatles stormed New York City. The English stream of punk rock bubbled up during the summer of 1976, an unusually hot summer and a high point of unemployment, inflation, and racial tension in cities like London, Birmingham, Manchester, and Liverpool. In England, more than the United States, punk rock was associated with a mainly white working-class youth subculture. More explicitly political and less artsy than some of the New York bands, groups like the Sex Pistols, the Clash, and the Damned succeeded in outraging the British political establishment and the mainstream media while at the same time achieving a modicum of commercial success in the late 1970s.

The most outrageous—and therefore famous—punk band was the Sex Pistols, formed in 1975 in London. They were the creation of Malcolm McLaren, owner of a London "antifashion" boutique called *Sex*, which specialized in leather and rubber clothing. (McLaren had begun his career in the music business in 1974, when he managed unsuccessfully the short-lived New York Dolls.) Upon his return to London, McLaren conceived the idea of a rock 'n' roll band that would subvert the pop music industry and horrify England's staid middle class. Glen Matlock (bass), Paul Cook (drums), and Steve Jones (guitar) were regular customers at the shop, and they were looking for a singer. McLaren introduced them to John Lydon, a young man who hung around listening to the jukebox at *Sex* and had never sung in public before. (Lydon's inconsistent approach to personal hygiene led Steve Jones to christen him Johnny Rotten, a stage name that stuck.) The Sex Pistols got their first gigs by showing up and posing as the opening band. Given the nature of Johnny Rotten's stage act—sneering and screaming obscenities at the audience, commanding them to applaud, and throwing beer on them when they didn't—it is perhaps not surprising that they were banned from many nightclubs.

The trajectory of this band's rapid ascent and implosion is complex, and we can present only a summary here. EMI Records, England's biggest and most conservative label, signed the Sex Pistols for around sixty thousand dollars in 1976, releasing their first single, "Anarchy in the UK," in December. The single was a Top 40 hit in the U.K. but was withdrawn from record shops after Rotten uttered an obscenity during a television interview. At an annual meeting of shareholders in December 1976, the chairman of EMI, Sir John Read, made the following statement (as recorded in the Report of the EMI General Meeting, 12/7/76):

> Sex Pistols is the only "punk rock" group that EMI Records currently has under direct recording contract and whether EMI does in fact release any more of their records will have to be very carefully considered. I need hardly add that we shall do everything we can to restrain their public behavior, although this is a matter over which we have no real control.

The resulting uproar caused EMI to terminate the Sex Pistols' contract in January 1977, and all but five out of twenty-one dates on a planned concert tour of the U.K. were promptly canceled. In March the bassist Glen Matlock was replaced by John Ritchie, a nonmusician friend of John Lydon, who went by the stage name <u>Sid Vicious</u>. The American label A&M Records then signed the Pistols for over $200,000, only to fire them the very next week. In May Virgin Records signed them and released their second single, "God Save the Queen (It's a Fascist Regime)." Despite being banned from airplay, the song went to Number Two (cited as a blank on the U.K. charts). The band was featured in a 1978 film called *The Great Rock 'n' Roll Swindle*, a title that some critics thought captured perfectly the essence of the band's exercise in manipulation. The Sex Pistols broke up that same year, during their only U.S. tour, a tour undertaken to support the release of their only studio album, *Never Mind the Bollocks, Here's the Sex Pistols* (1977). In 1979 Sid Vicious was imprisoned in New York on charges of stabbing his girlfriend to death, and he died of a heroin overdose while out on bail. In 1986 the surviving members of the group sued Malcolm McLaren for cheating them of royalties and were awarded around $1.5 million. Though they did not represent "the end of rock 'n' roll," the Sex Pistols did manage to do away with themselves quite efficiently.

The Sex Pistols.
Frank Driggs Collection.

reminiscent of the work of Bruce Springsteen, often regarded as a working-class rock 'n' roll hero of the 1980s (see Chapter 13), and this realism suggests that American punk rock was not a totally nihilistic movement.

If the Ramones and the Sex Pistols epitomized punk rock's connections to the rebellious energy of early rock 'n' roll, another band, Talking Heads, represented the more self-consciously artistic and exploratory side of the alternative rock scene of the mid-1970s. Talking Heads was formed in 1974 by David Byrne (born in Scotland in 1952), Chris Frantz, and Tina Weymouth, who met as art students at the Rhode Island School of Design. They first appeared at CBGBs in 1975 as the opening act for the Ramones, though they attracted a somewhat different audience, made up of college students, artists, and music critics. In 1976 they were signed to a recording contract by Sire Records, and their first album, *Talking Heads: 77*, achieved critical acclaim and broke into the Top 100 on the *Billboard* album charts. The band's style reflected their interest in an aesthetic called minimalism, which stresses the use of combinations of a limited number of basic elements—colors, shapes, sounds, or words. This approach was popular in the New York art music scene of the 1960s and 1970s, as represented in the work of composers such as Steve Reich, Terry Riley, and Philip Glass, who made use of simple musical patterns, repeated and combined in various ways. The Talking Heads' instrumental arrangements fused this approach with the interlocking, riff-based rhythms pioneered by African American popular musicians, particularly James Brown (see the discussion of funk music below). Clarity is another important aspect of the minimalist aesthetic, and the Talking Heads' songs were generally quite simple in structural terms, with strong pop hooks and contrasting sections marked off by carefully arranged changes in instrumental texture.

In their visual presentation and stage demeanor, the Talking Heads were from another universe than the other CBGBs bands—they dressed in slacks, sweaters, and vests, projecting the image of cerebral but nerdy college students. David Byrne's stage demeanor was described by reviewer Michael Aron for *Rolling Stone* magazine (11/17/77):

> Everything about him is uncool: his socks and shoes, his body language, his self-conscious announcements of song titles, the way he wiggles his hips when he's carried away onstage (imagine an out-of-it kid practicing Buddy Holly moves in front of a mirror).

Just as the punk rockers' antifashion became a new kind of fashion, so David Byrne's studied awkwardness established a new kind of cool, one still much in evidence on college campuses today.

The center of attention on most Talking Heads recordings was David Byrne's trembling, high-pitched voice and his eclectic songwriting. Byrne often delivered his lyrics in a nervous, almost schizophrenic stream-of-consciousness voice, like overheard fragments from a psychiatrist's office. A good example of this approach—as well as the only single from the Heads' first LP to appear on the singles charts (peaking at Number Ninety-two)—was the song "Psycho Killer," inspired by Norman Bates, the schizophrenic murderer in Alfred Hitchcock's film *Psycho*. Although it now seems like an ironic commentary on mass media portrayals of "the serial killer," this song had a darker, more immediate resonance when it was released in

1977, during the Son of Sam killing spree, in which a deranged man shot thirteen people in New York City.

The recording opens with Tina Weymouth's electric bass, playing a simple riff reminiscent of mid-1970s funk or disco music (see below). She is soon joined by two guitars, playing crisply articulated, interlocking chord patterns. David Byrne's voice enters in the thirteenth bar, enunciating the lyrics in a half-spoken, half-sung style, over a simple melody that uses only a few pitches and stays mainly on the tonic note. The first verse (A^1) gives us a glimpse into the psychosis of the narrator:

> *I can't seem to face up to the facts*
> *I'm tense and nervous and I can't relax*
> *I can't sleep 'cause my bed's on fire*
> *Don't touch me I'm a real live wire*

This verse is followed by two statements of the chorus (B), which references the title of the song, dips abruptly and somewhat schizophrenically into a second language (French), and ends with a stuttered warning to the listener:

> *Psycho Killer, Qu'est-ce que c'est* [What is it?]
> *Fa fa fa fa fa fa fa fa far better*
> *Run run run run run run run away*

The chorus blends into a four-bar vocal interlude, with Byrne's voice leaping up an octave and emitting a distressed "Ay yai yai yai," and a two-bar instrumental section that reestablishes the basic groove. In the second verse (A^2), Byrne shifts from singing to speech, becoming more agitated as he expresses his anger at people who talk a lot, despite having nothing to say, and at his own inability to communicate with others:

> *You start a conversation, you can't even finish it.*
> *You're talking a lot, but you're not saying anything.*
> *When I have nothing to say, my lips are sealed.*
> *Say something once, why say it again?*

The chorus (B) is heard two more times, followed by the interlude, and then by a new section (C), in which Byrne struggles to confess his crime in an awkward, strangled variant of French:

> *Ce que j'ai fais, ce soir la* [The things I did on that night]
> *Ce qu'elle a dit, ce soir la* [The things she said on that night]
> *Realisant mon espoir* [Realizing my hope]
> *Je me lance vers la gloire . . . Okay* [I throw myself toward glory . . . Okay]

Eventually Byrne switches back into English, focusing obsessively on a single pitch and revealing more of his character's motivation for committing an unspecified though presumably horrific act:

> *We are vain and we are blind*
> *I hate people when they're not polite*

After final repetitions of the "Psycho Killer" chorus (B) and interlude, the band moves into a concluding twenty-four-bar instrumental section (or coda), in which the basic groove is elaborated with distorted textures, wavering pitches on the guitars, strange vocal sounds from Byrne, and the panning of one guitar back and forth from left to right speaker, like the unanchored movement of a madman's thoughts. The last sound we hear is the squeal of feedback from one of the microphones, fading into silence and darkness.

LISTENING CHART "PSYCHO KILLER"

Music and lyrics by David Byrne, Chris Frantz, Tina Weymouth; performed by Talking Heads; recorded 1977

FORM	LYRICS	DESCRIPTIVE COMMENTS
Intro (12)	Instrumental	Bars 1–4: The electric bass plays a simple two-bar pattern two times.
		Bars 5–8: The bass drum enters with a steady pulse, and electric guitar plays sustained chords.
		Bars 9–12: The second electric guitar enters, completing the basic groove—the two guitars play choppy, rhythmically interlocking chords (à la James Brown).
A¹ (8)	*I can't seem to face up . . .* *I'm tense and nervous . . .* *I can't sleep . . .* *Don't touch me . . .*	Vocal enters; simple melody, centered on tonic pitch; instrumental accompaniment is based on interlocking riffs.
B (8)	*Psycho Killer, Qu'est-ce que c'est?* *Fa fa fa fa fa fa fa fa fa far better* *Run run run run run run run away* *Oh-oh-oh-oh . . .*	New harmonies, sustained chords on guitar mark beginning of chorus; bass and drums continue pulse.
B (8)	Lyric repeats	
Interlude (6)	*Oh . . . Ai yai yai yai yai (4)*	Byrne sings nonsense syllables, makes muffled vocal sounds in background.
	Instrumental (2)	Bass, drums and guitars play basic groove for last two bars.
A² (8)	*You start a conversation . . .* *You're talking a lot . . .* *When I have nothing to say . . .* *Say something once . . .*	Byrne moves from singing into speech mode; uses vocal quality to evoke psychotic persona.
B (8)	*Psycho Killer, Qu'est-ce que c'est?* *Fa fa fa fa fa fa fa fa fa far better* *Run run run run run run run away* *Oh-oh-oh-oh . . .*	
B (8)	Lyric repeats	
Interlude (2)	*Oh . . . Ai yai yai yai yai*	First part only.

C (20)	Ce que j'ai fais, ce soir la	Rhythm section plays marchlike pulse in unison for first eight bars, while Byrne speaks the lyrics.
	Ce qu'elle a dit, ce soir la	
	Realisant mon espoir	Guitar plays sustained chords (four bars).
	Je me lance, vers la gloire . . . Okay	Rhythm section reestablishes basic groove (four bars).
	Ya ya ya ya ya ya ya	
	We are vain and we are blind	Groove continues (four bars).
	I hate people when they're not polite	
B (8)	Psycho Killer, Qu'est-ce que c'est?	
	Fa fa fa fa fa fa fa fa fa far better	
	Run run run run run run run away	
	Oh-oh-oh-oh . . .	
B (8)	Lyric repeats	
Interlude (4)	Oh . . . Ai yai yai yai yai	Byrne sings nonsense syllables, makes vocal sounds in background.
Coda (3 × 8 = 24)	Instrumental	Bass, drums and guitars elaborate on basic groove for last twenty-four bars, building in intensity. Last eight bars feature stereo effect, guitar moving back and forth from left to right speaker.

Rather like David Bowie's Ziggy Stardust, the persona projected in "Psycho Killer"—tongue-tied, nervous, emotionally distant, and obsessively intellectual—provided David Byrne with a durable stage persona. In a review of the 1984 Talking Heads concert film *Stop Making Sense,* one critic remarked on Byrne's ability to project "a variant on his basic 'Psycho Killer' self for each song; he demonstrates over and over that a public self is a Frankenstein self, a monster put together from bits and pieces of image tissue." Throughout the late 1970s and 1980s Talking Heads recorded a series of critically acclaimed albums, most of which reached *Billboard*'s Top 40 and achieved either gold or platinum status. The commercial success was linked to the accessibility of Talking Heads' music, which mixed in influences from rhythm and blues and funk music, and from West African music, with its complexly interlocking but catchy polyrhythmic patterns. David Byrne went on to become a major figure in the world beat movement of the 1980s and 1990s, introducing American audiences to recording artists from Africa, Brazil, and the Caribbean.

"TEAR THE ROOF OFF THE SUCKER": FUNK MUSIC

Punk rock was a reaction against the pretentiousness of progressive rock and its multimillionaire superstars, hidden behind designer sunglasses, limousine windows, and mansion walls. *Funk music* represented yet another back-to-basics impetus, the impulse to dance. Most album-oriented rock music was aimed at a predominantly white male audience and was designed for listening rather than dancing. (While rock fans certainly engaged in free-form movement, the idea of organized social dancing was anathema to the "do your own thing" ethos of the counterculture and to the "high art" aspirations of some rock musicians.) In urban black communities across America, however, dance remained a backbone of social life, a primary means for transmitting traditional values and for generating a sense of novelty and excitement. And for the first time since the twist craze of the early 1960s, funk music—and its commercial offspring, disco—brought this intensive focus on dancing back into the pop mainstream.

The word "funky"—probably derived from the (central African) BaKongo term *funki,* meaning "healthy sweat"—was already in wide use by New Orleans jazz musicians during the first decade of the twentieth century. Today "funky" carries the same ambivalent meaning that it did a century ago—strong body odors (particularly those related to sex), and a quality of earthiness and authenticity, quintessentially expressed in music. If the concept of soul symbolized the spiritual, uplifting side of black consciousness, then funk was its profane and decidedly down-to-earth counterpart.

By the early 1970s the term "funk" was being used as a label for a genre of popular music characterized by strong, dance-oriented rhythms, catchy melodies, call-and-response exchanges between voices and instruments, and heavy reliance on repeated, rhythmically interlocking patterns. Most funk bands, echoing the instrumentation of James Brown's hits of the late 1960s, consisted of a rhythm section (guitar, keyboards, electric bass, and drums) and a horn section, which effectively functioned as part of the rhythm section and occasionally supplied jazz-influenced solos. Although funk music was initially targeted mostly at the predominantly urban black audience for soul music, funk groups such as Kool and the Gang, Ohio Players, and Chic were able to score Number One pop hits during the 1970s. Funk represented a vigorous reassertion of African American musical values in the face of soft soul's dominance of the R&B/pop crossover market, and it paved the way for the more commercialized sounds of disco music in the mid-1970s (see next section).

As we have suggested, James Brown was one of the prime inspirations for funk musicians. During the early 1970s Brown continued to score successes with dance-oriented hits, including "Super Bad" (Number Thirteen pop, Number One R&B in 1970), "Hot Pants (She Got to Use What She Got to Get What She Wants)" (Number Fifteen pop, Number One R&B, 1971), "Get on the Good Foot" (Number Eighteen pop, Number One R&B, 1972), and "The Payback" (Number Twenty-six pop, Number One R&B, 1974). Brown's ranking on the pop charts declined gradually throughout this period, however, in large part owing to competition from a new generation of musicians who played variations on the basic style he had established the decade before. This approach—the core of funk music—centered on the creation of a strong rhythmic momentum or groove, with the electric bass and bass drum often playing on all four main beats of the measure, the snare drum and other instruments playing equally strongly on the second and fourth beats (the backbeats), and interlocking ostinato patterns distributed among other instruments, including guitar, keyboards, and horns.

Another important influence on 1970s funk music was the group Sly and the Family Stone, an interracial "psychedelic soul" band whose recordings bridged the gap between rock music and soul music. Sly Stone (Sylvester Stewart) was born in Dallas, Texas, in 1944, and moved to San Francisco with his family in the 1950s. He began his musical career at the age of four as a gospel singer, went on to study

Sly and the Family Stone. Frank Driggs Collection.

trumpet, music theory, and composition in college, and later worked as a disc jockey at both R&B and rock-oriented radio stations in the San Francisco Bay Area. Sly formed his first band (the Stoners) in 1966 and gradually developed a style that reflected his own diverse musical experience, a blend of jazz, soul music, San Francisco psychedelia, and the socially engaged lyrics of folk rock. The Family Stone's national popularity was boosted by their fiery performance at the Woodstock Festival in 1969, which appeared in the film and soundtrack album *Woodstock*.

Between 1968 and 1971 Sly and the Family Stone recorded a series of albums and singles that reached the top of both the pop and soul charts. Recordings like "Dance to the Music" (Number Eight pop and Number Nine R&B in 1968), the double-sided hit singles "Everyday People"/"Sing a Simple Song" (Number One pop and R&B in 1969) and "Thank You (Falletinme Be Mice Elf Again)"/"Everybody is a Star" (Number One pop and R&B in 1970), and their last big crossover hit, "Family Affair" (Number One pop and R&B, 1971) exerted a big influence on funk music. The sound of the Family Stone was anchored by the electric bass of Larry Graham—positioned prominently in the studio mix—and by an approach to arranging that made the whole band, including the horn section, into a collective rhythm section.

By 1973 funk music had burst onto the pop music scene, pushed to the top of the charts by a large and heterogeneous audience, united by their thirst for rhythmically propulsive dance music. Crossover gold records such as Kool and the Gang's "Jungle Boogie" (Number Four pop and Number Two R&B in 1973) and "Hollywood Swinging" (Number Six pop and Number One R&B in 1974), The Ohio Players' "Fire" (Number One pop and R&B, 1974) and "Love Rollercoaster" (Number One pop and R&B in 1975), and the multimillion-selling "Play That Funky Music" (Number One pop and R&B in 1976) by the white band Wild Cherry were played constantly on AM radio and in nightclubs and discotheques. These bands kept the spirit and style of James Brown and Sly Stone alive, albeit in a commercialized and decidedly nonpolitical manner. The image of black "funkmasters," dancing in Afro hairdos, sunglasses, and brightly colored clothing on television shows like *American Bandstand* and *Soul Train*, occasionally came uncomfortably close to racial stereotyping. Certainly, the record industry's packaging of black "authenticity"—as symbolized by strongly rhythmic, body-oriented music—had a great deal to do with the sudden crossover success enjoyed by bands such as Kool and the Gang and the Ohio Players (who had struggled for success as an R&B band since 1959). However, if the success of funk music in the mainstream pop market capitalized to some degree upon long-standing white American fantasies about black culture, white funk bands such as Wild Cherry and the Average White Band were also able to place records in the R&B Top 10.

Although they did not share the huge commercial success of the groups just mentioned, the apotheosis of 1970s funk music was a loose aggregate of around forty musicians (variously called Parliament or Funkadelic), led by George Clinton (a.k.a. Dr. Funkenstein). Clinton (b. 1940), an ex-R&B vocal group leader and songwriter, hung out with Detroit hippies, listened to the Stooges, and altered his style (as well as his consciousness) during the late 1960s. Enlisting some former members of James Brown's band (bassist William "Bootsy" Collins and saxophone players Maceo Parker and Fred Wesley), he developed a mixture of compelling polyrhythms, psychedelic guitar solos, jazz-influenced horn arrangements, and R&B vocal harmonies. Recording for the independent record company Casablanca (also a major player in the field of disco music), Parliament/Funkadelic placed five LPs in the *Billboard* Top 40 between 1976 and 1978, two of which went platinum.

The band's reputation was in substantial measure based on their spectacular concert shows, which featured wild costumes and elaborate sets (including a huge flying saucer called "the Mothership"), and their innovative concept albums, which expressed an alternative black sensibility, embodied in a patois of street talk, psychedelic imagery, and science fiction–derived images of intergalactic travel. George Clinton took racial and musical stereotypes and played with them, reconfiguring black popular music as a positive moral force. On his albums, Clinton wove mythological narratives of a primordial conflict between the "Cro-Nasal Sapiens" (who "slicked their hair and lost all sense of the groove") and the "Thumpasorus People," who buried the secret of funk in the Egyptian pyramids and left Earth for the Chocolate Milky Way, under the wise leadership of "Dr. Funkenstein." Parliament concerts featured a cast of characters such as "Star Child" (a.k.a. "Sir Lollipop Man"), the cosmic defender of funk, and "Sir Nose D'VoidOfFunk," a spoof of commercialized, soulless, rhythmically challenged pop music and its fans. Clinton's blend of social criticism, wacky humor, and psychedelic imagination is perhaps best captured in his revolutionary manifesto for the funk movement: "Free Your Mind, and Your Ass Will Follow."

"Give Up the Funk (Tear the Roof off the Sucker)," from the million-selling LP *Mothership Connection*, was Parliament's biggest crossover single (Number Five R&B, Number Fifteen pop in 1976). It exemplifies the band's approach to ensemble style, known to fans as "P-Funk": heavy, syncopated electric bass lines; interlocking rhythms underlain by a strong pulse on each beat of each measure; long, multisectioned arrangements featuring call-and-response patterns between the horn sections and keyboard synthesizer; R&B-styled vocal harmonies; and verbal mottoes designed to be chanted by fans ("We want the funk, give up the funk; We need the funk, we gotta have the funk"). Arranged by Clinton, bass player Bootsy Collins, and keyboardist Bernie Worrell, the recording is constructed out of these basic elements, alternated and layered on top of one another to create a series of shifting sound textures, anchored in the strong pulse of bass and drums.

Clinton and other former Parliament/Funkadelic musicians continued to tour and record throughout the 1980s, but public and critical disdain for 1970s popular culture—especially disco and the dance-oriented music that preceded and inspired it—had a negative impact on the band's fortunes. During the early 1990s the rise of funk-inspired rap (e.g., Dr. Dre) and rock music (e.g., Red Hot Chili Peppers) established the status of George Clinton and his colleagues as one of the most important—and most frequently **sampled**—forces in the recent history of black music. Discovered by a new generation of listeners, Clinton is still performing as of this writing, having appeared to great acclaim at the 1999 reincarnation of the Woodstock festival.

"NIGHT FEVER": THE RISE OF DISCO

If funk music heralded the return of black social dance music to the mainstream of American popular music, the era of *disco*—roughly 1975 to 1980—represents the commercial apotheosis (and sudden, though temporary decline) of this trend. Like punk rock, disco music represented a reaction against two of the central ideas of album-oriented rock: the LP as Art and the rock group as Artists. Unlike punk, disco deemphasized the importance of the band—which, in disco music, was usually a concatenation of professional session musicians—and focused attention on the producers who oversaw the making of recordings, the **DJ**s who played them in nightclubs, and a handful of glamorous stars, who sang with the backing of anonymous studio musicians and often had quite short-lived careers. Disco also rejected the idea of the rock album as an architecturally designed collection of individual pieces. Working night after night for audiences who demanded music that would keep them dancing for hours at a stretch, DJs rediscovered the single, expanded it to fill the time frame offered by the twelve-inch long-playing vinyl disc, and developed techniques for blending one record into the next without interruption. (These turntable techniques paved the way for the use of recordings in popular genres of the 1980s and 1990s, such as hip-hop, house, acid jazz, and techno.)

The term "disco" was derived from "discotheque," a term first used in Europe during the 1960s to refer to nightclubs devoted to the playing of recorded music for dancing. By the mid-1970s clubs featuring an uninterrupted stream of dance music were increasingly common in the United States, particularly in urban black and Latino communities, where going out to dance on a weekend night was a well-established tradition, and in the increasingly visible gay communities of cities such as New York and San Francisco. The rise of disco and its invasion of the Top 40 pop music mainstream were driven by several factors: the inspiration of black popular music, particularly Motown, soul, and funk; the rise in popularity of social dancing among middle-class Americans; new technologies, including synthesizers, drum machines, and synchronized turntables; the role of the Hollywood film industry in promoting musical trends; and the economic recession of the late 1970s, which encouraged many nightclub owners to hire disc jockeys rather than live musicians.

The archetypal early disco hit is Donna Summer's "Love to Love You Baby" (Number Two pop, Number Three R&B, 1975), recorded in Germany and released in the United States by Casablanca Records, the independent label that also released LPs by Parliament/Funkadelic. "Love to Love You Baby" reflects the genre's strong reliance on musical technologies of the mid-1970s and the central importance of the record producer in shaping the sound texture of disco recordings. Producer Giorgio Moroder's careful mix takes full advantage of multitrack recording technology (which allows Summer's voice to appear in several places at the same time), clear stereo separation of instruments, keyboard synthesizers with the ability to play more than one note at a time and to imitate other musical instruments, and electronic **reverb,** which plays a crucial role in establishing the spatial qualities of a recording. The original recording is much longer than the usual pop single—almost seventeen minutes long—and was produced specifically for use in discotheques, where customers demanded unbroken sequences of dance music. (The version that made the *Billboard* singles charts was edited down to under five minutes in length, to fit the framework of Top 40 radio.) The performance is clearly seductive in intent, an impression created not only by the lyrics themselves but also by Summer's languorous and sexy whispers, moans, and growls. (This impression is reinforced by the nicknames bestowed on Donna Summer at the time by the popular music press, including "First Lady of Lust" and "Disco's Aphrodite.")

The recording opens with an intake of breath and Summer's voice singing the hook of the song ("Ahhhh, love to love you baby") in an intimate, almost whispering voice, accompanied by the gentle sound of a closed hi-hat cymbal (a pair of cymbals opened and closed by the drummer's left foot). The next sounds to appear are the electric guitar, played with a wah-wah pedal (a foot-operated device that allows the guitarist to change the timbre of his instrument), and the bass drum, playing a solid four-to-the-bar beat. The core elements of early disco music are thus presented within the first few measures of the recording: a sexy, studio-enhanced female voice, and a rhythm track that is borrowed in large part from funk music and anchored by a hypnotic steady pulse. The overall arrangement is made up of two basic phrases, which are alternated, always returning to the hook. Working with his then state-of-the-art multitrack recording board, Giorgio Moroder gradually builds up layers of sound texture and then strips them away to reveal the basic pulse of the music.

By the late 1970s disco had taken over the popular mainstream, owing in large part to the success of the film *Saturday Night Fever* (1977), the story of a working-class Italian kid from New York who rises to become a championship dancer. *Saturday Night Fever*—shot on location at a Brooklyn discotheque—strengthened interest in disco stars like Donna Summer and Gloria Gaynor. The film also launched the second career of the Bee Gees, an Australian group known theretofore mainly for sentimental pop songs like "Lonely Days" (a Number Three pop hit from 1970) and "How Can You Mend a Broken Heart" (Number One in 1971). The Bee Gees reinvented themselves by combining their polished Beatle-derived vocal harmonies with funk-influenced rhythms, played by Miami studio musicians, and created a mix that appealed both to committed disco fans and a broader pop audience; their songs from the *Saturday Night Fever* soundtrack, such as "Stayin' Alive" and "Night Fever," were among the most popular singles of the late 1970s. At a more general level, *Saturday Night Fever* also helped to link disco music and dancing to a traditional American cultural theme, that of upward mobility. Spreading from the urban communities where it first took flower, disco dancing offered millions of working-class and middle-class Americans, from the most varied of cultural and economic backgrounds, access to glamour that hadn't been experienced widely since the days of the grand ballrooms.

The strict dress codes employed by the most famous discotheques implied a rejection of the torn T-shirt and jeans regalia of rock music, and the reinstatement of notions of hierarchy and classiness—if you (and your clothes) could pass muster at the velvet rope, you were allowed access to the inner sanctum. Walking through the front door of a disco in full swing was like entering a sensory maelstrom, with thundering music driven by an incessant bass pulse; flashing lights and mirrors on the ceiling, walls, and floor; and—most important—a mass of sweaty and beautifully adorned bodies packed onto the always limited space of a dance floor. For its adepts, the discotheque was a shrine to hedonism, an escape from the drudgery of everyday life, and a fountain of youth. (The death throes of this scene are evocatively rendered in the 1998 film *The Last Days of Disco*.)

A few examples must suffice here to give a sense of how thoroughly disco had penetrated popular musical taste by the late 1970s. One important stream of influence involved a continuation of the old category of novelty records, done up in disco style. A band called Rick Dees and his Gang of Idiots came out of nowhere to score a Number One hit with the goofy "Disco Duck" (1976), followed by the less successful zoo-disco song "Dis-Gorilla" (1977). The Village People—a group built from scratch by the French record producer Jacques Morali and promoted by Casablanca Records—specialized in over-the-top burlesques of gay life and scored Top 40 hits with songs like "Macho Man" (Number Twenty-five, 1978), "YMCA" (Number Two, 1978) and "In the Navy" (Number Three, 1979). For those who caught the inside references to gay culture, the Village People's recordings were charming, if simple-minded parodies; for many in disco's new mass audience, they were simply novelty records with a disco beat. Morali's double-entendre strategy paid off—for a short while in the late 1970s, the Village People were the bestselling pop group in North America.

For a few years everyone seemed to be jumping on the disco bandwagon. Barbra Streisand teamed up with disco artists, including the Bee Gees' Barry Gibb, who produced her multiplatinum 1980 album *Guilty*, and Donna Summer for the single "No More Tears" (Number One in 1979). Disco met the surf sound when Bruce Johnston of the Beach Boys produced a disco arrangement of "Pipeline," which had been a Number Four instrumental hit for the Chantays back in 1963. Even hard rock musicians like the Rolling Stones released disco singles (such as "Miss You," Number One in 1978). On the other side of the Atlantic a genre called Eurodisco developed, featuring prominent use of electronic synthesizers and long compositions with repetitive rhythm tracks, designed to fill the entire side of an LP. (This sound, as developed by bands like Germany's Kraftwerk, was to become one important root of techno.) And black musicians, who had provided the basic material of which disco was constructed, were presented with new audiences, opportunities, and challenges. Motown diva Diana Ross scored several disco-influenced hits (e.g., "Love Hangover," Number One in 1976, and "Upside Down," Number One in 1980). And James Brown, who was knocked off the pop charts by disco music, responded in the late 1970s by promoting himself as the "Original Disco Man." (His R&B hit "It's Too Funky in Here," released in 1979, is a clear gesture in this direction.)

Few styles of popular music have inspired such passionate loyalty, or such utter revulsion, as disco music, and it is worth taking a few moments to consider the negative side of this equation. If you were a loyal fan of Led Zeppelin, Pink Floyd, and other album-oriented rock groups of the 1970s, disco was likely to represent a self-indulgent, pretentious, and vaguely suspect musical orientation. The rejection of disco by rock fans reached its peak during a 1979 baseball game in Chicago, where several hundred disco records were blown up and a riot ensued. (This mass passion is reminiscent of the Beatle record burnings organized during the 1960s by fundamentalist Christian preachers.) After all, disco is only music—what on earth could inspire such a violent reaction?

Some critics connect the antidisco reaction of the 1970s with the genre's links to gay culture. The disco movement initially emerged in Manhattan nightclubs such as the Loft and the Tenth Floor, which served as social gathering spots for homosexual men. According to this interpretation, gays found it difficult to get live acts to perform for them. The disc jockeys who worked these clubs responded to the demands of customers by rummaging through the bins of record stores for good dance records, often coming up with singles that had been successful some years earlier in the black and Puerto Rican communities of New York.

That disco was to some degree associated in the public imagination with homosexuality has suggested to some observers that the phrase "Disco Sucks!"—the rallying cry of the antidisco movement—evinces a strain of homophobia among the core audience for album-oriented rock, young, middle- and working-class, and presumably heterosexual white men. Certainly disco's associations with a contemporary version of ballroom dancing did not conform to contemporary models of masculine behavior. The tradition of dancing to prefigured steps, and to music specifically designed to support dancing, which had found its last expression in the early 1960s with dance crazes like the twist, had fallen out of favor during the rock era. It may therefore have seemed to many rock fans that there was something suspect—even effeminate—about men who engaged in ballroom dancing.

Still, it can safely be assumed that the audience for album-oriented rock wasn't entirely straight, and that heterosexuals did patronize discos with large homosexual clienteles, at least in the big cities. The initial rejection of disco by many rock fans may have had as much to do with racism as with homophobia, since the genre's roots lay predominantly in black dance music. In addition, the musical values predominant among rock fans—including an appreciation of instrumental virtuosity, as represented in the guitar playing of Jimi Hendrix, Eric Clapton, or Jimmy Page—would not have inclined them toward a positive regard of disco, which relied heavily on studio overdubbing and consisted mainly of fairly predictable patterns designed for dancing. And the fact that millions of sports fans of all descriptions today enthusiastically mimic the movements of a popular—and, for some listeners, explicitly gay—disco record like the Village People's multimillion-selling single "YMCA" complicates the picture even further. Although disco cannot simply be identified as "gay music," there is no doubt that the genre's mixed reception during the late 1970s provides additional evidence of the transformative effect of marginalized musical styles and communities on the commercial mainstream of American popular music.

LISTENING TO "BAD GIRLS" AND "GOOD TIMES"

Dance-oriented music dominated the American pop charts in the late 1970s. The titles of the Number One pop records from the end of 1977 through the summer of 1979 would read, with few exceptions, like a track listing for a "Disco's Greatest Hits" album. Disco's spectacular hold on the Number One spot ended with two splendid examples of the genre: "Bad Girls," performed by Donna Summer, and "Good Times," performed by Chic. A brief consideration of the similarities shared by these records, and of the differences between them, will offer us a useful look at the essential characteristics, as well as the diversity, of disco music.

What Makes Both These Records "Disco"?

1. ***The BEAT!*** This is dance music, of course, and the pounding beat defines the music as disco. Indeed, the beat is established immediately on both "Bad Girls" and "Good Times," and it never lets up, persisting right through the fade-outs that end these recordings. The beat constitutes the essential hook on all disco records. It is characteristic of disco that every pulse is rhythmically articulated by the bass and/or the drums. There is no such thing as stoptime in this music, and the signature *thump!— thump!—thump!—thump!* of disco creates and maintains an irresistible dance groove; disco dancers literally never have to skip a beat. Consequently, although there are many changes in the musical texture during "Bad Girls," the rhythm never lets up, regardless of whatever other instruments or vocal parts enter or leave the mix. On the other hand, the fact that there are only slight alterations in texture throughout "Good Times" helps assure that attention remains focused on the rhythm itself, and the minimal feel of this particular recording offers an excellent example of how hypnotic a basic rhythm-propelled track can be.

2. ***A steady, medium-fast tempo.*** Like most social dance music, disco recordings maintain an unvarying tempo throughout. Above and beyond this obvious characteristic, however, the tempos of most disco records tend also to be fairly similar to one another, to accord with the active dance styles preferred by the patrons of discotheques. The tempo of "Bad Girls" is slightly faster than that of "Good Times," but obviously the same kinds of steps and body movements would fit both records equally well. Recordings intended for use in discotheques often bore indications of their tempos in the form of beats per minute (*b.p.m.*), to assist the club disc jockeys in arranging relatively seamless sequences of dance numbers, and if the DJ had an adjustable-speed turntable, it was possible to adjust the tempos of individual records slightly so that the dance beat wouldn't vary at all from one to the next—then, even when the song changed, the dancers still would never have to skip a beat.

3. ***Straightforward, repetitive song forms.*** With the emphasis on dancing, it would obviously be pointless for disco records to employ complex,

Chic and Donna Summer: kings and queens of disco. Frank Driggs Collection

intricate song forms, such as those developed by some artists in the late 1960s and the 1970s. Such niceties suggest an entirely different kind of listening environment and, if they weren't just missed entirely by disco fans, might prove distracting and even annoying on the dance floor. Both "Bad Girls" and "Good Times" are based clearly on a verse-chorus kind of form. Furthermore, in both, the chorus is heard first, and this serves a number of purposes. Each song's chorus begins with the title words ("Bad girls," "Good times"), identifying the song immediately and functioning as a concise, and extremely effective, verbal and musical hook. Counting the initial statement, the chorus in each of these recordings is heard a total of three times, which results in a readily accessible, repetitive kind of structure that assures memorability.

4. ***Straightforward subject matter and lyrics.*** No Dylanesque imagery or poetic obscurities, please—again, for obvious reasons. There is no doubt what either "Bad Girls" or "Good Times" is about. This is not to say that the lyrics to disco songs are without interest, however; see the further discussion, especially in reference to "Bad Girls," below.

5. ***Limited harmonic vocabulary.*** In essence, the harmony of "Good Times" simply oscillates between two chords, with the change occurring on the downbeat of every other measure. "Bad Girls" has only a slightly wider harmonic vocabulary, but it too gives the sense of being built around two basic, alternating chords much of the time; these two chords underlie the entire chorus and do not shift when the choruses give way to the verses. Both records thus achieve a highly focused, almost hypnotic, effect in the harmonic realm that is analogous to—and abets—their virtually obsessive rhythmic character. (The conceptual debt that recordings of this type owe to the late 1960s music of James Brown should be obvious; see Chapter 10.)

Note: The five characteristics listed above—emphasis on the beat; steady, relatively fast, tempo; avoidance of formal complexity; direct lyrics; and a limited chord vocabulary—clearly do not apply only to typical disco music. They also would serve well in a general way, for example, in describing much typical early rock 'n' roll. The point to be made here is that, in the context of album-oriented rock, the output of singer-songwriters, and several other manifestations of 1970s pop music, the "return to basics" (that is, the return to danceable music)—with a new twist—that disco represented came across, to many, as both novel and refreshing. It is also important to emphasize here that disco music proved, in certain ways, to be forward-looking. The most immediate example of this is the fact that the chords and rhythmic patterns of "Good Times" were borrowed wholesale to constitute the instrumental backing for the single that broke rap music into the commercial mainstream for the first time: "Rapper's Delight," by the Sugarhill Gang (see Chapter 14).

Some Distinguishing Characteristics of "Bad Girls" and "Good Times"

We have already noted the greater textural variety of "Bad Girls." Donna Summer's lead vocal, responding voices, brass instruments, and even a police whistle appear, disappear, and reappear—sometimes expectedly, sometimes not—over the course of the recording, creating a feeling that is evocative of the action, excitement, and occasional unpredictability of a busy street scene. It also seems appropriate that "Bad Girls" is more elaborate from a formal point of view than "Good Times." The verse sections of "Bad Girls" fall into two distinct parts, the second part marked by a pause in the vocals and the interjection of short, accented chords on the brass instruments. (This part has a formal effect somewhat similar to that of a bridge section in other song structures.) In addition, after the third and final verse, there is a coda in place of the expected concluding chorus. In this coda, the lead vocalist abandons at last her position as observer of the scene and actually joins the "bad girls" with a shout of "Hey, mister, have you got a dime?"—acting, in effect, upon her earlier realization (in the third verse) that she and the "bad girls" are "both the same," even though the others are called "a different name."

The vocal styles used in the two recordings are decidedly different. Donna Summer's emphatic, expansive style clearly derives from roots in R&B and gospel; her background, like that of so many African American pop stars, included church singing. Summer's personal intensity solicits our involvement in, and concern with, the story of the "bad girls." In short, "Bad Girls" is a brilliantly performed pop record that is enhanced by an elaborate and clever production. Yet the question suggests itself: can any recording so irresistibly danceable, with such an upbeat rhythmic feeling, really convey a downbeat social "message"— especially about an issue as thorny and complex as prostitution? Won't people be too busy dancing to notice? And doesn't it sound as if these "bad girls" are really just out for, and having, "good times"?

In a way, the inverse situation applies to "Good Times." This apparently carefree anthem is intoned by a small group of voices singing in unison in a clipped, unornamented, basically uninflected kind of style that comes across as intentionally depersonalized. Is there ultimately something just a little too mechanistic about the voices, and the obsessive chords and rhythms, in these "good times"? Some rock critics have suggested that the song has an ironic edge to it, and they could certainly support this idea by pointing to those occasional darker phrases that pop up in the lyrics like momentary flickering shadows: "A rumor has it that it's getting late," and "You silly fool, you can't change your fate." On the other hand, it might be claimed that those looking for hidden depths in a song like "Good Times" are those who have simply lost the ability to enjoy a superb party record.

On the one hand, the popular music of the 1970s provides rich evidence of the continuing vitality of venerable musical forms and techniques—including the African-derived polyrhythms of funk music and reggae, the twelve-bar blues form in rock music, and the Euro-American ballad form in country music—and of the capacity of marginalized communities and musical traditions to revitalize the commercial mainstream of popular music. On the other hand, the 1970s also saw the consolidation—on an unprecedented worldwide scale—of corporate control over the production of musical products. By the close of the decade, a handful of major transnational companies were responsible for the majority of record sales—in America and worldwide—and were busy swallowing up smaller companies. At the same time that the major record companies sought to make the market more predictable, however, the audience for popular music fragmented into dozens of specialized taste communities, creating a complex musical landscape bound to elude the predictive efforts of even the most experienced record producer or corporate CEO. The margins and the mainstream; corporate control and consumer unpredictability; ancient traditions and new technologies—these are the themes that will now carry us into the decades of the 1980s and 1990s, as we conclude our journey through the history of American popular music.

CHAPTER THIRTEEN

THE 1980s

Digital Technology, MTV, and the Popular Mainstream

From the viewpoint of the American music industry, the 1980s began on a sour note. Following a period of rapid expansion in the mid-1970s, 1979 saw an 11 percent drop in annual record sales nationwide, the first major recession in the industry in thirty years. Profits from the sale of recorded music hit rock bottom in 1982 ($4.6 billion), down half a billion dollars from the peak year of 1978 ($5.1 billion). The major record companies—now subdivisions of huge transnational conglomerates—trimmed their staffs, cut back expenses, signed fewer new acts, raised the prices of LPs and cassette tapes, and searched for new promotional and audience-targeting techniques. The pattern of relying on a small number of multiplatinum artists to create profits became more pronounced in the 1980s. By the mid-1980s, when the industry began to climb out of its hole, it was clear that the recovery was due more to the megasuccess of a few recordings by superstar musicians—Michael Jackson, Madonna, Prince, Bruce Springsteen, Whitney Houston, Phil Collins, Janet Jackson, and others—than to any across-the-board improvement in record sales.

A number of reasons have been adduced for the crash of the early 1980s—the onset of a national recession brought on by the laissez-faire economic policies of the Reagan administration; competition from new forms of entertainment, including home video, cable television, and video games; the decline of disco, which had driven the rapid expansion of the record business in the late 1970s; and an increase in illegal copying ("pirating") of commercial recordings by consumers with cassette tape decks. In 1984 sales of prerecorded cassettes, boosted by the popularity of the Sony Walkman personal tape player and larger portable tape players called "boomboxes," surpassed those of vinyl discs for the first time in history. (The introduction of digital audio tape, or DAT, in the early 1990s, and of writable compact discs, or CD-Rs, at the turn of the century, provided consumers with the ability to make near-perfect copies of commercial recordings, a development that prompted the music industry to respond with new anticopying technologies.)

The 1980s also saw the rise of technologies that would revolutionize the production of popular music. The development of *digital sound recording* led to the introduction of the five-inch *compact disc* (CD), and the rapid decline of the vinyl disc. The sounds encoded on a compact disc are read by a laser beam and not by a diamond needle, meaning that CDs are not subject to the same wear and tear as vinyl discs. The first compact discs went on sale in 1983, and by 1988 sales of CDs surpassed those of vinyl discs for the first time. Although CDs cost about the same as vinyl LPs to manufacture, the demand for the new medium allowed record companies to generate higher profits by pricing them at thirteen dollars or more, rather than the eight or nine dollars charged for LPs. Digital technology also spawned new and more affordable devices for producing and manipulating sound—such as *drum machines* and *sequencers*, and *samplers* for digital **sampling**—and the *musical instrument digital interface* (MIDI) specification, which standardized these technologies, allowing devices produced by different manufacturers to "communicate" with one another. Digital technology—portable and relatively cheap—and the rapid expansion of the *personal computer* (PC) market in the early 1990s allowed musicians to set up their own home studios and stimulated the growth of genres like *hip-hop* and *techno*, both of which rely heavily on digitally constructed sound *samples, loops*, and *grooves*. For the first time, satellite technology allowed the worldwide simultaneous broadcast of live concerts, and the development of fiber optics allowed musicians in recording studios thousands of miles apart to work together in real time.

Deregulation of the entertainment industry led to an explosion in the growth of cable television, one by-product of which was the launching of *Music Television* (MTV) in 1981. MTV changed the way the industry operated, rapidly becoming the preferred method for launching a new act or promoting the latest release of a major superstar. (The advent of videos designed to promote rock recordings is often traced to the band Queen's mock-operatic hard rock extravaganza "Bohemian Rhapsody," released in 1975. However, such early music videos were essentially advertisements for the sound recordings and not viewed as products that might be sold on their own merits.) Although the first song broadcast on MTV bore the title "Video Killed the Radio Star," it is more accurate to say that MTV—and its spin-off VH-1, aimed at an older, twenty-five- to thirty-five-year old audience—worked synergistically with radio and other media to boost record sales and create a new generation of rock superstars. It also strongly influenced the direction of popular music in the early 1980s, sparking what has been called a second British Invasion by promoting English artists such as Eurythmics, Flock of Seagulls, Adam Ant, Billy Idol, and Thomas Dolby. (In July 1983 eighteen of the singles in *Billboard*'s Top 40 chart were by English artists, topping the previous record of fourteen, set in 1965 during the first British Invasion.) By the mid-1980s the impact of MTV had been felt throughout the music industry.

MTV's relentless focus on white rock artists reminded many critics of the exclusionary practices of album-oriented rock radio in the 1970s. Out of more than 750 videos shown on MTV during the channel's first eighteen months, only about twenty featured black musicians (a figure that includes racially mixed bands). At a time when black artists such as Michael Jackson and Rick James were making multiplatinum LPs, they could not break into MTV, which put Phil Collins's cover version of the

Supremes' "You Can't Hurry Love" into heavy rotation, but played no videos by Motown artists themselves. Executives at MTV responded to widespread criticism of their policy with the argument that their format focused on rock, a style played by few black artists. Of course, this was a tautological argument—the restrictive format of MTV was the cause, and not merely a by-product, of the problem.

The mammoth success of Michael Jackson's *Thriller*, released by Columbia Records in 1982, forced a change in MTV's essentially all-white rock music format. The three videos made to promote the *Thriller* LP through three of its hit singles—"Billie Jean," "Beat It," and "Thriller"—set new standards for production quality, creativity, and cost and established the medium as the primary means of promoting popular music. "Thriller"—a horror movie *cum* musical directed by John Landis, who had previously made the feature film *An American Werewolf in London*—metamorphosed into a sixty-minute home video entitled *The Making of Michael Jackson's Thriller*, with the original fifteen-minute video and lots of filler material, including interviews with the star. *The Making of Michael Jackson's Thriller* sold 350,000 copies in the first six months, yet MTV still refused to air Jackson's videos. Finally, after Columbia Records threatened to ban its white rock groups from performing on MTV, the channel relented, putting Jackson's videos into heavy rotation. (*Thriller* will be discussed in more detail later; for now we will simply note that Jackson did not share the segregationist sentiments of MTV executives, going out of his way to include white rock stars such as Paul McCartney and Eddie Van Halen on his LP.)

The process of corporate consolidation (sometimes called "horizontal integration"), which has emerged at intervals throughout the history of American popular music, once again reared its head during the late 1980s and early 1990s. To a greater extent than ever before, record labels could no longer be considered standalone institutions but rather subdepartments of huge transnational corporations. By 1990 six corporations collectively controlled over two-thirds of global sales of recorded music: the Dutch *Polygram* conglomerate (owner of Mercury, Polydor, Island, A&M and other labels); the Japanese corporations *Sony* (Columbia Records) and *Matsushita* (MCA and Geffen Records); the British firm *Thorn* (EMI, Virgin, Capitol); the German *Bertelsmann* conglomerate (BMG and RCA Records); and *Time-Warner*, the only American-based corporation in this list (Warner, Elektra, and Atlantic Records). Similarly, the American market for recorded music now had to be seen as part of a wider global market that transcended national borders. In 1990 the largest market for recorded music in the world remained the United States, which, at $7.5 billion, accounted for approximately 31 percent of world trade, followed at some distance by Japan (12 percent), the United Kingdom and Germany (9 percent each), and France (7 percent). Even in the United States, however, the record company executives concerned themselves to an unprecedented degree with global sales and promotion.

This move toward global corporate consolidation of the music business was accompanied by a further fragmentation of the marketplace for popular music and the creation of dozens of new musical genres, marketing categories, and radio formats. Some of these were more novel than others, but all bore some relationship to musical forms of the past. Country music continued its six-decade journey from the margins to the center of popular taste, becoming the bestselling genre of music in the United States with rock- and pop-influenced country superstars such as Garth

Brooks, Clint Black, and Reba McEntire. Rock music, which had undergone a process of fragmentation in the early 1970s, shattered into a hundred specialized genres and subgenres, some with huge audiences (adult contemporary and heavy metal), and others supported by smaller but devoted groups of fans (hardcore, thrash, and techno, the respective children of punk rock, heavy metal, and Eurodisco). Rap music, which had emerged during the mid-1970s from the hip-hop culture of black, Latino, and Caribbean American youth in New York City, had by the late 1980s grown into a multimillion-dollar business. During the 1990s the relationship between the center and periphery of the music business, and between mainstream and marginalized types of music, became even more complicated, with self-consciously anticommercial genres like gangsta rap, speed metal, and grunge reaching the top of the *Billboard* LP and singles charts and generating huge profits for the music industry, and with musicians from Latin America (Ricky Martin) and French Canada (Celine Dion) ranking among the most profitable superstars in the United States at the end of the second millennium.

The core themes that we have traced throughout this book—the intimate relationship between social identity and musical style; the links between music, economics, and technology; and the interaction of various streams of musical tradition—were just as evident at the close of the twentieth century as they were at its inception. On the other hand, much has changed over the past hundred years; old, deep patterns of American musical culture have been profoundly shaped by the advent of new technologies and institutions, new social movements, and profound shifts in the self-definition and values of musicians and their audiences. In this chapter we will begin our consideration of the popular music of the 1980s and 1990s with a look at the changing nature of the musical mainstream.

DIGITAL TECHNOLOGY AND POPULAR MUSIC

During the 1980s new technologies—including digital tape recorders, compact discs, synthesizers, samplers, and sequencers—became central to the production, promotion, and consumption of popular music. These devices were the fruit of a long history of interactions between the electronics and music industries and between individual inventors and musicians.

Analog recording—the norm since the introduction of recording in the nineteenth century—transforms the energy of sound waves into physical imprints (as in pre-1925 acoustic recordings) or into electronic waveforms that closely follow (and can be used to reproduce) the shape of the sound waves themselves. *Digital recording*, on the other hand, samples the sound waves and breaks them down into a stream of numbers (0s and 1s). A device called an *analog-to-digital converter* does the conversion. To play back the music, the stream of numbers is converted back to an analog wave by a *digital-to-analog converter* (DAC). The analog wave produced by the DAC is amplified and fed to speakers to produce the sound. There have been many arguments among musicians and audiophiles over the relative quality of the two technologies: initially, many musicians found digital recording too "cold" (perhaps a metaphor for the process itself, which disassembles a sound into millions of constituent bits). Today, however, almost all popular recordings are digitally recorded.

Synthesizers—devices that allow musicians to create or "synthesize" musical sounds—began to appear on rock records during the early 1970s, but their history begins much earlier. One important predecessor of the synthesizer was the *theremin*, a sound generator named after the Russian inventor who developed it in 1919. This instrument used electronic oscillators to produce sound, and its pitch was controlled by the player's waving his or her hands in front of two antennae. The theremin was never used much in popular music, although its familiar sound can be heard in the soundtracks of 1950s science fiction films such as *The Day the Earth Stood Still*, and on the Beach Boys' 1966 hit "Good Vibrations."

Another important stage in the interaction between scientific invention and musical technology was the *Hammond organ*, introduced in 1935 by the inventor Laurens Hammond. The sound of the Hammond B-3 organ was common on jazz, R&B, and rock records (e.g., Santana's "Oye Como Va"), and its rich, fat sound is frequently sampled in contemporary popular music. The player could alter the timbre of the organ through control devices called "tone bars," and a variety of rhythm patterns and percussive effects were added later. Although the Hammond organ was not a true synthesizer, it is certainly a close ancestor.

In the early 1970s the first synthesizers aimed at a mass consumer market were introduced. These devices, which used electronic oscillators to produce musical tones, were clumsy and limited by today's standards, yet their characteristic sounds are viewed with some nostalgia and are often sampled in contemporary recordings. The first synthesizers to be sold in music stores alongside guitars and pianos were the *Minimoog*, which had the limitation of being able to play only one pitch at a time, and the *Arp* synthesizer, which could play simple chords. The *Synclavier*, a high-end (and expensive) digital synthesizer, was introduced to the market in 1976. The more affordable *Prophet-5*, introduced in 1978, was an analog synthesizer that incorporated aspects of digital technology, including the ability to store a limited number of sampled sounds.

The 1980s saw the introduction of the first completely digital synthesizers—including the widely popular Yamaha *DX-7*—capable of playing dozens of "voices" at the same time. The *MIDI* (Musical Instrument Digital Interface) specification, introduced in 1983, allowed synthesizers built by different manufacturers to be connected with and communicate with one another, introducing compatibility into a highly competitive marketplace. *Digital samplers*—for example, the *Mirage* keyboard sampler, introduced by Ensoniq in 1984—were capable of storing both prerecorded and synthesized sounds. (The latter were often called "patches," a nostalgic reference to the wires or "patch cords" that were used to connect the various components of early synthesizers.) *Digital sequencers*, introduced to the marketplace at around the same time, are devices that record musical data rather than musical sound and allow the creation of repeated sound sequences (loops), the manipulation of rhythmic grooves, and the transmission of recorded data from one program or device to another. *Drum machines* such as the *Roland TR 808* and the *Linn LM-1*—almost ubiquitous on 1980s dance music and rap recordings—rely on "drum pads" that can be struck and activated by the performer, and which act as a trigger for the production of sampled sounds (including not only conventional percussion instruments but also glass smashing, cars screeching, and guns firing).

Digital technology has given musicians the ability to create complex 128-voice textures, to create sophisticated synthesized sounds that exist nowhere in nature, and to sample and manipulate any sound source, creating sound loops that can be

controlled with great precision. With compact, highly portable, and increasingly affordable music equipment and software, a recording studio can be set up literally
anywhere—in a basement, or on a roof. As the individual musician gains more and
more control over the production of a complete musical recording, distinctions
between the composer, the performer, and the producer sometimes melt down
entirely.

Certain contemporary genres make particularly frequent and effective use of
digital technologies, particularly rap/hip-hop and various genres of electronic dance
music (electronica or techno). The technology of digital sampling allows musicians
to assemble preexisting sound sources and to cite performers and music from various styles and historical eras. During the 1980s musicians began to reach back into
their record collections for sounds from the 1960s and 1970s. It has been suggested
that this reflects a more general cultural shift toward a "cut-and-paste" approach
to history, in which pop music cannibalizes its own past. However, it is worth re-
membering that, while the technology is new, the idea of recycling old materials
(and thereby selectively reinventing the past) is probably as old as music itself.

Some interesting legal dilemmas are connected with the widespread use of digital sampling. American intellectual property law has always made it difficult to
claim ownership of a groove, style, or sound, precisely those things that are most
distinctive about popular music—like the timbre of James Brown's voice, the electric bass sound of Parliament/Funkadelic's Bootsy Collins, or the distinctive snare
drum sound used on many of Phil Collins's hit recordings (a sound constructed in
the studio out of a combination of sampled and synthesized sources). In recent years
many lawsuits have centered on these issues, in which musicians and producers
claim that their sound has been stolen by means of digital sampling. George Clinton has responded to the wholesale sampling of his albums by rap musicians by releasing a collection of sounds and previously unreleased recordings called *Sample
Some of Disc, Sample Some of D.A.T.* The collection comes with a copyright clearance
guide and a guarantee that users will only be "charged per record sold, so if your
single flops, you won't be in the red."

Of course, no technology is inherently good or evil—it's what humans do with
their tools that counts. On the one hand, many musicians mourn the replacement of
acoustic musical instruments—and the physical discipline and craft involved in mas-
tering them—by machines. Others tout the democratization of popular music made
possible by more affordable technologies. And still others point out that, no matter
how good the technology, only a small percentage of musicians are able to gain access to the powerful corporations that control the music industry. The odds that a
musician will succeed have not changed much, precisely because almost everyone
now has access to the new technology. While high-quality demonstration tapes
("demos") used to be a luxury available to only those musicians who could afford
to rent a professional recording studio, now every kid on the block has a demo.

A 1980s CD CHANGER

Although the single disc had gone into decline as a primary medium for distributing popular music—replaced first by the LP, and then by the CD and music video—
it nonetheless remained true that, as one record company executive put it, "nobody

goes around humming albums." Songs remained the basic currency of popular music throughout the 1980s and into the 1990s. As we did in our attempt to sketch the stylistic range of Number One pop singles during the 1970s (Chapter 11), we will again use the metaphor of the jukebox—or, more apropos to the 1980s, the multi-disc CD player—to discuss a series of recordings that illustrate the diversity of materials and performers that topped the charts.

We have chosen to focus on five recordings, each of which reached the Number One position on the pop charts during the 1980s. Taken as a group, they give us a sense of the diversity of styles embraced by the mass audience for popular music. As in our examples from the 1970s, the majority of these songs were written by the performers themselves. The two exceptions are Kenny Rogers's version of "Lady," a song penned by fellow pop superstar Lionel Richie, and Tina Turner's performance of "What's Love Got to Do with It," written by a pair of professional tunesmiths.

Taken individually, each of these recordings reveals a distinctive dimension of the subject matter that, more than any other, has dominated American popular music for over a century: love (and its profane cousin, sex). If during the 1980s consumers were faced with an ever broader choice of musical styles, they were also bombarded by a great diversity of mass-mediated images of intimate relationships. From the romantic chivalry of Kenny Rogers's "Lady" (1980) to the world-weariness of Tina Turner's "What's Love Got to Do with It" (1984) and the playful blues-derived bravado of Peter Gabriel's "Sledgehammer" (1986), popular music in the 1980s remained an important forum for public discourse about the nature of love and sexuality.

Performed by Kenny Rogers; written by Lionel Richie

"Lady" (1980)

The blend of country and pop music that had helped to create huge crossover hits for Nashville during the 1970s continued apace throughout the following decade, paving the way for country music's spectacular invasion of the mainstream during the 1990s. Texas-born Kenny Rogers (b. 1938)—a veteran of folk pop groups such as the New Christy Minstrels and the First Edition, and the star of made-for-TV movies such as *The Gambler* and *Coward of the County*—was one of the main beneficiaries of country pop's increasing mainstream appeal. As a renegade from pop music, Rogers was not considered authentic by conservative country music fans, but he did receive a number of awards from the Country Music Association, including Male Vocalist of the Year (1979). From 1977 to 1984 he sold an estimated $250 million worth of records, including a total of six gold and twelve platinum albums.

The song "Lady" appeared on *Kenny Rogers's Greatest Hits,* the bestselling country album of the 1980s, and was the tenth bestselling single of the entire decade. In addition, it was one of very few singles during the decade to appear on all of the major *Billboard* charts, topping the pop (*Hot 100*), adult contemporary, and country charts, and reaching Number Forty-two on the rhythm & blues chart. Only a few other recordings in the history of American popular music accomplished this feat, including Elvis Presley's "Hound Dog" and "Don't Be Cruel" (1956). In style and sensibility, however, Rogers's performance of "Lady" is light-years away from Presley's crossover hits. Whereas Presley found common ground between the blues and country music in the musical heritage of the South, Rogers was first and foremost a creature of the pop mainstream, and more particularly of a category called "adult contemporary" (that did not even exist as a marketing category in 1956), mainly romantic songs aimed at a twenty-five- to forty-five-year-old audience.

"Lady" was written and produced by another superstar of the 1980s, Lionel Richie. Richie, a former member of a vocal R&B group called the Commodores, is an African American singer and songwriter whose career overarches conventional genre boundaries. Although his own big hits of the 1980s were soul-tinged variants of adult contemporary music, Richie also placed two singles in the country Top 40 during the 1980s and was the composer of "Sail On," a song covered by a number of prominent country artists. (In the mid-1980s Richie became one of the few black musicians admitted to the Country Music Association during a period when country and black popular music had less overlap then ever before.)

"Lady" is a sentimental song that has much in common with popular songs of the nineteenth century, including Stephen Foster's "Jeanie with the Light Brown Hair" (see Chapter 2). The song follows a verse-chorus structure and uses the image of a knight in shining armor, ultimately derived from the Crusades of the Middle Ages, to profess the singer's deep and undying love. Lionel Richie, who produced the recording, followed a strategy of keeping it simple, avoiding "gimmicks," and foregrounding Rogers's sincere delivery of the lyrics.

The musical accompaniment for Rogers's husky voice is delicate, opening with a solo acoustic piano, and only gradually introducing additional layers of orchestration—an oboe, strings, a suggestion of pedal steel guitar (evocative of country music). Finally, just as the chorus arrives, the whole rhythm section joins in, energetically supporting the emotional climax of the whole song. This structure repeats with the same pattern of quiet reflection giving way to the more explicitly emotional chorus, which is repeated at the end.

In many ways "Lady" seems a throwback to the prerock era: a soft and sentimental song, couched in a determinedly bland arrangement calculated both to create an air of intimacy and to offend as few people as possible. The crossover success of "Lady" is particularly interesting in that it took place in the 1980s, a period when the country and R&B charts each overlapped frequently with the pop charts but rarely with each other. By the early 1980s it may have been that the one thing that country music and soul fans had in common was the old tradition of the romantic "torch song."

"Sweet Dreams (Are Made of This)" (1983)

Written and performed by Eurythmics

This Number One single from the early 1980s exemplifies one of the directions dance music took in the postdisco era. With its heavy reliance on electronically synthesized sounds, sequenced loops, and what has been described as a cool or austere emotional tone, Eurythmics' "Sweet Dreams" points the way toward later technology-centered music styles such as techno. Like some of the most successful techno groups of the 1990s (see Chapter 14), Eurythmics consisted of a core of only two musicians—the singer Annie Lennox (b. 1954 in Scotland) and keyboardist and technical whiz Dave Stewart (b. 1952 in England).

Eurythmics' first chart appearance in the United States came with the release of their second album, *Sweet Dreams (Are Made of This)*, in 1983. The title track was released as a single soon after the album, rocketed to Number Two on the English charts, and shortly afterward climbed to Number One on the American charts. The popularity of "Sweet Dreams (Are Made of This)" in the United States was boosted enormously by a video produced to promote the record, which was placed into heavy rotation by the fledgling MTV channel. In particular, the stylishly androgynous image of Annie Lennox—a female David Bowie, in a business suit and close-cropped orange hair—is often identified as an important ingredient in Eurythmics' success.

"Sweet Dreams" is a good example of commercial new wave music of the early 1980s, an outgrowth of the 1970s new wave/punk scene promoted by major record labels. It also exemplifies a more specific genre label that began to be used about this time: "synth-pop," the first type of popular music explicitly defined by its use of electronic sound synthesis. Although synth-pop died out by the end of the 1980s, it helped to establish the centrality of the synthesizer in popular dance music.

"Sweet Dreams" is built around a hypnotic digital loop: a repeated pattern established abruptly at the beginning of the record, as though the listener were dropped into the flow of a synthetic river of sound. A booming steady pulse, synthesized on a digital drum machine and reminiscent of disco music, underlies the melodic portion of the loop. Annie Lennox's singing alternates between an R&B- and soul-influenced **melismatic** style and the flatter, more deadpan tone that she adopts on the verses. The verses themselves consist of two four-line blocks of text, sung by Lennox in overdubbed harmonies. The singer seems to be expressing an unsettling—and titillating—combination of cynicism, sensuality, and—in the chorus—hope for the future. Some lines of the text ("some of them want . . . ") hint darkly at sadomasochistic relationships, suggesting that the singer's sophistication has perhaps been won at some emotional cost. In the call-and-response chorus—which uses multitracking technology to alternate Lennox as lead singer with Lennox as choir—the mood changes, and the listener is exhorted to "hold your head up," while the multitracked voices urge us to keep "movin' on."

Combined with Lennox's carefully cultivated sexual ambiguity—in a subsequent music video, "Who's That Girl," she plays male and female characters, and ends up kissing herself/himself—the lyrics and musical textures of "Sweet Dreams" suggest a sophisticated, even worldweary take on the nature of love, far removed from the naïve romanticism of Kenny Rogers's recording of "Lady."

Finally, although "Sweet Dreams" is sometimes regarded to as an example of the emerging technological sophistication of the early 1980s, the recording was made under less than optimum conditions. The studio rented by Stewart was a dingy, V-shaped warehouse attic, without any of the amenities of a professional studio (such as acoustical tiles or isolation booths for recording separate instrumental tracks). Their equipment was rudimentary—an eight-track tape recorder and a cheap mixer, two microphones, an early version of a digital drum machine available in England at the time, and a handful of old sound effects devices. "It sounded so sophisticated," reported Stewart in a 1983 feature in *Billboard,* "but often we had to wait for the timber factory downstairs to turn off their machinery before we could record the vocals." In fact, not all of the instrumental sounds on the recording are electronic in origin: the clinking counterpoint under the chorus of "Sweet Dreams" was played on milk bottles pitched to the right notes by filling them with different levels of water. In this sense "Sweet Dreams" both hearkens back to the "do it yourself" ethic of 1970s punk and new wave music and points forward to the experiments of 1990s techno musicians, who often introduce natural environmental sounds into their recordings.

"What's Love Got to Do with It" (1984)

Performed by Tina Turner; written by Terry Britten and Graham Lyle

By the time <u>Tina Turner</u> (née Annie Mae Bullock, b. 1939 in Tennessee) recorded "What's Love Got to Do with It," she had been in the popular music limelight for over twenty years. Her recording debut took place in 1960 as a member of the Ike and Tina Turner Revue. Tina's husband, Ike Turner, had begun his recording ca-

Tina Turner in action. Frank Driggs Collection.

reer much earlier, as a performer on Jackie Brenston's "Rocket 88" (1951), sometimes credited as the first rock 'n' roll record. Ike and Tina scored big crossover hits during the 1960s with "A Fool in Love" (Number Two R&B and Number Twenty-seven pop in 1960), "It's Gonna Work Out Fine" (Number Two R&B and Number Fourteen pop in 1961), and a gold record version of Creedence Clearwater Revival's 1969 hit "Proud Mary" (Number Four pop and Number Five R&B in 1971).

As recounted in her 1986 bestselling autobiography, *I, Tina,* Tina Turner eventually tired of the abusive behavior of her husband, leaving him in 1976 to start her own career. The first years were tough, but by 1981 the Rolling Stones and Rod Stewart, old fans of the Ike and Tina Revue, had hired her as an opening act on their concert tours. In 1983 she was offered a contract by Capitol Records. Her first album, entitled *Private Dancer* (1984), reached Number Three on the album charts, stayed in the Top 40 for seventy-one weeks, spawned five hit singles, and eventually went on to attain worldwide sales in excess of eleven million copies. In succeeding years Turner continued to build her career, releasing a series of platinum albums and appearing in movies such as *Mad Max beyond Thunderdome* (1985). In 1993 a film version of her autobiography was produced, entitled *What's Love Got to Do with It.*

The crossover hit "What's Love Got to Do with It" (Number One pop and Number Two R&B in 1984) stayed on the charts for twenty-eight weeks, and earned Grammy awards in 1984 for Best Female Pop Vocalist, Song of the Year, and Record of the Year. Turner did not like the song at first and did not hesitate in conveying this sentiment to Terry Britten, its coauthor and producer of the *Private Dancer* album. "[Terry] said that when a song is given to an artist it's changed for the artists," Turner reminisced. "He said for me to make it a bit rougher, a bit more sharp around the edges. All of a sudden, just sitting there with him in the studio, the song became mine" (Wynn 1985, p. 132).

The lyric of "What's Love Got to Do with It" sets up an ambivalent relationship between the overwhelming sexual attraction described in the verses and the singer's cynicism about romantic love, derided in the song's chorus as a "secondhand emotion." This dynamic in the song's text is reinforced by the musical accompaniment. Though the tempo remains fairly constant (a relaxed pace of 98 beats per minute), the instrumental arrangement alternates between the rich, continuous texture, dominated by flute- and stringlike synthesizer sounds, that underlies the verses, and a more bouncy, reggae-like groove established by the electric bass and guitars on the chorus, the lyrics of which begin with the song's title.

The whole arrangement itself is carefully constructed—an eight-bar instrumental introduction; a unusual thirteen-bar verse ("You must understand . . . "), comprising seven- and six-bar sections (A); an eight-bar chorus (B); then another verse (A) ("It may seem . . . "), followed by another chorus (B). The middle point of the arrangement in structural terms is a synthesizer solo of seven and a half bars, using the harmonies of the chorus (B'). This is followed by an eight-bar section (C) with new harmonies, where the singer reveals her fear of heartbreak more explicitly ("I've been taking . . . "). The arrangement concludes with three repetitions of the chorus (minus one bar, thanks to the early entrance of the chorus each time through), fading away at the very end.

For many in her audience, the character in this song—an experienced, cynical, yet still vulnerable woman—was Turner herself, a case where the boundary between the public and private lives of a recording artist seems to have dissolved almost entirely. (In the case of a David Bowie or—as we shall discuss—Madonna, a sense of ironic distance between the celebrity image and the individual behind it is carefully maintained. In Tina Turner's case, this distinction between image and identity is much less certain.) The combination of poignancy and toughness projected in Turner's recordings and live performances was linked by her fans to the details of her biography and helps to explain her appeal as the first black woman to attain major status in the predominantly white male field of arena rock music.

"Jump" (1984)

Performed by Van Halen, written by Eddie Van Halen, Alex Van Halen, Michael Anthony, and David Lee Roth

Heavy metal music, pioneered in the late 1960s and early 1970s by bands such as Led Zeppelin and Deep Purple, went into a period of relative decline during the late 1970s, partly as a result of the disco craze. By the early 1980s most hit singles—particularly those promoted on MTV—were oriented more toward postdisco dance music played on keyboard synthesizers than toward the electric guitar virtuosity of heavy metal bands. The music industry tended to ignore heavy metal music, regarding it and its core audience of adolescent white males as something of an embarrassment.

During the 1980s, however, heavy metal came back with a vengeance. A slew of metal albums topped the singles and album charts, ranging from the pop metal sounds of bands like Van Halen, Bon Jovi, Mötley Crüe, and Def Leppard to the harder sound of speed metal bands such as Metallica, Slayer, Anthrax, and Megadeath. One of the most important moments in the mainstreaming of heavy metal was the release of Van Halen's album *1984,* which featured the Number One pop single "Jump."

"Jump" was in some ways a remarkable departure from standard heavy metal practice. To begin with, its main instrumental melody was played on a synthesizer rather than an electric guitar. This may seem like a minor detail, but it was an important symbolic and aesthetic issue for hardcore metal fans, many of whom focus closely on the technical virtuosity of guitarists like Eddie Van Halen. From this perspective, the keyboard synthesizer (like disco music) is viewed as a somewhat questionable, perhaps even effeminate instrument. As Philip Bashe, an expert on heavy metal music, has put it, the fact that Eddie Van Halen played the bombastic opening theme of "Jump" on a synthesizer rather than a guitar was "a brave test of the Van Halen audience's loyalty" (Bashe 1985, p. 137). The success of the single was boosted by its corresponding music video, which was shot in home-movie style and featured the athletic prowess and oddball sense of humor of David Lee Roth—at that time Van Halen's lead singer.

On "Jump," the song itself, in the conventional sense of words-plus-melody, is not a core focus of attention for the musicians or their listeners. (Eddie Van Halen, when asked by an interviewer what his mother would think of the lyrics to his band's songs, said that he had no idea at all what they were!) The text of "Jump"—a casual come-on to a girl from a guy leaning against a jukebox—seems almost an afterthought, apart, perhaps, from the clever "go ahead and jump!" hook phrase, which sounds rather as though David Lee Roth were counseling the object of his affections to jump off a high ledge, rather than into his arms. The notion of love as risk taking—so strongly portrayed in Tina Turner's "What's Love Got to Do with It"—is present here as well, though from a decidedly male point of view.

The chief significance of a recording like "Jump," however, lies not in the song per se but in the musical textures created by the band and the studio engineer, and in the sensibility that they evoke. As we have mentioned, one of the main points of attention for heavy metal fans is the virtuosity of the genre's master guitarists, a tradition that they trace back to pioneers such as Jimi Hendrix and Led Zeppelin's Jimmy Page. Eddie Van Halen, widely recognized as a primary innovator in electric guitar performance, is famous for developing widely used techniques ("pull-offs" and "tapping") and for performing various operations on his guitars and amplifiers to modify their sound.

Although "Jump" relies heavily on the keyboard synthesizer for its effect, the sounds generated by Eddie Van Halen are in fact closely analogous to his guitar style. In particular, he uses the synthesizer to create something akin to "power chords," two-note combinations that, when played at high volume on an electric guitar, create the massive, distorted, bone-crunching sound associated with heavy metal bands. "Jump" opens with a synthesized power chord, as if to announce right from the beginning that the sheer sound of the music is more important than the specific instruments used to produce it. Thick textures and a strong pulse, played on keyboards, bass, and drums, propel us through the first two verses of the song. The arrival of the chorus is marked by a sudden opening up, in which the synthesizer plays long sustained chords, the electric guitar plays a sizzling counterpoint to the vocal melody, and the drums and bass play an interesting irregular rhythmic pattern that first suspends the beat and then, after four bars, unleashes it with even greater energy. After another verse- and-chorus section, we are transported into the midst of a virtuoso guitar solo that uses Eddie Van Halen's famed techniques. The guitar solo is followed by a longer synthesizer solo, which develops an elaborate melodic improvisation that closely parallels the style of Van Halen's guitar playing.

Although some hardcore metal fans criticized Van Halen for moving away from the guitar-centered model of heavy metal musicianship, the band succeeded in introducing synthesizers into the genre, and in helping to spread metal's popularity to a larger and more diverse audience. In 1983 only 8 percent of records sold in the United States were heavy metal; a year later that total had risen to 20 percent, making metal one of the most popular genres of popular music. This process continued in 1986 when the pop metal band Bon Jovi released the album *Slippery When Wet*, which held the Number One spot for eight weeks and went on to sell over twelve million copies worldwide. By the end of 1986 MTV had launched *Headbangers' Ball*, a show designed specifically for metal fans, which soon became the most-watched show on the channel. In the late 1980s heavy metal music accounted for around half of the Top 20 albums on the *Billboard* charts on any given week.

Written and performed by Peter Gabriel

"Sledgehammer" (1986)

Peter Gabriel (b. 1950 in England) first achieved celebrity as a member of the art rock group Genesis. After leaving Genesis in 1976, Gabriel released four solo albums, all of them titled *Peter Gabriel*. Partly in an effort to clear up the consumer confusion that followed in the wake of this unusual strategy, he gave his next album a distinctive-if brief-title: *So. So* was an interesting and accessible amalgam of various musical styles, reflecting Gabriel's knowledge of the new digital technologies, his budding interest in world music (see Chapter 14), and his indebtedness to black music, particularly R&B and soul music of the 1960s. The album peaked at

Number Two on the Top LPs chart, sold four million copies, and produced Gabriel's
bestselling single "Sledgehammer" (Number One pop, Number Sixty-one R&B in
1986).

"Sledgehammer" features a horn section led by the trumpet player Wayne Jackson, who, as a member of the Memphis Horns, had played on many of the biggest
soul music hits of the 1960s ("Knock on Wood," "Soul Man," etc.). Jackson had
deeply impressed sixteen-year-old Peter Gabriel during an appearance with the Otis
Redding Soul Revue at a London R&B club in 1966. Gabriel described "Sledgehammer" as

> an attempt to recreate some of the spirit and style of the music that most excited me
> as a teenager—60s soul. The lyrics of many of those songs were full of playful sex-
> ual innuendo and this is my contribution to that songwriting tradition. It is also
> about the use of sex as a means of getting through a breakdown in communication.
> (Bright 1999, p. 267)

The lyrics to "Sledgehammer"—packed with double-entendre references to sledge-
hammers, big dippers, steam trains, the female "fruitcake" and the male "honey-
bee"—are in fact a G-rated variant of the sexual metaphors that have long been a
part of the blues tradition (compare, for example, Blind Lemon Jefferson's 1926
recording of "That Black Snake Moan," discussed in Chapter 5).

The formal building blocks of "Sledgehammer" are twelve-bar and eight-bar
sections, with the former predominating in the first half of the arrangement. While
most pop music recordings are concerned to establish the beat or groove as quickly

as possible, "Sledgehammer" opens with an exotic touch, a digital keyboard sample of a Japanese flute called the shakuhachi, as a hint of Gabriel's budding interest in world music. The funk-influenced groove—with strong backbeats on the snare drum, the keyboard bass landing strongly on the first beat of each measure, and the guitar playing a bouncy upbeat pattern similar to ska—is introduced by the horn section, backed by synthesizers. After eight bars the horns drop out and the rhythm takes four measures to establish the groove that will carry us through the rest of the recording.

Following the introduction, Peter Gabriel sings two verses (beginning with the lines "You could have a steam train" and "You could have a big dipper"), each of which is twelve bars in length. Though his intent to evoke the blues form seems clear, he does not strictly observe the a-a-b lyric form of the classic blues (that is to say, he does not repeat the first line of the text in the verses). In addition, he dispenses with the traditional approach to blues harmonies, staying on the tonic chord for a full eight measures, moving to a related chord (which musicians call the relative minor) for two bars, and then returning to the tonic for the last two bars. (Although many traditional blues linger on the tonic chord in a manner similar to this, they rarely if ever move to the relative minor chord, a harmony more in keeping with Tin Pan Alley music.)

After singing two of these twelve-bar verses, Gabriel moves to the eight-bar chorus ("I want to be your sledgehammer"). Once again, the song takes an interesting turn in harmonic terms, shifting from the major key of the verse to a minor key based on the same tonic note. (More precisely, the B section begins on a chord closely related to the tonic major, and then shifts to the tonic minor chord itself.) Listen closely for the shift between the A and the B section, and see if you can hear the different color or feeling of the harmonies.

The arrangement continues with a four-bar instrumental section taking us back to the major-key harmonies of the verse; another verse ("Show me round your fruit-cakes"), shortened to eight instead of twelve bars; and two presentations of the chorus ("I want to be your sledgehammer"). The last section of the arrangement relies on a minor-key harmonic pattern closely related to that of the chorus, moving back and forth between the tonic minor chord and another, closely related chord; it begins with a keyboard synthesizer solo. Finally, a series of eight-bar sections ("I will show for you") are heard, in which Gabriel's vocal phrases alternate with a choir of gospel-style singers. The arrangement reaches a peak here, with Gabriel improvising solo phrases against the responses of the choir ("Show for me, Show for you"). Gabriel's attempt to "recreate some of the spirit and style" of 1960s soul music may be successful precisely because he does not try to produce an exact copy of the black musical styles that inspired him. Rather, he uses fundamental elements such as the twelve-bar blues form, call-and-response singing, strong funk-derived polyrhythms, and an R&B style horn section as the basis for a performance that reflects his own musical experience and taste, including references to world music and harmonies that take the blues in new directions.

The success of "Sledgehammer" was in no small part due to the massive exposure it received on MTV in the mid-1980s. The video version of "Sledgehammer" was an eye-catching, witty, and technically innovative work that pushed the frontiers of the medium. It won nine MTV Awards (more than any video in history), including Best Video and the prestigious Video Vanguard Award for career achievement in 1987, and was ranked the fourth best video of all time in a 1999 retrospective aired on MTV. The making of the video, which combined stop-motion techniques and live action, required Gabriel to spend eight painful sixteen-hour days lying under glass with his head supported by a steel pole. (Aardman Animations, the outfit that produced the "Sledgehammer" video, went on to work on the *Wallace and Gromit* videos and the talking car ads aired by Chevron in the late 1990s.)

One key to the success of any music video is the relationship it establishes between the sound of the original recording (which, except in the case of live concert videos, is always made first) and the flow of visual images. The video of "Sledgehammer"—directed by Steven Johnston—opens with enlarged microscopic images of human sperm cells impregnating an egg, which develops into a fetus, accompanied by the exotic sound of the synthesized flute. As the groove is established, we see Gabriel's face in close-up, moving to the groove, wiggling his eyebrows, ears, and mouth in time to the music. The stop-motion technique—in which the camera is halted and restarted in order to create the illusion of inanimate objects moving under their own power—creates a jerky stop-start effect that establishes a kind of parallel reality, carefully coordinated to match the rhythms of the music. The lyrics of the song are also reflected in the video images: when Gabriel sings "You could have a steam train," a toy locomotive circles his head on miniature tracks; when he sings "You could have a bumper car bumping, this amusement never ends," two smiling (and singing) bumper cars appear next to his ears, mountains of popcorn pile up behind him, and his hair turns to pink cotton candy. After a series of stop-motion sequences featuring everything from singing fruits and vegetables to dancing furniture, Gabriel is transformed into a "starman" and walks off into the night sky. Thus the video takes us from the microscopic origins of life to the vastness of the galaxy, with many diverting stops in between. As Gabriel himself admitted some years later, although the recording of "Sledgehammer" would probably have done well on its own, the ambitious and highly creative video of the song, played endlessly on MTV, introduced the song to millions of Americans who might otherwise never have purchased a Peter Gabriel record.

A TALE OF THREE ALBUMS

A brief look at three multimillion-selling albums of the 1980s will help document the variety of styles that characterized this period. Each of these albums represents the biggest commercial success in its artist's solo career. *Thriller*, in fact, ranks as the top-selling album in history as of this writing, having achieved worldwide sales in excess of forty million copies; it was the Number One album for thirty-seven weeks during 1983.

In the case of Michael Jackson, *Thriller* was the zenith of a career as a solo artist that had been gathering momentum throughout the 1970s, even while Jackson continued to be a pivotal member of the tremendously successful group the Jackson Five (which changed its name to the Jacksons with its departure from the Motown organization in 1976, a departure that caused no substantial interruption in its long-running success story). *Thriller* was state-of-the-art pop music, an album dedicated not so much to breaking new ground as to consolidating Michael Jackson's dominance of the contemporary pop scene by showcasing his versatility as a performer of a stylistically wide range of up-to-date material.

Like Jackson, Paul Simon got his start in the 1960s as a member of a group, in this case the famous folk rock duo Simon and Garfunkel (see Chapter 10). When Simon went on to a productive solo career in the 1970s, however, the duo disbanded. *Graceland* revived a career that had seemed to be in decline in the early 1980s (Simon's two preceding albums had neither the critical nor the commercial success that greeted most of his work of the 1970s) and—with its employment of African musicians, African music, and (occasionally) African subject matter, along with other "exotic" touches—suddenly thrust Simon into the forefront of the new category called world music.

On the other hand, Bruce Springsteen's *Born in the U.S.A.* seemed more concerned with this country's past in its depiction of adult working-class Americans whose better days are behind them, and the album's music is drenched appropriately in Springsteen's typical roots-based rock sound. The glitzy, consciously "modern" sound and production values of *Thriller* clearly were not for Springsteen; neither was he trying in any way to change the basic direction of his career and his music, as Simon was in *Graceland*. In *Born in the U.S.A.* Springsteen was simply continuing to make the kind of music, and to voice the kinds of concerns, that had characterized his career from its beginning in the 1970s. The unexpected megasuccess of the album (it sold over fifteen million copies, whereas the best selling album among Springsteen's previous efforts—*Born to Run* from 1975—had sold less than five million) took the artist himself somewhat by surprise and left him anxious to ascertain whether his newly enlarged audience was truly understanding the less-than-cheerful messages he wished to convey, as we shall see.

Thriller (Michael Jackson, 1982)

In fashioning *Thriller*, <u>Michael Jackson</u> (b. 1958) worked with the veteran producer Quincy Jones to create an album that achieved boundary-crossing popularity to an unprecedented degree. At a time when the pop music audience seemed to be fragmenting to a greater extent perhaps than ever before, *Thriller* demonstrated a kind of across-the-board appeal that established new and still unduplicated heights of commercial success. In a sense, Jackson here revived the goal that had animated his old boss at Motown, Berry Gordy Jr. (see Chapter 9): to create an African American–based pop music that was aimed squarely at the mainstream center of the market. That Jackson met his goal in such a mind-boggling fashion proved conclusively that there indeed still was a mainstream in the pop music of the early 1980s, and that Jackson had positioned himself unquestionably in the center of it.

To do this, Jackson had to be more than just "the sound of young America" (to quote Motown's memorable phrase from the 1960s). It is of course true that teenagers, preteenagers, and young adults made up a substantial portion of the 1980s market. But members of the baby boom generation, along with the many who came to maturity during the 1970s, were also still major consumers of pop music. And age was far from the only basis on which segmentation of the audience seemed to be taking place; fans of soft rock, heavy metal, funk, and new wave music, for instance, appeared to want less and less to do with one another. A disturbing subtext of all this was a tendency toward increasing resegregation along racial lines of the various audiences for pop. Heavy metal and new wave fans—and bands—were overwhelmingly white, while funk and the emerging genre of rap were associated with black performers and listeners.

Thriller represented an effort to find ways to mediate among the various genres of early 1980s pop music, to create points of effective synthesis from the welter of apparently competing styles, and to bridge the divides—actual or potential—separating different segments of the pop music audience. Jackson confronted the racial divide head-on by collaborating with two very popular, and very different, white artists: ex-Beatle Paul McCartney joined Jackson for a lyrical vocal duet on "The Girl Is Mine," while Eddie Van Halen of the heavy metal group Van Halen contributed the stinging guitar solo on the intense "Beat It." Both of these radically different songs, along with two others on *Thriller,* were written by Jackson himself; his versatility and his gift for crossing genres extended also into the domain of songwriting. It is also clear that "The Girl Is Mine" and "Beat It" were fashioned to attract different segments of the white audience. The mere presence of Paul McCartney was a draw for many listeners who had been fans of the Beatles in the 1960s, as well as for those who admired McCartney's 1970s band Wings; as a song, "The Girl Is Mine" combines a gentle melodic flow with a feeling of rhythmic vitality, effectively echoing the virtues of the best Beatles and Wings ballads. "The Girl Is Mine" captured this essentially soft rock ambience—and its audience—especially well: the single release of this song held the Number One spot on *Billboard*'s "Top Adult Contemporary" chart for four weeks. Moreover, "The Girl Is Mine" had sufficient crossover appeal to top the R&B chart (now called "Hot Black Singles") for three weeks as well. As the first single to come out of the *Thriller* album, "The Girl Is Mine" demonstrated immediately how well Michael Jackson's new music could break down preconceptions about marketability.

"Beat It," on the other hand, has nothing to do with soft rock and was a gesture obviously extended to "metal-heads," who must have been struck by the novelty of a collaboration between a celebrated heavy metal guitarist and an African American pop icon. But this door also could, and did, swing both ways. "Beat It" joined "The Girl Is Mine" on the list of Number One black singles in 1983.

Much of *Thriller* consists of uptempo, synthesizer- and bass-driven, danceable music that occupies a (probably conscious) middle ground between the heavy funk of an artist like George Clinton and the brighter but still beat-obsessed sound that characterized many new wave bands (of which Blondie would be a good example). Perhaps the outstanding—and, in this case, unexpected and highly original—example of the album's successful synthesis of diverse stylistic elements may be found in the title song. "Thriller" starts out depicting a horror-movie scene, which eventually turns out to be on the television screen being watched by two lovers, providing them with an excuse for cuddling "close together" and creating their own kind of thrills. In a conclusion that pairs an old white voice with a new black style, horror-movie star Vincent Price comes from out of nowhere to perform a "rap" about the terrors of the night. (This "rap" describes some typical horror-film situations, but its language is occasionally spiced up with current pop-oriented slang—as when Price refers to "the funk of forty thousand years.")

In the early years of long-playing records, the pop music album was typically a collection of individual songs, several (and sometimes all) of which had previously been released as singles. In our discussions of the 1960s and 1970s, we have remarked on the steadily increasing importance of the album over the single, as pop artists began more and more to conceive of the album as their principal creative medium. *Thriller* is a unique landmark in this evolutionary process. *Thriller* is not a concept album—unless the "concept" was to demonstrate that an album could be made to engender hit singles, rather than vice versa. For out of the nine songs on *Thriller*, seven were released as singles, one by one, starting with "The Girl Is Mine" (the only one to be released prior to the album itself), and all seven were Top 10 hits. (Both "Billie Jean" and "Beat It" were Number One pop hits; these two and "Thriller" sold over two million copies each as singles, while "The Girl Is Mine" was a million-selling single. The only songs from *Thriller* that were not turned into hit singles are "Baby Be Mine" and "The Lady in My Life.")

Visual media both old and new played a significant role in the *Thriller* saga. In May 1983 Jackson appeared on the television special *25 Years of Motown* and introduced what came to be known as his "moonwalk" dance while performing "Billie Jean" from *Thriller*; the performance was a sensation and doubtless added to the continuing popularity of the album. By this time, the videos for *Thriller* songs that Jackson had made were being shown regularly on MTV. Jackson's embrace of the relatively new medium of music video reflected his foresight in realizing its potential. While bringing his work to the attention of yet another segment of the music public, his videos in turn helped boost the power and prestige of MTV itself, because they were so carefully, creatively, and elaborately produced. Because Jackson was the first African American artist to be programmed with any degree of frequency on MTV, *Thriller* thus contributed to the breakdown of yet another emerging color line in pop culture. (Significantly, in the video of "Beat It," Jackson is seen breaking up a racially charged gang fight.)

Born in the U.S.A. (Bruce Springsteen, 1984)

Throughout the 1970s Bruce Springsteen (b. 1949) had been forging a progressively more successful career in pop music while continuing to cast both his music and his personal image in the light of the rebellious rock 'n' rollers of the 1950s and the socially conscious folk rockers of the 1960s. Springsteen's songs reflected his working-class origins and sympathies, relating the stories of still young but aging men and women with deadend jobs (or no jobs at all), who are looking for romance and excitement in the face of repeated disappointments and seeking meaningful outlets for their seething energies and hopes in an America that seems to have no pieces of the American dream left to offer them. Some of the song titles from his first few albums are indicative: "Born to Run," "Darkness on the Edge of Town," "Hungry Heart," "Racing in the Street," "Wreck on the Highway," and so on. Springsteen performed with his E Street Band, and their music was characterized by a strong, roots-rock sound that emphasized Springsteen's connections to 1950s and 1960s music. The band even included a saxophone—virtually an anachronism in the pop music of this period—to mark the link with the rhythm & blues and rock 'n' roll of earlier eras. (In this connection, it is worth noting that one of the songs on *Born in the U.S.A.*, "Cover Me," is based on a twelve-bar blues progression. Twelve-bar blues form was also all but an anachronism in the mainstream pop music of the 1980s, but it was part of Springsteen's musical heritage and style, and his continuing employment of this form represented another obvious homage to the roots of rock.) Still, the emphasis in Springsteen's music was predominantly on the traditional rock ensemble of guitars, bass, and drums, with keyboard instruments occasionally used prominently.

Bruce Springsteen. Frank Driggs
Collection.

The album immediately preceding *Born in the U.S.A.* represented a departure
for Springsteen: *Nebraska* (1982) featured him in a solo, "unplugged" setting that
underlined the particular bleakness of this collection of songs. Consequently, many
fans may have celebrated *Born in the U.S.A.*, which brought back the E Street Band
with an actual as well as a symbolic bang, as a kind of "return to form" for Springsteen. Certainly the album is dominated by uptempo, rocking songs, with Springsteen shouting away in full voice and grand style, and the band playing full tilt behind him. Still, listening at the record (or tape or CD) player with the album's lyric
sheet in hand, it is hard to see how anybody could have regarded *Born in the U.S.A.*
as anything other than a typically dire commentary by Springsteen on the current
state of the union. Indeed, the very first lyrics of the title song, which opens the album, set the tone decisively:

> *Born down in a dead man's town,*
> *The first kick I took was when I hit the ground.*
> *You end up like a dog that's been beat too much*
> *Till you spend half your life just covering up.*

"Born in the U.S.A." tells the story of a returning Vietnam veteran unable to get a
job or to rebuild his life, and its despairing message is characteristic of most of the
songs on the album.

But maybe many people weren't listening to the words. In the wake of this album's rapid and enormous popularity, Springsteen found himself and his band on
tour playing to huge, sold-out stadiums where—given the amplification levels and
the crowd noise—most people probably couldn't even *hear* the words. Confronted
with hordes of fans waving American flags, and the exploitation of his image in the
presidential election year of 1984 by political forces for which he had little sympa-

thy, Springsteen periodically found himself having to explain that he was not as-sociated with "feel-good" politics or uncritical "America first" boosterism. Was Springsteen a victim of his own success, forced into a stadium rock culture that ill served the purpose and meaning of his songs? (Had rock music gained the world, so to speak, only to lose its soul?) Or was there actually some fundamental di-chotomy between Springsteen's message and the energetic, crowd-pleasing music in which he was couching it?

There is of course no objectively "correct" answer to such questions. But when listening to *Born in the U.S.A.* as a recording, and as a whole, Springsteen's sincer-ity seems as apparent as his intensity, and it is hard not to sense, and hard not to be affected by, the prevailing dark ambience. In a general way, *Born in the U.S.A.* is a concept album: a series of musical snapshots of working-class Americans, all of whom seem to be somewhere around Springsteen's age (he turned thirty-five the year he released this album, the same age as his protagonist in the song "My Home-town"), many of whom are having economic or personal difficulties, and all of whom sense the better times of their lives slipping into the past. In the album's orig-inal LP form, each of the two sides starts out with a strong, aggressive song and winds down to a final cut that is softer in sound but, if anything, even darker in mood. The first side ends with the low-key but eerie "I'm on Fire," whose protag-onist seems about to explode from the weight and pain of his own "bad desire"; in terms of the listening experience, the spooky urgency of this song appears to speak to the cumulative hard luck and frustration of all the different characters described in the songs of Side One. Side Two starts off with an extroverted rebound in mu-sical energy and a cry of "No Surrender." But disillusionment and resignation come to characterize the songs on this side of the record as well, until the "fire" image reappears strikingly in the penultimate song, "Dancing in the Dark." Finally comes "My Hometown"; Springsteen, his voice drained of energy, sings of the decay of his place of birth and of possibly "getting out" with his wife and child, heading to-ward—it isn't clear what. In this poignant finale, Springsteen comes as close as any pop artist ever has to embracing and conveying an authentically tragic vision.

Amazingly, "My Hometown" was a major hit as a single recording, reaching Number Six on the pop chart in early 1986 (and Number One on the adult con-temporary chart). It was the last of seven consecutive singles to be culled from the album, all of which were Top 10 pop hits; in this respect, *Born in the U.S.A.* followed in the footsteps of *Thriller* as an album that spawned a parade of hit singles. The al-bum itself sold over fifteen million copies, as we have already noted, and stayed on the album charts for over two years. Like Michael Jackson, Springsteen produced a series of music videos to go with several of the songs released as singles from *Born in the U.S.A.*; these videos proved popular in their own right and further en-hanced the popularity of the album. Thus Springsteen stayed abreast of the chang-ing music scene at the same time that he tried to speak, through his songs, to the values and attitudes that for him lay at the core of all that was worthwhile and en-during in rock.

Graceland (Paul Simon, 1986)

Paul Simon's interest in music that was not indigenous to the United States mani-fested itself long before he recorded *Graceland*. When he was still singing with Gar-funkel, Simon (b. 1941) recorded "El Condor Pasa," a song that paired his own lyrics

Paul Simon. Frank Driggs Collection.

with a backing instrumental track based on an old Peruvian folk melody, performed in "native" style by a group called Los Incas. "El Condor Pasa" appeared on the 1970 Simon and Garfunkel album *Bridge over Troubled Water* and was released as a single that same year. The song was indicative of the path Simon would later pursue much more systematically and thoroughly in *Graceland,* in which many of the songs present Simon's vocals and lyrics over an accompaniment performed in South African style by South African musicians.

A considerable portion of the music for *Graceland* was actually recorded in South Africa, and that resulted in some awkward political issues for Simon. Like *Born in the U.S.A.,* this album became a focus of political attention for fans, skeptics, and, with reluctance, its creator. At the time, a United Nations boycott on performing and recording in South Africa was in effect as part of an international attempt to isolate and ostracize the government of that country, which was still enforcing the widely despised policy of apartheid (separation of the races). Simon could not deny that he broke the boycott, but he claimed that he was in no sense supporting the ideology of the South African government by making music with black South Africans on their native soil. In fact, the success of *Graceland* helped bring black South African musicians and styles to a much wider and racially more diverse audience than they had ever been able to reach before; this proved to be true within South Africa itself, as well as in America and many other parts of the world. It could well be argued that Simon ultimately made, through his racially integrated music, a forceful statement about the virtues of free intermingling and cultural exchange.

In any case, Simon came to a mutual understanding with the United Nations and the opponents of apartheid in relatively short order, and he stopped performing in South Africa until apartheid was dismantled several years later.

A truly "global" album from a geographical point of view, *Graceland* was recorded in five different locations on three different continents: in addition to Johannesburg, South Africa, tracks were cut in London, England; New York City; Los Angeles; and Crowley, Louisiana. Many of the selections on the album combine elements that were recorded at different times in different places, but others were the result of sessions where all the participants were present in the same place at the same time. While Simon flew to South Africa to work on several songs with musicians there, at another time he brought South African musicians to New York to work with him, and on yet another occasion Simon and the South African vocal group Ladysmith Black Mambazo recorded together in London.

What ultimately distinguishes *Graceland* from earlier forays into world music, whether by Simon or by other pop musicians, is the extent to which the album explores the concept of *collaboration*—collaboration among artists of different races, regions, nationalities, and ethnicities, which produced in turn collaboration among diverse musical styles and approaches to songwriting. This provides a conceptual basis for *Graceland,* to be sure, but Simon's album is quite different from the usual concept album. There is certainly no explicit or implicit story line that connects the songs, nor is there any single, central subject that links them all together—unless one is willing to view collaboration itself (primarily *musical* collaboration but also, in two instances, collaboration on lyrics as well) as the album's "subject matter." But the idea of an album designed to explore collaboration seems a perfectly logical, if unusual, concept to embrace in understanding *Graceland.*

The various approaches to the concept of collaboration that are found among the songs on *Graceland* run a gamut from "Homeless," in which both the words (in Zulu and English) and the music were cowritten by Simon and Joseph Shabalala of Ladysmith Black Mambazo, to a cut like "I Know What I Know," in which Simon added his own lyrics and vocal melody to preexisting music (originally not written for Simon) by General M. D. Shirinda and the Gaza Sisters. In the case of "Homeless," the song makes a unified and gently poignant impression; the images of poor people could refer to South Africa or to America, or to both, and the slow-moving, harmonious vocal music encourages us to take their plight seriously. In "I Know What I Know," on the other hand, Simon deliberately makes no attempt to match the tone of his lyrics to the culture or to the implied locale of the original South African music. Instead, the lyrics seem to portray an encounter between two worldly wise and cynical people at an upper-crust cocktail party (or some such gathering), and their mood and subject both stand in remarkable, ironic contrast to the jubilant, uninhibited sound of the danceable South African instrumental music and to the Gaza Sisters' voices. The result is a virtual embodiment, in words and sounds, of a profound clash of cultures—as if some characters typical of Simon's earlier, sophisticated urban songs of late twentieth-century anxiety (such as those found on an album like *Still Crazy after All These Years,* from 1975) were suddenly dropped into the middle of a busy South African village on a day of celebration.

That the uneasy mismatch of music and lyrics in "I Know What I Know" is neither accidental nor careless on Simon's part is signaled by the presence on the album of songs that, occupying a middle ground between "Homeless" and "I Know

What I Know," make cultural diversity an aspect of their stated subject matter and of their music. The third verse of "You Can Call Me Al" describes a man who is uncomfortable in a foreign culture:

A man walks down the street
It's a street in a strange world
Maybe it's the Third World
Maybe it's his first time around
He doesn't speak the language
He holds no currency
He is a foreign man
He is surrounded by the sound
The sound

The "sound" here is being produced by a group of black South African musicians playing with Simon and American session musicians in New York City; significantly, the multicultural group is joined on this cut by Morris Goldberg, who (Simon's liner notes pointedly inform us) is a *white* South African emigrant based in New York, and who contributes a striking pennywhistle solo. Members of this same diverse ensemble also play on "Under African Skies," the verses of which actually shift location from Africa to Tucson, Arizona, and back again. Here Simon is joined in vocal duet by Linda Ronstadt—from Tucson, Arizona.

In both the music and the words of *Graceland*, the meanings and implications can be allusive and elusive, often seeming to change color or to shift in midphrase. Yet the lilt of Simon's melodies and the dynamic rhythms provided by his diverse collaborators keep the album from ever sounding "difficult" or arcane. It is to Simon's credit that he never attempts to sound like anybody but himself, nor does he require his fellow musicians to adapt their style perforce to his; this is why the songs on *Graceland* are true collaborations, and such unusually successful ones. In the largest sense, one might say that *Graceland* is "about" the joys, complexities, and perplexities of living in an increasingly diverse, multicultural world. (This is a subject that also informs the words and music of Simon's next album, *The Rhythm of the Saints*, from 1990.)

That one need not venture to other continents, or even to other countries, to find "other" cultures is a point made, in effect, by the last two cuts on *Graceland*: "That Was Your Mother," in which Simon is joined by the Zydeco band Good Rockin' Dopsie and the Twisters, from Louisiana; and "All Around the World, or The Myth of Fingerprints," in which Simon plays with Los Lobos, the well-known Mexican American band from Los Angeles. On both of these selections, the prominent employment of accordion and saxophone creates aural links with the sounds of South African ensembles on other songs from *Graceland*, demonstrating musically that the world is indeed a shrinking place. (Conversely, Simon remarks in his liner notes how the South African instrumentalists he recorded in Johannesburg for the title song produced a sound that reminded him in certain ways of American country music.) At the end, then, Paul Simon comes home, only to find himself still, and always, a musical "citizen of the world."

Graceland, although not exactly the kind of smash-hit album that both *Thriller* and *Born in the U.S.A.* were (it never hit Number One on the album chart), eventually sold over five million copies. As the Grammy Award winner for Album of the

Year in 1986, it spectacularly revived Simon's then-flagging career and garnered a great deal of attention, not only for Simon himself, but also for many of the musicians who played on the album with him. *Graceland* did not prove to be a major source of hit singles, but a concert video featuring much of its music, taped in Africa with African musicians, was very popular. It is the album responsible, more than any other, for introducing a wide audience to the idea of world music, and for this reason alone the importance and influence of *Graceland* cannot be underestimated.

"BABY I'M A STAR": PRINCE, MADONNA, AND THE PRODUCTION OF CELEBRITY

The production of celebrity may be as central to the workings of the American music industry as the production of music itself. In the 1910s and 1920s Irene and Vernon Castle were made into national figures through a combination of theater tours, silent film appearances, magazine stories, and mass-produced "how-to" guides to ballroom dancing. In the 1930s and 1940s crooners such as Bing Crosby and Frank Sinatra were turned into media stars through increasingly sophisticated promotional techniques involving sound film, network radio, and the print media. During the postwar years network television became an indispensable tool for the promotion of popular music and the production of celebrity—it is, for example, hard to imagine the careers of Elvis Presley or the Beatles without the initial boost provided by network television appearances.

By the 1980s the "star-making machinery behind the popular song" (to quote a lyric by singer-songwriter Joni Mitchell) had grown to unprecedented proportions. Since the profitability of the music industry depended on the sales generated by a relatively limited number of multiplatinum recordings, the coordination of publicity surrounding the release of such recordings was crucial. The release of a potential hit album—and of those individual tracks on the album thought to have potential as hit singles—was cross-promoted in music videos, television talk show appearances, Hollywood films, and newspaper, magazine, and radio interviews, creating the overall appearance of a multifront military campaign run by a staff of corporate generals.

The power of mass-mediated charisma is rooted in the idea that an individual fan can enter into a personal relationship with a superstar via images and sounds that are simultaneously disseminated to millions of people. The space between the public image of the star and the private life and personality of the musician who fills this role is where the contemporary industry of celebrity magazines, television exposés, "unauthorized" biographies, and paparazzi photographers flourishes, providing fans with provocative tidbits of information concerning the glamour, habits, and character traits of their favorite celebrities. This field of popular discourse is dominated by certain well-worn narratives. In what is perhaps the most common of these storylines, the artist, born into humble circumstances, rises to fame, is overtaken by the triple demons of greed, power lust, and self-indulgence, falls into a deep pit (of despair, depression, drug addiction, alcoholism), and then repents his or her sins and is accepted (in a newly humbled status) by the media and millions of fans. Other celebrities manage to flaunt convention and maintain their "bad boy" or "bad girl" image throughout their careers, while still others are portrayed as good-hearted and generous (if a bit bland) from the get-go. Of course, these story lines are as much about the fans themselves—and the combination of admiration and envy they feel toward their favorite celebrities—as about the particular musicians in question.

While stars such as Bing Crosby, the Beatles, and Bob Dylan had played an important role in shaping their own public image, the 1980s saw the rise of a new breed of music superstar particularly adept at manipulating the mass media, and at stimulating public fascination with their personal characteristics, as well as with their music. Certainly, no analysis of celebrity in late twentieth-century America would be complete without discussion of <u>Madonna</u> and <u>Prince</u>. Like their contemporary Michael Jackson, Madonna Louise Veronica Ciccone and Prince Rogers Nelson were born in the industrial north-midwestern United States during the summer of 1958. (All three of these 1980s superstars were only six years old in 1964, when the Beatles stormed America, and barely ten years old during the first Woodstock festival.) Despite the proximity of their geographical origins, Ciccone and Nelson followed quite distinctive career paths. To begin with, Ciccone was a dancer and photographic model who moved into music almost by accident, while Nelson had been making music professionally since the age of thirteen, as an occasional member of his father's jazz trio. Madonna first emerged out of New York's thriving dance club scene, while Prince's career developed in the regional metropolis of Minneapolis, Minnesota. Madonna's hit recordings—like most pop recordings—depended on a high degree of collaborative interaction between the singer, the songwriter(s), the producer, the recording engineers, studio session musicians, and others. But many of Prince's hit recordings, inspired by the early 1970s example of Stevie Wonder, were composed, produced, engineered, and performed solely by Nelson himself, many at his own studio in Minneapolis (Paisley Park, Inc.).

Despite these obvious differences, however, Madonna and Prince have much in common. Both are self-conscious authors of their own celebrity, creators of multi-

Superstars of the 1980s:
Prince and Madonna.
Frank Driggs Collection

ple artistic alter egos, and highly skilled manipulators of the mass media. Both experienced a meteoric rise to fame during the early 1980s and were dependent on mass media such as cable television and film. And both Madonna and Prince have sought to blur the conventional boundaries of race, religion, and sexuality and periodically sought to rekindle their fans' interest by shifting shape, changing strategy, and coming up with new and controversial songs and images. Early, sexually explicit recordings by Madonna and Prince played a primary role in stimulating the formation of the Parents' Music Resource Center (PMRC), a watchdog organization founded in 1985. During the second half of the 1980s, the PMRC—bolstered by its alliance with the Parent/Teachers Association (PTA)—pressured the recording industry to institute a rating system parallel to that used in the film industry. Although popular musicians ranging from Frank Zappa to John Denver argued against the adoption of a ratings system, the industry began to place parental warning labels on recordings during the late 1980s.

Madonna

From the late 1980s through the 1990s Madonna's popularity was second only to that of Michael Jackson. Between 1984 and 1994 Madonna scored twenty-eight Top 10 singles, eleven of which reached the top spot on the charts. During the same ten year period she recorded eight Top 10 albums, including the Number One hits *Like a Virgin* (1984), *True Blue* (1986), and *Like a Prayer* (1989). Over the course of her career, Madonna has sold in excess of fifty million albums and has been one of the most reliable sources of profit for Warner Entertainment, corporate owner of the Sire record label, for which she records. She also paved the way for female dance music superstars of the 1990s such as Paula Abdul.

As a purposefully controversial figure, Madonna has tended to elicit strongly polarized reactions. The 1987 *Rolling Stone* readers' poll awarded her second place for Best Female Singer and first place for Worst Female Singer. (In the same poll she also scored third place for Best-Dressed Female and first place for Worst-Dressed Female.) Jacques Chirac, the former president of France, once described Madonna as "a great and beautiful artist," while the political philosopher Camille Paglia asserted that she represented "the future of feminism." The author Luc Sante's distaste for Madonna (as articulated in his article, "Unlike a Virgin," published in *The New Republic*, 8/20/90) was based largely on aesthetic criteria:

> Madonna . . . is a bad actress, a barely adequate singer, a graceless dancer, a boring interview subject, a workmanlike but uninspired (co-)songwriter, and a dynamo of hard work and ferocious ambition.

Other observers are ambivalent about Madonna, perhaps feeling—as the satirist Merrill Markoe once put it—"I keep trying to like her, but she keeps pissing me off!" (Sexton 1993, p. 14). In the academic field of popular culture studies, scholars have created a veritable cottage industry out of analyzing Madonna's social significance, variously interpreting her as a reactionary committed to turning back the advances of feminism, a postmodern performance artist, a politically savvy cultural subversive, and a "container for multiple images." Whatever one's view of these various characterizations, the fact that it is difficult to find anyone who (a) has never heard of Madonna, or (b) harbors no opinion of her at all, is an indication that her career strategy has by and large been most effective.

Madonna Louise Veronica Ciccone was born into an Italian American family in Rochester, Michigan, a suburb of Detroit. She moved to New York City in 1977, worked as a photographic model, studied dance, and became a presence at Manhattan discotheques such as Danceteria, where the DJ, Mark Kamins, played her demo tapes. (It was Kamins who introduced Madonna to executives at Sire Records, the label of the Ramones and Talking Heads, and who in 1982 produced her first dance club hit, "Everybody.") In 1983 Madonna's breakthrough single "Holiday" (Number Sixteen pop, Number Twenty-five R&B) established certain elements of a distinctive studio sound, rooted in the synth-pop dance music of the early 1980s (see the discussion of "Sweet Dreams (Are Made of This)" earlier in this chapter). In addition, Madonna took a page from Michael Jackson's book, enlisting the services of manager Freddie DeMann, who had guided Jackson's career in the years leading up to the megasuccess of 1982's *Thriller.* DeMann oversaw the production of Madonna's first two music videos, "Borderline" and "Lucky Star," the latter of which featured glimpses of the young star's navel, setting a precedent for subsequent, ever more explicit sexual provocations. The choice of Freddie DeMann also points toward an important aspect of Madonna's modus operandi—the ability to enlist a collaborative network of talented professionals, including producers, recording engineers, designers, and videographers.

In 1984 her second album—*Like a Virgin,* produced by Nile Rodgers, who was involved with the writing and production of a number of disco-era hits, including Chic's "Good Times" (see Chapter 12)—shot to top of the album charts, eventually selling more than ten million copies. The album spawned a series of hit singles: "Like a Virgin" (Number One for six weeks in 1984 and early 1985), "Material Girl" (Number Two in 1985), "Angel," and "Dress You Up" (both Number Five in 1985). *Like a Virgin* was promoted on MTV with a series of videos and formed the basis for an elaborately staged concert tour (the "Virgin Tour"), all carefully coordinated as part of a campaign to establish Madonna as a national celebrity. In 1985 Madonna also played a leading role in the film *Desperately Seeking Susan,* receiving generally positive reviews. In an industry where women are often treated as attractive but essentially noncreative "objects," Madonna began early on in her career to exert an unusual degree of control, not only over her music (writing or cowriting many of the songs on her early albums and playing an active role in the production process), but also over the creation and promulgation of her media image. Even seemingly uncontrollable events—like the ubiquitous tabloid accounts of her tempestuous and short-lived marriage to actor Sean Penn—seemed only to feed Madonna's growing notoriety.

During the second half of the 1980s Madonna began to write and record songs with deeper—and more controversial—lyric content. These included "Papa Don't Preach" (1986), in which a pregnant young woman declares her determination to keep her baby and urges her father to lend his moral support; "Open Your Heart" (1986), the video version of which portrays Madonna on display at a sleazy peepshow attended by dozens of men; "Express Yourself" (1989), in which she appears alternatively as a cross-dressing figure, dominating a tableau of male industrial workers, and as a submissive female stereotype, crawling under a table with a collar around her neck; and "Like a Prayer" (1989), the video of which included images of group and interracial sex, burning crosses, and an eroticized black Jesus. (This last video was censured by the Vatican and caused the Pepsi-Cola Corporation to cancel a lucrative endorsement deal with Madonna.)

The controversy-and-commercialism ante was upped even further in 1992 with the publication of *Sex,* a 128-page coffeetable book featuring nude and S&M-garbed photographs of Madonna and other celebrities, and the synchronized release of the album *Erotica,* which peaked at Number Two on the *Billboard* album chart and produced five major hit singles. The year 1994 saw the release of a warmer and more subtly sexual album, *Bedtime Stories,* which spawned "Take a Bow," her biggest single hit ever (Number One for seven weeks in 1994). Toward the end of the 1990s Madonna once again refined her public image, winning a Golden Globe award for her leading role in the film *Evita* (1996) and releasing an album of love ballads (*Something to Remember,* 1996) aimed at a more mature audience. But in 1998 she returned to the disco-derived synth-pop sound that had dominated her early recordings, with the release of *Ray of Light,* which debuted at Number Two on the album charts.

Madonna has frequently challenged the accusation—leveled at her by critics on both the left and the right—that her recordings, videos, and concert productions reinforce old, negative stereotypes of women. In a 1991 interview Madonna responded to these criticisms:

> I may be dressing like the typical bimbo, whatever, but I'm in charge. You know. I'm in charge of my fantasies. I put myself in these situations with men, you know, and everybody knows, in terms of my image in the public, people don't think of me as a person who's not in charge of my career or my life, okay? And isn't that what feminism is all about, you know, equality for men and women? And aren't I in charge of my life, doing the things I want to do? Making my own decisions? (Sexton 1993, p. 286)

Madonna's rhetorical question pulls us into the middle space between the public image and the private life: between the international superstar, Madonna, and Madonna Louise Veronica Ciccone, a talented and ambitious Italian American woman from the suburbs of industrial Detroit. Throughout her career, Madonna Ciccone has released tidbits of information about her private life, attitudes, and values that invite her fans (and her detractors) to imagine what the woman behind the "star-making machinery" is "really" like.

LISTENING TO "LIKE A VIRGIN" (1984)

The core dichotomy of Madonna's public persona—the innocent, emotionally vulnerable, cheerful girl versus the tough-minded, sexually experienced, self-directed woman—was established in the hit single that propelled her to superstar status: "Like a Virgin" (Number One pop and Number Nine R&B in 1984). "Like a Virgin" was not written by Madonna herself but by a pair of male songwriters, Billy Steinberg and Tom Kelly. As Steinburg himself put it, this is not a song about a virgin in any narrowly technical sense—rather, it is about the feeling that someone who has grown pessimistic about love gets from a new relationship. (We have already encountered this theme in Tina Turner's rendition of "What's Love Got to Do with It.") "Like a Virgin" is a good example of the mileage that Madonna and her producer, Nile Rodgers, were able to get out of a fairly simple set of musical elements.

The form of "Like a Virgin" is straightforward. After a four-bar instrumental introduction that establishes the dance groove, there is an eight-bar verse, which we are calling A^1 ("I made it through the wilderness . . . "); a ten-bar version of the verse with somewhat different harmonies, which we call A^2 ("I was beat, incomplete . . . "); and a chorus featuring the hook of the song, which we call B ("Like a virgin . . . "). The only additional structural element is an eight-bar interlude near the middle of the arrangement. The basic structure of the recording is thus

A^1A^2B
A^1A^2B
Eight-bar interlude
A^2BBB (etc., with a gradual fade out)

As in much popular music, the timbre, texture, and rhythmic momentum of "Like a Virgin" are more important to the listener's experience than the song's structure. The studio mix—overseen by Madonna's longtime collaborator Shep Pettibone—is clean, with clear stereo separation, heavy reliance on synthesized sound textures, and the singer's voice strongly foregrounded over the instruments. (As on many dance-oriented hit singles of the 1980s, the characteristic lead guitar sound of rock music is absent here.) Synthesizers are indispensable to the overall effect of this recording—this is a studio sound that simply could not have been created ten years before. Throughout the recording, however, the producer and engineers are careful not to make the instrumental parts too busy or complex, so that Madonna's voice remains the undisputed center of the listener's attention.

As we have discussed, Madonna's persona on recordings and videos and in concert depends on the ironic manipulation of long-standing stereotypes about females. Her vocal style in "Like a Virgin" reflects this aspect of her persona clearly and deliberately, ranging from the soft, intimate breathiness associated with Hollywood sex symbols like Marilyn Monroe to the throaty, tougher sound of 1960s singers like Ronnie Spector, the lead singer on the Ronettes' "Be My Baby." (The contrast between these two vocal personas is reinforced in the video version of "Like a Virgin" by an alternation between images of one Madonna as a bride dressed in white, about to be taken to bed by her groom, and another Madonna dressed in a tight black skirt and top and blue tights, dancing sexily in a gondola moving down the canals of Venice.) During the verses Madonna uses a breathy, somewhat reedy "little girl" voice, occasionally interspersing little squeals, sighs, and intakes of breath at the ends of phrases. Throughout the recording, Madonna shifts back and forth between the two personas, the innocent virgin and the experienced, worldly wise woman, each signified by a distinctive set of vocal timbres.

Of course, how a song's lyrics are interpreted is strongly influenced by their musical setting and by the visual images that accompany the words and music in a video or live concert. When Madonna revived "Like a Virgin" for her 1990

Blonde Ambition tour, the song was placed in a more complex and provocative context, with Madonna clad like an ancient Egyptian princess, reclining on a huge bed, and framed on either side by black male dancers wearing cone-shaped brassieres. Whatever one's interpretation of the sexual and religious symbolism of Madonna's performances and its relationship to her own experience growing up as a Catholic, it is clear that she has a talent for recycling her repertoire in controversial and thought-provoking ways.

Prince

Between 1982 and 1992 Prince (a.k.a. the Artist) placed nine albums in the Top 10, reaching the top of the charts with three of them (*Purple Rain* in 1984, *Around the World in a Day* in 1985, and *Batman* in 1989). During the same decade he placed twenty-six singles in the Top 40 and produced five Number One hits. Over the course of his career, Prince has sold almost forty million recordings, making him one of the most popular music superstars of the last two decades of the twentieth century. More importantly, Prince is one of the most talented musicians ever to achieve mass commercial success in the field of popular music.

Prince Rogers Nelson was born in Minneapolis, Minnesota, the child of parents who migrated from Louisiana to the north and identify themselves as African Americans while acknowledging a mixed-race heritage that includes Italian and Native American ancestry. Prince has stated that growing up in a middle-class Minneapolis neighborhood exposed him to a wide range of music, and that his early influences included everything from James Brown and Santana to Joni Mitchell. As he testified in a 1985 interview on MTV (also transcribed in *Rock & Soul*, 4/86):

> I was brought up in a black-and-white world and, yes, black and white, night and day, rich and poor. I listened to all kinds of music when I was young, and when I was younger, I always said that one day I would play all kinds of music and not be judged for the color of my skin but the quality of my work.

When he was seven his mother and father separated, and Prince spent much of his adolescence being shunted from one home to another. Various statements by Prince suggest that the instability of that period in his life, and the ambivalence of his relationships with his estranged parents, have formed the source material for some of his best-known songs.

One of the first things that strikes one about Prince's career is his amazing productivity. Throughout the 1980s and 1990s, when most superstars released an album every two or three years, Prince's output averaged over an album per year. During the 1980s he composed, performed, and recorded more than seventy-five songs each year. Only about three hundred of these songs have been released; the studio vault at Paisley Park is said to contain more than one thousand unreleased songs, more than ten thousand hours of material. Prince's compositions have been recorded by a wide range of artists, including George Clinton, Miles Davis, Joni Mitchell, Madonna, Bonnie Raitt, and Celine Dion. In addition to recordings released under his own name, Prince has developed a variety of satellite projects, groups or artists who have served in part as outlets for his music (for example, the Time, Apollonia 6, and Sheila E).

In stylistic terms, Prince's recorded output has encompassed a wide range of musical inspirations, from funk and guitar-based rock 'n' roll to urban folk music, new wave, and psychedelic rock. While the dominant impression of Prince's musical approach is that of a thoroughgoing open-mindedness, he has from the beginning sought to exert tight control over his music and his business. Prince owns his own studio (Paisley Park Studios, in Minneapolis) and produces his own recordings; plays most of the instruments on his albums; and struggled for years to wrest control of his music from Warner Brothers, eventually signing an agreement with Capitol-EMI that let him retain control over the master tapes recorded in his studio. (The basis of this dispute seems to have been that Warner Brothers could not release and promote Prince's new material as quickly as he wanted. As of this writing, Prince is rerecording and rereleasing all of the material that was originally released by Warner.) By the late 1990s he was releasing music exclusively—and extensively—on his own independent label, NPG Records, through his Web site, and via his direct-selling telephone hotline, which receives some seven thousand calls a month.

Descriptions of Prince's personality in the popular press present a series of opposed images: he is portrayed as a flower child and as a dictator; a male chauvinist who can form close personal relationships only with women; an intensely private person and a shrewd self-promoter; a sexual satyr and a steadfastly pious man, who has dedicated many of his albums to God. These discussions of Prince draw many comparisons with earlier figures in the history of popular music: the extroverted and sexually ambiguous rock 'n' roll star Little Richard; the guitar virtuoso Jimi Hendrix; the groundbreaking and idiosyncratic bandleader Sly Stone; and the brilliant songwriter and multi-instrumentalist Stevie Wonder. Prince has been critical of the tendency of journalists and record company publicists to identify him only with black artists. In response to the question "What do you think about the comparisons between you and Jimi Hendrix?" he responded, "It's only because he's black. That's really the only thing we have in common. He plays different guitar than I do. If they really listened to my stuff, they'd hear more of a Santana influence than Jimi Hendrix" (Karlen, 1985)

Prince's British biographer Barney Hoskyns christened Prince "the Imp of the Perverse," referring to his apparent delight in confounding the expectations and assumptions of his audience, music critics, and the record industry. Certainly, Prince's relationship to the "star-making machinery" of the entertainment industry is as complex as his racial identity, sexual orientation, and musical style. As a public celebrity, Prince occupies a middle ground between the hermitlike reclusiveness of Michael Jackson and the exuberant exhibitionism of Madonna. Throughout his career, Prince has granted few press interviews yet has for the most part managed to keep himself in the limelight. In the early 1990s Prince changed his name to a cryptic and unpronounceable symbol that blended male and female elements, engaged in a series of public battles with Warner over control of his music, and produced a compact disc recording that could only be played in the order in which it was originally programmed, a reassertion of the principle of the rock album as a complete artistic work. It is hard to imagine another celebrity who would willingly relinquish his nom de plume, publicly (and successfully) defy the will of the transnational corporation that had initially helped to launch his career, and deny his fans the right to consume his songs in whatever order they might choose.

Perhaps the best example of Prince's skill at manipulating the boundary between the public and the private are the film and soundtrack album *Purple Rain* (1984), which established him as a pop superstar. *Purple Rain* was the bestselling album of 1984, bumping Bruce Springsteen's *Born in the U.S.A.* out of the top position on *Billboard*'s pop album chart, holding the Number One position for twenty-four weeks, and producing five hit singles, including "When Doves Cry," "Let's Go Crazy" and "Purple Rain." Since 1984 the album has sold more than thirteen million copies, making it one of the ten bestselling albums of all time. The film did reasonably well at the box office, although it did not succeed in establishing Prince as a matinee idol. Reviews varied widely, some critics regarding the film as a self-indulgent, poorly written, badly acted attempt to promote a music album, while *Rolling Stone* numbered it among the best rock movies ever made. The film and the album were cross-promoted by Warner Entertainment, which spent $3.5 million for television ads, and by MTV, which ran footage from the celebrity-packed premiere party in Hollywood. The single of "When Doves Cry" was released a few weeks before *Purple Rain* appeared in theaters and helped to boost the film's popularity, which in turn helped several other songs on the soundtrack to reach the Top 40.

The plot and characters of *Purple Rain* draw heavily on the details of Prince's life, both personal and professional. Prince stars as "the Kid," a young, gifted musician struggling to establish himself in the nightclub scene of Minneapolis. His main competition in the musical arena is Morris Day, the real-life leader of one of Prince's "satellite" projects, the Time. The Kid is attracted to a beautiful young singer named Apollonia (another of Prince's real-life protégés), who in the film is also being pursued by Morris Day. The Kid's parents—the only characters in the film portrayed by professional actors—are to some degree based on Prince's mother and father. Another subplot has to do with the Kid's inability to accept creative input from the musicians in his band, the Revolution. The film concludes on a relatively upbeat note as the Kid adopts one of his father's compositions, incorporating a rhythm track created by members of the Revolution, and creates the song "Purple Rain," which wins over his audience, the band, Apollonia, and even Morris Day.

As with any semiautobiographical work, it is not easy to draw boundaries between the fictional character (the Kid), the celebrity persona (Prince), and the private individual (Prince Rogers Nelson). The character of the Kid—talented, self-absorbed, obsessed with exerting control over his music and his career, troubled by family conflicts and an inability to sustain intimate relationships—seems consonant with the accounts offered by Prince's family and professional associates. Apart from the Academy Award–winning soundtrack, a major source of the film's attraction for Prince's fans no doubt lay in the idea that this was a form of public psychoanalysis, a tantalizing opportunity to catch a glimpse of the "man behind the curtain." If *Purple Rain* is a film with genuinely confessional aspects, it is also a product of the increasingly sophisticated marketing strategies applied by entertainment corporations during the 1980s.

LISTENING TO "WHEN DOVES CRY" (1984)

"When Doves Cry"—a last-minute addition to the *Purple Rain* soundtrack—is an unusual pop recording in a number of regards. To begin with, the album track runs almost six minutes, a length that, although not without precedent, was much longer than the typical Top 40 hit of the 1980s. (A shortened version was released as a single.) Pop music recordings of the 1980s—such as Madonna's "Like a Virgin"—were typically the product of collaboration among the singer, songwriter(s), producer, studio engineers, session musicians, and others. "When Doves Cry," on the other hand, is essentially the work of a single person—Prince wrote the song, produced the recording, sang all of the vocal parts, and played all of the instruments, including electric guitar, keyboard synthesizers, and the Linn LM-1 digital drum machine. The lyric of "When Doves Cry," with its striking imagery and psychoanalytical implications, certainly does not conform to the usual formulas of romantic pop song. In addition, this recording crosses over the boundaries of established pop genres, fusing a funk rhythm with the lead guitar sound of heavy metal, the digitally synthesized and sampled textures of post-disco dance music, and the aesthetic focus and control of progressive rock and the singer-songwriter tradition. In this sense it is a good example both of Prince's desire to avoid being typecast as a traditional R&B artist and of the creative eclecticism that led music critics to come up with labels such as "dance rock," "funk rock," or "new wave funk" to describe his music.

The instrumentation of "When Doves Cry" is also somewhat unusual, as it lacks a bass part. Usually the bass helps to establish the tonality (or key) of a given piece of music and combines with the drums to provide the rhythmic bedrock of a recording. Prince's decision to "punch out" (exclude) the bass track that he had already recorded—apparently a spur-of-the-moment experiment during the process of mixing—gives the recording an unusually open feeling. In addition, Prince's composition avoids the tendency, pronounced in many rock and pop recordings, to establish a clear distinction between a verse and a chorus, each having its own distinctive melody and harmonies. "When Doves Cry" does use the verse-and-chorus form, but the melody and supporting harmonies are almost identical in the two sections, making the distinction between them much less fixed. While many pop recordings use the verse-chorus structure to build to a final climax, followed by a relatively rapid fade-out, the musical intensity of "When Doves Cry" rises and falls continuously, creating a complex succession of peaks and valleys. (One critic has interpreted this "ebbing and flowing of pleasure" as embodying a female rather than male pattern of sexual excitement and has connected this musical approach to Prince's embracing of female qualities in his own personality.) Finally, the studio mix is also unusual, relatively spare and dry, and quite unlike the lush, reverb-laden studio sound of most 1980s dance music recordings (including Madonna's hit singles). Prince does use studio effects such as echo and digital processing, but they are tightly controlled and focused.

The arrangement of "When Doves Cry" can be divided into two major sections. Section One, about three and a half minutes in length, is basically a presentation of the song, with its alternation of verse (A) and chorus (B). Section Two consists of a series of eight-bar phrases in which the background texture is subtly varied while instrumental solos (guitar and keyboard synthesizer), sung phrases (both solo and overdubbed in harmony), and other vocal effects (breathing, screaming, sighing, groaning) are sometimes juxtaposed or layered on top of one another, and sometimes alternated one after the other. Perhaps the best analogy for the overall effect of this recording is that of a weaving, made up of patches of subtly shifting textural effects and tone colors, held together by the strong threads of a funk-derived dance groove, and strung on a formal loom made up of eight-bar sections. This is a recording that rewards repeated listening, not least because one musician has created every sound that you hear throughout.

"When Doves Cry" opens abruptly with a virtuoso burst of lead guitar, establishing from the very first moment Prince's mastery of the hard rock idiom. (We could say that Prince was able to do for himself what Michael Jackson needed Eddie Van Halen's help to accomplish on his *Thriller* album.) As the main dance groove is established on the Linn LM-1 digital drum machine, the guitar plays five more bars. We then hear a strange yet recognizably human sound, a pattern created by running Prince's voice through a digital processor and turning it into a repeating loop. As the keyboard synthesizer introduces a chord pattern that interlocks rhythmically with the drum machine (completing the basic groove that will carry us through most of the recording), Prince's voice moves across the stereo space of the recording from left to right and then fades out. Only sixteen bars into the recording, it is clear that this is not your normal pop single.

The first half of the arrangement (Section One) begins by placing equal weight on the verse and the chorus material (sixteen bars each) and then gradually deemphasizes the verse (A), which finally disappears altogether (see the listening chart). The chorus is always followed by an eight-bar groove section, in which the underlying drum machine–and–synthesizer dance rhythm is brought to the fore. The presentation of the song, with its weakly contrasted verse-chorus structure, makes full use of studio technology, and of Prince's remarkable abilities as a singer. In the first verse he sings alone, in a middle-register voice. The second verse introduces a second copy of Prince, another middle-register voice that overlaps slightly with the first one; as this concludes, the two Princes sing together, first in unison, then in overdubbed harmony. In the chorus ("How can you . . .") these two voices are joined by a third, low-register, growling voice; eventually ("Maybe you're . . . "), we are presented with four Princes singing in harmony with one another, plus a fifth Prince who interjects solo responses.

The second half of "When Doves Cry" (Section Two) presents an even more complex palette of timbral and textural variations, playing with combinations of the drum machine–plus–synthesizer groove, sustained orchestral sounds, instrumental solos (including a keyboard solo that resembles eighteenth-century music), and an astonishing variety of vocal timbres. If you listen closely you should be able to distinguish as many as a dozen unique voices in the studio mix, positioned to the left, right, and center, some heavily modified by digital technology, and others closer to the natural sound of Prince's singing voice. In addition to the complex patterns of harmony and call-and-response singing, Prince uses a variety of vocal effects, including a James Brown–like scream, rhythmic breathing, sighs, and groans. These sounds lend a sense of physical intimacy to the recording and enhance its aura of sexuality.

If "Like a Virgin" can be interpreted as a musical analogue to Madonna's "split personality," "When Doves Cry" may represent an even more complex set of psychological relations between the public persona and private personality of a pop superstar. In a 1996 television interview, Prince Rogers Nelson revealed that he, like millions of other children, had created an alternative personality, an imaginary companion who had not only helped him through the dislocations of his youth but also continued to offer him guidance as an adult. It may not be too much of a reach to suggest that the "multiple Princes" of "When Doves Cry"— a song that wears its Oedipal heart on its sleeve, so to speak—are not only an experiment in musical polyphony but also a conscious representation of the continuous inner dialogue that has shaped Prince's career. (In interviews, Prince has described how his "spirit" has advised him to change course, abandon projects, and even alter his name.) In its rich layering of instrumental textures and vocal personalities, "When Doves Cry" imparted to the public image of Prince a complexity and psychological depth that is in fact not typical of mass-media celebrities. And in the process, it established his reputation as one of the most creative and influential musicians of the 1980s.

LISTENING CHART   "WHEN DOVES CRY" (ALBUM VERSION)

Composed, performed and produced by Prince; recorded 1984

FORM	LYRICS	DESCRIPTIVE COMMENTS
Intro		Lead guitar solo, no accompaniment
Section One [0:03–3:19]		
Groove (8)		Dance tempo established on drum machine; guitar stops at end of bar 5; digitized loop of Prince's voice enters in bar 6 (L side).
Groove (8)		Keyboard synthesizer enters, playing main riff; Prince's voice loop moves [L to R], then fades (bars 1–4).
A (8)	*Dig if you will . . .*	Keyboard drops out; solo voice and drum machine only.
A (8)	*Dream if you can . . .*	Second solo voice enters (overlaps with first voice); two voices combined (overdubbed), bars 5–8; vocal harmony in bars 7–8 ("They feel the heat").
B: (8)	*How can you . . .*	New vocal timbre added (growling bass voice); solo voice responds in bar 4 ("So cold"); new synthesizer
+		pattern added (offbeats).
(8)	*Maybe you're . . .*	More overdubbed voices added; four-part vocal harmony; solo voice responds in bar 4 ("She's never satisfied").
Groove (8) [1:34]		Drum machine and keyboard synthesizer.
A (8) [1:50]	*Touch . . .*	Vocal sounds in background (groans, sighs).
B: (8) [2:05]	*How can you . . .*	New vocal timbre added (bass voice, growling); vocal responses in harmony.
+		
(8) [2:20]	*Maybe you're . . .*	More overdubbed voices added; four-part vocal harmony.

Groove (8) [2:35]		Drum machine and keyboard synthesizer; voices drift in and out (high falsetto timbre); vocal harmony riff (bars 7–8).
B: (8) **[2:50]**	*How can you . . .*	Synthesized string sounds added in background; four-part vocal harmony with solo voice responses.
+		
(8) **[3:05]**	*Maybe you're . . .*	Four-part vocal harmony with solo voice responses.

Section Two [3:20–5:51]

Interlude (8)	Synthesizer riff drops out; drum machine plus synthesized string sounds; Prince's "voices" overlap ("When doves cry").
Groove (8)	Groove reestablished; lead guitar solo begins; solo and duet voices drift in and out.

[NOTE: The single version of the song fades out and ends at this point.]

Groove (8)	Guitar solo; solo and duet voices drift in and out.
Groove (8) [4:06]	Guitar solo; solo and duet voices drift in and out; James Brown–style scream begins bar 5.
Groove (8)	Guitar solo ends; vocal sounds float over the groove (breathing, sighs, screams, groans).
Groove (8) [4:37]	Vocal sounds float over groove.
Groove (8)	Stoptime in rhythm section with vocal harmony response; keyboard solo begins bar 5.
Groove (8)	Keyboard solo continues with vocal riff background; groove reestablished in bar 5.
Groove (8)	Prince's "voices" overlap ("When doves cry"); synthesized strings.
Groove (8)	Prince's "voices" overlap ("Don't cry").
Coda	Rising melodic pattern on keyboard; synthesized strings in background.

The decade of the 1980s saw important shifts in the music business, starting with a precipitous decline in record sales unprecedented since the Great Depression; the introduction of digital technologies, including samplers and the compact disc; the increasing reliance of corporations on a small number of multiplatinum albums by megastars, promoted on the new medium of music video; and the continued splintering of the market for popular music into dozens of specialized audiences and genres. In Chapter 14 we will follow the development of alternative music movements such as hip-hop, hardcore, alternative rock, techno, and world beat from the 1980s into the 1990s, paying particular attention to conflicts over authenticity and commercialism (or "keeping it real" and "selling out").

CHAPTER FOURTEEN

"SMELLS LIKE TEEN SPIRIT"

Hip-Hop, "Alternative" Music, and the Entertainment Business

During the first decades of the twentieth century the market for popular music was clearly divided into a stylistic core—Tin Pan Alley love songs and ragtime- and jazz-influenced dance music, with the occasional touch of Latin American exoticism—and a periphery, including types of music that came to be known as race music, hillbilly music, and ethnic music. By the end of the twentieth century, it had become almost impossible to sustain a clear-cut dichotomy between the center of American popular music and its margins.

For one thing, the most economically successful popular music (in terms of record sales and radio airplay) no longer presented a coherent stylistic thumbprint. The bestselling albums of the 1990s featured an extraordinary variety of artists, ranging from "adult contemporary" divas such as Celine Dion, Janet Jackson, and Mariah Carey (the biggest-selling pop and R&B recording artist of the decade) to country music stars like Clint Black, Reba McEntire, Shania Twain, and Garth Brooks (the biggest-selling male artist of the decade), the R&B vocal quartet Boyz II Men, gangsta rappers such as Snoop Doggy Dogg, 2Pac Shakur, and the Notorious B.I.G., hard rock and heavy metal bands like Aerosmith and Metallica, punk-influenced alternative rock bands such as Nirvana, Pearl Jam, and the Red Hot Chili Peppers, the confessional "alternative singer-songwriter" Alanis Morissette, and hugely popular lush, romantic soundtrack albums for films such as *The Bodyguard* (1993) and *Titanic* (1996). Albums by new artists were very successful, as the record companies sought to identify and promote a new generation of pop superstars (in the process spending hundreds of millions of dollars on recording deals, in the hope of repeating the ever elusive Michael Jackson phenomenon). Five of the annual bestselling albums of the 1990s were in fact debut albums by previously unknown artists: Mariah Carey's eponymous debut album (1991); *The Sign* by the Swedish Euro-disco group Ace of Base (1994); the southern blues rock album *Cracked Rear View* by Hootie and the Blowfish (1995); Alanis Morissette's angst-ridden *Jagged Little Pill,* the best-selling album of the entire decade (1996); and *Spice* (1997), by teenybopper girl idols the Spice Girls.

Although the singles market as a whole continued to shrink, the 1990s did produce a number of the bestselling singles in history, including "One Sweet Day," an R&B-flavored love song by Mariah Carey and Boyz II Men, which held the Number One position for a record sixteen weeks in 1995; "Candle in the Wind 1997," retro-rocker Elton John's multiplatinum tribute to the late Princess Diana; and a Latin novelty number called "The Macarena," which swept the nation in a matter of weeks in 1996, inspiring a dance fad and supplementing the repertoire of songs performed by audiences at massive sporting events (a diverse corpus that also includes "Take Me Out to the Ballgame," composed in 1908 by Tin Pan Alley song-writers Albert von Tilzer and Jack Norworth, "We Will Rock You," by the 1970s arena rock band Queen, and the Village People's disco hit "YMCA").

Taken as a whole, then, the popular mainstream of the 1990s includes a jumble of old and new styles, slick pop and R&B, rock-influenced country music, and rough-edged, in-your-face alternative rock and rap music. It is these last two categories on which we wish to focus in this chapter. Throughout this book we have traced the relationship between mainstream popular music—the music that in any given era attracts the broadest audience, receives the widest dissemination via the mass media, and generates the bulk of profits for the music industry—and varieties of music that originate on the margins of the musical economy, where survival is predicated on patronage from particular regional or ethnic communities. Many of the strongest influences in the history of popular music have come from people historically excluded from power, wealth, and social mobility, including African Americans, the working class, rural southerners, and immigrant communities. More recently, ironically, the very notion of outsider, alternative, or marginal music has itself become a means of promoting music to a mass audience hungry for novelty, excitement, and a sense of authenticity.

In this chapter we will examine a group of genres and styles that originated outside the mainstream in one way or another. First, we will look at the history of *hip-hop*—the first street-based movement in black popular music since vocal-group R&B of the 1950s—and its transformation from a local outgrowth of minority youth culture in New York City into a multimillion-dollar global industry. Then, in the second half of the chapter, we will examine the concept of *alternative music,* a term that is used across a wide range of popular genres, including rock, rap, adult contemporary, dance, folk, and country music. We will begin this half of the discussion with a consideration of alternative rock, which emerged as a more-or-less underground movement in the early 1980s, combined the rebellious spirit and youth appeal of rock 'n' roll with the nihilism of punk rock, and during the 1990s led to the confounding spectacle of vociferously anticommercial artists playing at corporate-sponsored rock festivals and releasing multiplatinum albums for major record companies. We will then examine the meaning of the term "alternative" as it is applied to other genres, including urban folk music (Ani DiFranco), hip-hop (Lauryn Hill), and country music (k.d. lang), and we will take a brief look at the development of postdisco electronic dance music, or *techno*. Finally, our focus will turn to one of the few truly novel developments of the 1980s and 1990s: the emergence of so-called world music or world beat, a heterogeneous category that includes artists from Africa, the Near East, and Asia—the ultimate margins of the American music industry (and of the American musical imagination). While this category covers a great diversity of musical styles, we will focus on two examples of collaboration between American and non-Western artists.

Each of these musical genres or movements—hip-hop, alternative music, techno, world music—exemplifies the tensions and contradictions created when music is marketed to a mass audience specifically on the basis of its difference from or opposition to the popular mainstream, and taken as a whole, they give us a glimpse of the diversity and complexity of American popular music at the end of the twentieth century.

"DROPPIN' SCIENCE": HIP-HOP CULTURE AND RAP MUSIC

Of all the genres of popular music surveyed in this book, none has spurred more vigorous public debate than rap music. Rap has been characterized as a vital link in the centuries-old chain of cultural and musical connections between Africa and the Americas; as the authentic voice of an oppressed urban underclass; and as a form that exploits long-standing stereotypes of black people. In fact, each of these perspectives has something to tell us about the history and significance of rap music. Rap is indeed based on principles ultimately derived from African musical and verbal traditions. Evidence of these deep continuities may be found in features already discussed at length in earlier sections on African American music: an emphasis on rhythmic momentum and creativity; a preference for complex tone colors and dense textures; a keen appreciation of improvisational skill (in words and music); and an incorporative, innovative approach to musical technologies. Much rap music does constitute a cultural response to oppression and racism, a system for communication among black communities throughout the United States ("Black America's CNN," as rapper Chuck D once put it), and a source of insight into the values, perceptions, and conditions of people living in America's beleaguered urban communities. And finally, although rap music's origins and inspirations flow from black culture, the genre's audience has become decidedly multiracial, multicultural, and transnational. As rap has been transformed from a local phenomenon, located in a few neighborhoods in New York City, to a multimillion-dollar industry and a global cultural phenomenon, it has grown ever more complex and multifaceted.

The Origins of Hip-Hop, 1975-1979

Rap initially emerged during the 1970s as one part of a cultural complex called *hip-hop*. Hip-hop culture, forged by African American and Caribbean American youth in New York City, included distinctive styles of visual art (graffiti), dance (an acrobatic solo style called breakdancing and an energetic couple dance called the freak), music, dress, and speech. Hip-hop was at first a local phenomenon, centered in certain neighborhoods in the Bronx, the most economically devastated area of New York City. Federal budget cuts caused a severe decline in low-income housing and social services for the residents of America's inner cities during the mid-1970s. By 1977, when President Carter conducted a highly publicized motorcade tour through New York's most devastated neighborhoods, the South Bronx had become, as the *New York Times* put it, "a symbol of America's woes."

The youth culture that spawned hip-hop can on one level be interpreted as a response to the destruction of traditional family- and neighborhood-based institutions and the cutting of funding for public institutions such as community centers, and as an attempt to lay claim to—and, in a way, to "civilize"—an alienating and hostile urban environment. The young adults who pioneered hip-hop styles such as breakdancing, graffiti art, and rap music at nightclubs, block parties and in city parks often belonged to informal social groups called "crews" or "posses," each associated with a particular neighborhood or block. It is important to understand that hip-hop culture began as an expression of local identities. Even today's multiplatinum rap recordings, marketed worldwide, are filled with inside references to particular neighborhoods, features of the urban landscape, and social groups and networks.

If hip-hop music was a rejection of mainstream dance music by young black and Puerto Rican listeners, it was also profoundly shaped by the techniques of disco DJs. The first celebrities of hip-hop music—Kool Herc (Clive Campbell, born in Jamaica, 1955), Grandmaster Flash (Joseph Saddler, born in Barbados, 1958), and Afrika Bambaata (Kevin Donovan, born in the Bronx, 1960)—were DJs who began their careers in the mid-1970s, spinning records at neighborhood block parties, gym dances, and dance clubs, and in public spaces such as community centers and parks. These three young men—and dozens of lesser-known DJs scattered throughout the Bronx, Harlem, and other areas of New York City and New Jersey—developed their personal styles within a grid of fierce competition for celebrity and neighborhood pride. As Fab Five Freddie, an early graffiti artist and rapper, put it:

> You make a new style. That's what life on the street is all about. What's at stake is honor and position on the street. That's what makes it so important, that's what makes it feel so good—the pressure on you to be the best . . . to develop a new style nobody can deal with. (George 1985, p. 111)

The disco DJ's technique of "mixing" between two turntables to create smooth transitions between records was first adapted to the hip-hop aesthetic by Kool Herc, who had migrated from Kingston, Jamaica, to New York City at the age of twelve. Herc noticed that the young dancers in his audiences responded most energetically during the so-called breaks on funk and salsa records, brief sections where the melody was stripped away to feature the rhythm section. Herc responded by isolating the breaks of certain popular records—such as James Brown's "Get on the Good Foot"—and mixing them into the middle of other dance records. These rhythmic sound collages came to be known as "breakbeat" music, a term subsequently transferred to "breakdancing," acrobatic solo performances improvised by the young "B-boys" who attended hip-hop dances.

Another innovation helped to shape the sound and sensibility of early hip-hop: the transformation of the turntable from a medium for playing back recorded sound into a playable musical instrument. Sometime in the mid-1970s Kool Herc began to put two copies of the same record on his turntables. Switching back and forth between the turntables, Herc found that he could "backspin" one disc (i.e., turn it backwards, or counterclockwise, with his hand) while the other continued to play over the loudspeakers. This allowed him to repeat a given break over and over, by switching back and forth between the two discs and backspinning to the beginning of the break. This technique was refined by Grandmaster Flash, who adopted the mixing techniques of disco DJs, particularly their use of headphones to synchronize the tempos of recordings and to create smooth transitions from one dance groove to the next. Using headphones, Flash could more precisely pinpoint the beginning of a break by listening to the sound of the disc being turned backward on the turntable. Flash spent many hours practicing this technique and gained local fame for his ability to "punch in" brief, machine gun-like segments of sound.

A new technique called "scratching" was developed by Flash's young protégé, Theodore, who broke away and formed his own hip-hop crew at the tender age of thirteen. In 1978 Theodore debuted a new technique that quickly spread through the community of DJs. While practicing backspinning in his room, Theodore began to pay closer attention to the sounds created in his headphones as he turned the disc counterclockwise. He soon discovered that this technique yielded scratchy, percussive sound effects, which could be punched in to the dance groove. At first Theodore wasn't sure how people would react:

> The Third Avenue Ballroom was packed, and I figured I might as well give it a try. So, I put on two copies of [James Brown's] "Sex Machine" and started scratching up one. The crowd loved it . . . they went wild. (Hager 1984, p. 38)

The distinctive sound of scratching became an important part of the sonic palette of hip-hop music—even in the 1990s, after digital sampling had largely displaced turntables as a means of creating the musical textures and grooves on rap records, producers frequently used these sounds as a way of signaling a connection to the "old school" origins of hip-hop.

Although all DJs used microphones to make announcements, Kool Herc was also one of the first DJs to recite rhyming phrases over the "breakbeats" produced on his turntables. Some of Herc's "raps" were based on a tradition of verbal performance called "toasting," a form of poetic storytelling with roots in the trickster tales of West Africa. The trickster—a sly character whose main goal in life is to defy authority and upset the normal order of things—became a common figure in the storytelling traditions of black slaves in the United States, where he took on additional significance as a symbol of cultural survival and covert resistance. After the Civil War the figure of the trickster was in part supplanted by more aggressive male figures, the focus of long, semi-improvised poetic stories called "toasts." The toasting tradition frequently focused on "bad men," hard, merciless bandits and spurned lovers who vanquished their enemies, sometimes by virtue of their wits, but more often through physical violence.

Although the toasting tradition had largely disappeared from black communities by the 1970s, it took root in prisons, where black inmates found that the old narrative form suited their life experiences and present circumstances. One of the main sources for the rhymes composed by early hip-hop DJs in the Bronx was the album *Hustler's Convention* (1973), by Jala Uridin, leader of a group of militant ex-convicts known as the Last Poets. *Hustler's Convention* was a compelling portrait of "the life"—the urban underworld of gamblers, pimps, and hustlers—comprising prison toasts with titles like "Four Bitches Is What I Got" and "Sentenced to the

Chair." The record, featuring musical accompaniment by an all-star lineup of funk, soul, and jazz musicians, became enormously popular in the Bronx and inspired Kool Herc and other DJs to compose their own rhymes. Soon DJs were recruiting members of their posses to serve as verbal performers, or "MCs" (an abbreviation of the term "master of ceremonies"). MCs played an important role in controlling crowd behavior at the increasingly large dances where DJs performed and soon became more important celebrities than the DJs themselves. If DJs are the predecessors of today's rap producers—responsible for shaping musical texture and groove—MCs are the ancestors of contemporary rappers.

Hip-Hop Breaks Out, 1979–1988

Until 1979 hip-hop music remained primarily a local phenomenon. The first indication of the genre's broader commercial potential was the twelve-inch dance single "Rapper's Delight," recorded by the Sugarhill Gang, a crew based in Harlem. This record, which popularized the use of the term "rapper" as an equivalent for MC, established Sugar Hill Records—a black-owned independent label based in New Jersey—as the predominant institutional force in rap music during the early 1980s. The recording recycled the rhythm section track from Chic's "Good Times" (see Chapter 12), played in the studio by session musicians usually hired by Sugar Hill to back R&B singers. The three rappers—Michael "Wonder Mike" Wright, Guy "Master Gee" O'Brien, and Henry "Big Bank Hank" Jackson—recited a rapid-fire succession of rhymes, typical of the performances of MCs at hip-hop dances.

> Well it's on-n-on-n-on-on-n-on
> The beat don't stop until the break of dawn
>
> I said M-A-S, T-E-R, a G with a double E
> I said I go by the unforgettable name
> Of the man they call the Master Gee
>
> Well, my name is known all over the world
> By all the foxy ladies and the pretty girls
>
> I'm goin' down in history
> As the baddest rapper there could ever be

The text of "Rapper's Delight" alternates the braggadocio of the three MCs with descriptions of dance movements, exhortations to the audience, and humorous stories and references. One particularly memorable segment describes the consternation of a guest who is served rotting food by his friend's mother, seeks a polite way to refuse it, and finally escapes by crashing through the apartment door. The record reached Number Four on the R&B chart and Number Thirty-six on the pop chart and introduced hip-hop to millions of people throughout the United States and abroad. The unexpected success of "Rapper's Delight" ushered in a series of million-selling twelve-inch singles by New York rappers, including Kurtis Blow's "The Breaks" (Number Four R&B, Number Eighty-seven pop in 1980), "Planet Rock," by Afrika Bambaata and the Soul Sonic Force (Number Four R&B, Number Forty-eight pop in 1982), and "The Message", by Grandmaster Flash and the Furious Five (Number Four R&B, Number Sixty-two pop in 1982).

While most of the early hip-hop crossover hits featured relatively predictable party-oriented raps, "The Message" established a new (and, in the end, profoundly influential) trend in rap music: social realism. In a recording that links the rhythmic intensity of funk music with the toast-derived images of ghetto life in *Hustler's Convention*, "The Message" is a grim, almost cinematic portrait of life in the South Bronx. The rap on the first half of the recording was cowritten by Sylvia Robinson, a former R&B singer and co-owner of Sugar Hill Records, and Duke Bootee, a sometime member of the Furious Five. (Resident Sugar Hill percussionist Ed Fletcher composed the musical track, using a Roland 808 digital drum machine and keyboard synthesizer, embellished with various studio effects.) On top of the stark, cold electronic groove Grandmaster Flash intones the rap's grim opening hook:

It's like a jungle sometimes, makes me wonder how I keep from goin' under

The sudden sound of glass shattering (produced on the drum machine) introduces a rhythmically complex and carefully articulated performance that alternates the smooth, slyly humorous style of Grandmaster Flash with the edgy, frustrated tone of MC Melle Mel:

Don't push me 'cause I'm close to the edge
I'm tryin' not to lose my head
Ah huh huh huh huh

The two MCs—Melle Mel in particular—time their performances with great precision, speeding up and slowing down, compressing and stretching the spaces between words, and creating polyrhythms against the steady musical pulse. The lyric alternates between the humorous wordplay typical of hip-hop MC performances and various images of desperation—threatening bill collectors, a homeless woman "living in a bag," violent encounters in Central Park, a young child alienated by deteriorating public schools. The relationship between the grim reality of ghetto life and the tough-minded humor that is its essential antidote is summed up by Melle Mel's humorless quasi-laugh: "Ah huh huh huh huh."

The second half of "The Message"—a *Hustler's Convention*–style toast written and performed by Melle Mel—paints an even more chilling picture, an account of the life and death of a child born into poverty in the South Bronx:

A child is born with no state of mind
Blind unto the ways of Mankind
God is smiling on you, but he's frowning too
Because only God knows what you'll go through . . .

You'll admire all the number-book takers,
Thugs, pimps and pushers, and the big money makers
Driving big cars, spendin' 20s and 10s
And you want to grow up to be just like them, huh-huh . . .

Now you're unemployed, all null and void
Walkin' round like you're Pretty Boy Floyd
Turned stick-up kid, but look what you done did
Got sent up for a eight year bid [prison term] . . .

It was plain to see that your life was lost
You was cold and your body swung back and forth
But now your eyes sing the sad, sad song
Of how you lived so fast and died so young.

This recitation is followed by the sound of the Furious Five—MCs Cowboy, Kidd Creole, Rahiem, Scorpio, and Mel—meeting and greeting on a street corner and discussing the evening's plans. Suddenly a police car screeches up and officers emerge, barking orders at the young black men. "What are you, a *gang*?," one of the policemen shouts. "Nah, man, we're with Grandmaster Flash and the Furious Five." Flash enters from one side to defend his friends: "Officer, officer, what's the problem?" "You're the problem," the cop shouts back, "get in the car!" We hear the car driving away with the Furious Five in custody, arrested evidently for the crime of assembling on a street corner, and the track quickly "fades to black."

A whole stream within the subsequent history of rap music can be traced from this gritty record, ranging from the explicitly political raps of KRS-One and Public Enemy to the "gangsta" style of Los Angeles MCs like N.W.A., Snoop Doggy Dogg, and 2Pac Shakur. As the first honest description of life on the streets of the nation's urban ghettos in the 1980s to achieve wide commercial circulation, "The Message" helped to establish canons of realness and street credibility that are still vitally important to rap musicians and audiences.

Gold records like "Rapper's Delight" and "The Message" created opportunities for New York rappers to perform at venues outside their own neighborhoods and thereby widen their audience. They also alerted the major record companies to the commercial potential of hip-hop, eventually leading to the transition from the twelve-inch dance single as the primary medium for recorded rap (an inheritance from disco) to the rap album. The mid-1980s saw a rapid acceleration of rap's movement into the popular mainstream. In 1983 the jazz fusion musician Herbie Hancock collaborated with DJ Grandmixer DST on "Rockit," which made the R&B Top 10 and was played frequently on the still-young MTV channel. The following year, the popular soul singer Chaka Khan invited Melle Mel to provide a rap introduction for her hit single "I Feel for You," an adaptation of a Prince song that went to Number One R&B and Number Three pop.

The year 1986 saw the release of the first two multiplatinum rap albums, *Raising Hell* by Run-D.M.C. (which reached Number Three on *Billboard*'s Top Pop Albums chart and sold over three million copies) and *Licensed to Ill* by the Beastie Boys (Number One for seven weeks, with over seven million copies sold). That neither Run-D.M.C. nor the Beastie Boys hailed from the Bronx indicates the expanding appeal of rap music in the New York area. The key to the commercial success of these albums, however, was the expansion of the audience for hip-hop music, which now included millions of young white fans, attracted by the transgressive, rebellious sensibility of the genre. Both *Raising Hell* and *Licensed to Ill* were released on a new independent label called Def Jam, cofounded in 1984 by the hip-hop promoter Russell Simmons and the musician-producer Rick Rubin. During the 1980s Def Jam took up where Sugar Hill Records left off, cross-promoting a new generation of artists, expanding and diversifying the national audience for hip-hop, and in 1986 becoming the first rap-oriented independent label to sign a distribution deal with one of the "Big Five" record companies, Columbia Records.

Run-D.M.C.—a trio consisting of the MCs <u>Run</u> (Joseph Simmons, b. 1964) and <u>D.M.C.</u> (Darryl McDaniels, b. 1964), and the DJ <u>Jam Master Jay</u> (Jason Mizell, b. 1965)—was perhaps the most influential act in the history of rap music. Simmons, McDaniels, and Mizell were college-educated black men, raised in a middle-class neighborhood in the borough of Queens. Working with Russell Simmons (Run's older brother) and producer Rick Rubin, they established a hard-edged, rock-influenced style that was to influence profoundly the sound and sensibility of later rap music. Their raps were literate and rhythmically skilled, with Run and D.M.C. weaving their phrases together and sometimes even completing the last few words of one another's lines. The "beats" produced by Rubin and Jam Master Jay were stark and powerful, mixing digitized loops of hard rock drumming with searing guitar sounds from heavy metal. Run-D.M.C. was the first rap group to headline a national tour and the first to appear on MTV. They popularized rap among the young, predominantly white audience for rock music; gave the genre a more rebellious image; and introduced hip-hop sartorial style—hats, gold chains, and untied Adidas sports shoes with fat laces—to millions of young Americans. The now familiar connection between rap music and athletic wear was established in 1986 when the Adidas corporation and Run-D.M.C. signed a $1.5 million promotional deal.

Run-D.M.C. Courtesy BMI Archives.

The creative and commercially successful synergy between rock music and hip-hop pioneered by Def Jam Records and Run-D.M.C. is well illustrated in "Walk This Way" (Number Four pop, Number Eight R&B in 1986), the gold single that propelled *Raising Hell* nearly to the top of the album charts. "Walk This Way," a collaboration between Run-D.M.C. and the popular hard rock group Aerosmith, was a cover version of a song written and previously recorded by Aerosmith. (Aerosmith brought a large portion of the hard rock audience to the table, having sold over twenty-five million albums since the early 1970s.) The recording opens with a sample of rock drumming from the original recording, interrupted by the sound of a turntable scratching, and the main riff of the song, played by Aerosmith's guitarist Joe Perry. Run and D.M.C. trade lines of the song's verses in an aggressive, shouted style that matches the intensity of the rock rhythm section. The chorus ("Walk this way, talk this way . . . ") is performed by Aerosmith's Steven Tyler, who sings the lyrics in a high, strained voice, a timbre associated with heavy metal music. As the track progresses, Run, D.M.C., and Tyler combine vocal forces in the interest of collective mayhem, and the recording ends with a virtuoso guitar solo by Joe Perry.

The video version of "Walk This Way"—the first rap video to be put into heavy rotation by MTV—gives visual substance to the musical image of a tense conversation between the worlds of hard rock and rap, unified by the sizzling textures of hip-hop scratching and hard rock guitar, the contrasting but similarly aggressive vocal timbres of Run-D.M.C. and Steven Tyler, and the over-the-top male braggadocio of the song's text. (The lyrics to "Walk This Way," with references to horny cheerleaders and high school locker room voyeurism, suggest that one of the few things shared by the predominantly male audiences for rap and rock was a decidedly adolescent approach to sex.) The video opens with Run-D.M.C. performing in a small sound studio. The amplified sound of turntable scratching penetrates a wall that separates this intimate but restricted musical world from that of a hard rock concert, held on the stage of a huge arena. Disturbed by the noise, the members of Aerosmith use their guitars to punch a hole in the wall, through which Run-D.M.C. run onto the stage of the concert and basically take over the show. Initially met with scowls from Tyler and Perry, the rappers succeed in winning them over, and the video ends in discordant harmony, with the huge, largely white crowd cheering. It is difficult to think of a more explicit (or more calculated) acting out of the process of black-white crossover in the history of American popular music, and the video of "Walk This Way" doubtless played a pivotal role in the mainstreaming of rap music. (Run-D.M.C. was not the first rap group to incorporate textures and grooves from rock music. Early hip-hop DJs Kool Herc and Afrika Bambaata regularly used breaks from groups like the Rolling Stones and Led Zeppelin.)

The Beastie Boys, the rap trio whose album *Licensed to Ill* topped the pop charts a few months after the release of *Raising Hell,* were the first commercially successful white act in hip-hop. Like Run-D.M.C., their recordings were produced by Rick Rubin, released on Def Jam Records, and benefited greatly from the distribution deal signed by Russell Simmons with industry giant Columbia Records. Although they received a great deal of criticism for ripping off a black style, it is perhaps more accurate to suggest that their early recordings represent a fusion of the youth-oriented rebelliousness of hardcore punk rock—the style that they began playing in 1981—with the sensibility and techniques of hip-hop. In 1985 the Beastie Boys were signed by Def Jam Records, appeared in *Krush Groove*—one of the first films to deal with hip-hop culture—and toured as the opening act for both Madonna and Run-D.M.C. The following year *Licensed to Ill,* their first album, sold 720,000 copies in six weeks and thereby became Columbia Records' fastest-selling debut album up to that point. The most popular track on the album, the Top 10 frat-boy anthem "(You Gotta) Fight for Your Right (To Party)" (a hit in 1987), established the Beastie Boys' appeal for the most rapidly expanding segment of the rap audience, young white males. After leaving Def Jam Records in 1988, the Beastie Boys continued to experiment with combinations of rap, heavy metal, punk, and psychedelic rock, and they scored a series of critical and commercial successes in the 1990s, culminating with the release of their 1998 album *Hello Nasty.*

By 1987 a series of million-selling singles had proven rap's commercial potential on the pop and R&B charts; the hits included rap ballads (L.L. Cool J's "I Need Love," Number One R&B, Number Nine pop in 1987), women's rap (Salt-N-Pepa's "Push It," Number Nineteen pop, Number Twenty-eight R&B in 1987), humorous party records (Tone-Lōc's "Wild Thing," Number Two pop, Number Three R&B in 1987), and rap specifically targeted at a young adolescent audience ("Parents Just Don't Understand" by D.J. Jazzy Jeff and the Fresh Prince, the gold single that established the career of actor Will Smith, which reached Number Twelve pop and Number Ten R&B in 1988). A number of the small independent labels that had sprung up to feed the growing demand for hip-hop music—Jive Records, Cold Chillin' Records, Tommy Boy Records, and Priority Records—followed the lead of Def Jam, signing distribution deals with the multinational entertainment conglomerates.

If 1986 and 1987 saw the emergence of new markets for hip-hop music, 1988 brought possibly an even more important milestone: the launching of MTV's first show dedicated entirely to hip-hop music. Hosted by hip-hop raconteur Fab Five Freddie Braithwaite, *Yo! MTV Raps* immediately attracted the largest audience in the network's history and was soon being broadcast on a daily basis. The mass popularity of rap was also reflected in the appearance of *The Source,* the first periodical devoted solely to hip-hop music and fashion. Over the subsequent decade *The Source* became the largest-selling music periodical in America, surpassing by a wide margin even such long-established publications as *Rolling Stone.* In 1988 the National Academy of Recording Arts and Sciences added a rap category to the Grammy Awards, and *Billboard* added a rap singles chart. This mainstreaming of rap music had a number of interesting consequences. While some rappers and producers focused their energies on creating multiplatinum crossover hits, others reacted against the commercialism of "pop rap," reanimating the tradition of social realism that had informed recordings like "The Message" and creating a more hardcore sound that paradoxically ended up generating some of the biggest crossover hits of all.

The tradition of socially engaged rap, chronicling the declining fortunes of urban black communities, received its strongest new impetus from the New York–based group Public Enemy. Founded in 1982, Public Enemy was organized around a core set of members who met as college students, drawn together by their interest in hip-hop culture and political activism. The standard hip-hop configuration of two MCs—Chuck D (a.k.a. Carlton Ridenhour, b. 1960) and Flavor Flav (William Drayton, b. 1959)—plus a DJ—Terminator X (Norman Lee Rogers, b. 1966)—was augmented by a "Minister of Information" (Professor Griff, a.k.a.

Public Enemy. Courtesy BMI Archives.

Richard Griffin) and by the Security of the First World (S1W), a cohort of dancers who dressed in paramilitary uniforms, carried Uzi machine guns, and performed a martial arts–inspired parody of Motown choreography.

The release of Public Enemy's second album in 1988—*It Takes a Nation of Millions to Hold Us Back* (Number One R&B, Number Forty-two pop)—was a breakthrough event for rap music. The album fused the trenchant social and political analyses of Chuck D—delivered in a deep, authoritative voice—with the streetwise interjections of his sidekick Flavor Flav, who wore comical glasses and an oversized clock around his neck. Their complex verbal interplay was situated within a dense, multilayered sonic web created by the group's production team, the Bomb Squad (Hank Shocklee, Keith Shocklee, and Eric "Vietnam" Sadler). Tracks like "Countdown to Armageddon" (an apocalyptic opening instrumental track, taped at a live concert in London), "Don't Believe the Hype" (a critique of white-dominated mass media), and "Party for Your Right to Fight" (a parody of the Beastie Boys' hit "Fight for Your Right (To Party)," from the previous year) turned the technology of digital sampling to new artistic purposes and insisted in effect that rap music continue to engage with the real-life conditions of urban black communities.

"Night of the Living Baseheads" is an instructive example of the moral authority and musical complexity of many of Public Enemy's recordings. The lyrics for "Night of the Living Baseheads" combine images of corpselike zombies with a commentary on the crack cocaine epidemic that was sweeping through America's inner cities during the 1980s. The track opens with the voice of the black nationalist leader Louis Farrakhan, sampled from one of his speeches:

> Have you forgotten that once we were brought here, we were robbed of our names, robbed of our language, we lost our religion, our culture, our God? And many of us, by the way we act, we even lost our minds.

With these words still ringing in our ears, we are suddenly dropped into the middle of a complexly textured groove. The lead MC of Public Enemy, Chuck D, opens with a verbal explosion, a play on words derived from hip-hop slang:

> *Here it is*
> *BAMMM*
> *And you say, Goddamn*
> *This is the dope jam*
> *But lets define the term called dope*
> *And you think it mean funky now, no*

In hip-hop argot the term "dope" carries a double meaning: it can function as a positive adjective, broadly equivalent to older terms such as "cool," "hip," or "funky"; or as a reference to psychoactive drugs, ranging from marijuana to the new, more devastating drug being critiqued by Chuck D in "Night of the Living Baseheads," crack cocaine. The rhetorical tactic of announcing the arrival of a compelling performance (a "dope jam") and thereby laying claim to the listener's attention is common in rap recordings. Chuck D takes this opening gambit and plays with it, redefining the term "dope jam" as a message about drug use and its effects on the black community. At the end of each stanza of his rap, Chuck D uses another pun, based on the homonyms "bass" (the deep, booming tones favored by rap producers) and "base" (a shorthand reference to "freebase," or crack cocaine).

> *Sellin', smellin'*
> *Sniffin', riffin'*
> *And brothers try to get swift an'*
> *Sell to their own, rob a home*
> *While some shrivel to bone*
> *Like comatose walkin' around*
> *Please don't confuse this with the sound*
> *I'm talking about . . . BASE*

Chuck D presents here a chilling snapshot of the effects of crack on the human body ("Some shrivel to bone, like comatose walkin' around"), and uses the bass/base pun to draw a contrast between the aesthetics of hip-hop and the devastating scourge of crack cocaine ("please don't confuse this [base] with the sound [bass]"). After this first occurrence, the bass/base homonym returns periodically in a syncopated, digitally sampled loop that punctuates the thickly layered sonic texture created by the Bomb Squad. Chuck D goes on to scold black drug dealers for victimizing members of their own community ("Shame on a brother when he dealin' [drugs on] the same block where my [Oldsmobile] 98 be wheelin'"). A sampled verbal phrase ("How low can you go?") is used as a rhythmic and rhetorical device to set up the final sequence of Chuck D's rap, which concludes with the story of a crack addict, a former hip-hop MC fallen on bad times:

> Daddy-O once said to me
> He knew a brother who stayed all day in his jeep
> And at night he went to sleep
> And in the mornin' all he had was
> The sneakers on his feet
> The culprit used to jam and rock the mike, yo
> He stripped the jeep to fill his pipe
> And wander around to find a place
> Where they rocked to a different kind of . . . come on, y'all
> [Samples of voices]
> I'm talkin' 'bout BASE

The grim message of "Night" is enveloped in a jagged, stark sonic landscape, layered with fractured words and vocal noises, bits and pieces of music and other sounds sewn together like a crazy quilt. The producers incorporated digital samples from no fewer than thirteen different recorded sources, among them an early twelve-inch rap single, several soul music records, a gospel music group, a glam rock record, and the sound of drums and air-raid sirens. In musical terms, "Night of the Living Baseheads" is like a complex archeological dig, a site richly layered with sonic objects, the cumulative meaning of which depends on the cultural and musical expertise of the listener.

Although rap is often regarded primarily as a verbal genre, a recording like "Night of the Living Baseheads," with its carefully constructed pastiche of sampled sound sources, compels us to consider rap *as music.* Hank Shocklee has argued vociferously for a broader conception of music and musicianship:

> Music is nothing but organized noise. You can take anything—street sounds, us talking, whatever you want—and make it music by organizing it. That's still our philosophy, to show people that this thing you call music is a lot broader than you think it is. (Rose 1994, p. 82)

This philosophy is similar to that expressed by certain art music composers throughout the twentieth century who have used tape recorders, digital technology, and elements of noise in their works. But it could be argued that the most extensive and creative use of the technology of digital sampling has been made in dance music—hip-hop, R&B, house music, and techno—rather than in contemporary art music composition. Rather than creating a cold, disembodied form of self-expression—as many critics of the new technologies had feared—digital technology in pop music has often been used to create communal experiences on the dance floor. On the other hand, some critics bemoan what they see as a lack of creativity in much contemporary rap music, referring to the practice of sampling as "artistic necrophilia" and the end product as "Memorex music." Whatever one's position on these matters, Public Enemy's "Night of the Living Baseheads" stands as a pioneering example of the creative and social potential of digital sound technologies.

Commercialization, Diversification, and the Rise of Gangsta Rap (1990s)

The expanding nationwide appeal of rap music during the late 1980s and early 1990s followed a familiar pattern. At the same time that some artists moved toward the pop mainstream, developing styles that blended the verbal cadences of rap and the techniques of digital sampling with R&B-derived dance rhythms and vocal styles, a variety of alternative rap styles emerged, reflecting the attitudes, experiences, and dialects of particular segments of the hip-hop audience. Interestingly, these marginal variants of hip-hop—especially so-called *gangsta rap*—ended up generating millions and millions of dollars in profits for the record industry.

The year 1990 was a watershed year for the mainstreaming of hip-hop. M. C. Hammer (Stanley Kirk Burrell, b. 1962), a rapper from Oakland, California, hit the charts in March of that year with *Please Hammer Don't Hurt 'Em*, which held the Number One position for twenty-one weeks and sold over ten million copies, becoming the bestselling rap album of all time. Hammer's celebrity was boosted by music videos that highlighted his impressive abilities as a dancer, by his appearances in corporate soft drink advertisements, and even by a short-lived children's cartoon show, called *Hammerman*. At the height of his popularity, Hammer was attacked by many in the hip-hop community for his lack of skill as a rapper and for pandering to a mass audience. There can be no denying that Hammer's success pushed rap fully into the mainstream, continuing a trend started in the mid-1980s by Run-D.M.C. and the Beastie Boys. At the same time, Hammer's pop-friendly rap style opened the door for an artist widely considered hip-hop's icon of "wackness" (weakness), the white rapper Vanilla Ice (Robert Van Winkle, born 1968 in Florida). Ice's first album, *To the Extreme* (1990), monopolized the Number One position for sixteen weeks in early 1991, selling seven million copies. In hip-hop culture, a performer's credibility is correlated by fans not only with musical and verbal skill but also with the degree to which the artist in question possesses "street knowledge," that is, firsthand experience of the urban culture that spawned rap music. When it was discovered that Van Winkle, raised in reasonably comfortable circumstances in a middle-class neighborhood, had essentially invented a gangster persona for himself—a form of misrepresentation known in hip-hop parlance as "perpetrating"—many fans turned their backs on him. It is undeniable that race was also a factor in the rejection of Vanilla Ice, for he was widely regarded as being merely the latest in a long line of untalented white artists seeking to make a living off the fruits of black creativity. Yet some white rappers and producers—for example, the Beastie Boys—have managed to gain acceptance as legitimate hip-hop artists, largely by virtue of their ability to forge a distinctive style within the parameters of an African American tradition.

By the late 1980s a number of distinctive regional variations on the formula of hip-hop music were well established in cities such as Philadelphia, Cleveland, Miami, Atlanta, Houston, Seattle, Oakland, and Los Angeles. The music critic Nelson George noted this process of regionalization:

> The rap that'll flow from down South, the Midwest and the West Coast will not, and should not, feel beholden to what came before. Just as hip-hop spit in the face of disco (and funk too), non–New York hip-hop will have its own accent, its own version of b-boy wisdom, if it's to mean anything. (George 1998, p. 132)

During this period southern California became a primary center of hip-hop innovation, supported by a handful of independent labels and one of the few commercial AM stations nationwide to feature hip-hop programming (KDAY). The sound of "new school" West Coast rap differed from "old school" New York hip-hop in a number of regards. The edgy, rapid-fire delivery of Melle Mel and Run-D.M.C. remained influential but was augmented by a smoother, more laid-back style of rapping. The dialects of southern California rappers, many of them the offspring of migrants from Louisiana and Texas, also contributed to the distinctive flavor of West Coast rap. And if the verbal delivery of West Coast rap was sometimes cooler, the content of the MCs' recitations themselves became angrier, darker, and more menacing, the social commitment of Public Enemy supplanted by the outlaw swagger of artists such as Ice-T (Tracy Marrow), who in 1987 recorded the theme song for *Colors*, Dennis Hopper's violent film about gang versus police warfare in South Central Los Angeles. Both the film and Ice-T's raps reflected ongoing changes in southern California's urban communities, including a decline in industrial production and rising rates of joblessness, the continuing effects of crack cocaine, and a concomitant growth of drug-related gang violence.

The emergence of West Coast gangsta rap was heralded nationwide by the release of the album *Straight Outta Compton* by N.W.A. (Niggaz with Attitude). While rap artists had previously dealt with aspects of urban street life in brutally straightforward terms, N.W.A. upped the ante with recordings that expressed the gangsta lifestyle, saturated with images of sex and violence straight out of the prison toast tradition. The nucleus of the group was formed in 1986, when O'Shea "Ice Cube" Jackson (b. 1969), the product of a middle-class home in South Central Los Angeles, met Andre "Dr. Dre" Young (b. 1965), a sometime member of a local funk group called the World Class Wreckin' Cru. Jackson and Young shared an interest in writing rap songs, an ambition that was realized when they teamed up with Eric "Eazy-E" Wright (1973–95), a former drug dealer who was using the proceeds of his occupation to fund a record label, Ruthless Records. Soon, the three began working together as N.W.A., eventually adding D.J. Yella (Antoine Carraby) and M.C. Ren (Lorenzo Patterson) to the group.

When the group started work on their second album, *Straight Outta Compton*, the idea of establishing a distinctive West Coast identity within hip-hop was clearly in their minds. As M.C. Ren put it in a 1994 interview in *The Source*:

> When we did N.W.A . . . New York had all'a the bomb groups. New York was on the map and all we was thinking, man—I ain't gonna lie, no matter what nobody in the group say—I think we was all thinking about making a name for Compton and L.A. (George 1998, p. 135)

Released in 1989, the album was more than a local success, selling 750,000 copies nationwide even before N.W.A. started a promotional tour. The album's attitude, sound, and sensibility was clearly indebted to earlier hip-hop recordings—particularly Public Enemy's *It Takes a Nation of Millions to Hold Us Back*, released the year before—but was in some ways unlike anything heard before, featuring tracks with titles like "F—— the Police" and "Gangsta Gangsta," underlain by a soundtrack that mixed the sound of automatic weapon fire and police sirens with samples from funk masters such as George Clinton and James Brown, a bouncy drum machine–generated dance groove called new jack swing, and high-pitched, thin-sounding synthesizer lines. The raps themselves were harrowing egocentric accounts of gang life, hearkening back to the bleakest aspects of the prison toast tradition. The cover of the CD—with the posse staring implacably down at, and holding a gun to the head of, the prospective purchaser—reinforced the aura of danger, one of the main appeals of the group for the young suburban audience that pushed the album to multiplatinum sales.

The acrimonious breakup of N.W.A., beginning in 1989, had the effect of disseminating the group's influence over a wider territory. During the 1990s Ice Cube went on to make a series of platinum albums totaling almost six million in sales, including the brilliant *AmeriKKKa's Most Wanted* (Number Nineteen in 1990), a more explicitly political album recorded in New York with Public Enemy and the Bomb Squad, and *The Predator,* which reached Number One in 1992. Eazy-E sold over five million albums in the 1990s, all released on his Ruthless Records label, and M.C. Ren sold one million copies of his *Kizz My Black Azz* (Number Twelve in 1992). But the most influential and economically successful member of N.W.A. turned out to be Andre Young (Dr. Dre), who founded an independent record label (Death Row/Interscope), cultivated a number of younger rappers, and continued to develop a distinctive hip-hop production style, christened "G-Funk" in homage to the P-funk style developed in the 1970s by George Clinton, often sampled on Dre's productions. Dr. Dre's 1992 album *The Chronic*—named after a particularly potent strain of marijuana—sold over three million copies and introduced his protégé, <u>Snoop Doggy Dogg</u> (Calvin Broadus, born in Long Beach in 1972).

Snoop's soft drawl and laid-back-but-lethal gangster persona were featured on *Doggystyle* (1993), which made its debut at the top of the album charts. The gold single—"What's My Name?," a so-called clean remix of the opening track on the *Doggystyle* album—will give us a sense of Snoop Doggy Dogg's prowess as a rapper and of Dr. Dre's distinctive G-funk production style. (Like many rap recordings intended to cross over to the pop charts, "What's My Name" was released on the album in its original, unexpurgated version and in a "clean" version on a single designed for radio airplay and mass distribution. We will analyze the remix here, which reached Number Eight on the *Billboard* Hot 100 singles chart in 1993.) Although the track opens with a dense, scratchy sample reminiscent of a Public Enemy/Bomb Squad recording—actually a brief sequence from an old Parliament track, looped to create a syncopated pattern—the texture soon shifts to a smoother, more dance-oriented sound. A relaxed, medium-tempo dance groove is established by drum machine and keyboard synthesizers (including a weighty and sinuous keyboard bass part), over which a digitally processed, nasal-sounding human voice floats, singing a melismatic phrase:

> *Eee-yi-yi-yi-yi-yah, the Dogg Pound's in the hou-ouse*

A female choir enters, repeating the phrase "Snoop Doggy Dogg" in soul music style, and is answered by the sampled voice of George Clinton, intoning "Da Bomb" (a phrase commonly used to describe compelling grooves and other pleasurable experiences). After this brief mood-setting introduction, Snoop's drawling, laconic voice enters:

> *From the depths of the sea, back to the block* [the neighborhood]
> *Snoop Doggy Dogg, funky as the, the, the Doc* [Dr. Dre]
>
> *Went solo on that ass, but it's still the same*
> *Long Beach is the spot where I served my cane* [prison term]

Snoop Doggy Dogg. Courtesy BMI Archives.

These two stanzas immediately establish Snoop's local identity, his indebtedness to his mentor Dr. Dre, and his street credibility, referring to the time he spent in jail.

He then explodes into a rapid-fire, percussively articulated sequence of tongue-twisting wordplay:

> *Follow me, follow me, follow me, follow me, but you betta not slip*
> *'Cause Nine-trizzay's the yizzear* [1993's the year] *for me to f—— up sh——* [make an impact]

> *So I ain't holdin nuttin back*
> *And once again I got five on the twenty sack* [sentenced to five years in prison for possession of a twenty-dollar bag of marijuana]

Snoop declares his arrival in no uncertain terms, asserting that 1993 is the year for him to make a major impact on the music scene. He refers to a more recent conviction on marijuana possession charges and then shifts to a more threatening posture—aided by Dr. Dre's interjection of an automatic weapon-like sound effect:

> *It's like that and as a matter of fact* (Dr. Dre: *rat-tat-tat-tat*)
> *'Cause I never hesitate to put a fool on his back* [imitating Muhammad Ali]

(Dr. Dre: *Yeah, so peep out the manuscript* [pay close attention to the words]
You see that it's a must we drop gangsta sh—— [talk gangster talk])

Hold on, wha's my name?

The female choir reenters, introducing a bit of hip-hop history, a melodic line from Parliament's "Give Up the Funk (Tear the Roof off the Sucker)" (see the discussion of this recording in Chapter 12). Then Snoop continues to add verbal layers to his gangsta persona, boasting about his potential for lethal violence, referring to himself as "Mr. One Eight Seven"—a reference to the California penal code for homicide—and departing the scene of a bloody massacre by disappearing mysteriously into the night ("I step through the fog and I creep through the smog").

The following interlude between verses introduces a digitally processed voice chanting "Bow-wow-wow, yippie-yo-yippie-yay," a sly reference to country and western music and cowboy films. (References to cowboys and country music are not at all unknown in rap music; for example, Seattle-based rapper Sir Mix-A-Lot's "Buttermilk Biscuits," recorded in 1988, is a parody of square dance music.) In the third and final section, Snoop moves on to another favorite subject, his sexual potency. He begins with a catchphrase that goes back to the South Bronx origins of hip-hop and MCs like Kool Herc and Grandmaster Flash:

Now just throw your hands way up in the air
And wave them all around like ya just don't care

Yeah roll up the dank [marijuana], *and pour the drank*
And watch your step (why?) 'cause Doggy's on the gank [ready to injure anyone who disrespects him]

My bank roll's on swoll [swollen]
I'm standin' on hit, legit, now I'm on parole, stroll

With the Dogg Pound right behind me
And rollin' with my b—— [woman], *is where ya might find me*

Layin' that, playin' that G Thang
She want the G with the biggest sack [testicles], *and who's that?*

He is I, and I am him, slim with the tilted brim

Wha's yo name?

Read as words on a page, divorced of their musical context, "What's My Name?" is simply an updated version of "Stagger Lee," a traditional African American ballad about a powerful and amoral black desperado of prison toast fame. But the commercial success of "What's My Name?" had as much to do with the musical groove and texture of the recording as with the content and flow (rhyme and rhythm) of Snoop Doggy Dogg's verbal performance. "What's My Name?" is in fact a club dance record, more than half of which is taken up by instrumental music or singing. (It could be argued that most of the people that bought this record could not have interpreted portions of the text in any case, given the use of local references and gang jargon.) This recording is obviously less musically complex than Public Enemy's "Night of the Living Baseheads," judged from the viewpoints of textural complexity, tone color, or historical references. Dr. Dre's G-funk sound, while indebted to the innovations of Public Enemy's production team, the Bomb Squad, has an entirely different aesthetic and commercial goal. Dre's approach to the use of digital sampling is much less ambitious than Public Enemy's: he uses here only three prerecorded sources—George Clinton recordings from the 1970s and early 1980s—and generally seems to aim for a clean, crisp studio sound. (The less ambitious use of digital samples may have to do with the court cases discussed in Box 14.1, which by the mid-1990s made it much more difficult for hip-hop producers to experiment with prerecorded sources.) Despite its controversial verbal content, "What's My Name?" is a quintessential pop record, bristling with hooks, catchy melodies, riffs, and verbal mottoes, organized around a medium-tempo groove, and carefully calibrated for dance club consumption.

While the conflation of gangsta rhetoric and reality at least temporarily boosted the sales of rap recordings, it also had terrible real-life consequences, as the matrix of conflict between posses—one source of the creative energy that gave birth to hip-hop in the 1970s—turned viciously in on itself during the mid-1990s. Such conflicts—evoked constantly in gangsta rap—can develop at many levels: between members of the same posse ("set trippin'"), among posses representing different 'hoods, between gangs of different ethnicity (as for example between Chicano and black gangs in Los Angeles), among larger organizations (for example, national gangs like the Crips, Hoods, and Black Gangster Disciples), and between entire cities or regions of the country.

The mid-1990s saw the violent eruption of conflicts between East and West Coast factions within the hip-hop business. Standing in one corner was Marion "Suge" Knight, CEO of Los Angeles–based Death Row Records, and Death Row's up-and-coming star <u>Tupac (2pac) Shakur</u> (1971–96). In the other corner stood the producer and rapper <u>Sean "Puffy" Combs</u> (a.k.a. Puff Daddy, P. Diddy), CEO of the New York independent label Bad Boy Records, and the up-and-coming star <u>the Notorious B.I.G.</u> (Christopher Wallace, a.k.a. Biggie Smalls, 1972–97). By the time the stranger-than-fiction scenario played itself out at the end of the 1990s, Tupac Shakur and Christopher Wallace had been shot to death; Suge Knight, already on parole for a 1992 assault conviction, was reincarcerated after an attack on two rappers in a Las Vegas casino and had come under federal investigation for racketeering; Interscope, a subdivision of Time Warner Entertainment, had severed its formerly lucrative promotion and distribution deal with Death Row Records; Tupac Shakur's mother had sued Death Row for the rights to her dead son's tapes; and Dr. Dre and Snoop Doggy Dogg, Death Row's biggest stars, had severed ties with the label. In January 1998 Snoop told the *Long Beach Press-Telegram* (as quoted in RockOn-TheNet.com) that he was leaving Death Row Records for fear of his life:

> I definitely feel my life is in danger if I stay in Death Row Records. That's part of the reason why I'm leaving . . . there's nothing over there. Suge Knight is in jail, the president; Dr. Dre left and 2Pac is dead. It's telling me that I'm either going to be dead or in jail or I'm going to be nothing.

Chillingly, both 2Pac and the Notorious B.I.G. had recorded prophetic raps that ended with the narrator speaking from the grave rather than standing in bloody

---

Box 14.1 Hip-Hop, Sampling, and the Law

As we have seen, the tradition of incorporating beats from secondary sources is as old as hip-hop itself. However, the increasing sophistication and affordability of digital sampling technology had, by the late 1980s, made it possible for rap producers to go much farther, weaving entire sound textures out of prerecorded materials. This development triggered some interesting court cases, as some of the artists being sampled sought to protect their rights.

In 1989 the Miami-based rap group 2 Live Crew released a song called "Pretty Woman," which borrowed from the rock 'n' roll hit "Oh, Pretty Woman" (Number One pop in 1964), written by Roy Orbison and William Dees. Although 2 Live Crew had tried to get permission from the music publisher of the song, Acuff-Rose Music, to make a rap version of the song, permission had been denied. A lawsuit ensued over rapper Luther R. Campbell's (a.k.a. Luke Skyywalker's) raunchy send-up of the tune, and Campbell took the position that his use of the song was a parody that was legally protected as a fair use. The Supreme Court recognized the satirical intent of Campbell's version and held that 2 Live Crew's copying of portions of the original lyric was not excessive in relation to the song's satirical purpose.

Although the 2 Live Crew decision upheld the rights of rap musicians and producers to parody preexisting recorded material, control over actual digital sampling tightened up during the 1990s, as a result of a few well-publicized court cases. In 1991 the 1960s folk rock group the Turtles sued the hip-hop group De La Soul for using a snippet of the Turtles' song "You Showed Me" on a track called "Transmitting Live from Mars." The Turtles won a costly out-of-court settlement. That same year, an up-and-coming hip-hop artist named Biz Markie recorded a track that sampled the sentimental pop song "Alone Again (Naturally)," a Number One pop hit for the Irish songwriter Gilbert O'Sullivan in 1972. O'Sullivan was not pleased and pursued the case, eventually forcing Warner Brothers to remove Biz Markie's album from the market until the offending track was itself removed from the album. These decisions sent a chill through the rap music industry and encouraged producers to be less ambitious in their use of sampled materials. As the hip-hop historian Nelson George phrases it, "The high-intensity sound tapestries of Public Enemy have given way to often simpleminded loops of beats and vocal hooks from familiar songs—a formula that has grossed [M.C.] Hammer, Coolio, and Puff Daddy millions in sales and made old R&B song catalogs potential gold mines" (George 1998, p. 95).

---

triumph over his victims. (True to the logic of the popular music business, these voices were manifested in highly profitable posthumous albums with titles like *Life after Death, Born Again, Still I Rise,* and *Here After*).

Since the late 1980s the highly stylized narratives of gangsta rap have provided a chronicle of the dilemmas faced by urban communities—poverty, drug addiction, and violence—from a first-person, present-tense viewpoint. The recordings of artists like Ice-T, N.W.A., Snoop Doggy Dogg, 2Pac Shakur, and the Notorious B.I.G. combine a grim, survivalist outlook on life with a gleeful celebration of the gangster lifestyle. This celebratory nihilism, propelled by funk-derived, digitally sampled grooves and surrounded in the video versions of rap recordings with a continual flow of images of hip-hop fashion, champagne, expensive cars, and sexy women (characterized as "bitches" and "whores"), provokes an understandable ambivalence toward gangsta rap on the part of observers genuinely sympathetic to the plight of people struggling for economic and cultural survival in America's cities. How, such critics ask, could a genre of music that presents itself as being committed to "keeping it real" so deeply indulge itself in the escapism of consumer capitalism and in the exploitation of women as sex objects?

Part of the answer may lie in the fact that rap music is a part not only of African American culture but also of American culture as a whole. Rap reflects the positive qualities of American culture—its creative energy, regional diversity, and technological acumen—just as it expresses American society's dark side: the obsession with guns and violence, material wealth and status symbols, and long-standing traditions of racism, homophobia, and sexism. (And, as a number of observers have pointed out, folk tales of black outlaws like Stagger Lee have always existed in a dialogue with popular images of white gangsters like Capone and Derringer, and with violent Hollywood films like *Little Caesar, Scarface,* and *Natural Born Killers.*)

On the one hand, rap has provided an unvarnished view of the dystopia that infects many urban communities—what Cornel West, the prominent African American cultural critic, has called "the lived experience of coping with a life of horrifying meaninglessness, hopelessness, and lovelessness . . . a numbing detachment from others and a self-destructive disposition toward the world" (West 1993, p. 14). On the other hand, it is also clear that gangsta recordings, promoted by huge entertainment corporations to a predominantly white mass audience, may have served inadvertently to reinforce some old and pernicious stereotypes of black masculinity, dating back to the knife-toting dandy of the nineteenth-century minstrel show. Perhaps this is what Chuck D was referring to when in 1998 he told an interviewer, "Ten years ago, I called rap music black America's CNN. My biggest concern now is keeping it from becoming the Cartoon Network."

TECHNO: DANCE MUSIC IN THE DIGITAL AGE

During the 1980s, following on the heels of disco and paralleling the emergence of hip-hop, new forms of up-tempo, repetitive, electronic dance music developed in the club scenes of cities such as New York, Chicago, and Detroit, cross-fertilized with developments in London, Düsseldorf, and other European cities. These styles, generally traced to early 1980s genres such as garage and house music, and loosely lumped together under the general term *techno,* are in fact quite varied. There are literally dozens of subcategories, including jungle, drum'n'bass, funky breaks, tribal, 'ardcore, gabba, happy hardcore, trance, trip-hop, acid jazz, electro-techno, intelligent techno, ambient, and ever more subtly defined sub-subcategories (ambient house, dark ambient, ambient breakbeat, ambient dub, and so on), each patronized by a loyal cadre of fans. As Simon Reynolds puts it in his book *Generation Ecstasy:*

> For the newcomer to electronic dance music, the profusion of scenes and subgenres can seem at best bewildering, at worst willful obfuscation. Partly, this is a trick of perspective: kids who've grown up with techno feel it's **rock** that "all sounds

the same." The urgent distinctions rock fans take for granted—that Pantera, Pearl Jam, and Pavement operate in separate aesthetic universes—makes sense only if you're already a participant in the ongoing rock discourse. The same applies to dance music: step inside and the genre-itis begins to make sense. (Reynolds 1998, p. 7)

In essence, techno is the musical dimension of a whole youth culture, within which arguments about the difference between good music and bad music are informed by a set of shared assumptions and shared knowledge of the genre's history. Techno culture is focused on DJ/producers—who, unlike disco and hip-hop DJs, often attempt to remain anonymous, operating their equipment in the dark behind a web of wiring. (Most techno "groups"—such as the Orb, Orbital, Prodigy, and Moby—are in fact solo acts, or teams of two or three DJs.)

The main venues for techno are dance clubs and semipublic events called *raves*, partly modeled on the be-ins of the 1960s counterculture. A controversial aspect of raves—which started in England in the late 1980s and spread, in a more limited fashion, to the United States soon thereafter—is the prevalent use by participants of a psychoactive drug called Ecstacy (MDMA), which creates visceral sensations of warmth and euphoria. Matthew Collin, a British journalist who has written extensively about the drug-rave-music connection that emerged in his country in the 1980s, has described the drug's sensation:

> The world had opened up all around, the blank warehouse somehow changed into a wonderland designed just for us, glistening with a magic iridescence that I couldn't see earlier. New world. New sound. New life. Everything felt so right. A huge, glowing, magical YES. (Collin 1997, p. 3)

Unfortunately, this YES eventually mutated into a resounding NO, for one of the documented long-term effects of MDMA is an alteration of brain chemistry that makes it harder and harder to get high, leading to severe depression. Added to this was the banning of Ecstacy by the FDA in the United States, which drove the drug underground, exacerbated the problem of worse drugs being circulated under the guise of Ecstacy, and led to a number of fatal overdoses. In any case, by the mid-1990s increasing numbers of DJs and fans had rejected the use of Ecstacy. As one insider put it, "the *music* drugs the listeners."

The roots of techno are often traced to the Detroit area, home of Motown, the Stooges, and George Clinton. During the early 1980s a group of young, middle-class African American men living in the predominantly white suburban town of Belleville developed a form of electronic dance music that Derrick May, a pioneer of the genre, described as being like George Clinton and Kraftwerk "stuck in an elevator" with just a sequencer. Detroit techno was grounded in a different cultural scene from that which had spawned the Motown sound; young men like May and Juan Atkins were obsessed with symbols of class mobility, Italian fashions, and European disco recordings, and they developed a form of electronic dance music that featured futuristic imagery, samples from European records, and a dry, minimalist sound, underlain by a subliminal funk pulse.

At around the same time a genre called *house music* (named after the Warehouse, a popular gay dance club) was developing in Chicago. The Chicago house scene was pioneered by Frankie Knuckles, a DJ from New York who worked at the Warehouse from 1979 until 1983. Knuckles introduced New York turntable techniques to Chicago, manipulating disco records to emphasize the dance beat—the drums and bass—even more strongly. Many house recordings were purely instrumental, with elements of European synth-pop, Latin soul, reggae, rap, and jazz grafted over an insistent dance beat. By the mid-1980s house music scenes had emerged in New York and London, and in the late 1980s the genre made its first appearances on the pop charts, under the guise of artists like M/A/R/R/S and Madonna.

In the 1990s techno music began to diversify into the dozens of specialized sub-categories mentioned above. These branches of techno were often distinguished by their relative "hardness," a quality connected with the tempo or b.p.m. (beats per minute) of recordings. Some forms of techno were influenced by punk rock, others by experimental art music, and still others by black popular music, including funk and hip-hop. The sensual and emotional tone of the music also varied widely from the stark, futuristic sound of Belgian gabba and the energetic funkiness of jungle to the world music influences of tribal and the otherworldly sonic atmospheres of ambient. Although techno has produced few big commercial hits throughout its history, the recordings of musicians like Prodigy, Orbital, and Moby did make inroads into the charts during the late 1990s, and techno recordings were increasingly being licensed as the soundtracks for technologically oriented television commercials and films.

ALTERNATE CURRENTS

In the 1990s the marketplace for popular music continued to metastasize into hundreds of named genres, each correlated with a particular segment of the audience. From jangle pop to trip hop, psychobilly to thrashcore, the decade saw a splintering of genres that exceeded anything previously experienced in the history of American popular music. While many of these styles sprang from the ground up, as it were, nurtured by local audiences, regional networks of clubs, and low-profit independent labels, the entertainment industry had refined its ability to identify such "alternative" genres and their specialized audiences.

By the end of the 1990s, almost every major genre had sprouted an alternative subcategory. According to the *All Music Guide* (www.allmusic.com), a widely consulted Internet guide to popular music, the range of alternative genres included alternative dance (including techno, which often forms its own category, and groups such as Pop Will Eat Itself and Everything but the Girl), adult alternative pop/rock (Alanis Morissette, Dave Matthews Band), alternative country (k.d. lang, Dwight Yoakam, Lyle Lovett), alternative country rock (Uncle Tupelo, the Jayhawks), alternative contemporary Christian music (Sixpence None the Richer, Jars of Clay), alternative metal (Rage against the Machine, Korn, Limp Bizkit), alternative rap (De La Soul, Arrested Development, Lauryn Hill), and a variety of styles broadly lumped under the heading of alternative pop/rock (R.E.M., Sonic Youth, Living Colour, Soundgarden, Nirvana, Nine Inch Nails, Red Hot Chili Peppers, Phish, and many other groups). Some artists classified under the "alternative pop/rock" rubric sound similar, while others seem to have come from different musical planets entirely. Some record for small independent labels, while others sign contracts with major record companies. Some have a strong social, moral, or political outlook—right-wing or left-wing—that shapes their music, and others do not. And to all these sub-categories, still others could be added, such as "alternative singer-songwriters"

(Sinéad O'Connor, Ani DiFranco, Tracy Chapman). What, then, defines them all as "alternative" musicians?

Our difficulty in coming up with a one-size-fits-all definition of "alternative music" stems partly from the use of this term to advance two different and often conflicting agendas. On the one hand, the term "alternative"—like the broadly equivalent terms "underground" and "independent"—is used to describe (and to positively valorize) music that, in one regard or another, challenges the status quo. From this perspective alternative music is fiercely iconoclastic, anticommercial, and antimainstream; it is thought by its supporters to be local as opposed to corporate, homemade as opposed to mass-produced, and genuine as opposed to artificial.

An entirely different sense of the term underlies the music industry's use of "alternative" to denote the choices available to consumers via record stores, radio, cable television, and the Internet. This sense of the term is bound up with the need of the music business to identify and exploit new trends, styles, and audiences. In an interview conducted during the late 1980s, a senior executive for a major record company revealed that

> there's a whole indie section [of our company. There are] . . . kids—that will only buy records that are on an indie label . . . which is why we sometimes concoct labels to try and fool them. (Negus 1992, p. 16)

The notion of a huge entertainment corporation cooking up a fake independent record label to satisfy an audience hungry for musical expressions of authenticity and rebellion may seem a bizarre contradiction at first glance. From our long-term historical perspective, however, we can see this institutional development as the culmination of a decades-old trend within the music business. In the days before rock 'n' roll, genres such as race music, hillbilly music, and ethnic music were predominantly the bailiwick of small independently owned and operated record labels. By the 1980s and 1990s, however, the major record companies had fully internalized the hard lesson of rock 'n' roll and had come to view independent labels as the functional equivalent of baseball farm teams: small, specialized, close-to-the-ground operations perfectly situated to sniff out the next big thing. In an era when most so-called independent labels are distributed, promoted, and even owned outright by huge entertainment corporations, it became difficult to sustain a purely economic definition of alternative music as music that doesn't make money. To put it another way, the fact that a band's music, song lyrics, appearance, and ideological stance are anticommercial doesn't mean that they can't sell millions of records and thereby help to generate huge corporate profits.

Alternative Rock, 1980s–1990s

In the wake of punk rock's collapse—symbolized by the breakup of the Sex Pistols in 1978 (see Chapter 12)—a number of distinctive streams of "indie rock" or "underground rock" bubbled up in cities and towns across the United States. Strong underground rock scenes developed in towns such as Boston, Massachusetts; Athens, Georgia; Ann Arbor, Michigan; Minneapolis, Minnesota; Austin, Texas; San Francisco, California; and Seattle, Washington. Many of these communities are home to large populations of college students and to student-programmed college radio stations, both key ingredients for a regional underground scene. Starting out as local phenomena, supported by small but devoted audiences, touring within regional networks of clubs, and releasing recordings on tiny, hand-to-mouth independent labels, bands such as Sonic Youth, R.E.M., the Dead Kennedys, and Nirvana came to symbolize the essence of indie rock—local, anticommercial, guitar-based music blending the abrasive, do-it-yourself sensibility of 1970s punk with the thick, heavy sonic textures of heavy metal. In general, underground rock bands maintained a defiant stance toward the conformity and commercialism of the music industry. They were committed to songwriting that explored taboo issues (drug use, depression, incest, suicide); interested in social and political movements such as environmentalism, abortion rights, and AIDS activism; and identified with unconventional (and soon merchandised) styles of self-presentation that included "dressing down" in torn jeans, flannel shirts, and work boots. Despite their avowed opposition to mainstream rock music, genres such as indie rock, hardcore, and thrash were supported by a predominantly white, middle- and working-class, male audience.

As time wore on, some of these groups went on to achieve commercial success on an international scale, signing deals with major record companies and moving toward a more pop-influenced sound. Others, driven by the ideology of authenticity through nonconformity, remained small, intensely local, and close to their fan base. For the underground bands who made it big—leading to the emergence of alternative rock as a marketing category around 1990—there were many contradictions to face, not least the problem of maintaining an outsider identity as their albums rose to the top of the *Billboard* charts, received Grammy Awards, and were promoted on the mainstream mass media. For many of these groups, the sensation of being on the inside looking out was new and unnerving. For a few musicians, it proved fatal.

The most influential indie rock bands of the 1980s were R.E.M. (formed in 1980 in Athens, Georgia) and New York's Sonic Youth (formed in 1981). While both bands were influenced by the 1970s New York punk scene, they developed this musical impetus in different directions. R.E.M.'s reinterpretation of the punk aesthetic incorporated aspects of folk rock—particularly a ringing acoustic guitar sound reminiscent of the 1960s group the Byrds—and a propensity for catchy melodic hooks. Touring almost constantly and releasing a series of critically acclaimed and increasingly profitable albums on the independent label IRS, R.E.M. gradually grew from its roots as a regional cult phenomenon to command a large national audience. This process culminated in the release of *Document,* the band's first Top 10 album, in 1987. In 1988 R.E.M. signed a ten-million-dollar, five-album agreement with Warner Brothers, becoming one of the first underground bands of the 1980s to receive such a deal. By 1991, when alternative rock seemed to many observers to have suddenly erupted onto the pop music scene, R.E.M. had already been working steadily for over ten years to develop its idiosyncratic sound. That year the band released the album *Out of Time,* which shot to Number One on the album chart, sold four million copies, generated two Top 10 singles, and won a Grammy award for Best Alternative Music LP. (The alternative category had been established just the year before, an indication of the music industry's awakening interest in underground rock music.)

Sonic Youth, formed in New York City in 1981, pushed underground rock music in a quite different direction. Influenced by avant-garde experimentalists such as the Velvet Underground, Sonic Youth developed a dark, menacing, feedback-drenched sound, altering the tuning of their guitars by inserting screwdrivers and drumsticks under the strings at random intervals, and ignoring the conventional song structures of rock and pop music. On a series of influential (though commercially unsuccessful) recordings, released during the mid-1980s on the independent label SST, Sonic Youth began to experiment with more conventional pop song forms while maintaining the discordant sound with which they were so closely identified by fans and other musicians. By the early 1990s Sonic Youth, the former underground phenomenon, had signed with the major label DGC (owned by the media magnate David Geffen) and was being widely hailed as a pioneer of the alternative movement in rock. The magazine *Vanity Fair* went so far as to proclaim Sonic Youth's lead singer, Kim Gordon, the "godmother of alternative rock." The 1994 album *Experimental Jet Set, Trash, and No Star*, their third release on DGC, reached Number Thirty-four on the Top 100 album chart, proof that their national audience, like R.E.M.'s, had expanded beyond all expectations.

Around the same time that R.E.M. and Sonic Youth were formulating (and reformulating) their distinctive underground sounds, another influential branch of postpunk music was developing in clubs on the West Coast. *Hardcore* was an extreme variation of punk, pioneered during the early 1980s by bands in San Francisco (the Dead Kennedys) and Los Angeles (the Germs, Black Flag, X, and the Circle Jerks). These groups—and others, such as the Texas-based Butthole Surfers—took the frenzied energy of the Ramones and the Sex Pistols and pushed it to the limit, playing simple riff-based songs at impossibly fast tempos and screaming nihilistic lyrics over a chaotic wall of guitar chords. Audiences at hardcore clubs—typically adorned in tattoos, buzz cuts, and combat boots—developed the practice of *slam dancing* or *moshing*, in which members of the audience pushed their way up to a *mosh pit*, an area situated directly in front of the stage, and smashed into one another, sometimes climbing onto the stage and diving off into the crowd. Most hardcore recordings were released by independent labels like SST, Alternative Tentacles, and IRS, and the typical hardcore disc was produced to look and sound as though it had been made in someone's basement. Few of these bands managed to score contracts with major labels, a fact proudly pointed out by fans as proof of their genuine underground status.

"Holiday in Cambodia" by the Dead Kennedys, released on the independent label Alternative Tentacles in 1981, is a good example of the sensibility of early 1980s hardcore. The lyrics—written by the band's lead singer, <u>Jello Biafra</u> (Eric Boucher, b. 1959 in Boulder, Colorado)—brim with merciless sarcasm. The song is directed at the spoiled children of suburban yuppies, who Biafra suggests ought to be sent to forced labor camps in Cambodia—then in the grip of Pol Pot's genocidal regime—to gain some perspective on the magnitude of their own problems. The recording opens with a nightmarish display of guitar pyrotechnics, a series of Hendrix-inspired whoops, slides, scratches, and feedback, evocative of a war zone. The band—guitar, electric bass, and drums—gradually builds to an extremely fast tempo (around 208 beats per minute). Over this chaotic din, Jello Biafra's quavering voice sneers out the caustic lyrics:

> So you been to school for a year or two
> And you know you've seen it all
> In daddy's car, thinkin' you'll go far
> Back east your type don't crawl

Play ethnicky jazz to parade your snazz [coolness]
On your five grand stereo
Braggin' that you know how the niggers feel cold
And the slums got so much soul . . .

Well you'll work harder with a gun in your back
For a bowl of rice a day
Slave for soldiers till you starve
Then your head is skewered on a stake . . .

Pol Pot, Pol Pot, Pol Pot, Pol Pot . . .

And it's a holiday in Cambodia
Where you'll do what you're told
A holiday in Cambodia
Where the slums got so much soul . . .

The Dead Kennedys' variant of hardcore was lent focus by the band's political stance, which opposed American imperialism overseas, the destruction of human rights and the environment, and what the band saw as a hypocritical and soulless suburban lifestyle. Jello Biafra composed songs with titles like "California über Alles," "Kill the Poor" (a Jonathan Swift–like suggestion for the practical application of neutron bombs), and "Chemical Warfare." As the hardcore scene began to attract right-wing racial supremacists—a problem that the genre shared with 1970s punk rock—Biafra penned a song entitled "Nazi Punks F—— Off" (1981), in an attempt to distance the progressive hardcore skinheads from their fascist counterparts.

By the mid-1980s the hardcore movement had largely played itself out, though aspects of the music's style and attitude were carried on by bands playing *thrash,* which blended the fast tempos and rebellious attitude of hardcore with the technical virtuosity of heavy metal guitar playing. Thrash was a harder, faster version of the commercially successful *speed metal* style played by bands such as Metallica, Megadeath, and Anthrax. (The 1991 album *Metallica* was the ultimate confirmation of heavy metal's mass popularity and newfound importance to the music industry: it streaked to Number One on the album charts, sold over five million copies, and stayed on the charts for an incredible 266 weeks.) Unlike speed metal, thrash didn't produce any superstars—the Los Angeles band Suicidal Tendencies was the most recognizable name to emerge from the genre—but it did exert an influence on alternative rock bands of the 1990s. Although thrash never developed a mass audience, its fans remained dedicated, keeping the style alive as an underground club-based phenomenon through the 1990s.

Although underground bands began to appear on the charts during the late 1980s, the commercial breakthrough for alternative rock—and the occasion of its enshrinement as a privileged category in the pop music marketplace—was achieved in 1992 by Nirvana, a band from the Pacific Northwest. Between 1992 and 1994, Nirvana—a trio centered on singer and guitarist Kurt Cobain (b. 1967 in Hoquiam, Washington; d. 1994) and bassist Krist Novoselic (b. 1965 in Compton, California)—released two multiplatinum albums that moved alternative rock's blend of hardcore punk and heavy metal out of the back corners of specialty record stores and into the commercial mainstream. The rise of so-called *grunge rock*—and the tragic demise of Kurt Cobain, who committed suicide in 1994 at the age of twenty-seven—provide some insight into the opportunities and the pressures facing alternative rock musicians in the early 1990s.

Cobain and Novoselic met in 1985 in the town of Aberdeen, an economically depressed logging town some one hundred miles from Seattle. (Cobain's parents had divorced when he was eight years old, an event that by his own account troubled him deeply and left him shy and introspective.) Inspired by the records of underground rock and hardcore bands and the creativity of the Beatles, and frustrated with the limitations of small-town working-class life, they formed Nirvana in 1987 and began playing gigs at local colleges and clubs. The following year they were signed by the independent label Sub Pop Records, formed in 1987 by the entrepreneurs Bruce Pavitt and Jonathan Poneman. (Sub Pop started out as a mimeographed fanzine for local bands before mutating into a record label.) Nirvana's debut album, *Bleach* (1989), cost slightly over six hundred dollars to record—less than the cost of thirty minutes of recording time at a major New York or Los Angeles recording studio—and sold thirty-five thousand copies, an impressive amount for a regional indie rock release. In 1991 the group signed with major label DGC. Following a European tour with Sonic Youth, the album *Nevermind* was released in September 1991, quickly selling out its initial shipment of fifty thousand copies and creating a shortage in record stores across America. By the beginning of 1992 *Nevermind* had reached Number One, displacing Michael Jackson's highly publicized comeback album *Dangerous*. The album stayed on the charts for almost five years, eventually selling more than ten million copies.

One source of *Nevermind*'s success was the platinum single "Smells Like Teen Spirit," a Top 10 hit. One of the most striking aspects of "Teen Spirit" is its combination of heavy metal instrumental textures and pop songwriting techniques, including a number of memorable verbal and melodic hooks. The band's sound, which had been thick and plodding on its Sub Pop recordings, is sleek and well focused (thanks in part to the production of Butch Vig and the mixing of engineer Andy Wallace). The song itself combines a four-chord heavy metal harmonic progression with a somewhat conventional formal structure, made up of four-, eight-, and twelve-bar sections. The overall structure of the song includes a verse of eight bars ("Load up on guns . . . "), which we are calling A, and two repeated sections, or choruses, which we have labeled B (eight bars in length) and C (twelve bars). These sections are marked off by distinctive instrumental textures, shifting from the quiet, reflective, even somewhat depressed quality of A, through the crescendo of B, with its spacey one-word mantra and continuous carpet of thick guitar chords, into the C section, where Cobain bellows his unfocused feelings of discontent and the group slams out heavy metal–style power chords. This ABC structure is repeated three times in the course of the five-minute recording, with room created between the second and final iterations for a sixteen-bar guitar solo.

Nirvana's "Smells Like Teen Spirit," the first alternative rock single of the 1990s to enter the Top 10, is a carefully crafted pop record. The sleek, glistening studio sound; Cobain's liberal use of melodic and verbal hooks; the trio's careful attention to textural shifts as a means of marking off formal sections of the song; and the fact that Cobain's guitar solo consists of an almost note-for-note restatement of the

LISTENING CHART   "SMELLS LIKE TEEN SPIRIT"

Music by Nirvana; lyrics by Kurt Cobain; performed by Nirvana; recorded 1991

FORM	LYRICS	DESCRIPTIVE COMMENTS
Intro (16 = 4 + 8 + 4)		Bars 1–4: solo guitar plays progression (quiet); bars 5–12: whole band plays progression (loud, intense); bars 13–16: bass plays progression with guitar chimes (soft).
A (8)	*Load up . . .*	Lead vocal enters; quiet, somewhat depressed tone; gentle instrumental texture.
B (8)	*Hello, hello . . .*	Spacey one-word vocal, backed with continuous guitar chords; gradual crescendo.
C (12)	*With the lights out*	Vocal angry, growling; heavy metal power chords, loud and distorted.
Interlude (4)		Stoptime effect with guitar response.
Intro (4)		Last four bars of Introduction; bass plays progression with guitar chimes (soft).
A (8)	*I'm worse . . .*	
B (8)	*Hello, hello . . .*	Dreamy vocal (like Beatles); continuous bed of distorted guitar chords.
C (12)	*With the lights out*	Vocal angry, growling; heavy metal power chords, loud and distorted.
Interlude (4)		Stoptime effect, answered by guitar.
Guitar solo (16)		Guitar plays melody of sections A and B (little if any improvisation).
Intro (4)		Last four bars of Introduction.
A (8)	*And I forget . . .*	
B (8)	*Hello, hello . . .*	Crescendo, spacey one-word vocal.
C (20 = 12 + 8)	*With the lights out . . .*	Vocal angry, growling; heavy metal power chords, loud and distorted.

melodies of the A and B sections, driving these hooks even deeper into the listener's memory—all serve to remind us that the Beatles were as profound an influence on 1990s alternative rock as were bands like the Velvet Underground.

Although alternative bands like R.E.M. and Sonic Youth handled their rise to fame with relative aplomb, success destroyed Nirvana. The group's attitude toward the music industry appears to have crystallized early on, as this 1989 Sub Pop press release (reproduced at Sub Pop Records' Web site) indicates:

NIRVANA sees the underground scene as becoming stagnant and more accessible to big league capitalist pig major record labels. But does NIRVANA feel a moral duty to fight this cancerous evil? NO WAY! We want to cash in and suck up to the

big wigs in hopes that we too can GET HIGH AND F—— . . . SOON we will need
groupie repellant. SOON we will be coming to your town and asking if we can stay
over at your house and use the stove. SOON we will do encores of "GLORIA" and
"LOUIE LOUIE" at benefit concerts with all our celebrity friends.

The sardonic humor of this public relations document only partially masks the
band's intensely ambivalent attitude toward rock celebrity, a kind of "listen to us,
don't listen to us" stance. As *Nevermind* rose up the charts, Nirvana had begun to
attract a mass audience that included millions of fans of hard rock and commercial
heavy metal music, genres to which their own music was explicitly opposed. This
realization impelled the group to ever more outrageous behavior, including baiting
their audiences, wearing women's clothing, and kissing one another onstage. In
1992 Cobain married Courtney Love, the leader of an all-female alternative rock
(a.k.a. "foxcore") group called Hole. Rumors concerning the couple's use of heroin
began to circulate, and an article in *Vanity Fair* charged that Love had used the nar-
cotic while pregnant with the couple's child, leading to a public struggle with the
Los Angeles child services bureau over custody of the baby. In the midst of this ad-
verse publicity, Nirvana released the album *In Utero,* a return to the raw sound of
Nirvana's early Sub Pop recordings, which shot to Number One in 1993 and sold
four million copies.

In 1994, after the band had interrupted a concert tour of Europe, Kurt Cobain
overdosed on champagne and tranquilizers, remaining in a coma for twenty hours.
Although the event was initially described as an accident, a suicide note was later
discovered. He returned to Seattle and entered a detoxification program, only to
check out two days later. On April 8, 1994, Cobain's body was discovered in his
home; he had died three days earlier of a self-inflicted shotgun wound. While there
is a diversity of opinion concerning the ultimate meaning of Cobain's suicide—he
is viewed on the one hand as a martyr of alternative rock, and on the other as a
self-indulgent, hypocritical rock star—his death has widely come to be viewed as
evidence of the pressures faced by alternative musicians who are pulled into the
mainstream.

Although the term "alternative rock" is most often used to describe bands like
R.E.M., Sonic Youth, Dead Kennedys, and Nirvana—inspired by the 1970s punk
rock movement—some forms of alternative rock found their inspiration elsewhere.
The band Phish created a loyal following by extending the approach of the quintessential 1960s concert band, the Grateful Dead. Like the Dead, the members of
Phish embraced eclectic tastes and influences. A typical Phish concert would weave
together strands of rock, folk, jazz, country, bluegrass, and pop. A band devoted to
improvisation, Phish required a live performance environment to be fully appreciated. There are some obvious differences between Phish and the Dead—Phish being a smaller and in some regards a more technically adept band, with a range of
stylistic references arguably even broader than that of the Grateful Dead. Be that as
it may, bands like Phish, Blues Traveler, and Dave Matthews Band, inspired by the
counterculture of the 1960s and by the improvisational work of jazz musicians such
as Miles Davis and Sun Ra, provide an optimistic, energetic, and open-minded alternative to the nihilism and relentless self-absorption of many alternative rock
bands. The fact that Phish was often dismissed by rock critics—in part because their
music doesn't make sense in terms of the rock-as-rebellion scenario that dominates

Box 14.2   The "Seattle Sound"

Regional "sounds" have played an important part in the history of popular music, from the Chicago blues of Muddy Waters to the Memphis rockabilly style of Elvis Presley and the southern California inflections of gangsta rap. Seattle, where Nirvana honed their sound and built a local fan base, was already home to a thriving alternative rock scene by the late 1980s. (The Pacific Northwest, while at somewhat of a remove from the main centers of the recording industry, had twenty-five years earlier played a role in the development of garage band rock, an important predecessor of punk rock.) The group often singled out as an originator of the "Seattle sound" was Green River (formed in 1983), whose 1988 album *Rehab Doll*, released on Sub Pop, helped to popularize grunge rock, blending heavy metal guitar textures with hardcore punk. Green River was also the training ground for members of later, more widely known Northwest bands such as Mudhoney (formed 1988), which was Sub Pop's biggest act until Nirvana came along, and Pearl Jam (formed 1990), who went on to become one of the most popular rock bands of the 1990s. One of the first bands signed to the fledgling Sub Pop label was Soundgarden (formed 1984), a heavy metal band that many insiders expected to be the first group to break the Seattle grunge sound on the national market. However, Soundgarden's first across-the-boards success—the album *Superunknown*, which reached Number One on the charts and sold five million copies—was not released until 1994.

Today, the push to define a regional style often comes as much from the promotion departments of record companies as from the local artists and fans themselves. The documentary video *Hype!* (1996), a revealing portrait of the role of Sub Pop Records in the Seattle alternative rock scene, suggests that many Seattle-based musicians and fans rejected the grunge label as a commercial gimmick, especially when it was adopted by advertising agencies and upscale fashion designers. This tension between commercialism and authenticity continues to play a central role in the creation and promotion of alternative rock music.

such criticism—didn't impede their success as a live act. Unlike bands such as R.E.M., Nirvana, and Pearl Jam, however, their popularity as a touring act never translated into massive record sales. By the mid-1990s Phish was able to pack stadiums—selling out Madison Square Garden in merely four hours—but none of their albums has sold as many as a million copies.

The twelve-and-a-half-minute track "Stash," from the concert album *Phish: A Live One* (1995), exemplifies the band's loose-jointed, freewheeling approach to collective improvisation. (This is, it must be admitted, a relatively brief selection. For an even better sense of the band's improvisational prowess, we would advise that you listen to one of the longer tracks, perhaps the half-hour-long "Tweezer.") The song—in the sense of a verse-chorus structure with a more or less fixed melody and lyrics—takes up only a small proportion of the track, which is an extended collective exploration of the improvisational possibilities of a minor-key chord progression, carried along on a rhythmic groove indebted to Latin American music. Certain relatively fixed elements create a sense of structure—for example, the tangolike melody played by guitarist Trey Anastasio at the beginning of the track and periodically throughout. (The audience's familiarity with these structural points is evidenced by the fact that they fill in one part of the melody with collective, and reasonably precise, clapping.) At some points these structural elements seem to melt away completely, as the guitar, acoustic piano, electric bass, and drums develop a subtle interplay, taking the performance in unexpected directions. While Anastasio's guitar is generally the dominant instrument in the mix, Phish's approach to improvisation resembles the collective polyphony of early New Orleans jazz (see Chapter 3) more than the hierarchical structure of rock bands, in which the soloist becomes the more or less exclusive center of attention and the rest of the band plays a subservient role.

In an interview in *Addicted to Noise* (issue 1.07, June 1995), guitarist Trey Anastasio talked about fact that Phish has never in over a decade of touring had a hit album or single:

> Lately I've been thinking . . . the worst thing that could happen to a band is to have a hit single. . . . Because you weaken your fan base. People start coming in that aren't interested in the whole thing. And then they're expecting to hear that one song. . . .
>
> Kind of like life. You don't go from being 13 to being 30, you gotta go through everything in between. Music is life to a musician. Having a hit single is very similar to going up to someone in eighth grade and saying, "Wow, that thing you did in eighth grade was really great. We're going to skip you to college. Here you go! Good luck!" Take it slow. Life is long.

Life is long, but lives are sometimes short. It is in the end difficult to explain why musicians such as Duke Ellington, Ray Charles, Bill Monroe, Paul Simon, and the Grateful Dead managed to sustain a pattern of creative growth over several decades, while others—for instance, Robert Johnson, Hank Williams, Jimi Hendrix, or Kurt Cobain—burned out almost overnight, consumed by social pressures or personal demons. Anastasio's quote suggests that the key to musical longevity may be the ability to balance the passionate involvement of music making with a philosophical, even somewhat distanced perspective on the business of making a living from music.

Women's Voices: Alternative Folk, Hip-Hop, and Country

While the term is most frequently associated with rock music, there are "alternative" artists in almost all genres of popular music. In this section we will look at the work of three women who have established an alternative identity in their respective genres: Ani DiFranco (a folk singer-songwriter); Lauryn Hill (a hip-hop artist); and k.d. lang (a country singer). In each case, the music industry's application of the term "alternative" to these performers has to do with the fact that women's perspectives—and feminist values—play an important role in their recorded work. While DiFranco, Hill, and lang share this commitment, they differ in their relationships to the corporate music business, in their performance styles, and in the degree of commercial success they have enjoyed.

A folk singer dressed in punk rock clothing, <u>Ani DiFranco</u> (b. 1970 in Buffalo, New York) has spent her career resisting the lure of the corporate music business, releasing an album and playing upward of two hundred live dates every year, and

Ani DiFranco. Courtesy BMI Archives.

building up a successful independent record label (Righteous Babe Records) and a substantial grassroots following. DiFranco began performing publicly at nine, performing covers of Beatles songs at a local coffeehouse. By the age of nineteen DiFranco had written over one hundred original songs and relocated from her native Buffalo to New York City to pursue a musical career. In 1989 she recorded a demo album and pressed five hundred copies of an eponymous cassette to sell at shows. The tape—a spare collection of intensely personal songs about failed relationships and gender inequality, accompanied with acoustic guitar—quickly sold out, and in 1990 DiFranco founded the independent label Righteous Babe Records to distribute her recordings more effectively.

By the mid-1990s the mainstream media had begun to take notice of DiFranco's homespun, low-tech music. Her 1995 album *Not a Pretty Girl* garnered notice from CNN and the *New York Times,* though it did not appear in the *Billboard* charts. But 1996 brought *Dilate,* an eclectic work recounting a love affair with a man, which debuted in the Top 100 of the *Billboard* charts, an unusual achievement for an independent release. The live album *Living in Clip,* released in 1997, became her first gold album. In 1998 DiFranco released the studio effort *Little Plastic Castle,* her highest-charting album to date, which debuted at Number Twenty-two on the Top 200 chart. All of these albums were released on the Righteous Babe label, despite many offers from major record companies.

"Not a Pretty Girl," from the album *Not a Pretty Girl* (1995), is a typical Ani DiFranco recording, with self-revealing lyrics and an austere, minimalist studio sound, focused on DiFranco's voice and acoustic guitar. Because—as is often the case in urban folk music—the words are so important to the effect of this song, we must pay particularly close attention to their construction and how they are performed. The lyrics operate on at least two levels: first, as a response to an individual, a man who has wronged the singer in some way; and second, as a more general indictment of society's treatment of women.

The track opens in a reflective mood, with the solo acoustic guitar playing a four-chord progression. The musical form of "Not a Pretty Girl" is not dissimilar to that of many Anglo-American folk songs, and the song's text, as printed on the CD's liner notes, suggests the format of a traditional folk ballad, made up of a series of stanzas. However, DiFranco's performance of the lyrics—which escalates from a sung whisper at the beginning to an assertive growl in the middle, then ends with gentle wordless singing—creates an effect entirely different from that of seeing the words laid out on the page. DiFranco lays her lyrics over the structure of the song like ropes, tightening them here, loosening them there, and creating a sense of emotional intensity and musical momentum. She begins the first verse of the song in a whisper, her dislike for the man to whom the song is addressed emerging clearly only on the word "punk," which she spits out derisively. The way the accents in the text are distributed around the strong waltz rhythm of the music—with its *one-two-three* pulsations—creates the sense of a woman who is impatient with the injustices of the world and who insists upon being treated as a person, not a stereotype. (Each numbered line below represents a unit of four three-beat measures.)

I am not a
(1) **pretty** *girl,*
(2) that is not what I **do,** *I ain't no* **dam-**
(3) sel in **distress,** *and I don't* **need**
(4) to be rescued, so, so put me **dowwwwn,**
(5) **punk.** *Wouldn't you pre-*
(6) **fer** *a maiden* **fair?** *Isn't there a*
(7) **kit***ten stuck up a* **tree** *somewhere?*
(8)

At this point DiFranco's acoustic guitar is joined by electric guitar, bass, and drums, changing the texture of the recording to a blend of folk music and alternative rock. In the second verse DiFranco packs more syllables into each four-bar musical phrase, the words rushing out and then being held back, emphasizing the central point of the lyrics (i.e., that women who express themselves forcefully are too often dismissed as merely being "angry"). In the second half of the verse, the accents of her words coincide with the stressed beats of the music more frequently, creating a sense of urgency.

I am not an
(1) **an***gry girl, but it seems like*
(2) I've got **ev***eryone fooled. Every time I say*
(3) **some***thing they find hard to* **hear,** *they chalk it* **up**
(4) to my **an***ger, and* **nev***er to their own fear. I-*
(5) **ma***gine you're a girl, just trying to*
(6) **fi***nally come* **clean,** *knowing full*
(7) **well** *they'd prefer you were* **dirty**
(8) and **smi-i-i***ling. And I am*
(9) **sorry,** *but I am*
(10) **not** *a* **mai***den fair, and I am not a*
(11) **kit***ten stuck up a tree somewhere*
(12)

In the third verse the texture moves even further toward the rock side, and DiFranco further escalates the emotional tension. At the very end of the verse a slight shift in the lyric makes us more aware of the singer's mixture of defiance and vulnerability. Whereas, in the second verse DiFranco's character states emphatically that she is "not a kitten up a tree," at the end of the third verse that claim is pushed a bit off-center when she asks rhetorically, "Don't you think every kitten figures out how to get down, whether or not *you* ever show up?" Here we catch a glimpse of a wound that lies beneath the protagonist's emotional armor:

> *And **gen**erally my*
> *(1) **gen**eration wouldn't be caught **dead***
> *(2) **work**ing for the **man,** And generally I a-*
> *(3) **gree** with them, **Trou**ble is, you've got to **have***
> *(4) yourself an **al**ternate plan, And I have **ear** . . .*
> *(5) **ned** my **dis**illusionment, I have been*
> *(6) **work**ing all of my **life** And I am a **pa**-*
> *(7) triot, **I** have been*
> *(8) **fight**ing the good **fight.** And **what** if there are no*
> *(9) **dam**sels in dis**tress?** **What** if I knew*
> *(10) **that,** and I called your **bluff?** Don't you think every*
> *(11) **kit**ten figures out how to get **down***
> *(12) **Whe**ther or not you ever **show up?***

The final stanza of "Not a Pretty Girl" reinforces the more general message of the text, a critique of the physical norms by which society, and men in particular, so often judge women.

> *I am **not** a **pre**tty girl*
> *I don't really **want** to be **pre**tty girl*
> *I want to be **more** than a **pre**tty girl.*

The recording ends gently, with DiFranco's overdubbed voice singing two melodic patterns in a responsorial manner.

The impact of "Not a Pretty Girl" is closely tied up with its carefully controlled fluctuations in musical texture, verbal density, and emotional color. DiFranco artfully blends the progressive outlook of urban folk music with the rebellious energy of alternative rock. At the same time, her performance—a song-portrait of a woman whose experience of sexism has had profound emotional consequences—implies that matters of the heart cannot simply be reduced to political positions. This is where music can exceed the power of a speech or slogan, filling in the texture and nuance of emotions and demonstrating that social injustice is registered not only in the mind but also in the heart.

Lauryn Hill (b. 1975 in South Orange, New Jersey) is a hip-hop artist whose work is a self-conscious alternative to the violence and sexism of rap stars such as Dr. Dre, the Notorious B.I.G., and 2Pac Shakur. Hill started her recording career with the Fugees, a New Jersey–based hip-hop trio that scored a Number One hit in 1996 with their second album, *The Score*. Hill's debut solo album—*The Miseducation of Lauryn Hill* (1998)—extended the Fugees' successful blend of rap, reggae, and R&B. The album shot to Number One on the charts, selling seven million copies in a little over a year, and spawning the Number One hit "Doo Wop (That Thing)."

"Doo Wop" combines aspects of 1950s R&B—including a soulful lead vocal, four-part vocal harmony, and a horn section—with Hill's penetrating observations on male and female behavior. The cut opens with Hill and a few of her friends reminiscing about the good old days. Then the digital drum machine's groove enters, and Hill launches into the first half of her rap, directed to female listeners:

> It's been three weeks since you were looking for your friend
> The one you let hit it [have sex with you] and never called you again
> Remember when he told you he was 'bout the benjamins? [interested only in money]
> You act like you ain't hear him, then gave him a little trim [had sex with him] . . .
>
> Talkin' out your neck [being hypocritical], sayin' you're a Christian
> A Muslim, sleeping with the Gin
> Now that was the sin that did Jezebel in . . .

Hill admonishes the women in her audience to be more selective about their sexual relationships and to avoid being hypocritical about their personal conduct. She then turns to the men in her audience, opening up a rapid-fire volley of wordplay that strips the so-called gangstas of their tough-guy trappings, exposing them as mother-dependent, sneaky, woman-beating, sexually immature hypocrites:

> The second verse is dedicated to the men . . .
>
> Let's stop pretendin' they wanna-pack-pistol-by-they-waist men
> Cristal [champagne]-by-the-case men, still [living] in they Mother's basemen'
> The pretty-face-men-claimin'-that-they-did-a-bid [prison time] men
> Need-to-take-care-of-their-3-and-4-kids men
> But they face a court case when the child support's late
> Money-takin', heart-breakin', now you wonder why women hate men
> The sneaky-silent men, the punk-domestic-violence men
> The quick-to-shoot-the-semen . . . Stop acting like boys and be men!
>
> How you gon' win when you ain't right within?!

"Doo Wop (That Thing)" is essentially a moral parable, delivered in terms that leaven Hill's righteous anger with light-hearted and thoroughly up-to-date hip-hop jargon. She lowers her audience's potential defensiveness by admitting that she has found herself in similar situations and pleads with them to pay attention to the development of an inner life—*How you gon' win when you ain't right within?*—in order to avoid the twin traps of materialism and easy pleasure. The mixture of sweet soul singing and assertive rapping, R&B horns and a digital groove, moral seriousness and playful humor not only announced the arrival of a new and distinctive voice but also made the single "Doo Wop" a unique and important contribution to the hip-hop repertoire.

k.d. lang (b. 1961 in Alberta, Canada) has always occupied a marginal position in the conservative world of country music. Raised in an isolated rural town on the high plains of Canada, lang listened to classical and rock music as a young girl, discovering country music somewhat later, when she played a Patsy Cline–type character in a college play. She began her career in 1982 as a Cline imitator, going so far as to christen her band the Re-clines. During the early 1980s she released two albums on the Edmonton-based independent label Bumstead Records, but it was only in 1987, when Sire Records (former label of Patti Smith and the Ramones) released her *Angel with a Lariat*, that lang came to the attention of a broader audience. (The album was played on college radio stations and progressive country stations.) Her subsequent albums—1988's *Shadowland* and 1989's *Absolute Torch and Twang*— moved toward a more traditional honky-tonk sound, producing lang's first appearances on the country Top 40 chart, and a Grammy award for Best Female Country Vocal Performance. Even at that stage, however, lang never sat quite right with the Nashville establishment, who found her campy outfits (rhinestone suits and cat-eye glasses) and somewhat androgynous image off-putting.

A scandal over lang's appearance in a commercial for the "Meat Stinks" campaign of the People for Ethical Treatment of Animals led stations in the cattle-producing areas of the Midwest to boycott her records and generated an impressive volume of hate mail. In 1992 lang officially announced her homosexuality, a move that rather than hurting her career, led to lang being christened an "icon of lesbian chic" (*New York* magazine). During the 1990s lang moved in the direction of adult contemporary pop music, becoming an "alternative" star in that category as well. *Ingénue*, a 1992 album that owed little to country music, sold over a million copies in the United States and over two million in Canada. A single from *Ingénue*,

k.d. lang. Courtesy BMI Archives.

"Constant Craving," reached the pop Top 40 and won the Grammy award for Best Female Pop Vocal Performance. Although she was not able to repeat this commercial success, lang continued throughout the 1990s to maintain a dedicated following.

"Nowhere to Stand," from the 1989 album *Absolute Torch and Twang* (1989), is a traditional song in musical terms, with a series of four-line verses and a repeated chorus, all in triple meter. In fact, apart from lang's public image, the only thing that marks this as an alternative country song is the content of the lyrics, which are an indictment of the "traditional" practice of child abuse. The song begins quietly with lang's country-tinged alto voice, accompanied by acoustic guitar. The message of the song is not explicit in the first two verses, the second of which is accompanied by a solo fiddle:

> *As things start to surface, tears come on down*
> *Scars of a childhood in a small town*
> *The hurt she pushed inward, starting to show*
> *Now she'll do some talkin', but he'll never know*
>
> *Tables have turned now, with a child of her own*
> *But she's blind to the difference, what's taught is what's known*
> *Numbed by reaction, and stripped of the trust*
> *A young heart is broken, not aware that it's just*

The intensity of lang's performance builds through the second verse, but only in the chorus—which enters suddenly, a measure early—do we become aware that this is not the typical lovelorn country song and that something hidden, and deadly serious, is being revealed to us:

> *A family tradition, the strength of this land*
> *Where what's right and wrong is the back of a hand*
> *Turns girls into women, and a boy to a man*
> *The rights of the children have nowhere to stand.*

The characterization of child abuse as a "family tradition, the strength of this land"—in which moral values and gender identity are taught with "the back of a hand"—drives lang's message home without resorting to explicit descriptions of violence. The verse that follows sketches the psychological legacy of domestic violence as a deeply buried memory, "like a seed that's been planted and won't be denied," and the recording reaches its emotional peak in the second, final chorus. Lang's juxtaposition of traditional Anglo-American song form and country music sensibility with a lyric that in essence questions the sanctity of the family—used by politicians and cultural commentators as the ultimate symbol of traditional values—creates a tender but powerful critique of American (and Canadian) culture.

Ani DiFranco, Lauryn Hill, and k.d. lang have all achieved the status of alternative artists in their respective genres, and it is worth taking a moment to consider why. The lyrics of DiFranco's "Not a Pretty Girl" don't depart totally from the norms of urban folk music, a genre long identified with social and political criticism. What makes this track an alternative folk recording is the introduction of instrumental textures and vocal style from punk rock, and the fact that it was released on a small independent label, managed by the artist herself. Hill's "Doo Wop (That Thing)" is classified as an alternative hip-hop recording not because it incorporates aspects of

R&B and soul music—many mainstream hip-hop records do this—but rather because the song's lyric challenges aspects of the materialistic and sexist ideology promoted on many of the most commercially successful rap recordings. k.d. lang's "Nowhere to Stand" hews quite closely to the norms of country and western music in its form, its vocal and instrumental style, and its emotional tone. Its status as an alternative country song has more to do with the singer's public persona (the only Jewish Canadian vegetarian lesbian in country music), and with the subject matter of the song, the secret of child abuse in "traditional" families.

While these three songs present an interesting series of contrasts, it is also worth noting the strong parallels among the careers of DiFranco, Hill, and lang. All three are innovative singer-songwriters, whose "alternative" perspectives are deeply informed by historical knowledge of the particular genres in which they have chosen to work. DiFranco refers to herself as "just a folk singer" and performs at tribute concerts for urban folk pioneers like Pete Seeger, while Hill demonstrates her "old school" credentials by evoking, and verbally citing, the sound of postwar rhythm and blues, and k.d. lang uses the 1960s country style of Patsy Cline to convey her social messages. All three artists are committed to creating popular music that engages with contemporary social issues, particularly the rights of women and children. And finally, in a business where the boundaries of acceptable nonconformity are narrowly drawn, and where even today any hint of a feminist perspective is generally enough to propel an artist into the "alternative" category, DiFranco, Hill, and lang have all been able to achieve a degree of commercial success while not compromising their passionate and distinctive voices.

Globalization and the Rise of World Music

During the 1980s the boundary between mainstream and marginal music became ever fuzzier, and the twin pressures to expand the global market for American popular music and create new alternative genres and audiences within the American market grew ever stronger. One of the most interesting results of these processes was the emergence of a category called *world music*. The term was first systematically adopted in the late 1980s by independent record label owners and concert promoters, and it entered the popular music marketplace as a replacement for longer-standing categories such as "traditional music," "international music," and "ethnic music." These sorts of records were traditionally positioned in the very back of record stores, in bins containing low-turnover items such as Irish folk song collections, Scottish bagpipe samplers, German polka records, recordings by tourist bands from the Caribbean and Hawai'i, and perhaps a few scholarly recordings of so-called primitive music from Africa, Native America, or Asia. International records were generally purchased by immigrants hungry for a taste of home, by cross-cultural music scholars such as ethnomusicologists, and by a handful of aficionados. In general, while transnational entertainment corporations became ever more successful at marketing American pop music around the globe, most of the world's music continued to have little or no direct influence on the American marketplace.

To be fair, we can point to some examples of international influence on the American pop mainstream before the 1980s—Cuban rumba, Hawai'ian guitar, and Mexican marimba records of the 1920s and 1930s; Indian classical musician Ravi Shankar's album *Live at the Monterey Pop Festival*, which reached Number Forty-three in 1967, as the counterculture was at its peak; "Grazing in the Grass" (1968), a Number One hit by the South African jazz musician Hugh Masekela; or "Soul Makossa" (1973), the Top 40 dance club single by the Cameroonian pop musician Manu Dibango, often cited as a primary influence on disco music. But these cosmopolitan influences were typically filtered through the sensibilities of Western musicians and channeled by the strategies of American and European record companies and publishing firms. A quintessential example of this is the Tokens' rock 'n' roll hit "The Lion Sleeps Tonight" (Number One in 1961), an adaptation of a hit single by the urban folk group the Weavers, entitled "Wimoweh" (a Number Fourteen pop single in 1952). "Wimoweh" had in turn been an adaptation of a 1939 South African recording by a vocal group made up of Zulu mine workers, Solomon Linda and the Evening Birds. By the time the Evening Birds' song reached the ears of Americans, it had undergone several bouts of invasive surgery, including the insertion of a pop-friendly melodic hook and English lyrics, and removal of all royalty rights pertaining to the original performers.

This sort of rip-off—a basic operating procedure for many years in the fields of American rhythm & blues and country music as well as in the international music market—reflected the global imbalances of power that had initially been created by Western colonialism. Later world fusion or world beat projects—including Paul Simon's pioneering albums *Graceland* (see Chapter 13) and *The Rhythm of the Saints,* the annual WOMAD (World Music and Dance) festival, initiated in 1982 by Peter Gabriel, and various recordings by David Byrne and Ry Cooder—helped to redress this imbalance to some degree. Nonetheless, the unequal economic relationship between "the West" and "the rest" continues to haunt such cross-cultural collaborations up to the present day.

The 1980s also saw musicians from Africa, South Asia, the Near East, Eastern Europe, and Latin America touring the United States with increasing frequency and appearing, if rarely, on the *Billboard* pop charts. The first indication that musicians from the so-called Third World might gain increased access to the American market was the release in 1982 of the album *Juju Music,* by a Nigerian group called the African Beats, led by the guitarist King Sunny Adé. Featuring an infectious brand of urban African dance music that blended electric guitars, Christian church hymns, and Afro-Caribbean rhythms with the pulsating sound of the Yoruba "talking drum," *Juju Music* sold over 100,000 copies and rose to Number 111 on *Billboard*'s album chart. The African Beats' next album, *Synchro System,* reached as high as Number 91 on the chart; however, the group was soon thereafter dropped by Island Records and never again appeared on the American pop charts.

In an article published in 1982 in the *Village Voice* by the popular music critic Greg Tate, entitled "Are You Ready for Juju?," the author explicitly identified King Sunny Adé as a potential replacement for Bob Marley, the Jamaican reggae superstar who had very recently died. On one level, this seems perfectly logical, and it probably reflects the strategic thinking of Island Records, who released the Adé albums. Adé might well have had a shot at equaling Marley's success, but the fact that he sang in Yoruba—a language spoken by precious few American listeners—rather than Marley's richly spiced version of Jamaican English doomed him to failure from the beginning. (Very few American Top 40 hits have not featured English lyrics. This is an insurmountable barrier for many international musicians, although this may change as the linguistic makeup of the United States continues to diversify.) Adé did succeed in establishing a market for so-called Afro-pop music, opening the door for African popular musicians such as Youssou N'dour (Senegal), Salif Keita (Mali), Thomas Mapfumo (Zimbabwe), and Ali Farka Toure (see below).

By 1990, when the heading "world music" first appeared above a *Billboard* record chart, it was as a subcategory of the broader heading "adult alternative albums." Interestingly, this latter category also included New Age music, a genre of instrumental music designed to facilitate contemplative and mystical moods, and sometimes loosely linked with the religious and healing practices of Native American, African, and Asian cultures. The larger category "adult alternative albums" suggests an effort on the industry's part to identify forms of alternative music that would appeal to an affluent baby boomer audience, rather than to the younger audience attracted by rock bands such as Nirvana. (Since 1991 the National Academy of Recording Arts and Sciences [NARAS] has limited its Grammy awards for world music, New Age, folk, Latin, reggae, blues, polka, and various other alternative genres to albums only, presumably on the assumption that such genres are unlikely to generate hit singles.) The world music sections of most record stores usually do not include Latin dance music (salsa) or reggae, genres that sell enough records to justify their own discrete territories.

What, then, is world music? In a strictly musical sense, it is a pseudo-genre, taking into its sweep styles as diverse as African urban pop (juju), Pakistani dance club music (bhangara), Australian Aboriginal rock music (the band Yothu Yindi), and even the Bulgarian State Radio and Television Female Vocal Choir, whose evocatively titled 1987 release *Le Mystère des Voix Bulgares* (*The Mystery of the Bulgarian Voices*) reached Number 165 on the *Billboard* album chart in 1988. Bestselling albums on *Billboard*'s world music chart have featured the Celtic group Clannad (whose popularity was boosted in the United States by their appearance in the soundtrack for a Volkswagen advertisement), Spanish flamenco music (played by the Gypsy Kings, a hotel band from France), Tibetan Buddhist chant (presented by Mickey Hart, drummer for the Grateful Dead), and diverse collaborations between American and English rock stars and musicians from Africa, Latin America, and South Asia. The overlap among various types of "adult alternative" music—including New Age, world music, techno, and certain forms of European sacred music—is reflected in the commercial success of albums like *Vision* (1994), a mélange of "12th-century chant, world beat rhythms, and electronic soundscapes," as one press release put it. (It's hard to imagine better confirmation of the historical saw that "the past is another country.") The attraction of world music for its contemporary American audience is bound up with stereotyped images of the "exotic," whether these be discovered on imaginary pilgrimages to Africa and the Himalayas, or in time travel back to the monastic Christianity of medieval Europe. Nonetheless, there are limits to the degree of musical exoticism most listeners are willing to tolerate. This may explain the almost total absence on the *Billboard* charts of music from East Asia, which many American listeners find particularly challenging.

We are all familiar with the assertion that music is a universal language, by which people usually mean to suggest that music can transcend the boundaries separating diverse nations, cultures, or languages. This statement, however comforting, does not stand up to close scrutiny—even within American culture, one person's music may be another person's noise. Nonetheless, the music industry has wasted no time in chaining the rhetoric of musical universalism to the profit motive, as for example in this mid-1990s advertisement for the E-mu Proteus/3 World, a digital device programmed with hundreds of samples of world music:

Enrich Your Music with a Global Texture. As borders dissolve, traditions are shared. And this sharing of cultures is most powerful in the richness of music. . . . E-mu has gathered these sounds and more—192 in all. Use them to emulate traditional world instruments or as raw material for creating one-of-a-kind synthesized sounds of your own. (Théberge 1997, p. 201)

Music, with its ability to flow over the boundaries of society and the borders of nations, holds open the possibility that we may glimpse something familiar and sympathetic in people strange to us—that the inequalities of the world in which we live may for a moment be suspended, or even undermined, in the act of making or listening to music. Still, the suggestion that installing a digital device in your home studio in order to emulate the "gathered sounds" of faraway people has anything to do with "sharing cultures" reveals a critically impoverished vision of cross-cultural communication. There is no denying that music has the potential to traverse the boundaries of culture and language and thereby add to our understanding of people very different from us. But the ultimate responsibility for interpreting its meanings, and determining its impact, lies with the listener.

Two World Music Collaborations: Ali Farka Toure and Nusrat Fateh Ali Khan

By the 1990s collaborations between American and foreign musicians had become more common, spurred on the one hand by folk and alternative music fans' search for a broader range of musical experiences, and on the other by the globalization of the music industry. Two particularly interesting examples of this sort of transnational collaboration are the album *Talking Timbuktu*, which won the Grammy award for Best World Music Recording in 1994, and a sampler album inspired by the film *Dead Man Walking*, which reached Number Sixty-one on the album charts in 1996.

Talking Timbuktu was produced by the singer and guitarist Ry Cooder (b. 1947 in Los Angeles), whose career as a session musician and bandleader had already encompassed a wide array of styles, including blues, reggae, Tex-Mex music, urban folk song, Hawai'ian guitar music, Dixieland jazz, and gospel music. The sound and sensibility of *Talking Timbuktu* are derived from the music of Ali Farka Toure (b. 1950), a guitarist and traditional praise singer (*griot*) from the West African nation of Mali.

Encountering a track like "Diaraby," an American listener is likely to be struck by the music's close affinities with the blues. This is no accident. To begin with, the blues styles of Mississippi, Texas, and other southern states were strongly influenced by the traditions of African slaves, many of whom came precisely from the Sahel region of West Africa, homeland of Ali Farka Toure's people, the Bambara. The high-pitched, almost wailing sound of Toure's singing; the percussive, ostinato-driven guitar patterns; and the use of song as a medium for social and personal commentary—all of these features represent an evolution of centuries-old links between the West African griot tradition and the blues created by black musicians in America's Deep South. In point of fact, it turns out that Toure's style was directly influenced by American blues musicians such as John Lee Hooker, whose records he discovered after his career was established in Africa.

Talking Timbuktu features contributions by the blues guitarist and fiddler Clarence "Gatemouth" Brown and various prominent session musicians. The result, as exemplified by "Diaraby," sung in the Bambara language, hews close to its African roots, with the American musicians playing in support of Toure. The lyric of the song is itself reminiscent of the bittersweet emotion of some American blues:

> *What is wrong my love? It is you I love*
> *Your mother has told you not to marry me, because I have nothing. But I love you.*
> *Your friends have told you not to marry me, because I have nothing. But I love you.*
> *Your father has told you not to marry me, because I have nothing. But I love you.*
> *What is wrong my love? It is you I love.*
> *Do not be angry, do not cry, do not be sad because of love.*

The sound and sensibility of "Diaraby" provide additional evidence, if any were needed, of the deep links between African and American music. This is not music functioning as a universal language, but rather a conversation between two dialects of a complexly unified Afro-Atlantic musical language.

The track "The Face of Love" is a different sort of collaboration, featuring the lead singer for the Seattle-based alternative rock band Pearl Jam, Eddie Vedder (b. 1966 in Chicago), and the great Pakistani musician Nusrat Fateh Ali Khan (1948–97), and produced by Ry Cooder. Khan was a leading performer of *qawwali*, a genre of mystical singing practiced by Sufi Muslims in Pakistan and India. (Sufism was founded in Iran between the ninth and twelfth centuries C.E. A response to orthodox Islam, Sufism emphasizes the inner kinship between God and human beings and seeks to bridge the distance between them through the force of love.)

Nusrat Fateh Ali Khan and Ensemble. Photo by S. T. Sakata.

Qawwali singing is traditionally accompanied by a double-headed drum called the *dholak* (or a *tabla*, used in Indian classical music) and a portable keyboard instrument called the harmonium, which creates a continuous drone under the singing. In traditional settings the lead singer (or *qawwal*) alternates stanzas of traditional poetic texts (sung in unison with a choir) with spectacular and elaborate melodic improvisations, in an attempt to spiritually arouse his listeners and move them into emotional proximity with the Divine.

During the 1990s Nusrat Fateh Ali Khan became the first *qawwali* artist to command a large international following, owing to his performances at the annual WOMAD festivals curated by the rock star Peter Gabriel, and to a series of recordings released on Gabriel's Real World label. Khan began to experiment with nontraditional instruments and to work with musicians outside the *qawwali* tradition, leading some critics to charge that the music had moved away from its spiritual roots. "All these albums are experiments," Khan told the interviewer Ken Hunt in 1993. "There are some people who do not understand at all but just like my voice. I add new lyrics and modern instruments to attract the audience. This has been very successful" (see the web version of *All Music Guide*).

Most American listeners first heard Khan in the soundtracks to *The Last Temptation of Christ* and *Natural Born Killers*, though without knowing it, since he was part of the overall blend. (Khan was unhappy about being included in the soundtrack for *Natural Born Killers*, since it did not reflect the spiritual goals of *qawwali*.) The 1996 film *Dead Man Walking*—the story of a nun's attempt to redeem the soul of a convicted murderer on the verge of execution—was the first to foreground Khan's contributions. Many reviews of *Dead Man Walking* stressed the contribution of Khan's voice to the haunting, mystical, and spiritual atmosphere of the film. The song "The Face of Love" is based on a simple melody, sung first by Khan with lyrics in the Urdu language, and then with English lyrics by Pearl Jam's lead singer Eddie Vedder:

Jeena kaisa Pyar bina [What is life without love]—
Is Duniya Mein Aaye ho to [Now that you have come to this world] *(2x)*
Ek Duje se pyar karo [Love each other, one another]

Look in the eyes of the face of love
Look in her eyes, oh, there is peace
No, nothing dies within pure light

Only one hour of this pure love
To last a life of thirty years
Only one hour, so come and go

In this case the sound of the music (particularly the drone of the harmonium) and the mysticism of the Sufi poetic text resonate with the transcendental atmosphere of the film—the contemplative mood of a man sentenced to die by lethal injection. The filmmaker does not make an explicit argument for or against the death penalty, and the music, with its subtly shifting textures, embodies the complexity and ambivalence of the film's subject. Although Eddie Vedder could not be expected to possess the formidable vocal improvisatory technique that Khan unleashes briefly in the middle of this track, he nonetheless manages to blend the timbre of his voice (and his acoustic guitar playing) with the mood and texture of the *qawwali* ensemble. In addition, Vedder's English lyrics do evoke the theme of mystical love so central to *qawwali* singing. This is not an example of music's functioning as a universal language, for most members of the film's American audience neither understood the words that Khan sang nor possessed any knowledge of the centuries-long history of Sufi mystical traditions. Nonetheless, it could be argued that this is a case where the well-meaning effort of artists to reach across cultural and musical boundaries does produce something like an aesthetic communion, a common purpose embodied in musical texture and poetry, provisional though it might be.

Khan's appearance on the soundtrack of *Dead Man Walking* led to his being signed by the indie label American Recordings, managed by Rick Rubin, formerly the mastermind behind the rappers Run-D.M.C. and the Beastie Boys. The American music industry's market positioning of world music as yet another variant of alternative music is indicated by that label's roster of artists, which included not only Nusrat Fateh Ali Khan but also the "death metal" band Slayer, the rap artist Sir Mix-A-Lot, and the country music icon Johnny Cash.

We have completed our historical journey through American popular music, from the emergence of minstrelsy up through the invention of the phonograph and radio, the Jazz Age, the swing era, the birth of rock 'n' roll, into the age of rock music, rap, digital technology, and global pop. In our concluding chapter, we return to the underlying themes that were presented at the beginning of this book: the relationship between music and identity, the effect of technology on music, the operations of the music business, and the complex, shifting relationship between the mainstream and the margins of popular taste and the marketplace for popular music.

CHAPTER FIFTEEN

CONCLUSION

"The more things change, the more they stay the same." In some ways this French aphorism seems perfectly suited to the state of American popular music at the beginning of a new century. Just look at two of the bestselling pop singles of the entire rock era, both released during the 1990s. "One Sweet Day" (Number One for sixteen weeks in 1995) was a sentimental song, performed by a female crooner (Mariah Carey) backed by a four-voice African American vocal group (Boyz II Men) and the lush sound of orchestral strings. "Macarena (Bayside Boys Mix)" (Number One for fourteen weeks in 1996) was a nutty little Latin novelty number that ended up sparking a nationwide dance craze. Reading this, we could be forgiven for thinking that such tastes in popular music characterized the 1930s, or 1940s, or 1950s, as well as the 1990s.

At the beginning of our survey of the development of American popular music we suggested that this history is best thought of, not as a single story told in a single voice, but as a variegated and continually shifting landscape, characterized by the complex interaction of various styles, performers, audiences, and institutions. We provided surveying tools to help orient ourselves, a set of thematic sightlines that run right across the expansive terrain of America's popular music. These included the relationship between music and identity; the evolving role of musical technology; the institutions and strategies of the music business; and the notion that the marketplace for popular music can usefully be divided into a center or mainstream, on the one hand, and various margins or peripheries, on the other. In this concluding section we will revisit these themes—glancing back, as it were, over the broad landscape of American music history—and discuss some trends that are likely to influence the future development of popular music in the United States.

MUSIC AND IDENTITY

We have encountered dozens of examples of the complex relationship between *music and identity*. One of the most prominent of these has been the long, complicated history of white fascination with black music—and of the relationship between black and white musicians, and between African American and European American musical traditions. Many metaphors have been used to describe this relationship—homage, borrowing, syncretism, crossover, exchange, exploitation, rip-off—but none of them adequately captures the shifting, sometimes tensely ambivalent and sometimes joyously synergistic relationship between these two great musical streams, and the cultures that gave them birth.

The role of *race and ethnicity* in American music must be situated within a broader context. The very fact that Americans speak of black and white music as though these were self-evident, well-defined entities stems from a particular history of racial segregation—and from the so-called Jim Crow laws designed during the early twentieth century to prevent racial commingling in the American South. This way of classifying human beings into racial categories is not universal and in fact differs substantially from perceptions of human diversity in many other parts of the world. Of course, if race is more a social fiction than a biological fact, it is a fiction that has taken on a powerful life of its own, helping some people to achieve their goals and radically disadvantaging others on the basis of their supposed ancestry. If we accept the statement that "music has no color"—an assertion made in full sincerity by great musicians of all colors—we nonetheless cannot escape the fact that racial stereotypes carry just as much force in contemporary popular culture (say, in many of the gangsta rap videos) as they did when white performers first "blacked up" for a nineteenth-century minstrel show.

A pernicious by-product of any relentless focus on differences and interactions between black and white music and musicians is the tendency to forget about our third stream, a diverse Latin American tradition that has reasserted itself again and again throughout the history of American popular music. (We need only recall the "Latin tinge" of early jazz, ballroom dance crazes such as the tango and cha-cha, and the Latin rock recordings of Carlos Santana, who created one of the most distinctive sounds of the 1960s counterculture and resurfaced some thirty years later to receive the first Grammy of the twenty-first century.) Some people have suggested that Latin American music be referred to as brown, rather than black or white, music, but this only highlights the absurdity of attempting to squeeze music into the pigeonholes of race. (Once you've opened up the Crayola box, it's hard to get it closed again.) At the close of the twentieth century, many of the top-selling albums in the United States were by Hispanic artists, a reflection of America's growing Latino population, and of the mainstream success of Latino artists such as Ricky Martin. This phenomenon pushes us toward a wider view of American culture, as a transcontinental zone of cultural interaction that reaches from Canada to South America.

In the end, much of the music that we have examined does not admit easily of straightforward racial or ethnic classification—think, for example, of Elvis Presley's two-sided hit "Don't Be Cruel"/"Hound Dog" (the only record ever to top the pop, country, and R&B charts at the same time); Ray Charles's rural twang on "I Can't Stop

Loving You"; the Beatles' emulation of Chuck Berry's country-tinged rock 'n' roll style; or the wildly eclectic juxtaposition of funk, rock, and European synth-pop in hip-hop breakbeats. To argue that there is a broad body of music that can reasonably and simply be labeled American is not, however, to deny the continuing existence of racism in American society, or the effect of racial identities on popular music.

Sexuality and gender are other aspects of identity that are also central to the history of American popular music. During our journey we have encountered many strikingly stylized images—or stereotypes—of American men, including the comfortable middle-class husband and father of Gene Austin's "My Blue Heaven" (1927); the footloose hobo of Jimmie Rodgers's "Waiting for a Train" (1928); the unemployed yet optimistic ex-GI of Louis Jordan's "Choo-Choo Ch' Boogie" (1946); the mythological super-male of Muddy Waters's anthem "Hoochie Coochie Man" (1954); and the interracial (and decidedly adolescent) male bonding of Run-D.M.C. and Aerosmith on "Walk This Way" (1986). We have met many memorable women along the way as well—Stephen Foster's ethereal "Jeanie" (1854); the malevolent super-female of Big Mama Thornton's "Hound Dog" (1953); the mature, world-weary persona of Tina Turner's "What's Love Got to Do with It" (1984); and the young feminist in Ani DiFranco's "Not a Pretty Girl" (1995), whose critique of sexist stereotypes combines the personal with the political.

A large proportion of American popular music has been concerned, in one way or another, with relationships between men and women. This polyphonic public conversation has represented many voices, attitudes, and viewpoints: the tragically misdirected jealousy of "After the Ball," America's first million-selling song (1892); the romantic abandon of Gershwin's "Embraceable You" (1930); the tense call and response formed by Hank Thompson's "The Wild Side of Life" (1952), on the one hand, and Kitty Wells's "It Wasn't God Who Made Honky-Tonk Angels" (1952) on the other; the mature resignation of Carole King's "It's Too Late" (1971); the old-fashioned chivalry of Kenny Rogers's "Lady" (1980); the Freudian angst of Prince's "When Doves Cry" (1984); and the hip moralizing of Lauryn Hill's "Doo-Wop (That Thing)" (1998), a didactic song that urges both men and women to clean up their acts. The history of American pop music is a history of popular attitudes toward romance, love, and sex.

Since so much popular music deals with love and sex, it is not surprising that public authorities of various sorts have been concerned to monitor representations of sexuality. There are many examples of censorship in the history of American popular music—for example, the cover version of Big Joe Turner's "Shake, Rattle, and Roll" by Bill Haley and the Comets, or the production of "childproofed" versions of hip-hop and alternative rock hits, with the offensive references "bleeped" out. One area of particular concern has been the expression of perspectives on love that deviate from the normative views expressed by political and religious authorities. For example, the depiction of nonheterosexual relationships has been treated gingerly by the entertainment industry. However, the fact that homosexual and bisexual relationships were rarely explicitly represented in popular music did not prevent Cole Porter's love songs—many of which were written with other men in mind—from being interpreted (and performed) as straight love songs. Similarly, the Village People—for a while in the 1970s the bestselling group in America—were an inside joke for millions of gay people, a put-on that millions of straight Americans caught up in the disco craze apparently didn't get. (This reminds us that the meaning of a given song is always deeply informed by the cultural and musical experience and the values of the listener, as well as by the intentions of the composer or performer.)

Although Americans, unlike the English, are often characterized as being oblivious to *class distinctions*, the expression of working-class, middle-class and upper-class identities and experiences runs right through the history of American popular music. Some of these expressions of class identity have to do with historical shifts in the American economy. Thus, the comfortably middle-class protagonist of "My Blue Heaven," a song recorded in 1927, seems to occupy a universe entirely different from that of the wanderers and hobos described in the depression-era songs of Jimmie Rodgers and Robert Johnson. The perspective of these artists is echoed in later recordings like Merle Haggard's "If We Make It through December" (1973), Grandmaster Flash's "The Message" (1982), and Bruce Springsteen's "Born in the U.S.A." (1984).

Class identity has often bubbled just below the sleek surfaces of American pop music. In Chuck Berry's "Maybellene" (1955), the protagonist's automotive pursuit of a young woman is given a distinctive flavor by the distinction between his working-class V-8 Ford and the girl's more expensive Cadillac Coupe de Ville. (The use of a French name—always a marker of elite culture—drives the point home, we might say.) The Crystals' 1962 hit "Uptown" sketches the social geography of New York City, tracing the daily path of a young man who works "downtown," where he "don't get no breaks," and comes home every evening to his lover's "uptown" tenement, where he feels like a "king." Although Americans do not tend to wear their class affiliations on their sleeve, popular music is full of references to wealth, poverty, and the effect of economic matters on the human heart.

Generational identity has, perhaps naturally, been a constant theme in an industry that relies to a great degree on the exploitation and creation of new styles, or at least the appearance of novelty. Popular music has played a major role in creating youth cultures and in shaping Americans' conceptions of adolescence. Beginning with the jazz craze of the 1920s and continuing through the rock 'n' roll era and the myriad youth movements and fads that have followed in its wake, generational identity has been crucial to the workings of the American music industry and to the identity formations of musicians and audiences. The music industry now draws a broad distinction between kids in the twelve to sixteen age bracket—the patrons of teenybopper acts like the Backstreet Boys, the Spice Girls, and Britney Spears—and young adults in the seventeen- to twenty-five-year-old range, whom the industry relies on to buy millions upon millions of rock, rap, and alternative music CDs. Popular music provides us with a unique window onto changing conceptions of adolescence, ranging from the mild rebellion of the Beach Boys' "Fun, Fun, Fun" (1964) to the Beastie Boys' rowdy party anthem "(You Gotta) Fight for Your Right (To Party)" (1987) and Nirvana's sardonic, depression-tinged "Smells Like Teen Spirit" (1991).

TECHNOLOGY AND THE MUSIC BUSINESS

We have traced shifts in technology for the recording, reproduction, and mass dissemination of sound, from the phonograph (1877), the radio (1922), the electric microphone (1925), and sound film (1927), through magnetic tape recording and the long-playing disc (1940s), and FM radio (1950s), to the innovations of the 1970s and 1980s (home video, cable television, portable tape players, the compact disc, and digital sound generation). At each stage in the development of popular music, new technologies have opened up creative possibilities for musicians and have created a wider range of choices for consumers. Of course, there is no guarantee that a given technological innovation will automatically provide greater freedom and flexibility for musicians and consumers, or lead to more creative, interesting and satisfying music. (We have noted elsewhere the nostalgia that crops up from time to time for older, more "human" technologies, a sentiment that motivates many alternative music scenes and the contemporary "lo-fi" movement.) We are accustomed to thinking of technology as an agent of change. In some cases, however, the new digital technologies have allowed musicians to excavate the musical past. The techno musician Moby did precisely this on his bestselling 1999 album *Play*, when he sampled segments of performances by Georgia Sea Islands singer Bessie Jones, Texas blues singer Boy Blue, and the Shining Light Gospel Choir, recorded in the field some forty years earlier by the folk music scholar Alan Lomax. What goes around comes around, but never in precisely the same form.

During the 1990s technology continued to affect how popular music is made, reproduced, marketed, and enjoyed by listeners. A new standard for digital music making was introduced in 1992 with the Alesis *ADAT*. The core of the ADAT system was an eight-track digital synthesizer/recorder that could expand to 128 tracks by adding additional units. This meant that a consumer could set up a basic home digital studio at relatively small expense, while professionals could use the same basic technology to build highly sophisticated digital sound facilities. *Electronic Musician* magazine declared in 1992 that "ADAT is more than a technological innovation; it's a social force."

Of course, the *music business* is intimately linked to issues surrounding the new technologies, as it has been throughout the history of American popular music. During the 1990s corporations battled over new media and formats for personal music recording and consumption. In 1991 the Philips Corporation introduced the *compact disc interactive*, or CD-I player, which could plug into a TV or a computer and play music and video from an interactive on-screen menu. That same year Polygram Records released *Louis Armstrong: American Songbook*, a disc that could be played on a regular CD player but that also contained additional text and interviews, lyrics cued to the music, and two unreleased tracks, all of which became available when the disc was played on a CD-I player. In 1992 the Sony Corporation began sales of the *MiniDisc*, a recordable magneto-optical disc encased in a plastic cartridge with the same seventy-four-minute capacity as the compact disc, but at half the size and with greater compression. The MiniDisc was intended to replace both the CD and the compact cassette. Sales of cassette tapes had been decreasing since 1989, and Sony felt that the compact cassette system was approaching the end of its format life. By the close of the 1990s *CD-R (CD recordable)* and *CD-RW (CD rewriteable)* technology was widely available to consumers, making it possible for anyone with a home computer to create personal compact disc recordings and put together personalized albums of songs.

The year 1995 saw the introduction of a new format called *DVD (digital video disc)*. Like a digital compact disc, DVD relies on an analog-to-digital converter that encodes information as patterns of bumps on the mirrored surface of a disc. However, whereas a CD can hold about 650 megabytes of information (or roughly seventy-four minutes of music), each side of a DVD can hold about 4.7 gigabytes of information—almost eight hours of music or two hours of high-quality video. (This is made possible by a compression system called MPEG—an abbreviation for Moving Picture Experts Group—which allows files to be squeezed down to only one-fortieth of their original size.) Although the creative possibilities of DVD are still just beginning to be explored as of this writing, it is clear that this technology will allow artists to create all sorts of interesting multimedia projects combing text, sound, and visual imagery.

Finally, the impact of the Internet—essentially a collection of millions of computers linked together by a global network—has already been profound, and it promises to change the means by which popular music is disseminated and consumed. The most popular and controversial new medium associated with the Internet is **MP3,** a variant of the MPEG compression system. MP3 allows sound files to be compressed to as little as one-twelfth of their original size. Let's assume that you would like to download a four-minute track of music from a Web site featuring original music. In its uncompressed, digitally encoded form, this track would require 40 megabytes of data, creating a file that would take hours to download over a modem. With MP3 compression, this file could be squeezed down to only 4 megabytes, while still retaining the sound quality of a CD.

The introduction of MP3 technology spurred a series of bitter struggles between entertainment corporations and small-scale entrepreneurs, echoing past conflicts between major and indie record labels, though on an even larger scale. In 1997 a firm called MP3.com was founded by Michael Robertson, who started by making three thousand songs available for free downloading over the Internet. By the year 2000 MP3.com had become by far the most successful music site on the World Wide Web, with over ten million registered members. As with digital sampling, this new way of disseminating musical materials raised a host of thorny legal problems, centered on the issue of copyright. While MP3 files are not inherently illegal, the practice of digitally reproducing music from a copyrighted compact disc and giving it away for free without the artist's or record company's permission arguably is illegal.

In January 2000 a lawsuit was filed against MP3.com by the Recording Industry Association of America (RIAA), the trade association whose member companies—Universal, Sony, Warner Brothers, Arista, Atlantic, BMG, RCA, Capitol, Elektra, Interscope, and Sire Records—control the sale and distribution of approximately 90 percent of the off-line music in the United States. The suit charged Robinson with copying forty-five thousand compact discs produced by these companies and making them available for free. MP3.com immediately issued a countersuit against the RIAA, but a court injunction forced them to remove all files owned by the corporations.

The year before, in 1999, an eighteen-year-old college dropout named Shawn Fanning had developed an Internet-based software program that allowed computer users to share and swap files, specifically music, through a centralized file server. Once again, the RIAA filed suit, charging Napster with tributary copyright infringement (meaning that the firm was accused not of violating copyright itself but of contributing to and facilitating other people's violation of the law). In its countersuit the firm argued that because the actual files were not permanently stored on its servers but rather transferred from user to user, Napster was not acting illegally. A federal court injunction finally forced Napster to shut down operations in

February 2001, and users exchanged some 2.79 *billion* files in the closing days of Napster's existence as a free service.

At the time of this writing Napster has paid a multimillion-dollar settlement to music publishers for past copyright infringements and signed licensing agreements with the corporations represented by the RIAA, and is preparing to reopen as a fee-based service. As the history of American popular music might lead us to expect, however, this will almost certainly not mark the end of the struggle between the entertainment conglomerates, on the one hand, and Internet entrepreneurs, fans, and independent musicians, on the other. By 2002 a number of successors to Napster had arisen, including FastTrack, Gnutella, and Audio Galaxy. These services' claim to exemption from copyright law is based on the fact that there is no central server on which files are even temporarily stored, and thus no "place" in cyberspace to which the act of copyright violation can be traced, apart from the millions of computers of the network's users. From the viewpoint of these users—including many musicians attempting to promote their recordings outside the corporate framework—such "peer-to-peer" file-sharing networks are the ultimate expression of musical democracy, a decentralized system made up of millions of individuals expressing free choice. From the RIAA's viewpoint, peer-to-peer music sharing is a case of mass theft, a maddeningly complex cybernetwork that challenges the ability of corporations (and the courts) to apply traditional conceptions of music as a form of property. The MP3 debates have raised fundamental questions about American culture, particularly in regard to the not always harmonious relationship between representative democracy and corporate capitalism.

These controversies—and others surely yet to come—ultimately stem from the fact that digital technology allows the *content* of a recording to be liberated from its original *medium*, the ultimate expression of "schizophonia" (a concept we introduced in connection with our discussion of the phonograph in Chapter 2). To some extent, all recording technologies have done this: a long-playing (LP) record, for example, transforms sound waves into physical impressions on the surface of a vinyl disc. But the transformation of musical sound into streams of numbers means that music can be transmitted, reproduced, and manipulated in a "virtual" form, free of the physical constraints of *any* particular technology (compact disc, magnetic tape, etc.). This development has raised questions that will no doubt shape the course of American popular music for years to come: What does it mean when a consumer licenses the right to use the *contents* of an album, rather than buying a single copy of it in a store? How can copyright be enforced—indeed, what is the meaning of the term "copyright"—when thousands of consumers can download the same piece of music simultaneously over the Internet? How will the transformation of music into pure *information* affect musicians and consumers? If "Video Killed the Radio Star"—to cite the first song promoted on MTV—will the Internet kill the record store? What will the music industry of tomorrow look like?

CENTERS AND PERIPHERIES

As we have charted the growth of the marketplace for recorded music—which had by the close of the twentieth century reached an annual sales total of fourteen billion dollars nationally and forty billion dollars worldwide—it has become increasingly difficult to sustain the distinction that we initially drew between the *main-*

Box 15.1 Popular Music and Television Advertising

One of the most lucrative markets for record companies is the licensing of recordings for use in films and television, media that have long used popular music to evoke a mood or an era and to target particular demographics. Television advertising is a particularly lucrative field—during Superbowl XXXIV (2000) the cost of purchasing one minute of airtime rose to four million dollars, a completely unprecedented figure. As companies compete to impress themselves upon the consciousness of consumers and to establish something like a distinctive corporate style, they become discerning in their licensing of popular music, new and old. In 1999 a retail clothing chain called the Gap licensed the following recordings for a series of advertisements, correlating musical genres and periods with particular fabrics and styles of jeans:

AD TITLE	MUSIC
Khakis Rock	Crystal Method: "Busy Child" (American techno, 1997)
Khaki Soul	Bill Withers: "Lovely Day" (folk/soul, 1970s)
Khaki Country	Dwight Yoakam: "Crazy Little Thing Called Love" (country, 1999)
Khakis Swing	Louis Prima: "Jump, Jive, An' Wail" (jump band R&B, 1956)
Everybody in Vests	Madonna: "Dress You Up" (dance club hit, 1984)
Everybody in Cords	Donovan: "Mellow Yellow" (folk rock, 1966)
Khaki a-go-go	James Clarke: "Wild Elephants" (U.K. techno, 1999)
Everybody in Leather	Depeche Mode: "Just Can't Get Enough" (synth-pop, 1981)
That's Holiday	Boston Pops Orchestra: "Sleigh Ride" (Christmas song by Leroy Anderson and Mitchell Parish; composed 1948, recorded 1949)
That's Holiday	Vanilla Ice: "Ice Ice Baby" (white rap, 1990)

This one advertising campaign presents something like an impressionistic mini-survey of recent American music history, ranging from a Christmas "evergreen" to postwar jump band ballroom dance music, 1960s folk rock, hip-hop (of a sort), techno, and country music (a cover version of a song first recorded by the rock band Queen). The soundscape of American television is literally saturated with these sorts of cut-and-paste musical references, a multimillion-dollar source of profit for the recording industry.

stream of popular music and its *margins*. In part this is because at the outset we were able to conflate two quite different concepts: on the one hand, the idea of a *musical* mainstream and margins, involving cultural and stylistic distinctions that have grown more and more blurry over time; and, on the other, the idea that the market for popular music has an *economic and institutional* center and periphery. In the early twentieth century these two dichotomies fit together rather neatly, for the mainstream of popular music—mainly Tin Pan Alley love songs and jazz- and ragtime-tinged dance music—coincided to a great degree with the central institutions of the music business (publishing firms, phonograph companies, and somewhat later, radio networks). But by the end of the century, the two dichotomies, as well as the correlation between them, had broken down almost completely. What started out as marginal genres—like R&B, country and western, urban folk music, soul music, disco, heavy metal, and rap—came in turn to occupy the mainstream, right alongside (and frequently displacing) "adult contemporary" music more directly descended from the Tin Pan Alley tradition. And this process was mirrored in turn by the economic evolution of the music business. When BMI was founded in 1941 as an alternative to ASCAP, it represented marginalized genres such as race and hillbilly music. Today both of these performing rights societies license the widest imaginable range of music, from folk to country to hip-hop. Independent record labels, which once operated on the fringes of the industry, are today more and more closely tied in with (and sometimes even invented by) the major record companies. At the beginning of the twentieth century, New York City was unquestionably the geographical center of the American popular music industry. One hundred years later, the spread of digital technology seems to be completing a process of total decentralization, as anybody with a computer, anywhere, can with increasing ease produce and market his or her own recordings.

The rise of international pop superstars such as Julio Iglesias, Ricky Martin, and Celine Dion, and the emergence of world music as a distinct category with its own Grammy award and *Billboard* chart, suggest that the center/periphery concept must now be recast in truly global terms. Although the United States is still the largest market for recorded music in the world, its preeminence as the nexus of the music industry is no longer indisputable. At the beginning of the twenty-first century five major conglomerates are responsible for as much as 90 percent of the sales of music worldwide, and only one of these corporations is officially headquartered in the United States. With the unification of the European market and ongoing changes in Asia (including the rise of India and China as major centers for the production and consumption of popular music), it seems likely that the United States will remain an important, even indispensable part of the global music system, but not its dominant center.

Even if the United States can no longer cling to a mythology of manifest destiny in relation to the rapidly growing and diversifying global entertainment industry, there can be no doubt that the sounds and sensibilities of American popular music will continue to exert an enormous impact all over the world. Millions of people worldwide have come to know the United States through its popular culture, as disseminated in movie theaters, on television and radio, and on cassettes and discs. This image of America is a song-map: a set of narratives about being "Born in the U.S.A." and "Living in America," and a network of imaginary pathways connecting "Georgia on My Mind" to the "St. Louis Blues," juxtaposing street knowledge "Straight Outta Compton" with the urban delights of "Spanish Harlem," and pitting the seductively mirrored "Hotel California" against the plain white city hall of "Muskogee," Oklahoma. Similarly, the popular narrative of America as a center of novelty, excitement, and mobility has been disseminated by mass-reproduced sonic images of Americans "rollin' on the river" on the "Proud Mary," "Waiting for a Train," "Leavin' on a Jet Plane," driving around in a "Merry Oldsmobile" or a "Little Deuce Coupe," and wandering footloose, "Like a Rolling Stone." Although music is by no means a universal language, the recurring themes of American popular music—love and sex, home and travel, materialism and morality, optimism and despair—have resonated with millions of listeners worldwide. (This may be why country and western music is extremely popular in Africa, a fact that surprises many Americans)

We have reached the endpoint of our journey, but there is every reason to expect that the energy and creativity, the crassness and commercialism of American popular music—that messy product of almost four centuries of cultural miscegenation—will continue to impress themselves on the world's consciousness, provoking equal measures of admiration and disapproval. Whether one views this process as an extension of cultural imperialism or as proof positive of the unique value of American musical culture, there can be no denying that popular music—forged by sons and daughters of Africa and Europe, shaped by the diverse musical cultures of the Americas, hustled and hyped by generations of entrepreneurs, molded and remolded by the force fields of identity, technology, and the music industry—constitutes an epochal contribution not only to American culture but also to a wider, still-emerging world culture. Rock on!

GLOSSARY

This glossary consists of terms requiring specialized definitions that recur throughout the book. Such terms appear in the text in **boldface**. Important terms of local significance—that is, those relevant principally to particular chapters or to sections of chapters only—are *italicized* in the text and defined in context, and may also be located using the index.

a cappella   Vocal singing that involves no instrumental accompaniment.

A&R   Abbreviation for "artists and repertoire." This is the department of a record company whose responsibility it is to discover and cultivate new musical talent, and to find material for the artists to perform—naturally, with an eye toward commercial potential. As many artists today write and record their own material, the latter function of A&R has atrophied to some extent.

arranger   A person who adapts (or arranges) the melody and chords of a song to exploit the capabilities and instrumental resources of a particular musical ensemble. For example, a simple pop tune originally written for voice and piano may be arranged for a jazz "big band" with many horns and a rhythm section.

ballad   A type of song consisting usually of verses set to a repeating melody (see **strophic** form) in which a story, often romantic, historic, or tragic, is sung in narrative fashion.

blue notes   Expressive notes or scalar inflections found primarily in blues and jazz music. The blue notes derive from African musical practice; although they do not correspond exactly to the Western system of **major** and **minor** scales, it is helpful to imagine them as "flatter" or "lower" versions of the scale degrees to which they are related, and thus one speaks of "blue" thirds, fifths, and sevenths (see Chapter 5).

blues   A genre of music originating principally from the field hollers and work songs of rural blacks in the southern United States during the latter half of the nineteenth century. Themes treated by blues lyrics included the oppressive conditions suffered by African Americans; love gone wrong; alienation; misery; and the supernatural. The lyrics are often obscured by a coded, metaphorical language. The music of the blues is rich in Africanisms and earthy rhythms. Originally an acoustic music, the blues moved to the urban North in the mid-twentieth century, becoming electrified in the process (see Chapters 5 and 7).

bridge   A passage consisting of new, contrasting material that serves as a link between repeated sections of melodic material. A bridge is sometimes called a **release** (see discussion of Tin Pan Alley song form in Chapter 4).

cadence   A melodic or harmonic event that signals the end of a musical line or section, or of the piece as a whole.

chord   The simultaneous sounding of different pitches.

chorus   A repeating section within a song consisting of a fixed melody *and* lyric that is repeated exactly each time that it occurs, typically following one or more verses.

coda   The "tail end" of a musical composition, typically a brief passage after the last complete section that serves to bring the piece to its conclusion

composer   A person who creates a piece of music. Although the term may be, and often is, used to describe the creators of popular songs, it is more commonly applied to those who create more extended, formally notated works of music.

counterculture   A subculture existing in opposition to and espousing values contrary to that of the dominant culture. The term is most often used to describe the values and lifestyle of young people during the late 1960s and early 1970s (see Chapter 10).

counterpoint   The sounding of two independent melodic lines or voices against one another.

dialect   A regional speech variant; one may allude to regional musical "dialects" to describe stylistic variants of the same basic musical genre, as with Mississippi Delta blues or East Texas blues.

dissonance   A harsh or grating sound. (The perception of dissonance is culturally conditioned. For example, the smaller intervals employed in certain Asian and Middle Eastern musics may sound "out of tune" and dissonant to Western ears; within their original context, however, they are regarded as perfectly consonant.)

distortion   A buzzing, crunchy, or "fuzzy" tone color originally achieved by over-driving the vacuum tubes of a guitar amplifier. This effect can be simulated today by solid state and digital sound processors. Distortion is often heard in a hard rock or heavy metal context.

DJ   Disc jockey (deejay); one who plays recordings on a radio program.

feedback   Technically, an out-of-control sound oscillation that occurs when the output of a loudspeaker finds its way back into a microphone or electric instrument pickup and is reamplified, creating a sound loop that grows in intensity and continues until deliberately broken. Although feedback can be difficult to manage, it becomes a powerful expressive device in the hands of certain blues and rock musicians, most notably the guitarist Jimi Hendrix. Feedback can be recognized as a "screaming" or "crying" sound.

groove   Term originally employed by jazz , rhythm & blues, and funk musicians to describe the channeled flow of swinging, "funky," or "phat" rhythms.

hook   A "catchy" or otherwise memorable musical phrase or pattern.

lyricist   A person who supplies a poetic text (lyrics) to a piece of vocal music; not necessarily the composer.

major   refers to one of the two scale systems central to Western music (see **minor**); a major scale is arranged in the following order of whole- and half-step intervals: $1-1-\frac{1}{2}-1-1-1-\frac{1}{2}$. (This pattern is easy to see if one begins at the pitch C on the piano keyboard and plays the next seven white notes in succession, which yields the C major scale: CDEFGABC.) A song is said to be in a major tonality or key if it uses melodies and chords that are constructed from the major scale. Of course, a song may (and frequently does) "borrow" notes and chords from outside a particular major scale, and it may "modulate" or shift from key to key within the course of the song.

melisma   One syllable of text spread out over many musical tones.

minor   Refers to one of the two scale systems central to Western music (see **major**); a minor scale is arranged in the following order of whole- and half-step intervals: $1-\frac{1}{2}-1-1-\frac{1}{2}-1-1$. (This pattern represents the so-called natural minor scale, often found in blues and blues-based popular music; it is easy to see if one begins at the pitch A on the piano keyboard and plays the next seven white notes in succession, which yields the A minor scale: ABCDEFGA. The two other minor scales in common usage—the melodic minor and harmonic minor scales—have ascending and descending forms that differ somewhat from the natural minor scale.) A song is said to be in a minor tonality or key if it uses melodies and chords that are constructed from the minor scale. Of course, a song may (and frequently does) "borrow" notes and chords from outside a particular minor scale, and it may "modulate" or shift from key to key within the course of the song. In comparison to the major scale, the minor scale is often described as having a "sad" or "melancholy" sound.

MP3   A variant of the MPEG compression system, which allows sound files to be compressed to as little as one-twelfth of their original size.

payola   The illegal and historically widespread practice of offering money or other inducements to a radio station or deejay in order to insure the prominent airplay of a particular recording.

polyrhythm   The simultaneous sounding of rhythms in two or more contrasting meters, such as three against two, or five against four. Polyrhythms are found in abundance in African and Asian musics and their derivatives.

producer   A person engaged either by a recording artist or, more often, a record company, who directs and assists the recording process. The producer's duties may include securing the services of session musicians; deciding on arrangements; making technical decisions; motivating the artist creatively; helping to realize the artistic vision in a commercially viable way; and not unimportantly, insuring that the project comes in under budget. A good producer often develops a distinctive signature sound, and successful producers are always in great demand. They are often rewarded handsomely for their efforts, garnering a substantial share of a recording's earnings, in addition to a commission.

R&B   Rhythm & blues. An African American musical genre emerging after World War II. It consisted of a loose cluster of styles derived from black musical traditions, characterized by energetic and hard-swinging rhythms. At first performed exclusively by black musicians and aimed at black audiences, R&B came to replace the older category of "race records" (see Chapter 7).

ragtime   A musical genre of African American origin, later exploited to great advantage by white performers, that emerged in the 1880s and became quite popular at the turn of the century. Ragtime is characterized by melodic accents that fall on "off" or weak beats; it is highly **syncopated.** Scott Joplin is the recognized master of this genre, having composed numerous rags for the piano (see Chapter 2).

refrain   In the verse-refrain song , the refrain is the "main part" of the song, usually constructed in AABA or ABAC form (see discussion of Tin Pan Alley song form in Chapter 4).

release   *See* **bridge.**

reverb   Short for "reverberation"—a prolongation of a sound by virtue of an ambient acoustical space created by hard, reflective surfaces. The sound bounces off these surfaces and recombines with the original sound, slightly delayed (reverb is measured in terms of seconds and fractions of seconds). Reverberation can occur naturally or be simulated either electronically or by digital sound processors.

riff   A simple, repeating melodic idea or pattern that generates rhythmic momentum; typically played by the horns or the piano in a jazz ensemble, or by an electric guitar in a rock 'n' roll context.

rockabilly   A vigorous form of country and western music ("hillbilly" music) informed by the rhythms of black R&B and electric blues. It is exemplified by such artists as Carl Perkins and the young Elvis Presley.

sampling   A digital recording process wherein a sound source is recorded or "sampled" with a microphone, converted into a stream of binary numbers that represent the profile of the sound, quantized, and stored in computer memory. The digitized sound sample may then be retrieved in any number of ways, including "virtual recording studio" programs for the computer, or by activating the sound from an electronic keyboard or drum machine.

scat singing   A technique that involves the use of nonsense syllables as a vehicle for wordless vocal improvisation. It is most often found in a jazz context.

slap-back   A distinctive short reverberation with few repetitions, often heard in the recordings of rockabilly artists, such as the Sun Records recordings of Elvis Presley.

soli (plural of solo)   Band textures achieved by having a small group of players within the band play certain passages of music together. Soli playing contrasts with **tutti** sections, wherein the entire ensemble plays (see the discussion of swing bands in Chapter 6).

strophes   Poetic stanzas; often, a pair of stanzas of alternating form that constitute the structure of a poem. These could become the **verse** and **chorus** of a **strophic** song.

strophic   A song form that employs the same music for each poetic unit in the lyrics.

syncopation   Rhythmic patterns in which the stresses occur on what are ordinarily weak beats, thus displacing or suspending the sense of metric regularity.

tempo   Literally, "time" (from Italian). The rate at which a musical composition proceeds, regulated by the speed of the beat or pulse to which it is performed.

through-composed   A form of song composition in which each successive section of a piece is fundamentally different from any of the preceding sections.

timbre   The "tone color" or characteristic sound of an instrument or voice, determined by its frequency and overtone components. Timbre is the aspect of sound that allows us, for example, to differentiate between the sound of a violin and a flute when both instruments are playing the same pitch.

tonic   Refers to the central or "home" pitch, or chord, of a musical piece—or sometimes of just a section of the piece.

tremolo   The rapid reiteration of a single pitch to create a vibrating sound texture. This effect can be produced by acoustic instruments or by electronic means.

tutti   Literally, "together" (from Italian). A passage in a musical piece wherein all the instruments of the ensemble (band or orchestra) are playing simultaneously.

verse   In general usage, this term refers to a group of lines of poetic text, often rhyming, that usually exhibit regularly recurring metrical patterns. In the verse-refrain song, the verse refers to an introductory section that precedes the main body of the song, the **refrain** (see discussion of Tin Pan Alley song form in Chapter 4).

vibrato   An expressive musical technique that involves minute wavering or fluctuation of a pitch.

waltz   A dance in triple meter with a strong emphasis on the downbeat of each bar.

BIBLIOGRAPHY

This list includes all works cited in the body of this book, along with a small number of others that may be recommended for further reading on individual topics and issues central to the material covered in the preceding pages. No attempt is made to offer a comprehensive bibliography here, or to list books of a general introductory nature in the area of American popular music.

Armstrong, Louis. *Satchmo: My Life in New Orleans*. New York, 1954.

Austin, William W. *"Susanna," "Jeanie," and "The Old Folks at Home": The Songs of Stephen C. Foster from His Time to Ours*. New York, 1975.

Bashe, Philip. *Heavy Metal Thunder*. Garden City, N.Y., 1985.

Basie, William, and Albert Murray. *Good Morning Blues: The Autobiography of Count Basie*. New York, 1995.

Beatles, the. *Anthology*. San Francisco, 2000.

Berlin, Edward A. *King of Ragtime: Scott Joplin and His Era*. New York, 1994.

Berry, Chuck. *The Autobiography*. New York, 1987.

Bright, Spencer. *Peter Gabriel: An Authorized Biography*. London, 1999.

Camus, Raoul. "Bands." In *The New Grove Dictionary of American Music*, vol. 1. New York, 1986.

Castle, Irene, Robert Lipscomb Duncan, and Wanda Duncan. *Castles in the Air: As Told to Bob and Wanda Duncan*. Reprint. New York, 1980.

Chapple, Steve, and Reebee Garofalo. *Rock 'n' Roll Is Here to Pay: The History and Politics of the Music Industry*. Chicago, 1977.

Charles, Ray, and David Ritz. *Brother Ray: Ray Charles' Own Story*. New York, 1978.

Chilton, John. *Let the Good Times Roll: The Story of Louis Jordan and His Music*. Ann Arbor, 1994.

Clarke, Donald. *The Rise and Fall of Popular Music*. New York, 1995.

Cockrell, Dale. *Demons of Disorder: Early Blackface Minstrels and Their World*. New York, 1997.

Collin, Matthew. *Altered State: The Story of Ecstasy Culture and Acid House*. London, 1997.

Deffaa, Chip. *Blue Rhythms: Six Lives in Rhythm and Blues*. Urbana, Ill., 1996.

Dodworth, Allan. *Dancing and its Relation to Social Life*. New York, 1885.

Emerson, Ken. *Doo-dah! Stephen Foster and the Rise of American Popular Culture*. New York, 1997.

Frith, Simon. *Sound Effects: Youth, Leisure, and the Politics of Rock 'n' Roll*. New York, 1981.

Furia, Philip, with Graham Wood. *Irving Berlin: A Life in Song.* New York, 1998.

George, Nelson. *Hip Hop America.* New York, 1998.

George, Nelson, et al., eds. *Fresh: Hip-hop Don't Stop.* New York, 1985.

Gillett, Charlie. *The Sound of the City: The Rise of Rock and Roll.* New York, 1996.

Goodwin, Andrew. *Dancing in the Distraction Factory: Music Television and Popular Culture.* Minneapolis, 1992.

Guralnick, Peter. *Sweet Soul Music: Rhythm and Blues and the Southern Dream of Freedom.* New York, 1986.

——— *Last Train to Memphis: The Rise of Elvis Presley.* Boston, 1994.

——— *Careless Love: The Unmaking of Elvis Presley.* Boston, 1999.

Hager, Steven. *Hip Hop: The Illustrated History of Break Dancing, Rap Music, and Graffiti.* New York, 1984.

Handy, W. C. *Father of the Blues: An Autobiography.* New York, 1941.

Howe, Irving. *World of Our Fathers: The Journey of the East European Jews to America and the Life They Found and Made.* New York, 1976.

Jablonski, Edward, and Lawrence D. Stewart. *The Gershwin Years: George and Ira.* New York, 1996.

Jackson, Mahalia, and E. M. Wylie. *Movin' on Up.* New York, 1966.

Karlen, Neal. "Prince Talks." *Rolling Stone,* April 1985.

Keil, Charles. *Urban Blues.* Chicago, 1966.

Keil, Charles, and Steven Feld. *Music Grooves.* Chicago, 1994.

Laing, Dave. *One-Chord Wonders.* Philadelphia, 1985.

Levine, Lawrence. *Black Culture and Black Consciousness: Afro-American Folk Thought from Slavery to Freedom.* New York, 1977.

Lhamon, W. T., Jr. *Raising Cain: Blackface Performance from Jim Crow to Hip Hop.* Cambridge, Mass., 1998.

Malnig, Julie. *Dancing till Dawn: A Century of Exhibition Ballroom Dance.* New York, 1992.

Malone, Bill C. *Country Music, U.S.A.* Rev. ed. Austin, Tex., 1985.

Morgan, Thomas L., and William Barlow. *From Cakewalks to Concert Halls: An Illustrated History of African American Popular Music from 1895 to 1930.* Washington, D.C., 1992.

Morse, Dave. *Motown and the Arrival of Black Music.* New York, 1971.

Negus, Keith. *Producing Pop: Culture and Conflict in the Popular Music Industry.* London, 1992.

Oliver, Paul. *Blues Fell This Morning: Meaning in the Blues.* Cambridge, England, 1990.

Palmer, Robert. *Deep Blues.* New York, 1981.

——— *Rock & Roll: An Unruly History.* New York, 1995.

Peterson, Richard A. *Creating Country Music: Fabricating Authenticity.* Chicago, 1997.

Petkov, Steven, and Leonard Mustazza, eds. *The Frank Sinatra Reader.* New York, 1995.

Pleasants, Henry. *The Great American Popular Singers.* New York, 1974.

Porterfield, Nolan. *Jimmie Rodgers: The Life and Times of America's Blue Yodeler.* Urbana, Ill., 1979.

Reynolds, Simon. *Generation Ecstasy: Into the World of Techno and Rave Culture.* New York, 1998.

Roberts, John Storm. *The Latin Tinge: The Impact of Latin American Music on the United States.* New York, 1979.

Rose, Tricia. *Black Noise: Rap Music and Black Culture in Contemporary America.* Middletown, Conn., 1994.

Schafer, R. Murray. *The Tuning of the World.* New York, 1977.

Schwartz, H. W. *Bands of America.* New York, 1975.

Sexton, Adam, ed. *Desperately Seeking Madonna.* New York, 1993.

Shaw, Arnold. *Honkers and Shouters: The Golden Years of Rhythm and Blues.* New York, 1986.

Stephenson, Richard M., and Joseph Iaccarino. *The Complete Book of Ballroom Dancing*. New York, 1980.

Stowe, David W. *Swing Changes: Big-Band Jazz in New Deal America*. Cambridge, Mass., 1994.

Taylor, Timothy D. *Global Pop: World Music, World Markets*. New York, 1997.

Théberge, Paul. *Any Sound You Can Imagine: Making Music/Consuming Technology*. Middletown, Conn., 1997.

Toop, David. *The Rap Attack 2: African Rap to Global Hip Hop*. London, 2000.

Tucker, Mark, ed. *The Duke Ellington Reader*. New York, 1993.

Walser, Robert. *Running with the Devil: Power, Gender, and Madness in Heavy Metal Music*. Middletown, Conn., 1993.

West, Cornel. *Race Matters*. Boston, 1993.

Whiteman, Paul, and Mary Margaret McBride. *Jazz*. Reprint. New York, 1974.

Wynn, Ron. *Tina: The Tina Turner Story*. New York, 1985.

INDEX

The annotation "f" indicates a reference to a figure on the specified page.

CD 1

1. "Jeanie with the Light Brown Hair"—Thomas Hampson (Foster). ℗1992 Angel Records. Courtesy of Angel Records under license from EMI Music Special Markets

2. "Castle House Rag"—James Reese Europe's Society Orchestra (Europe). Under license from BMG Special Products

3. "Tiger Rag"—The Original Dixieland Jazz Band (Original Dixieland Jazz Band). Courtesy of The RCA Records Label

4. "El Manicero"/"The Peanut Vendor"—Don Azpiazú & His Havana Casino Orchestra (Moises Simon). Courtesy of The RCA Records Label

5. "My Blue Heaven"—Gene Austin (Whiting/Donaldson). Courtesy of The RCA Records Label

6. "April Showers"—Al Jolson (B.G. DeSylva/Louis Silvers) (1921 Version). Originally released 1921 Sony Music Entertainment Inc. Under license from The Sony Music Custom Marketing Group, a division of Sony Music, a group of Sony Music Entertainment Inc.

7. "April Showers"—Al Jolson (B.G. DeSylva/Louis Silvers) (1932 Version). Originally released 1932 Sony Music Entertainment Inc. Under license from The Sony Music Custom Marketing Group, a division of Sony Music, a group of Sony Music Entertainment Inc.

8. "I Got Rhythm"—Ethel Merman (Gershwin/Gershwin). Courtesy of MCA Records under license from Universal Music Enterprises

9. "Embraceable You"—Nat King Cole (Gershwin/Gershwin). Courtesy Capitol Records under license from EMI Music Special Markets. Nat King Cole® is a registered trademark of King Cole Partners, Inc.

10. "St. Louis Blues"—Bessie Smith (William C. Handy). Originally released 1925 Sony Music Entertainment Inc. Under license from The Sony Music Custom Marketing Group, a division of Sony Music, a group of Sony Music Entertainment Inc.

11. "That Black Snake Moan"—Blind Lemon Jefferson (Blind Lemon Jefferson). Courtesy of Milestone Records/Fantasy, Inc.

12. "Blue Yodel No. 11"—Jimmie Rodgers (J. Rodgers). Courtesy of the RCA Records Label/Nashville

13. "Gospel Ship"—The Carter Family (Traditional/Arranged by A.P. Carter). Originally released 1935 Sony Music Entertainment Inc. Under license from the Sony Music Custom Marketing Group, a division of Sony Music, a group of Sony Music Entertainment Inc.

14. "Wrappin' It Up (The Lindy Glide)"—Fletcher Henderson (Henderson). Courtesy of MCA Records under license from Universal Music Enterprises

15. "Paper Doll"—The Mills Brothers (Black). Courtesy of MCA Records under license from Universal Music Enterprises

16. "In the Mood"—Glenn Miller & His Orchestra (Joe Garland). Courtesy of The RCA Records Label

17. "Cool Water"—Sons of the Pioneers (Bob Nolan). Courtesy of MCA Nashville under license from Universal Music Enterprises

18. "New San Antonio Rose"—Bob Wills & His Texas Playboys (Bob Wills). Originally released 1940 Sony Music Entertainment Inc. Under license from The Sony Music Custom Marketing Group, a division of Sony Music, a group of Sony Music Entertainment Inc.

19. "Choo Choo Ch' Boogie"—Louis Jordan (Gabler/Horton/Darling). Courtesy of MCA Records under license from Universal Music Enterprises

20. "(I'm Your) Hoochie Coochie Man"—Muddy Waters (Dixon). Courtesy of MCA Records under license from Universal Music Enterprises

21. "Hound Dog"—Big Mama Thornton (Leiber/Stoller). Courtesy of MCA Records under license from Universal Music Enterprises

CD 2

1. "The Wild Side of Life"—Hank Thompson (Carter/Warren). Courtesy of Capitol Nashville under license from EMI Music Special Markets

2. "It Wasn't God Who Made Honky-Tonk Angels"—Kitty Wells (Miller). Courtesy of MCA Nashville under license from Universal Music Enterprises

3. "I'm So Lonesome I Could Cry"—Hank Williams, Sr. (Williams). Courtesy of Mercury Records under license from Universal Music Enterprises

4. "Shake, Rattle and Roll"—Bill Haley and the Comets (Calhoun). Courtesy of MCA Records under license from Universal Music Enterprises

5. "Sh-Boom (Life Could Be a Dream)"—The Crew Cuts (Edwards/Feaster/Feaster/Keyes/McRae). Courtesy of The Island Def Jam Music Group under license from Universal Music Enterprises

6. "Maybellene"—Chuck Berry (Berry). Courtesy of MCA Records under license from Universal Music Enterprises

7. "Long Tall Sally"—Little Richard (E. Johnson/R. Blackwell/R. Penniman). Courtesy of Specialty Records, Inc.

8. "That'll Be the Day"—Buddy Holly (Holly/Allison/Petty). Courtesy of MCA Records under license from Universal Music Enterprises

9. "My Girl"—The Temptations (Robinson/White). Courtesy of Motown Records under license from Universal Music Enterprises

10. "You Can't Hurry Love"—The Supremes (Holland/Dozier/Holland, Jr.). Courtesy of Motown Records under license from Universal Music Enterprises

11. "Good Vibrations"—The Beach Boys (Love/Wilson). Courtesy Capitol Records under license from EMI-Capitol Music Special Markets

12. "Papa's Got a Brand New Bag (Part 1)"—James Brown (Brown). Courtesy of Universal Records under license from Universal Music Enterprises

13. "Crocodile Rock"—Elton John (John/Taupin). ℗1972 This Record Co. Ltd.

14. "Love's Theme"—Love Unlimited Orchestra (White/Schroeder). ℗1974 The Island Def Jam Music Group

15. "What's Going On"—Marvin Gaye (Gaye/Cleveland/Benson). Courtesy of Motown Records under license from Universal Music Enterprises

16. "Oye Como Va"—Santana (Tito Puente). Originally released 1970 Sony Music Entertainment Inc. Under license from The Sony Music Custom Marketing Group, a division of Sony Music, a group of Sony Music Entertainment Inc.

17. "The Harder They Come"—Jimmy Cliff (Cliff). ℗1972 The Island Def Jam Music Group

18. "Give Up the Funk (Tear the Roof off the Sucker)"—Parliament (Clinton/Collins/Brailey). ℗1978 The Island Def Jam Music Group

19. "Bad Girls"—Donna Summer (Sudano/Summer/Hokenson/Esposito). ℗1979 The Island Def Jam Music Group

20. "Night of the Living Baseheads"—Public Enemy (Sadler/Ridenhour/Boxley). ℗1988 The Island Def Jam Music Group

21. "Holiday in Cambodia"—Dead Kennedys (Dead Kennedys). ℗1980 Cherry Red Records Ltd. Courtesy of Cherry Red Records Ltd.

22. "Not a Pretty Girl"—Ani DiFranco (Ani DiFranco). ℗1995 Righteous Babe Records, Inc. Ani DiFranco appears courtesy of Righteous Babe Records, Inc.